Showered in Shale

One man's circuitous journey throughout the country in pursuit of an obsession: British Speedway

Jeff Scott

methanol
press

First published in Great Britain by
Methanol Press
2 Tidy Street Brighton East Sussex BN1 4EL

Second Impression August 2006

Published to accompany British Speedway

For a complete catalogue of current and forthcoming publications please write to the address above, or visit our website at
www.methanolpress.com

Text and photographs copyright © Jeff Scott, 2006

ISBN 0-9553103-0-X
ISBN 978-0-9553103-0-0

A catalogue for this book is available from the British Library

(Long suffering) Editor: Michael Payne
Word Wrangler: Graham Russel
Proof Reader: Caroline Tidmarsh
Design: Rachael Adams <www.scrutineer.co.uk>
Additional Photography: Julie Martin, Graham Platten and Steve Dixon
Photographs Edited by: Rachael Adams and Julie Martin

Cover Design: Rachael Adams
Cover Photographs: Julie Martin

UK Distributor:
Central Books
99 Wallis Road London E9 5LN
020 8986 4854
www.centralbooks.com

Contents

*	Introduction	7
1	Reading v. Isle of Wight: High-flying Bird suffers a Bunyan	9
2	Poole v. Belle Vue: Clash of the Champions	17
3	Oxford v. Arena Essex: The latest 'Final Farewell'	23
4	Edinburgh v. Stoke: A Coach trip to the Monarchs	33
5	Berwick v. Hull: Of popes and Bandits	41
6	Glasgow v. Edinburgh: The Kindness of Strangers	51
7	Swindon v. Eastbourne: Rockin' with the Robins	63
8	Under-21 British Championship Final, Rye House: In Pursuit of Dreams	71
9	Rye House v. Hull followed by the Elmside Raiders v. Newport GMB Union Mavericks: Of Fences and Start Gates	85
10	Wolverhampton v. Eastbourne: Crash, Bang, Wallop, What a Picture, What a Photograph	93
11	Arena Essex v. Eastbourne: An Evening with Ronnie Russell in Thurrock	113
12	Mildenhall v. Weymouth: Fun Frying in the Fens	125
13	Poole v. Eastbourne: The Love of a Lifetime	141
14	Peterborough v. Eastbourne: Showtime at the Showground	155
15	Reading v. Edinburgh: Down Memory Lane at Smallmead	165
16	Isle of Wight v. Edinburgh: Big Track on a Small Island	175
17	Weymouth v. Travis Perkins Select: Cool For (Wild)Cats	187
18	Sheffield v. Berwick: Professional Motorsport in the Heart of the City of Sheffield	195
19	Workington v. Stoke: A Night with The Comets	203

20 Stoke v. Workington: Pottering in the Potteries — 215

21 Scunthorpe v. Hull Angels: Sunday in Scunny and the Marmite Question — 231

22 Somerset v. Rye House: Off with the Rousing Rebels — 243

23 Newport v. Kings Lynn & Newport v. Oxford: The Club that Tim Built — 253

24 Exeter v. Edinburgh: A Trip to the Ring of Steel — 271

25 Kings Lynn v. Newport: The Jewel of Norfolk — 283

26 Ipswich v. Poole: Family Speedway in Suffolk — 297

27 Eastbourne v. Wolves: Perspectives from Eagles and Wolves — 311

28 Newcastle v. Somerset: Barney in Byker — 321

29 Hull v. Workington: End of an Era in Hull — 335

30 Sheffield v. Newcastle: Something Special in Sheffield — 349

31 Coventry v. Arena: Of Bee's, Memories and Referee's — 361

32 Belle Vue v. Eastbourne: Televising the Aces on their Dirt-Naked System Track — 379

33 Oxford v. Eastbourne: The World according to Waggy — 393

34 Buxton v. Scunthorpe: That Buxton Feeling — 407

35 Peterborough v. Eastbourne – twice: The Pride of the Panthers — 419

36 Reading v. Isle of Wight: The Penultimate Evening of the Racers — 429

37 Isle of Wight v. Reading: The Magic of the Island — 437

38 Sittingbourne v. Armadale & Sittingbourne v. Boston: Sport of the 500's — 447

39 Referee's Practice day — 461

40 Brighton Bonanza: Behind the Scenes — 471

* Afterword — 499

* Acknowledgements — 503

**"You're only given a little spark of madness.
You mustn't lose it."**
Robin Williams

To my mum and dad and in memory of Michael Donaghy (1954-2004)

Introduction

This book investigates the question 'What is Speedway?' Not in the usual way by means of a club history or the (auto)biography of a rider, but through a snapshot of my personal experiences as I journeyed round every place that staged the sport in Britain during 2005.

I chose to write this for two reasons: first, to take on the challenge of trying to get round every track in the country in a season, and second because speedway strikes me as the complete opposite of the contrived experiences of today that are considered 'authentic' and 'real'. I consider this mendacity the bane of modern life. The continuous shift to false representations of reality engulfs us, whether at work, on the telly, in the shops, in our sports stadiums, and it has even crept into our relationships with family, friends and partners. Luckily, I believe – and choose to believe – that speedway is, somehow, resolutely 'make-over resistant' and I hope it always remains so. Nonetheless, speedway has often re-invented itself and people will continue to pretend or to try to make it something it is not. That is their right and this process has already started with some success. I see this book as an antidote to that process but sadly, though, I nonetheless expect an inevitable loss of community and authenticity will result. The rich variety of the present will inevitably be replaced by an ersatz much more glossy and slightly false showbizzy version of the same. I believe that such a devolution will be seen by many of the more entrepreneurial, successful business personalities that the sport has begun to attract as a necessary, small sacrifice of culture, if it means their financial success. I fear this future is just around the corner. Possibly. But just in case it is, I thought I'd try to freeze a moment in time of what we presently have before it disappears or morphs into something else.

Still, enough of that.

For anyone unclear about what speedway is, the online reference resource *Wikipedia* has a useful definition of the basic concept of speedway:

"Speedway is a form of motorcycle racing which takes place on dirt (shale) short tracks. Speedway uses motor bikes without brakes or gears and riders have to powerslide the bikes into the turns."

"An international individual speedway championship has taken various forms since its beginnings in the 1930's… Speedway is presently most popular in Central and Eastern Europe, Scandinavia, the United Kingdom, and to a lesser extent these days Australia and New Zealand; it has some popularity in the USA as well… Most European countries run their own domestic speedway leagues. A team speedway meeting usually features 15 heats but in a team oriented format, and each rider is programmed to ride 4 or 5 times. In team races, there is a set order that riders will race although… these orders are regularly adjusted. Team races use four riders per heat with traditional scoring (3-2-1-0)"[1]

However, while this definition takes some beating, it doesn't really answer many fundamental questions that one might have about the sport or its enduring, though declining, appeal. For me the sport represents one of the last true bastions of white working-class culture in the country and is a sport I grew up with. I believe speedway also says a lot about people, relationships and community. And passion, belief, and dedication. I could make quite a list here. So, with rose-tinted spectacles, I thought I should savour the sheer variety of the sport while still possible. I have recorded my impressions, frequently painful ones as you'll find, and have tried to meet as many of the people involved in the sport as I could – many of them frequently overlooked, ignored, or unheard from in traditional speedway books – and I tried to find out what they think and feel about it all.

I'm not sure what else I can tell you. Obviously I set out with preconceptions and misconceptions. I have managed to retain many of these and have had others challenged. I have ridden my own hobbyhorses and watched others ride theirs.

It was a great privilege to have an excuse to go to all these tracks and an even greater pleasure to meet everyone I did. I had intended to do a 'proper' chapter on each club and even visited some more than once.[2]

Perhaps, all this blather aside, my editor Michael Payne provides the best guidance to what might be in store for you:

"This book is a series of chapters that chronicles the visits of the author to motorcycle racetracks, 'Speedway', in the UK during a period of time in the spring, summer, and fall of 2005."

"The narrative introduces us to a general overview of the history of Speedway as a sport in the UK, the reality of the sport at the local racetracks visited, and a survey of the current conditions of the sport. This latter object is achieved through vivid character sketches of key individuals who work in the sport industry at the local racetracks or watch the races there, as well as through the reflections and experiences of the author as he makes his visits."

"As someone who at seventeen managed to break his arm, a double compound fracture, by falling off a motorcycle that was at rest, I bring a certain reserve to the subject. True, I went on to travel by Vespa from Rome to North Africa and then to Madrid, but I still experience a phantom ache in my arm every time I think about riding one. That this book provokes me to consider even the possibility of riding one again speaks highly of the ability to connect the sport and the enthusiasm and affection you have for it with the reader. It is a deeply personal emotion, profoundly individual, and resonates from your life experience."

Well, there you have it. I hope that you enjoy your journey.

25th May 2006 Brighton

---

[1] This is a good, succinct, and simple definition of the sport that we know and love. It manages to capture its essence without getting bogged down in a fret of detail and jargon. It might be fun, though, to come up with a deliberately confusing set of clarifying tenets on the sport, presented in the style of those tea towels produced for tourists that ostensibly try to clarify and explain the rules of cricket ("You can't be out until you're in.") and so on.

[2] Actually the 'proper' chapter on Poole is 13, Reading should really be 15, and similarly Oxford should be 33.

Chapter 1: High-flying Bird Suffers a Bunyan

27th March Reading v. Isle of Wight

"It's such a competitive sport, and the difference between winning and losing is so small" Chris Louis

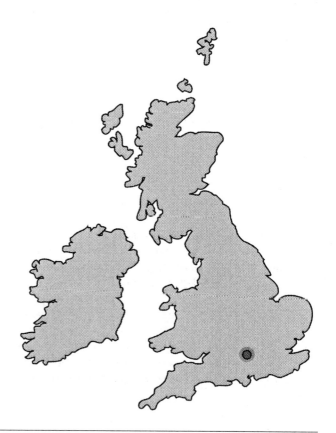

3.2 Offences
3.2.2 d) bribing or attempting to bribe any Competitor or Official
3.2.2 f) acting other than in an orderly, gentlemanly and sporting manner at all times
3.2.2 g) acting fraudulently in any manner, including giving/receiving orders to "throw" a heat or position in a heat

Easter Sunday takes me to Smallmead Stadium in Reading for my first chance to see the Racers ride this season. It's their second meeting and something of a collector's item, since it takes place on a Sunday. The match programme might also be considered something of a collector's item because the inflation that affects all sports has seen its price rise to £1.50. Still, I look to the bright side since the use of the car park is still free[1] and the attraction of speedway on a Bank Holiday weekend has already brought huge numbers of cars to the car park; well over an hour before the official start time. Like the club's

[1] BSI have now bought Reading Speedway club from Pat Bliss. They immediately signaled their ambitions by moving the club into the Elite League. They have invested in gifted riders and backroom staff accordingly. They have also, as a marketing initiative, changed the club name from the Reading Racers to the Reading Bulldogs – a name most closely associated with speedway in Bristol. BSI work closely with the local media to present their product captivatingly and have commissioned prime time satellite television adverts! Of all these immediate changes, the alteration of the club name has caused frequent complaint but these criticisms ignore previous precedent, since not only do club names change over time but also fails to appreciate that club names do not have 'exclusivity' within speedway (for example, in the Premier League, there are the Tigers of Glasgow and Sheffield). BSI have increased the match programme price to £2.50. Admittedly this is quite handsome and arguably the best looking speedway programme in the country, which is part of BSI's ongoing campaign to up the current standards of presentation throughout speedway.

The derelict back straight grandstand. © Jeff Scott

stadium, the car park has definitely seen better times. It's been pitted and potholed for years, especially if you venture away from the side of the stadium that also has the pits entrance and head towards the more careworn area and the bright lights of downtown Reading.

While it's noticeably crowded tonight compared to the savagely reduced numbers that the club has normally attracted over the past few years, it's still nothing like the heyday nights of Smallmead's early years. An arrival at this time in the late 1970s would have made you struggle to enter through the many turnstiles, never mind get to stand in your favourite spot on the terraces. I always used to stand on the high bank of the crowded second bend with George Grant, who introduced me to the sport, and who always claimed how you could definitely get the best view of all the action from there. Namely the start itself, the first corner battle, and the continuing duel for position through the second bend and up the straight. It would be many years before I moved to watch from elsewhere though, for the last few years, the small crowd numbers have afforded everyone at Smallmead the luxury of choice of anywhere they like in the stadium except the condemned stand. Recently you've even able to watch from the previously prized position directly in front of the home straight, close to the start line. Well as close as the dog track fence, which separates you from the wire track fence. It's an experience that would definitely have been an impossibility in my childhood with its packed seats and a tarmac so log-jammed with people that it was difficult to find your way through. Also the ludicrously popular bars and crowded restaurant of the main grandstand could not be entered then, unless you wished to risk that you would miss a good part of the meeting. Not that this was an option as I rarely had anything other to spend than my entrance and programme money[2]. Altogether this was an enriching childhood experience, first there was the thrill of the smell and noise of the speedway, then there were also the encounters with the first proper 'foreigners' of my youth in the form of the riders, albeit at a safe distance from behind the safety fence.

I'm sold my entrance ticket at the turnstiles by the Reading Promoter, Pat Bliss, who helps out on the gate, as she often does when it's busy. It's one of those taken-for-granted but slightly touching things that make you follow speedway, especially outside the Elite League, and is rather like going to watch Reading Football Club play football and you then find Steve Coppell at the turnstiles. Pat chats briefly about the large crowds, "I am pleased", and she shares my surprise at the fascination that an early fixture in the less-than-glamorous Premier Trophy Regional Group stage exerts over the notoriously fickle Reading speedway public.

[2] The culinary delight of the night was the occasional nibble of George's traditional but, to me, oh-so-exotic sweet and sour chicken, which he sometimes bought from the Chinese restaurant we visited on the way home. I was always fascinated by this brief taste of the Orient on the way back home to Tadley. It was a doubly exotic experience since it involved eating out, if only a takeaway, which my family never really did even with English food – let alone try to sample the cuisine of other nations. Also we always favoured my mum's delicious home-cooked food over the wasteful expense of dining out, even at the local chippie.

She's even happier when she converses about the weather, that perennial staple of British conversation, since she hopes to get the meeting over quickly because "it's cold for Easter but then it is March". Finally I make my way into the stadium proper, but only after I have also spent an inordinate time in admiration of the temporary looking awninged entranceway that adds a touch of the caravan park to the entry turnstiles, where all the talk of the terraces is food. More exactly, how to prepare, freeze and get the best from your spaghetti bolognaise[3]. It doesn't quite get my taste buds going, but it is a distraction and is definitely a topic of conversation that would have sounded completely alien in the 1970s, but now that we're so sophisticated and picky about our culinary requirements seems touchingly recherché.

The start is delayed in deference to the large crowd of eager spectators who have still to pass under the awning, through the turnstiles and onto the slight incline that takes you up towards the fourth bend of the track. From there the splendour of the stadium is laid out magnificently before you. The skyline may have changed, with the nearby country-park-style campus of the smoked-glass-fronted office buildings and the silver towers of the nearby Courage's brewery, but the basic site has not[4]. There's almost a party atmosphere, well at least in the announcer's imagination, as he breathlessly informs the waiting crowd of a double-header birthday on Tuesday 29th March. The Racers' Chris Mills will soon be 22 while a discreet veil is drawn over the actual age of team manager Ivan Shears since, "it's an official secret how old he is". We're also allowed to learn that the Isle of Wight's Krister Marsh was 29, just a few days ago on 23rd March. A further bit of quick research reveals Matej Zagar and Ulrich Ostergaard are also Arians, so we could be well on the way to one of speedway's most unusual statistics, a record number of Aries competing in tonight's fixture? In a sport that loves statistics, I'm surprised that this hasn't been considered a crucial but influential factor before! Just to be on the safe side, especially as it's the sign of the ram, I resolve to keep a close eye out for any headstrong or aggressive riding that would typify those born under this sign. I resolve to check later on the dates of Jason Crump's and Nicki Pedersen's birthdays[5].

When the first race eventually does start, Craig Boyce shows remarkable speed to the first corner and commands the rest of the race from that position. The Reading mascot, a lion sponsored by the local paper the *Evening Post*, tries to drum up some enthusiasm from the crowd by the start line, just before he heads off round the plastic-covered dog track in search of other youngsters to goad into a state of frenzy. The reserves race sees one of the rarer nations represented with Matt Tresarrieu who flies the flag for the French nation and follows in the tyre tracks of his brother Sebastian, who rather synchronistically and recently used to ride for the Isle of Wight. The inexorable branding of all contemporary activities, which even includes speedway clubs, has now been extended to the team uniforms worn in the Premier League. Reading ride in a blue uniform, which prominently displays their sponsorship by *Ideal Video*, but Matt is so new to the team that he's yet to get fitted out with this essential accoutrement. This doesn't in any way affect his riding, since the Racers' pair storm into the lead and win easily and Reading leap into an early 8-4 lead. The home crowd greatly appreciates the heat win and, for the second race of the night so early in the season, the response is truly rapturous. The tractor immediately comes out and pulls the bowser round the circuit twice to thoroughly water the track. This sets the tone for an evening of extensive and frequent grooming of the track surface, almost the equivalent of a pathological need to pamper your beloved pet fastidiously; or it would be, if you restricted this fastidiousness and attention to only one night a week. The loudspeaker blares its announcements but, in keeping with the slightly unkempt ambience of the stadium, the speaker close to where I stand by the start line mostly utters inaudible crackles. The enforced break gives Rory, which I'm going to guess is the mascot's name, the chance to work his way back to the grandstand. It also gives the disc jockey in the booth the chance to

---

[3] Much of the advice the man next to me reports to his partner comes from that noted authority, Ainsley from Ready Steady Cook who's apparently a confirmed advocate of the taste benefits of reheating from frozen (?).

[4] Except for the back-straight grandstand, which has a "Welcome to Reading Stadium" sign. Though this stand looks remarkably forlorn and remains definitively shut, due to safety reasons and so no longer fills with match-day crowds deafened by the guttural amplified roar of the bikes' engines as they repeatedly flash by.

[5] To my surprise I find that they'd confirm my interesting born under the sign of Aries and prone to aggression on the track theory, if only Crumpie wasn't born in Bristol – that's Bristol England not Australia Jason – in August. Nicki is, naturally, an Aries through and through. Even more strangely, given his inconsistency on the big occasion, it turns out ex-Reading Racers' rider Lee Richardson isn't a Gemini after all!

play some of his back catalogue, particularly those that don't usually get to be heard at wedding receptions I imagine he covers when he's not at the speedway. The music drifts back from the bend speakers so we can delight to the sounds of Seal ruminate on his complex 'Solitary Brother' before we're treated to another tune with the repetitive chorus of 'There's No Limits' which eventually serenades the tractor from the track.

The next race sees Ulrich Ostergaard draw close to the start line, but a slight delay then gives all of us the chance to study his sponsorship by 'Cabin Newsagents', an early entrant and attractive contender for the 'Mundane Sponsor of the Season' award. We only have to wait for two drawn heats before, immediately after heat 4, the tractor once again circles the Smallmead bowl on an emergency track grade. It takes three laps and the subsequent thorough rake of the uneven clods of shale it deposits randomly about the surface, which thereby gives the crowd some more time to swarm the bar area or ponder some of the great unanswered speedway questions of our time, such as "When did established riders stop selling their previous seasons leathers to newer, more impecunious but similar sized riders?" The advent of the sponsored team suit, allied to the arrival of the innovative kevlar material to replace leathers, appears to have created an automatic obsolescence into these garments that the strength and durability of the material of its construction should logically defy. Whoever might decide to purchase the discarded Ostergaard uniform in the future remains even more uncertain than for other riders, since he appears much taller than the standard and diminutive default size that typifies many of the speedway brethren.

Another drawn heat attracts the tractor out for a couple of further celebratory laps. Heat 6 turns out to be highly controversial and, even though it's only the second meeting of the season, it effectively ends Reading's challenge for any honours in 2005. On the third lap of the race, Danny Bird brilliantly overtakes Jason Bunyan with characteristic style and speed on the second bend, to only (almost immediately and unceremoniously) come to grief as he attempts to exit the next bend. This is because Bunyan appears to deliberately cut the corner to catch up but instead dramatically collides with Bird and sends him hurtling into the fence with great velocity. My own impression from an uninterrupted and close view of Bunyan's riding is that Bunyan caught Bird with a degree of accuracy and forcefulness that it is difficult to see as entirely accidental. It's often said that no rider would deliberately attempt to injure another, out of mutual respect but also because they could possibly interfere with their own immediate financial livelihood if they happened to injure themselves as well. Nonetheless, given Bunyan's many years of experience (which, for the Isle of Wight, has him line up as a heat leader), it is hard not to see his actions as deliberate; albeit probably not premeditated, but as lawyers might say: "thoughtlessly and dangerously conceived in the heat of the moment". Afterwards Bunyan, his team and the Isle of Wight management all strenuously deny any 'intent' on his behalf. This appears at variance with his unusual manner of riding that particular bend in that particular race, especially in conjunction with his subsequent path/unusual trajectory through the bend into the race leader. But then, accidents do happen, and there's no doubt that Bird has been involved in quite a severe one as he lays prostrate on the Smallmead racing surface.

What isn't in dispute is that the referee deems that Bunyan is responsible for the crash and thereby excludes him for 'unfair riding'. The strong reaction of the home crowd would leave him in little doubt that he wouldn't receive many Christmas cards that year from the Racers' fans, or Bird himself. Things certainly look very serious for quite some time and Bird lays apparently motionless by the fence for well over 20 minutes, surrounded by the St John Ambulance. The situation is serious enough for the on-track medical staff to call for a full-time ambulance crew from the Royal Berks Hospital in the city centre. Throughout this period of anxiety and fretfulness in the crowd, there are very few public announcements and the ones that there are made can't be heard where I stood. Things look so serious for Bird that the mascot has taken off his giant-sized lion's head to watch, as he stands in attendance near to the fallen rider. From other crowd members we gather that Bird has "a suspected broken leg", which would be the least of the injuries that you would have expected him to sustain, especially given the severity of the crash and his subsequent violent impact into the fence.

Adversity often throws you together with other people and, in this instance, mutual concern at the extent of Bird's injuries led me to meet my neighbouring fans. The man next to me, Paul Evans, had his own version of a commonly repeated personal history of association with the sport. In that he had watched religiously until he was 12 before he then stopped for 26 years. This was his second season back as a fan and the bug had deeply bitten him again, to such an extent that he was "totally hooked". Because he was a Wembley Lions fan as a child, one of the first tracks he'd deliberately revisited was the re-opened and resurgent Wimbledon. He felt, though, that it bore absolutely no resemblance to how he remembered it as a child, with the longer track of his memory now shrunk to a small, tight track. He also found the quality of the racing and the almost complete lack of regular overtaking a disappointment compared to other contemporary tracks and, of course, his recollections from childhood. In his recent second incarnation as a speedway fan, he'd already visited lots of the speedway tracks easily accessible from the M4 motorway: Oxford, Newport and Swindon. He was particularly enamoured with Swindon which he felt had a "great track and a great promotion". Paul has good bona fide connections to the sport as his father rode for Rye House, not to mention that his mum and dad actually met for the first time at speedway. There's no doubt that his claim to be "a true child of speedway", given his parents' credentials and connections, is true. However, he now regrets his 26 years away from the sport (a mistake his elder brother didn't make), so now he's keen to make up for his own lost years and watches with his brother as often as they can manage. Paul claims, "reasonably manage" but later concedes that it could become an obsessional but extremely fulfilling activity for them.

For Paul the contrast of speedway with football was huge. Speedway is "good value for families", especially when you take advantage of the 'kids for a quid' offers, and he sincerely feels that it is "a sport for the people". The friendliness of the people and the riders is the sort of attitude he still finds as a sponsor of a soccer team in Ryman's League, but completely doesn't exist within the higher echelons of contemporary football. The cost of seats and refreshments at Chelsea is a scandal and national disgrace in his opinion. His partner, Alison Edwards, has also grown to enjoy speedway enormously, but she strongly believes that the quality and variety of the food sold at tracks throughout the country is an area where the sport fails. Because she has a professional involvement in catering, the insult that is serving your customers poor food is particularly noticeable to her, especially since people often travel great distances to attend speedway meetings. If you're an away fan or casual visitor, it's likely that you'd arrive hungry and be happy to spend your money on well-prepared food. At best when she visits tracks with Paul, she found some adequate food but very little choice. At tracks where they struggle to survive, she believes that perhaps if the food improved it would generate more revenues and maybe attract more families keen to sample the racing and satisfy their taste buds. Ali acknowledges that it's not always possible to improve the food and drink, particularly where the clubs are tenants within the stadium and therefore don't control the provision of the food

or receive the profits. Her overall impression, as a comparative newcomer, is that of facilities stuck in the distant past with complementary old-fashioned attitudes to customer satisfaction. That said, Ali and Paul enjoy the fact that the sport appears "retro" in its stadiums, the style of its presentation and community ethos but also know that basic business sense dictates that to correct the catering provision requires little ingenuity or effort.

Ravenous from all this talk of food, I climb up to the bar area only to find huge queues of fans who have already had the same idea, only they had it earlier than me. From the vantage point of the small window in the gent's toilet, I can see that the headless lion by the dual carriageway, as he hops from paw to paw and waits for the ambulance to appear on the elegantly named A33 Relief Road. As I watch, the mascot directs the arriving vehicle to the side of the stadium, so they can gain access to Bird who still lies in pain on the track. By the time I'm back in my place, the ambulance crew has carefully and gingerly loaded the stricken rider onto the stretcher and rushed him off for treatment at the hospital. Paul says he's heard that Bird has sustained a "suspected broken tibia and fibula in his left leg". This, if correct, would probably signal the end of the season for Danny, even if you allow for the prodigious recovery rates of speedway riders from injury.

In heat 7 Reading's top notch Aries (Matej Zagar) storms to another easy win, but after that the home side's challenge hits the buffers because they concede three successive 5-1s and so trail by six points after ten heats completed. The only real interest for the home fans now is the chance to vent their considerable ire towards Jason Bunyan in extremely vociferous fashion, which they do without respite, when he finally returns to the scene of the crime in heat 8. Zagar rides to a faultless win in the next race but is not offered effective support by the inexperienced Chris Johnson. The home crowd grows restless and an exuberant wheelie of celebration by Zagar hardly stirs any response from them. If the wheelie had been judged for artistic merit and interpretation, it definitely would have scored very highly since Zagar executes his celebration one handed and with both feet on the handlebars. I'm not sure where but last season a celebrating rider had the misfortune and embarrassment to hit the track tractor on his victory lap, an event that left him red faced and in pain[6]. Zagar is too skilful a rider to commit this basic error, but the tractor is nonetheless out for yet another grade of the track.

Danny Bird's injury deprives the Racers of his services in the vital heat 13, a race that sees Boyce stamp his authority on the race to inflict

---

[6] Jamie Smith of Somerset broke his leg after he collided with the track grader at King's Lynn on 29th March 2006 on his second lap of celebration. It was an accident in which the rider was fortunate to escape without more serious injury.

Zagar's only defeat of the night. Bunyan is again very loudly booed but it doesn't affect the score. Immediately after this heat, there's a collection for Danny Bird among the large crowd to which people give very enthusiastically. The reasons for this instant response seem partly to do with sympathy for his injuries and the undoubted future loss of his earnings, but it's also a function of the sport itself, mainly because I believe that it remains more closely in touch with its audience. It's a closeness that appears to unite those all involved throughout speedway, whether in the crowd, behind the scenes or its participants on the track.

To reduce the difference in the scores and to create the slim outside chance that Reading will recover enough to win the meeting in the last two races, Zagar lines up as a tactical substitute in heat 14. This dreadful rule has gained some currency in the sport and, it's widely suspected, it was created in order to artificially generate some excitement in matches for Sky Sports television coverage; particularly where, early in proceedings, it's already apparent that the contest will be one-sided. While all fans will invariably be pleased when the team they support benefits from this ruling, the great majority of loyal and die-hard speedway fans actively dislike this artificial manipulation of results. Many people consider it as another measure cynically introduced due to the self-interest of the Elite League promoters because of their peculiarly close relationship with Sky Sports television and the need for 'entertainment' at all costs during its live coverage. It's definitely a regulation that works against speedway's public perception as a serious sport. The rule works for the purpose for which it was intended though, since it does undoubtedly but artificially enhance any dreadfully one-sided fixture that the Sky Sports programme planners accidentally or contractually chose to televise live[7].

In the event, Zagar wins very easily and is ably supported by his keen grass tracker and locally based team-mate with the boyish features, Andrew Appleton. The 8-1 heat score does in fact reduce the deficit to a more competitive 42-45. This creates some additional interest in the final heat, which has now become effectively a last heat decider. Any momentary quickening of the pulse immediately ceases, among the Smallmead faithful, when Craig Boyce splits the home pair to deny Reading an unlikely and undeserved victory. Zagar follows Prince's sage advice to party like its 1999, when he celebrates his victory lap with some more ecstatic wheelies, just as the crowd, mostly disconsolately, simultaneously starts to file from the stadium. Zagar has scored 20 points out of the home team's 46 points, which emphasises his importance and throws into sharp relief the need the club has for support from riders, like Bird, to ensure that it challenges for honours. Bird's injury spells a season of frustration ahead and, no doubt, this realisation contributes to the sombre mood of the fans as they exit the stadium and troop into the car park. From a financial point of view for the Racers, his injury is also extremely bad news since this is the largest crowd I can remember here in many years and now is highly unlikely to be repeated in 2005.

29th March Reading v. Isle of Wight (Premier Trophy) 46-47[8]

---

[7] Whatever the real reasons, the measure undermines the 'integrity' of the match scores – particularly relevant in the context of the allocation of the additional bonus point awarded because of the aggregate score – since it introduces the potential anomaly that the double points of a second placed rider scoring more (four points) than the winner (three points). This defeats common sense and fair play in one fell stroke.

[8] The next day I check the Reading Racers' official website for news on Bird's injuries. In the manner that the Matrix, in the film of the same name, always and instantly corrects itself to seamlessly restore the facsimile appearance of order, so it is that the language of officialdom throughout speedway always exudes excessive diplomacy, usually anodyne, and often to the point where it deliberately insults your intelligence. Or appears at variance to what you thought you saw. The Reading site opts for masterly understatement in the match report:
"Bird got into a tussle with former Racer Jason Bunyan on the third bend of heat 6, with Bunyan appearing to leave Bird no room coming off the fourth turn and the Reading rider crashing heavily into the fence".

Showered in Shale

Chapter 2: Clash of the Champions
April 13th Poole v. Belle Vue

"We're just about to see the incident, why don't you talk us through it" Jonathan Green (to practically every rider every televised Sky meeting)

6.7 The cleaning of motorcycles is not permitted at Speedway meetings except where specifically designated facilities are provided. In all cases the use of water without the addition of chemical products is recommended

What could be better than an early season trip to Wimborne Road to watch the Pirates, the reigning League champions, take on the Belle Vue Aces, who many pundits predict will replace the Pirates as Elite League champions this season. It's another trip to a speedway meeting with my publisher friend Stefan Usansky, proud citizen of Manchester who lives away from that city on missionary work in the South of England. He's one of nature's gentlemen, invariably optimistic although he is a fanatical Manchester United season ticket holder, but few hold this dedication against him since his partisan blindness for all things Red is balanced by his love of sports in particular and his keen membership of Lancashire County Cricket Club. As a native of Manchester he's always been an Aces' fan and for the last few years I've gone with him to watch the Aces when they visit Arlington. His visits haven't been a good luck charm for Belle Vue on their travels but they also haven't been short of incident. A meeting a few years ago (Stef's first visit to speedway in a criminally long 36 years), saw a bike catch fire right by us at the start, and Stefan was mystified since he couldn't see the flames as the methanol burnt. It was also fun to watch him suffer as the temperatures dropped considerably – as they always do at Arlington –

after the early warmth of a late summer's evening had lured Stef to wear some colonial-style shorts. Our visit last season enabled us to see a fantastic speedway race between Jason Crump and Nicki Pedersen that was worth the admission money on its own, as they vied for the lead and rode handlebar to handlebar throughout. Arguably the race of the season in 2004 and maybe the best match race I've ever seen or, at least, can genuinely recall.

Stefan is a good friend and an excellent travelling companion, full of firmly held opinions allied to a good sense of fun, inquisitiveness about people and compassionate acceptance of their foibles or failings. We fight our way through the surprisingly dense rush-hour traffic from Southampton to Poole and find ourselves in good time for the start of the meeting, as we queue in bright sunshine to pass through the turnstiles. The entrance area has a bright modern aspect that's unusual for speedway tracks but, simultaneously, very bland as it's modelled on the look of the cramped, inferior sports club facilities that you often find within contemporary hotels with pretensions to be better than they are.

Although it is only mid April you could have mistaken it for a summer's day, especially since thick clouds have just started to clear away to leave almost perfect conditions for an evening to watch and enjoy the speedway. Stef has keenly anticipated his visit to Wimborne Road Stadium since he always loves a winner, but also because of my description of Poole as the 'Manchester United of speedway'. Perhaps I should have called them the 'Chelsea of speedway' but decided to spare myself Stef's traditional rant about the Russian provenance of Chelsea's owner's money and how these allegedly ill-gotten gains corrupt the sport. Bathed in the aura of the comparison with his beloved Red Devils as we enter the very imposing glass-fronted home-straight grandstand, he's immediately impressed and comfortable on his first-ever visit to the stadium. It's already very busy, the tables are crowded and the bar area, with its large and dramatic image of a speedway rider above it, has attracted quite a few early drinkers. With a love of the catering at sports grounds everywhere, Stef finds it hard not to sample the delights of the cuisine on offer or to pass up the lure of the chance to join another queue. His sunny mood matches the evening and, upon reflection, it was a delightful evening of casual conversation, competitive speedway racing and unassuming company[1].

After he's appreciatively stuffed his face, we are free to explore the grandstand and so we go up the nearby stairs to investigate the view of the track you get from there. Stef leads the way and at the top of the stairs, when asked about programmes by the staff there, Stef politely thanks them for their interest and said we already have ours. Once we

---

[1] We were unaware at that time that Stefan was already seriously unwell though, at the time of writing, he is, thankfully, in remission.

arrive upstairs, we discover that you get a wonderful panoramic view of the whole speedway track and the well-covered greyhound track for that matter. You could also walk the length of the glass-fronted home straight to the end that overlooks the home side of the pits and study the frenetic activity there, from within the warmth of the grandstand or, if you choose, outside on the fire escape steps. But, the most notable thing about upstairs was our surprise to find a large buffet spread out on many tables, to which a waitress invites us to help ourselves, after she has pointed out the nearby paper plates. It's one of those unexpected moral dilemmas: whether to immediately tuck in, when you know that you're there by accident or under false pretences; and you can imagine them scolding you when they discover you are gatecrashers and embarrassingly throwing you out with your half-eaten sausage roll. As we'd accidentally stumbled upon what was apparently a party, or at least a fun gathering, it seemed churlish not to join in the spirit of it. At least Stef thought so, although I was more reluctant. Though he'd just eaten, ever practical and uncomplicated, Stef really needed no second invitation to tuck into the available food with vigour and relish, albeit slightly pickily. These characteristics typify him and probably explain his slim figure, particularly notable for a man of his age after years of high exposure to a lifetime's worth of business lunches.

Since we do not wish to abuse our good fortune, we decline the offer of more 'free' programmes ("how many can you fill out at one meeting anyway?" Stef pondered) or the chance to pick up a baseball cap emblazoned with the club's sponsor's logo[2]. Instead, we do briefly gorge ourselves on the selection of chicken drumsticks, mini quiches, cocktail sausages, crisps and quartered sandwiches. We soon gather that the whole upstairs area and buffet is set aside for the exclusive use of the Pirates' sponsors and their specially invited guests. No one would deny that it's an impressive facility at which to gather and entertain your clients, but especially so if you're a sponsor of Poole Speedway club. Their impressive dominance on the track over the past few years, and throughout their history if you listen to their fans, is even more well planned and executed off it, especially if you judge them on the basis of the event we just inadvertently gatecrashed. You can dine and watch extremely comfortably, easily overlook all the action on the track and in the pits as well as, if you happen to miss the odd exciting moment when the food and drink distracts for a moment, you can see it instantly replayed on one of the many television screens dotted throughout the dining area. I'm not sure that I'll get to see such impressive facilities anywhere else on my travels to other speedway tracks. It all reflects so well on Poole Speedway and their main sponsor, RIAS, that we're now curious, and guilty enough, to bother to find out what on earth they do as a business, when they're not kindly sponsoring the Pirates or providing a second tea for Stef. I vaguely remember that the previous major sponsors at Poole specialised in lifts and a brief look at speedway sponsors throughout the country instantly tells you that they cover a heterogeneous and improbable mix of business specialisations. Fortunately, I can safely say that I'm not within the target demographic of the RIAS group and, subsequently, I find that their adverts state they're "specialists in home and car insurance for the over-50s". Stef has no excuse for his ignorance, but he vainly tries to find one anyway. For once, the sponsor appears to have chosen their sport well, especially given both the age profile of the sport's traditional followers, and Poole is surrounded by places where the wealthy aspire to retire to in their later years. You just know from the prosperous streets of the town that the local area is filled with proud homeowners, only too keen to take the theft of personal property and their insurance responsibilities seriously.

As the fixture nears its start, we make our way round to the covered grandstand on the home straight of the stadium. It's already very crowded but we're lucky enough to get a couple of seats almost parallel with the start line. Inevitably, there's a good mix of generations, and a casual glance at our near neighbours definitely illustrates that this is a family-oriented sport. Behind us we have an OAP father and two grown-up sons who are his spitting image, while in front we have an old man with his son and grandson. Seated in front of them, we can see a grandmother and her grandson. Stef doesn't appreciate my comment that we might also be mistaken for father and son, and he quickly points out our different surnames (how will they guess these?) as well as our obvious physical and facial dissimilarities. For some reason, this instantly reminds me of his story about when he received an excitable junk mail letter from *Reader's Digest* that advised

[2] Though later the lure of a free car sticker advertising the local 2CR radio station is too hard to resist.

him "out of all the Usanskys in Kidlington, you have been chosen to win a special prize", if only he subscribed to said publication. Given that Usansky is such a rare surname ("we were the only freaking Usanskys in Kidlington – the only other people I've met with the Usansky name were my mother and brother"), *Reader's Digest* could definitely learn a lot from the RIAS marketing department.

When I finally get the chance to read the programme, I learn that the home-team promoters, billed as "Mike and Matt" (which sounds like a comedy team from a third-rate holiday camp, or some hospital radio disc jockeys), expect to be "pushed to the limit" tonight by the "powerful" visiting Aces. That's my expectation too, as an interested but neutral visitor, and hopefully we will see many exciting close races.

The announcer makes a point of "welcoming our friends from Manchester", though a casual glance round the crowded grandstand or a survey of the fans who stand on the open terraces, doesn't reveal many Aces' fans who were prepared to journey to the south coast during mid week. Given the supposedly legendary support and rich history that promoter Ian Thomas always stresses, you'd have expected more of an effort for the so-called clash of the speedway giants. In fact, there's not a famous but distinctive sombrero to be seen or Mancunian accent to be heard, except for Stef's, within earshot or elsewhere throughout the evening. The sight of the start-line girls strutting their stuff in their unfeasibly skimpy clothes on a cold evening – they wear Poole crop-top kevlars set off with coloured flags to help identify the riders' helmet colours – inevitably draws Stefan's attention and sympathy. His concern increases further with each additional race and the rapid fall in the temperatures, as the night progresses, compounds his anxieties. The bare stomachs of the start-line girls notwithstanding, the Pirates race to an easy 5-1 heat victory in the first race with hardly a challenge from the visitors after the first 10 yards. Though the race is notable for its small details, as Bjarne Pedersen trails his steel-shoed foot into each corner to create a shower of sparks throughout the race. In the next race, the veteran rider Andy Smith fully justifies his surprising pre-season selection as the Aces' reserve, when he uses all his experience and track craft to gradually negotiate his way past both Poole riders for a craftily deserved victory.

The next race is processional throughout, particularly after the Aces' Kenneth Bjerre quickly decides not to continue to challenge his Poole counterparts after the second bend of the first lap. The heat after provides the first real excitement and perhaps the race of the night, when Ryan Sullivan out-gates fellow Aussie and defending World Champion, Jason Crump, which is the signal to commence a four-lap neck-and-neck tussle for superiority. Sadly, like the Jack Nicholson film of that name, it's *As Good As It Gets* for the rest of the fixture from a racing point of view, since Poole have already created a 10 point deficit that the Aces never look likely to close and even less likely to overhaul. Not that this is anything like a disappointment to the stands thronged with partisan Poole supporters. They positively revel in each heat victory, no matter how predictable or processional; particularly the OAP in front of us who leaps to his feet with great agility in exaltation, after almost every race, to wave his Poole programme board delightedly. The entire crowd appears to watch in the full expectation that their riders will definitely win every single race. These, I suppose, are the expectations that continual success fosters, even in the most modest fan; but it is an attitude and atmosphere that will create undue pressure on the Pirates' riders, should the results or the collective mood ever turn sour. As a group of fans they celebrate uproariously and without restraint, but also without the vainglorious gloats and chants that often afflicts more popular sports like football. As the points pile up in the Pirates' favour, Stef's broad Mancunian accent appears to become more and more pronounced.

In heat 6, to my mind, the Flag Marshal stands so far onto the track, almost on gate 2, as he waves the chequered flag with gusto that he impedes, and thereby prevents, Andy Smith's charge to the line for an attempted third place. Though, the referee apparently doesn't notice this or, if he does, chooses to ignore it. There's a glimmer of hope for the miniscule number of Aces' fans at Wimborne Road when, at the start of the next race, Bjerre manages to out-gate Sullivan, though this ends after just two bike lengths when his machine rears and his resulting loss of speed costs him valuable race positions. During the subsequent heat, Simon Stead overtakes Ricky Ashworth spectacularly on the third lap to keep the scores within the bounds of respectability and retains the possibility that the fixture still remains a viable contest, but still the home fans get to celebrate deliriously when Kasprzak wins comfortably.

The beautiful pink, red and blue hues of the sky are something special to savour, when we look out over the stadium towards the brightly lit skyline that is the nearby Poole town centre. Ferjan's victory from the start over Crump, while on a supposedly face-saving tactical ride, is enjoyed by the crowd who don't appear that they will ever tire of winning, no matter how routinely processional the race turns out. I'm thankful for the interval break that gives Stef the chance to take a brief but enjoyable stroll down memory lane. He fondly recalls when he went to watch the Aces race at Hyde Road on a Saturday night as a teenager, when "it was always full with crowds of around 10,000". The whole Hyde Road area was a magnet for Stef and his friends with its theme park, fun fair, dance halls and the wrestling – all located in the same place. Often "as a gang of us" they'd try to combine as many sports events as they could together into the same day. They'd watch Manchester United play on a late summer or early autumn afternoon before they would go to the speedway at Hyde Road, or *The Zoo* as it was known locally. In the summer they'd participate in the athletics with Sale Harriers before they would head off to watch the Aces, and also preferably manage to sneak in to see the last few rounds of the wrestling. "The speedway was always 7.30 to 9 pm-ish, whereas the wrestling was 7.30 to 10 p.m., so we'd sneak in to watch the last few bouts". With eyes that dance and glisten, Stef notes, "your memory starts to plays tricks – it was always sunny when I used to go – but my abiding recollection is the smell, the enormity of the stadium with stands on both sides and round the bends at Hyde Road and always the sheer enthusiasm of the supporters". His favourite was Peter Craven "who held the track record for years" and he recalls the hostile but ultimately good-natured booing of Ove Fundin or Barry Briggs whenever they happened to visit. The whole experience and that time of his life in general "still holds very special memories". Stef thinks he started to go often to Hyde Road around 1958 and 1959, which was also when he won the Manchester Schools Athletics Championship for running in the 220 yards race, before he adds the small but important qualifier "for my age group!"[3]

---

[3] This is a typically pedantic and very Stefan-like comment. He has a scrapbook of newspaper clippings from that era that detail his sporting achievements. These were many and various – football, swimming and athletics mostly – and the scrapbook always falls open at another page of his sporting exploits ("wonder boy Usansky") from the *Manchester Evening News Football Green* or the *Manchester Evening News Football Pink*. The reports mostly reveal his speed, close control and skill scoring a hat trick. These newspaper reports, accidentally, are also littered with reports from long ago fixtures that featured the great Aces of Belle Vue. Stef never rode a speedway bike nor had the inclination to try with so much else to compete at throughout his teenage years. When I encountered Stef for the first time when he was already 'old' (at 42) in 1988, and these scrapbooks detailing his athleticism now appear an even more incongruous contrast with the man I've come to know, when I see them years later. They do explain a lot about his love and fanatical interest in practically all sports – "though I just can't stand horse racing" – as both a keen doer and a keen watcher.

While the Aces perform poorly compared to our expectations, Stef ponders the itinerant life of the travelling speedway rider before he notes, "these speedway riders work really hard – having to race, prepare their bikes and do all the travelling". As if to prove how hard they work, back on the track Jason Crump and Bjarne Pedersen put on a tremendous display of competitive racing in a closely fought heat 13 that they spend practically locked together throughout its duration, before the home advantage finally tells to stir still more sustained delight from the crowd. Poole is the type of place that attracts large crowds, by contemporary speedway standards, and it appears that there are almost an equal number of fans to cars in the car park when we overlook it from the apex of the final bend. We've retreated here from the warmth of the stand to the comparative cool freshness of the clear evening, to watch heat 15 and in order to make a quick getaway ahead of the majority of the voluble Poole fans. In the cold air of the open terraces, Stefan's concern for the poor warmth provided by the skimpy clothes of the start-line girls increases still further. Watched from this position, we get a very different perspective on the racing (and the girls), which definitely looks much more stately when viewed from this angle, particularly compared to the sheer speed of the riders that you notice from the grandstand. But then appearances are deceptive, though it does give us the chance to get showered in shale but not the bright stream of sparks that repeatedly fly from Pedersen's steel shoe as it scrapes along the track surface.

In the car, Stef's impressions of the contemporary version of the sport that he's seen, has only given him a comparison between the not exactly typical of speedway facilities at Arlington and Wimborne Road. Poole wins this comparison hands down in his opinion "it's a much better atmosphere than Eastbourne, everything about it's better in fact – bigger crowds who are more enthusiastic and have better facilities". I'm not sure that he's really comparing like with like. Nonetheless, he's adamant that even when there were some extremely boisterous and vocal Belle Vue fans present at Arlington, unlike tonight at Wimborne Road, the atmosphere just didn't compare to the vibrancy that he experienced in the Poole grandstand tonight. Even when he discounts accidentally gatecrashing the sponsor's buffet, however much it was enjoyed by Mr Usansky, he notes, "it's much more like a football crowd here, just without the obscene chanting or threat of violence! So many people just don't know that speedway still exists, well may be Belle Vue, but not Poole or Eastbourne, so they never get to enjoy it or know what it's like".

13th April Poole v. Belle Vue (Elite League A) 53-41

Chapter 3: The latest 'Final Farewell'
21st April Oxford v. Arena Essex

"He keeps mutating the strain of what it takes to be the world's best speedway rider" Gary Havelock (on Tony Rickardsson)

RANDOM SCB RULES

2.1 Tactical Ride (TR): A Tactical Ride in which the Programmed riders points scored are doubled towards the teams score. NB. The riders starts from the Starting Gate.

Tactical Substitute (TS): as above except... NB. The rider starts from a 15 metre handicap

---

The rare chance to see the great Tony Rickardsson ride in the UK this season is too difficult to resist. He has a temporary assignment to race for the Arena Essex Hammers in place of the injured Mark Loram. It's symptomatic of the problems of British speedway and indicative of the status of our Leagues that the world's best speedway rider no longer chooses to compete full time in this country. The ostensible reasons given for this decision – the need to spend more time with his family, the demands of his travel schedule and, most significantly, the need to concentrate on the Grand Prix series – just after Rickardsson finished riding for Poole mostly sound plausible enough but don't quite ring true in the context of the short duration of any speedway career. Although there's no doubt that Rickardsson has sufficient financial independence to no longer have to chase every penny. Also as a gifted driver, ignoring his skill on a bike, he's had a number of flirtations with an alternative career racing high-performance cars. When push comes to shove, British speedway has become a stagnant backwater that no longer holds his attention or interest. It's a decision that should worry fans and promoters alike, since its symptomatic of the relative decline in the status of speedway in this country compared to Sweden or Poland and

maybe a sign of the future when it comes to the attitudes of the sports superstars[1].

Whatever the reasons, Rickardsson is quite open about the fact that this is a temporary assignment for him at the start of his season, since it provides the ideal way for him to gain match fitness in preparation for his tilt at his sixth world championship victory. It makes good sense to sharpen his already considerable skills and technique as well as sort out his bike set up's in Britain at a time when the Polish and Swedish league seasons have yet to start. His decision is Arena's gain and, for a limited period, that of the British speedway public; who get an infrequent opportunity to watch him race in the original *team* version of the sport that most people consider its true form.

I, too, am delighted to get the chance. I take my kicks where I can and so I leave for Oxford where I've managed to combine the trip with a rare job interview in the publishing industry, where I enjoyed a long career before my redundancy. I arrive in Oxford so early for the interview that I have time to go the Tesco's superstore adjacent to Sandy Lane, home of the Oxford Silver Machine. A short distance away across the car park I spot what appears to be your typical speedway rider's transit van, albeit that this one is grey rather than the more ubiquitous white colour. Under the pretext of a stroll to stretch my legs, I wander past to look at the two blokes who chat animatedly by the van's rear doors. Since I'm without my glasses, I'm not quite certain if one of them is the world number 3, Greg Hancock. Even though we're so close to Sandy Lane that you can see the floodlights and glimpse the top of the grandstand roof, I decide that it's definitely not him. Mostly because he looks so unlike my mind's-eye image of him from the television and the speedway press, but also because he appears so small and it seems peculiar to arrive nearly six hours before the fixture's start time. After my near brush with what is effectively speedway royalty, I drive to fill up at the petrol station. Then it occurs to me that I've never seen Greg in his civilian clothes before, I have no real idea of his height and then remember the clincher that he lives with his wife and baby son Wilbour in Sweden. If he lived in Britain, even if he were exceptionally keen to arrive at the track early, there would be no way he'd wish to hang about for six hours beforehand. However, if he'd only flown in that morning, it would make sense that he'd arrive early to ensure that he doesn't encounter any flight delays or traffic problems. On this assumption of his professionalism and because I'd only kick myself it was him, I decide to return to learn if it is the man himself and try for a brief chat. Back in the car park, the van is now locked, the blokes have vanished and, after a complete inspection of the

[1] Particularly as speedway in Poland is so lucrative and, like Sweden, both have started to move beyond just staging fixtures on their historic 'fixed' race nights of Sundays and Tuesdays. This trend to extend racing programmes has become very visible in 2006 and, unless the situation is properly managed by the respective speedway federations, will soon present riders with fixture clashes and the need for a supposedly difficult, but in reality, easy choice about where to ride.

exterior of the van, there's none of the usual signs that say 'Joe Bloggs Speedway rider', or any indication at all of whose van it is. No garish logos, traditionally from various not-quite-famous, provincial or obscure sponsors, festoon every panel of the van. Such a scheme is one that many speedway riders appear to favour, always a mosaic of contrasting signs as though the van had been decorated in a style favoured by a spatially challenged manic who fancied themselves as an artist.

Now I've retrieved my glasses, the fan in me has taken over and my thirst for a brief encounter with celebrity has banished all thoughts of my interview. My attempt to determine if the man in question was actually Greg has been made easier by actually being able to see properly. Inside the store, I quickly spot the world number 3 just as he was to be served next at the checkout near the restaurant and the customer toilets. My initial thought was that he'd obviously had a lot of time on his hands, since the small number of items he intended to buy would have normally let him stand in the '10 items or fewer' checkout queue rather than the slower checkout he'd chosen. I greet him with the immortal lines, "excuse me, are you Greg Hancock?" It's a rhetorical question since I can now definitely see that it is indeed him; but I decide it's a polite question since I'm not quite sure what the correct etiquette is to interrupt speedway riders as they shop, off duty, for a few basic necessities. The checkout girl looks at me with disdain, while Greg smiles broadly and replies, "I am, indeed!" She doesn't quite know what to make of this famous person she's never heard of in her checkout aisle, so instead she gawps at us both and then quickly scans the items in the Hancock basket.

I can't say that I'd ever given it too much thought as what would fill the average (or above average) speedway rider's shopping basket; probably just the same as any other man on the street, except that there would probably be no alcohol and definitely no medication. Especially since the list of banned substances is now so long and the manufacturers of most health products appear to pride themselves on their inadvertently administered 'help' to ensure that sports people often fail their random drug tests. Speedway riders also have a tradition that they bear their complex and painful injuries manfully, so there would definitely be no aspirins, Vick's nasal spray or Night Nurse in any modern rider's basket, no matter how great his pain or snotty the cold. Since he's a recent father you might reasonably expect the Hancock basket to contain a few nappies but given that the mother and baby are, no doubt, still safely at home in Sweden, there are none. In fact, as his purchases move down the conveyor belt in *The Generation Game* fashion, it's clear that Greg has avoided the cuddly toy and deliberately only chosen practical items. Rather predictably, he's chosen food and drink, in his case, a large bottle of still water, a standard pasta salad (rather than one from 'The Finest'™ selection they have at Tesco) and a fashionable wrap-style sandwich from the 'Healthy Eating' range. These choices probably reveal the cultured palate he gained through his cosmopolitan childhood in America as well as a concern with his weight. But as you look at him dressed in jeans, green jumper and black trainers, you would not imagine that he had any weight issues, since he appears to be a remarkably slight and slim gentleman. Too lean, perhaps, which is a surprise given his itinerant lifestyle potentially means lots of exposure to junk and airline food while he travels to a different country and different racetrack almost every day throughout the summer. And, especially praiseworthy, since he will shortly be 35, which is the sort of age where traditionally your normally svelte waistline starts to go unexpectedly awry, even for charming Taureans like Greg.

But back to Greg, who quickly packs his own plastic bag, after politely refusing with a broad smile and a "no", the checkout girl's mandatory offer of help. Her suggestion was given in a surly monotone that dares you to accept the offer, especially if you're under the pensionable age. He's bought four of the same roll-on deodorant — one of those more sportily packaged varieties — in bright colours (blue and black) that attract the casual male shopper. It's certainly attracted Greg to buy them in bulk, which may be because there was a special offer that was difficult to overlook or possibly because to ride a speedway bike professionally is generally extremely sweaty work. Then again, perhaps, he's bought some of his team-mates an unusual gift of deodorant which, given his reputation as a nice chap, would probably be out of concern and respect more than anything else. Come to think of it, there's quite a fashion for sleeveless tops, or no top at all, below the kevlar race suits for the riders. This is partly a function of practicality but also a desire to strut your stuff like a peacock or to territorially mark out your small area of the pits. At least this chance encounter has established that Greg is as dedicated to the elimination of potential body odours off the track as he is dedicated to success upon it.

While I still ponder the mystery of his bulk purchase, Greg pays in cash and flourishes his Tesco club card. This is final proof, if proof were needed, about the down-to-earth normality of the sport's practitioners. The very idea that Greg's collects club-card points for his discount vouchers shows commendable parsimony, particularly as he lives in Sweden, but still boggles the mind when this loyalty card is in the hands of a top sportsman. Could we seriously imagine that David Beckham or John Terry own a club card? Take that back, we can't even imagine that they would shop for food or other small essential items, except, obviously, if Becks needs to buy clothes or a secret top up mobile phone for some illicit text messages or if John Terry needs *The Racing Post* to check the form before he lashes out obscene quantities of cash down at the bookies. Greg has shown himself to be such a man of the people that I can't prevent myself and enquire why he's here, "I'm just shopping for a bite to eat later and I'm going to eat in the café with my friend over there" he says, as he nods towards the other bloke I'd seen earlier who now sits at a table by the window that overlooks banks of gridlocked trolleys. I take the chance to explain about my research, travel plans and my intentions for my book. Greg asks a few questions and seems genuinely interested in what I might cover. He's been asked a few times to write his autobiography but has so far refused. He modestly notes, "I'm not planning to just yet as I don't have anything to say". I beg to differ, before we then both agree that the family nature of the sport is a big factor in its general appeal. Greg has always consciously tried to "remember the people", especially since some riders find it easy to forget these simple courtesies when they become more successful and absorbed in their own concerns. "I've been everything – spectator, fan and rider" so, no matter what sort of evening's racing he's had, Greg doesn't forget that everyone plays their own vital part in the whole equation. He's honest enough to admit that he increasingly has to remind himself about this, since to find the time for the fans every night can easily get lost in the mix of everyday life, never mind the many demands and the inevitable complexity of your international travel schedule when you're a successful rider. Greg has successfully managed to balance all these demands very capably, but the key for him is to avoid injury, mostly because, for each individual rider, ultimately "success in the Grand Prix is everything". He acknowledges to me that he's mostly seen and done it all before in his speedway life, but stresses that he is fortunate since he still retains the hunger and desire to want to do it all over again!

As I have observed his career from afar, Greg has always appeared genuine, friendly and a real ambassador for the sport. When I mention this, he thanks me for my praise but notes, "everyone is different" and it all "depends on how you're brought up". In his case being open and considerate, where possible, is "just the way I was brought up". Even during our impromptu chat in Tesco's, when he has other things to do, appears indicative of this approach to life. He hopes I enjoy my visit to the track tonight and that I collect lots of good material for my book. He happily signs an autograph and then, as we part, nods at my suit and enquires, "if you're coming to the speedway, how come you're dressed so smart?" I explain about my job interview and he stops, once more, to ask a few pertinent questions about what the job is, what the responsibilities will involve and the reputation of the company. It can't really matter to him but he does seem genuinely interested, he then wishes me "good luck!" with a smile and cheerful wave as he strolls off to his table with his Tesco carrier bag. As I leave the shop, I feel confident that accidentally meeting Greg in Tesco's has been a lucky coincidence and positive omen for the interview. After our chat though, I'm now cutting it fine to arrive at the interview exactly on time, where I will listen to a middle manager with a grandiose job title.

Later that evening the main grandstand terraces of Sandy Lane is bathed in the late spring sunshine. I'm relieved that I've had my interview and aptitude test and have now changed into more comfortable attire[2]. The stadium fills up with a large contingent of Oxford fans and a variety of other fans in their local team's colours, which also includes Reading, Swindon and not just the luminous red of tonight's visitors Arena Essex. There's the inevitable interesting mix of generations and characters that take up their favoured positions to watch the pre-meeting introductions and parade of the riders. Undoubtedly the attraction of Tony Rickardsson has drawn additional spectators to the stadium and thereby causes the extra buzz in the atmosphere rather than the mere thrill of the visit of Arena, who notoriously aren't the best travellers away from the their home base of Thurrock. Tonight is supposed to be Tony's last scheduled UK appearance this season, since it's the end of his short stint with Arena and just before he seriously gets on with the task of his attempt to try to equal Ivan Mauger's record of six World Championship titles[3].

While we wait I scan the Oxford programme and I notice that the promoter Nigel 'Waggy' Wagstaff favours a comprehensive approach to his meeting notes. He gives the fans a lengthy outline of news and events, as seen from his own particular point of view, in a column rather wonderfully called the 'Engine Room'. The warm welcome the visitor's receive is partly traditional and partly based on the optimism that the rare arrival of a team that Oxford would expect to beat necessarily encourages. Although tonight the ease of this task has been somewhat complicated by a serious early season injury to one of Oxford's star riders, Billy Hamill. In the programme we learn that the search for an adequate replacement has proved difficult and that instead, as he makes a virtue out of necessity and economic good sense, Waggy would prefer to try to develop young rider talent with a long-term eye to the future. Waggy also outlines, in some detail, his latest marketing initiative which takes the form of a competition for children who, in order to enter, will try to get posters that advertise the speedway pasted throughout the local area. The eventual lucky winner will become the Oxford team mascot for the evening, wear a replica shirt for the night (only!), also get their chance to meet their favourite riders before the meeting, and finally sit with Waggy at his post-meeting press conference. So there's quite an incentive to enter. Both in terms of the prize and a bona fide excuse to stay up late, for the enthusiastic Oxford-supporting youngster as well as for their parents, who will get the chance to accompany the winner. Waggy's writing style in the programme, except for its length, is a master class in the genre. He easily manages to combine the optimism and defensiveness of a teenage text message with a healthy degree of spin, while he avoids difficult topics and almost appears honest and straightforward.

It's the third home meeting of the season and the programme includes a rather unique insert that details the 'History of Oxford Speedway'. Tonight we've reached 1950 an era of "excellent racing" and exceptionally "large crowds" that thrilled to the action on the track, especially in the local derbies with Swindon or that delighted in the specially produced "excellent souvenir programmes".

---

[2] I subsequently learn in a pleasantly emollient but rather sweaty bottomed letter of rejection, that I'm over-qualified for the position in question and the management team (both of them) worried that my opportunities for career progression would be stymied in that business unit by my own understandable great, but as yet unexpressed, ambitions. What bollocks.

[3] Though mostly gained under a different format to the one-off finals Ivan was so successful at winning.

I stand by the start gate where I'm lucky enough to bump into a chatty couple, Arlene and Peter Digweed. She's been a speedway fan for many years, since she was 18, and Peter has been one for so long that he's inevitably developed many strong opinions on the sport. Though it's quickly apparent that he's closer in outlook to the racing days outlined in the insert on the 1950s than he is to the present. He claims with delight, "to be still living in 1966", and still tries to live in a contemporary version of the past without modern-day complications and distractions like mobile phones or computers. Given his relish for an uncomplicated past, he definitely views speedway as his sport, particularly because it already has its best days behind it. The fact that he believes it takes place in stadiums that look like they belong behind the Iron Curtain, and have the facilities and services to match, also adds to the appeal for him. Both love the spectacle and Arlene confesses, "I just love men in leathers". They describe the riders as a breed apart, who mix heroism and madness in equal parts since they "risk their lives five or six times a night for peanuts". Peter bemoans that most speedway stadiums depend on other minority sports to actually survive and that a great spectator sport like speedway finds itself in the hands of the greyhound or stock-car people and so often struggles with poor facilities. Sandy Lane is a case in point; the dogs are its main activity with occasional speedway thrown in as an afterthought. Peter also feels that members of the average crowd now attracted to the sport are slightly peculiar. To illustrate this point he theatrically looks around him at the crowded grandstand before he notes, too loudly for my liking, "there's always a high percentage of weirdoes in the crowd". He identifies these mainly as "real nerds and OAPs in baseball caps", although idiosyncratic dress or poor teeth also play their part in his critique of the look he claims is favoured by the typical speedway fan, though in the next breath he stresses, "it's a classless sport that's open to everybody". To my untutored eye, everyone in the crowd looks just the same as you'd find at practically any other speedway meeting. There's the traditional mix of ages, all casually dressed in clothes that they find comfortable or who sport shirts and anoraks that proclaim their allegiance either to speedway or their particular team. It's a place where you can come as you are – a broad predominantly white church that attracts all denominations, ages and backgrounds, individuals and families. The close-knit community among the riders definitely carries over onto the terraces. Or, is it the other way round?

Peter warms to his theme; he finds the ownership of rider contracts by the promoters to be iniquitous ("didn't we abolish slavery years ago under Wilberforce?") and worries about how the modern obsession with the naked pursuit of money negatively alters the dynamics of the sport. Many different people are still involved "just for the love of it" and would be reluctant to sever their attachment. Even the riders, once they have it in their blood, often struggle to retire or find fulfilment afterwards. Nonetheless, despite this fierce loyalty and attachment, he's worried about the way the sport has changed, which he views as typified by the deleterious effects of the Grand Prix series. Peter notes that the owners of the series, the BSI, "aren't involved as a charity". They're obviously keen to exploit their assets, which must have an impact on riders and fans alike as well as ultimately upon the future structure of the sport in England. The pressure on the riders to succeed and the importance of success to maximise sponsorship support and financial reward leads to greater aggression and risk taking, "I worry about the impact of money in an already dangerous sport".

Peter believes that the fans have begun to resentfully notice the impact of the changes to the management and structure of racing in the UK, especially at the Elite League level. Teams have changed from their traditional race night, the riders often have less loyalty to the club than themselves and the criteria by which the Elite League Champions are decided, by play-offs, has been altered for the worse to suit the demands of live television. These changes will ripple throughout the lower levels of the sport; most likely to become the model that they adopt in future seasons and, even if the present status quo were maintained, would have many detrimental consequences. Finally the increased commercialisation of speedway everywhere – led by a rampant but apparently completely unfettered BSI – will lead to a situation where local people can no longer afford to attend meetings. Peter has already witnessed this at the 2004 Prague Grand Prix where long-time local fans, from an area famous as a hot-bed of speedway interest, were unable to pay the required £60 ticket prices. Or, in Hamar for the Norwegian Grand Prix where the event only managed to attract 4,000 people to a venue that had a capacity that was more than double that amount. Even the economics of an ordinary Elite League meeting like this one have become more mysterious. Peter has it on good authority that Waggy pays £1500 per meeting to rent the stadium and £750 for an ambulance and must cover all his other costs of staff, equipment, advertising, riders' money and expenses from crowds that average around 1,000 people per meeting. With adult admissions at £14 per head and programmes at £2 a copy, you will need great sponsorship, exceptionally skilled accountants or deep pockets to even pay your bills, never mind run a speedway club profitably. There's often talk that speedway is run at loss to provide a tax write-off for other businesses owned by the promoter or their associates. If so, this appears a rather mad and deluded long-term business strategy, particularly if the regular League racing in this country is consistently run on that basis. It is also difficult to identify more than a few Elite League clubs that consistently make their activities profitable, which is a situation that spells trouble for the longevity and health of the sport in this country.

Rather than concern myself any more about the intricacies of contemporary British speedway finance or the ins and outs of the balance sheet, I decide to concentrate on the exciting racing prospects ahead this evening at Oxford. The packed stadium buzzes with fans who crowd into every possible viewing space. The rider parade takes place on the tarpaulin-covered dog track as each team and their team manager line up to be individually introduced to the fans. And quite a line up it is with three ex-World Champions in the field. Of course the reception for the visitors is muted in comparison to the cheers for the home side, but it's all done in that very civilised speedway fashion that doesn't descend into the sectarian and visceral hatreds of football. The Arena manager, Ronnie Russell, shakes hands with his opposite number Waggy. It's a clash of sartorial styles, as Ronnie's kind of Butlins redcoat cum military chic meets Waggy's more louche, ageing wide boy and lothario look. The captains Leigh Lanham and Greg Hancock toss for gate positions and we're off to the races. Unusually for the Sandy Lane track, in my experience, the surface is looking extremely smooth, well prepared and ideal for a speedway fixture. The action is spectacular in heat 1, for all the wrong reasons, as Travis McGowan manages to hit the back-straight fence at full tilt when he attempts a daring manoeuvre to overtake. He then spins along uncontrollably with the momentum for around 15 yards before he comes to a painful halt and is excluded. Once again, he proves the legendary toughness of the riders when he's quickly onto his feet and walks slowly back to the pits. He's lucky to do so since his bike looks completely wrecked by the severity of the crash. It's a comparatively short distance to limp, particularly since he travelled so far after the initial impact. It's too good an opportunity for Peter to resist, so he retells that hoary speedway joke that alludes to the rider's penchant for injury, namely that the winning time in a 100 yards sprint between speedway riders is usually around five minutes.

Tonight's match referee is Phil Griffin but the heats follow each other so quickly I have to double check the programme to ensure that Frank 'Speedy Gonzales' Ebdon doesn't actually push the buttons. The reserves heat has Arena take a maximum advantage before Oxford reply with the same outcome in the next. The next race has Rickardsson glide to a faultless and easy victory where he wins by a considerable distance, in the fastest time of the night, and thereby enables Arena to regain their earlier lead. I'm not exactly sure what the odds were on an away Arena victory, but Oxford is one of the few, if not the only, track in the country where you can actually place a bet at the stadium. There's always a chap with an old-fashioned board with the various odds written in chalk, who stands by the brick wall adjacent to main section of open-air terraces located below the home-straight grandstand. It's a 'service' offered by a local bookmaker and is definitely a chance to lose your hard-earned cash because speedway bets, as practised here, require you to specify the final score and not just the victorious team. Speedway matches are so unpredictable that it seems to me like a particularly foolhardy way to be parted from your cash. As ever, the major difficulty rests with the punter but, for once, it's difficult to see how the bookie can consistently set (and rig) the odds in their favour.

As if to prove the unpredictability of this task, Gary 'Havvy' Havelock wins heat 5 in an imperious manner. While he is an ex-World Champion from the early 1990s, it is safe to say that his Elite League performances of the last few years could be characterised as steady and unspectacular, though disappointing might be less generous but more accurate. He also has a slight bad boy reputation that, I imagine, is due to his age, experience and independent caste of mind, that definitely makes him reluctant to suffer in silence in the face of real or imagined slights. He is also one of the riders who want to formalise the rights and responsibilities of the promoters in relation to their essential staff (the riders) through the Speedway Riders

Association; an organisation that appears comparatively unacknowledged by the promoters, who inevitably prefer to divide and rule through individual negotiation with riders. There has also been some reluctance among the riders themselves to embrace the association, especially the younger ones, who fail to fully appreciate or have time to appreciate the advantages of collective agreements and responsibilities. Perhaps, there is also an element of not wishing to appear a 'troublemaker' during the nascent stage of your speedway career. Particularly since the promoters hold such unfettered power and can determine the longevity of your career on nothing more than a whim, masquerading as planning or contingency.

Whatever the reasons, Havvy inspires strong emotions and you get the clear impression that he really doesn't give a monkey's cuss for the opinions of people he doesn't respect. This is fair enough, but at some clubs over the past few years, the lack of reverence for him has come from the fans themselves. It's a situation that's been compounded by his recent rather itinerant career path, where he moves from club to club with a slightly greater frequency than the norm without ever setting the world on fire. To stand out as frequently itinerant, almost pathologically so, in a sport where the norm is frequent changes of team personnel and the loyalty between promoters and riders appears extremely low to non-existent, is definitely something special. Also very special, though, is his intense pride when he represents his country at a team level. This gives the lie to his reputation for insouciance, since Havvy gets picked surprisingly often for the England (Team GB) team, despite not because of his apparent form, before he then usually proceeds to justify his selection when he rides very well and motivates the team tremendously. Whether it's patriotism or just that he's genuinely inspired on the right occasion, no one can doubt his inspirational impact on the England team's performances; especially with his work behind the scenes and the support he gives his fellow riders in the pits.

This widely held perception of an indifferent or inconsistent attitude to his league racing contrasts sharply with his on-screen persona as a perspicacious and intuitive pundit for Sky Sports television. He thrives in this medium, despite his deliberate defiance of the journalistic convention to speak clearly and take a balanced approach. Havvy prefers to just call it as he sees it, often with caustic comments as he rides his own hobbyhorses in his own distinctive manner and accent. He's always insightful, provides a riders perspective and is often pleasingly irreverent, as often, in contrast, the other guests appear wooden or non-committal. Tonight on the track, however, when it comes to Havvy's riding skill, commitment and performance, we could be witnessing a renaissance in his career or, alternatively, simply the one swallow that makes this summer. He wins so skilfully and with such panache that you'd be forgiven for the thought that it is he, rather than Tony Rickardsson, that has aspirations to become a world champion for the sixth time. After he works his way through the field and then shadows the home rider, Niels Kristian Iversen, before Havvy carefully seizes his moment to overtake the leader with cunning and bravery on the last bend to win the race at the finish line.

This victory and the presence of Rickardsson in the side appears to inspire the Arena team to ride like they could well mount a challenge to be Elite League champions this season. Rickardsson wins his next two races decisively; he easily beats Hancock and then eclipses the strong Jensen-Iversen partnership. The results make the cumulative score 24-30 by heat 9, which is then slightly reduced by a Hancock victory. Again riding out of his skin, Havvy repeats his earlier triumph in carbon copy style; this time as he skillfully rounds Stefan Andersson for another victory on the line, after a fascinating dual between them throughout the preceding four laps. By the end of heat 13 the score has reached an unbelievable 33-46, with Rickardsson winning again ably supported by the resurgent Havvy who easily relegates Hancock to third place, even though it was a tactical substitute ride for him.

With an extremely rare away victory almost assured, the real collector's item of an overall aggregate win also appears a certainty for Arena. That is until the speedway gods intervene in heat 14, when Povazhny somehow temporarily loses control when he leads comfortably, after he manages to hit the only available bump on tonight's unusually smooth track. A definite aggregate win would have been assured by the then prospective 1-5 heat win, which this unfortunate glitch now turns into a completely unmerited tactical ride assisted 8-1 for the home team, just when Arena appeared ready to cruise to a shock result. However, this still leaves heat 15 and luckily for any of the crowd who would have been tempted to have a flutter at the bookmakers, their stall has already closed for the evening. I would have confidently wagered serious money on the certainty that Rickardsson and Havvy would storm to another victory together. As it was, the swallow that was the summer of Havvy's earlier impressive races ended with the resumption of his normal service, since he trails in a long way back in third place. Even more shockingly, Rickardsson finishes stone last and appears to have deliberately slackened off and decided to miss the chase, immediately after he finds himself relegated to the back of the pack in the first corner. Such a decision is the inevitable consequence of Rickardsson's lack of commitment to a team he has only joined temporarily and solely to further his own ambition to practice. His brief sojourn in the UK, to get his match race fitness and engines up to speed, was over for 2005. It's a weird note to finish on and you can't help but wonder about the advisability of hiring riders on short-term limited contracts, never mind the possibility if that we may ever see him race a full season of British speedway again in his career[4]. Still, despite the fact that they lost the last two heats by a margin of 13-2, Arena nonetheless manage to hang on for a deserved but rare away victory by 48-46, that causes the Oxford fans to grumble as they file out through the gates of the stadium. Nonetheless, it has been a pleasure for us all to witness Rickardsson in action in a British speedway league fixture.

21st April Oxford v. Arena Essex (Elite League A) 46-48

[4] Though we would get the chance to see him race again in the country, fleetingly, at the Cardiff Grand Prix in June. In 2006, he came back again to practise and gain race fitness when he joined Oxford. While it wouldn't seem possible, he raced even fewer fixtures for Oxford than he did for Arena before he suddenly ended his sojourn unexpectedly early. Surely, these short-term contracts further devalue the sport in this country and must be addressed by the sports governing body?

Chapter 4: A Coach Trip to the Monarchs
22nd April Edinburgh v. Stoke

"The most natural grader is a speedway bike" David Norris

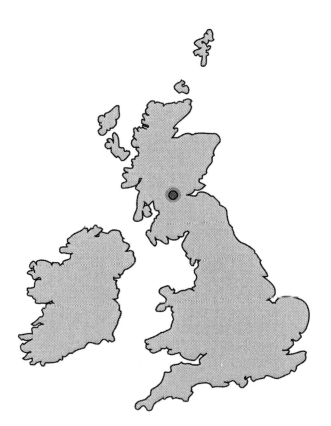

RANDOM SCB RULES

13.5 A Competitor failing to attend a meeting, arriving late, ceasing to participate, leaving the meeting without the Referees permission or failing to maker a bona fide attempt to race shall be guilty of an offence

My brief, late April, tour of Britain's most northerly race tracks starts on a cold, damp Friday night in the centre of the historic city of Edinburgh. The modicum of research I've undertaken has luckily enabled me to gather that a visit to Armadale, the present home of the Edinburgh Monarchs, would get off to a poor start if I were to operate under the assumption that it was actually located within the city. After a journey that has taken me all the way from Brighton to such a beautiful place, I decide against an evening that ends with a night in a B&B in Armadale itself or any attempt to travel there on public transport. I forgo, shrewdly it turns out, the delight of a convoluted Friday night trek in favour of the opportunity to travel to the meeting with the Edinburgh Supporters Club on their specially hired coach. After I exploit the new fangled technology that is the World Wide Web I manage to contact Ella MacDonald, who I don't know from Eve, and is the lady who organises these valuable weekly trips during the season from the city centre to the stadium. On the phone she kindly reassures me that as a stranger to these parts, with acknowledged poor directional sense, it's highly unlikely that I'll manage to miss the supporters' bus at its pick-up place in Waterloo Place. The reassurance that "everyone's always found

it before" is some consolation but would be meagre consolation should this not be easily done. To overcome my fear of missing the coach I decide to turn up massively in advance of the scheduled departure at 6.30 p.m. to ensure this superbly economical (£7 return) and convenient service doesn't leave without me.

On the night, I'm even earlier than I anticipated which gives me the opportunity to check out the street's location. As Ella suggested, it is where it has always been – unmistakably positioned at the end of Princes Street, slap bang in the middle of the Edinburgh that tourists always militate to, i.e. right by Waverley Station. My impression of the city centre has usually focused around the lovely feel and genuine olde-worlde atmosphere of its rich variety of beautiful buildings and the stunning general architecture of the place. Whether it's the sea, the backdrop of Arthur's Seat, the warren of steep streets with their quirky back passages and tenements, or the hill top castle that nestles on the sheer-faced crag that forms the natural border of the old city – it's truly a magnificent setting. In fact I would claim Edinburgh to be the most beautiful city setting in Britain in which to stage speedway meetings, if only the track wasn't actually located some distance away in Armadale.

After I've promenaded up and down Waterloo Place for quite some time in search of Edinburgh speedway fans or the coach, I took to generally lurking anxiously and I eventually spotted some other speedway folk. The first was a man with a limp and a stick, who sported a sleeveless jacket festooned in old-fashioned style sewn on badges. The impressive variety of these badges was a personal chronicle of the bygone era of his many previous travels to watch speedway meetings throughout Britain and Europe. These original but now somewhat faded badges were drawn from an era when the World Championship was settled each season by a do-or-die one-off Final. Great examples decorate the jacket and these include one that advertises the '1985 World Final – Odsal' or the more glamorous but less popular two-day affair of '1987 World Final – Amsterdam'. The overall rather fetching retro effect screams from a different era when qualification for the championship was tortuous, hard won and prized; from a period well before the present cumulative, invitation-only 'same old riders each time' Grand Prix system; which was still but a far-off twinkle in various avaricious eyes. On this stunning jacket there are badges of various shapes and sizes emblazoned with 'Gulf Oil' and its Scottish but less common variant 'Gulf Oil – Monarchs'. It's a garment worn with pride and distinction with its wide range of contemporary or defunct teams, which almost represents a geography and history lesson in itself but also includes my personal favourites for this impressive collection, the '1929-1989 Diamond Jubilee Exeter' and 'BLRC – Belle Vue'.

I meander a few steps behind the man wearing speedway's equivalent of

Joseph's Technicolor Dream Coat, in order to follow him to the coach. This is a bright idea but, very slowly, he leads me to a pub in Waterloo Place. Eventually a gaggle of likely looking lads, well men, gather further up the street before they board the coach Ella insisted would "be difficult to miss." Ella's observation is again completely accurate and our transport for the evening appears, if anything, to have been drawn from a vintage era well before that of the badged jacket. If an antique dealer had to describe the supporter's club coach it would, no doubt, be flatteringly presented, as 'a classic of its kind' while a local advert in the newsagents would probably highlight it as 'spacious and reliable'. In fact it's a blue, delightfully old-fashioned Volvo coach with an indeterminate but aged registration number (NIC 7057). Inside it's replete with around 65 worn but comfortable seats, including a proper back seat at the rear of the coach and throughout its length it's lined with minuscule luggage racks, useful for those with small objects like handbags or a newspaper to stow away for the duration of the journey.

I quickly get the impression that everyone else on board is a regular, particularly since everyone is clearly pretty familiar with each other's company. There is an inordinately long wait before we make a move to start our journey so, as a visiting stranger, I drink up the general conversation. There's studiously observed silence from some supporters but the majority involve themselves in some impressive speedway discussions on a whole variety of topics that includes the evening's prospects; previous and recent meetings between the sides; a brief run through great all-time speedway meetings actually attended by these supporters or, indeed, meetings you'd have wished to have attended in hindsight, and some heated analysis of the varying abilities of the riders who'll be on display tonight. There is also some discussion of the weather (cool but dry tonight is the consensus) along with random rhetorical observations like, "where's Alan, he's usually here by now?"

By the time we eventually set off there are probably forty plus people on the coach, mostly men of a certain age (and outlook) with a smattering of women supporters – which includes Ella who sits rather magisterially at the front of the bus – along with the four teenagers who inevitably occupy the back seat. To generalise not altogether wildly, the coach is filled with an affable group of mostly over 50s; people who look, if I slightly exaggerate and tar all the males with the same brush, proudly balding or thinner on top with what is often kindly described as fuller, more prosperous figures.

Most of the chatter on the bus, now we're under way to Armadale, focuses on the huge number of injuries that clashes between Edinburgh and Stoke have historically thrown up. An impressive roll call of past crashes and racing incidents ensues with various speculations upon who might be considered to be really at fault, closely allied to almost surgical levels of medical knowledge about the complex interrelations of bones that go to make up the human body. Obviously, given that this is the Edinburgh supporters' coach the litany of 'dishonour' will necessarily be slightly biased and tend towards the partisan rather than the objective. This analysis of recollected injuries quickly results in a consensus, which identifies a triumvirate of extremely guilty culprits among rival visiting riders: notably Mark 'Buzz' Burrows, Alan 'Moggo' Mogridge and the "biggest culprit" Paul Pickering who, it is alleged, deliberately "just spears them." Though they reckon that tonight should be a comparatively quiet night for the St Andrew's Ambulance staff and the local hospital A&E department, particularly since Burrows now rides in the Conference League and 'Pickers' is sadly already out for the season with his own early season arm and shoulder injuries. This would usually leave 'Moggo' as the sole focus for the home supporters' abuse and opprobrium at tonight's fixture but for the distraction of the eagerly anticipated appearance at Armadale of James Grieves, as a guest rider for Stoke. Even the casual listener can easily pick that there's quite a bit of previous animosity between Mr Grieves and the home support that hasn't been at all dimmed by his recent move over the border to ride for Newcastle Speedway. Universally acknowledged as the rider the Edinburgh fans 'most love to hate' was, I gathered, a role Grieves invariably relishes. This is usually reflected in his superlative performances when he rides against the Monarchs and, invariably, these are occasions used by Grieves as another opportunity to trade gestures with the more excitable elements of the Edinburgh crowd. Grieves had already recently and immaculately continued his traditional role as a thorn in the Monarchs' side the previous week, when he inspired Newcastle to an early season Premier Trophy victory with a flawless five-ride 15 point maximum.

The onboard debate about this defeat among the supporters could have focussed on the incontrovertible fact that Grieves comfortably rode to victory in every race but, instead, prefers to concentrate on the perceived poor organisational skills of the Newcastle club. The skills of the Diamonds' speedway management are widely adjudged to be woeful ("a bunch of wallies"), in sharp contrast to many other speedway clubs with respect to prompt starts in order to avoid the forecast threat of rain. After they apparently failed to open their gates until 40 minutes before the 5.30 p.m. start, the Newcastle club then indulged in an inordinately lengthy introductory parade of the riders before the first race finally started at 5.50 p.m. to be followed by the second at 6.30 p.m. Short of conducting a centre-green rain dance, this protracted approach is viewed as unacceptably thoughtless behaviour throughout a lengthy discussion among the supporters within my earshot. This "mindless" attitude occupies the group much more than any analysis of the defeat itself or any perceived shortcomings among the Monarchs' team. To be fair to the always friendly but in this instance pilloried Newcastle promotion, this initial organisational 'oversight' is compounded on the night by further unexpected delays caused by medical attention that results from Robert Ksiezak's suspected broken leg in heat 2.

The coach slowly wends its way through the city centre rush hour traffic, passing many magnificent looking streets and buildings along the way, before we finally pick up a bit of speed as we head out along the A8. A convoy of white stretch limousines, you always imagine filled with people off for an evening of extremely riotous behaviour, pass in the opposite direction. All the while, I'm ensconced on an ageing Volvo coach delightfully surrounded by knowledgeable and enthusiastic people who idly discuss a variety of speedway topics. We pass the many planes that crowd Edinburgh Airport airfield at this time of night and then pass the rather desolate countryside that leads us in 40 minutes ("we made good time tonight") to the stadium at Armadale.

The rural feel of the latter part of the trip is compounded by the bitingly cold wind that very noticeably whips across the car park adjacent to the stadium where we finally park the coach. I rush to enter the stadium to escape the wind and in the hope of some warmer shelter somewhere inside. This expectation is quickly dashed by my brief inspection since there appears to be limited options and there's definitely no appreciable difference in the wind despite being inside the comparative shelter of the stadium grounds. My choice of outside viewing positions comprise of some open exposed standing areas on bends 1 and 3, a covered area on the back straight (with a warm crowded bar) or, my choice, the covered main grandstand already favoured by a large proportion of the crowd. This stand has a couple of rows of seats plus about ten rows of terraces and is located on the first bend to give a great view of the track as we look back towards the start gate. The wind and ambient temperature still remains astonishingly cold, despite the comparative shelter and the heat provided when surrounded by the warming presence of other people. From the vantage point of this grandstand, you can see the armada of riders' white vans that have congregated together over the far side by the even more exposed bend 4 pits area, and you also get a clear view of the executive housing estate that has rapidly sprung up behind that bend.

This housing development signals further trouble on the horizon for the stadium in general – which runs greyhound meetings on Mondays and Thursdays – but especially for the speedway club. After the previous struggle to find an appropriate site to stage the sport locally after their enforced departure from the environs of the city, Armadale represented an excellent choice. By embracing the virtue of this remote (if not secluded) location, the club immediately reduced the ever-present possibility of noise complaints – inevitably generated by any speedway club with close proximity to residential property – and thereby hoped to ensure its continued survival after many years of a peripatetic existence. In the near future, their strategic choice of remote environment will definitely be threatened when the Armadale local authorities start to give far greater weight to possible noise complaints from the influx of new voters and community charge payers, who will be drawn to the local area by this executive development. The primacy of the opinions of the voters over that of the speedway club is further complicated by fact the Monarchs only have permission to stage speedway meetings on the basis of a lease that will expire in the near future. An application for a new lease or an extension of the existing lease will have to be made to the local authorities and is a course of action that will probably provoke objections or changes in the terms of consent. It goes without saying, and is quickly obvious, that the investment in the facilities at the stadium reflects the possible fact that there might not be a long-term future for the Monarchs racing at this particular stadium. Despite this situation the commitment towards and enthusiasm of supporters, riders and the promotion for the Monarchs to continue remains undimmed.

However, the club have made some recent investments in the fabric and furniture of the place and are still developing some aspects of the stadium, to make the very best of what they've already got. After my visit I read in the Speedway Star that the club will shortly introduce a second hospitality area to the stadium. This rather grandiose description hides the reality of the situation, since it's a development that was described to me as, "basically a portacabin with a carpet". It's probably my own lack of observational skills but I can't say that I actually spotted the existing corporate hospitality area. Unless it was that small group of tables, covered with plastic tablecloths, which serves as an outside dining area for the carpeted portacabin located adjacent to the bend 1 and 2 grandstands? Tonight the coldness of the weather, along with the wind that whistles through the track, would be enough to put off the hardiest souls from some relaxing alfresco dining on the terraces. Irrespective of the cold weather, if the welcome is anything like that I experienced from the fans in the stadium and on the supporters' coach, any visitors to the stadium can't help but be impressed with the genuine sincerity of the fans. I imagine that if you combine this reception with a warm summer's night, then the opportunity to eat, drink, be merry and watch the speedway would be irresistible to lovers of speedway everywhere, irrespective of the appearance of the dining area. The need to attract local businesses to sponsor and use their facilities is the aim of every speedway club. If this somewhat spartan dining area (and the additional one) is what is required to get local businesses and businessmen pumped up, excited and raring to be associated with all things Monarchs, then I'm sure that they will enjoy every success. It's definitely a refreshing contrast to the usual corporate entertainment offer that comprises a three-course meal with traditional music and bagpipes that my hotel advertised as available for interested businesses, albeit in the pleasant surroundings of Edinburgh Castle rather than Armadale.

For basic warmth, I hankered after some thermal underwear or the thermos I don't yet own which, with some basic garden furniture like a collapsible garden chair, would indicate that I'd finally become a properly equipped and true speedway fan. Unless it's some insult to national pride or a slight on the fans' resilience, perhaps the track shop could consider a range of Monarchs branded thermal underwear to supplement the usual range of hats, T-shirts and sweatshirts? I know that I would have paid any price for these after a few heats that evening and, if my reaction is anything to go by, I'm sure other visiting fans would flock to take advantage during many times of the year. No one would be able to see the Monarchs' logo beneath

your clothing anyway. There would be considerable demand among the 'soft' visitors – the Isle of Wight photographer commented on similar arctic conditions during his late May visit – except during those brief but balmy summer nights for which Armadale is famed and the outside dining suitable. At the track shop, located in a small portacabin type shed where a very friendly lady serves me, I instead content myself with the purchase a photograph of a smiling rider chosen at random. For future edification and delight I enquire who it actually pictures, only to be told "och, it's our skipper." I'm then treated to a fulsome tribute to the impact and general abilities of one of Speedway's rarities – a successful Dutch speedway rider – Edinburgh's very own favourite cloggie, Theo Pijper[1].

Theo is a significant local figure with the Monarchs' fans, which is illustrated a few weeks later when despicably sneaky thieves steal and wreck all his valuable speedway equipment. The press claims that he'll have to postpone his planned November wedding to his local fiancée and spend the money instead on expensively re-equipping himself to continue to ride, and perhaps exaggerates his dedication and intentions. But also indicates that Carrie, his bride-to-be[2] is extremely understanding of her man's abiding passion for the sport. Luckily, however, despite the future Mrs Pijper's long-standing keen personal interest in speedway and especially all things Monarchs' speedway, the fans – in solidarity and outrage – rally round superbly with local collections that amount to around £2000 in total. An impressively high figure that is a measure of the fans' generosity and simultaneously manages to avert disaster on the track and in affairs of the heart[3]. This isn't really a surprise given the legendary generosity of the Scots people in general who, as a nation, consistently head the league tables of regional per capita charitable donations for the whole of the UK. It's also another example of the 'one big family' ethos that characterises speedway and its followers!

There's a very healthy-sized crowd dotted throughout the stadium that all appear impervious to the bitter cold. They're mostly clustered together under the roofed back-straight grandstand, shelter in the nearby bar or, like myself, huddle in the grandstand with an excellent view of the

[1] If we lived in the Netherlands, Theo's surname might cause some amusement. The word Pijpen means "to give a blow job" and the word Pijper would describe the one doing it. Strangely, even the Glasgow fans don't appear to have picked up on this meaning and the opportunity for playful banter that his surname provides.

[2] Who was previously renowned as a star of one of those legal compensation commercials that recommend you sue people after you've unexpectedly sustained injuries after tripping over, falling, getting knocked off your bike etc. These ambulance chasing 'no-win no-fee' legal firms always claim a track record of successful claims and that no case is ever too small for them to proceed with fighting. Hopefully, Carrie still had enough contacts in the industry to advise Theo with the insurance claim for his speedway equipment, though from the reports it appears that he might not have been insured.

[3] The track collection was particularly praised by Mike Hunter in his subsequent *Speedway Star* report as a great achievement, especially given the weather conditions on the night of the collection – namely it was cold and damp with only a small crowd in attendance. In a manner that would inevitably be ruled out as far-fetched in a Hollywood movie or too schmaltzy in *The Waltons*, Theo is later gratefully quoted, though it's best to imagine this in a Dutch accent with a hint of Scots twang, "one wee boy came up to me on Friday with a card in an envelope and some money inside, and handed it to me. He said he'd been saving up his money for me all week. I wish I had never lost the bikes but the support I have had has helped me to get through it."

slightly sloped downhill section of the track from the start gate to the first bend. Among the spectators there is a broad mix of men and women, of all ages with a good number of families and even a dog. We patiently listen as the announcer gives a very thorough and knowledgeable introduction to the riders and stars of both teams with lots of vocal support throughout from the crowd. The returning Peter Carr, in his 25th season as a rider, is introduced as "the king of Armadale", which is a description that mostly brings cheers with some less appreciative but muted boos. To judge from the volume of the response, the local favourites of the Armadale crowd appear to be Rusty Harrison and Daniel Nermark. To loudly confirm this throughout the meeting, a large girl just behind me goes completely mental every time Daniel appears to ride on the track, and she beseechingly urges on her very own "Danny Boy". She screams like a woman possessed at every opportunity or generally hops about and leaps up and down, so energetically that it must keep her remarkably warm.

It's an enthusiasm shared by the announcer who, after heat 1, notes, "Daniel rode an intelligent line to block James Grieves". Daniel's technique is also possibly aided by the bellows of the banshee behind me, so loud she may even be audible to the riders, who repeatedly urges him to even greater success with cries of "go on, Daniel!" By the end of heat 2 the Monarchs have already gained the lead and a points advantage that proves beyond the capabilities of the visiting Potters team to recoup during the rest of the meeting. His confidence in a probable Monarchs' victory allows the announcer to admire the style and technique of Stoke's Rob Grant, who is praised for a "leg trailing style just like his dad" when he finishes in a distant third place in that race. The crowd are further driven into a frenzy of apathy with the news "it's only £20 to sponsor a heat as a birthday surprise". I'd be surprised if there were any takers, keen enough to brave the chill wind to journey to the speedway office to register their interest for future weeks but, sometimes, you've got to take your pleasures where you can even on the coldest of nights. Fellow spectators inform me, as is later corroborated by Ella, that this week isn't anything like as cold as the freezing temperatures that greeted Sheffield's visit the week before.

On the track in heat 5, the announcer grumbles that the Edinburgh fans' bête noire, James Grieves, "in the first tacky ride wins the ultimate reward". This actually refers to the benefit of six points gained for his team rather than his impending beatification or ascent to heaven as a result of his exhilarating ride. While it's theoretically still alive as a contest until late on, by heat 8 Pijper is already being congratulated by the man with access to the microphone for "three rides, three wins: his patch is as purple as his kevlars." With hyperbole like this from the announcer, all that's needed is for the club poet, Mose, to compose a few slightly contrived verses to properly round off this evening of linguistic gymnastics. Subsequently, the "awesome pairing" of Pijper and Nermark has the announcer, on secondment from planet excitable, waxing lyrical before we learn during an investigative interview with Russell 'Rusty' Harrison that "my Elite League riding helps my Premier League form, especially in heat 15". All this additional practice doesn't stop the sharp-as-a-knife Robbie Kessler providing what is called afterwards the "passing move of the night" when he easily sweeps past Harrison. Thereby making Rusty look just that, when Kessler relegates him to second, and the metaphorical spoon drawer, despite all that sharpening up in the Elite League.

If this was a fairy story, the meeting would end with a 'they lived happily ever after' or, much more suitable to this rather dimly lit stadium, 'time for bed'. However, the Monarch's 10-point victory only results in some further and very enjoyable second-half practice races, which feature young riders from the club's Conference League team, the 'Dale Devils'. The crowd greeted this racing just as enthusiastically if not more so than the racing put on by the senior riders and still appeared oblivious to the heightened awareness of the numbing cold that the tentative racing of the second half brought on for myself. So, as a soft Sassenach, I retreated from the freezing gloom of the dimly lit stadium grandstand and, instead, retired to the warmer climes of the crowded and boisterous back-straight bar to survey events and politely await the chance to rush back to the warmth of the supporters' club bus.

On pain of death and severe excoriation, Ella had earlier emphasised our planned prompt 9.30 p.m. departure to return to the city centre. Everyone was quick to retreat to the comfort and shelter the coach provided except one laggard who irked everyone by his display of selfishness. Interestingly, it was the one rather glaringly incongruous supporter who had already stood out, to my eyes, from all the other fans on the outward journey[4]. The departure of the coach was severely delayed by his drunken arrival back over 15 minutes late, and he justifiably merited the sharp, critical words that Ella deservedly dished out to him on his eventual arrival. If it was possible, 'Two Cans' was even more studiously ostracised, despite the increased volubility and banality of his conversations that had, in the interim, been heightened by his Dutch courage. Frightened to actually put whatever irrelevant case he thought he had directly to Ella, 'Two Cans' complained to the other person close by, obviously also 'in drink' as they say, with the laughable but endlessly repeated refrain "I don't have to put up with that shit, she's talked to me like that two weeks now". Hopefully, he has got the hint that even polite and genuine speedway fans don't exactly welcome the chance to travel with the aggressively stupid. Some of the other pensioner age fans on the coach now risked missing their onward late night public transport travel connections home, due to the 'Two Cans' desire for more alcoholic refreshment that he couldn't handle maturely.

On the delayed but quicker journey home, in the dark interior of the coach we travel mostly in mumbled silence or stop intermittently to drop off people along the route before we again rejoin the late evening throng of people and traffic that crowded the city centre. Edinburgh, if possible, looked even more resplendent than when we departed; with the castle on the hill superbly lit up in the distance, as it magnificently towered over the city, before we passed the delightfully under-lit gothic Scott Monument tower in Princes Street Gardens in the final minute of our journey. I leave the coach determined to watch the Monarchs race again this season but also to try to fully enjoy the experience in the friendly company of their passionate and loyal supporters.

22nd April Edinburgh v. Stoke (Premier Trophy) 53-43

---

[4] A short rather pale man with alopecia, he initially drew my attention to his social inadequacy through his deliberately incongruous appearance, set off by his Millwall baseball cap – rarely enough seen in England but rarer still in Scotland. Throughout the trip to Armadale, he ostentatiously drank from the cans he'd brought with him – the only person to do so, hence his soubriquet 'Two Cans' – and also exhibited an exaggeratedly confrontational attitude through his inappropriate conversational choices. For example, he repeatedly held up a newspaper clipping that highlighted the behaviour of what he termed Celtic "scum", who supposedly ignored a minute's commemorative silence at a recent football game. He supplemented his sectarian ramblings with further observations about the so-called "terrible abuse of the Celtic fans" during the silence for Princess Margaret's death. Without apparent irony, he further commented, "I thought not stirring up sectarian hatred applied to Catholics too". As genuine and proper people from the broad church of speedway, the Edinburgh fans treated him with the contempt he deserved by completely ignoring him. He cut a rather forlorn, albeit bigoted, figure. He was one of only two really repellent individuals I personally encountered on all my travels.

"The Grand Prix's better than ever with the new format shown exclusively on Sky" Nigel Pearson

10.21 Brakes shall not be fitted to any motorcycle ridden at a Speedway Meeting or practice thereof

Royal Berwick-upon-Tweed is justifiably known as one of Britain's most beautiful royal towns. The term picture postcard perfect can be used without any further need for justification. It's a town deeply steeped in history, particularly Anglo-Scottish history, having, by the latest count, changed hands 13 times. Presently it's considered part of England although everything about it seems to say that it's in Scotland. From the architecture, the local mix of accents – Scots crossed with Northumbrian – as well as the general look and atmosphere of the town. Anyone fortunate enough to visit Berwick by train gets the chance to savour a ride that takes in a route recently voted the most scenic rail journey this country possesses. It's a trip that takes in some truly breath-taking sites as the track hugs the edge of the North Eastern coastline between Newcastle and Edinburgh, the major city it's geographically closest to, which adds weight to its Scottish credentials. It's a brilliant way to appreciate the spectacle of the town since it gives any visitor a magnificent perspective upon the estuary and the sea; while the panoramic view laid out before you includes the town castle, its surviving battlements as well as an array of magnificent vertigo-inducing bridges: the Old, the Royal Tweed and the Royal Border.

Upon my arrival I experience a gesture typical of the kindness of strangers for which speedway is justifiably renowned. I arrive only minutes before tapes up at 7 p.m., so David from the bed and breakfast in town (recommended to me by the speedway club) kindly picks me up at the station to give me a lift over to Berwick Rangers Football Club home of the Berwick Bandits. The B&B is actually run by his wife Pam, a keen speedway fanatic, while he works at sea as a fisherman. My train is delayed and with the careworn automated voice that offers "apologies for any inconvenience that this may have caused to your journey" throughout the scenic journey, still echoes in my mind as we rush by car across the picturesque town centre. So I have no time to appreciate the spectacular historic buildings, the renowned killing zones of the old walled town[1] or Britain's most unusual parish church without a steeple, tower or church bell. There's no doubt that it's deservedly one of the most attractive provincial speedway towns in the country.

We cross the river and arrive just in time at the home of the Bandits – Berwick Rangers Football Club. The football club reinforces the unique Scots connection because they are the only English town that compete in the Scottish football leagues. It has a rather quaint but pleasantly old-fashioned small entry gate and turnstile. Apart from a grandstand on either side of the football pitch cum centre green, the rest of the stadium is exposed to the elements. It's easy to imagine it would be character building to watch the football here in the depths of the winter but luckily I visit when it's a very temperate April evening for the fixture against the Hull Vikings. It's a head-to-head Premier Trophy encounter that pits the Kirkland-Carpet-sponsored Bandits against the Hull CPD Vikings.

Just as I walk in through the turnstiles, the riders are already busy 'gardening' as they sit astride their machines in preparation for the tapes to rise on heat 1. Almost immediately, the tapes fly up and they roar directly towards me to where, as I'm late, I've stupidly hurried to the wall at the apex of bends 1 and 2. Seconds later I retreat, but only after the passing riders have repeatedly and painfully showered me with shale, since my enthusiasm temporarily overcomes my commonsense or observational skills. The heat ends and I get to properly consider this rather delightful setting. The football pitch itself is ringed by the track and there are two covered stands – a large grandstand on the home straight and a smaller but nonetheless impressive one on the back straight of the track. There is also a raised area of grass banking in the far right-hand corner (or Bend 3) with what I later discover is, in fact, an unusual but very civilised canopied temporary bar area. However, the most immediately distinctive feature of the stadium is the deep black colour of the shale and distinctive shape of the track itself. It's a track with narrow straights that run into unsymmetrical bends, with the widest

---

[1] Though these impressive walls have never actually seen a shot fired in anger since they were built after the conflicts over the town's ownership had finally subsided.

of the two being the final bend, which features some steep banking. It's the kind of gradient that would favour any rider who regularly rode its contours. To confirm its unique configuration, and because the riders travel clockwise when they race, there's an uphill incline on the home straight with its matching but opposite downhill slope on the back straight. All in all, this layout must surely be a considerable advantage to those familiar with the track.

In the spirit of research I've closely studied all things Berwick in the *Speedway Star*, so I'm already aware that the club has weathered its pre-season difficulties with ambulance availability. The need for an on-site medical vehicle is a vital safety feature and legal requirement under SCB regulations. Failure to have this service available would have been terminal for the club's future in the sport. Along with the many column inches dedicated to this crisis, I'd also paid close attention to Berwick's early season home results and reports in the *Speedway Star*. Despite all my study, absolutely no mention had been made of the most significant feature of the track, its banked bend (I imagine everyone just assumes you already know about this aspect). There had been extensive grumbles about the early season track preparation at Berwick, which was held to be completely unconducive to frequent passing, which is so often viewed as the vital characteristic of the sport. There had been no mention, however oblique, about the contribution or otherwise of the steeply banked bends to the apparent dearth of such quintessential speedway manoeuvres. They say that the older you get the more vehemently you claim that policemen always look younger. The speedway equivalent of this complaint is to highlight the supposed absence of entertainment caused by a lack of overtaking. There is another long-standing perception among those unfamiliar with the sport, namely that whichever rider arrives at the first bend in front of the others will invariably win. From the reports on the early season fixtures I expected this to be the case at Berwick.

It's a sincerely held point of view that goes from the gentle susurration of chatter in the trade press to hurricane force levels of complaint on the "unofficial" Bandits' website. This use of modern technology to criticise his club enrages Peter Waite, the diminutive, friendly and financially careful promoter of the Bandits. Peter has no time for these opinions and consequently spends considerable time and energy on a one-man campaign that frequently rails against the iniquities of the Internet in the pages of the match programme and also in the pages of the *Speedway Star*. His one-man vendetta pursued to hold back the frontiers of technology innovation and to limit the areas of free speech in a democracy or, at least, try to ensure that users only ever comment favourably on the Bandits doesn't enjoy much success. You have to admire someone who embarks on such a fruitless and so evidently self-interested a campaign. Luckily for Peter, out of diplomacy and a lack of interest I won't deign to look at the offending material and vulgar comments on this site but will instead form my own judgements. Ironically, if Peter hadn't created such a song and dance about these slights with his frequent complaints, it wouldn't have even entered my mind to think of this as a possible criticism of the quality of the racing offered at Berwick Speedway. However, now that I'm on the lookout for processional racing and possible explanations for its occurrence here, my initial impression is that the layout of the circuit at Berwick, and the narrowness of the straights themselves, might not be conducive to much devil-may-care and madcap overtaking by the riders that regularly use it.

When you watch the Bandits, another feature that is impossible to ignore is the massively amplified roar and vibration of the speedway bikes as they pelt past the cavernous grandstands, which are themselves very close to the track itself. For any fan inside the stadium, as opposed to the local residents outside it, if you judge its reception by the strictly enforced race night curfew of 9.30 p.m., it's a delightful experience as the riders repeatedly roar round the circuit. Another concession to the embattled eardrums of the neighbouring populace is the strict prohibition of the use of air horns at the stadium. This is a major step, since it's practically impossible to visit any British speedway track without the frequent and loud sound of blaring air horns. The total ban is a great relief to those of a nervous disposition or those outside galled by the traditional ambient noise created by some zealous people at a speedway meeting. However, for the surrounding houses, the repeated use of the microphone by the announcer is a nuisance noise source that isn't regulated or controlled on a speedway race night at Berwick. The programme lists these serial interjections as being the work of either Dennis McCleary, who has multiple responsibilities as "Announcer/Timekeeper/Incident Recorder/Programme", or Dick Barrie who is responsible for "Centre Green Presentation". My guess is that it's Dick who entertains us throughout the evening. After

Lacey and Muriel – the friendly Berwick turnstile ladies. © Jeff Scott

The shy Bob Johnston takes a break from his duties. © Jeff Scott

The always helpful programme seller Davina Johnston. © Jeff Scott

heat 1 is awarded after a heavy fall by Paul Thorp ("the only ex-World Finalist on view tonight"), Dick tries to enthuse the quiet crowd of around 500 people with the hope that the "cashmere girls"[2] are perhaps all budding Anthea Redferns keen and willing enough "to give us a twirl". Maybe these twirls are something the home crowd longs for or anticipates on a weekly basis but, especially given the large number of children and women who attend this meeting, I'd imagine this really isn't high on their list of reasons as to why they watch the speedway.

Heat 3 provides the first instance of any rider using his experience of the track to skilfully swoop up the banking of the bend, past another rider and into the lead. It's a manoeuvre that Michal Makovsky executes with considerable aplomb, ease and style. Prior to the interruption of this exciting manoeuvre, Dick (most likely) is getting carried away with his own hyperbole and the proximity of his mouth to the microphone. His audible excitement is caused by his fevered anticipation at the immanent first (re-)appearance of Yorkshireman Scott Smith on his home debut. Scott has been awarded a short-term contract with Berwick to replace the recently "axed Simon Cartwright". It's nearly all too much of a thrill for Dick, and leads him to the astonishingly (almost Nigel Pearsonesque) exaggerated claim that "no more exciting rider to watch exists in British Speedway". It's a statement that is completely open to dispute and which, obviously, immediately fates Scott to race excitingly to a well-earned last place. Though it's more than understandable that Scott feels a bit rusty after he spent 18 months away from the sport. Given the announcer's penchant for obscure insight, he strangely ignores the chance to inform us that Scott has spent his time away from his career in speedway at work on his jewellery business which he has built up around the various antiques markets found in God's own county of Yorkshire. The offer of a contract to ride for Berwick, from the reputedly extremely parsimonious Peter Waite, has Scott eagerly accepting the chance to indulge again in the long-distance travel lifestyle of the itinerant speedway rider, in preference to the more prosaic lure of regular visits to market towns such as Doncaster, Rotherham and Barnsley.

After his delight at the news of Scott Smith's return, the announcer is so excited that he tries out his early entry for the Speedway all-comers announcement of the 2005 season! It's a speedway gem and concerns his explanation of the Hull team's reaction to the convoluted justification put forward by the Bandits to secure the "rider replacement facility" they have been granted because of the absence of the Polish registered rider, Piotr Dym, from the Berwick side for tonight's fixture. Piotr's unavailability results in the superb collectors item of a statement over the tannoy that "following the sad death of the Pope, in honour of his

[2] How quaintly named are the start-line girls at Berwick? Especially in comparison to some other tracks more down-to-earth descriptions, but much nicer weather, for their female track staff.

memory, all Speedway fixtures in Poland were cancelled for a period of ten days." These "postponed fixtures are being staged this weekend" so, as a result, Piotr is "unavailable for tonight's Premier Trophy fixture". Hull are said to be "disappointed" though you just know that they didn't include that particular expression in their comments. The disbelief, frustration and anger that this turn of events supposedly registered with the Hull team causes the wry comment that "I don't know if they think Peter Waite murdered the Pope." The small crowd of Hull supporters who've made the journey up to the Shielfield Park Stadium with their flag, to stand on bend 2, collectively groan.

The races come thick and fast, as though referee Tony Steele thinks he's Frank Ebdon or is on a promise later if only he can rush through all tonight's heats in record time. The races are keenly contested and we're rewarded with some close contests and a brilliant overtake by Garry Stead in heat 9. In an evening of generally fast times that follow on from the quickest time of the year so far, 66.3 seconds, set by Adrian Rymel in heat 4. Rymel wins easily for the Bandits in heat 10: it's a victory, which afterwards involves a lap of honour, some celebratory wheelies and includes singling out various excited fans for a congratulatory wave.

They breed a committed group of fanatical fans on the Borders. By now I've ventured to stand behind a small group of Berwick fans close by the back-straight stand. Closest to me is a group that comprises of two older looking males, one in his late 50s and the other of around pensionable age, who stand together with a woman in her late 20s. They really stand out from the other assembled fans due to the wild exuberance of the celebrations that the apparent thrill of the racing repeatedly inspires in them. Especially excitable is the bespectacled, grey-haired older man who has the respectable look, but not the demeanour, of a retired bank manager or doctor, smartly dressed as he is in collared shirt and jacket (but no tie). By the time heat 13 arrives, his extreme celebrations are quite something to behold. Another daring overtake by that man Adrian Rymel again, on the banked final turn of the last lap to win on the line, provokes an orgasmic sound and breathless exclamation of, "yes! yes! – go on Adrian – woo, yes! yes!" This is elegantly combined with two high spawning salmon-like leaps into the air with arms outstretched in celebration and wonder. It's a wild dance that appears incongruous for a man of his age. By heat 14, with victory assured quite some time ago in the evening for Berwick against a labouring and slightly out of sorts Hull side, our gymnastic fan executes some more cartoon-character type shouts and leaps. His latest ecstatic celebration is brought on by yet another exciting passing manoeuvre[3] brilliantly executed by Michal Makovsky with great dash, daring and determination on the exit of the banked bend on lap 3. For the second time in five minutes "yes! yes! woo – Michael – yes!" screams Mr Grey Hair, only fractionally less orgasmic this time.

Makovsky again salutes the crowd throughout his celebratory lap and goes out of his way, when he almost slows to a standstill, to greet the excited group of young kids that stand on bend 2. The frequent comments about the processional nature of the entertainment at Shielfield Park Stadium have, obviously, touched a nerve with the announcer along with many others who work for the club. Apropos of nothing, but still waxing very lyrical and philosophical, we're somewhat tenuously informed, "that perhaps those who have complained about the standard of the racing should remember that you need good opposition!" I must say that based on the evidence of tonight that the meeting has been fantastically entertaining though the opposition has been subdued. It has also involved some spectacular passes by both teams' riders, so it's definitely "yah boo sucks" to the many Internet critics, though I haven't been to the fixtures that they complained about witnessing. Later as I leave the stadium, Peter Waite greets me warmly and asks that I specifically mention "all the exciting passing and overtakes here tonight!"[4]

After yet another victory lap of celebration, Michal Makovsky stops by the fence on his bike and casually chats to the fans. We hear over the tannoy that a fan has given Chris Schramm £10 "towards his diesel money" for the long journey up to each meeting from his home at Maldon in Essex. At 8.45 p.m. the meeting is announced as "officially closed" though, after

[3] If this is how overtaking is regularly celebrated maybe, after all, they are extremely rare occurrences in these parts?

[4] It would be hard not to mention these manoeuvres, as they happen so often.

a short break, the races then continues with a quick series of second half 'Junior' races until the final curfew of the night at 9.30 p.m. The easy familiarity between the crowd and the riders continues when many of the team arrive on the terraces in their mud-covered kevlars to sign autographs, chat and generally mingle with gaggles of the enthusiastic local fans. The easy approachability of these Berwick stars of the track is very noticeable and the riders are happy to mix with fans of all ages but, particularly, the younger women. Of whom there are suddenly many more! Michal Makovsky appears particularly in his element, since he spends most of his time smiling broadly and surrounded by a horde of admiring fans. I join some of the various patiently waiting queues of well-wishers and autograph hunters that excitedly and spontaneously form by the riders. The riders find the time for a few well-chosen words for each, most often on the evenings racing but they appear to answer any questions from anyone who cares to ask them. The evening's star performer on the track was Adrian Rymel, who won four races; though he informs me, when the crowd of female admirers temporarily subsides, that "the track is sweet if you ride it like that, very easy, I could ride all night." The Bandits' German reserve rider Joachim Kugelmann is more circumspect in his comments, despite an excellent performance when he rode the previous evening as a guest for Edinburgh ("I like very much that track"), and stresses, "I'm still nervous here after a bad crash in my first meeting, it's still in my head." While the flamboyant entertainer that is Michal Makovsky very modestly notes, "it's not always like that, but it was enjoyable."

Chris Schramm, who I'd seen ride earlier in his career when he was part of the Reading team, chats for much longer. He has an unenviably long drive from Maldon, which his dad quite correctly notes is a huge distance to come for only "four minutes work" each week. Chris is keen to succeed and make the most of his temporary contract with the Bandits. If he rides well and secures a regular place in the team it will be well worth the effort, despite the fact that he usually arrives home exhausted at 5.30 am after a 'home' meeting. He's nearly twenty-one and he enjoys racing at the Shielfield Park track, "though it's frightening how fast the fence comes up on you here, it takes some getting used to". Despite his comparative youth, in his career he's already ridden for a variety of clubs and these include Reading and Newport (where he claims "I really didn't get on"). Chris is at pains to point out that dedication and effort are essential components to career success, especially as "many British riders are getting annoyed with the number of foreigners coming in at the expense of the Brits. I don't mean the foreign lads here, of course, but generally". It's a precarious career, where injury or the wrong average can result in almost any rider getting unceremoniously kicked out of a club, so it's essential for them to have an alternative career (and income!) to support their speedway racing. Chris is a self-employed builder who works until 8 p.m. every evening when he's not racing. Many supporters on the terraces throughout the country only ever get to dream of racing speedway competitively. Chris appreciates his good fortune, that he has actually managed to live out this commonly held dream, but remains keen to make the most of it, "you have to, while you can, you never know when it'll end!" I make a small donation to his diesel money before I leave him to the attentions of a crowd of young female admirers.

While the Junior riders repeatedly power round the track in their keenly contested but apparently innumerable second-half races, Tony Steele has swapped the comparative calm of his referee's box for the truly deafening roar and vibration of the main grandstand. Tony appears to have success overcoming both the noise and language difficulties, since he has a lengthy and earnest conversation with Michal Makovsky. Back in the warmth of a crowded box by the glowing electric fire, Tony chats affably to me to reveal his sincere enthusiasm for the sport, "good speedway is timeless, there's nothing like it on the planet". Tony has the speedway bug big time and estimates he attends 50 meetings a year as the referee and around 100 a year as a spectator. It's this level of interest and research that contributes to Tony's reputation of Britain's leading speedway official. He modestly omits to mention that many of the 50 meetings a year that he officiates at during the season are often the showpiece events from the Grand Prix or the World Cup. Tony always prefers to experience and watch his speedway live and notes he isn't a big fan of the meetings shown on Sky because, "it's not a sport you can watch from the house, you have to be there!" He speaks, as only a truly engaged supporter of speedway racing can, when he notes that when you watch live in the flesh, you're "so close to the action, living every second and feeling like you're riding the bike yourself."

Tony is a friendly, thoughtful and intelligent man who gently qualifies my view that the whole experience of speedway in this country remains quintessentially British. He highlights that, for a long time now, the riders have ceased to be solely drawn from this country though we both agree that the essential theatricality involved when you stage any speedway meeting remains something of endless fascination. "The ground, the people and most of the activities are typically British or still appear so. It's the most fascinating thing to me, as a referee, just seeing what goes on from two hours beforehand with all the preparations with the tidying, catering and equipment. There's all this slow build up to this extremely manic action and then there's final fever pitch of heat 15. Then, within 10 minutes, it goes from the noisiest to almost complete silence."

Tony has been hooked on speedway for 37 years, really ever since he saw a sign that said 'Greyhounds and Speedway'. He noticed this advert from the upstairs of a passing bus and was told by his dad "don't worry about that, they don't have it any more." Nonetheless determined, he's watched ever since he went to the Leicester Lions fourth match in 1968 and, when you casually chat with him, you just know he's completely fanatical about this sport! Other duties and people call Tony's attention, so I watch some more of the second-half races from the comparative warmth of the large home straight grandstand before I head to the exit and the long walk back to my B&B.

Luckily I bump into Peter Waite just as I leave the stadium and he insists, with true Scots hospitality, that I must go to *The Grove* pub just half a mile up the road. "It's where everyone always goes afterwards – win or lose. See you there." As a complete stranger to any place, the direction "just close by" can be very difficult to find no matter how confidently you set off into the darkness of the surrounding streets and houses. After a walk of some confusion, I ask a man in his 50s as he leaves one of the houses if he knows the whereabouts of said establishment. It turns out I'm actually very close. Another 50 yards, more patience and less panic would have allowed me to easily find my own way, particularly as just around the next corner was a huge number of that archetypal symbol of the itinerant Speedway rider – the trademark and essential tool that they all apparently possess, namely a large white van. There's a whole armada of them that line the verges of the road on both sides by the pub. Ironically the kindly stranger turns out to be the friendly Terence who, rather self-deprecatingly, describes himself very formally as "Mister Makovsky's mechanic and driver." It's a role that he has fulfilled with enthusiasm for some years. It takes him to tracks all over the country when he's not trying to make ends meet as a self-employed builder. Terence tantalisingly says, "oh – the stories I could tell you for your book" but then doesn't elaborate further except for a theatrical wink. Instead of salacious stories, he instead limits himself to anodyne observations, such as, "you have to score 10 or more to make it pay as a rider" or "Michal's a lovely man who was once Czech Under-21 Champion and was the full Czech champion in 1999". Before I can glean any more 'insights' we enter the noise, atmosphere and confined space that is the exceptionally crowded Grove on a Saturday night. Inside the pub, it appears everyone ever connected with Berwick speedway has succumbed to the convivial lure of this particular pub. After an evening of speedway, the subsequent option to spend some more time in an extremely packed room with your friends, contemporaries or other like-minded people is apparently a very easy choice.

The Grove turns out to be one of those delightful, old-fashioned pubs still stuck in a time warp that is decorated and laid out in a way they all were in, say, the late 1960s. It's got a well-worn but comfortable atmosphere that the marketing department of any self-respecting brewery head office would instantly despair over the existence of in any pub property portfolio, let alone their own. If it were, they would turn despair into disaster by an immediate and catastrophic redevelopment of *The Grove* into another 'cool destination venue' cum drinking ghetto. The redesign would doubtless religiously echo whatever the latest ubiquitous contemporary theme is presently used to attract the fickle but always desirable demographic that is the high-spending younger clientele. Not that this pub has any difficulty in attracting lots of younger customers or high spenders of any age. There are numerous young men in the crowded bar of *The Grove* (these include most of the riders from both sides) and lots of young women attired in a manner appropriate to the warmth of the bar, but that quickly makes me feel my age.

The packed bar has an atmosphere of unaffected bonhomie with an almost surreal variety of happy punters, who dramatically differ in age, dress sense and outlook but not class. It's a rich mix that exists less and less nowadays due to the soulless standardisation and age stratification that affects so many drinking and entertainment establishments throughout the country. It's a trend that is increasingly noticeable in our provincial towns and town centres close by to these uber-pubs, especially on the comparatively more boisterous and lawless weekend nights. They stubbornly resist this tide of apocryphal change here at *The Grove*, since everyone is happy just to get on with a drink, a smoke and a chat. It's a notably loud but apparently happy throng of people happily crushed together or who sit packed onto the padded benches and scattered stools. The large bar itself is continually crowded and the bar staff have the look and demeanour of locals who've been doing this for years – overworked, harassed but still very chatty and friendly as they go about their service. The clientele includes locals of all ages, particularly the younger set, mixed in with loads of people from the speedway track – fans, riders, mechanics and staff. Another one of the delights of the sport is the chance to meet, greet and bleat with the riders in the bar afterwards. The conviviality of *The Grove* provides the ideal combination of a proper local pub combined with the comfortable camaraderie of speedway folk rather than the more usual experience of the track clubhouse bar. I'm definitely a stranger but I'm made welcome nonetheless as an honorary member of this pub and its extended speedway family.

Terence kindly points out various riders from the club, who are extremely difficult to recognise in their civilian clothes. There's Adrian here and Chris there – who drinks one of those ridiculous looking and slightly gauche modern blue-bottled drinks that are anathema to more old-fashioned drinkers – along with Michal who amiably chatters in the corner. The cardigan girls, if indeed it is they, have discarded their work clothes in favour of skimpier much more plunging attire. They have been joined by lots of other young ladies keen to enjoy themselves fully on a Saturday night. It's a visible reminder of the continued endurance and appeal of the combination of youth, daring, risk and speed that is typified by speedway riders. It's an exciting lifestyle that appears, from the clothes and décolletage on display, to have set the hormones raging among the young ladies' section of the clientele here at *The Grove* tonight. It's a phenomenon that I observe repeated at many tracks around the country throughout any season. Terence also kindly nods towards the young lady, who is temporarily seated but has luckily had to squeeze very closely past me many times throughout our conversation, and warns, "she's the promoter's daughter". It's good to have more of the picture though clearly, as she closely squeezed past, my face must have betrayed an inadvertent flicker of emotion that Terence noticed. She's quite visibly one of the many attractive young women in the room, dressed as if ready to go to a party, who stand out for their looks and due to the incongruity of their contrast to this old-fashioned, old boys' pub they find themselves in. Evidently though, apart from myself, it's just another normal night at *The Grove* for everyone else.

Terence pointedly mentions that it's still commonplace for speedway fans and riders alike to negatively ascribe the ills of contemporary British speedway to the increasing presence of "foreigners". Bucking this trend, the majority of Berwick riders actually live and work in the town and are openly accepted as a vibrant part of the local community. Traditionally speedway riders lived in and were known in their communities for their riding and after-race activities and, uniquely, this is still the case in Berwick, albeit these are in fact the visiting "foreigners", who mostly live close by in the community, socialise together and frequently travel together around a strange country to try to make their living. Some of the riders from Central Europe – the Czech Republic, Poland and the like – are initially flung together and share accommodation in the town. Joachim (from Germany) stays in a local and friendly B&B well used to looking after riders, mechanics, visiting fans and, tonight, myself. Indicative of this situation, behind us is Josef 'Pepe' Franc, deep in conversation with his father, who has arrived over for a visit. He used to ride for Berwick but remains in the area even though he now plies his trade with Newcastle Speedway.

I can't deny that this genuinely friendly atmosphere has a kind of magic and also nostalgia for anyone of a certain age, who fondly recalls the local hostelries of their youth or early adulthood. It's a style of pub that's gone by the board in a welter of themes and drinks promotions that their modern equivalents provide as a substitute for community. Even at *The Grove*, they serve those fashionable brightly coloured drinks and have a pool table, although these appear to be the only limited concessions to the banal trends in contemporary pub furniture and other self-consciously metropolitan styling mores. In keeping with the retro outlook and décor, I indulge in an old-fashioned cellophane-wrapped but homemade white cheese-and-pickle bun before the landlady kindly calls a taxi for me. This requires a brief trip to the saloon bar, which is a haven of calm in comparison but seems even more of a throwback to a different era and an almost lost way of life and drinking. It's definitely darker and smokier, while full of older generation males in a strangely sparse kind of way, as each preserves their own personal drinking space. Some are unshaven and others are dressed in that 'Saturday night best' look popular in the late 50s; others sport an array of jackets and waistcoats or comfortable jumpers. Though they look exactly like archetypal speedway fans, I imagine they're not, particularly since they've retreated from the heaving hubbub of the next-door public bar for the safe haven of the saloon. While I wait patiently, they slowly discuss local matters of import or note among themselves, and watch the world idle by in their own more leisurely fashion. The stranger briefly in their midst hardly merits a glance before I leave to wait outside in the cool night air of Tweedmouth for my missing taxi back to Royal Berwick.

23rd April Berwick v. Hull (Premier Trophy) 57-37

Chapter 6: The Kindness of Strangers
24th April Glasgow v. Edinburgh

"Both teams really want to win here tonight" Jonathan Green (to Kelvin Tatum, practically every week at the start of the programme)

12.6.2 Competitors must wear complete undergarments if the suits are unlined

There's nothing like making life complicated, though my journey from Berwick to the Glasgow versus Edinburgh derby meeting at Ashfield Stadium became circuitous even by my standards. It was a trip that involved the proverbial planes, trains and automobiles but, in my case, more in the order of trains, automobiles and planes. Rested from a comfortable night at the friendly Cara House B&B in historic Castlegate, an establishment justifiably recommended by Berwick Speedway club, I headed off to their dining room to enjoy a Scottish breakfast fit for a speedway rider. I know that this definitely was the case since no sooner did I tuck into my Cornflakes than Berwick's German speedway rider Joachim Kugelmann surfaced from his room to join me and the other guests. His arrival at breakfast was unexpected, on my part if not his, and a welcome bonus for my research for this book. I'd already learnt a lot from the owners of the establishment, David Thompson, who'd been very helpful when we met for the first time the day before, and his very well-informed, enthusiastic and speedway-mad wife, Pamela. When I called to confirm my booking, David has just returned from his full-time work as a fisherman, I formed an early impression of Pamela's speedway fanaticism, or good fortune at her geographical location, it all depends on your point of view, since that night she was away for the evening at Workington to watch her beloved Berwick Bandits ride, pretty poorly as it happened.

I chatted with Pamela about speedway while she cooked all the breakfasts. I quickly learnt from her that Joachim had stayed at Cara House with David and Pamela "from the start" of his time in Berwick. He had become well settled into the team and into the routine of a speedway rider living here in the centre of Berwick[1]. When Joachim wasn't riding or maintaining his bike, he tried to establish some sort of all-comers' record for time spent asleep. In fact, according to Pamela, he was "an expert at sleeping", but you knew from the way she spoke that she was delighted to have him in the house and proud to have him as a temporary member of their family. Berwick is the sort of close-knit, more family-oriented place and speedway club where all the riders, mechanics, management and fans socialise together. Whether it's at the stadium, in the town itself or, most likely, at the friendly Grove pub close to the track. After the racing, as I'd discovered the night before, the pub becomes packed with speedway people and the many riders who mostly live in the Berwick area. This is unusual for speedway in the modern age, which, unlike yesteryear, has become increasingly more international in its outlook, composition and travel arrangements. Pamela believes, apart from the Berwick riders who congregate in the town, the majority of contemporary speedway riders, "just want to get off and clean their bikes in their workshops as, at the end of the day, it's just a job for them". Some fans are often disillusioned to find that their heroes are keen to leave immediately after they've finished their day's work; which is, after all, to have ridden at the speedway track. This attitude often punctures the illusion, mystique and allure that the popular image of the 'speedway rider' still inspires among many fans, mostly it has to be said, often through over-investment in the image and perception of the gladiatorial and high-risk nature of their work. The discovery that they are human, and not superior beings, is often hard and disillusioning to take on board for some people. However, the exception that proves the rule is the Berwick team, who get on with their work but still like to remain together afterwards; this includes Chris Schramm, who lives hundreds of miles away in Essex, and even riders who've left the team but still live in the area, like Josef Franc.

Chez Thompson accommodates a familiar stream of speedway visitors – fans, family and riders. Chris Schramm stays sometimes along with his mum and dad, but it's only Joachim who's a permanent resident at Cara House. When Joachim has the time, he goes into town and plays pool with Pamela but doesn't play her at darts, a sensible decision for his male pride, since she's represented East Berwickshire with her arrows. He's definitely part of their family and, as Pamela correctly notes, "they're all somebody's sons!" Evidently she treats him like a son, since she nags him to eat more when he finally shuffles in for breakfast. He's adapted well to the lack of continental fare in this country and from this kitchen. He evidently feels at home, enough to get his own breakfast, unlike the other more temporary guests like myself, who tuck into the endless supply of food that Pamela magics up. Because I have lived and worked in Europe, I know that breakfast can mean many different things to many different people[2]. Surprisingly to my mind, for a speedway rider, Joachim demonstrates a remarkable lack of pace or urgency in all his actions. Maybe he's just supremely laid back or isn't used to waking so early in the morning. It is, after all, almost 9 am and the morning after a night of work and subsequent relaxation at *The Grove*.

All the while she's in the kitchen Pamela talks about a wide range of speedway related topics. We even get to discuss the announcers at various tracks; Dick Barrie at Berwick doesn't meet with her approval as he's a "pain in the arse", and she describes Michael Max, presenter at Glasgow Speedway, as "notoriously so biased". Whatever their relative merits, I'm sure they are in the ear of the listener, I enjoyed Dick's interjections and I look forward to later when I can hear Michael at work and judge for myself. He was very enthusiastic when I spoke to him on the phone prior to my trip. Pamela continues to cook the breakfast and prepare the sandwiches for her excursion to Glasgow, since she and David will go to the same meeting that I will, albeit for them in Joachim's van, since he will be a guest rider at reserve for Edinburgh this afternoon.

[1] Shortly afterwards Joachim was to fall out with the mercurial Berwick promoter Peter Waite, allegedly over a full-time contract, which thereby cut short his Berwick career. So far, he has not returned to UK racing.

It's a repeat booking that follows a successful display for them on the other extremely cold evening, when I saw him ride well for the Monarchs at Armadale against Stoke. Joachim has excellent English and he is extremely polite and articulate when he intermittently chats, but mostly restricts himself to a few speedway platitudes while he just eats his breakfast. I can't say that I blame him, because he's only just awoken and his day's work stretches ahead of him. Pamela is excited about the meeting and is eager to leave for Glasgow, particularly so that Joachim has all the time he needs in the pits to properly prepare, both mechanically and mentally. They would give me a lift to Ashfield Stadium but, unfortunately, the van is already full.

When I eventually leave, I see Joachim's distinctive speedway rider's big white transit van outside, just like so many others except for the German registration plates and the left-hand drive. I take my time because the first train of the day that stops at Berwick station and then heads north to Edinburgh, isn't until after 11 am. This is pretty incredible and leaves any visitor with the strong impression that Berwick, while picturesque and beautiful, is well off the beaten track despite its excellent rail connections. I was already aware last night of the fact that Berwick was very much a provincial town, because the last train to there from nearby Newcastle left at 6 p.m., although this is a luxury compared to the summer timetable when it leaves at 5.30 p.m.![3] Still, instead I enjoy the morning sunshine and a promenade along the town's battlements – never actually used in battle though hugely forbidding – and through its many arches with apparently every dog owner in the town.

I make a brief stop at Somerfield for vital supplies of food and drink for the long day ahead along with a copy of the paper to check the reports on Sunderland's football game yesterday. There's no mention of speedway, in general, or the Glasgow-Edinburgh derby, in particular, in any of the papers as usual, not even the specially produced regional Scottish editions of these national newspapers[4]. Whatever the reasons, I'm eager to savour the journey to Edinburgh Waverley station where I will join the Edinburgh Supporters Club bus trip to Ashfield Stadium in Glasgow. As a first-time visitor to Glasgow speedway, if not to the Edinburgh supporters' coach, it strikes me as the ideal way to build up the pre-meeting atmosphere. Also, the introduction and subsequent history of these coach trips to Glasgow are intimately related to the move of Glasgow speedway to Ashfield stadium. Previously, given the relative proximity of the cities, many people would drive to the meeting, but concerns (real or imagined, I can't establish which) led to a marked reluctance among Monarchs' fans to risk theft from or of their cars when parked outside the stadium during the derby fixtures. I can't comment on the veracity of this, plus there is always the often distorted view that Edinburgh people have of Glasgow to take into account, and vice versa – although later I did learn of a Glasgow fan who had his wheels stolen from his car when it was in the Armadale car park – nonetheless the supporters' club coach trips have become a regular, and welcome, fixture of the derby meetings.

---

[2] There's the famous, possibly apocryphal, Malcolm Rifkind story, that when he was Foreign Minister in the early days of the Thatcher government, he breakfasted with the Belgian Foreign Minister, who took a Weetabix, carefully split it in two with a knife before he then buttered it. Joachim shows no inclination to butter his Weetabix, Shreddies or Cornflakes.

[3] Competition on the East Coast mainline between Virgin and GNER means that you can now arrive as late as 9 p.m. on a Saturday night. However, you still have to want to leave on a Sunday morning.

[4] Speedway appears to have disappeared from the nation's consciousness and I would propose that the sport adopt the notorious Millwall slogan 'everyone hates us but we don't care' for the speedway cause. However, ignoring that speedway fans don't behave in the manner of Millwall supporters, the sport isn't so much hated as ignored. In this context it appears to be indifference, class snobbery, forgetfulness or the basic fact of the speedway's decline, rather than antipathy, that explains the continued lack of regular national coverage for the sport. However, worse still, when covered it is either often treated with condescension and indifference or, more worryingly, the sheer range and variety of the speedway competition (Elite, Premier and Conference Leagues) in this country is wilfully misrepresented by Sky Sports television to further their own narrower commercial interests. Primarily because Sky Sports solely promotes the Elite League or the Grand Prix and so, therefore, has no real or active interest in the greater number of riders and teams that compete in the Premier or Conference Leagues, except where it occasionally provides more raw speedway talent for the upper echelons. To some extent this is a function of the contract negotiated and is therefore beyond the remit of the television company. However, it remains the responsibility of the sports governing body and one in which they have significantly failed to fulfil their strategic or pragmatic responsibilities. It is an abdication that has a high price since it continues to cost national credibility and, more importantly, ensures that the decline of the sport in this country continues, albeit on a managed basis, because there are not even any Sky monies to ensure an environment that provides an effective infrastructure or investment in British speedway talent. The present disequilibrium ensures the rich clubs get richer (or become more Elite) and the grassroots is effectively left to fend for itself.

On the bus, there's an atmosphere of a coaching holiday since everyone is very friendly and gets on well, while the number of times that the sweets tray is passed around the seats is delightful. Also, on this leg of the trip there is still a wide choice from the boxes of 'Quality Street' brought along to pass the time on this journey. Ella MacDonald, the organiser of this coach trip, kindly charges me a slightly discounted fare for a one-way trip to Glasgow. The conversation is lively, entertaining and sometimes heated. Everyone is keen on their speedway and very much looks forward to an Edinburgh victory in yet another derby contest between the two rival clubs. I sit close to that doyen of so many things to do with the Edinburgh Monarch's speedway club, the friendly Mike Hunter, who's mostly content to listen to the banter around him or offer the odd helpful, insightful or acerbic comment. Mike is one of the directors of the Monarchs and its press officer as well as the author of the enjoyable but, arguably, the most even-handedly honest and impartial reports in the *Speedway Star*. However, I mostly chat to Brian Scott, who has followed speedway since 1960 when he was 13 years old, and Agnes who, although she declines to tell me her age, has followed the sport since 1968. She had supported Berwick up until 2000 before she switched her allegiance to the Monarchs for reasons I don't quite establish. One thing is for sure, she greatly admires the sport and particularly "admires anyone who gets on a speedway bike". She and Brian both relish and enjoy the thrill of watching the riders, home and away, and as the coach winds its way to Glasgow, they carefully analyse the relative strengths of each team. Hope springs eternal and they forecast an Edinburgh victory, albeit probably for reasons of partisanship rather than form. Yet because they speak so well of the Glasgow riders it might, after all, be a prediction based on a careful evaluation. What's not in dispute, in that they agree among themselves, is that while there have been heroes in the past who might have become Spitfire pilots, in the modern age, they feel the closest that anyone could approach this level of daring-do and exhilaration would be to become a speedway rider. Agnes suggests that I try to meet Gary Lough at Ashfield, the author of a book on Edinburgh's 2003 Championship winning season. It's a self-published personal account of his travels in support of the Monarchs entitled *10th yer Baws*! It's a title that all sounds rather mysterious, peculiarly regional and passionate to my sheltered southern English perspective.

When we arrive at Ashfield Stadium, home of the Glasgow Tigers, it's already exceptionally hot and sunny, especially when you consider that it's late April and we're in bonny Scotland! There's a long queue to enter the stadium. I look round at the local neighbourhood that surrounds the stadium, well, as much as I can see from the window of the coach or as I wander round the perimeter wall. It doesn't look like the jungle of urban crime and depravation that the story behind the advent of these trips had led me to expect. In fact, this appears to be just another urban area, slightly old fashioned, but with a nearby corner shop, pub and, because it's Sunday, quiet and deserted factory buildings. Most noticeable of all are the large tower blocks that dot and blot the nearby surrounding skyline and the visible horizon. This type of housing development was popular in large towns and cities throughout the more communally minded 1960s and 1970s. Given the density of this type of housing and the sheer numbers of people that must live there, it's significant that the number of local services and amenities in this vicinity do appear shockingly poor. While I stand in the queue, I can't help but notice that the only obviously vibrant area of this neighbourhood is the speedway club, with its queues of fans and its large but busy car park to the right of the stadium entranceway, where there are even parking attendants to supervise the high volume of cars. This, in turn, indicates to me that the proximity of the high-rise blocks to Ashfield Stadium doesn't necessarily attract a significant number of locally based spectators to the speedway club on its doorstep. However, just as housing styles change, so do people reclaim urban areas and regenerate them. In the nearby area, there are the signs of new modern estates of detached houses with garages and gardens, which must be good for the overall social fabric of the area. But these developments are not necessarily good news for the speedway club, since the new residents probably won't be predisposed to the sport or will have strong preconceptions about the dirt and noise they believe or imagine that it will create.

While I wander round to the turnstiles I chat with Mike Hunter, who's both curious and very helpful about my book. He suggests that to save on time, expense and duplication that I focus my travel plans so that I get to see every unique League stadium in the country rather than attempt to see every single team, in all the British leagues, ride at their home stadium. Mike correctly points out that many teams run different teams in different leagues from the same venue. It's a very common-sense suggestion, for which I definitely thank him and, afterwards, immediately apply. When asked what he thinks the essential appeal of speedway is, Mike believes it's "different things for different people" and jokingly claims, "to have forgotten why I like it". Mike has always been very interested in sport and, to his mind, speedway easily combines the "best of individual and team competition". You can have pride in your team "like soccer but without the bad sides" and at the same time follow your favourite individual riders, while the sport's love of statistics actually enhances your appreciation of riders' performances. Mike has always had a predisposition for the statistics of racing and was hooked from the start by the "magical experience" as well as his fascination of the layout of the race card within the match programme. Mike has also always been attracted to the glamour of the racing, its cut and thrust, as well as the atmosphere and the colours of the race jackets, leathers or helmets. He definitely doesn't like injuries or home defeats but relishes the bond of shared interest and experience that unites speedway supporters throughout the country. Thankfully, he notes, there are no prima donnas within the sport, like soccer attracts in the form of Rio Ferdinand and his ilk, and this applies whether you're talking about in the pits or on the terraces. The casual freemasonry of all speedway fans has a reputation that's well deserved and he believes is something to be extremely proud of; while everyone usually has their own friends, though you can still always stand side by side with your opponent's fans without fear and in the full expectation of a warm welcome.

In our queue, as if to illustrate this very claim, there's a mix of fans but all the talk, in Scots accents, anticipates the closeness of the derby clash. Once I'm through the turnstiles, I find myself in the darkened corridors under the main stand. It has the look and feel of the sports grounds and stands of my childhood, when I followed Sunderland football team with my father, and still appears to have the sorts of facilities that the corporatisation of sports stadiums throughout the UK now deems unsuitable to the match day experience. I like it though, with its dingy toilets and makeshift programme stall, for its careworn, lived in but unpretentious atmosphere. When you emerge into the light on the side of the track, you are immediately greeted with the sight of a small, compact stadium, though it is the rather smooth-looking track that most immediately confronts you. According to the programme they have paid increased attention to the track recently, even going so far as to gratefully borrow the "blade" of Doc Bridgett from the Edinburgh club to help overcome the ravages of the wet weather upon the notoriously rough surface of the Glasgow track. Whatever's been happening, it looks lovely, the centre green grass grows very lush and luxuriant, while the strength of the sun provides a suntrap on the open terraces in front of the tiered, covered seats of the large stand.

HEAT	PRIZE (Not in confirmed order)	COST
1	Mountain Bike	70.00
2	Portable TV	50.00
3	Portable DVD Player & accessories	80.00
4	Portable Gas BBQ	50.00
5	Mini Hi Fi	25.00
6	Portable Stereo	20.00
7	Car Vacuum Cleaner	30.00
8	Scotch Whisky	40.00
9	Tool Box	50.00
10	Luggage Set	40.00
11	TV DVD Combi	80.00
12	DVD Player	30.00
13	Personal CD / MP3 Player	30.00
14	CD Clock Radio	30.00

The seated grandstand already looks full to the rafters of its corrugated roof. The fans have a great view of the track from there as well as an excellent perch above the start-line area. In front of this stand to the right is the pits area and to the left there are some more covered terraces, these are standing only with old-fashioned sturdy crush barriers, presently deep in shade. This stand is at a height lower and less elevated than the main stand. A strong smell of chips wafts from the refreshment stall on the terraces. Further away on the bend is the popular stadium bar, housed in a low white flat-roofed building with a red stripe of paint at the top and windows that look out across the length of the straights of Saracen Park. A small viewing terrace in front of the bar basks in the bright sunlight where a few people stand, blinking into the distance as they hold their pints or in the children's case, their soft drinks and crisps. The programme makes a great play of the availability of discounted bottles of Stella for all the thirsty fans at this derby encounter. The meeting time for this fixture has been switched from its original start time to accommodate the Old Firm clash, between Glasgow Rangers and Glasgow Celtic, in the world of football. It's always a match that inspires extremely strong passions; which is a polite way to allude to the visceral sectarian hatred that has become a prevalent feature of these frequent confrontations. The contrast with the world of speedway couldn't be greater, though there's still occasional strong expressions of loyalty or doubt about the ancestry and sexuality of your rival's fans, but all very much all in an atmosphere of passionate bonhomie. There is no violence, no hint of violence or even, it appears, the possibility of the mildest confrontation.

The crowd offers the usual mix of generations and gender, with many families at the meeting and throughout the stadium I see both sets of fans stand easily together. I search for Michael Max, who Agnes has told me I'd not fail to recognise as he's a big man, although I'm not sure if she means tall or wide. The nearby stadium staff direct me to look in the pits area since that's where they'd just seen him. Nonetheless, Michael proves very elusive to find, particularly since his duties cause him to dash throughout Saracens Park on race day. When I finally catch up with Michael he's friendly and ebullient about the delights of watching speedway. To his mind "no one's indifferent: you either love it or loathe it" and there's nothing that compares to, "two guys slugging it out on the track, with respect for each other". He views his job as the presenter at Glasgow Speedway as a real privilege and in marked contrast to his other (full-time) work during the week at Partick Thistle Football Club. The opportunity to watch great racing is "the biggest buzz in the world", especially as it has the powerful ingredients of "no brakes, respect, side-by-side racing while going hell for leather". While I listen to Michael describe his delight in the sport, it's easy to get caught up in his enthusiasm. He has no doubts that the race meeting this afternoon will be excellent on their "well-prepared track". Not that there aren't some clouds on the horizon. The club's license to stage speedway at this venue is due for renewal in two years time, and that will involve a local council decision that must take account of the local residents' thoughts and opinions. While the speedway racing is limited to a couple of hours a week during the summer months, Michael admits that it's no secret that "nuisance and noise objections are becoming more prevalent"; the question of dust is also a factor here but he fails to mention this concern. It's a trend that's likely to continue as more new houses start to be built around the area and the council will, inevitably, have to take full account of these voters' opinions. Nonetheless, he stresses that he'll always enjoy the speedway, no matter where it's staged, and he hopes that I have a great visit to the club this afternoon. He offers to help in any way he can afterwards, since he will be otherwise engaged throughout the rest of the afternoon. I ask Michael how easy it is to get a bus or a taxi to the airport, since I booked my flight back before they decided to delay today's original staging time because of the local Rangers-Celtic football derby. He tells me not to bother with a cab because he'll sort something out, but only if he knows where I'll be later. I tell him I'll be on the covered standing terraces with the Edinburgh fans I travelled with. At this news he grimaces theatrically, but then says he'll be back in touch shortly.

Back on the terraces, Agnes introduces me to the very helpful author, Gary Lough. It had initially surprised me that Gary Lough had found time off from his schedule training Paula Radcliffe to instead fanatically follow Edinburgh speedway, but it turns out that he's not the Gary Lough who is Paula's frequently berated husband. However, while he's no help at all on a long-distance run, he's full of information and encouragement about speedway book publishing[5]. By now, all around us, quite a crowd of visiting Edinburgh fans have congregated together on the terraces. I even spot the girl who shouted loudly and ecstatically, behind me during another very cold evening last Friday at the speedway at Armadale. I also chat briefly with Pamela and David from Cara House who've already been at the track for some hours with Joachim. The grandstand looks completely full and the back straight stand, on the opposite side to our position, has also attracted a healthy crowd.

While the riders are introduced to us on parade, I glance through the match programme, which has a helpful section on the cumulative Ashfield performances of the visiting Monarchs' riders. If, unlike the stock market, past performance can possibly sometimes indicate future performance, then it appears we can expect Rusty Harrison and Theo Pijper to perform the best for Edinburgh this afternoon. When I spoke with Michael Max earlier, I had mentioned that the Glasgow rider I'd most like to meet would be their captain, Shane Parker. He's quite a character within the sport, renowned for his Australian patriotism, though domiciled in England; his commitment to the welfare of riders is well known throughout the sport, especially through his chairmanship of the Speedway Riders Association, as is his notoriety and penchant for streaking. We're luckily not likely to be forced to see this spectacle at this afternoon's match, despite the very sunny weather, since he usually reserves his naked rides on a speedway bike, except for his sensible use of a crash helmet, for special occasions and testimonial fixtures. One such possible occasion this season might be his own testimonial meeting later in the summer. The programme has a helpful letter from Shane that details his plans for the event, while it also provides a number of sponsorship opportunities. These range from the chance to sponsor some of the prizes for the riders that win an individual heat. From this list, it appears the average rider is quite motivated by the sort of goods you'd traditionally see on the conveyor belt at the end of *The Generation Game* in the 1970s. Well, there are no cuddly toys or fondue sets, but there are BBQs, mountain bikes and that essential rider's accessory, the pressure washer. Of even more interest to the cost-conscious fan, which national Scots pride would surely represent well in this afternoon's crowd, is the list of how much it costs to sponsor a rider at the meeting. The rocket fuel of methanol comes out at £5 per rider; while oil is double that, with

[5] He used Juma Publishing in Sheffield to publish his book. They printed 500 copies for him at a cost of £2300 and he's now achieved enough sales to be very close to his break-even figure of 330 copies sold. The reception he's had has been very positive among the Edinburgh fans, as you'd expect, but also farther afield at some of the other clubs, where track shops have stocked his book. His motivation for writing the book was to celebrate the Championship year when he travelled home and away to follow the team throughout the country and often stayed in the same hotel as the team. But mostly it was written to debunk the opinions and forecasts of the so-called experts who wrote at the start of the season in the *Speedway Star*. These forecasts were drawn from well-informed people at every Premier League track the Monarchs would visit throughout the season and, to a man, they all singularly failed to predict Edinburgh's eventual triumph as champions. It's also a personal account of his fellow Monarchs' fans as well as a number of his strong personal opinions on the sport and its riders. He has his favourites and, it's safe to say, he has some intense dislikes of others. It's a long list that, but to name but a few it includes Simon Stead, James Grieves, Derek Sneddon and Josef Franc. Luckily none of them will ride this afternoon. Writing the book itself became a bit of a marathon during the winter of 2003 and spring of 2004, though he was delighted to do it to commemorate the victorious season.

tyres (£30) and insurance (£20) boost the cost of participation, or at least sponsorship, per rider to £60. Shane invites whatever help your budget can afford and all you have to do is contact him or, his brilliantly named helper, Elaine McSkimming.

Without further ceremony the meeting gets under way with an easy victory, after a well-timed overtaking manoeuvre on the last bend on the first lap, for Glasgow's heat leader George Stancl. Matthew Wethers finished last; previously he rode for Edinburgh before his increased average dictated that there was no place for him in the team for the 2005 campaign. Agnes praises the Australian; she notes that he's a very approachable young man whom she appreciates as a "good rider with no fear in him". Agnes also suggests that I should immediately venture over to the pits to try to persuade a Glasgow rider to take me to the airport, because she knows that some of them frequently travel from there or stay at their sponsor's Glasgow Airport Travel Inn. It's a good suggestion but you need to be as confident and personable as Agnes to try this mid-way through a speedway meeting. Heat 3 sees an early contender for bizarre fall of the season. Glasgow's James Birkenshaw manages to fall off in front of us in a manner that allows the bike to hit him full on the head afterwards. He has the sportsmanship and instinctive presence of mind to clear his bike from the track to allow the other riders to continue with the race, but then immediately collapses on the centre green in a crumpled heap. Michael Max observes with masterful understatement that James "came off in a horrible manner". He's helped back to the pits by the St John Ambulance staff, but he sensibly withdraws from the meeting with broken toes, possible head injuries and pain in his shoulders. I'd definitely consider never to ride again, rather than just withdraw from the fixture, if a bike had just landed like that on my head. But, then that's why I watch the spectacle from the safety of the crowd.

And the crowd this afternoon typifies all that's good about speedway fans, in general, as well as the Glasgow and Edinburgh fans in particular. They consistently applaud any exhibition of skill on a bike, no matter which team the rider actually races for, just as they also indulge in the witty exchange of banter throughout the afternoon. Glasgow initially fall behind by a considerable distance but slowly start to reduce the deficit through a cunning tactical ride by Shane Parker in heat 6. Michael describes his desperate burst to overtake on the last bend, as the riders rush to the finish line, as "a brilliant second". Shane leads by example and follows this with another win in the next heat. This provokes an Edinburgh fan in a white jacket at the front of our stand to repeatedly give Shane the finger during the race. The fan even makes this gesture again as Shane passes on his celebration lap of honour, which provokes Shane to reverse, stop by the fan and lecture him loudly with some pointed advice on manners and etiquette. After he's had a word, Shane returns to the pits but continues to shake his head in theatrical fashion.

The standard and quality of the racing throughout the afternoon is just what you need for a lively and exciting speedway contest. With the sides evenly matched, the riders compete for each position on the track with such zeal and professionalism that it suggests that much more than the Premier Trophy is at stake. A real rivalry or a desire for local honour and bragging rights infects the crowd and the riders. The seated grandstand crowd loudly applauds every Glasgow riders heat victory and the match from heat 6 is evenly poised with only a few points to separate the two closely matched teams. The bright sunshine and the smooth track conditions facilitate some exciting and good competitive racing. Heat 10 is a sensational race as Stancl rides handlebar to handlebar throughout with 'Rusty' Harrison who, Michael Max later informs us, wishes in future to be addressed by his full and proper name Russell. Stancl just sneaks past 'Rusty'/Russell on the last bend of the last lap to win the race and tie the overall scores. The crowd goes wild and Michael Max again permits himself to comment on the "brilliant speedway" we all have just witnessed. Shane Parker is out to ride again in heat 11 and hilariously finds the time and skill to show the gesturing spectator in the white jacket his own finger, when he passes him on the final bend while in the process of winning the race. Both sets of fans laugh at his audacity and Shane makes a point to stop by once again on his victory lap. Though this time he stops to acknowledge the sportsmanlike reaction of the Edinburgh fan in question, who is now only too happy to applaud Shane's humour, skill and victory. With his work for the SRA, Shane tries to represent the collective interests of the riders when it comes to safety, contracts and remuneration. But he also doesn't allow this work to distract from his own fundamental realisation that speedway is primarily about the need to offer entertainment and spectacle.

Immediately afterwards I experience firsthand the generosity of the crowd at Glasgow speedway, when presenter Michael Max surprisingly conducts a loudspeaker appeal about my predicament and how I need to get to the airport in time for my flight home. "That race was magic but we also have a very special guest in the crowd this afternoon, who is trying to work his own bit of literary magic but needs a lift to the airport immediately after the meeting ends, can anyone help?" After he has explained the situation, in the manner of an auctioneer, he then conducts the crowd in a show of hands of those who could volunteer to offer a lift. A surprisingly large number put up their hands and Michael identifies a man in the crowd for me to rush over to and sort out arrangements with. The generous man in question is Ian Maclean, with who I will get a lift to the airport straight afterwards, well from his daughter Marian, an off duty police officer. We arrange that I'll return to sit by him in the stand for the final race of the afternoon, so that we can make a quick departure. As someone who travels the country going to football matches and, even though I know that speedway fans are special, it's a small act of generosity that astonishes and touches me. Not only has the club, in the larger than life form and attitude of Michael Max, gone out of their way to help, but they've then also offered outstanding support and courtesy. Never mind that Ian would volunteer to take a complete stranger, albeit a speedway supporting one, to the airport. In the United Kingdom, despite its undeserved reputation for meanness, it's the Scottish people who consistently are the country's most generous individual donors to charitable causes. I offer my own small but very touching example of this generosity and will to help others than themselves.

The Edinburgh fans I travelled with on the coach are also touched by Michael's announcement and Ian's kind offer, but then quickly return to celebrate the matters in hand when Edinburgh again race into the lead, but only after the referee decides to award the result of heat 12. The firm but fair, 'no quarter given' nature of the riding, along with Trent Leverington's exclusion, provokes Michael Max to publicly acknowledge, "there's always a little edge to the local derbies". During the interval I head to the bar for liquid refreshment and the chance of a quick bask on the terrace in the bright sunshine, after the chill of the cool shade of the terraces. Inside the bar heaves with deep queues of customers, while all the many tables are already crowded with smokers, drinkers and families. The old-fashioned décor of the bar is straight from the trade union clubs of my childhood; slightly austere, ramshackle and a little bit run down though remarkably fit for the purpose for which they were always intended – drinking. The attitude of the punters and the luxury of the toilets displays a pragmatism mixed with a desire to live for the moment, and maybe perhaps to indulge oneself over a relaxing Saturday cigar to go along with your pints and the whisky chasers, while the horse racing continues to blare out on the ignored telly.

I fail to get a drink, since the queues are way too big to join and, since I want to watch the remainder of this local derby fixture, I return to my place in the shade. By my side is a 70-year-old man who's been coming to speedway for the 56 years since he first went in 1949. He still loves his racing and has loved it ever since his "first night", but wishes that the "promoters would put something back into the sport by running training schools, just like they used to". He speaks with approval of ex-riders who still run schools to pass on the benefit of their experience and insight, but worries that it's an attitude that's in terminal decline. By his side is another fan, Steven, who misses the contretemps he regularly had with the always combative James Grieves during derby meetings between the two clubs, when James rode for the Glasgow side for many years. Grieves is now at Newcastle but Steven fondly recalls their mutual antipathy for each other which often "nearly resulted in fisticuffs in the bar afterwards". It's a style of engagement apparently engendered by them both having "similar natures" but had escalated to the extent that James Grieves would specifically "look me out in the crowd". Whatever the merits or otherwise of this conduct, it shows the intimate bond that still exists between the terraces and the heroes on the track although it's an approach I intend, like the majority of fans, to strenuously avoid. Especially since James Grieves has also trained to kick box to increase his upper body strength and thereby further improve as a speedway rider.

In the next race George Stancl's upholds his deserved reputation for frequent mechanical gremlins to randomly strike his equipment at every fixture. This necessarily, it seems, involves an engine failure or some other problem for his bike in

James Birkinshaw in full flight. © The programme

practically every meeting he rides. The tradition continues in the next race when his bike packs up on the last bend of the last lap. The home fans groan in frustration and the Edinburgh fans delight in loudly drawing his attention to alleged gaps in his preparations in the workshop and pits, while he slowly wheels his machine past them and back to the comparative sanctuary of the pits. The next race is drawn and I say my goodbyes to the Edinburgh fans before I head to a rare vacant seat, reasonably close to Ian, in the main grandstand. It's a great place from which to view the meeting, as it has an elevated view of the track and proceedings throughout the stadium. The last nominated heat requires the two Glasgow riders to win in order to force a draw in the match, it would be quite an achievement to snatch a point, particularly since the home side has never led at any point during the match. They nominate their big guns – captain Shane Parker and George Stancl on his, hopefully, rejuvenated bike. They roar from the start line, just as the tapes rise, and their victory never really looks in any doubt. This is the signal for Ian, Marian and myself to rush away, with an alacrity that wouldn't disgrace the riders, through the darkened corridors of the stadium and head over to Marian's car, which is parked in the special season ticket holders' area of the car park. Ian is also in some hurry to get to the airport to catch a flight down south to Luton in England.

They're a very keen speedway family – Ian has attended meetings since 1952, while Marian has carried on the family tradition for over 30 years herself, ever since she was two years old. Her brother also travels up from London regularly in order to get his fix of action on the shale and, similar to myself, he has often successfully gained a lift back from away fixtures by just going into the Glasgow side of the pits after a meeting to ask cheerfully who might be able take him back home. Though this sounds a risky approach if your request falls on deaf ears! Marian's fondest speedway memories come from when she watched Glasgow race in the 1980s, during their "big time" era, when they raced in "a lovely big stadium to packed crowds". Ian struggles to define exactly to his own satisfaction the glamour and appeal of the sport. He decides it's a combination of factors; but mostly it's "a social thing", the basic opportunity to "enjoy interaction with all the other supporters" and its innate "friendliness" is such that you can just as sensibly take your grandmother as take your child. Unlike many other sports, you can always have a friendly drink in the bar with the riders and rival fans, as well as chat with them on the terraces. Ian's of the confirmed opinion that to really enhance and enjoy the spectacle of the racing, speedway should ideally be experienced at night under the floodlights. However, he's been happy to watch speedway in Scotland wherever and whenever it happens.

At various times, it appears that he has supported practically every speedway team that has ridden in Scotland. He originally watched the

Ashfield Giants, before they closed in 1952, and he then supported the Lanarkshire Eagles at Motherwell until they were "dumped out of the league in 1954". After that he keenly followed Edinburgh from 1960 until they closed in 1970 and went on to watch Cowdenbeath and Fife speedway clubs. "It was the inclusion of George Hunter in the 1971 Glasgow team that lured me back to speedway, though George only rode at Hampden Park for not quite two complete seasons, but I was hooked again and have been a Glasgow fan ever since" before he goes on to proudly recalls that he went to practically all their away fixtures on the supporters' coach. The star of this period of his speedway fanaticism, in the 1970s, was the late George Hunter (who rode only briefly for Glasgow and ten seasons for Edinburgh), though Ian also had a lot of admiration for both Kenny McKinna and Merv Janke. However, Ian's all-time favourite rider is Steve Lawson whom he saw ride for 15 years and whom he recollects "always winning, home and away". Steve still holds the record for the most points in a season, for which he apparently still appears in the Guinness Book of Records, before he bravely took the decision to retire in 1992, while at the top of his chosen sport[6]. The next two seasons, from 1993-94, were the Glasgow Speedway club's glory years, when the club managed to win the league and the cup for two years in succession. This period has fond memories for Ian and Marian but sadly, Ian ruefully notes with a cast of mind familiar to all loyal but long-suffering fans in practically any sport, "since then it's all been downhill".

The journey to the airport ends too quickly since we've hardly yet spoken about Glasgow Speedway club. I rush towards the check-in desks to find that my flight is, after all, severely delayed. While I sit in the sunshine of the rather snazzy glass-fronted departure area, I get the chance to ponder how different the surroundings at the airport are from those where I'd just come from at Ashfield stadium. Earlier, I'd felt part of a vibrant, welcoming community and here, in a modern space ostensibly designed to project an atmosphere of calm, comfort and safety, I feel isolated and anonymous. The gulf between these two experiences in the late afternoon spring sunshine symbolises how far we've come and how much we've lost as a society. Except, of course, for some of the few tiny pockets of resistance and community that still remain, like speedway and other dying pastimes, traditions and ways of life. Activities that still manage to connect people to a place; their passions to their lives; their dreams to their communities, but without the relentless consumerism and anonymity of so many aspects of contemporary life in our modern society[7].

24th April Glasgow v. Edinburgh (Premier Trophy) 46-46

[6] Ian suggested that I look out a publication and video on Steve's career, rather enigmatically entitled *Steve Lawson: The Story So Far*, if I want to get more information on and insight into this great rider.

[7] After a considerable delay, after we'd waited in an atmosphere of increased impatience; the flight to Gatwick was turbulent and crowded. Despite our close proximity and our shared experience, no one spoke to each other or showed any interest in their fellow travelling companions. The contrast with the speedway had continued from the terminal to the plane and any sense of community remained starkly absent from this safe, comparatively stylish but ultimately sterile environment.

"These boys are tough. If they can walk and breathe, unless they're carried off the track, they'll be in the rerun" Steve Johnson

"Eastbourne are going to have to regurgitate their chances" Kelvin Tatum

RANDOM SCB RULES

8.1.1 Competitors must be physically and mentally fit and will be excluded from participating unless otherwise pronounced fit by an SCB nominated Medical Officer. Such conditions leading to exclusion include (inter alia):
a. organic or functional loss of a lower limb or hand
b. corrected visual acuity of less than 6/6 with both eyes open together
c. serious neurological or psychiatric disorder
d. epilepsy or unexplained sudden loss of consciousness
e. anyone with an alcohol or drug dependence problem
(If in any doubt, contact the SCB Medical Advisor)

I arrive at the Abbey Stadium in Blunsdon, home of the Swindon Robins Speedway club, on one of those will it won't it evenings of showery springtime weather so beloved of supporters who travel to early season Speedway meetings. When I arrive it's well over two hours away from tapes up in the first heat but there are already quite a few even keener souls than myself parked up in the large car park adjacent to the stadium at Blunsdon. I imagine that they're waiting to rush the gates to reserve their favoured spot on the terraces from which to watch the night's proceedings. There's very little activity by the entrance gates although it sounds like the speaker and microphone systems undergo an intense test in preparation for the night's events. It will probably be the usual heady mix of partisan comment, factual information and wry observation that is the lingua franca of most Speedway meeting presentations. Most likely, the music will be selected from the collection of someone who fancied themselves, at one time, as a DJ to have built up a collection of all time classics and chicken in the basket staples just perfect for their mobile discotheque that specialises in local church hall events. The selection will usually be eclectic, retro and always pleasantly catchy in a 'that years hits played at the funfair' kind of way. The chance to

either wander the car park or stare through the limited gaps in the perimeter fencing at the empty stadium and track proves irresistible pre-meeting entertainment for myself only. The other early arrivals shelter in their cars and busy themselves with catching up on the papers or rootling in the car boot to check that they have all the essentials for an evening's comfortable viewing. Notably, a garish team anorak, some variety of fold away garden seating, a Tupperware box which includes a selection of sandwiches, maybe wrapped in tin foil or cling film, and a couple of special biscuits. Mine would have been a Bar Six if they were available any more. On track preparations remain shrouded in mystery despite my attempts to peer through gaps in the perimeter fence. May be everything that could have been done, has already been done because now, on an overcast afternoon, nothing is apparently happening. The complete lack of activity (other than aurally) throughout the stadium is notable by its obviousness. Nothing stirs, except inside the parked cars or in the pits area, which we can't actually see from here through the gaps in the fence.

It was ever thus and, no doubt, is part of the magical appeal that the general non-speedway going Swindon public remains so able to resist on a regular basis with yet more elaborate displays of indifference. Maybe they're more meaningfully occupied at home having tea with their partners, kids or grandkids. Or more likely in the encroaching culture that is the modern way, probably all still at work in the impressive array of office buildings and warehouses of the many International companies that increasingly litter the country, which noticeably fill the large trading estates in the Swindon area that you have to pass when you drive to the Abbey Stadium in Lady Lane, Blunsdon. A journey that in my case includes, accidentally, passing near to the large 70s Kremlin like nerve centre that is the Head Office of the WH Smith & Sons Ltd organisation, housed in the nearby infamous Greenbridge Industrial estate. Unfortunately as a business and national institution, W.H. Smith & Sons has, to all intents and purposes, mirrored the parallel, but more measured, decline in the popularity of speedway from the giddy heights of its heyday. However, in the case of Smith's this deterioration has been accomplished with far greater professionalism and élan as they moved on and attempted to keep with the times, even going so far as to use focus groups and consultants. The many reported attempts to reposition its core offerings and range to appeal to new customers is in sharp contrast to the lack of consultants reports and analysis at BSPA towers, where some hand wringing and frequent cosmetic changes will suffice. The idea that father knows best still holds sway in a way that would be unthinkable in most other sports organisations, let alone modern businesses. However, thinking about it for a moment, they have both accomplished roughly the same thing when it comes to a decline from a position of pre-eminence, albeit in different ways, but at considerably less cost for speedway in the case of the British Speedway Promoters'

Association's management of change. Whereas Smith's might be acknowledged as a national institution that has sadly lost its way, the continued plight of speedway over the last twenty-five years has been singly ignored or treated with stunning indifference at a national level. The trauma and anxiety, the 'where did it all go wrong' conversations have all been held but only in the rather rarefied and hermetically sealed environment that is planet speedway. Sadly we have just been left to get on with it ourselves and suffer our grief in private away from the spotlight of national consciousness. It's a level of decline that would have had the sports media fraternity completely up in arms if we'd been talking about tennis, cricket and rugby or, heaven forefend, football.

Back at the stadium, away from my attempts to figure out who exactly to hold responsible for the spectacular demise of British speedway, we're all still condemned to lurk at the portals of the beast that is Abbey Stadium. Most weekday nights, it's home to the greyhound racing that is the primary revenue raising activity hereabouts. It's only usually on the regular Thursday race night you can stand around with eager anticipation of an evening's excitement watching the racing on a big shale track (as opposed to the sandy one the dogs run on). Tonight's rather ornithological encounter will pit the Robins of Swindon against the Eagles of Eastbourne. As we finally enter in a rush through a rather deluxe entrance area set off by the kind of canopy you'd expect to see at a provincial casino, two camouflaged military helicopters fly past overhead, possibly from the army but definitely not from the navy given how far in land we are. At this first hint of life and movement at the stadium entrance, there's a mini-scramble, or as much of one as can be nimbly managed by a large group of people of a certain age, for the best (or maybe just their regular favourite) place from which to view proceedings. Inside it looks a bit more spick and span than it did on my last visit when Swindon raced in the Premier League, which reflects that, the present promotion are hungry, ambitious and keen for success. Or, that they have access to lots of cans of red paint that they're not afraid to use liberally about the place. It's Swindon's second season in the so-called top flight having made the step up into the more rarefied atmosphere of the Elite League, which comes along with its many international superstar riders, regular TV coverage and, hopefully, increased revenues through additional sponsorship and fans.

At Blunsdon they take some aspects of their arrival into the highest echelon of the sport very seriously and speculate to accumulate through investment in the stadium fabric, architecture and facilities of the place for the, probably, long haul into a brighter future. Most notably, the track was dug up in the close season to install a brand spanking new drainage system, and thereby overcome a traditional predisposition to track sogginess from the intermittent wet weather of a Wiltshire summer. The contour of the steep grass banking by the entrance also plays its part here since it funnels all the rainfall that there is onto the track surface every time the heavens open. The pits also had some long overdue attention, and have been newly built, repositioned and equipped with new showers – I recall reading in the *Speedway Star* some in-depth discussion of this shower provision as though it were equivalent to the eighth wonder of the world. All this, plus the aforementioned healthy lick of paint, compliments the installation the previous season of the ubiquitous Elite League air fence. This is reputedly a particularly vital enhancement for rider safety given the high speeds easily reached by the riders at the Blunsdon racetrack.

All this talk of stadium developments and specifically air fences, naturally quickly leads to consideration of Swindon Speedway's all-time favourite son – the legendary Barry Briggs. Well it does by the grandstand 'snack bar' as I casually chat with Graham Price. Even if his local accent doesn't totally give the game away, Graham proudly displays his allegiance to all things Swindon since he sports a fine example of their spectacularly garish red Robins race jacket (or anorak in old money) with matching colour coordinated cap. According to Graham, Briggs was a giant on the track in his generation, and would be for any generation, even if you ignore that Graham is biased since Barry is his favourite rider from any era. Even while he was a rider and especially since his retirement, Briggo has demonstrated a remarkable entrepreneurial flair for the introduction of dramatic and successful innovations into the sport he excelled at. Most notably, he exclusively imported Russian ESO bikes; there is also the air fence business nowadays run by his son, plus the no less important, but taken for granted, innovation of his stylishly and aeronautically designed dirt deflector with its unique practical shape. Not that this inventive precocity has been motivated solely by altruism, since Briggs has financially been a winner off the track as well as on. Widely acknowledged as a shrewd and wealthy businessman, Graham delights in the recognition provided by Briggo's deserved millionaire status. But then, during our brief conversation, Graham strikes me as the genuine kind of man with an outlook that means he consistently but rather gently sees the positives in most situations. He's another one of that generation of people I've met throughout the country on my travels who started to watch the sport in the dim and distant mists of time, in his case 1953. I admire his longevity, which he modestly counters by looking around and saying "that's nothing – you should meet my brother, he's around here somewhere, who's been coming since 1949!"

Graham, who still has the speedway bug in his blood as strongly today as when he first caught it, prides himself on all the enjoyable years he's spent watching the Robins and, he stresses, really wouldn't want to miss any meeting, if at all possible, no matter who the opposition was on the night. Nonetheless, he still hankers nostalgically for the golden era of the 1950s and 1960s when speedway held its head high as a truly national sport ("we were second-most popular after football, then") and we had a much richer vein of talented, top-class English riders. Graham's view is not xenophobic, since he whole-heartedly believes that League racing is "more exciting nowadays with all the foreigners racing", plus he feels the modern Grand Prix competition really benefits from a richer mix of nationalities. Some aspects of the sports appeal still endures over the intervening years – the atmosphere, the speed (especially pronounced if you watch every week at Swindon); along with the inevitable intensity and competitiveness of the on-track action and the basic fact that "each race is different, anything can happen." I leave Graham to savour his cigarette and the almost non-existent early evening snack bar queue; an unusual sight in itself, as it defies the immutable law of huge queues, irrespective of the time of night or food quality that apparently applies countrywide to takeaway stalls at speedway meetings. Although it's still an hour to the off, the crowd has steadily built to an already decent proportion with loose clumps of chatting fans scattered here and there throughout the stadium but especially throughout the home-straight grandstand. There is quite an array of garden furniture already placed strategically on the concourse with their owners, mostly older generation people, who enjoy drinks from flasks or sandwiches from snack boxes. The track shop is totally packed having already attracted much active browsing through the piles of 'new' early season merchandise. I witness yet another purchase of the ubiquitous bright red Robins race jacket while I browse inside. There are so many people that wear these Robins jackets that I'm convinced there must be some discount when you enter the stadium if you wear one. It certainly makes a statement about the loyalty the club inspires, if not the fashion sense. Though, even to the casual observer, many of the jackets are subtly different which indicates that changing fashion mores impact even this most practical of garments.

The biggest part of the crowd has clustered down by the pits area and patiently lines the temporary-looking tall wire fence placed on the tarpaulin-covered dog track. They casually watch and in some cases strain for a glimpse of the riders and mechanics, who go about their pre-meeting preparations. The British desire to stand in a queue is only rivalled at speedway meetings by a similarly strong desire to stand and watch men fiddle with machines in the pits, but apparently only if viewed through a fence. When approached from the grandstand side of the stadium, via the tyre-laden tarpaulin of the dog track, the curious can only really easily view the increasingly feverish activity that's on the Robins side of the pits. There's an impressive age range of interested punters, from kids to balding reconstituted teenagers plus a few ladies who have strayed along to this area, mostly with the mandatory display of Robins-branded attire bought over the years which ranges from the gaudy to the comparatively subtly understated. There is also a minor outbreak of long-haired, bearded men in attendance by the pits and in the stadium: maybe it's a local variation on 'the kids for a quid' promotions with some sort of discount, hopefully restricted to males, for the 'conspicuously hirsute'?

While the bikes are warmed up and loudly roar into life in the pit lane, close by on the track Jon Cook, the visiting Eastbourne manger, is deep in earnest conversation with his team's owner Terry Russell. Who, by the quirky and slightly anomalous rules that typify modern British speedway, actually has ownership of both of the clubs who will race in tonight's meeting. While it's a cliché of sports commentary and sports reports to claim that there's only one winner, Terry will be the only one with a guarantee that this will actually be the case tonight! In speedway, there is little public debate or, indeed, public complaint about a situation where for Terry Russell it's a case of 'heads I win, tails I win'. If this were Premiership football – which is itself not normally renowned for probity in its dealings or transparency in its governance if Tom Bower's recent book Broken Dreams is to be believed – owning, say, Arsenal and Bolton wouldn't even be contemplated never mind allowed by the fans, the press or the sports governing authorities. However, this being Speedway there's not a peep of negativity or concern. Nothing, it seems, is even mentioned about this rather unique state of affairs with regards to ownership. With the sleeping dogs pointedly remaining completely catatonic, this is no doubt on the pragmatic basis that willing punters prepared to invest and support Speedway are, nowadays, somewhat thin on the ground[1].

Just prior to the rider parade and tapes flying up for the first race, the concourse of the main grandstand and the first turn is thronged with a large partisan crowd, if judged by the sea of red Robins jackets. The air is thick with local Wiltshire accents and the sound of Queen's 'We are the Champions' blasts from the stadium's tannoy speakers without any hint of irony. While, Swindon are undoubtedly the best team in Wiltshire (in fact the only team in Wiltshire), the claims to perfection and world dominance advanced by Freddie and his pals is a little far fetched when applied to Swindon Speedway club. Especially in the context of last winning League Championship honours in 1967, although the trophy cabinet has seen some action this millennium with some of the 'lesser' trophies available to teams who compete in the sport. These are sometimes unfairly characterised as the speedway equivalent of the LDV Vans or Milk Cup competitions in football in comparison to the status of the League champions' mantle; though it's all clearly pretty irrelevant to the strong affection that the club is consistently held in by the Wiltshire people. This is also the case throughout the country with speedway teams but has a long tradition particularly here in this county, where all things Swindon inspires undying loyalty. To build the sense of anticipation and excitement, we're then treated to the well used but apposite musical accompaniment of the tune of 'When the Red, Red Robin goes bob, bob, bobbing along' played over the tannoy, just as the riders march out for their introductory parade. The aural repertoire at Blunsdon sadly doesn't extend to include other tunes with an ornithological emphasis such as the legendary 'Birdie Song'. Nor is there any tune specifically appropriate to the visitors played during the evening. Maybe in the spirit of wit and lateral thinking that characterises the music of speedway

---

[1] Although, to be fair, serial investors in speedway clubs like Terry Russell, Chris Van Straaten and Tony Mole do appear to have good business acumen as well as being committed investors for the long term with continued great belief in the probable future vibrancy and health of the sport. As well as strong faith in the various communities in which their many clubs are based.

meetings, we could at least have had a song from The Eagles or something suitably mock heroic like the theme tune from the film *Where Eagles Dare*.

As it is everywhere else, the Blunsdon presentation is all about the need to enthuse the home fans and we're quickly all suitably delighted to learn that the excellent Leigh Adams will celebrate his 34th birthday tonight. Leigh has really become a local hero, since he is the out-and-out number one rider for the Robins as well as consistently topping the British Elite League averages on a regular basis over the last few years. Though he often comes across as remarkably serious and taciturn, this lack of a charismatic personality has been no obstacle to the Australian's growth in popularity at Swindon where he scores highly, lives locally and has quickly become an adopted son of the loyal Wiltshire fans.

The meeting has barely started before the events of heat 1 fatally compromise and undermine this season's league challenge by the Eagles, even before it has hardly had the chance to get going. On the first lap, David 'Floppy' Norris careens into the bend 2 air fence, while he enthusiastically chases the home-track hero Leigh Adams. It's another one of those innocuous looking crashes at speedway that has long-term repercussions way beyond the apparent seriousness of the injuries sustained by the rider. Norris is diagnosed as suffering from concussion and inevitably withdraws from the meeting with what the announcer, slightly unsympathetically, characterises as "a knock on the head". Sadly, for the rider, the Eagles' team and fans, he is never quite the same again throughout the rest of the 2005 season when astride his speedway bike. Injuries to the head and the delicate nature of the human brain means that while Floppy recovers his equilibrium and composure away from the speedway track he continues to suffer on it. The torque and vibration of a highly charged and extremely powerful speedway machine repeatedly plays havoc with three vital bones he damaged in his neck during this crash throughout the coming months.

By rights, Floppy's withdrawal should have signalled the start of a rout by the Robins over the weakened Eagles but, instead, we're treated to a great fighting team display allied to a virtuoso performance by Nicki Pedersen in a narrow 48-44 Swindon victory. On a fast track that favours competitive riders he overcomes the natural home track advantage and knowledge of Swindon's excellent top two riders, when he beats Leigh Adams three times and Lee Richardson twice during the evening[2]. In terms of entertainment, many of these races are well worth the price of the admission money alone, which includes a thrilling race in heat 8 when Andrew Moore rides his reputedly aluminium-framed bike with

[2] Lee has quite a sporting pedigree with his father Colin who also rode speedway, and his grandfather Eric was a former Sunderland footballer. Often plagued by inconsistency and for the early part of the 2005 season by engine problems, Lee's sporting pedigree doesn't provide much help on this particular evening.

considerable brio.

The atmosphere of the terraces is partisan but welcoming as we all concentrate on the competitive and keenly fought speedway meeting that unfolds throughout the evening. Stood next to me is Simon Jones and his 14-year-old son Ben, both of whom are recent converts to watching speedway fixtures at Blunsdon. Simon has had a lifelong fascination with motorbikes so, since he moved to Swindon from Cirencester, he needed very little excuse to attempt to instil that love of bikes and speed into his son through the weekly thrill and the spectacle of watching the Robins race. It's a great way to spend quality time together on a weeknight as they watch a sport they both enjoy, while mum (a life-long Swindon resident and fan) has to work. In the short time they've come to the speedway, Simon feels much more part and parcel of his local community, particularly when he chats to others about the Robins' recent meetings than he ever did in Cirencester, even after he lived there for years. "You really feel like they're your team and that you're a real part of the town itself".

Also next to me on the terraces, but at the other end of the speedway-attendance continuum, is the extremely knowledgeable, informative and voluble Eagles fan Sid Greatly. He has, as usual, followed the Eastbourne team practically everywhere they ride around the country and he proudly wears his distinctive trademark Eagles' blue and yellow race jacket. Sid is a veritable mine of information with many very strong opinions on all aspects of speedway, not just the Eastbourne Eagles. During the course of the evening, I take a brief random stroll down memory lane with Sid. He's aged well but is definitely of advanced years. The sprightly Sid has watched speedway since 1946 when he was taken along by his father. He's never looked back, and since then believes he's travelled well over a million miles going to speedway meetings. Sid cheerily notes "if I had the choice of having my life over, I'd do it all again!" Naturally a huge amount has changed in the sport over the last 59 years he has spent watching but his enthusiasm remains completely undiminished. The most notable change in that time, for Sid, is the fall off in speedway's general popularity, which is visibly reflected everywhere in the decline of the crowds, plus there have been numerous changes in the machines themselves as well as with the attitude and approach of the riders. Sid doesn't set great store by comparisons "it wasn't better in the past, it was just different." He initially followed in the footsteps of his speedway-loving father, so Sid supported the famous Dons of Wimbledon for over 40 years and recalls regular crowds of 25,000 people who attended fixtures at Plough Lane. He has legions of fascinating stories and peculiar insights from the past, which includes the flooding incident inside Wimbledon's Plough Lane Stadium that enabled some impromptu canoeing at the track. Wimbledon had many great riders over the years and Sid counts his good fortune since he regularly witnessed them ride. He has many favourites from different eras of racing and these include the diminutive Dave Jessup who rode brilliantly throughout his career but, to Sid's mind, always struggled in wet conditions at Plough Lane to the extent that (allegedly) he rarely bothered to unload the bike when it rained. He holds the promoter Ronnie Green, who lived in Hastings, in the highest respect but, in marked contrast, although he's pleased the Wimbledon club once more rides again, ultimately he completely despairs at the present Conference League incarnation of the club. "It's nothing like it was. It's sad to see it like that, compared to before; but I best not think about what they've done as it's all too upsetting".

Sid is easily transported back in time, to when he started to attend which was, in retrospect, a golden era to watch the sport in general and in London in particular. Sid regularly went to all his many local London tracks. It was a time you'd get 28,000 on a Wednesday night at New Cross to go along with the large crowds in attendance at Hackney and Haringey. Never mind the 70,000 he remembers that once attended Wembley for a League match. The stand-out star rider of this whole era of speedway watching is Ronnie Moore who, at 72, is the exact same age as Sid and whom he describes as "cool and calm, the best rider ever who'd always team ride." Sid also owns an impressive collection of speedway memorabilia that properly reflects his life-long passion and obsession. A particular source of pride and joy is Ronnie's exploits in *Once a Jolly Swagman* from his New Cross days in the 1950s. As the superstar rider of his day and in an era when the sport attracted huge crowds, Ronnie was very well rewarded financially by the standards of that time. Very deservedly so, according to Sid, as Ronnie frequently started his home and away(!) league races with a 20-yard handicap which, inevitably being the rider he was, he exhilaratingly overcame. Around 1951 or 1952 there was frequently talk of

Ronnie being paid a king's ransom, in the order of £68 for 2 rides or £110 for the night, in rightful acknowledgement of his effect on the box office that news of his appearance (and skill at riding) always generated. Though, like many people of his age, Sid's reminiscences are becoming tinged with sadness over time with the recent deaths of others. In this case the 1950s rider Ray Harris, aged 85. Just before I disappear into the Wiltshire night, Sid shies away from further considerations of mortality to wistfully remember his heroes frozen in time in his imagination, "you know Martin Dugard was the Ronnie Moore of the modern era". I leave contented feeling I've witnessed a gripping evening's racing seen, as it should be, under almost ideal conditions. Namely close, fast, entertaining and under floodlights, everything really but the warmth of a darkening summer night. Along with the added privilege of a trip down memory lane with casually met affable fellow speedway fans. In this case typified by long time speedway fanatic Sid Greatley or by Simon Jones and his son, typical of the kind of evangelical people who inevitably surround you and engage you in conversation at speedway meetings throughout the country.

28th April Swindon v. Eastbourne (Elite League A) 48-44

SKY CHATTER

"I'm pleased we're laughing 'cos it's useless really" Kelvin Tatum, (on starting-gate failure at Coventry)

RANDOM SCB RULES

0.5.3b. [Medical Officer to] ensure all competitors are physically fit, both before and during a Meeting and shall so certify if required by a Referee
8.6 a. Medical Equipment: A Stretcher, oxygen supply, apparatus to immobilise limbs and vertebrate column and First Aid medicants and materials

---

Since I lived on the Hertfordshire-Essex border and also worked in Harlow, I have always had a soft spot for the speedway club based in Hoddesdon, the home of the Rye House Rockets. Hoddesdon is a small town just outside Harlow down the A414 and much handier for the A10 than its neighbour. The borders of countries and counties are often hard to characterise but, in this part of the world, it is Essex rather than Hertfordshire that attracts the lion's share of unfair criticism and even worse jokes, particularly about its womenfolk. Maybe the reason is just snootiness or it might be because many of the new towns that rapidly sprung up in the post-war period throughout the South East were originally primarily used to house people from the poorer, East End parts of London.

Whatever the reasons, this unfair condescension has remained to this day in many people's minds and, like all bad reputations, it's something that the county of Essex just can't shake off no matter how hard it tries to emphasise its heritage, countryside or intellectual credentials. When I worked in Harlow I heard all the jokes and got to experience

firsthand the fun that was a night out on the town there. It was a town that was sort of like the Wild West, but without the Indians, and where the cowboy boots would always be white with stiletto heels. Even foreign visitors temporarily relocated to Harlow got caught up in the snobbery. The most notable example of which came from an American ex-colleague, who claimed that you could immediately tell the type of town you were in by the way it chose to advertise its local hotels. A peculiar yardstick by which to judge a town I'll agree, but it was a perspective that came from the wrecked derelict car used on a roundabout close to our workplace and the railway station that advertised (very entrepreneurially I thought) the delights of one particular local hotel. It was a family-owned establishment that I'm sure would have been much more comfortable to stay in than the rather austere local Moat House type hotel close by the M11 motorway. Such was the awareness of the comparatively lowly status of parts of Harlow, that it made some people stress that they came from Old Harlow, where they had million-pound houses years ago, rather than the less salubrious "new" Harlow[1]. However, if there was one thing everyone could agree on locally, it was that Harlow prided itself on the fact that it was a much nicer place to live than its near neighbour Hoddesdon. I always enjoyed the many times I stayed in Hoddesdon, not only because I had friends who lived there, or that I walked the dog by the canal, but also because of the peculiar claim, taken as gospel truth locally, that the town reputedly had the highest number of Ferrari owners per head of population in the UK. So many in fact that the council had to embark on a policy to remove all sleeping policemen in the town, due to the potential lost votes caused by unnecessary damage to cars, particularly those low-slung, sleek sports beasts beloved of the wealthier mid-life males from the area. My affection wasn't just because Charlie Hurley, Sunderland's 'Footballer of the [20th] Century' had lived there for years or even the occasional contract killings in pub car parks ("slayings" as the tabloids would have us properly call them). Most importantly, it was Little Lennie Silver[2] who helped breathe more life into the area when he restored speedway to the town at its rightful home of Rye House. Well, that's not strictly the reason, but it really adds a helluva lot more appeal to the area down by the canal, just a short way from that quaintly unique but narrow toll bridge by the sewage works.

Rather than follow the helpful directions printed in the bumper-sized special start of the season *Speedway Star*, I instead thought that I'd simply reminisce and drive to the stadium via Harlow. I was completely confident that, although it was a few years ago, I easily knew my way there without thinking, especially since I thought I recalled the general

[1] Modern Harlow was built as a new town in 1947 and designed by Sir Frederick Gibberd. He laid out the town with separate neighbourhoods and each contained a health centre, local shops, schools and community facilities. The town boasts a collection of modern sculpture collected by Lady Gibberd. The story of 'old' Harlow covers the ages from Roman to Victorian times and includes its Saxon and Georgian periods.

[2] Len as affectionately described by Colin Pratt

area. It was a lovely sunny day to drive through the outlying areas of Harlow, particularly as it looked the lush green garden city of the future that the town planners had always intended it to be. My intention was to cut through the Pinnacles trading estate, near where my previous employer's warehouse used to be, before I headed past the quaint, old railway station where the abandoned booking hall has subsequently become an Italian restaurant. From there it should be a short drive, albeit one that will incur a 50p toll over the toll bridge, just after you've skirted past the entrance and grounds of the impressive Down Hall Hotel. Unfortunately, confidence and my admiration for the many new buildings that appeared to have sprung up on the trading estate in the last few years distracted me. Harlow has always been a town that attracted main or regional distribution centres, due to its proximity to the various motorways that head in all directions, and to London. Something that definitely belies the usual image of this part of the Hertfordshire-Essex borders in the popular imagination is some of Britain's loveliest and most underestimated countryside in England; full of lost gems, especially given that so many of its towns and villages appeared in the Domesday Book. However, I quickly find myself lost in the village of Royden. While it looks shockingly familiar to me (having been to the pub there on a number of occasions) I swiftly realise that I'm totally lost and unsure of the best way to get myself to the annoyingly close speedway stadium.

As it's a sunny Saturday afternoon, Royden appears to be completely deserted apart from the odd passing car. Maybe they're all away, shopping at Bluewater or in the shade at home; wherever they are they're definitely not wandering the country lanes so that I can ask them for directions. I retrace my steps and luckily spot a middle-aged man who fastidiously tends his flowerbed in front of his house. Pleased to have found someone, I stroll over to interrupt the careful husbanding of his flowerbeds and ask for directions.
"Excuse me, do you happen to know the best way to the speedway from here?"
"Do I know the best way to the speedway?" (He repeats the question back to me as if he needs to weigh its meaning.)
"Yes. I used to live round here, but I've got lost."
"Well it's not a question you hear so much round here anymore, but as it happens, yes I do, as I used to ride there in the 1960s."

Of all the people to find and stop to ask directions, I've stumbled across Geoff Maloney, a fit man apparently in his 50s but who turns out to be 60. He needs no second invitation to have a brief stroll down memory lane to fondly recall the thrill and camaraderie of his riding days. Geoff started late in the sport, aged 22, and then rode from 1967 to 1974 with Rayleigh and Rye House. It's a part of his life that still remains very significant for him and he still regularly keeps in touch with his friends in the sport, especially his good friend Bengt 'Banger' Jansson; who is one of my favourite riders from his racing days at Reading when I was a teenager, although Bengt is generally most fondly remembered within the sport for his contributions to Hackney Speedway. Geoff attends some of the Veteran Speedway Riders Association events whenever he can to catch up with friends, recollect old times and renew acquaintances. It's like a select but very friendly club. The next event he'll attend is the 'Hackney Reunion' later in the summer, though not technically a Veterans' event it's a keenly anticipated get together for fans and riders from this popular but now defunct club. The Len Silver connection is strong there, since he was its famous, ebullient and always hard-working promoter. According to Geoff, he was a man on a mission a man who continually strove for new ways to promote the sport, attract fans to Hackney on a Friday night and generally tried to draw the entertainment and thrill of speedway racing to wider attention. Geoff has great admiration for Len's skills and, as a member of the old school of speedway promotion, it's a tradition that he still carries on at Rye House, as anyone who visits the stadium will notice.

While the Hawks no longer ride, the memory and camaraderie lives on. The 'Hackney Reunion' Dinner Dance will be held at a wildlife park in the local area, which will also be the site for a permanent speedway museum. The museum has yet to be built and there's a fund-raising campaign to generate the £50,000 or so it requires. Donations have almost reached half way[3] and there have been tireless fund-raising and consciousness-raising efforts that most frequently involve the

[3] The appeal is now on the cusp of success and by the time this book is published should have already been achieved.

ubiquitous ex-rider George Barclay and his wife, Linda, who have evangelised about the concept at speedway meetings and social events throughout the country. Geoff thinks that a permanent memorial to the sport and its riders is a great idea too, particularly given the importance that speedway used to have in the country. He is saddened by its decline from the post-war period boom of interest and attendances. While there was a subsequent renaissance during Geoff's riding days in the late 1960s and early 1970s, this was itself a period when the sport had arguably already passed its heyday, especially when compared to those regular attendances of the early post-war years. Not that he saw it like that then but the various cadres and dynasties created by dynamic, controversial or entrepreneurial larger-than-life characters, particularly on the promotional side – Geoff recalls the dominance of Allied Promotions or people like Len Silver, Reg Fearman and Wally Mawdsley – have effectively declined or disappeared in the contemporary version of speedway. The fact that Len still continues as an active promoter is the exception and not the rule; the new breed of promoter and the diminished number of the 'old school' type promoters are sources of sadness for Geoff. Though he still keeps up with the modern version of the sport, mostly through gossip with friends and through the media, he is well informed about the increasingly dominant present-day club owners like Terry Russell and Tony Mole as well as the ambitious but arriviste Chief Executive Officer of the BSI, John Postlethwaite. Nonetheless, his primary worry remains exactly where the next British World Champion will come from. The sport has become flooded with foreign riders and there's a dearth of similarly talented riders from these shores. Those that there are, with few exceptions, don't quite have the right approach and attitude to ensure that they really succeed. It's a situation that Geoff believes is not helped by the fact that in order to be the best in the world you have to be a dedicated and an extremely skilful rider, but you also need that "little bit extra to succeed". The vital ingredient, in his opinion, if you are to reach the top in speedway is a "bit of anger and aggression". There are ultimately no awards for niceness and many if you display the necessary ruthlessness and steely determination. Tony Rickardsson has it; the unpopular in some quarters, Nicki Pedersen definitely has it; while the present World Champion, Jason Crump, is admired by Geoff for the grit he demonstrates and through his sometimes robust technique. He sends me on my way with his good wishes and a request to pass on "Geoff says hello" to Len Silver should I bump into him this evening.

Armed with accurate directions, my short drive takes me over the toll bridge and into an already extremely crowded stadium car park, where the marshals creatively manage the large volume of cars and the limited available space. The Under-21 British Championship has been well promoted by Len Silver and many fans have been attracted from around the country by the early season chance to watch the young British potential stars of the future, all gathered in one location for the night. The championship has run since 1969, when it was originally called the 'Junior Championship of Great Britain'. It was run as a second-half event at Wimbledon that year before it became an event in its own right the next year. It ran for many years at Kingsmead Stadium in Canterbury, which, like Hackney and many other places, has now ceased to be an active part of the contemporary version of the sport. In 2004 Len Silver, avowedly keen on youth development and ever capable as a promoter, ran the event so successfully at the Rye House Stadium that it was almost a foregone conclusion that he would stage the event again the next year. The fact that the event is on a Saturday night, the regular race night for the Rye House 'Rockets' team, works well to maximise the number of parents, family friends and fans able to attend. There's already a good-humoured and large queue of eager fans, who patiently wait outside the entrance turnstiles in the warm late afternoon sunshine, albeit with a steady buzz of expectant conversation. When you finally arrive inside the stadium you immediately come across the small programme stall where some of the UK's youngest programme sellers serve you. Both of the young girls, Shannon Gutteridge and Danni Smith, are friendly and meticulous in the way that only earnest young people can be. They answer my jovial but obvious questions with patient and unselfconscious directness and honesty. They give some straightforward directions to the track shop, which is only 30 seconds away but hidden from sight, though they're keen to stress, "we don't have time to chat as we have work to do".

The track shop is located just by the entrance to the bar and refreshments area and is a short distance from the only impressive building at the stadium, the main grandstand which overlooks the start line and provides an excellent view of the rest of the circuit. There is a whole variety of speedway merchandise laid out on tables, with the usual range of programme boards, books, pens, clothing, replica models as well as an impressive array of Rye House branded paraphernalia. The baseball caps appear to be particularly contemporary in style and extremely good value at £6, but I decide against a purchase, mostly on the basis that I don't actually support Rye House. The lure and ease of digital photography tempts me to take a couple of pictures of the track shop and I notice the severe reluctance of the lady serving to be included in any shot. She ducks behind the jamb of the doorway in an attempt to avoid being captured for posterity, in sharp contrast to the young girls on the programme desk who were happy to pose for a photo for my book[4]. The manager of the shop, Andy Griggs, is happy to pose by his merchandise, after he observes, "we don't get many people taking photos of the track shop around here." He's a very well-informed and friendly man, who's easy to talk with while a large crowd of customers carefully examine the range of goods on offer at the shop but only infrequently buy them. The shop has an ideal location, as everyone has to pass it if they wish to go to the main grandstand, the pits, the bar or attempt to purchase some of the renowned refreshments on offer at the stadium. Andy informs me that the most popular items in the shop are, obviously enough, the more reasonably priced goods branded in some way with the Rye House Speedway logo or name, but he's keen to stress that the fans at Rye, unlike some other clubs he names, aren't narrowly partisan but enthusiasts for the sport in general and extremely knowledgeable. Consequently, he can confidently hold a much wider range of items, including books, videos and DVDs, and expect reasonable demand. He's happy to sell any books, particularly those that mention or feature Rye House.

Andy looks forward with great excitement and very high expectations about the Rye House Rockets squad's potential to achieve success in the forthcoming 2005 Premier League season ahead, even though they have yet to race the first League fixture of the season[5]. This season the Rockets have a very strong side, which features many promising young British riders, some of whom are very much in evidence tonight, while five of the team have qualified to ride in tonight's Under-21 Championship. This is primarily a function of Len Silver's policy towards youth development, both at the Premier League level but also a direct result of the Raiders team who compete in the Conference League. Andy sincerely believes that the

[4] Only after a short delay while I explained to them that I needed to search for a responsible adult to give their permission before one said, " it doesn't matter, please hurry up as we have programmes to sell!"

[5] The opening fixture of their campaign is two days later on the Bank Holiday Monday against the defending champions Hull. Andy suggests it would be a potentially close meeting that I really shouldn't miss, especially as I can fit it in before my trip to Wolverhampton on the same day.

fans at Rye House are especially fortunate to have the promoter and the track that they presently have, "Len prepares a brilliant track and its very fair for everyone with lots of passing". Andy is sure that I will enjoy my evening and any subsequent visits to the Hoddesdon track.

I walk through the bar and building adjacent to the track shop in search of the best vantage point from which to watch tonight's fixture and also to savour the pre-meeting atmosphere. As I head towards the grandstands, I notice that the interior of the catering area has the type of wood finish that you'd expect in a Scandinavian chalet or sauna; though this is no disincentive to its extreme popularity and already the queues are quite something. The aroma of the cooking food smells tempting; the quality and variety of the catering at Rye House is something that Len Silver is always keen to lay great emphasis upon when he advertises the forthcoming events and stadium facilities at Hoddesdon in his frequent *Speedway Star* adverts. The signature dish of the club appears to be fish and chips; they're very popular throughout the evening and have a quality that Len claims is without parallel although, that said, he never reveals exactly what rival outlets he actually compares them to. Morning meetings at Rye House have the added culinary attraction of bacon butties to satisfy the early morning craving for hot food (and salt replenishment) and later during the 2005 season Len makes great play in his adverts of his rather unique claim to be, "the first and the only track in the country to offer kebabs". Which is quite a claim to fame, shrewd marketing and very canny as the sales of food and drink in facilities that he owns (rather than rents) will always make a hugely significant contribution to the total level of net profits delivered by the speedway club.

There is no more experienced promoter in the country and Len has forgotten more than most promoters remember when it comes to gaining attention for the various activities at a speedway club. Greyhounds also run regularly at the stadium and, I gather from reading the *Speedway Star* that he also owns a successful travel agency that specialises in skiing holidays among others. For the last few seasons, he has utilised his travel agency contacts to great effect with an invitation for all the riders in his squad to enjoy a ski trip that also serves as a motivational close-season team-building exercise. Which is great for club morale, economical to organise at discounted rates and it also provides some valuable additional free advertising for his travel business in the pages of the speedway press or via the Internet forums[6].

I decide not to stand in the only substantial grandstand in the stadium, that overlooks the start line, nor in the other covered grandstand that has a distinctively temporary or half-built appearance. This stand is a structure constructed from a bizarre tangle of scaffolding poles, albeit with comfortable wooden planks that serve as the seats. It is located by the referee's box along the part of the home straight that leads towards the first corner, before it's intersected with the pits lane exit to the track. Rather than cross this pathway I hang back and sit in one of the few available spaces that remain, eat my sandwiches and study my match programme, while I half-listen to the various conversations of the fans that surround me. You can't really see that clearly into the pits from here, even if you stand by the pits lane, because of the distance and the wall that obscures the view. Many of the riders pace the track circuit to inspect the surface or stand in groups deep in conversation in a small area, which I later gather is the riders' viewing area, and is separated from the fans by some crash barriers.

All around me there are a lot of people here who already know each other and the dominant local accent sounds to my ears to be a London one. To judge from their conversation, there's also a strong Harlow contingent on these terraces along with, an inevitable sight at any speedway meeting, a very strong representation of members of the older generation. There is a preponderance of adults with their children in replica football shirts, which isn't a garment that you notice so much of at speedway fixtures round the country in comparison to team anoraks or other speedway branded items. But here this evening, it appears that there's a greater display of allegiance to football clubs rather than team jackets or the speedway replica shirts that have slowly started to catch on among the Elite League fans. Very noticeably, the London clubs dominate with West Ham, Tottenham and Chelsea shirts on display in comparison to any items of clothing that bear speedway insignia. Most peculiarly, even some of the older generation wear these alien replica shirts; maybe it's just the way that London pride still manifests itself in this part of Hertfordshire.

People who appear to be officials of the speedway club, in mostly matching overalls, purposefully stride up and back from the pits to the track regularly without apparently really doing anything. Apart from that, the only visible sign of last-minute preparations is the tractor that frequently circles the track. There are also a lot of young men, mostly riders partially dressed in their kevlars and their mechanics plus a smattering of obsessive fathers, who take turns to frequently pop up from the pits to ostentatiously lean on the crash barriers of their viewing area to watch the tractor as it passes. Maybe the sight of the tractor provides the required inspiration or levels of concentration they'll shortly require. Or, else they gaze off into the distance lost in thought, stare knowingly or wistfully at the track, before they exchange a few words with the older adults that surround them, before they head back to the pits once more. It's noticeable that compared to a traditional team meeting, there are a larger number of helpers than usual, hangers on and advisors for the 16 riders that comprise the field for this evenings Under-21 Championship event. Since there is absolutely nothing else to entertain us, many in the audience avidly watch the various people mill about the pathway that leads from the pits to the track or the viewing area.

I decide that it would best to change my seat for a viewing position on the banked open terraces of the first bend corner, where it joins the apex of the second bend. While I sit there, numerous people go past clutching their large portions of fish and chips, which indicates that the catering outlet located inside the wood-panelled interior of the main grandstand area does a significant and profitable trade with many hungry speedway fans. I choose a spot a few rows back on the open terrace, which has a sort of cinder material base and uses vertical wooden planks to keep the steps in place. All this area of the terraces appears well maintained and thoughtfully designed to maximise practicality but to minimise costs of construction and maintenance.

[6] On a personal note, a few weeks after my visits to Rye House, the Chairman of the BSPA, Peter Toogood, very kindly circulated a letter to all the UK promoters to advise them of my proposed travel itinerary of research visits for my book throughout all speedway tracks in the country. Although his club didn't appear on this itinerary, as I'd already visited by then, Len immediately wrote to me by return (along with the courteous Tony Mole who was the only other promoter to reply directly). In his letter, Len welcomed my book and the possibility of a research visit but went out of his way to note that, since he assumed it was a "commercial project", he would, unfortunately, be unable to permit me to have free entry to his facilities, unless I had press accreditation. Though his assumption isn't completely correct as a contribution to the Speedway Riders Benevolent Fund will be made for each copy sold and, anyway, it's unlikely the book will make a profit. Nonetheless, his letter demonstrates exactly why Len Silver succeeds as a promoter, when so many of his contemporaries have failed or have ultimately disappeared. Clearly this success has come through close control of his own financial destiny allied to his own keen sense of the importance of marketing and public relations. On a final note, I never sought free entry from Mr Silver – though it would be greatly appreciated in the future – but still visited his track twice. Also in repeated calls I struggled to find any suitable dates or times, via his extremely protective assistant, to avail myself of his kind offer of an interview and assistance with the compilation of this book. This is my loss and, hopefully, one that can be put right in the future, especially since so many people I've met have spoken so highly of his knowledge, energy and vision for the sport!

While I eat my sandwiches, I take the chance to study the programme to try to get a much better idea of all the young men that will compete for the crown of British Under-21 Champion. The pre-meeting favourite is Edward Kennett who rides at the track for Rye House and so will have some sort of home-track advantage over some of his rivals, except for his four Rye House team mates who also compete and should be able to slightly mitigate this advantage. Edward's main edge though is based on a combination of his confidence and his ability, which is considerable for someone of his age. It's a skill that he's had to work and practise hard to acquire, through the junior ranks at Eastbourne, a place where he has also had to bear comparisons with his famous uncle Gordon. This season he's left the familiar and comfortable surroundings of the Eastbourne track to go on loan to ply his trade with their local Elite League rivals Poole; however, it's his regular Rye House Premier League meetings that have most helped him to progress, since he rides for them competitively every week of the season.

Another Eastbourne asset at the meeting is Dan Giffard, whose team of cheerleaders and supporters I accidentally meet when I ask if they mind if I take their photograph, as the sight of three women who in turn avidly read the match programme or, alternatively, gaze track wards completely captures the casual but slightly earnest atmosphere of the terraces around me. Dan's team of keen supporters is composed of Mrs Christine Filmer, her daughter Laura and her aunt Anne; all of them are convinced that they'll witness Dan lift the trophy later that night. He rides as a heat leader for the Wildcats of Weymouth in the Conference League; ever since he recovered from some serious, career-threatening injuries he sustained when he rode in a Premier League fixture against King's Lynn at Stoke in 2003. Last season at Weymouth, he had already started to rekindle the consistent form and early promise that he initially demonstrated in 2001 and 2002, prior to his injuries. Victory here would take that process of consolidation to another and higher level, as well as widely signal his rejuvenation and reconfirm his future potential to a much wider audience. As an unattached fan with no loyalties to any particular rider in the championship, I promise his team of cheerleaders that I will shout along with them for Dan! Christine confidently suggests, "you can even get his photo later when he's holding the cup", though, in fact I manage to get his photo a few minutes later when he chats, and smooches, with Laura over the crash barriers of the riders area, with her marooned on one side of this temporary fence and Dan on the other side. Hopefully, these last-minute tips, gestures of affection and words of encouragement will make the vital difference to his luck and performance tonight.

While we wait for the pre-meeting parade, I learn from the match programme that a great friend of the U21 Championship and a real advocate for giving youngsters a regular platform to express their speedway skills within the sport is that experienced British speedway character, Peter Oakes. He is the brains and dynamic impetus behind the recent emergence of the Under-15 Academy League, he is the GB Under-21 team manager and has been publicly acknowledged by Len Silver as a driving force behind the continued success of the reincarnation and rejuvenation of these championships. Peter has had many, many years' involvement in the sport as a promoter, team manager (though presently co-manager with Coventry), writer, journalist and commentator. I still have some of his books from when I was a fanatical speedway teenager and, on my travels, I've rather bizarrely often been mistaken for Peter Oakes by some mystified riders[7]. The match programme includes his insightful overview and brief history of the Championship. The message that quickly comes across, loud and clear, is that while many previous winners of this competition have gone on to confirm their abilities and find fame, if not necessarily fortune, within the sport; many others have most definitely not done so. For every illustrious

[7] I imagine that this is on the basis of the common assumption that any book that somehow involves the attempt to cover all the speedway clubs in this country must be written and conceived by Peter Oakes or, at least, somehow connected to him. This misperception is particularly prevalent among foreign speedway riders, unable to identify the subtle but marked nuances of various English accents, particularly if they have just started to make their living in the UK. At some point over the previous months, I gather that practically all riders will have received a call from Peter to request an update for his database of information, which he uses to compile the entries in his peripatetic Who's Who-type guidebook to British speedway. For many lesser-known riders this appears to be their only, often mysterious, contact with interested journalists outside that regularly organised on their behalf by the promoters of their clubs with the local or speedway trade press. Peter writes very well and during the close season often produces a must-read column for the Speedway Star, which is effectively as close as what passes for 'gossip' between the officially sanctioned club and BSPA statements on the one hand and the wilder speculations of the unofficial speedway Internet forums on the other. The majority of his information comes from his extensive network of contacts built up over the years and remains, to all intents and purposes, authorised comment in all but name.

name that has appeared on the championship trophy, there are many other riders that have not lived up to the potential of their late teenage years. The reasons vary but, as Peter succinctly puts it when he describes these riders, "they probably never had a better night throughout their careers than when they were crowned British Junior Champion". I won't list the names that Peter includes as examples of this phenomenon, but it does illustrate a truth of everyday life that the fragility of everyone's lives, hopes and dreams can change dramatically without reason or warning; sometimes for the better and other times for the worse. Once you have reached a pinnacle in your chosen field or your life, there is no sure guide to the future.

But rather than wax philosophical, it's worth noting that if you manage to finish as one of the top riders in this event, it ensures that you are able to take part in the further qualifying rounds of the world equivalent of this championship for the Under-21 age group. These rounds take place throughout Europe and pit the riders against the best of each country from their generation. It's quite an incentive, perhaps, much greater than the actual financial benefit of the win tonight, which I heard rumoured later, is a cheque for only £400. This appears a small and rather exploitative financial reward given the supposed prestige of the event and the size of the crowd attracted to watch them race for the title. However, at least they can actually take part in an impartial and fair qualification process to potentially become World Under-21 Champion. Which is much more than can be said for the current senior version of the more prestigious World Championship Grand Prix series[8].

Tonight at Rye House, the dreams and aspirations of the cream of British speedway talent, no matter how precarious these might ultimately turn out to be, still have a meaningful qualification competition to ride in as well as an environment in which they can flourish and grow. This is as it should be; they can leave any anxiety, disillusionment or cynicism about Grand Prix qualification for the future when, hopefully, progression and independent, professional administration of the Grand Prix will have become the confirmed order of the day. The goal for everyone who takes part in this meeting is, ultimately, to ride on MERIT in the Under-21 World Championship Final, which is to be held later in the summer at Wiener Neustadt in Austria on August 17th. Everything about the organisation of this Championship event appears to go smoothly and with an ease that belies the hard work and efforts that it really must have taken to achieve that impression. There's a strong hint of military-style regimentation and planning about the place; which is, perhaps, as it should be since it comfortably fits with the wartime generation and ethos from which the promoter drew his own formative experiences of life. It is also echoed when Len Silver leads a troupe of his staff onto the circuit in precise military fashion, literally marching in formation and smartly attired in their distinctive uniforms as they walk onto the track as though on a parade. The ceremonial atmosphere is complimented by the many Union Flags that line the perimeter of the whole stadium and flutter or, given how little breeze there is, gently sussurate against the darkening sky. The display of flags and the march of the track staff echoes an outlook that is keen to simultaneously commemorate the national importance of this championship but also to send a signal with regard to the strong level of general pride and patriotism felt by the promoter. You just know that Len Silver is proud to be British, keeps British values and tries to reflect these beliefs, as best he can in a commercial environment, throughout his club. The man himself heads up his contingent of staff – all the assorted track rakers, tractor drivers and safety marshals – each of whom adheres to the discipline of the group, which is further confirmed by everyone being smartly dressed in a jacket and tie. No doubt, all their clothes are also immaculately pressed although I can't actually confirm that from the distance I am away on the terraces. He might be diminutive in stature but you know that Len is definitely in command.

[8] There has been some recent debate about the issue of rider selection for the World Championship Grand Prix series, particularly as it applies to the closed entry qualification and nomination operated by the latest contractual rights holders Benfield Sports International. However, it should be noted, that all changes to this competition always have to be sanctioned by the FIM. Many critics highlight that entry to the GP series is now effectively by invitation only and it thereby remains a predictable and a closed tournament. In order to address these claims, that there is no incentive or qualification procedure for upcoming and experienced speedway stars from any country to take part in this key event on the basis of merit, changes have been made by BSI to ensure that some riders can qualify for the 2007 version of the GP series. Though the majority of competitors for the 2007 series will still not qualify by this method. In addition to the 3 "qualifiers", the Top 8 from the 2006 series will automatically qualify and thereby 5 will be selected. This is the same selection procedure that denied Hans Andersen a place in the 2006 GP series.

It's an impression reinforced by Len's introductory comments and welcome to the assembled crowd over the tannoy, while all the riders embark on a circuit of waving nonchalantly as they go round the track together on the back of a fancy, American style, blue pick-up truck. It appears speedway meetings all over the country are typified by a quick bout of compulsory, but often half-hearted, waving by the riders to the assembled fans and neutrals before they return to the pits to ready themselves to engage and challenge each other to a contest of skill, bravery and commitment on bikes without brakes. After they've all clambered off the back of the pick-up truck, they're all individually introduced to us, which is an ideal opportunity for me to gauge the relative popularity of the riders tonight in this neck of the woods. The biggest cheer by far is for Edward Kennett although, around me, the biggest cheer is for Dan Giffard from his own special group of cheerleaders seated directly behind me on the tiered terraces. Now that the event is nearly underway, I decide to recheck their anticipation levels about a likely Giffard victory, only to be told about Kennett that they now feel, "he's too good, that one!" If the spirit of the blitz type atmosphere that has been created by Len and his staff were to continue then there should be some stirring Vera Lynn music at this point but, instead, we make do with some music from what I imagine, and would bet serious money, that Len still calls "the Hit Parade". One thing is certain, none of the ambitious young riders here tonight will be just going through the motions, as if it's yet another speedway meeting of no real consequence. They will all be determined to do well for themselves, their families, supporters and sponsors.

The first heat gets underway, with practically every other rider in the Championship crowded into the small viewing area, demarcated from the terraces by the crash barriers, to analyse the race and pick up guidance for their future part in tonight's contest. Since I sit so close to the pit lane path and riders' viewing area, I'm ideally placed to watch the comings and goings, the joy and the upset as the night progresses. It's also noticeable that there are a number of senior riders who help out various riders in the pits; whether they undertake mechanical duties, offer words of encouragement, advice or just general support it's all very impressive and typical of the collegiate, community emphasis of British speedway. The senior professional rider at Rye House, Brent Werner, is most definitely here to help out; his shaven bald head is most distinctive; since it glints in the glare of the floodlights, while he continually dashes about here and there. It is also Brent's testimonial year at Rye House this season. We've already been informed that later there will be a raffle; that will go round among the fans here in attendance tonight, in order to raise some more funds for his benefit. We'll all get the chance to win one of Brent's helmets signed by all of the competitors who ride tonight; so quite a commemorative prize for some fortunate fan to get really excited about. Hopefully it will be me!

After each completed heat the riders immediately return to just in front of us, to be greeted by their mechanics for a quick bit of TLC for the bikes. This inevitably involves a quick spray of each bike's engine with some form of, I assume, lubrication or protective aerosol. Before the rider then dismounts to limp quickly back to the pits, employing the distinctive gait that all riders adopt when, for the duration of the meeting, they wear a steel shoe on their left foot. I relish that I have an ideal vantage point from which to observe all the riders get pushed off before each race, consider their demeanour upon their return, and generally get to study closely how they and their parents or helpers react to the gradually rising pressure of the event, when they intermittently gather to watch in the riders' viewing area. It's also an excellent vantage point from which to experience each race; since the riders all shoot towards us at great speed, to compete for space and position, from the tapes for that all-important bend 1 of the first lap. Plus, we're well placed to watch the riders jockey for position, as we're right on top of the first bend action and can get to clearly view all the various manoeuvres and tactics that they strategically employ, in the blink of an eye, during turns 1 and 2 to gain that vital inch of track, race position or racing line.

Heat 2 includes Dan Giffard's first appearance of the evening and he wins it easily, which delights our tiny partisan corner of the stadium. The next race results in a win for Rye House Rocket, Daniel King, who takes full advantage of his local track knowledge with a superb exhibition of controlled passing. This skill enables him to easily sweep past the two riders already ahead of him before he continues on for a comfortable victory. It's a manoeuvre that leaves Essex-based Chris Schramm in second place, who unusually for a Saturday night doesn't find himself racing at his Premier League club's home meeting in faraway Berwick. It's the second successive Saturday I've watched him race and, subsequently I noticed his tipple of choice in the bar afterwards; so I hope that tonight they've got a few of those blue alcopop drinks in stock at the Hoddesdon bar, should he need to celebrate victory in this Championship tonight.

We're then distracted by the arrival of the promised chance to win Brent Werner's signed white-coloured crash helmet in one of his many testimonial raffles planned for this season. The lady who sells the tickets works on the testimonial committee for this event, well actually there are many events including the showpiece event of the Testimonial itself to be held in October. I place my money in the bucket carried by her excited but efficient young helper and cross my fingers that I've just bought the lucky winning ticket.

Heat 4 has Chris Johnson fall, but still have the wherewithal and enough of the sporting gene to clear the track of himself and his bike, to thereby avoid any delay to the other competitors in the race, before he then collapses, dramatically, in agony on the centre green. He writhes and lies there with the St John Ambulance staff for the remainder of the race before they are joined by concerned members of the Johnson pits team, all of whom sprint with great determination over to also attend to him. Under the rules of the sport, only a rider's team mates or mechanics can go to his aid on the track; so any spectating parents or girlfriends will have to endure additional anxiety while they sit or stand tight at the edge of the track to receive any news, rather than to rush over to get it themselves. I suppose if your loved ones are involved in a dangerous sport like speedway, this extra delay just has to be accepted, though it goes against your natural instincts.

Edward Kennett then has his first win of the night in a strange race that concludes with the only one other finisher, his team mate Tommy Allen; while William Lawson has a long walk back to the pits, pushing his bike, after an engine failure in the race leaves him in a far from happy mood. Dan Giffard wins the next race to cause another ripple of anticipation and optimism to run through his cheerleaders in our section of the stand. In heat 8, Kennett then matches this excellent start to the competition with his second rather easy victory. We are immediately treated to his reappearance in the very next heat which, when I looked ahead through the programme beforehand, stood out as though it would be the one of the key heats of the meeting; since it pitched many of the fancied riders against each other. Almost immediately, as the riders depart the tapes in a close group, we witness a fiercely contested race in just three corners of action. Initially the main protagonist Kennett almost physically moves his rival Tom Brown aside who then, in turn, manages to immediately re-pass Kennett on the exit of the second bend of the first lap before he then falls at speed on the third bend after Kennett powered back underneath him, without contact, for the lead. It's a racing incident that typifies the type of determination that Geoff Maloney earlier saw as an essential component of any rider's outlook and make up; particularly if they intend to have a career where they rise to the challenge and excel, in order to really become the 'first among equals' among their peers and contemporaries. Tom Brown is subsequently excluded and is demonstrably very unhappy with Kennett, whom he physically confronts, with flailing arms and wild gestures, when he also shares his thoughts on the topic in an extremely heated manner. In the re-run of the race Kennett then has an engine failure on the final lap and has to sprint for almost a complete circuit, pushing his bike all the way round to the finish line for a well-earned solitary point gained behind James Brundle and Adam Roynon.

Laura has another quick smooch and final word of encouragement with Dan, over the crash barriers of the riders' area before the next race. It's essential that he aim for his third consecutive victory in order to try to keep parity with the other Championship favourites. The dropped points we've just witnessed from one of the favourites, Edward Kennett, make a win for Dan even more vital to establish a small cushion before their head-to-head meeting in heat 15. Sadly the next race, heat 10, was to prove to be the turning point of his Championship campaign. Giffard just about led by a whisker when all the riders came out of the first bend but, just immediately behind him, there was a mass pile up cum crash that involved every other rider in the race, except Dan. It was a dramatic collision of men and machines that was, in my opinion, since it happened right in front of me, caused by Steve Boxall in the yellow helmet. The referee, Ronnie Allen, saw it differently or erred on the side of indecision when he then ordered a re-run of the heat with all four riders, without the expected exclusion of Boxall as the primary cause of the stoppage. There is an apparently immutable law in these situations, where the rider who led in the initial attempt to race, then doesn't make anything like a similarly good start and, usually, the rider putatively at fault also then goes on to win. So it would prove, when Boxall took full advantage, helped by Giffard who left the tapes as though he had suddenly decided to compete on a solid lead bike. Unable to manage a third consecutive victory, the solitary point gained by Giffard left him tied overall with Kennett on seven points while Boxall led the Championship on eight points from his three rides. Such, then, is the mix of skill and good fortune that goes to make up life, never mind a speedway career.

The heats continue to pass with ruthless efficiency, which is a compliment to the organisational abilities of the Rye House promotion, the referee and track staff. An older man, whom I assume to be the Clerk of the Course, appears instrumental in ensuring that this speed is maintained throughout the night. He constantly chivvies everyone along, usually with a loud shout of, "when you're ready boys!" The referee makes another apparent error in heat 13, albeit one that would be almost impossible for him to realise or see from the distant referee's box at Rye House. In front of everyone in my section, Adam Roynon clearly crossed the inside white line of bend 2 with both wheels of his bike on his second lap; for which he should, if the rules are correctly upheld, be excluded. Fortunately the subsequent result and points from this heat ultimately have no meaningful influence on the final destination of the Championship trophy.

The vital, eagerly anticipated and decisive heat 15 quickly arrives. Kennett powers to an easy victory from Daniel King and Richard Hall, while disaster befalls Dan's hopes of a significant evening when he finishes in last place. It's a result that stuns his cheerleaders into silence, with glum faces all round but, since it's then the interval break, we then all get extra time to contemplate the reality of the situation. Laura goes off to speak with Dan and I speak with the man next to me who has continually explained events on the track throughout in some detail to his young son. He lives in Hoddesdon and is so close to the track that he can hear the noise at home, if the wind is in the right direction. He's always loved the smell and atmosphere of the sport and we're both in agreement that we're all lucky to be able to watch tonight's meeting in ideal conditions, since it's a pleasantly temperate evening and the majority of the meeting has taken place under floodlights[9].

In a previous era and incarnation of speedway at Rye House, the man warmly recollects how he used to help grade the track and push the bikes out on the Sunday afternoons of his almost-forgotten teenage years. He started coming at 15 and is now keen to, hopefully, infect his son with the bug slightly earlier than he ever was. The length of the meeting and the number of races appear to overwhelm his son too much for him to enjoy or fully comprehend, since he repeatedly claims that he only really likes to see crashes rather than the races. The crashes do clearly fascinate him, if you judge his ability to graphically describe them in detail and he openly admits to disappointment at the lack of drama so far during this meeting. They'd come much more often but his father dismisses the idea because "it's too expensive for families like us to attend regularly". Since he needs to distract his son from the boredom induced by his recollections, they wander off to enjoy the entertainment of queuing to get some of the very popular fish and chips that have passed us continuously throughout the evening.

I've struggled to master the basic functions of my camera, so I ask the ladies if I can have another attempt to capture them all together, to which Christine jokingly replies, "only if you can make me look like Rachel Hunter!" This could prove beyond my capabilities, although it's a mystifying request, since she already looks attractive enough just as herself.

Even though it prolongs the anticipation and excitement for the fans, I'm still old-fashioned enough to think that the winner on points after the 20 heats has earned the right to be declared the overall winner. In this competition, and it's a blight that increasingly appears to be widely infectious in contemporary speedway, there are often further races between the top point scorers to determine the ultimate winner. The format at this championship is that the top two riders automatically qualify for the final while the next four best-placed riders compete in a semi-final, with the first- and second-placed riders from that penultimate race then progressing to the final. All very silly, but the upshot of this qualification format is that Dan still has an outside chance and might still qualify for the semi-final. But only if he wins his last race and the remainder of the results go his way in the other heats. While his cheerleaders bite their nails in nervous anticipation, the referee continues with his campaign to inject some artificial excitement into proceedings with some more bizarre decisions, this time in heat 19. In the first re-run of the heat, Richard Hall clashes with Tommy Allen and forces him into the fence on the second bend of the first lap. Allen manages not to fall but travels around ten painful yards without the aid of his bike. The referee puts on the red exclusion light to (correctly in my view) exclude Hall before he then changes his mind, to instead exclude the unfortunate Allen in the green helmet. Who says referees never change their minds? Hall then goes on to win the repeat re-run race to qualify for the semi-final run off whereas Allen, who looked a certainty to at least make the semi-final if not go to the final directly if he'd won, misses out on the chance for potential glory. Dan returns to form to win the vital heat 20 to go thereby into the semi-final run off. It's a race too far for him because it's a heat where he, sadly, makes another shockingly poor start and can only finish third, and so fails to make the final cut. In the final Kennett justifies his status as pre-tournament favourite when he wins easily to wildly ecstatic celebrations from the crowd and his entourage. It's a deserved victory against his contemporaries; especially since his only dropped points of the night were solely due to mechanical failure.

The centre-green presentations, with Len in command, take place to warm applause and loud congratulation. Edward Kennett definitely appears destined to be one of those young men who'll go onto greater things within the sport, rather than just this night and its memories representing the absolute pinnacle of his career. That would be my opinion and, no doubt, many of the other people here in Hoddesdon who witnessed his almost flawless riding throughout the night and, ultimately, the rather imperious manner of his victory.

30th April U21 British Championship (Rye House) Edward Kennett

---

[9] I believe that these are the ideal conditions because your eyes naturally concentrate on the races on the track without unnecessary distraction and, thereby, it makes the whole spectacle appear much more gladiatorial. Quite why this happens is hard to explain. But it's definitely an effect that, under the floodlights, is always created. Mostly because the lighting appears to empty the surrounding world of detail only to concentrate and imbue the racing with enhanced significance – the colours, the sheer speed and the spectacle of the competition of four men on highly powered bikes comes alive, captures you and absorbs you. Time does strange things when you observe these floodlit speedway races, since the spectacle simultaneously appears timeless, caught in the moment and some how more significant in the overall scheme of things. All this appears, I believe, despite – rather than because of – the fact that the actual event of each race is basically founded on repetition with an equally strong element of undifferentiation between the competitors. The result is an almost elemental clash of four men, four bikes over four laps; where the riders' bodies, bikes and helmet colours simultaneously become almost dehumanised by the intensity of the competition and pursuit of victory, which somehow also grants it added significance and lustre.

Chapter 9: Of Fences and Start Gates

May 2nd Rye House v. Hull followed by the Elmside Raiders v. Newport GMB Union Mavericks

"The best referee is the referee you don't even notice" Sam Ermolenko

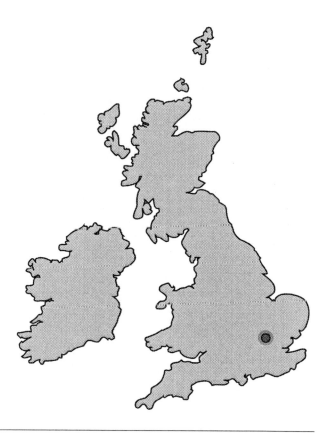

RANDOM SCB RULES

14.9.5 A TRAINEE REFEREE's duties are limited solely to underpinning the Meeting Referee (except as permitted in SR 13.9). In order to further their training programme, if so ordered by the Meeting Referee, a trainee may at the following Meetings, carry out the full duties of the Referee, although at any time and at the sole discretion of the Meeting referee, may order the Trainee Referee to undertake specific duties, both before, during and after a meeting:

a) Non Official Elite League and Premier League Competitions

b) Conference League Meetings

c) At the second leg of Official Elite League & Premier League Team Competitions, once the aggregate score is beyond doubt

d) With prior agreement of the Staging promoter and both Team Managers

The temptation to see three meetings on the same Bank Holiday Monday proves difficult for me to resist, even immediately after my visit to Hoddesdon two days before. Still, such is the appeal of speedway and virulence of the bug. I set off very early so that I will arrive at the stadium in time to avail myself of the free bacon butties that I mistakenly believe Len Silver will offer to patrons today, as an incentive to return for another meeting at Rye so soon after the last one. Even though I don't get lost, Bank Holiday traffic and the queues of shoppers lured to Bluewater delay me enough so I arrive only a short while before the tapes go up on the first Premier League meeting of the season at the club. The ground is wet from a persistent drizzle in the area that has only now stopped. This doesn't appear to have discouraged people from attendance in the hope that the meeting will still be held.

Once again, the car park marshal enjoys his work as he organises the parking. He's one of those retired men who, if he were your father, would always get out of the car to elaborately and exactly direct you to your parking spot. Very helpful

and sincere, but he confuses me with all those "back at little bit, a little bit more, left-hand down" kind of instructions. Luckily most people, who manage to drive their cars to the split-location car park outside Rye House speedway stadium, can also just about manage to park them in a safe and orderly fashion. It's still impressively crowded given the early start to the meeting, so I have to park very close to the canal, directly opposite where they've built some "Luxury Canal Side Executive 3 & 4 bedroom houses", or at least that's what it says on the large builder's sign that advertises the various deluxe benefits of a life lived close to the water. There's no mention of their proximity to either the large and very visible stadium that stages regular greyhound and speedway meetings or the nearby sewage farm. Both of which I'm sure will get right up their noses when they actually start to feel the inevitable urge to assert their recently bought territorial prerogatives. I must say that, to my untutored eye, the developer appears to have crowded far too many houses onto a comparatively small patch of land. This results in a clutter of houses, gardens and driveways that works against the supposed 'executive' pretensions of the development.

Despite the proximity of the start time, there's still quite a queue of late arrivals that file in through the efficiently run turnstiles at the entrance gate. The young girls who sold the programmes on Saturday night are back again this morning and they do a brisk trade. Both Shannon Gutteridge and Danni Smith have really mastered the details of the transaction down to a fine art and handle all the requests and comments of the punters with confidence. With a practical 'so much to do and so little time to do it' attitude, albeit a delightful one, they react to the foolishness of my surprise that I encounter them again so soon with practised insouciance. Just as you would treat a particularly dim-witted older relative, they coolly reply, "we do it every week!" and that's said with a very long emphasis upon the word "every", as though it's triple underlined in red.

Andy Griggs at the track shop has time for a few words and is quite keen to stock my book, particularly if it covers Rye House as well as other clubs. Despite the comparatively early hour, he still has quite a number of fans eager to buy speedway merchandise from the various tables of his track shop and I again notice that the Rye House baseball caps appear to sell briskly. No doubt, partly because of local loyalties but also for reasons of style and practicality on a cool morning with, if you glance at the sky, the possible threat of further rain. They look extremely modern in style and would be just the sort of good value purchase, at £6, that allows you to show your allegiance to the club; and, may be even of some practical use later, whether it rains or, as forecast, turns out to be a lovely sunny day.

They say that the sign of a good advert is that it makes you only listen to what you want to hear. The offer of complimentary bacon butties would seem to be a case in point, since the catering kiosk inside the main grandstand already has huge queues of hungry punters who're happy to pay for said fried comestibles. Though only after they've had the chance to study and fully savour the sauna-style wood finish of Rye stadium refreshments area. I ask someone in the queue about the "free bacon butties" only to have them laugh freely at my naïveté and justifiably claim, "Len Silver definitely isn't the kind of man who gives freaking anything away for free!" However, he is the sort of man who you know will do anything to ensure that all aspects of the club run professionally and in an orderly almost military fashion, plus you'll never be left in any doubt whatsoever that he's in charge of the place and that it's definitely his club. No sooner have I left the alpine chalet ambience of the refreshment area, in favour of a spot on the wooden construction open-air standing terraces by the start line, than the introductory theme music blares from the speakers. This is all part of the show and match day spectacle that Len prides himself on and, at Hoddesdon, it includes the march of the staff out onto the track in strict military fashion. While the music from Those Magnificent Men in their Flying Machines plays, it would be more accurate to say it feels like a military tattoo, though the way Len marches at the head of his troupe suggests that he's probably seen some form of military service. Well, his age would indicate that anyway, although with compulsory National Service I'm sure that, unlike the modern-day Police force, there would have been no minimum height requirement that would have precluded Len's enrolment. However, though he looks more like Lofty from *It Ain't Half Hot Mum*, it doesn't stop Len from exhibiting the gait, attitude and demeanour of a much taller man.

Len Silver is dressed in a smart blue jacket and sports a pressed collared shirt with a tie to match. The track staff mostly have matching blue boiler suit overalls, while many of them also sport the new-look Rye caps. Though the meeting is slightly delayed, all the staff parade out onto to the track and then quickly assume their positions dotted around the inside of the centre green. As Master of Ceremonies Len starts off with a polite greeting, "Hello ladies and gentlemen and children, welcome to Rye House Speedway!" Then he apologises for the news that the immediate delay is due to the absence of a vital piece of safety equipment, namely an ambulance. Dressed in their distinctive green clothes and bright yellow fluorescent tops, the St John Ambulance medical staff have also already marched out behind the track staff but they legally aren't allowed to minister to the sick at a speedway fixture without transport to carry the badly injured away to hospital, should the need unfortunately arise. Len is affable but not definitely happy, "they said they were 10 minutes away and that was 15 minutes ago!" Still, I know there was a lot of traffic on the roads and if you haven't got your blue lights flashing and the siren on, then you will have to take your time in the traffic en route just like everyone else. Len paces up and down the track, while he passes on his observations via the tannoy system and he promises that "we'll get on with our packed programme of racing in this great Bank Holiday double-header meeting that has the Rockets racing against the Vikings, followed by the Raiders against the Mavericks!" To the ironic cheers from the crowd, you can just about see the top of the ambulance above the perimeter fence as it finally arrives and makes its way round the outside of the circuit.

During the enforced delay, the terraces have become even more crowed with late arrivals that range from couples, young and old, single males with impressive amounts of camera equipment and families with a variety of pushchairs. It's a friendly atmosphere in the warm sunshine and the catkins from the overhanging trees at the back of the stand gently flutter in the breeze. This vantage point is a great place from which to view the racing or the activity in the newly painted white referee's box, where we have the luxury of two match officials for today's fixture. First up on the buttons, for the Premier League clash, will be the experienced Chris Gay and his colleague Barbara Horley, whom I understand is either a trainee or newly qualified, will officiate at the subsequent Conference League encounter. She'll benefit from the expert supervision and tutelage of Chris Gay, who I'm sure will exhibit his trademark approach to hold the tapes, for what appears to be longer than necessary and that invariably threatens to burn out some clutches, before he finally releases them; but not until he's definitely ensured that no rider has gained any advantage by illegal movement before the start.

The delay allows me to speak to my neighbours, Emy and Ronnie Lewis, who tell me that they always stand in pretty well the same place for every meeting at Rye House. They used to stand on the back straight, but had to move because the "dust got too much". Now they've settled under the slightly overhanging branches of the trees and towards the back of the

Len drives the tractor © Jeff Scott

The safety fence is demolished © Jeff Scott

Billy Legg doesn't break a leg © Jeff Scott

wooden terraces. They think speedway is the "best sport ever, a real family sport" and have watched it together for well over 50 years. They love the thrill and the fact it "makes your heart flutter". Emy is unequivocal, "I love it" and both agree that Len Silver puts on a wonderfully professional event, especially the other night for the British Under-21 Championship, which was "an absolutely terrific evening". They have attended speedway for long enough to really be able to judge these things and know what they're talking about when it comes to Len's professionalism and showmanship.

When the racing starts, the odd fall or exclusion is the only thing that delays an exciting and quick run first half of the meeting. The first heat of the league season at Hoddesdon has Sunderland-born Stuart Robson use all his experience to overtake the even more vastly experienced Paul Thorp on the last bend of the third lap. Almost immediately we hear a snatch of Elton John's Rocket Man and the crowd enthusiastically greet Robson on his victory lap of honour. The very informative and engaging announcer, Craig Saul, provides the result, along with some intermittent bursts of comment and colour, just as he does throughout the rest of the day. A win for Craig Branney in the next race appears to immediately exhaust the creative powers of the person in charge of the jingles at Rye. These creative juices start to flow again when Chris Neath wins the next race and we're all treated to a brief snatch of Robbie Williams's Let Me Entertain You. These wittily chosen jingles are only played to celebrate Rye House race wins and, fortunately, it turns out they have a large stock prepared in advance, since the home riders win a significant number of the races that remain of this fixture. The first few heats finds Len Silver avidly marking up his programme after each race, like a true fan of speedway; but apart from that, he kicks his heels on the centre green. To be not in control and uninvolved clearly isn't something that comes easily to him. Before you know it, he's then to be found on the bright red tractor that tows the bowser round the circuit to give it a thorough water, just after heat 4 and Rye's first 5-1 win of the afternoon. It's an absorbing race that has Brent Werner burst past the Viking's Garry Stead at the last moment on the finish line, to secure a valuable second place. Behind me on the terraces, Emy is pretty ecstatic at this show of skill and over to my left in the permanent grandstand, that is the substantial one made of concrete rather than the one constructed from wooden planks and poles, some large girls dance wildly in celebration. They wave and leap about manically when the riders pass on their victory lap and, afterwards, while Len thoroughly waters the track; we learn that the raffle at the Under-21 event raised £327 towards Brent Werner's testimonial fund. We're also informed that tickets for Rye's "Northern Tour" on the coach to Edinburgh, Berwick and Glasgow have already sold out.

The meeting remains close during Heats 5 and 6, which has Len repeatedly out on the tractor to attend to the track surface between races.

It quickly appears that passes are at a premium on the Hoddesdon circuit and the superior track knowledge of the home team is significant and extremely useful. This becomes yet more evident in heat 7, when Werner wins from Branney, and thereby lets the jingle man dust off Bruce Springsteen's Born in the USA, no doubt for the first of its many plays throughout the season. Even the announcer is happy to veer towards the more mannered but obvious cliché by calling Werner "the American Express". Rye easily pull away into an unassailable lead during the middle portion of the meeting with consecutive 5-1s in heat 9 and 10, before we witness a very competitive heat 11 during which Hull try to use their tactical substitute to claw themselves back into the match. Again Werner is in the thick of the action when he soon passes Paul Thorp before he stalks Emiliano Sanchez, British speedway's only Argentinean rider, for a couple of laps and then bursts past on the very last bend. I can hear why Emy loves the sport so much, since she seems to live and feel every turn of Brent Werner's wheel, and she screams "go on, go on" extremely loudly for someone of her age never mind her small size and calm demeanour. In unison with Emy, the home crowd goes wild at this demonstration of skill from the Rockets' riders, but mainly because Hull's hopes to get back into the fixture fade from the promise of a tactically assisted 1-8 to an eventual 3-5 result in this heat. I'm not sure that I agree with or enjoy the tactical replacement or substitution rules and this is reflected in the bizarre and silly-looking heat and match scores that they invariably generate. Still who am I, or any other of the loyal, paying fans for that matter, to stand in the way of what the British Speedway Promoters' Association deem as necessary progress?

With their last throw of the dice, the Hull riders contribute to an even more thrilling heat 13, which sees the lead change and re-change many times among the triumvirate of Thorp, Robson and Garry Stead. These are the most experienced riders at the meeting and all of them race in this heat. Even with Werner quickly relegated to last place, the quality of their racing reflects their skill and long service in the sport. Robson's final burst round the outside of Stead straightaway followed with his inside pass of Thorp was alone worth the admission money. The next race has the added but manufactured excitement of the appearance of Thorp in a black-and-white helmet colour, as he's a tactical substitute, and so starts the race handicapped by 15 metres. Though he races from the back, by the third bend of the third lap he's caught up with the flame-haired Tommy Allen, who then crashes spectacularly into the fence under limited pressure from the evergreen Thorp. As a neutral, this looks to be perfectly fair riding by Thorp, who puts pressure on the inexperienced Allen, without any touch or real interference but to which Allen responds with complete panic before he comprehensively demolishes the fence. This isn't how the partisan home support views the incident and they loudly boo Thorp for what they clearly perceive to be his unfair and dirty tactics. This blind bias towards your own riders, despite the evidence of your own eyes, doesn't reflect well on the home supporters, particularly when the team is already so far in the lead. In the re-run the promising and determined Daniel King races to victory with cheers for him and even more loud jeers for Thorp. He's clearly not happy with his treatment from the home crowd and makes this point, when he pointedly stops by the main grandstand to shake his head theatrically and gesture in admonishment at the loudest section of his detractors.

The formality of the last race is completed and ensures a comfortable victory over the reigning champions and includes yet another win for Chris Neath, which gives him a faultless five ride maximum. He then indulges with three celebratory victory laps that include two laps where he executes some flamboyant wheelies. The crowd really appreciate it and cheer loudly in the now very warm sunshine and I suddenly notice that I've become covered in dust from the catkins that has moulted from the trees in the light breeze.

During the interval Len continues to give the track the benefit of his attention on the tractor, to such an extent that the announcer praises him with the truism that, "the work of the promoter is never done". However, the words have barely left his mouth before Len is back off the tractor and holds the microphone to tout his half-time entertainment plans to the crowd. In actual fact, pretty well all expense has been spared; though his wartime experiences, his showmanship and strong degree of parsimony allow him to inject an almost breathtaking enthusiasm into the tension that surrounds the spectacle of "the lucky £2 coin thrown to the young people by the pit gate". The surprisingly large gaggle of kids that this attracts scrabble off to compete to pick up their exalted prize, while Len instructs the attentive crowd into the black arts of

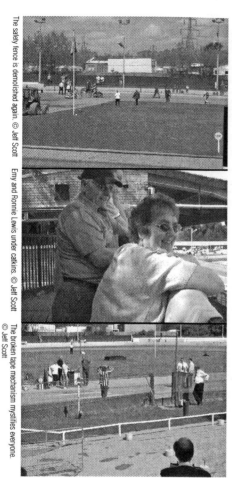

speedway track preparation. After he apologises for some of the dust created by the earlier heats, we learn in this ad hoc master class that, "watering has to be done very carefully to make it safe for the riders". It's a difficult task that Len only appears to trust himself to do, so far. Len then points us to the sponsorship details contained in the programme for those in the crowd keen to help boost Brent Werner's finances through his testimonial, while the crowd mills about or takes advantage of the legendary catering available in the stadium. I notice the referee Chris Gay stretches his legs between fixtures and he wanders anonymously among the crowd, unaccosted in a manner that wouldn't ever be possible for an official at an equivalent football match.

The Conference fixture starts and in heat 2, the Mavericks' Billy Legg attempts to set a record for the shortest race ever run before sustaining a debilitating injury. He revs his bike aggressively at the tapes but, as they rise, his bike rears into the air and throws him off the back of the machine. He's hardly travelled any distance before he comes to an immediate and grinding halt from which he sustains an extremely heavy and painful fall. The ambulance is immediately called out onto the track to attend to the fallen rider, who writhes in considerable agony on top of his own bike. Like many of the riders at the Conference League level, he's still in the very early stages of his career and will learn from his mistakes. This appears to be an especially painful lesson to learn but, at age 16, it's likely to one that he'll not forget in a hurry. Given the traditional sensitivities of his age, never mind his desire to prove himself as a rider, in other circumstances I'm sure he'd feel very embarrassed to leap from the start gate so dramatically and then fall so quickly. The sombre announcement that "Billy Legg has sustained a suspected broken leg" sounded comically incongruous to me, except for his pain obviously, but it appears I'm in a minority of one that finds this vaguely funny. In fact, to my right, an older lady wails so loudly I begin to suspect that, rather in the manner of a sympathetic pregnancy, that she must have sustained a sympathetic broken leg! As Billy is bundled into the ambulance to be taken to the hospital and plays no further part in the meeting, the crowd applauds warmly, while the announcer philosophically observes, "it looked an innocuous fall". I subsequently don't feel quite so bad that I laughed at Billy's misfortune (sorry Billy) when I learn that his leg isn't actually broken as it was suspected at the time.

The re-run of the race is equally bizarre though this time, at least, all the riders manage to exit the tapes without immediate mishap. By lap two, the Mavericks' Sam Hurst retires for no apparent reason and that leaves the Raiders' riders the simple task to complete the remainder of their laps for an assured 5-0 victory. But then nothing is so simple or can be taken for granted at this level of racing, since Daniel Halsey then has to push his bike home for a lap and a quarter after an engine failure on the last bend of the third lap. Still, they're young and the exercise, it could be claimed, will be good for them. Gary Coltham, a 15 year old, is delighted to win the race and the Raiders take an apparently invincible 10-1 lead after just two of the fifteen heats. This lead increases further with another easy victory for the home pair of the alliteratively named Barry Burchatt and "Broxbourne-born" Harland Cook. The lead stretches further still, despite the many riders who show extreme care throughout these races, with each lap they complete characterised by much tentativeness and with exaggeratedly careful management of their throttles, as though they're handling a poisonous snake. Burchatt tries to celebrate his victory with some wheelies, but he is still so new to the sport that he can't make the front wheel lift at all. Well, an inch or two, for a yard or so, is about as much as he finds possible to achieve before gravity overcomes his front wheel with a thump. But he does, at least, try repeatedly.

The topsy-turvey nature of Conference League encounters is further confirmed when the Mavericks then take their turn to win some heats easily. The sheer volume and intensity of the heats we've witnessed in the meeting so far, appears to cause the starting-gate equipment to go on the blink and the tapes begin to malfunction by rising inconsistently, or not at all. There's much scratching of heads and hips are collectively thrust out by the track staff, while they gather round and minutely examine the equipment like they can collectively repair it with will power alone. It's amazing how often a seemingly simple but vital piece of equipment can go wrong at a speedway meeting. And, inevitably, given its crucial importance to any speedway fixture, it is always the start-gate mechanism that goes wrong. When this particular piece of equipment at Rye malfunctions, it goes completely awry, big time! We then enter a tear in the space-time continuum and for the next half hour we take part in speedway's equivalent of *Groundhog Day*, since the tape mechanism is simultaneously tested to exhaustion while it stubbornly continues not to work properly. Things are of such seriousness that Len Silver immediately discards his important duties on the tractor and microphone to quickly arrive on the scene to mastermind repairs. You just know that Len will take his supervisory duties with conspicuous and earnest seriousness, whether whatever it happens to be that he has to manage, be it animate or inanimate. No sooner does an irked Len consider the predicament than the announcer's call immediately goes out for reinforcements to help with some emergency remedial action. Steve Naylor is told "to report to the gate immediately" and, when he arrives, Len waves his arms and speaks to him animatedly, but sadly just out of earshot of the fans on my section of the terraces. We're all thoroughly entertained and can roughly gather the nature of Len's sentiments without the actual benefit of sound. The crisis is such that Chris Gay abandons the control panel to emerge from the referee's box to watch the ongoing problems unfold before him at trackside and he then chats to the gaggle of supervisors, who all offer conflicting, yet ineffective advice on the attempted repairs.

Eventually, after considerable further delay, the start-gate mechanism is sufficiently fixed for heat 5 to finally be re-run. The confidence inspired by his earlier win has clearly affected Burchatt. On the back straight of the second lap, he tries to overtake the Conference League rider with the most eloquent moniker, Karlis Ezergalis, when there really is absolutely no space to sensibly attempt to do so. This provides him with a box seat in the subsequent demolition derby, since he manages to single-handedly decimate an impressively lengthy section of the safety fence. The medical staff race over to the stricken rider; so does Len Silver, as fast as his little legs can carry him, he then stops momentarily for a cursory glance at the fallen Burchatt before he attends to his first love and immediate object of his concern, the wrecked fence. The damage is considerable and, after another quick bend over the prostrate Burchatt, Len energetically throws himself into the supervision of the repairs. This requires a complete rebuild for the damaged section of the wire and wooden construction that serves as the safety fence at Rye House. Apparently, as a safety feature, the Hoddesdon fence is designed to be extremely flexible and thereby gives the impression when it shatters upon contact, that it's made out of nothing more substantial than balsa wood. The announcer alludes to the incident as "an alarming-looking tangle" while the referee, Barbara Horley, rightly excludes Burchatt for his pains.

It's a decision that a blind man on a galloping horse could have made easily but the news of the exclusion wakes and summons the monster from the sexist land that time forgot. This corpulent middle-aged man, probably called to the speedway from the depths of his usual sanctuary of his potting shed, launches into an inordinately lengthy barrage of foul language and vile assertions directed at the referee in her box. The monster in question wears his Rye House cap in a manner which befits his outlook – completely backwards. To briefly dispute an incorrect decision by a referee is part and parcel of the equation for fans and officials alike in many sports. The proximity of the open terraces to Barbara the match official, while she stands by the window in the raised white box enables a full, frank exchange of opinions. The monster evidently believes that the stupidity of the referee is caused by her gender and immediately suggests that she should "get back to the freaking kitchen sink where you belong". It's a suggestion that isn't said in that ironic post-modern manner beloved of young, aspiring comedians in their debut on Channel 4, but with deadly earnestness. The monster himself is not exactly a picture of intelligence or attractiveness. He comes across as the sort of Neanderthal bloke that will always discount his own beer gut and all-round physical unattractiveness, while he criticises the 'charms' of women unfortunate to cross his path. He gets angrier and angrier, and takes the silence of the surrounding crowd as assent to the brilliance of his tiresome attempts at wit and mono-browed insights. Frankly, he's an embarrassment to both men and the club he fervently supports.

The monster finally shuts up when the race is re-run and Harland Cook wins, but to judge from his subsequent attempts at celebration, he will also have to be kept back, along with Barry Burchatt, for some further remedial celebratory wheelie practice after the meeting. The start of heat 6 is then plagued with more extremely tiresome mechanical gremlins, which leads the announcer to helpfully observe, for any partially sighted crowd members, "once again a few problems with the starting gate". After the track staff have faffed about for some while longer, remedial repairs are finally affected and we then get to witness a one-rider master class in "How to fall off your bike when unchallenged". This is capably led by Newport's Sam Hurst. He takes to heart what should definitely be the Conference League's theme music, "I get knocked down but I get up again", when he embarks on an elegantly choreographed sequence of fall, remount, fall, and attempted remount before he eventually earns himself a deserved exclusion from the referee.

Another lengthy tapes malfunction again gathers a crowd of rubberneckers from among the track staff. Finally, they bow to the inevitable and announce that, like the Norwegian parrot, the gate "wouldn't vroom if you put a thousand volts through it". Well, actually, they say they will abandon the use of the starting tapes in favour of the dreaded, and invariably contentious, procedure of "green light starts". This has the happy result of energising the fixture back up to warp speed until heat 11 sees Scott Pegler seek to out-do the scope and scale of the earlier demolition work by Barry Burchatt. In fact, after he clips Robert Mears, Scott does a much better job of wrecking the fence. It has been torn up to such an impressive extent that the chatter among the crowd on the terraces begins to hum with talk about the possibility of abandonment. After 20 minutes of zealous repair efforts, it's the final straw for my afternoon's entertainment at Rye House, despite the warm sunshine that bathes my section of the open terraces. Sadly, I have to depart from the only meeting I will leave early all season. The delays have been so long and inordinate that my anxiety about the volume of Bank Holiday traffic, along with the thought that I will be late for my appointment at Wolverhampton, keeps me from watching the conclusion of this meeting.

2nd May Rye v. Hull (Premier League) 50-44

2nd May Raiders v. Mavericks (Conference League) 25-16 (final 50-40)

Chapter 10:
Crash, Bang, Wallop, What a Picture, What a Photograph
2nd May Wolverhampton v. Eastbourne

"Love him or hate him, this sport would be poorer without him!", "When Nicki puts his goggles on, there's only 3 other riders and him", "Out by the fence and giving it full gas", "He's fearless, he's fabulous, you can't ignore him" Gary Havelock [all on Nicki Pedersen]

"I don't like anyone getting maximums down here" Nicki Pedersen

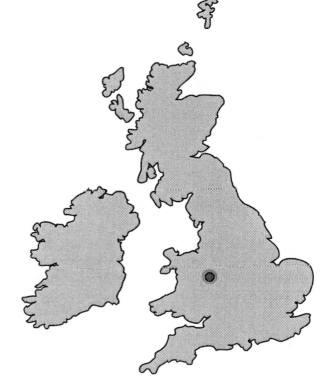

RANDOM SCB RULES

3.1.2 Every person shall be deemed to have submitted to these Regulations upon application to the SCB for a Licence or Registration. Additionally Competitors are at all times responsible (from time of entry to Meeting until its closure) for the actions and omissions of any accompanying person(s) and are liable for the consequences of such action of behaviour

I dash from the Hoddesdon circuit to my car before the protracted meeting is over because I worry it could be a long and congested 145 mile drive in the Bank Holiday traffic from Hertfordshire to the Black Country and the Monmore Green Stadium. It's the self-styled "Theatre of Thrills" and home of the Parry's International Wolves. I don't want to be late for my appointment to meet the hugely experienced Peter Adams, who wears many hats at the club in his roles as co-promoter, speedway manager and team manager. I will also meet Chris van Straaten with whom I'd discussed my visit a few days previously. He is another of the long-serving speedway stalwarts that comprise the club's triumvirate of co-promoters and, until recently, was the chairman of the sport's governing body, the BSPA. From my call, I understand that they've both agreed to meet with me to briefly discuss all things speedway and Wolverhampton Speedway in particular for my book. That is if I get there early, a few hours before the Bank Holiday evening Elite League 'A' fixture against the Eastbourne Eagles.

To find the stadium is a fairly straightforward task if you follow the glamorously named Black Country Route from the motorway, which is in fact the A454. It is very well signposted to the stadium in Sutherland Avenue, an area that is a strange mix of reasonably attractive parkland combined with a number of light industrial buildings. I arrive early. The substantial gates to the stadium car park remain forbiddingly shut and the huge expanse of empty car park looks particularly desolate. There appears to be very little sign of life, it's eerily silent, but then it is a Bank Holiday. I buzz the intercom, explain myself and the gates very slowly swing open to allow me into the vast car park. I'm followed by another car full of fans that have also arrived very early for this meeting. Since I have a wide choice of parking spaces, I park very close to the shuttered turnstile entrance to the stadium, which announces itself as 'Ladbrokes Stadium Monmore' in large letters on the side of its roof. The entry prices appear to be exceptionally good value for the Elite League, especially the charge of £7 for the so-called 'concession' fans – mostly the unemployed, students and old age pensioners – of whom the latter still resolutely remain the most important, loyal and largest demographic group at most speedway tracks. I've wanted to visit the Wolverhampton track for many years. They always seem to have a substantial number of fanatical fans, dressed in the team colours of old gold and black and sporting various Wolves branded items of clothing, who travel to loudly support their team whenever they ride at Eastbourne. I'd also heard stories of massive crowds, informed fans and a generally fantastic atmosphere at Monmore Green Stadium from Kevin Donovan, the man who I used to stand next to at Arlington. He'd taken his girlfriend to watch them ride against Eastbourne, a trip that had the added bonus and attraction of a rather wild Nicki Pedersen who then rode for the Wolves. Nicki had attracted everyone's attention earlier in the season with a hard riding but thrilling display of riding at Arlington – where he easily gained the mantle of the visiting rider that everyone loved to hate, mostly because of his ability, skill and obvious aggression. The visit to Monmore hadn't been great, if you were an Eastbourne fan, but despite the result for weeks afterwards Kevin waxed lyrical about how extremely passionate, friendly and knowledgeable the Wolves' fans were about the sport and their team. The general interest was so intense that he'd been amazed to find "even the birds are really mad for it up there!"

The mobility of speedway riders in general and the top riders of this contemporary generation in particular is remarkable. In the Elite League the process is especially pronounced and, to be fair, often exaggerated by team changes caused by injuries to riders. However, loyalty from the promoters towards the riders has also drastically dwindled, while the reality remains that all riders are self-employed and have to constantly seek the best deal for themselves each season. This leaves the loyal fans of any one club to often bemoan the whirlwind of rider changes within their team during the season as well as from year to year. The situation is further complicated by the ownership rules that apply to the rider's individual contracts. These contracts often remain the property of a promoter or ex-promoter for whose team the rider no longer appears, but for whom they still receive a loan fee when the rider appears for another club. A case in point is Nicki Pedersen, whose contract is still owned by Wolverhampton Speedway. It's not the type of restrictive contractual situation that would apply to ordinary jobs, under current UK and European employment law, let alone in other sports. It would be unimaginable in football, for example, where such practices would cause a national furore in the press and on television. But this is speedway and different ways of business often appear to apply and will continue to do so until challenged or, most likely, until it suits the contract owners themselves to change[1].

Unusually, Eastbourne have a reputation within the sport, over the last few years, for consistency and loyalty in their choice of team personnel and, compared to most other clubs in their League, they are a model of constancy with their staff. However, the nature of the speedway beast inevitably forces some changes to team line ups and, as a result, this now finds Nicki Pedersen as Eastbourne's top rider since he joined the club in mid 2003, the year he became World Champion. His own journey around the Elite League clubs in this country illustrates my point because since he left the Wolves, after the completion of the 2000 season, he has then travelled via King's Lynn and Oxford to end up at the Eagles. This has catapulted him from a heroic figure status always lauded by the Wolverhampton faithful to his present pariah status of 'Public Enemy Number 1'. Many of the Eastbourne fans have had a similar emotional journey with Nicki (but in the opposite direction from that experienced by the previously adoring Wolves' crowd) who now inspires great loyalty and devotion from the Arlington faithful in equal measure to the previous levels of opprobrium. Within the sport, Nicki Pedersen is arguably the most controversial current rider who presently works in the sport, often seen to be as popular as a rattlesnake in a lucky dip by the fans of rival teams, and there is a broad consensus about his supposed reputation for hard riding that means he's invariably portrayed as a villain. Only marginally more popular than Danish cartoonists to Muslims and just as often disparaged, off the track Nicki can be charming, diffident and gentle. But once that crash helmet is on and he's racing on the track, he competes to win at all costs. From a fan's perspective, the races he's involved in will always be exciting and often controversial because of his 'hard riding' style. However, they say that the definition of an alcoholic is someone who drinks the same as you do, but is someone you don't like; so similarly, the definition of a hard or unfair rider would be someone who's just as aggressive as your team's riders, but who rides for another team.

Whatever your opinion, it certainly makes very good box office and speedway as a sport is usually keen to stress the thrill and entertainment that the racing tries to provide. Nonetheless, I expect the partisan Wolverhampton crowd will be even more vociferous and pumped up for this evening's encounter. As I walk through the open gates by the shuttered turnstiles, the noticeable silence is broken only by the sound of the tractor that repeatedly pulls the bowser round the circuit to intensively water the track. The tractor is painted in the old gold and black of the home team and the bowser is similarly coloured with the logo 'Wolverhampton Speedway' painted in black letters on its side. Although it's a bright, sunny afternoon, rain is forecast later and it's noticeable that there are already a few rain clouds that have begun to threaten on the horizon. I'm so early that Chris van Straaten hasn't yet arrived at the track, so I take the chance to explore the large modern home-straight grandstand. I walk up the airy stairwell to look at the track from the first floor of the grandstand. There's also a large bar and refreshment area, which is presently closed as the stadium's entrance gates have yet to open, though some of the staff have sat down to have a chat and a hot drink together before their preparations for the evening's work begin. The refreshment area itself appears to stretch the length of the home straight and provides an excellent view of the whole circuit, which comprises of greyhound and speedway tracks, through the large glass windows. The grandstands in modern greyhound stadiums definitely cater to their punters who want to be able to uninterruptedly watch the evening's racing without the need to venture outside or even leave their seat, except maybe to get some refreshments or to use the adjacent facilities. The dog track itself is covered with tarpaulin held down with tyres to prevent shale polluting the racing surface.

[1] At some future point speedway contracts will definitely undergo their own re-evaluation and revision, equivalent to the revolutionary impact of the Bosman ruling in football, but this will only happen through force, when the contractual situation is legally challenged by a brave and suitably disgruntled rider.

Quite a large area of the perimeter of the stadium fence is thickly lined with trees, especially on the back straight, and their height indicates that they've been around for some while. This gives the whole stadium environment an unexpectedly rural feel and it contradicts the preconceived image that the mention of Wolverhampton generally conjures up. This rural feel and impression even applies to the pits area, which lies adjacent to some low-roofed office buildings, since it boasts a large grassy area sandwiched between the pits and the fence that guards bends 1 and 2 of the dog and speedway tracks. Both sides of the pits areas have grey-roofed open-fronted sheds in front of a line of tall trees. The final element of this rural effect is the route from the pits to the track itself that passes behind a large tree hedge that wouldn't look out of place in a suburban garden but seems slightly incongruous at a speedway track. Later, I notice that some of the riders make quick use of its convenient screening effect.

There's a flat-roofed building next to the pits, which I'm told is where I should find both Chris van Straaten and Peter Adams. When I get there it turns out they have finally arrived, but are locked in together in earnest discussion about something urgent that's just come up and that definitely won't permit Chris to speak with me. Though when reminded, he appears to have completely forgotten my call and our subsequent arrangement. I do, however, learn that in quarter of an hour or so Peter will kindly have a few minutes available to chat over a coffee on the benches near to the office. In the meantime, I head over to the Wolves' track shop, which is located by the grandstand in an ideal position for people who pass by either towards the pits or to stand on the open, tiered terraces in front of the grandstand. When you watch on television, this part of the stadium is always absolutely packed with loudly enthusiastic fans, as you imagine the rest of the stadium is at any Wolves' speedway fixture. However, this impression partly depends on an optical illusion, because when I look around it soon becomes clear that this appears to be the only place you can actually stand within the stadium to watch the action on the track. This, perhaps, makes sense since the stadium is primarily used as a dog track and so this is where the key action will always happen when the greyhounds race. Though the atmosphere is better with the crowd all packed together and it enhances the notorious Black Country camaraderie, it's not always been like this. The old stadium used to wrap round the third and fourth bends, with a covered stand on the back straight; indeed, many local fans jokingly call it the slowly disappearing stadium as the number of places to stand has gradually shrunk over time.

The avuncular and helpful Dave Rattenberry owns the track shop. He sets out the vast array of stock on the tables he has arranged for this purpose with his capable assistant, John Rich, under the temporary stand they construct each week and then cover with tarpaulin. From the impressive piles of coloured boxes and containers they have already unloaded, they set out an attractive display of every conceivable type of speedway accoutrement or memorabilia imaginable. There's a huge range of Wolverhampton merchandise with a great emphasis upon upper body clothing in a wide variety of sizes, particularly for the larger framed fan. There are anoraks, "hoodies" as the government has now taught us we should call them, sweatshirt tops and T-shirts that completely line the back wall of their shop area. The tables heave with old programmes, badges, pens, rider and team photographs, programme boards, some quite cute teddies and all the usual accessories, inevitably covered in the Wolverhampton or Wolves' logo. These include air horns, since they can be used without limit at Monmore Green Stadium because there is no curfew and no near neighbours to bother with noise disturbance. I glance through some of the old programmes and the recent magazines, and take the chance to point out a photo from 1974 that I'd previously noticed in the latest edition of *Backtrack*,[2] which features a very youthful looking Chris van Straaten when he was team manager of Stoke. We chortle at how long and almost hippyish his hair looks before Dave and John both rather seriously remind me that that sort of unkempt look was ubiquitous but still seen as ultra-fashionable back then.

Along with all the clothes that line the back tarpaulin wall is a bookstand that displays many recently published books. Dave believes that there are too many books published nowadays, especially ghost written or collaborative 'autobiographies' of famous riders, and some biographies, which often don't sell that well at the tracks where the riders hadn't regularly ridden. Uncontroversially, the best seller at Monmore is a history of the club written by Mark Sawbridge who has "phenomenal knowledge and is a very nice lad". Dave wishes me well with my book of my travels throughout the country and claims that it should have some appeal to the network of track-shop franchises that he runs around the country. He used to run more than he does nowadays but there was a falling out with Oxford and "that Wagstaff" over money. Money was the root of all evil at Coventry as well, although Dave notes that they additionally cover you in ordure at Brandon. That still leaves him a healthy network of shops that includes Buxton and Stoke. It must be quite some business, or, at least, one Dave Rattenberry is very proud to manage if John Rich's blue shirt is anything to judge by. It has a prominent multi-coloured stitched logo of a rampant rider broadsiding, surrounded by a circle of letters. The top half proclaims in white stitched letters 'DR Promotional Leisurewear' while yellow stitching at the bottom notes the unusual combination of 'Embroidery and Track Shops'. Like so many others with any connection to any club on race day, they're both huge fans of speedway. They note the great support that the fans traditionally give at the Wolves to go along with the excellence of the race track that is usually prepared at Monmore. They're also keen to sing the praises of the consistently high quality meetings you witness at the Stoke and Somerset racetracks, which they predict I'll enjoy when I visit.

The shop appears to act as a magnet for everyone who arrives at the stadium. The announcer Shaun Leigh stops by for a few words before he leaves for the commentary box to conduct some vital technical checks and preparations. He also has his own regular circuit of clubs where he works as announcer every week. These tracks are located in the Yorkshire-Lincolnshire triangle of Hull, Scunthorpe and include Sheffield, where he also does the stock cars, which is particularly handy as he lives only a quarter of a mile away from the stadium. On an afternoon in praise of good quality speedway entertainment, Shaun singles out for praise the country's newest track Scunthorpe, located "in the middle of a field", and the "very nice" promoters there, Rob and Norman. The referee for tonight's fixture, Chris Durno, echoes this opinion and describes it as a "great set up; anything you want them to do, they do". He has also been drawn to the shop, via the speedway office, where he has learnt some dramatic news. Everyone there then has what could best be described as an old wives' meeting, with lots of oohs and ums, as they discuss the news that Wolves will ride tonight without their Number 1 rider Michael Max and his younger brother Magnus Karlsson since they both remain stranded in Sweden. They have different surnames because, a few years ago, after Michael had rode for many years as a 'Karlsson', he then decided to revert to his mother's maiden name of Max, ostensibly, but somewhat mysteriously, to try to distinguish himself from his speedway racing brothers Peter and Magnus. There's unanimity at the shop that this state of affairs is precisely the logical consequence and peril that modern promoters inevitably run when they rely so heavily on so many foreign-based riders

[2] The always captivating retro speedway magazine covers the speedway era from the 1970s to 1990, and is published by the enterprising Tony McDonald

within their team. The exact circumstances of their non-appearance haven't been exactly or satisfactorily established, but they all have been told the same story, albeit until now no one has yet shared it with me. It appears that the brothers returned to Sweden, in order to enjoy a rare long weekend, but failed to allow for unforeseen events when they decided to schedule their return on a Monday, the day of their next Wolves' meeting, rather than to more sensibly return on a Sunday flight. Unfortunately for them and the Wolves' fans, their plane had developed unexpected 'technical problems' so, despite having cleared customs and immigration control, they were left without sufficient time to find an alternative route after their flight was then cancelled. This leaves the Wolves' promotion, management and team well and truly up a gum tree and faced with the prospect that they will have to compete with a massively depleted team for this evening's fixture with Eastbourne. Since they drew the away leg of the equivalent fixture at Arlington, where I believe they were unlucky not to actually win, they would have had understandably high hopes of a home victory that would also secure the additional bonus point. These would be vital points, even at this early stage of the season, particularly as they would follow on from a few away defeats and the embarrassment of an Elite League home loss to Belle Vue. The bumper Bank Holiday crowd of fans due to arrive through the stadium gates in a few minutes will definitely be quite right to feel short changed and cheated with a home team line up deprived of these key riders.

No wonder, Chris and Peter were locked in an important meeting in the office and suddenly unable to see me earlier. A few minutes later I do get to sit down with Peter who still takes the time to have a coffee, cigarette and a chat despite all that's happened. If the truth were told, he appears distracted and harassed as well as a little wary of my intentions. We chat about my research and travel plans before I produce my list of prepared questions that I'd like to ask him. Peter honestly states straightaway, "I don't like answering questions off the cuff". He'd much prefer to consider them before he answers, then chat on the phone another time or meet up before the next Wolves' fixture at Arlington later in the year. He's totally reluctant to talk about the missing riders, his thoughts on their absence and what he intends to do this evening before he soon heads back to the speedway office. It's a shame we can't talk, especially as Peter is one of the people I'd most looked forward to a talk with on my travels. Particularly because he always appears so thoughtful and analytical, albeit slightly taciturn, when he appears on national television or has his opinions committed to print.

Instead I decide to venture up to the referee's box, where Chris had invited me to consider the Monmore Green Stadium track from his lofty perspective. When I arrive Shaun is in mid-fiddle with his announcer's equipment, while Chris has his blue SCB rulebook ostentaciously held open for a closer inspection of the relevant section that includes the exact regulations that apply to suddenly absent riders. He does this simultaneously while he conducts an animated and lengthy discussion on his mobile phone, about the various possible scenarios that apply to these unusual circumstances. Chris confirms what I had suspected, but that Peter Adams guarded 'public' demeanour mostly disguised, that he is "like a bear with a sore head" and was "absolutely scathing" to Chris about his missing team members. He's strongly suggested that the referee "report them to the SCB" and wants Chris to ensure that they "implement the maximum penalty fines allowable under the circumstances" at them[3]. Chris explains that he's consulted with other referees on the notorious referees' grapevine, just to ensure that his interpretation of the rules with regard to substitute riders is correct. Every referee is agreed that since Max and Karlsson have been nominated in the Wolves' team already, then it's impossible at the last minute to replace the Number 1 rider Max with a guest or rider replacement. The Wolves have been left with little other available options but to replace Max with a young, promising but inexperienced Conference League rider from Stoke, Jack Hargreaves, and to replace Karlsson, who was programmed to ride at reserve, with locally based Tony Atkin, who literally dropped everything to answer the emergency call to shoot across to Monmore Green to fill in at the very last minute. This team line up will leave the home side severely depleted and, according to Chris, leaves Adams "desperate for a thunderstorm to cancel this meeting". With the mention of rain, we both instinctively glance out at the tractor that still continues to intensively water the track with the bowser. Whatever happens, the referee notes with some understatement, "it's going to be interesting". Wolves will attempt to mitigate the disappointment of the crowd by warning the fans of the late change to the team; both via the club call line and by posting information notices on the turnstiles. However, the majority of fans will be already on their way to the stadium confident that the meeting will definitely be held on an intermittently sunny, fine but cloudy evening.

Chris takes some time to explain many of the details involved in the work of a qualified SCB referee. Like many people who work in speedway, it is a labour of love that involves many hours of dedicated work with little financial reward. The officials are another vital part of the essential staff every track requires, the grassroots of the sport if you will, without which speedway in this country wouldn't be able to continue to function. Later I learn that the referees receive travel expenses and a small nominal payment for their work, – very different from the compulsory SCB fee of £100, in advance, for the services of their officials. Chris deliberately notes that, "so many people who do menial tasks at a speedway track do so without pay, usually because they're very passionate". He describes the lengthy qualification procedure that any would-be 'trainee' referees have to endure to become qualified and able to take charge of a meeting. This apprenticeship involves many hours of travel throughout the country at their own expense, while they shadow experienced qualified referees as well as undertaking rigorous study of the ever-changing rulebook. Ultimately, you will get to take part in a qualifying sequence of three meetings that you referee under supervision. This effectively constitutes your pass-or-fail examination. Many people never get this far, but instead immediately drop out at the first hurdle when they learn about the long hours of travel and the wear and tear on their cars. Even then, for those that manage to continue their apprenticeship, the attrition rate is high. The attrition is mainly due to the "ruthless and quite brutal" rigour of continual study allied to the stringent tests, which cause many of the trainees to "crash and burn". Out of the cohort of eleven trainees Chris started with, only four survived to qualify and it often comes down to the "survival of the fittest" and those adaptable enough to the "long hours, stress and loneliness". Each trainee referee adapts to the training programme in their own manner and takes a different length of time to serve their apprenticeship, usually a couple of years, before they pass. Chris passed in June 2002 and relishes his work as a referee. But the job makes huge demands on your family and spare time with many referees only able to do the job if they are self-employed or if they use all their holiday entitlement in order to fulfil all their refereeing obligations. Chris suggests that at another meeting I join him for an entire evening to get a real insight into a job the fans, promoters and riders consistently underestimate and take for granted[4].

The view from the referee's box is panoramic and, according to Chris, an ideal example of the type of facility you would

[3] The next day Chris van Straaten was quoted as saying, "We are a little bit disappointed that we were without our riders". It is worth noting that the straightforwardness of the Wolverhampton management prevented them from booking in high calibre replacement guests for their riders, which they could have done if Michael Max and Magnus Karlsson had feigned injury or illness.

want to work in as a referee – one in which you cannot be distracted by the crowd. At Wolves you're perched way above the heads of the fans and enjoy an uninterrupted view without the possibility of the supporters "getting stuck in" with their strongly felt opinions. However, unlike the other speedway track facilities that Chris praises – Belle Vue, Coventry and Oxford – this box is disadvantaged not only by its small size, but it's also located 30 or so yards ahead of the start/finish line which can make those ragged starts and close finish decisions very difficult. This wasn't always such an insurmountable problem for disputed close finishes since you could always unofficially consult the "scrupulously fair line marshal for his second opinion in particularly close calls". Now, however, this is something that Chris van Straaten has the power to put a stop to, and, as a consequence, the referees now must make the final decision without the benefit of this different but fair perspective.

Outside the entrance gates have finally opened and there's already quite a crowd of people gathered round the track shop, on the nearby benches or who congregate in their favourite spot on the terraces. Many more of the fans have made their way to the pits area and are either in the pits to chat with the riders and mechanics, or else they linger on the grass and watch the activity. There's a much bigger crowd by the home pits area and many of the riders happily sign autographs or pose for photographs with the fans. In most circumstances, small but kindly gestures can make all the difference to your perceptions of a place. A cheery "how are ya?" in broad Australian strine from Wolves' Captain Steve Johnson, directed to myself for no reason other than to greet me as I pass him, makes me instantly feel right at home. I'm already feeling particularly privileged since I have been invited along as a guest of Jon Cook, Eastbourne's friendly and knowledgeable promoter. We'd chatted about my book and he felt that, with Chris van Straaten's permission, because of its unique layout Wolverhampton would be the ideal track to closely observe all that happens in the pits as well as on the track itself. I stroll over and let Jon know I've arrived. He doesn't feel well and wants the meeting to proceed, despite the threat of rain, as he'd rather not have to travel back to the Midlands again for a rescheduled meeting. We watch the intensive watering continue and he shrugs philosophically, "with the team they've got tonight, it's nothing more than we would do if it was at our place and we wanted to ensure it got abandoned if it rains". He explained where I could stand – just by the motorway-style sleeper dividers that separate the pits from the grass bank that leads to the track fences – once the pits had been cleared of the fans 30 minutes before the fixture starts. This would give me the ideal vantage point to follow exactly what happens on the Eastbourne side of the pits, or the Wolves' pits adjacent to it and, for the races themselves, I can easily wander across the grass bank to get to see them. I'm delighted to be so close, if slightly in awe of the riders and mechanics who now busily prepare their bikes. I hesitate to interrupt them or Jon, particularly after he says, "right I'm off to do my job of managing".

Rather than intrude on the preparations I chat with the man beside me on the grass. Tony Charsley has travelled up from Stoke on public transport, as he does regularly, to watch the Wolves. He lives across the road from the Stoke track, which he notes has "brilliant racing but a crap stadium". He's been hooked on speedway ever since he went to his first meeting, New Cross versus Wimbledon in 1949, and feels that it's something that just gets into your blood. He's always admired the riders for not whinging when they fall, they "just get up and get on with it", unlike many other sports in his opinion, particularly football where he believes that they've become fitter not better. Tony has always had a penchant for stylish riders, especially Gordon Kennett, someone he thinks should have been World Champion. But then there have been so many riders with lots of skill and ability that never became the World Champions during the era they rode in. He wistfully and quickly reels off the names of Olly Nygren, Jack Parker, Brian Crutcher "who retired at 26", Chris Morton and the Moran brothers. His all-time favourite is Ronnie Moore, who was " a gentleman, did nothing dirty but lacked that killer instinct". Tony still loves the thrill of the racing and passing, even on modern tracks with modern equipment, though he thinks the tracks aren't as good as they once were because they lack "the dirt" of yesteryear. It's a problem both created and compounded by the present riders having highly tuned, powerful machines that "just don't like the dirt".

[4]For alternative insight into the politics and the paperwork as well as the trials and tribulations involved to become a qualified SCB official, I'd recommend the self-published pamphlet *A Ref's Tale* by Dave Osborne. I later take Chris up on his kind offer and enjoy an informative evening in his company at Coventry.

Around us, people still surround the riders and mechanics, who continue with their preparations, but still courteously find the time to pose for photos or sign autographs. Nicki Pedersen is extremely popular and is in huge demand but is also clearly very practised at public relations. As he kneels by a particularly recalcitrant and grumpy small boy who is very reluctant to pose for the photograph his father so obviously desires, Nicki gently but repeatedly pleads with him to "smile for Daddy". Eventually, the boy's resolve lightens at Nicki's gentle but persuasive persistence before father and son finally go off happily back to the grandstand terraces.

At 7 p.m. sharp, the time has come for the riders, mechanics and team managers to concentrate on the Elite League fixture at hand. The pits area is cleared of all members of the public and I feel suitably privileged to stay to watch proceedings first hand. The only other person who remains but doesn't help in the Eastbourne side of the pits is an extremely tall man who turns out to be Dean Saunders, not the notorious footballer, but in fact the proud sponsor of Davey Watt via his construction company Saunders Surfacing Contractors. He has just started his sponsorship this season. He believes it's good for the company and it also fulfils his long time interest in motorcycling of all kinds. Dean is an ex-bike rider himself. He rode moto-cross for 20 years before he broke his shoulder three years ago, and so started to get involved in speedway through someone he knows, Keith at Rye House. His surfacing business is successful but demanding, so he views sponsorship of Davey, and his recent involvement with speedway, as the ideal antidote to the everyday pressures and stress of his work. Apparently the management of all his vans, lorries and trucks, and the need to ensure that all the construction work was done yesterday, was never quite fully relieved as a keen Watford Football Club season ticket holder. Dean has just started to learn the ropes involved in sponsorship and is Davey's key secondary sponsor. He's still new enough to enjoy the sight of his company's initials on Davey Watt's bike cover and upon his race suit where it appears on the arm, leg and epaulette. No one can deny that Dean takes considerable pride in the image Davey projects.

The friendly welcome Dean received at Eastbourne amazed him – from the promotion to the riders themselves – particularly compared to his previous experience as a sponsor, when he tried to gain access to the pits at Poole speedway for whom Davey rode last season. Dean was refused entry to the pits at Poole on the basis that even sponsors that had contributed as much as £25,000 to Tony Rickardsson's campaign apparently didn't expect to receive access. In fairness, access to the pits is a privilege and I'm delighted to have this rare treat at Wolves, thanks to Chris van Straaten's kind hospitality and Jon Cook's good offices. On a busy race night, it's the prerogative of any club to determine who has access and if the Poole riders and staff want to be stand-offish and "keep themselves to themselves" that is, ultimately, their choice.

Dean points out that tonight Davey will miss the services of his usual mechanic, his young Australian compatriot and King's Lynn rider, Trevor Harding. Now that Dean draws my attention to this, it's very noticeable that everyone else in the Eagles' pits tries to help Davey get things ready with his bike. As I watched earlier, I could see that each rider had their own individual way to psyche themselves up and mentally prepare for the meeting. The most unique style of preparation belongs to Eastbourne Captain David 'Floppy' Norris who deliberately appeared to try to maintain a rather aloof distance from the clamour of the many fans. Not that he didn't also pose for photos or sign programmes, but his whole body language communicated a reserve that says 'do not interrupt for too long'. Now that he's found his own space, Floppy embarks on a weird series of callisthenics that mostly involves waving his arms around in a vigorous circular manner. It all appears very unorthodox and conducted as if he wants to fly off as much as stretch his arms to prepare for the racing. He does all this in his civilian clothes of jeans, trainers and dark jacket style anorak, before he changes into his kevlars, but throughout he bizarrely wears his racing gloves. All very Alan Partridge 'smart casual'.

Close by to Floppy, Dean 'Deano' Barker appears totally unconcerned or to engage in any form of warm-up exercise while Steen Jensen's routine involves either the melodramatic adjustments to his racing gloves, as though he were a fighter pilot, or alternatively, that he strikes the sort of elegant, aerodynamic but completely stationary poses on his bike that you imagine he later hopes to reproduce on the track when his bike is travelling at high speed. Perhaps, it's some advanced form of sports visualisation exercise? Whatever his intentions, for now Steen is content to twist his body into the various shapes required for this simulation, all of which can be accomplished without any need to start his bike.

In contrast, Nicki Pedersen sits quietly, isolated in the far corner of the pits, while he's wholly absorbed in the painstaking and fastidious cleaning of his goggles with some sort of fluid and a cloth. He then takes a similarly deliberate approach to the maintenance of his crash helmet and conducts a close, rigorous inspection of the tear-off's mechanism that is an essential accessory for all contemporary speedway riders. In fact, the highest-level speedway riders have a huge array of paraphernalia that, in the pits during the televised BSI World Championship Grand Prix series, definitely requires that you have many available pegs upon which to rest all four of your brightly shone but differently coloured helmets. It's a milieu that Nicki is familiar with but I can't help but notice the calm quietude of his person, attitude and preparations for this Elite League meeting, which is in sharp contrast to his aggressive on-track persona or public perceptions of his outlook and personality. Nicki then does some serious stretches and other bending exercises that are part of a well-rehearsed routine that slightly interrupts his contemplative and comparatively spiritual manner. His great flexibility isn't something I'd ever considered or appreciated beforehand. I watch him bend and place both of his hands completely flat on the floor; an action that I know from yoga requires great discipline, suppleness and flexibility. This might go some way to explain part of his exceptional ability to remain on the bike, after violent knocks and bumps with other riders or sharp manoeuvres at high speed. That is all part and parcel of his combative race technique. It's a skill all gifted riders have, and they often make it look frighteningly easy and controlled, but it clearly requires great ability allied to dedicated training. He then shatters the impression of Zen calm created by these preparations to have a pee by the adjacent tall hedge before he performs some impressively loud throat noises as a prelude to a brief bout of advanced spitting.

The two-minute warning then sounds for the first race and, as the riders for heat 1 make their way to the start line, the Eastbourne pair for the next race – Watt and Jensen – start to line up on their bikes on the track that runs from behind the pits and the hedge, that Nicki has just decorated, down to the track gate entrance on the second bend. They patiently wait there on their machines, and don't watch the first race but just wait for it to end. They're pushed off towards the track as the other riders, who have just completed the first heat, return to the pits. In fact, David Norris has immediately set a new track record when he convincingly won heat 1, but I remain in ignorance of this fact until after the meeting, solely due to the acoustics of the tannoy system that appears only directed towards the impressively packed crowd of fans on the grandstand terrace. My inability to understand the garbled announcements is a slight disappointment but is more than made up for by my close proximity to the pits and the great view of the entire track from my vantage point on the bend.

The activity is feverish but purposeful in both teams' pits areas. The bikes need adjustment or repair in the short time that remains before they go back out for their next race. It's probably an obvious point, but not one that I'd fully appreciated until now, that the riders apparently pay absolutely no attention whatsoever to the race card or the heat and cumulative score in the match programme, except as it applies to their own next race. They have the evidence of their own eyes when it comes to the race order in any heat, though the razzmatazz of Shaun's deliberately bombastic delivery of the exact details of the race results not only can't be heard in the pits but also is mostly irrelevant for the riders. But for all true speedway fans, it's THE essential tool to understand, record and register the events of the meeting. Since there is a personal financial incentive I'm pretty confident that each rider will be aware of his own individual score and what is required for their own next race. However, the riders, if sufficiently interested, mostly rely on their mechanics or, most likely, their team managers to keep them apprised of the cumulative match scores should they feel the need to know. The information they essentially require from the copius details that each race card lists is very straightforward and basic; the gate they're programmed to race from, their fellow riders and, hopefully from a fan's perspective, the actual tactics that they'll employ together in the race. Especially since it is notionally still a team sport that requires their joint endeavours to ensure success for their side. Still, whomever they hear the news from, it's clear that the riders just concentrate on their bikes and their own race. Anyway, it would be very difficult to ride, and hold onto a pen and programme with their gloves on.

One thing that the riders all pay a considerable amount of attention to, if possible – apart from the attentions of attractive solicitous female fans – is to watch what actually happens during the racing. Or, more accurately, particularly how the track is riding and how that might affect the racing set ups for their own equipment. Wolverhampton, as Jon Cook correctly identified beforehand, is an ideal track to watch the racing and still pay full attention to the rider's equipment in the pits area.

When they're not already on their bikes, the riders from both sides hover by the track fence and watch the action. They stand together in their respective team groups with various other people that include sponsors, press, friends and the team managers who clutch their programmes authoritatively. I keep myself to myself and hesitate to interrupt any of the riders or other staff. Eastbourne have arrived mob handed in this respect, since both Jon Cook and Trevor Geer share these duties and studiously gawp at their programmes. Steen Jensen actually engages me in a conversation, after he probably mistakes me for someone with a modicum of expertise or insight. He's not the tallest rider ever, but stands by the barrier to peer at the track, dressed in his shale splattered kevlars, before he sagely mentions to me the "funny inside line" they have at Monmore Green that apparently prevents the easy passing of other riders. It didn't seem to hold him back in his first race, when he followed his teammate Davey Watt home for second place in heat 2, but the rumour of its existence clearly bothers and concerns him. Like all sports the mental side is crucial and the diminutive 20-year-old Dane now appears unduly preoccupied with the reputation of this possible impediment to his future success to ever truly regain psychological mastery of the circuit. In order to try to help with some psychology myself and distract him from his continual anxious squinting at the inner ring of the track, I try to boost his nervous if not yet deflated self-esteem, with compliments about his performance so far tonight. As well as the week before, when I saw him ride quickly to frequently pass other riders at Reading for the Isle of Wight in the Premier League. Like here, it was his first visit to that track and his performance showed some pluck and much skill. Slightly morosely, Steen dismisses my encouragement, though he notes, "my gating was shit there". I didn't expect to talk, but throughout our brief encounter Steen comes across as approachable and very modest, albeit with a very fragile confidence in his own abilities.

I stand in the thick of things and it's completely fantastic, although I speak to no one. Stranded at the airport, the absence of the two Swedish riders for Wolves appears to initially make a big difference to Wolves' performance since, after a heat win by Floppy in heat 5, Eastbourne already lead by six points. I continue to watch from my ideal vantage point in front of the pits by the concrete wall that separates the grassy area from the greyhound track, which in turn is separated from the speedway track by a wire safety fence, and the Eastbourne riders frequently join me to watch. Most notably Davey Watt, who spends his time spitting with such violence and frequency that I begin to suspect that he is afflicted with some severe expectoration problem. I later learn that it's a common affliction, since the shale and the dust flies into your mouth with great velocity when you race and can't really be prevented from doing so, even when you lead throughout. I subsequently notice that most riders deliberately cover their mouths before they put on their helmets to race. However, Davey has won one race and only trailed behind Nicki Pedersen who rides far ahead in the distance, as usual eschewing any form of team riding, in the other. So along with the apparent lack of dust because of the earlier intensive watering, it's difficult to see where his early coughing stage of pneumoconiosis has developed.

Even after the earlier extensive watering, the quickly drying and unusual track conditions, in the absence of the forecast rain, also appears to play its part in catching the home side out. Indeed, the earlier decision to over-water the surface has resulted in an extremely grippy track as it dries and, if judged by how the riders race, the inside line appears very bumpy and thereby forces the riders to go out much wider than usual towards the potentially hazardous chain link fence. As on many tracks, the riders seem to hug close to the fence just as they reach their highest speeds on the straights. To the untrained eye this looks somewhat perilous on the tight circuit at Monmore Green, where the chance to unexpectedly catch your footrest in the fence appears to loom at any moment. Whether it's the grippy surface, a footrest in the fence or sheer inexperience is difficult to gauge, but the most junior rider on the night, 16-year-old guest Jack Hargreaves, hits or gets caught in the safety fence during heat 6. The velocity of the crash throws him and his bike dramatically into the air and

Steen Jensen, who trailed Hargreaves, makes a full-on impact into the fallen Jack and his bike. The carnage of man and machine causes the race to be stopped in the interests of safety by the referee and Hargreaves is excluded as the primary cause.

There is quite some delay and so I find myself next to Adam Shields to whom I mention that they're taking a long time to restart. A man notoriously of few words, he pauses before he says "yup" in a manner that combines brevity and disdain before he meanders back to the pits to tinker with his bike. It's a sharp contrast to the affable Jensen, who is the first to disentangle himself from the carnage on the track and slowly bob back, albeit gingerly, to the pits. But it's an extremely long time, before Hargreaves moves from where he lies prone on the track surface. There's a large crowd of St John Ambulance staff, track personnel, Peter Adams, and assorted riders in attendance and I'm glad to see that Floppy himself immediately runs over to where the young Hargreaves receives attention. I'm impressed by this gesture of sportsmanship and, afterwards, I notice Floppy speak with Davey Watt's sponsor, Dean Saunders, as he returns to the pits. But then Dean swiftly shatters my illusions when he reports that Floppy had gone over to help them clear the track because he'd suspected that the Wolves' team hoped to possibly rather cynically delay proceedings in the hope of possible rain. During the delay, I take the opportunity to watch the Wolverhampton pits where the activity and attention they pay to their equipment remains, throughout the duration of the delay, at a feverish pitch for most riders and mechanics. The Eastbourne team appear more confident and laid back in their attitude. I also notice Belle Vue's Joe Screen, reputedly one of the nice guys and most gifted but modest riders of his generation, while he visits all and sundry in the pits on a precious nights off from competitive speedway. This confirms, once again, the easy camaraderie and genuine interest that seems to naturally exist among most of the riders in the sport, that is when they're not racing each against each other. He spends quite some time deep in conversation with a smiling Dean 'Deano' Barker before he follows Top Cat's advice to mingle, mingle, mingle. After a long delay the racing eventually resumes.

Back in the pits while he waits for the re-run, Nicki sits quietly on his stool with his mouth pressed against what looks like a giant hand-held hairdryer. I assume it's some sort of a contraption that delivers pure oxygen. Whatever it does, Nicki sucks on it strongly before he storms to an easy win in the re-run of the race, which the home crowd greets with loud boos and a variety of readily understandable arm gestures. Clearly, the crowd no longer holds him in great affection or high esteem. This doesn't seem to concern Nicki at all, because after every race he's content to sit quietly in the corner of the pits or intermittently suck on his hairdryer, while his mechanics efficiently prepare his bike for its next race. He temporarily breaks off from his studious concentration to exchange a few jovial pleasantries with Joe Screen before he resumes with some fastidious cleaning and preparation of his helmet. On the track, the Wolves have stormed away to win the next heat, in which they used the Tactical Substitute rule to great effect, and thereby have almost restored the scores to parity. The next heat is shared before Nicki stimulates further ire from the Wolves' fans when he has the temerity to line up at the start gate for his next race. I'm lucky to have a great view of the riders as they leave the start and seek to gain that vital yard advantage as they all enter the first bend. In this race, heat 9, three riders make the start – Johnson, Pedersen and Lindgren – and arrive together almost in a line at the first corner. As they broadside into the bend, they bunch together before the Swede and the Dane find themselves badly tangled together. Pedersen and Lindgren are flung unceremoniously from their machines with great velocity into the inflated cushion of the air fence. It's difficult to judge the exact sequence of events that lead to the crash, but it appeared to me that both riders had ridden aggressively with neither of them prepared to give any quarter, before they both lifted slightly and Pedersen collected Lindgren, who was on his outside since he started from gate 3.

Whatever the exact sequence of events, Lindgren immediately leaps to his feet to gesticulate at Pedersen and to take great exception to his violent introduction to the safety fence. What was a full and frank exchange of views and contrary opinions between the two riders would just have been routine if it had then remained at that level of confrontation, after what was definitely a dramatic but, in the normal scheme of things, an unexceptional first-bend racing incident. However, when Nicki Pedersen is involved, things are often handled very differently, since his reputation appears to colour subsequent events and interpretations. So it proves in this instance, because things instantly degenerate when Lindgren decides to throw some punches at Pedersen, which has the effect of instantly summoning an angry pack of riders and mechanics from both teams to the incident. As luck would have it everything happens right in front of me.

A frequent complaint about professional wrestling is that a sport, which appears 'real', is patently fixed. The common complaint about ice-hockey fights is that while the level of aggression and battle is often tremendous, the lack of traction prevents any real damage, although I can't help but think that ice-hockey sticks still hurt. Speedway itself is even sometimes accused or rumoured not to be all that it appears to be. But with regards to this fight at Wolverhampton among the riders and mechanics, I can safely say that this is one of the most extreme few minutes of genuine fighting and real violence that I have ever witnessed first hand. I find this ironic because one of the reasons I am writing the book in the first place is because of the 'family values' that the whole working-class culture of the sport usually enshrines. Well, perhaps it still genuinely harbours these values among the fans but now, among the riders, I'm not so sure as I witness what pure adrenalin and the heat of the moment can unfortunately create.

At its simplest, Lindgren and Pedersen couldn't have been surrounded more quickly by other actual and would-be combatants if you'd offered a million-pound prize for the first 10 arrivals at the scene. Riders and mechanics literally sprint from the pits across the grass to very impressively vault the greyhound wall, safety and air fences to join the fracas in varying degrees. As a team-building exercise for the Eastbourne Eagles it is arguably excellent as, like the three musketeers, it is 'all for one and one for all' when the fists and the boots began to fly. First to the scene and with a great turn of speed for a man of his age, and his usually leisurely demeanour, is the Eagles' co-team manager Trevor Geer. His role of potential peacemaker is short-lived after the simultaneous arrival of the man-mountain figure of the security guard from the Wolves' side of the pits, who is closely accompanied by Lindgren's own mechanic. I initially mistake 'the Hulk' for a person who'd been hired by the Wolves as a security guard to prevent violence and, by his persuasive actions mediate among the combatants, to thereby maintain order at this speedway fixture. He is very closely followed by David Norris. But, as it turns out, he is Lindgren's own unhinged avenger and berserker with bulging muscles and a closely shaven head. My transient illusion that he is there to stop trouble is swiftly shattered by his unique approach to mediation; which not only involves some impressive gymnastic skills, that brings him trackside promptly, but also the skilful use of his personal 'mediators' at the end of his arms and legs. Dean Barker, distinctive by his combative attitude and rage-filled features, manages to restrain Lindgren's smaller sized mechanic from inflicting any permanent damage on a helmeted Pedersen by eventually wrestling him to the ground. But a strong desire to intervene and to protect his father from being attacked by the apparently crazed 'security guard', who himself takes offence to Trevor Geer's arrival to intercede between the riders and Lindgren's mechanic, sees Chris 'Geernob' Geer foolhardily throw himself at the Hulk. This despite the huge differences in size, strength and weight that are instantly apparent to the casual observer. Unfortunately, this valour and bravery doesn't really translate into effective action, although it does have the instant effect to switch the Hulk's attention from the father to the son. Without so much as a by-your-leave, the security guard then launches into kicking Geer's unprotected head as he tried to get up from the track, one of the most ferocious and repeated kickings that I have ever had the misfortune to witness. Anywhere, never mind at a speedway meeting! The blows to Geer's head are sickening in their ferocity and even footballs aren't usually kicked that hard. The extreme naked violence of the thug and the bully happens in full force in front of me and everyone else, including the distant but still vociferous Wolves' home crowd on the grandstand terraces.

It's hard for me now to establish the actual order of events or exactly recall all the details, particularly as so much went on so quickly, but it appeared it took an age to restore any semblance of order to the trackside and pits areas. Such a blurry recollection of the exact order and sequence of extreme events is often experienced by the police when they interview victims of violence for a statement, who most often can closely describe the weapon in great detail but not the actual perpetrator.

My impression is that the bystanders on the Eastbourne side are Davey Watt, Steen Jensen and, bizarrely, as the cause of the altercation Nicki Pedersen. He quickly withdraws from the action. Everyone else from the Eastbourne team joins the mêlée to a greater or lesser degree as well as the subsequent chase around the pits and close to the office area.

My familiarity with the Wolves' team and mechanics isn't comparable, so I can't name them so accurately as I can the Eastbourne riders, nonetheless, some of their riders also definitely take an active role in the initial disturbance and subsequent chase that spills all over the vicinity of the pits area for the next five or so minutes. At the forefront of the action for the Eagles, though definitely not its instigator, is David Norris along with Dean 'Deano' Barker who throws himself about the place with more gusto and desire that his recent rather tepid performances on the track belied. He is definitely the kind of man you'd like to be on your side in a fight or, in this case, trying to mediate a ferocious fight. Deano throws himself on people much bigger than himself, which is most people, except for other speedway riders or Freddie Lindgren's mechanic who he unhesitatingly tackles to prevent him from landing further punches on Pedersen. This has the effect of momentarily attracting Hulk's attention before he gets down to the serious business of treating Geernob's head as a football. Throughout David 'Floppy' Norris switches from his standard default setting of wry and petulant moodiness to a man seized with an inferno of self-righteous anger. This involves him in some impressive gestures and aggressive finger pointing, much shouting, contorted features, and teeth bared in anger as well as also trying to restrain others. Floppy is also the first and loudest of the pack of Eastbourne staff that chases the Hulk from the scene of the crime, and presumably his employment by the club as a 'security man', through the pits and out of the stadiums[5]. Again my exact recollection of events is sketchy but after the extreme violence of his assault the Hulk, with the definite assistance of Floppy, decides to make just an even quicker exit than he did on arrival at the crash scene.

Floppy demonstrated a considerable speed on his feet and a voluble but commendable desire to locate a policeman, although he has temporarily forgotten the immutable law that, like London buses, there's never a policeman when you need one and that no amount of shouting will ever help find one. The violent chain of events clearly causes Floppy to also forget the famed ethos that speedway prides itself on, namely that it never requires the attendance of police or stewards to marshal or separate groups of fans that you often find essential at other sports. And so he runs round frantically at high speed, shouty and, at times, almost manic in his fruitless search for the law. The closest person to a legal representative available is the match official Chris Durno, in the role of judge, jury and peacemaker, who swiftly arrives from the referee's box. Chris who, by the time he reaches the pits to restore good order, has substantial confusion to mediate with all agitated

[5] Later in the season, the Hulk is astonishingly spotted in the Wolves' pits.

and loudly shouting people, who all immediately claim to be the injured or slighted party.

The reactions of the management of both sides are interesting and instructive. Trevor Geer, for such an apparently taciturn and mild-mannered man, immediately runs to the initial incident but after that refrains from further involvement, though his son ensures the Geers remained well represented. Jon Cook tries to act as a peacemaker throughout, but also chases around madly with Floppy and Deano in hot pursuit of the perpetrator and the subsequent fruitless hunt for assistance from the absent long arm of the law. In my opinion, Lindgren's mechanic sparked the whole incident by his initial decision to intervene on the track and attempt to twat Pedersen. The incredible fighting machine from 'security' displayed a huge capacity for extreme violence matched only by his ability to scarper with the lightning speed of Ben Johnson when Floppy demanded legal retribution from the boys in blue. However, his turn of speed had nothing on that shown by Chris van Straaten who disappeared into his office with an alacrity that must be useful during the emergency evacuation of an aeroplane. They say when the going gets tough the tough get going and Chris immediately got going, albeit back to his own office. The speed with which he removed himself from the scene would have severely restricted his ability to have an informed opinion of what happened based on the evidence of his own eyes rather than the reports of others. Though he is one of the most experienced, influential and respected members of the speedway's hierarchy and governing body, it's still bound to disappoint when the action moves to within yards of his office, definitely within his jurisdiction, and he simply disappears in a 'now you see him now you don't' type manner, albeit without the obligatory wisp of smoke. Perhaps he'd already gone to look for the large carpet to privately sweep the whole incident under that both clubs and the SCB would later require. From his television appearances, Peter Adams strikes me as man very much in control of himself and his reaction to things that happen around him, though he also impresses you as someone you wouldn't like to mess with verbally or physically. During and afterwards, wearing his distinctive, bright old gold and black coloured Wolverhampton jacket, he didn't appear that ruffled or upset. They say when all around you lose their heads that it's best to keep your own, which Peter does with some assurance. He appears unconcerned at the absence of law enforcement officers when Floppy angrily requests such assistance from him and also phlegmatically confirms the impressively clean pair of heels shown by the departed assailant, when the Eagles' staff demand that he be found and lynched for his actions. That said Peter had earlier shown himself to be in control of his public demeanour even when annoyed and this approach serves him well in the aftermath of the fight, when he appears simultaneously nonchalant and unconcerned. But then the Wolves' riders and staff would expect him to publicly represent their best interests in every conceivable situation. That said Peter also strikes me as the sort of man who would frankly let you have his opinions in unmediated fashion afterwards in private. Later that night he demonstrates his maturity and experience, when he skilfully and methodically channels the waves of annoyance and anger that surround this situation, never mind the disadvantageous absence of his Swedish riders, to positive effect for his team.

Chris Durno then summons the teams and their managers to the equivalent of a post-coital cigarette in the form of a confidential dressing down. He administers this during an earlier than anticipated interval break to allow everyone the chance to calm down before the re-run of the race resumed the fixture. However, on the grandstand terraces, the milk of human kindness doesn't course quickly through the veins of the enraged Wolves' faithful when it comes to forgiving Nicki Pedersen or indeed forgetting the supposedly barbaric transgressions of their Public Enemy Number 1. The fact that Nicki sits quietly and calmly on his stool in his corner of the away pits, hairdryer-shaped ventilator close at hand while he patiently shines his goggles, further inflames feelings of outrage. So much so that many of the visiting fans feel the force of these objections to such an extent that some of them decide to seek protection and make a tactical retreat to the safety of the normally restricted grassy areas by the pits.

My proximity to the away pits area allows me to watch Nicki Pedersen nonchalantly wait for the end of the enforced early interval. He also takes the opportunity to remind his mechanics and teammates to focus on the job in hand and rallies them with a shout of "hey, boys; forget about it, let's get ready!" The re-run of heat 9 sees Denmark's very own version of Danger Mouse greeted with loud boos and a variety of insults and gestures by the start line, whereas Freddie Lindgren is lauded with similar vigour through noisy cheers and applause, almost as loud as the jeers for Pedersen. Lindgren seems determined to prove his worth on the track and victory appears to be within his grasp when he overtakes Pedersen on the third bend of the last lap. But, instead, Pedersen uses his undoubted skill and determination in combination with the track knowledge he has gained through his time spent with Wolves, to just sneak a deserved victory right at the finish line. It's a win that he definitely relishes and he celebrates with a brief onanist gesture to the loudly aggrieved hordes of disappointed Wolves' fans. Watt and Shields then combine for a 4-2 heat victory in the next race to extend Eastbourne's slight lead to three points with five races left. I watch the next heat beside the very affable Steen Jensen, who seems nonplussed at the need we have in this country to fight over something as silly as a speedway race. His only comment on the incident, "freaking Swedes", reflects the traditional Danish antipathy towards Sweden as much as what actually happened. Steen is keen to emphasise that he'd never fight and already looks forward to when the fixture is over so he can practise his skills and riding technique elsewhere on some of the country's larger tracks. Trevor Geer and Peter Adams now make a point to take the time to be seen to chat as normal between the races. This is still the basic appeal of the sport where no quarter is given on the track but, mostly, everyone remains firm friends off it. In fact, everything seems to have returned to its usual equilibrium in both pits – except for Deano who sits by himself and looks very thoughtful and disconsolate, while he stares at his gloved hands. Earlier he'd been zealous when he defended his own corner and that of his teammates during the melee - which he'd instantly joined as he attempted to throw punches and hold much bigger people than himself back or restrain the wildly flailing Lindgren – but now he looks exhausted and almost depressed. His two races that, so far, haven't troubled the scorer can't really help his apparently sour outlook.

A few minutes later, as we watch Eastbourne get another 3-3 to retain their slender lead, I find myself with Jon Cook who also looks far from happy. In this race Floppy finally finishes a comfortable second, but not before an unforced error costs him the lead that causes him to eventually finish behind David Howe. Even though I have watched many races, I have no idea why he made this unfortunate manoeuvre until Jon remarks matter of factly, "he was going too fast to try to cut back like that". It's amazing what experienced and tutored eyes can spot that the ordinary fans like myself won't see at all. As the riders approach the tapes for heat 12, Jon goes out of his way to sincerely apologise for his invitation that has led me to attend this particularly stormy meeting as his guest and that of the Eastbourne club. Jon persists with his apologies, "I'm sorry that you had to witness that" before he sighs and continues with "I would have loved all that in the old days but I'm really getting too old for that now!" I complement his team and staff, since they clearly stuck together and showed their resilience in the face of perceived external threats. It's just the sort of spirit that you'd want in your team, especially when so many of the top Elite league riders only briefly travel into the country for a meeting before they immediately leave again to ride for one of their many other speedway teams. Such camaraderie has a rather old-fashioned quality and the willingness to look after your colleagues is the sort of behaviour that you often pay expensive consultants to try to pretend to instil in your staff in normal business life.

The result of the next race doesn't much improve Jon's outlook since Deano and Davey Watt return to the pits after they finish a considerable distance behind the Wolves' riders to concede a 5-1 result that reduces the overall lead 38-37. The apparent newly confirmed but found in adversity team spirit then crashes spectacularly in a loud, blazing argument between the two riders. They say it takes to two to tango or to argue, but Deano is quite happy to conduct the argument with little or no response from Davey Watt except for the occasional word. Not that this lack of response stops Deano, who hurls any item of his racing gear that is to hand around the pits and repeats, in no uncertain terms, his dissatisfaction with Davey's abilities, team riding skills or overall spatial awareness on the track. Rather than intervene Jon Cook exasperatedly remarks, "I'm just not listening to this!" before he walks away. The argument eventually blows out in the face of the limited response from Watt to Deano's considerable display of contempt and ire. Glenn, Deano's mechanic, shrugs when I mention that his boss doesn't seem too happy with things before he notes, "it doesn't help that he's riding very poorly at the moment; he's only got seven points in three meetings". Davey Watt's sponsor, Dean, spends the next little while in conversation with him while he prepares for his next race, when he'll partner his less volatile fellow countryman Adam Shields. Afterwards, Dean complains, "Barker just doesn't have the right attitude".

Someone who does have the right attitude by almost any estimation, or at least considerable determination, is Nicki Pedersen who celebrates with another win in a rather pressured but vital heat 13. The crowd boos him beforehand and again afterwards, which he repays in kind with wild but rude gestures of celebration. The next heat is drawn to set this contest up for a thrilling last heat finale. Again Pedersen storms to a victory that, once more, he celebrates with that distinctive but joyfully delivered gesture to the crowd. The Eastbourne riders then proceed with some delight on to their victory parade. The lap of honour provides another chance for the Wolves' fans assembled on the grandstand terrace to rush forward to better vent their considerable frustration at the outcome of this fixture. The Eastbourne riders smile and wave even more exuberantly than normal in response to this very public display of righteous and aggrieved disgruntlement. As soon as The Eagles return to the pits, the victory smiles quickly fade as they're immediately called away by an extremely stern Jon Cook to their dressing room for an urgent team meeting. Suddenly the Eastbourne side of the pits is totally deserted and the tension of the evening still hangs in the atmosphere, albeit without any of the key protagonists present. By the time I find my way back through the crowds that still throng from the pits area to the track shop, the consensus among the home support appears to be that if only their Swedish riders could have organised their travel properly, they'd have won the fixture easily. As it was, on the night, their nemesis was Nicki Pedersen and he made all the difference to the final 46-47 score line in which he rode unbeaten in all five of his races. Dave and John in the track shop feel that it's typical of Wolves to get so close without actually being able to supply the required metaphorical killer blow, no matter how literally they tried to land actual blows earlier in the meeting!

2nd May Wolves v. Eastbourne (Elite League A) 46-47

Meeting Aftermath

They say a picture paints a thousand words. At the very least, picture choice forms an impression on the viewer and might well influence the perspective taken upon the object or events portrayed. David Icke used to claim that he liked to read *The Times* once a week and watch the BBC News just as frequently, so that he could find out what he was supposed to be thinking. It also goes without saying that while there are lies, damned lies and statistics; this popular phrase appears to omit that there are some quite mendacious ends to which you can apply photographs.

In the days that followed the Wolves versus Eagles fixture this suspicious outlook would prove to be a useful and instructive way to look at the print and visual coverage of the events I had witnessed.

If you ignore how close the meeting was and the excitement of the racing itself, there's no doubt that it was overshadowed by events in the pits and track after heat 9. Afterwards there was no shortage of opinions – in the local papers, on the Internet forums and later in the week in the pages of the *Speedway Star* – from the many fans who had attended the meeting and many more who had not.

Call me naïve but I honestly expected the print and photographic coverage to reflect what I had seen with my own eyes.

The newspaper coverage in Wolverhampton by the *Express & Star* newspaper was predictably selective in its reporting and picture selection, while the *Brighton Evening Argus* was arguably less partisan and the *Speedway Star* the most factual. This is eminently understandable. Given its allegiances as an advertiser in the club programme ("Follow Wolves Speedway in the *Express & Star* with Malcolm Cinnamond"), you would not expect the Wolverhampton paper to sharply denigrate the management of the Wolves organisation and particularly the control of their staff. Also given its target readership in the local area, it didn't make commercial sense to do anything other than apportion equal blame to both sides. It's also very understandable that they would tend to give emphasis to event summaries and commentary from the home promoter Chris van Straaten rather than the comparatively much-more-difficult-to-contact visiting promoter Jon Cook. Similarly, the *Argus* will have a natural predilection to view things more from an Eagles perspective than a Wolves one.

Pictures

If you ignore the eyewitness accounts of the mêlée, the choice of the three pictures for the back page of the next afternoon's *Express & Star* paper would definitely create the impression that there was only one team involved in the instigation of the fight. This particular selection of photographs, culled from the very large number of the incident apparently taken that night by Wolves' track photographer John Hipkiss, lends its own conclusions. The paper's editorial department chose to give prominence to one in which it would appear that David Norris attacked a very much larger security man (captioned "David Norris with security" in the *Express & Star* and "pointing the finger" in *The Argus*). The next photo used by the *Express & Star* was captioned "Dean Barker on top of Freddie Lindgren's mechanic" in Wolverhampton (and "brawling" in Brighton), while another which had Barker throw a punch was captioned "and Barker hits out" but was only used in Wolverhampton. The picture selection by both regional papers was effectively similar, which reflects the newsworthy content of the images chosen but also, I believe, an awareness of their presentational impact. Though it still seems peculiar that the photos taken on the night by John Hipkiss did not contain equally dramatic shots that would appear to hold Wolverhampton riders and staff equally instrumental or culpable for the fracas.

The pictorial portrayal of the events of the evening in the *Speedway Star* was different in emphasis from that which appeared in these local regional papers. Obviously, the *Speedway Star* has different responsibilities and a much wider audience. After all, it is the industry publication that covers the sport nationally and is not an individual sponsor of Wolverhampton or Eastbourne Speedway, nor is it beholden to the clubs for its speedway coverage in the way that both the *Evening Argus* and the *Express & Star* are respectively. Quite properly, the *Speedway Star* does have the interests of the sport of speedway in this country at heart for emotional, strategic and commercial reasons. The most significant aspect of their visual coverage of the fixture was the balanced choice of pictures used from those again taken on the night by John Hipkiss. Two of those chosen actually featured the race itself as well as a shot of the fallen riders, Nicki Pedersen and Freddie Lindgren. The final frame they used is the by now familiar Dean Barker wrestling shot.

Reports

The prominent *Speedway Star* report, written by the regular Wolverhampton match reporter David Rowe, noted the "shameful brawl". We also learnt that the security guard and Lindgren's mechanic were not excluded from the stadium on the night on the basis of an argument of reciprocity that the Wolverhampton management used to defend their staff, because of the similarly violent actions of Eastbourne's Chris Geer. Though the report did note that Geer was the "victim of an alleged assault as numerous personnel in the pits over-reacted" and that "the violence erupted on several occasions and threatened to reach the terraces at one stage before order was restored". Quite properly it noted that it was "an incident that did the sport no favours"[1].

The match report by Tim Hamblin in the *Express & Star* firmly laid the blame for the speedway aspect of the drama at Nicki Pedersen's door ("Pedersen had committed speedway's professional foul") before later highlighting "a graceless 'hurry up' gesture" by Pedersen after the rerun. Strangely the *Evening Argus* did not mention the happenings of this heat in its round up of the fixture.

The Things They Said

When questioned in the *Speedway Star*, *Evening Argus* or the *Express & Star*, the main protagonists had a variety of perspectives on events.
Chris Durno: "there was a brawl and a lot of people were involved who were not wearing riding leathers but riders are responsible for their mechanics."

---

[1] Only the *Evening Argus* would report that Trevor and Chris Geer made precautionary visits to hospital afterwards. Also, I wasn't aware until I read this article that "the cream of the country's Under-15s in the pits ready to launch the British Academy League" reportedly witnessed events. All quotes with kind permission for the *Evening Argus*.

Jon Cook: "It escalated when Wolverhampton security staff waded in and attacked two members of our staff. It was disgusting. It was the most disgraceful incident I have seen in speedway."
"It was a ridiculous situation really. Freddie Lindgren accepted afterwards in the riders' meeting that his reaction had been wrong".

Chris van Straaten: "The referee came in and calmed things down. Things did get very heated."
"The referee is sending a full report to the ruling authorities and if Wolverhampton, or its individuals, are found to be at fault then we will face those consequences".

David Norris: "I've been involved in fights at the track since I was 16 but usually it is handbags at dawn. But this was in another ballpark. It was like WWF had suddenly got serious. I thought Chris was dead because he didn't move. I could not restrain the man myself and ended up chasing him into the crowd but he got away. What he did was just not right...afterwards I couldn't ride well at all. I'm emotional, a softie. I could not sleep. I felt responsible because Chris works for me and he could have ended up with brain damage. It could have ruined his life and it would have affected mine seriously. I just thank God he is still alive....the majority of the Wolverhampton fans would have been as upset as everyone else. The beef I have is with the security people."[2]

Nigel Pearson, BSPA press officer (who wasn't present): "The SCB have the power to expel riders. They will read the referee's report and no doubt take other statements before deciding on what action to take."

Internet Statements
The Official Wolves' site went for the less-is-more approach:
"Tempers boiled over following a first bend tangle between Lindgren and Nicki Pedersen in Heat 9, with representatives from both clubs involved in some unsavoury scenes. Referee Chris Durno called an early interval and restored order, and the action which followed was out of the top drawer."

The Eastbourne official site went for a more righteous, legalistic but wounded approach:
"We will cooperate fully with any investigation and would like to place on record our support for the actions of the match referee in difficult circumstances. We would like to state our shock and outrage at the actions of a member of the Wolverhampton speedway security team and trust that the appropriate actions will be taken by his employer... The catalyst to the whole incident, a Wolverhampton Speedway Mechanic, was dealt with by the Referee on the night, and we trust that once Wolverhampton speedway have acted against their Security steward, both teams can move on and enjoy successful seasons"

Sadly the speedway public was never to learn the finding of the enquiry or how these were faced. It was clear from the official statements issued by both clubs that they would co-operate fully with the SCB investigation into the matter and that they would each send in full reports of their version of the evening's events. These would be statements based on the evidence of their own eyewitness accounts as well as the comments of other witnesses. They would also have photographic evidence to review, with the obvious caveat of possible selectivity, as well as the video footage of the evening's racing and intervening mêlée. I haven't had the opportunity to subsequently review what I saw with my own eyes and, as I write about it afterwards, it's clear that all accounts are personal and that your memory plays tricks. The scrum of

[2] When I spoke with Chris 'Geernob' Geer months later at the Brighton Bonanza, he recalled: "they started attacking Nicki Pedersen – I really like him – but when I saw the old man was hurt, I just got involved without thinking about it. They say the bloke was a giant but he seemed like a midget to me. I felt like killing him. I didn't feel a thing though my eye swelled where I got kicked and punched in the head and my shoulder popped out. When I was down only David [Norris] stood in for me. Afterwards I was in a daze cos I didn't know I was concussed or what I was doing really. Later Nicki sent me a nice text thanking me for standing in for him – as I say I like him – though I did it without thinking of any of the consequences. That's speedway though, all sorts goes on sometimes, like when the fans were spitting on David at Poole. You just have to try to ignore it, if you can, I just didn't that time".

people and the speed of the melee that unfolded makes it inevitable that I will have missed some things, be ignorant of others, and probably given undue emphasis to some others. The referee's perspective on events in his report to the SCB will contribute to their understanding and events and their final judgment. Though the referee, Chris Durno, is at a disadvantage here since he left the referee's box in order to visit the pits to try to restore calm and order. This inevitably means that he might have missed some aspects of the drama as it rapidly unfolded[3]. What I do know for certain is that the results of the SCB enquiry into that evening were never released to the public in any form that I'm aware at the time (over one year later) of editing this book for publication[4]. Although this sort of event is something that the sport shouldn't be proud of, even more shameful is the secrecy with which the enquiry results have remained shrouded. This reflects very poorly on the governance and administration of the sport. It must presently be awfully hard to open the SCB office doors with so much swept under its carpet, if its management of such a major public event forms any basis of judgment.[5]

[3] The SCB official Chris Durno was informed by Chris van Straaten afterwards that he couldn't have seen anything from his position in the referee's box and that he believed the mêlée that he missed was "only handbags".

[4] I'm led to understand that the SCB subsequently issued three heavy fines to Wolverhampton and one lighter fine to Eastbourne.

[5] With so much strenuous forgetting going on, it's probably best that I also start to also suffer from this collective or retrospective amnesia. But before events do drift into the mists of time, I would like to recall a number of conversations I had the next day about the evening's ruckus. These comments are necessarily selective since I had limited access to Wolves' personnel. However, they still help towards further understanding, particularly given the continued absence of any public report on the SCB's official findings and actions regarding the incident. Dean Saunders, owner of SSC and sponsor of Davey Watt, noted that "Cookie calmed everyone down in a team meeting afterwards" and said that in the changing room "Floppy and Deano argued with Wattie", though this almost certainly wasn't about the fracas. What occurs in any changing room, never mind a speedway one, would no doubt boggle the mind, bore the uncommitted or thrill the partisan. Whatever was or wasn't said, it's best that these things remain a mystery.

When I spoke a few days later with Jon Cook, he apologised again and mentioned that he'd spent the next two days "sorting out the ramifications of the evening". He was required to compile a lengthy report for the SCB after "reviewing a DVD of the whole incident, so I know the context of every frame". After he watched the DVD many times, he became upset that the *Express & Star* could be so selective in its choice of pictures and he intended to complain to the editor. He strongly felt that the picture choice deliberately made Eastbourne look guilty, which he surmised was in order to protect Wolves' speedway and the behaviour of some of their staff. Jon also worried that the images could slant perspectives of people who wouldn't ordinarily give the sport any consideration or national coverage. The photos have also provoked the interest of "a lot of unsavoury people in speedway for all the wrong reasons". In summary, Jon notes that "Dean got involved after Chris Geer was kicked in the head twice" but did concede that Chris, David Norris's mechanic, "perhaps shouldn't have got involved".
So, everyone agrees, that the least said the soonest mended for the teams, the people involved and the sport itself.

I will leave the last rhetorical comment to Jon Cook, "in what other sport could participants be assaulted by the staff employed by the home team and the police not become involved?"

Chapter 11: An Evening with Ronnie Russell in Thurrock
25th May Arena Essex v. Eastbourne

"I really like the new system, I wish it had been around when I was riding" Mark Loram (repeatedly about the new format of the 2005 GP series)

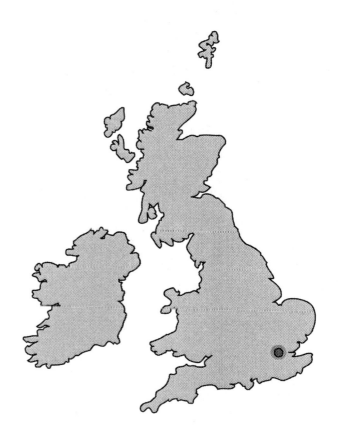

13.6.2 All Applicants must be of good repute and the SCB at its sole discretion may refuse to issue, cancel or suspend any Officials Licence

So finally I get to see some speedway racing, in true Essex style, with a trip to watch the mighty Husqvarna-sponsored Arena Essex 'Hammers' at their home track in Thurrock. It's actually one of UK speedways most stunning locations, albeit in a post-industrial sense. The raceway is located almost directly under the lee of the magnificent Queen Elizabeth Bridge or that bloody Dartford Crossing, as it's known to the long suffering drivers of the M25. I'm not sure if this section of the motorway was included in that recent peculiar book of photography *M25 Travelling Clockwise* by an airport taxi driver on the history and great sights of the M25 – but it should have been. It has a particularly beautiful view in both directions high above the Thames, though you tend not to appreciate this when grumbling if stuck in a jam or when you adhere to the 50 m.p.h. speed limit on the bridge. When crowded with traffic, provided that you look at it and are not in it, then this sight has a certain urban beauty. This sight is even more attractive at dusk, especially when the distant car lights blink and speckle the horizon in the advancing gloom.

If I were a commercial letting agent and the stadium that houses the Arena Essex raceway was for sale, I'd definitely highlight how convenient it was for the Thames and many other local amenities. It's handy for one of the few service stations that the orbital motorway boasts, numerous refineries and riverside cargo-handling facilities as well as a few other office buildings apparently marooned in the area. Most obviously though, if the key to success with any property is 'location, location, location', then it's very handily situated in Greater London. Actually, it's not. But if the handy rule of thumb holds true – that everything inside the M25 ring road is in reality all part of the sweeping tide of mini conurbations that nowadays defines Greater London, then Thurrock is close enough since it's just on the cusp. As close as you can get without quite being there; kind of like the Elite League season that the 'Hammers' have enjoyed to date, part of the league but just not quite of it, so far.

Anyway, once you've finally managed to negotiate, what is to the irregular user, the terror of the unofficial dodgem-car circuit cum racetrack that is the nearby large roundabout system, you've almost nearly made it to the Raceway. When you journey anywhere in the country where the local drivers dominate, particularly if you're not quite sure where you're going, it' always appears frighteningly fast. This is compounded if you experience the mania that regularly descends during the rush-hour traffic. However, the stadium is literally just off the freeway as, no doubt, Arena's American rider Josh Larsen has it when he describes it to his friends. If you avoid the attraction of an unnecessarily expensive pit stop in the nearby services, you're nearly home and dry. All that remains is to drive through some imposing gates and down a longish undulating road, which is most likely, a tributary of the famous A1306 Arterial Road. It's then a short distance to the stadium buildings on the near horizon past land that screams out at you as the ideal site for a car-boot sale or an overnight lorry park. It probably serves as both. The area has begun to be littered with the wrecked remains of lorries unfortunate enough to come to grief on the M25 motorway and towed to here for reasons and purposes unknown.

In preparation for my visit I'd rung ahead which gave me the chance to enjoy the Monty Pythonesque voice used for the recorded messages about the details of the next meeting. After a few calls, I'd spoken to a charming South African man, Gerald Richter who assures me that the gate marshal will expect my arrival on the night. Gerald is sceptical about the sanity of my project to visit every UK speedway track presently in existence as research for my book, "you'd really have to love speedway to want to do that". I park by the couple, who have decided to relax inside their ageing brown Marina and enjoy the sunshine of a hot May afternoon. They sit in their car with the doors open for the additional ventilation of a windless afternoon and together savour some pre-entry sandwiches and a flask of tea. They had first choice of an empty car park, so they've chosen THE prime location in which to park. Right next to one of the many whitewashed tyres that all stand out brilliantly against the dark gravel, and are dotted throughout this apparently barren area of wasteland. Their car is also close by the edge of the road and points in the direction of the M25, probably in anticipation of a quick getaway after the meeting.

The man at the gate is affable and helpful, he calls ahead on the phone and I hear him say "that writer's here for Ronnie". I have arrived early, as previously arranged, to meet the enthusiastic, down-to-earth promoter and team manager Ronnie Russell. From the pages of the *Speedway Star* as well as from his voluble appearances on the live televised meetings shown on Sky Sports, you just know that Ronnie is an enthusiast for all things Arena Essex. You also just know that he's patriotically English too! He can certainly talk for Britain and tirelessly promotes the forthcoming meetings at the stadium at every opportunity. RR cuts a strikingly distinctive figure. He looks most like a middle-aged version, albeit much slimmer, of a now forgotten lead singer from 1980s ska band Bad Manners – Buster Bloodvessel. Though I'm pretty sure Buster has never entered Ronnie's consciousness or served as any sort of role model for him. Especially when you consider that RR is always smartly dressed whenever you see him on TV (and later tonight) in that collared, well-ironed blue shirt worn in a way that cries out to you with a, 'I grew up when there was still National Service' attitude much more than I'm just off to bowls.

Strangely for a compulsive and capable self-publicist, during the slow-news period winter months of the close season Ronnie has spectacularly managed to embroil himself in a heated debate he can't possibly win, or recover from, with any glory. This has been played out in the most public of all forums within the sport, the letters and news pages of the *Speedway Star* or, less visibly, on the Internet forums. The dispute centred upon his intention to increase future admission charges for old age pensioners. Given that the popularity of speedway has severely declined from the pomp of its heyday, OAPs remain the backbone of the sport as we know it and, morbidly worryingly for the immediate future, will continue to be the largest age group from which the future lifeblood of the sport will be drawn. Ronnie has tried to justify this rather alienating proposal in a number of unsatisfactory ways. The central plank of his justification concerned the supposed systematic abuse by pensioners of the concession system of reduced entry fees, through a failure to provide proper documentation or, he implied, the use of forged documents. Maybe this concern with entitlement and correct paperwork is another manifestation of the National Service training thing again? Another spurious justification for this decision that Ronnie tried to advance was to claim a general intention throughout the sport to raise prices for pensioners through the abolition of concession entry fees, despite the subsequent conspicuous failure by any other promoters to implement these ill-conceived plans. The final and most tenuous excuse trotted out by RR was the complete failure of the old codgers to realise that increases in inflation and the cost of living generally would affect speedway in line with all other goods and services.

The whole situation became needlessly complicated and was undoubtedly a public relations disaster, no matter how tortuously Ronnie tried to explain or justify his stance on price increases. In a bizarre and rather delightful statement, Ronnie tried to run with a version of the economic facts of life that combined a variation of Harold Wilson's 'pound in your pocket' speech with a very complicated parable that involved OAPs at the supermarket checkout who still continued to do their weekly shop and bought food they needed to live on, even when prices went up dramatically![1] With a lot less hullabaloo than its initial suggestion, all his plans were suddenly dropped with some vague reference to Ronnie having been seriously misled by other promoters about their intentions.

The heat of the day scorches as I pass the main entrance way and grandstand while the racetrack bakes in the sunshine. There's quite a display of flagpoles with a nice patriotic array of Union flags, St George's flags and some of the chequered

[1] Ronnie was quoted as saying "The end of the senior citizen concession is part of a move throughout the sport. The old girl in front of me in the queue at Sainsbury's doesn't pay less for her shopping than I do. This is part of a move to what is happening in the rest of the world."

variety they wave at the Formula 1 drivers on the finish line. When it's not a speedway night, the stadium is mainly used for banger racing. First stop in my search to locate RR is the well-used and slightly tatty portacabin that forms the private office cum inner sanctum and nerve centre of operations on race night. Ronnie is the tenant and not the landlord at the Arena Essex Raceway, so the pervasive attitude appears to be very much make do and mend. Like the cupboard at Old Mother Hubbard's, the office is bare as RR is to be found down at the pits, where he chats amiably with Eastbourne's Adam Shields while he fastidiously cleans his bike. It's a work night and, although there are many hours to go before the meeting starts, Ronnie only has a "quick 10 minutes" to spare.

If you forget that we're geographically situated outside the unofficial border that is the M25, as soon as Ronnie opens his mouth you just know that really you're in London, the East End of London to be precise, most likely within the audible sound of Bow bells. Ronnie is charming, affable and helpful. He's infectiously enthusiastic about the sport and the riders. If time permitted, he could talk endlessly about his philosophy and opinions or recount many stories he's gained through years of involvement with speedway. Ronnie is at pains to stress that it's been an experience lived from both sides of the fence, both as a spectator and as a promoter. I'm enjoyably swept along on a tide of reminiscence, insight and opinion for nearly an hour. We're only fleetingly interrupted by a "quick word" with Paul Hurry about possible fixture clashes between his European long-track racing commitments and Arena Essex speedway fixtures ("lovely bloke. You should see his arm it would really horrify you"). Or by a "quick call" much later from Eve, his "lady wife" (RR speaks about many things with an old-fashioned manner), who punctures his reverie enough to remind him that it's race night and time for him to bustle off energetically to get on with tonight's "Showtime" once more. And "Showtime", I soon realise, when I watch him bounce about everywhere later that night as well as from the level of genuine excitement he generates during our conversation, is something that RR relishes and excels at. This evening's contest with the local rivals the Eastbourne Eagles is also yet another chance to go head to head with his more successful elder brother Terry, rival promoter of both Swindon and Eastbourne among his many other connections to speedway in this country. RR's tremendous respect for "my brother Terry" frequently peppers his stories and conversation.

For this evening's encounter, RR has rather excitingly managed to sign the current World Champion Jason Crump as a replacement number 1 for the absent Mark Loram. Mark was sadly injured, at the start of the season at Eastbourne, in a freak low-speed accident. Now he has secured the coup of a gifted guest rider like Jason Crump, Ronnie has an extra spring in his step and additional jauntiness to his demeanour.

The natural showman and promoter in him kicks in, buoyed up by the thought of all the extra Arena fans that might flood back through the turnstiles tonight excited at the prospect to watch Crump ride for Arena. Though it will be a delight still strongly tinged with sadness at what might have been, if only Mark hadn't had the misfortune to get so badly injured early in the season.

The injury has been a personal catastrophe for Mark, which has been compounded for the club by their continued failure to regularly find adequate temporary replacements. Well, to Ronnie's joy they did have an amazing temporary replacement in the form of Tony Rickardsson for a short while – "amazing", "what a rider", "what a professional" – who excelled in the Hammers' colours and managed to excite the often difficult-to-please home crowd. Ultimately (and very sadly for British speedway) Tony treated these rides as an extended chance to gain some early season practice, sharpen his consummate skills, perfect his bike set ups and achieve some additional match fitness for his forthcoming Grand Prix campaign and his tireless pursuit of the record six wins, held by Ivan Mauger. Uncontroversially Ronnie believes, "he's the best rider of his time, that's all you can ever say. You can't really compare, there have been so many greats – the legendary Ivan Mauger, the great Hans Nielsen and so on – they were the ultimate for their time, it's as far as you can say". According to RR, all these truly great riders have key qualities that helped them stand out from the rest – the ability, the mental energy and focus, the professionalism, the killer instinct that prevents them from being as easily beaten as some other riders – "your number 1 is different from the rest of the team, they're so special!" Since then he has spent endless hours on his mobile phone in a fruitless search for suitable alternative replacements. So much time that, at one stage, the mobile company blocked his phone because they thought it had been stolen, in light of the sudden high volume of overseas calls. Despite the best but inadequate efforts of the various guests Ronnie did secure, no one has managed to step into Mark's vacant steel shoe and his absence has badly affected results on the track. The frustration of his search for Mark's adequate replacement, in combination with the poor results and the dwindling crowds has so far made it the "worst season ever" for Ronnie as the promoter of Arena Essex speedway.

However, Ronnie is an indomitable type since he has been around the promotion game for quite a while now. Well, since 1982 give or take a few years when he had a sabbatical, which he found "very hard as it had been my total life", before he finally returned to speedway again with Arena in 2000. Her indoors, Eve, claims he's like a "drug addict", always on the lookout for his next fix. Never mind all the time and money he's "poured into it" over the years. RR has been that way about speedway ever since it got into his blood when he first went to see a meeting with his Dad. This was in Bow, East London, and the visitors were the Poole Pirates. The thrill of the sport caught his childish imagination, mostly due to the innate glamour and resonance of the striking image of the skull and crossbones on the race bibs of the Poole team. Ronnie was also fascinated with the spectacle of people who rode sideways at speed. After that he was hooked, though his formal involvement only started in 1963 when, after he'd endeared himself to the local track staff, which enabled him to start in the sport as "a pusher-outer". Since then it's been a glittering career in speedway promotion, often with his brother, which has taken in various tracks and includes spells at Crayford, Rye House and Arena. Where he finds himself now is very much where he wants to be. Arena Essex is the place he's laid his hat and therefore it's very much his home.

Since the turn of the 21st century, under his command, it's been drive and ambition all the way for the Arena Essex team. The first thing RR did was to purchase an inflatable air fence and thereby put his track ahead of the curve when it came to this aspect of rider safety. It was a decision that resulted in a reduction in his insurance premiums as the team immediately plummeted from top to bottom of the most unwanted title in the sport – the Race Crashes league rankings compiled on a yearly basis by the insurers. "Without disrespecting the teams in the Premier League, which is very difficult, like the first division nowadays in football", Ronnie only ever had eyes for the main prize to finally see Arena ride in the Elite League. He's never looked back though he admits he misses the "good crack together" that you'd have as a team of riders and mechanics during a three- or four-day "Northern Tour". However in the highest division, where Arena now find themselves, you no longer get that kind of tour experience or camaraderie. The modern-day reality is that the top riders work throughout Europe and fly here, there and everywhere. So it's likely that any Elite League team squad will only be together on the nights that they actually have a fixture.

Although the Elite League is "more professional in terms of equipment and attitude" it has resulted in a couple of very tough years financially for the Arena promotion, particularly since they stepped up a division. However, the dynamics of the modern version of the sport has changed and one of the most positive, in Ronnie's forceful view, is the coverage by Sky Sports, "the most fantastic thing to happen to speedway in many years". This, as if his acknowledged speedway habit and desire to succeed meant that he needed any further evidence, was a key factor in the move up in leagues from the Premier to the Elite League for Arena Essex. It's been a decision that has helped significantly increase the interest from and level of payments received from the club's sponsors. For example, the air fence adverts and sponsorship raised £80,000 in 2004 in the Elite League compared with only £11,700 raised without the air fence in the Premier League the previous year.

According to Ronnie, the sport has always attracted a very broad cross-section of society as spectators, riders, referees and it's the same with the sponsors. People watch the sport on the telly and it ignites a latent or previous interest which often means that they then decide that they want to be part of it again. That's what RR sincerely believes but also continues to hope. The medium of television is so powerful that Ronnie marvels that he was recently recognised as "Essex" when he was on holiday at Paignton in Devon. Never one to let the grass grow under his feet, he's recently attracted a firm of city stockbrokers to possibly take an interest in Arena and has ambitious plans to exploit the interest potential of 23,000 West Ham United season ticket holders (and thereby attract one group of "Hammers" fans to support another local "Hammers" team). Ronnie indicates that he could even get one of the buses he already runs locally to Arena fixtures every week, if it transpired that transport (or alcohol consumption) was a problem for newly interested fans to get to Thurrock from the East End.

Not that RR paints a rosy picture of the precarious finances of the average rider or promoter. After he's slipped a metaphorical onion casually from his pocket, Ronnie bemoans the uniquely shocking financial structure of the sport with regards to the distribution of profits from the Labour and Capital employed. It's a situation where the traditional relationship of the 'Wages of Labour' to the 'Profit of Capital', eloquently described by Marx in his *Economic and Philosophical Manuscripts of 1844*, has become inverted. The net result is that "so much of your money is given to your employees". Marx might have provided some great analysis, but he has absolutely nothing to say when it comes to what RR describes as the "unaffordable bit of the cake" which the riders then inevitably fritter away, "all their money goes on engine tuners and equipment" while they perpetually search for that magic vital but elusive ingredient required for instant success. Like the revolutionary but often useless equipment bought by obsessed club golfers in the hope of improved performance; it's a mostly fruitless quest for perfection that is invariably and pathologically shared by speedway riders everywhere. They optimistically and continually try to distinguish themselves from their rivals through obsessive tinkering with their equipment in the attempt to ensure their bikes go just that little bit faster.

It's enough to drive a bitter man to tears, but RR rises above these petty vicissitudes. He's delighted with the team's main sponsor – Husqvarna – so much so that he omits to mention to me that they manufacture the world's largest lawnmower! Which is definitely another unique claim to fame as well as another close association with success and innovation for the Husqvarna Hammers. Apart from the sponsors, Ronnie is delighted with the fans, of course, and quickly acknowledges that they're "committed" and "deeply knowledgeable". Though he still needs to chase the essential growth through the turnstiles that can apparently only come when you attract the "floating audience" to or back to speedway. Hopefully, the promise of regular TV coverage allied to the Husqvarna leadership position in the horticulture market will suffice to fulfil this ambition[2]. To achieve the required growth in spectator numbers, while you overcome the structural problem caused by the iniquitous business model between promoters and riders within the sport that Ronnie despairs of, you basically have to put on a damn good show week in and week out.

After only a few minutes in his company, you know that, if anyone is, Ronnie is a showman and an optimist. It just needs more hard work and the talking of the talk for it to all come together. This committed man sincerely hopes that the 'ifs, ands, buts and maybes' might shortly start to stack up in Arena's favour again. Basically, if Mark recovers quickly from injury and comes back racing shortly, Ronnie is sure that it'll boost the fans while, most importantly, add that vital intangible but absent ingredient back into the side. If that significant 'X' factor returned, he believes that it would give the team some increased oomph and generate the buzz for that elusive but vital "word of mouth" he always seeks.

It's suddenly only 90 minutes to go to the off and I've had a whistle-stop tour of the world of speedway according to Ronnie. His energy and enthusiasm is exhaustingly infectious. He's keen to get off to fry the many fish that is the typical race night lot of a person who combines the duties of promoter and team manager! The need to look the part is another crucial aspect of the process, so with a firm shake of the hand and a determination in his demeanour, he's off for tonight's latest fix. We're not at all far from take-off as RR bustles away to change from his casual civvies into his smart clothes which he'll wear, as ever, with his optimistic but plain speaking outlook[3].

Phew, is all I can say – to the evening's heat and the whirlwind that is Ronnie – as I lurk in the shadow of the main stand for a minute's rest. The car park has started to fill slowly and the crowd begins to filter in clutching their boards and garden chairs. A few of the early birds loiter by the rather well-stocked track shop situated in the main grandstand building. This is the only outlet open in a slightly sad parade of shuttered shops, though it boasts a panoramic view of the track and a sign that rather grandly proclaims it to be the 'Bangers & Speedway Souvenir Shop'. The shop definitely has even more than the usual array of merchandise crammed into a very small space and, for the next 30 minutes while I linger there, it attracts anyone who's anyone from the world of speedway who happens to be around in that part of Essex for this fixture against Eastbourne. Practically every passer-by stops for a chat, a question or to complain about the resolutely closed bar, particularly since it's a scorching evening when even the mind of the most loyal member of the temperance society would turn to the need for the cool refreshment of an alcoholic beverage. The general consensus is that the shut bar typifies the

[2] The number two growth pastime in the UK after cooking is gardening nowadays – a sad indictment in itself when, in the not-so-distant rose-tinted past, it was frequently claimed that fishing used to be the number 1 sporting pastime of choice with attending speedway fixtures a very close second

[3] Ronnie, not that he mentioned it, has been previously awarded the George Medal for bravery for his selfless actions on March 20th 1974 when he helped foil the attempted kidnap or killing of Princess Anne on the Mall. Ronnie happened to pass in the other direction at the time of the incident and spontaneously intervened without thought for his own safety. When you meet him you definitely don't need to be told that he's an old-fashioned, brave and chivalrous type of man.

poor organisational skills you can regularly expect as part of the Arena experience, in this case where sobriety rules and thirsts remain unquenched. "Laughable" is as polite a summary as I hear. Something about trips and breweries also gets frequently mentioned. So I can't help but realise that Ronnie really does need the bags of energetic determination he already has, but in even greater abundance if he's to staunch and turn round this apparently habitual level of casual grumbling. The knock-on impact of Mark's injuries to the results of the team on the track can't have exactly helped brighten the mood of this particular 'knowledgeable crowd'. All these serial moans and grumbles – from the "you're not going to believe what they've gone and done now" school of thought – makes me wonder if those West Ham season ticket holders haven't already started to attend Arena meetings in force.

Back at the track shop, the very friendly and impressively tattooed Tom has a kindly or measured word for practically everyone who passes. This includes the lady dressed to kill that night – with tasselled black boots and a sash that proclaims her rightful crown as 'Miss Arena Essex' – who kindly poses for a photograph for my book ("you'll have to speak to my agent") before she totters off to the pits area, where I later notice her as she amiably chats, cajoles or flirts with the assorted mechanics and riders[4]. With the shop besieged by swarms of punters and served by the affable Tom, a disembodied voice from a shady storeroom cupboard asks, "what's your book all about then?" The voice belongs to the renowned veteran speedway photographer Alf Weedon, who rests in the shady tranquillity of his cupboard with a well-deserved cup of tea. Alf still works for a living as a photographer at Arena speedway, despite his age and because of his experience. While his body may have aged, Alf is still far from anybody's fool. What this legendary character within speedway circles hasn't seen, photographed or whom he hasn't known in the sport for over the last half century would fit on the back of a postage stamp.

Alf will be at it again – photography that is – later in the evening but for now he conserves his energy in the store cupboard. Back home in Ilford, the fruits of the many, many years' labour have resulted in a unique, but personal, photographic archive of the sport. I can't believe that anyone hasn't yet bought this tremendous resource for posterity – Alf later confirms that it is for sale to the right home for the right price. There are over 200,000 photographs, stored as negatives, glass plates or cut film. It is the type of archive the country should buy for posterity and the use of future generations with funds from National Lottery[5]. Historically, photography was one among many ventures for Alf within speedway circles, along with the eponymous track shops he used to run. Alf even ran the Reading Racers' concession for donkey's years at Smallmead, the home of my first experience of the sport and speedway track shops. Those days are behind him, along with the glory days of the sport, according to Alf. There have been many changes. Mostly not for the better, often dictated by the modern disease that is the increasingly avaricious pursuit of money. This primary goal has long since overridden all the others and has, Alf believes, taken a lot of the historic "friendliness" away from the contemporary scene. The prevalence of this trait, when allied to a dearth of "real characters" in contemporary speedway, has been a huge loss and has severely diminished Alf's enjoyment. To Alf's mind, "it all changed for the worse when Bruce Penhall retired".

We're distracted from further discussion of the decline and fall of British speedway by the arrival of an impressively large bundle of the latest version of the speedway bible, otherwise known as the *Speedway Star*. Alf immediately grabs a copy and starts to flick through it and offers exclamations of surprise, critical comments and low rumbling noises while he studies the contents. This week's issue is available at the Arena track shop three nights ahead of its official Saturday publication day, hot off the presses and published from an office in Surbiton. I'm proudly told at Arena, just as I am over

---

[4] It later transpires that I have just encountered the notorious and kindly 'Scary Sheila'. Away from the track she's actually called Sheila La-Sage (pronounced, Sheila informs me as 'Lee-Sarge'). Her commitment to speedway, and especially all things Arena Essex, is legendary and boundless but brings her a well-deserved reputation for her energy and sincerity. Her heart is most definitely in the right place, she works tirelessly on behalf of the club and, for me, she definitely typifies the enthusiasm and friendliness of speedway fans in general and the Arena fans I met in particular.

[5] The collection is eventually reputedly sold at a bargain price to Tony McDonald at *Backtrack* magazine.

the next few weeks at all the other Wednesday night racetracks within the rough vicinity of London (Poole, King's Lynn and Wimbledon), as though it's gospel, "we're the first to get to sell this week's issue every week". Among speedway aficionados and the speedway cognoscenti – well those who make their living from speedway, in whatever capacity – this magazine is more generally known as "the comic". Among the ordinary fans that aren't privileged enough to be on "the inside", it has real cache as a source of information and often has the revered status that tablets from the mountain had in biblical times. The diet of weekly news, comment and results attracts a steady stream of interested readers at Arena raceway unafraid to pay full price – even when it would be much cheaper by yearly subscription and would arrive every Thursday in the post. But, then you wouldn't have the thrill to get your fix of news hot off the presses or, more importantly, to actually get to read it at a speedway meeting.

As if these riches weren't already enough, and with talk of West Ham fans earlier, the genial Tony McDonald arrives in his family motor with further riches from the stable that brought us *Confessions of a Speedway Promoter*. John Berry's trenchant, page turner but slightly self-serving account of the many larger-than-life figures he encountered from the sport during the salad days of his years in speedway promotion at Ipswich. Tony has arrived with bulk supplies of the latest edition of the long-established *Vintage Speedway Magazine* and, my personal favourite, his most recent venture the retro 1970s to 1990 companion speedway publication *Backtrack*. Alf briefly emerges from the shadows of his cupboard to exchange a few words with Tony and also seizes copies of both magazines with some alacrity. A lengthy feature in *Backtrack* particularly catches Alf's interest, since it covers the era of the famous promoter Wally Mawdsley's halcyon days, when he was bent on rapid expansion and set up new tracks hither and thither throughout the country. Alf notes, "the riders respected him" before he adds, unlike the somewhat breathless article, that ultimately Wally didn't enjoy long-term success because he eventually "almost shut down as many tracks as he set up". But, then again, if you metaphorically sit by the river as long as Alf has, you get to see a lot of things change and that includes other people's careers as they wax and wane.

Alf insists that I quickly run an errand for him to the referee/announcer's box, which is located on the home straight, up some steps in the stand and overlooks the start gate and has a panoramic view of the rest of the track. I'm to pass on the latest track shop news to the announcer for tonight's meeting ("it changes every week you see, or it mainly does" Alf notes). The basic message is that, to all intents and purposes, the shop is a treasure trove that stores a veritable cornucopia of speedway memorabilia and enough branded items to gladden the heart of any true Arena fan. Alf is keen to herald the addition of this season's new, bright-red Arena Essex team shirts, the sourcing and arrival of which I quickly gather is a source of some joy to him. They are finally now in stock and Alf expects that considerable pent-up demand is to be expected for Tom behind the counter of the track shop. In the announcer's box, Bob Miller faithfully promises to work the crowd into a frenzy of consumerism about all the available goodies later during the meeting. He also hopes for a referee with good eyesight and thorough understanding of the rules for tonight's meeting and he jokes about his previously unsuccessful attempts to influence the referee's decision while they sit next to him in the close confines of the Arena box. Bob laughs when he recalls a recent meeting where, after a racing incident, the referee's ("laughable") decision was doubted by absolutely everyone else in the stadium and the box (including the referee's wife) but sadly without any success. On my return to the track shop, a women in an Arena tracksuit top questions why there is no "lady's cut" version in the newly available team shirts. I leave Tom to finesse the situation with a series of increasingly unconvincing but polite arguments about shape and gender.

Afterwards, with many other fans, I lurk by the pits area, at the bottom of the slope near where the riders park their vans. It's an ideal spot to engage the riders in a spot of casual conversation, to ask for a photograph or their signatures. Every one of the riders must eventually pass by as they journey between the pits and the changing rooms, either dressed in their civilian clothes or their smarter looking kevlars. The rare visit by reigning World Champion Jason Crump, tonight as a guest rider for Arena, sparks considerable interest among the various men, women and children that loiter along the route. As does the ever popular Mark Loram, who's here although he's injured, and the personable but taciturn David Norris who rides despite

Ronnie Russell. © Jeff Scott

The legendary Alf Weedon. © Jeff Scott

The back straight. © Jeff Scott

the fact that he still struggles with limited vision as a result of the concussion he sustained a month previously at Swindon. While we wait to pounce on the riders, some people eat doorstep-sized sandwiches, a boy plays football with a tennis ball, and a loose collection of fans and riders informally mingle in the casual way that so typifies the casual ethos of the sport.

As Ronnie had remarked earlier "in this sport everyone's like a family, you get to know everyone, well, more like an extended family". And all families argue as we know, but tonight that's not the case as Ronnie, smartly attired and carrying a tightly rolled flag, strides purposefully towards the pits and track area. Alf Weedon follows shortly afterwards in a bright blue anorak to fulfil yet one more of the many thousands of evenings' work he's undertaken in his capacity as an official photographer. Later, from the banks of the back straight, I glimpse him as he strides purposefully round the pits area or when he flashes away with his camera from his place on the centre green.

Throughout the evening, as the meeting progresses, you could be forgiven for the thought that Ronnie does practically everything at the club – except ride the bikes and drive the tractor to grade the track. Generally, he's everywhere and his energy appears boundless as he cajoles and encourages in the pits, has a quiet word here and there, or slaps the riders on their backs as they depart and return, with what I assume, to be encouragement and praise. Though no longer built for speed, Ronnie also regularly runs on the track to check on any fallen riders; plus he manages to find the time to explain to the fans, via the pits microphone, almost as bluntly as he had in his office earlier, the reasons behind his regrettable decision to release Piotr Swist from the team. Based on the evidence of tonight's performance, Piotr does nothing to contradict Ronnie's perception that the problem is the standard and preparation of his equipment rather than his ability or the level of his experience.

Throughout the fixture there are pleasantly balmy but not too warm conditions, though Arena still manage to narrowly lose at home for the fourth time this season, albeit in a fashion that suggests that the closeness of the final score definitely flatters them. Particularly since Eastbourne have tracked a slightly weakened team on the night. Jason Crump guests superbly and rides to a faultless maximum of fifteen points, though he had been pushed very hard in two different races by a still very much under par Norris. The subsequent match report in the *Speedway Star* illustrates that the rail companies haven't quite cornered the thriving excuses market with their superb 'wrong type of snow' or 'leaves on the line' justifications. Unbelievably this report claims that the Arena boys were, unfortunately, effectively blind-sided by the wrong type of track surface (!). Terry Catley, the regular home meeting reporter, notes that in the days prior to the meeting the "top dressing" hadn't "fully settled in" and had an "adverse effect" on the team. Maybe the peculiarities of the surface were what encouraged Steen Jensen to execute one of those rarely witnessed speedway manoeuvres on the final bend of the race, when he lead heat 9. His elegant double pirouette, yards from the finish line, only served to frighten the passing riders and relegate himself from first to last place in one smooth but difficult action.

Tonight's crowd is the usual mixture of families and varying ages, with very few audible grumbles within my earshot about yet another defeat and disappointing home performance. RR had presciently remarked earlier that while fantastically knowledgeable "all speedway fans see it as their right to expect their team to always win at home". Maybe over the past few seasons, RR has been on a secret campaign to re-educate the Arena crowd to forget or lower their inflated expectations through the appearance of regular home defeats. We're treated to a lovely sunset with a spectacular dusk that has the lights attractively glint back towards the crowd from the Queen Elizabeth Bridge magnificently spanning the Thames. We're also treated to a professionally run and presented race meeting that entertains throughout while it remains reasonably close, and features a few stand-out races with some excellent examples of the currently dying art of team riding. As we collectively drift from the stadium to the car park, I finally hear some home fans bemoan their lot as Arena Speedway fans. But then, even with high hopes, Thurrock isn't going to become the speedway equivalent of Rome overnight without a lot of effort, determination and dedication. Or luck. If the capricious speedway gods, along with that always fickle mistress of public sympathy and sentiment, run in Ronnie's favour it will hopefully soon all change for the better. However, until then, Ronnie Russell isn't afraid to dream big and unreservedly views himself as the man to deliver those dreams for everyone connected with Arena Essex Speedway club.

Chapter 12: Fun Frying in the Fens
19th June Mildenhall v. Weymouth

SKY CHATTER

"The bikes roar" "We're looking at a 5-1 situation here" "We're looking at a 4-2 situation here" "We're looking at a 3-3 situation here" Some hardy perennials from Nigel Pearson at most meetings he covers

RANDOM SCB RULES

13.6 In all forms of sport a number of Officials are necessary to ensure the smooth running of proceedings, Speedway is no exception

---

It's one of those scorching hot midsummer days in June that cause people to flock to Brighton for a day by the beach. Instead of relaxing contentedly, they spend a few hours grid-locked in traffic on the roads that lead down to the seafront. It's always easier to get round by foot or bike than join the queuing hordes of the city's visitors and very few self-respecting Brightonians venture into their cars for anything other than to leave town. I'm lured away myself by the chance to go and see the Mildenhall 'UK Fire' Fen Tigers ride at Mildenhall Stadium based at West Row in Suffolk. On the subject of fires, a massive car fire on the A23 close to Hickstead causes everyone who heads north to go on a mammoth cross-country diversion and so terrorise the inhabitants round their own usually sleepy local lanes. This delays my journey to Mildenhall's home track, which was built in a potato field in the mid-1970s at the height of the last speedway boom in this country[1].

---

[1] The club started as a training school track on April 8th 1973 on farmland owned by Terry Walters. The co-promoter was Bernie Klatt who was employed as a chef at the nearby United States Air Force base.

ADULT £9

CHILD/OAP £4

FAMILY £22
(2 ADULTS AND UP TO 4 KIDS UNDER 14yrs OLD)

Times have changed and the Fen Tigers presently ride in the Conference League. It's a league succinctly described in their match programme as a "first step on the for many of the riders in their racing careers". Some of these ambitious riders never manage to progress beyond the first rung and, therefore, never get to climb this metaphorical 'ladder', which is missing from their careers and accidentally from this sentence in the programme. Whereas, some of the more experienced riders in this league head towards the twilight of their careers, down said ladder, and are counted as 'old hands' because they have already had careers elsewhere in different, higher level leagues. In essence it's a testing ground for the talent of tomorrow to cut their teeth, develop and spread their wings, depending on your choice of analogy. This afternoon's meeting is a fixture against the Weymouth Wildcats from the lovely Victorian seaside town on the south-west coast of the country. They, too, are a recently resurgent track with a rich and chequered previous history, and 2005 is their second year in their most recent incarnation under the tutelage of promoter and team manager Brian White.

In the summer, if all roads lead to Brighton then the same can't reasonably be said of West Row, which is a small village, tucked away in the Fenlands of Suffolk. Its surprisingly close to a number of major towns within a 20-mile radius but, at the same time, appears to be set in the quiet sort of Turneresque, undisturbed countryside that would strongly appeal to tourists in search of ye olde English village. In fact before you get to within a few miles of the environs of West Row, you'll have already passed a large number of curiously or quaintly named villages that might well tempt you to investigate them before you've ever managed to reach the sleepy calm and charm of West Row. Who could resist the chance to visit the Wilbrahams, a place that sounds like a country music trio if ever a destination did. In fact its two villages, Great Wilbraham and Little Wilbraham, that combine to produce the Wilbrahams monicker and immediately conjures up 'typical country' images of white-painted thatched cottages, village ponds, overgrown church graveyards and a low-beamed village pub filled with polished riding accessories. This afternoon's journey to the speedway takes me through Mildenhall High Town, a place that takes exceptional civic pride in its educational facilities if the sheer number of roadside signs that advertise these facilities is any indicator of its widespread local esteem. The baking afternoon heat makes life in the country appear to move even slower than my clichéd view might lead me to expect, particularly since we're having an early summer mini heat wave, so much so that by 1 p.m. the thermometer has already reached a dizzying 31 °C. That's 'very hot' for those of you that prefer your temperature reading in the old Fahrenheit money of a traditional English summer. The picture of rural, idyllic charm is somewhat interrupted by the imposing perimeter fence of the ex-US airbase, RAF Mildenhall, which covers miles upon miles of the countryside with huge, mostly unused runways in this neck of the woods. Its a very visible symbol of the Cold War with its barbed wire topped security fences, various assorted outlying buildings and those huge aircraft hangers built to house the next generation of planes capable of showing Johnny Russian his maker pretty damn quick. The gradual thaw of that particular conflict effectively stopped the search for reds under the bed or the need to fly reconnaissance missions to search for troop and missile movements behind the Iron Curtain; nonetheless, the airbase has stubbornly remained an imposing presence.

The still, empty atmosphere of the place is redolent of a time when, perhaps, *Enola Gay* or its European equivalent would sometimes need to take off from these huge, lengthy runways with its deadly payload on board. I grew up in Hampshire relatively near to RAF Farnborough, so I imagine that the reality of the 'real and present danger' was either terminal boredom or all those practice missions undertaken (that destroyed the soul if nothing else) usually in accident-prone jet fighters like the lethal Starfighter, which allegedly crashed almost as many times as it ever saw active service. Apart from the US servicemen stationed in this part of Suffolk, who possibly stirred resentment when they turned the local women's heads with the offer of stockings (or whatever the post-war equivalent commodity was), this particular area was an ideal part of the world in which to base a speedway track. There was the danger, the real peril of injury or death, the thrills and the noise and all without the need to do anything other than travel along to a converted potato field a few miles from the airbase. Should you desire, you could also pose about the stadium or bar and coolly smoke your US-manufactured Marlboros or filter-tipped Peter Stuyvesants. It was an age when you could have done this without fear of cancer, political correctness or pesky environmental factors that unnecessarily impinge on your overriding sense of fun.

Anyway, that's all a pretty long-handed way to say that the stadium nestles (or it would if it weren't so flat around here) in the countryside quite close to a whopping great big airbase that's seen better days. The one thing you can usually say for military establishments, stuck in the middle of nowhere, is that they generally ensure that the roads are wider, stronger and better maintained than they would otherwise have been. Especially, if it's expected that these highways and byways will have to cope with the transport of highly explosive ordinance or befuddled but often suicidally dangerous American servicemen, who venture out of their hermetically safe compounds to drive with the locals on the 'wrong side' of the road. Strangely, there mustn't have been much fraternisation by the airmen here, or maybe it was always a British airbase, just paid for by the Americans as part of their peace efforts, since the roads that lead to the track are really quite narrow, albeit pretty straight, with only occasional blind spots.

I grew up near narrow country roads, so I realise that the biggest possible danger on country lanes is, usually, the extremely fast, confident but appalling drivers that are the local residents. Not that you'd ever suspect this, if you listened to them describe the heinous driving of strangers later that evening in the pub with the horse brasses and the roaring fire (even in summer), mostly to the sympathetic barmaid with the low-cut top.

As I drove to the track a couple of drivers overtook me, with only millimetres to separate our respective paintworks, at criminally high speeds that wouldn't have disgraced them at Silverstone. Or with such consummate ease, skill and bravado on the odd blind corner that would have seen them well placed in the rally Tour of Britain, should it ever venture out of Wales for the challenges of the flat Suffolk countryside. Best of all – and this bit is true – I was overtaken by a completely dusty white transit van with the words "I WISH SHE WAS AS DIRTY AS THIS" wistfully drawn in the dust on the back doors. Out of curiosity, I nearly decided to forget about my decision to watch the Tigers versus the Wildcats and, instead, follow the van with its enigmatic message, admittedly on the mistaken assumption that I could ever have kept up with it, to its final destination just to get a glimpse of the driver and the woman in question. Or, maybe, even to wash it before she got to see the message. But, then, that's the mystery, was the lady in question – and undoubtedly she was quite a 'Lady' by this dusty account – supposed to see this message or not? And how would she react? The permutations of all these complicated questions nearly made me miss the turn into the large field that doubles as a car park for the speedway and greyhounds customers. Or, alternatively most evenings, as a field to dice with death in when the local dads attempt to teach their sons and daughters to drive with some special off-road practice just before they near their 17th birthdays. And you

The friendly, late Brian Snowie sorts things. © Jeff Scott

Weymouth riders rest in the pits. © Jeff Scott

John Barber swelters at work. © Jeff Scott

just know that every young person who lives in this part of the country really wants to pass that test as soon as they can.

I pull into one of the large selection of available unmarked parking spaces on offer in this huge field and then, so I think, show great common-sense to park under the shade of the trees. Later the car will be like an oven as – surprise, surprise – the position of the sun in the sky will change during the afternoon. However, at the moment I parked, the temperature in the shade, according to the German technology available to me in my car, is now 33 °C, which is exceptionally hot in Fahrenheit. The technology, should I have GPS, would also tell me that I had parked by the stadium in West Row, and we were actually much closer to the edge of the earth's atmosphere (6 miles or 10.6 km away) than we were to a nice refreshing dip in the sea. Although I suffer with the heat, now that I've arrived I'm hopeful that a cooling iced lolly or a '99' is only yards away from me once I've passed through the shade of the slightly derelict turnstiles. However, my self-congratulation is misplaced since, in my rush to search for the soothing effects of an ice lolly, I've not shown enough common-sense to remove my can of Coke which I regret later when it explodes in the car, and don't yet know that there are neither lollies of any description nor any 99s. Unaware my anticipation has run away with me, I make my way, careful to remain in the shade of the trees, to the apparently deserted entrance and its turnstiles.

In fact, the staff at the gate are very friendly, helpful and chatty, though without noticeably strong accents, when they direct me down the side of the grandstand towards the pits area where they're confident that I'll be able to find the object of my intentions. Which, for the purposes of this afternoon's research for my book, is the promoter and team manager of Mildenhall Speedway, Mick Horton. I spoke to him on his mobile a few days previously, so I hope that he's remembered to expect me, since he was a bit vague when I called. The always lively Internet speedway forums are particularly alive with gossip – when aren't they? – about Mick and the transfer of promotional rights at Peterborough Speedway to his brother, alleged forced upon him by financial necessity. I notice that the match programme advertises a forthcoming Mildenhall fans forum – which is, I must say, a pleasantly democratic and communicative way to approach a dialogue with your supporters, in contrast to practically every other professional sport you can name – in the bar, after the next home meeting, on June 26th against local rivals Boston. I wonder if someone will be brave enough to clarify all these rumours with a direct question? People at speedway can be very direct when the fancy takes them, that's my experience anyway, so I imagine that it's probably going to get discussed eventually, only not by me on my visit.

Apparently the pits are to be found round a few corners, after I walk down the length of the pleasantly shaded road that runs behind the main grandstand. I find myself stood by the large open doors of a large warehouse type building, very close to a car park crowded with riders' transit vans, many with the words 'Speedway Rider' emblazoned on the side. I ask directions from a topless, white-haired older man (Peter Thorogood), who rests in a comfortable chair by a table in the cool shade of this huge outbuilding. As I stand in the large open doorway while he territorially quizzes me about what possible business I want to see Mick for and then, after he's satisfied himself, he says that I'm only just a few yards away. When I squeeze through the narrow gaps between the parked vans I bump into Laura Filmer, the very dedicated girlfriend of Weymouth rider Dan Giffard who appears to travel everywhere with him. I'd not seen her since I sat near to her, when she watched Dan compete in the British Under-21 Championship at Rye House Stadium in Hoddesdon. This afternoon Dan is one of, if not, the star rider for the visiting Wildcats. Nicola's brother Adam Filmer will also ride for Weymouth as a reserve, so she'll get the chance to cheer them both on when they ride together in heat 6. They are the Weymouth pair that should appear in the match programme, if only a printer's error hadn't inadvertently transposed last week's Buxton pair with the geographically oriented surnames, Lee Derbyshire and Scott Chester, in their places. This erratum itself begs the question of the popularity and fashion that names enjoy over time; indeed, you rarely encounter many young Cedrics or Dorises nowadays but instead there's a great preponderance of Hayleys, Waynes, Chardonnays and Chelseas. A casual glance through any speedway match programme provides an instant snapshot of this changing nomenclature. Last week Mildenhall fans, the very few of them that bothered to turn up that is, witnessed a couple of Scotts, who coincidentally both rode at number 6 for their respective teams.

This afternoon's visitors Weymouth, though, are a team that, the helpful topless Father Time figure in the shed informed me, have never managed to win at Mildenhall in their 13 previous visits. Not even close apparently, although I can't corroborate this since I've forgotten the trusty-but-handy-every-match-ever-ridden-encyclopaedia that has yet to be invented, but should have been by now. Sort of like the book done every year by Peter Oakes only much more comprehensive. I do know, though, that not all of these visits have just been in the Conference League, since this is only the second-ever Conference fixture between the two sides. It will also be my first opportunity to see many of the young men that aim towards or are predicted to become the future stars of British speedway. This includes the latest young speedway sensation, 15-year-old Lewis Bridger about whom much was written in the *Speedway Star* during the close season. It was coverage that particularly focussed on the disappointment felt by the management of Conference League favourites Wimbledon, who confidently expected to sign the youngster to ride at their unique track, but were then distressed to find that he saw his future elsewhere at Weymouth. The match programme describes Lewis as a "precocious" talent and potentially he will be Weymouth's not-so-secret weapon because his present assessed average enables him to ride at reserve for the Wildcats in this afternoon's fixture.

Down the pit lane that leads onto the track I find Mick Horton, dressed sensibly for the weather in colonial-style shorts, deep in conversation with Trevor Swales, the team manager of Elite League Peterborough who, rather incestuously, was until this season previously also the Mildenhall team manager. Mick immediately makes it abundantly clear that he's a very busy man, that he has a tremendous number of unspecified tasks still to be completed and definitely doesn't have the time for our previously arranged conversation, in depth or otherwise, with me this afternoon. However, he does take the time to highlight that he believes that Conference League speedway is the genuine grass roots of the sport. He also believes that unless speedway at this particular level manages to thrive, then it's going to result in even more extremely bad news when it comes to the future provision of a stream of home-grown British speedway talent, particularly for the Elite and Premier League teams who compete at the so-called 'higher' levels within the sport. Mick has no doubt that the present trend to fill teams with unproven foreign riders will continue rather than decline over time, unless the Conference League teams manage to successfully provide some form of apprenticeship for talented British youngsters. The training and advancement of young talented riders critically depends upon tracks such as Mildenhall, which has, according to Mick, a commitment to youth development.

It's a vision of the future shared by many other advocates within the sport, people like Under-21 GB team manager Peter

Oakes who is closely involved with the Academy League, as well as the many riders from the past or the present day who, on an ad-hoc basis, voluntarily give up their free time and help out or train the youngsters. Different riders prefer to help at different tracks but, at Mildenhall, Mick is quick to highlight that Premier League rider Jason Bunyan often mechanics in the pits, while ex-World Champion Michael Lee and Elite League star Henning Bager often quietly come along to "help out the youngsters" at West Row. It's almost a tradition within speedway, in contrast to some other major sports, that some of its stars – contemporary or otherwise – freely give of their own time in order to mentor and advise the youngsters and thereby boost young rider progression in this country.

Mick is possibly correct in his surmise that there's often not this regular and voluntary commitment from ex-participants in other more glamorous and lucrative sports, like football, rugby or motor racing. But, then, I think that speedway justifiably claims to be a community-oriented sport for the whole family, an opinion that is confirmed a short while later when I see Mick pause from his team management duties for a moment, in order to chivalrously carry the pushchair of a young mother up some steep steps in the pits. Not the sort of behaviour you'd expect from an Arsene Wenger or Clive Woodward, to my knowledge. That's practically all the time Mick has to talk this afternoon, other than to reiterate his promise that if there should be sufficient local interest and also if decent crowds regularly attend this season's Conference League racing at Mildenhall, then he'd have the confidence to carry out his intention to try to race in the Premier League next season. It's hardly surprising news since he wrote something along similar lines in the programme, only in slightly more guarded language, when he mentioned, "as we look forward to the Premier League". Nonetheless, there is a loyal base of support for this move among Mildenhall fans in the stadium and on the Internet forums, plus there are enough possible lucrative local rivalries within a reasonable geographic area (Rye House, King's Lynn, etc.) to make this an attractive and commercially sensible proposition. It would be great if this change in leagues for the senior Mildenhall team allowed them to continue with a rider development strategy and still include a junior team in Fen Tigers colours in the Conference League team.

After Mick shoots off, I remain to chat in the pits lane with the amiable Brian Snowie, who is the club's commercial and marketing manager but, also, its keen-as-mustard youth scout. Brian takes both jobs and their responsibilities extremely seriously. He's keen to ensure that I get the information I need for my book research and he's concerned that I still have an enjoyable afternoon, despite Mick's unavailability. It's very considerate of him and I quickly gather that he's the type of sincere man only too pleased to talk with anyone; particularly if it's about club sponsorship – whether of a meeting or a race – but it's clear that his real, deep seated passion lies in the discovery of latent talent in young men who are keen to dedicate themselves to success at speedway. Brian has considerable experience as a spectator since he first watched the sport at 15 and then followed his local team, the Norwich Firs. The East Anglia and Suffolk areas have a rich tradition of speedway clubs and Brian took full of advantage to watch as many meetings as possible in the next 47 years.

To his mind, too many "teenagers are knocked back" in their ambitions for whatever field of activity that they've set their hearts on, not just speedway. It's a difficult time for teenagers in so many aspects of their lives, but one during which it's vital for any speedway club to make a lasting impression on their imaginations as they transition from late childhood into adult life. Unless we value our youth, their dreams and their training, Brian believes that the sport will suffer as the teenagers continue the contemporary trend to channel their energies into other possibly more convenient, fashionable or attractive things. Brian specifically helped to start the training schools for the Tigers to try to address and resolve this "drastic situation", which is a "necessity for the club" but one in which they frequently find themselves hampered by a "lack of recognition by the BSPA". In his opinion, speedway is not like other sports, mostly because it has still retained its community emphasis and has continued to be open and accessible to everyone. Not only can you often associate with the riders at the end of the evening in the pits and the bar but also, in general, it remains a family sport with no pretensions or trouble on the terraces; although he admits that when the adrenalin pumps in the heat of the moment that there can be the odd altercation in the pits. He's convinced that "once you get speedway in your blood" you'll always want more exposure to its innate 'excitement' and the thrill of racing without brakes. Within the present Mildenhall team he's particularly excited about the future potential of three young lads – and Brian then proceeds to enthuse to me at length about the potential of Lee Smart, Andrew Bargh ("his dad used to ride, he's a New Zealander") and Chris Johnson. Andrew will belatedly make his home debut today, after serving a suspension due to the manner in which his transfer from Wimbledon was handled. Brian stresses I should really keep an eye on all of them when they race today, "they're the future and they're going to be good". Keen that I should stress the importance of youth for the sport in my book, Brian immediately strikes while the iron is hot and kindly introduces me to the very tall and personable Chris Johnson, while he warms his bike up in the pits[2].

Chris is happy to chat for a few moments about how he began to ride in the sport, mostly after he watched Ben Howe ride and admired his talent, so the chance to emulate his accomplishments completely appealed to him when it presented itself. Also, best of all, his mum encouraged him to wholeheartedly try to fulfil his dream and ambitions within speedway.

The pits area is noticeably crowded with other young men all too keen to succeed in the sport, most of whom concentratedly make last-minute but crucial adjustments to their bikes or warm them up with ostentatious vigour. The home team have their own permanent section in the pits, while the visitors from Weymouth have no designated area, so instead congregate together in an open section on the edge of the pits, very close by to where the temporary fence separates them from the crowd in the grandstand. It's a proximity that means the fans can easily share their advice, suggestions, abuse and critical comments through the fence, if they can manage to be heard above the sheer volume of noise. There are also a number of parents scattered throughout the pits area, mostly dads but some mums, and a fair selection of young women I assume to be riders' girlfriends, which includes Dan Giffard's, Laura, who is the only person I can recognise.

There is a gallery cum balcony above the pits area, up some steps, that overlooks the home riders and has quite a few

---

[2] I am saddened by the news of Brian Snowie's death after a lengthy illness on March 31st 2006. Promoter Mick Horton commented on the sad news, "he was dedicated to the club and a tireless worker for the Fen Tigers. We will all miss him a great deal". A minute's silence was held on April 8th before the Mildenhall v Newport Premier Trophy fixture. When I met him, Brian spoke with genuine enthusiasm about his work and delighted when young riders progressed or tried to harness their potential. Even more noticeably, he also went out of his way to welcome me (a complete stranger) to the club and help me as much as possible all afternoon. He struck me as the kind of genuinely sincere man that was a credit to himself and his upbringing. But also one who typifies speedway and the many people who selflessly and voluntarily dedicate themselves to helping others succeed within the sport. He leaves wife Vicky and son David.

lucky, and undoubtedly proud, privileged spectators who are treated with an unrivalled view of the action, both in the pits and out over the first bend on the track. The track circuit itself is brown coloured and fits neatly within the greyhound track that surrounds it. The dog track is now where the original, faster and reputedly more exciting original speedway track was located when the club first opened on the ex-potato field in 1973. I have no previous experience to guide me so, to my eyes, this is how it's always been.

Trevor Swales bustles around the pits, though he no longer works for the club as team manager, he still provides the spares van sales service at Mildenhall. My impression has always been that, while speedway bikes aren't as expensive to purchasecompared to the high-specification machines required for road races, they're still very expensive items to buy and maintain for any cash-strapped young person. This is particularly so with the need for more than one available bike, the modern emphasis on the importance of the correct set ups, and the understandable desire for the latest 'right' parts and gizmos. All this is before you even consider the cost of tuning the engines or running the van you'll need to transport yourself and all your gear around the country. It's not the sort of career or hobby that you can indulge in lightly from a time, cost or injury perspective particularly as, without sponsorship, pay levels at the outset are so low. At the Conference Level, as at all other levels, you are generally paid per point with an additional 10p per mile as a contribution towards your petrol money for journeys undertaken to meetings. Given that the reputed usual rate of pay in the Conference League is £10 per point, riding at this level isn't going to fund a comfortable retirement, let alone cover the necessary equipment expenditures or provide an acceptable standard of living. Counter-intuitively, Trevor apparently sincerely claims to me that this is a "cheap sport to compete in", albeit with the important caveat, "in comparison to any other motor sports you can name". Which, on a barriers-to-entry basis, is true enough within the motor sports category but often speedway finds itself in competition with other 'cheaper' and more popular sports with minimal or less onerous equipment requirements. Let alone that these comparisons ignore that you inevitably always have to compete against other modern entertainments and lifestyles that more easily attract a young person's commitment and discretionary spend. However, it's an argument that Trevor has practised many times and believes, which he tries to support with the slightly flawed proposition, "how many other jobs pay you while you learn your profession?" Well Trevor, in the world of paid work, the vast majority; but it's more correct to claim that the idea of performance-related payments are generally not so usual during your apprenticeship in the world of individual and team sports. We're just going to have to agree to differ although I must say it's definitely another unique perspective on the pound in the youngster's pocket. Trevor concludes his thesis with advice for prospective speedway riders' parents, "don't put your son on the stage, Mrs Smith, if you don't know what you're letting yourself in for".

It's now so close to the start of the fixture and the pre-meeting parade that I immediately have to leave the pits area as only authorised and insured staff can remain. I have the choice to watch the racing from either the main covered grandstand by the start line, which has a considerable amount of room for anyone keen to stand there, or from the main other shady area on the first bend, which has the added appeal of a bar and refreshments in close proximity. This area also has the track shop but, most of all, on a scorchingly hot day, it offers the chance of a comfortable sit down with uninterrupted view from any one of the large selection of tables and chairs located there. And, in my case, the ideal place from which to take some notes on the people and the meeting itself as I avoid from the intense sunshine and sultry heat of the afternoon.

I decide that this would be the perfect spot to watch from, but first pop to look round at the merchandise in the track shop. Although it is in the deep shade, the ever-friendly John Barber struggles to cool himself down in the baking temperatures. Together with his brother Nick, he runs a whole series of track shop franchises throughout the country including the tracks at Eastbourne, King's Lynn, Ipswich, Workington, Peterborough, Somerset and Mildenhall. Consequently, they're very busy every day of the week at tracks throughout the country, except Monday and Tuesday, during the speedway season. They also have an unrivalled knowledge of what's in demand and popular and what is not. From my previous chats with Nick and Jon, I know that they're huge enthusiasts for the sport, always have a cheery word and are very well informed about the intricate machinations of the sport and at the various clubs. To help boost the sales of other authors, I've bought every new speedway title, too many probably but, once again, I spot another new book on display that I haven't yet added to my collection. Unique is a word bandied around with abandon in publishing circles but this one, a novel set against a speedway background, is definitely out there on its own. Well, in fact, it's the first work of speedway fiction of the 21st century (though there were many others historically) and, though like London buses, I know that ex-Ipswich promoter John Berry is planning to publish his novel this Christmas. You just couldn't make it up really[3]. Imagine the unrestrained excitement and joy on the face of any young speedway fan who finds a work of speedway fiction in their stocking or under the tree! The novel I've just brought is called *Full Throttle* and the authors come from the Isle of Wight, though I gather it's more of a work of teenage rather adult fiction. I'll look forward to reading it with interest though John isn't that optimistic about its likely sales potential, despite its very reasonable price. John meanwhile, continues to suffer in silence with the incredibly high temperature while he slowly serves the steady stream of customers who arrive at his shop – they're mostly after pens (as ever!), photographs and a programme board – while we chat amiably. To his mind Mildenhall is a lovely little racetrack at which to watch speedway, though he believes the only slight let down is that they aren't "getting the crowds that they deserve". Last week's crowd was especially low; so low that they almost had to introduce the crowd to the riders, mechanics and parents. The quality of the racing and the promotion deserves more, but it's likely that the sheer heat of the day will, this afternoon, keep many of the required casual spectators at home.

At the entrance to the stadium, Roger Last echoes this opinion on the disappointing attendance figures; he should definitely know as they all have to pass him at the turnstile where he works as a volunteer, along with everyone else who works here on a race day. When he's not on the gate at Mildenhall, he works "driving lots". To his estimation the crowd has built up to a regular gate of around roughly 400 people, a figure which is about average here and considerably more than the 150 hardy souls who actually showed up for last week's hastily, arranged fixture with Buxton. A "very poor team" in Roger's view whereas this afternoon's visitors, Weymouth, are one of the most attractive in the League; nonetheless he estimates that the unseasonably hot weather has kept many possible casual punters otherwise occupied. The distant sound of the bikes revving and the announcement of the rider's parade causes me to rush back up the steps to try to find a spare table set out on the nearby grandstand.

Fortunately the crowd is so sparse that one table still remains vacant and I'm delighted to find such a luxurious spot from which to watch this fixture. Not only is there an uninterrupted view of the whole circuit and the starting gate, but it's also in the shade and I've even got something to rest my programme and notepad on. Still, it's within earshot of a father and his two energetic young boys in front of me, a mother and her daughter to the side and, most interestingly of all, a group of men who stand together on the back wall to watch the action. They're all in their 50s and 60s and continually talk throughout the meeting; its all the usual speedway chatter and just the sort of thing I love to eavesdrop on. I resolve not to try to speak with them, if possible, but just to listen. They're very clearly Mildenhall fans and, from the outset of their conversation, it's obvious that they're extremely partisan and militantly keen to witness a comprehensive annihilation of Weymouth. Not that the fixture starts that well for the home team, since David Mason wins heat 1 for Weymouth though he's chased closely the whole way by the diminutive 'old hand' Jon Armstrong. The blokes behind bellow their words of encouragement throughout the race, predominantly with a succession of excitable shouts of "go on Jon boy, go on!" Sadly, for them, these instructions are to no avail. Mildenhall take the lead after the next race, which is notable for the fact that the talented 15-year-old Lewis Bridger very nearly catches Bargh (pronounced Barge) at the finish line, despite the fact it's his first-ever race on the West Row track as well as the additional 15-metre handicap he suffered when he inadvertently broke the tapes in the initial attempt to run the race. Within just one race, Lewis immediately confirms why he's rated so highly as an exciting and exceptional prospect for the future. Not only does he nearly win the race but also he rides with a determination and verve that will please crowds everywhere, if it continues. Even if you ignore his age, it's still a stunning performance when you consider that it's the first-ever race of his career on the Mildenhall racetrack! The young boys in

[3] Let's hope this time that John Berry doesn't include any song lyrics at the start of each chapter, like he did throughout his recent deliberately contentious, informative and enjoyable book *Confessions of a Speedway Promoter*. One thing that definitely isn't unique nowadays is the decision to publish a speedway book. It's an area in which there has been over-production and often variable quality. Nonetheless I still hope that my book will be a departure from the usual autobiographies, handbooks or club histories.

front don't appreciate the significance of Lewis's performance but, instead, are delighted just to recognise that a rider in Mildenhall colours has narrowly won the race and, accordingly, celebrate this particular fact wildly. Before they then plaintively ask their father "who was it that won?" before they appear instantly much the wiser once they're told it was Andrew Bargh.

Events on the bend in front of us on the third lap of the next race cause the blokes behind me to angrily denounce the referee in vehement terms. Jack Gledhill and Chris Johnson touch bikes together while they compete for a vital inch of space on the track when they enter the bend, though in my opinion Gledhill was already slightly ahead, which results in a crash for Johnson, in stately rather than hurtling fashion, into the safety fence. We all had an ideal vantage point to watch this collision, which happened immediately in front of us all, Johnson definitely appeared at fault to me, and also to the referee, who subsequently excluded him as the primary cause of the stoppage. While you could applaud him for determination and effort, you'd have to say that he learnt a vital but painful lesson for the future about positional awareness. It's safe to predict that it's not a popular decision among the Mildenhall faithful directly behind me, so much so in fact I start to get concerned about the heightened blood pressure of some of them. There was a good selection of expletives but the more measured among them instead settled for noting that it was "a very bad decision" before, quite politely, they advise the referee on his future optical requirements. One of the members of this group, with a real will to hyperbole, and maybe an eye on a future job writing worried leader columns for a mid-market tabloid newspaper, immediately sensed a worrying descent into anarchy ("where will it all end, if the laws aren't applied?"). A speedway meeting wouldn't be the first choice of venue for his predictions of a decline in moral values to happen or, for that matter, serve as your first choice of location from which to stage a revolution but it's obviously good to warn of such a slippery slope. In fact, another vociferous member of this ageing group of Mildenhall fans rather dramatically then claims, "it's really anarchy if you can just bang someone out of the way when you're behind them". We all have our opinions, but these appear to overlook the evidence of our own eyes and actual events on the track. The subsequent re-run of the race without Johnson enables Weymouth to level the overall match score with a 4-2 victory to the great consternation, further mutterings and gnashing of teeth from the blokes behind. Though they needn't have worried or complained so bitterly about moral decay within modern society, since it transpired that it was really the last time that Weymouth were in contention throughout the rest of the fixture.

The general mood of injustice quickly translates into its uglier cousin of schadenfreude, after Lewis Bridger suffers an engine failure in the next heat. The blokes, or one of them, delights in this misfortune and keeps triumphantly screeching, "and he's only got one bike!" As an impartial spectator I definitely hope that this isn't true, because I'd like to see as much exciting racing as possible rather than just witness an easy Mildenhall walkover.

Something you almost immediately notice when you first watch the Conference League speedway are the differences, some subtle but others not, particularly in the standard of skill exhibited by the young riders in comparison to that seen in the other leagues. The bikes sound that bit rougher but, most noticeably, the riders (understandably) appear to ride the track a lot less confidently and smoothly than their much more practised contemporaries from the more 'senior' leagues. Though this is exactly how it should be, in a league originally invented to allow riders to hone and practise their techniques. Nonetheless, you can't help but notice that some riders try to feel their way round the track that little bit more, to the extent that you can almost see them thinking about what they should do next. It's all very absorbing stuff, to watch people learn their craft and, over time, witness their progression and improvement. I think it probably leads to a greater empathy between the fans and the riders at the Conference League level, since you can more readily sympathise with their various trials, struggle and obvious toil; rather than just witness the effortless performance of the riders, as it often appears to be elsewhere.

Heat 5 results in another victory for Weymouth's 'old hand' David Mason who, rather touchingly and with strong echoes of past speedway fashions, cuts a very distinctive figure since he very visibly sports retro cowboy-style tassles on the sleeves of his kevlars. I mean to try to find him later to congratulate and quiz him on this unusual look but the forget to do this. So, sadly, I'm also unable to check if this afternoon his rather self-conscious choice to wear a mélange of styles, lifted from recent contemporary culture, also includes the blond-dyed Mohican punk hairstyle I notice that he sports at a later meeting.

The meeting heats up metaphorically and literally for the riders and the spectators. The heat theme continues with almost a dead heat on the finish line between Dan Giffard and Jon Armstrong that the referee awards to Armstrong by the width of a sweaty hair in heat 6. Throughout the meeting, the small girl on the next table keeps her ears theatrically covered, to protect them from the noise, during each heat and otherwise she hectors her mother for, in the sad absence of goodies from the freezer, some nice cooling fish and chips from the nearby snack bar. Despite the extreme warmth, the frequent wafts of the smell of cooking tantalises, though I just about manage to resist. Extreme feelings continue to run very high among the partisan blokes behind me, although the interestingly named Mildenhall reserve Scott Campos attracts their ire rather than their congratulation when he comprehensively finishes last in heat 7. When you're hungry or desperate for success anything less than perceived excellence gets short shrift from these guys who, old-fashionedly shout, "go home Campos!" with much venom and vigour but with absolutely zero humour.

The third successive last place, in heat 8, for Weymouth rider Paul Candy provokes considerable derision at his perceived lack of abilities among the ageing Mildenhall faithful, oblivious to the fact that every rider has to try to learn their craft somewhere. The derision his performance attracts isn't helped by his nickname, which is listed in the match programme as the 'Taunton Tornado'. Which leads the fans behind me, who, for once, exhibit some rare wit to go with their standard response of complaint, criticism and opprobrium, to re-christen Paul Candy as the "Taunton Tortoise". Based on this afternoon's performances, this appears to be a much more apt nickname. Elsewhere in the stadium, Laura Filmer finally gets the chance to cheer for her brother and her boyfriend in heat 9, when they compete in the same race for the first time this afternoon. Not that there's really anything for her to get excited about, since boyfriend Dan trails in third place and, for the third successive time already, brother Adam eventually finishes in last position. After the completion of heat 10, Mildenhall find themselves leading 34-26 and we break to have what the programme describes as "Interval – weather permitting". It's so extremely hot; I think that we'd all break en masse into the nearest cinema without permission, if we could.

Nonetheless, severe warmth aside, it's a welcome chance to stretch the legs and join a huge queue for the refreshments. Instead I head for the toilets deep inside the bowels of the grandstand where it's exceptionally cool and it would be worth spending some more time there, if it didn't look so suspicious. The enthusiastic young boys from in front of me have already beaten me to the loos and are in philosophical form when they ask me, "why is everyone's wee yellower than ours?" to which I deign to reply, "you better ask your father". Hopefully, he'll have explained it all to them by the time I return although, maybe, I should rush back myself out of my own curiosity at his explanation. As I leave the cool shade of the loos, I spot Lewis Bridger who walks gingerly (because of his steel shoe) down the dimly lit stairs, to get an ice-cold soft drink from the vending machine. When I stand next to him, dressed in his kevlars, he looks surprisingly big for a 15-year-old. I introduce myself with the comment that "I hear that you're going to be World Champion, Lewis" to which he immediately retorts, "Who told you that?" When he learns that a couple of people had mentioned that to me in the pits earlier and that it's listed in the match programme, the exact provenance of this claim only elicits a brief shrug of his shoulders. I enquire after his seized engine, an enquiry about which perks him up, to the extent that he enthusiastically explains at length what actually happened when the con rod went through his engine. It all sounds very complicated to me and as though it may be a highly unusual and expensive occurrence but, given my ignorance, who can say? I'm impressed that Lewis mistakenly thought I might have some mechanical expertise and would understand his explanation of events. I then mention my research for my book which gets a blank reaction and, after I request an interview with him at another more convenient time, he hands my card to the slightly older young chap he's with and says, "I'll give that to my mechanic". I ask him to email me so I can ask him some more questions at another convenient time that's not mid-way through a speedway meeting. He says he will before I quickly take an out-of-focus photograph, though sadly I never get the interview he promised. His performance up to that point in the meeting, since he'd dropped his only point through mechanical failure, would definitely appear to indicate that he has considerable natural talent on a bike, irrespective of his age, and a very bright future.

Speedway is the sort of community-based sport where you can still possibly leave the possessions you've brought with you behind, while you briefly go away and still reasonably expect to find them there when you return. Even if the bag has valuables in it like your camera, mobile and fruit like mine did. Though, just in case I was being presumptuous in my assumptions of honesty, I'd asked one of the group of blokes behind if he could keep an eye on it for me in the meantime. I returned from a different direction but still couldn't manage to sneak up to try to steal my own bag. Among the group of men behind me there's a smattering of casual bright yellow tops and one of them has a Mildenhall badge on it, so I imagine that they're probably the team colours although I can't be certain. The man who'd guarded my bag for me was Dave Mann, who bucks the general trend this afternoon when he wears a rather smart and more formal collared shirt. I'm not sure who's said what about whom earlier, so I chat to him as though I haven't listened to them at all. Dave hasn't missed a Mildenhall meeting since 1982 or 1983, though he's not exactly sure which year it was and, I quickly gather, he's extremely well informed about all things to do with Mildenhall speedway. For him, after he's pondered the question for a few moments, the biggest appeal of speedway at West Row is "that it's a small track that rides like a big track". I understand this to mean that there's plenty of close, competitive racing with a good deal of overtaking, which is a claim pretty well borne out by what we've witnessed so far that afternoon. Dave's not really bothered about the experience and supposed skill standard of the riders, he's much more interested in the "racing itself", particularly the "tight close racing" regularly seen at Mildenhall.

He's also strongly of the opinion that the "sport is slowly coming back nowadays" and that there's the start of a resurgence of interest in it across the country; predominantly because it's a family sport and your heroes on the track are "real people" that you can relate to in an everyday and ordinary way. They don't have airs and graces or consider themselves to be too special to mix with the fans, in fact, you can usually always meet them in the bar afterwards. His preferred type of rider is usually drawn from "those that can take it as well as dish it out". To his mind Eastbourne's Martin Dugard was a good rider but failed this crucial litmus test of reciprocity. As a fan of Martin's I sprang to his defence, only to hear at great length about an incident long ago with Mildenhall's Mel Taylor. Dave recalls that when Mel reciprocated at Mildenhall for Martin putting him in the fence earlier in the season at Eastbourne; Dugard was apparently less than happy at this outcome and, in Dave's recollection, his toys quickly left the pram. My defence of Martin clearly touched a nerve as Dave then also recollects that it was an era when you could choose your gate position, and he believes that Martin always carefully chose the one that his father Bob "had specially prepared beforehand". I couldn't comment, but to Dave's mind this was a common feature of the Eastbourne Eagles versus Mildenhall Tigers encounters at Arlington.

We then traipse back up from memory lane to the present day, Dave notes, to nods from the listening group of blokes, that at Mildenhall the "trouble is we can't track a team, we've 28 riders signed on but we can only manage 6 here today". This does sound like a peculiar problem and they then delightedly rehearse some of the better lame excuses that the riders invent in order not to ride, "even the ones that live two minutes away from the stadium often can't be bothered to turn up!" Though they often despair, nonetheless they still continue to come along each week and also travel to away meetings where, apparently, the atmosphere among the faithful on the bus is consistently second to none.

I sit back at my table where the boys have ceased their earlier philosophical journey of discovery but, instead, are now on a quest to establish my exact allegiances. "We're Mildenhall, who are you supporting?" My answer that I support nobody and that I'm just there to see good racing appears to strain their credulity and also confuses them as it's not a proper answer. They then keenly pester their father in the hope of an accurate answer, while I busy myself for the next few minutes of the extended interval with some study of the match programme. The programme is always a mine of information about any speedway club that you happen to visit and this one is definitely no exception. In fact, it's got my favourite feature of the season inside its pages from any track, but more of that in a moment. From this issue of the programme, in no particular order, I learn that the assistant team manager rejoices in the excellent, almost Dickensian, name of Blayne Scroggins. That James Purchase is missing today after he aggravated an old shoulder injury; while for Mark Thompson an accurate diagnosis of his recent injuries haven't been reached, though he's definitely trapped a nerve in his wrist but still awaits the results of further X-rays. One things for certain, if you run an accident and emergency department at your hospital and you're located reasonably close to an active speedway track, you're going to see quite a fair few lads in your X-ray department over the duration of a season!

The club also goes out of its way to recommend the 'Bird in Hand Motel' in Beck Row, Mildenhall, as its "recommended hotel", but it is actually holding its "End of Season Presentation" on November 12th at the Bell Hotel in Mildenhall. I can only assume that this is down to the size of the venue, the quality of the catering or, perhaps, that most people who will attend this event already have a bed for the night at their own homes nearby. Whatever the explanation, its a mystery and one that I'm not going to resolve before I drive home tonight, via the Wilbrahams, once more. Before the interval ends I intend to make a point to purchase another raffle ticket, to go with one I already got when I entered the stadium, especially now that I've discovered the main prize is "a Father's Day surprise", though the other prizes are shrouded in mystery and only referred to as, "plus five other prizes". The programme also has a couple of very grainy, poor quality photographs that look as though they'd been shot on the moon and sent back via satellite. One photo is of the Loomer Road Stadium in Stoke, the venue for this year's Conference League Fours, and another is of Jon Armstrong as he rather woodenly welcomes Andrew Bargh to the club with a staged presentation of a Mildenhall race bib. The grainy photos betray the sort of lack of attention to detail that would severely count against the club, should this particular match programme be selected as the one example of the club's work throughout the season for the *Speedway Star's* end-of-season programme reviews. These reviews are all too strange and bizarre to go into too much detail about. Other than to say that each track's programme is meticulously analysed against a set of criteria that treats each club's programme as though they should be judged as if they were a cross between the Magna Carta, the Dead Sea scrolls and a document newly found in the holy tabernacle. Additional attention, okay I will go on about it, is paid to pagination, the use of colour, typography and numerous other features, which include "depth of work" and "punctuation style". Each facet, and there are 10 of them, is then marked out of 100 to give an overall cumulative score out of 1000. It's as though each programme is a work of art and finds itself at the cutting edge of design typography and layout à la Neville Brody in 1986 with his innovative-looking magazine *The Face*. To be fair, I must say that the remainder of the photographs are all that you'd expect, especially the one of Chris Johnson's slight quiff[4]. Hopefully the judges, if they choose this programme, will be unduly lenient.

For me though, the absolute highlight of this programme, apart from the enthralling A-Z of Mildenhall Speedway[5], is the weekly 'Speedway Mastermind' quiz. This week it is a head-to-head contest between Lee Smart and the visiting Dan Giffard who answer questions posed, via mobile phone, by Martyn Cornwell. Some of them are pretty arcane questions and I reproduce them, with permission, here exactly as they appeared (with answers at the end of the chapter)

1. Who is the Governor of the Bank of England?
    Lee Smart (LS): I don't have a clue. Mum and Dad look after the money.
    Dan Giffard (DG): Whoa! A nice easy one to start then. No idea I'm afraid.
2. What do the initials NATO stand for?
    LS: You said this would be easy. Two wrong straight away.

[4] Ironically a few pages later in the programme is a large advert from the E'clip'Z Unisex Hair Salon in Newmarket that has, maybe, attracted Chris with its "competitive rates".

[5] Which had already reached the letter "F" by this edition and features the riders: Fareham, Ian (notable for a "handful of under par performances"); Farthing, Lee, ("a regular if not spectacular scorer") and Felgate, Chris ('after half a dozen outings failing to make any impression, soon lost his place"). None of theses riders ever quite became household names like Michael Lee, Terry Betts or John Louis but, in this part of Suffolk, their contribution to Mildenhall Speedway, its rich pantheon of stars and subsequent folklore hasn't been forgotten.

Fans fill out their programme in the shade. © Jeff Scott

Lewis Bridger, 15, with drink. © Jeff Scott

Inquisitive boys in front of me. © Jeff Scott

DG: What's NATO? (Oh dear, Dan)
3. Who was Henry VIII's first wife?
    LS: I was rubbish at history. Anne?
    DG: The only thing I did at school was draw speedway bikes on my pencil case. This is hopeless.
4. What colour is Noddy's hat?
    LS: Noddy? When I get up *Balamory* is on. PC Plum is great. I reckon its red or blue, I'll go for red.
    DG: What, the cartoon Noddy? God, I haven't seen that for years. I reckon it's yellow.
Question 5 is a speedway question, which gets both lads off the mark. The answer is Paul Lee, if you'd like to guess the question?
6. Before the Euro, what was the currency of Italy?
    LS: I have absolutely no idea.
    DG: I know this. Ah what's it called now? I'm gonna kick myself. Nope it's gone.
Question 7 turned to darts where again the lads done good. The answer to this one is 25 if you'd like to guess that question?

Martyn then thanks both riders for "being good sports, guys" before he notes, after some recent five and four point scores by other riders in the quiz, "things are back to normal". He wishes both well and, in a slightly post-modernist touch, suggests that they both score more points on the track this afternoon. Which they do, since they each only scored two points in the quiz! But then that's hardly surprising, since both Lee and Dan are speedway riders and you'd expect that they will have spent time to learn how to excel on a speedway bike or in the workshop, rather than revision for this quiz and, most likely, other exams.

Luckily, with the distant roar of the bikes from the pits, the questions are over and the only ones left to be asked are all to be answered on the track. Lewis roars to victory in heat 11 on borrowed equipment, which prompts the men behind me to observe "he looks old". This is difficult to tell in my view, since he wears a crash helmet. But maybe they saw him earlier or mean that he rides with maturity? Whatever the explanation they follow it up with the subsequent observation that "he's got really big hands". And we all know what they say about that so it seems a peculiar observation?

By now, I've become mesmerised by the start-line girls' pre-race routine[6]. Less so because of how they dress – despite the heat their clothing remains practical rather than skimpy – but more because it appears that the choreography of their routines involve much more movement once they've actually left the track than before the race when

[6] From the "Mildenhall-Grid-Girls" website I learn, there's Hayley in Red, Sam in Blue, Alice in Green and Clare in Yellow. Clare's "fav rider" is "Erm Me Big Bruv Lee Smart (SMARTY)".

they're on its surface, where they have to notionally guide the spectator's eye to which colour helmet and rider rides in which lane. Before start-line girls were invented, or imported from America more like — the idea not the girls who are probably drawn from local villages such as Mildenhall or West Row — as fans we somehow used to figure these things out ourselves with a brief glance at the riders' helmets themselves to determine who went where. Or, we could look in the match programme. In modern speedway, we have the distraction of the start-line girls at practically every meeting you attend, no matter the occasion. I can recall that during my teenage speedway-watching years that there were girls used then to add lustre and glamour to proceedings, but only ever at 'major' events. If you glimpsed a start-line girl, you definitely knew that you were about to witness a special or significant meeting. In the stifling heat of a Suffolk summer's afternoon, they have even arrived in Mildenhall for this Conference League fixture with Weymouth. Anyway, their routine mostly involves some synchronised waves while they're on the track and in the relevant start lane before they all walk off the track in unison in an orderly file. Then, just before they sit down, they perform a few rather dramatic and exaggerated but obviously choreographed movements that would be out of place at an experimental dance performance, before they all elegantly sit down in synchronised fashion. Quite why their routine has this complexity on the centre green, just when all eyes should be focused on the riders severely revving the bikes at the start of the race, is mystifying. Once they've sat down I notice that the girls barely watch the racing but instead chat among themselves and definitely don't keenly fill in their match programmes. In fact, they don't seem to have programmes so, maybe, they know who is in which lane for each race by ESP?

Heat 13 sees Chris Johnson take third place from David Mason, which gives David ample time to study the imaginative "Johno" nickname plastered in large letters on his backside. Dan Giffard manages to easily outscore his earlier Mastermind quiz score in one tactical substitute ride when he wears the black and white helmet. The start-line girls cope with this unexpected last minute change in helmet colour and the normal colour scheme of things easily enough before they then perform their distinctive little dance cum pirouette on the way to resting their weary legs. Dan Gifford splendidly nearly makes up all of his 15-metre handicap from the start before he loses on the line by the width of a dart to Andrew Bargh. He scores four points for his valuable efforts. Not that it really makes much difference to the match as the cumulative score including that heat moves to 47-39 before Mildenhall seal it with a last race loss of 2-4 for an eventual 49-43 overall points victory. It's been a great afternoon's racing in difficult conditions, solely due to the weather not the track, and great entertainment off it, as I sat in the shade among the sparse but passionate crowd. The young boys in front of me celebrate the Mildenhall victory wildly before they suggest to their father in unison that some sweets might be in order to really help them savour the moment properly. I return to roast and marinate in my car for the duration of the journey home, but not before I've made a mental note to return to this part of Suffolk as soon as possible. Driving conditions ease considerably once I make it away from the roads near the track, but I've only gone a short distance when I'm nearly killed by an aggressively driven transit van, which is notable for what appears to be a sparkling and newly cleaned rear door.

19th June Mildenhall v. Weymouth (Conference Trophy) 49-43

Quiz Answers
1. Mervyn King
2. North Atlantic Treaty Organisation
3. Catherine of Aragon
4. Blue
5. The missing question was "What's the connection between the Mildenhall and Weymouth track record?" The answer was that Paul Lee held the track record at both these locations, though this has now been (literally) overtaken by events.
6. Lire
7. In darts, how much is the outer ring around the bull's-eye worth?

Chapter 13: The Love of a Lifetime
22nd June Poole v. Eastbourne

SKY CHATTER

KelvinTatum (to Neil Middleditch) "What is the safety issue exactly, Neil?"
Neil "Do we know how long it's going to take them to sort out a piece of elastic?"

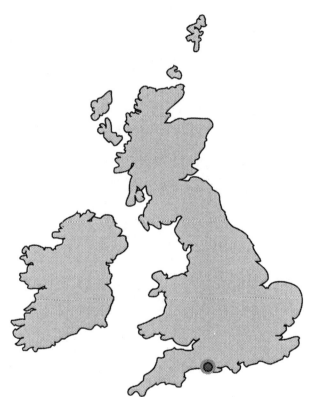

RANDOM SCB RULES

6.8.1 Advertising posters are not posted in inappropriate places or to trees in particular, neither distribute leaflets or pamphlets onto parked cars

---

The coastal town of Poole in Dorset is, arguably, the smartest and most up-scale place in the country to play host to the sport of speedway. It's a very desirable town, surrounded by beautiful countryside, which nestles on the coast with a reputation for great weather and a relaxing lifestyle as well as some of the most expensive houses in the whole of the country (even when you include London and the rest of the South East). More people wish to move to the area than there are available houses for sale, so consequently prices are at a premium for every type of property. Many people retire to live here and many wish to do so though it just about manages to avoid the sleepy atmosphere that affects other South Coast retirement towns, like Eastbourne and Worthing.

It's a beautiful, hot sunny day with a cloudless clear blue sky as I arrive in the blisteringly bright stadium car park behind the fire station. Unfortunately, I don't park my car in the nearby multi-storey car park so thereby miss one of the country's most innovative speedway adverts, where the Poole Pirates have one placed on the mechanical arm of the exit barrier!

From where I have parked there is a very noticeable clearness of light on the distant skyline, the kind that you frequently get in the bright sunshine when you're close to the sea and its shoreline. Maybe it's the refraction of the light on the seawater or the effect created on your perspective by the skyline and the horizon as they meet in the far distance out at sea; whatever the reason, there's a change in the atmosphere and a sense that the sky is somehow lifted higher above the ground than when you're inland. However, despite these advantages, as a town Poole suffered from the urban blight known at the time as the contemporary architectural style of the 1960s and 1970s. If you stand outside the Wimborne Road stadium, you can easily see some excellent examples of this rather brutalist genre. There's the nearby multi-storey car park and its adjacent shopping centre, which were, very obviously, constructed during an era that relished concrete as a construction material and preferred to use it in bold geometric shapes. As it happens, the town's history is rich and varied and, although it doesn't appear in the Domesday Book, it gained its reputation as a small fishing village in the 12th century. Queen Elizabeth I gave the town its charter in 1568 and by the 1800s it was a large place by the standards of the time. Its population grew with the increased amenities but it received a considerable further boost with the creation of the new seaside resort of Bournemouth. This drew new industries, such as pottery, brick making and brewing, along with the people to undertake these activities to the area, which added to the traditional trades of shipbuilding and rope-making that formed the town's general reputation.

By the time of the first-ever fixture at Poole Speedway, on what had been a tarmac cycle track since the thirties and was the home of Poole Football in 1948, all of these traditional industries had pretty well disappeared with exception of the pottery. When Poole Speedway opened, the track already had stands on both sides but it retained an atmosphere that was described as "a little bit rural" during these formative years. From the outset, the sport fired the imagination of the local people and has, since it began, inspired a very strong sense of loyalty and belonging within the town. The first-ever race at the track has become the stuff of legend and possibly subject to some exaggeration over time, with almost everything that could happen happening in that initial contest between Poole and Yarmouth. In front of a packed crowd of 8,000 people, on a cinder track, the very first race featured Paddy Hammond and Reg Craven for Yarmouth who rode against Charlie Hayden, the first Poole captain, and Alf Elliott for the home side. All four riders lined up at the start, but by the first turn Hammond had suffered an engine failure and the subsequent crash saw all the other riders fall or crash through the fence. Craven sustained a severe fracture to his skull in this incident and died in hospital six days later. Despite this tragedy, it's always recalled in popular memory as a thrilling race meeting, which electrified the entire crowd and thereby, ever since, became a defining moment that set the tone for how the club saw itself and the standard of meetings to be expected at Poole Speedway. The club prides itself on the size of its support within the local community as well as the warmth and legendary friendliness of its supporters. Success on the track came quickly to the club and its first trophy arrived in 1951, while its supporters also received widespread acclaim for their reputation for cheering the performance of the visiting teams' riders.

I had arrived at the Wimborne Road stadium as the guest of the modern club's press officer, Gordon 'Gordie' Day, for the always eagerly anticipated clash between the Pirates of Poole with their local south-coast rivals the Eagles of Eastbourne. It's the fixture that usually has the most charged atmosphere and intense significance for both sets of fans and is a rivalry that has each loudly proclaim faux sympathy for the natural handicap of rampant inbreeding that apparently besets the other set of rival fans. I wait in the cool shade of the swish, modern and rather magnificent glass-fronted stand that dominates the home straight at Poole Stadium, just around the time that the staff are starting their preparations in the nearby 'Pirates Bar' and food outlet. Gordie arrives shortly afterwards and is a friendly, bearded, middle-aged man who works full time for the club, in an official capacity as their media and PR man. It's quickly apparent that he's infectiously enthusiastic about all things Poole, frighteningly knowledgeable about the club and generally has an easy charm that you'd expect from the PR man's PR man. I'm already chuffed to be welcomed by Poole Speedway as their guest and to be shown the behind the scenes preparations for a race night, never mind to have the added bonus of Gordie's company and insights.

In additional to his official tasks and duties, Gordie has taken it upon himself to become the custodian of the club's history and with it has the task to guard, as best as he can, the flame of the club's success for future generations. Gordie embarked on the marathon task of "recreating an archive of Poole history" because he found many of the "stars of yesteryear" had, what he politely calls, an "imperfect memory of events". Particularly when you compared their recollections of events to what the records indicate as the reality of what actually took place. Although it's a slow process, it's also a labour of love inspired by his devotion to the club since his father first took him to watch Poole at Easter 1951. Subsequently, during his attempt to restore the materials required for this archive, Gordie has discovered the club's own record keeping and its storage of memorabilia was far from satisfactory, though this set back hasn't deterred his efforts or determination to succeed.

Gordie is a willing and very capable evangelist for the club, which he claims comes easily to him since, "I'm a Poole man". He has an intense pride in the club but then that's because "speedway is to Poole, what football is to the people of Manchester, Madrid or Milan". It's a phrase Gordie uses with ease and confidence, which, I imagine, comes from his confidence in its truth as well as the number of times he's used it before. There is no doubt that the speedway club in Poole is effectively part of the lifeblood of the place and inspires a widespread and enduring fanaticism throughout the area. Gordie proudly relates that the sport is "very big in the town" and many local people are filled with the "Pirates' Pride and Passion". Despite this devotion and fanaticism for Poole Speedway, he always finds it "amazing that Poole people still cheer the opposition" but then "care and consideration" are also part of the core values automatically upheld by the vast majority of the club's loyal fans. These devotees still regularly come in sufficient numbers to worship at their Dorset speedway shrine, around 7,000 in total every fortnight, and are rightly seen as the numerical equals to the regular attendances of their nearby rivals, albeit one with a different sports code, Bournemouth Football Club.

In fact Gordie stresses that as a club, or as part of people's lives, Poole Speedway club arguably inspires greater love and devotion than the Cherries at Dean Court. To support his claim, Gordie reels off an impressively long litany of achievement and success for Poole, though it's a huge list of achievements, which nonetheless Gordie is able to remember and recall with ease. There have been a litany of "doubles and trebles" scattered among a rich history of success that includes eleven league titles and three cup-winning seasons.

Poole Speedway club has always been very special to Gordie and has been part of his own life, ever since he "cried so much at the noise" during that first addictive visit in 1951 to Wimborne Road with his father. After that particular day, there

has never been any another activity with such enduring significance for his imagination or for his life; indeed there's never been any doubt that he'd "always want to come back". Like many others from the area – and I believe in all seriousness – Gordie quietly but earnestly notes, "we're all in love with the same girl and her name is Poole Speedway!" This love of a lifetime has inspired devotion from a very large number of suitors in the Poole area; I'm sure that Gordie still has rival suitors despite the time, care and attention he has conscientiously lavished upon her over the years!

At the age of 60, it's his 54th season and enthusiasm remains resolutely undiminished while he carries out his many duties throughout the stadium. It's a "full-time job" that involves "dealing with sponsors and riders; all the admin of invoicing and contracts as well as [his own speciality] working with the press". On a race night, these responsibilities revolve around a very strong element of pastoral care for the riders and the various employees of the track. He also has to ensure that the many administrative tasks, that pack the hours that lead up to a race day, all go smoothly. Throughout all this intense activity, Gordie is keen to stress that, "we still like to enjoy ourselves though!" As we wander to the far side of the stadium to try to sort out the exact whereabouts of the key for a locked gate, we briefly pop into his office handily located on the apex of the first bend. Gordie also has to search for a solution that will allow the electronic scoreboards to actually work at tonight's meeting, since the laptop which contains the required software program to operate them is, unfortunately, absent having "been borrowed" since last week. It's precisely these unexpected tasks and problems that it's Gordie's responsibility to quickly resolve. The required software program isn't easily or widely available, since it had originally to be specially commissioned and developed by the club because the complexity of the metrics required, to accurately run a speedway scoreboard and its score system, is very specialised.

The idea that you might answer your own software requirements is symptomatic of the trend, at Wimborne Road, to try to control, wherever possible, your own affairs and destiny. This equally applies to all activities throughout the stadium and includes their own track shop for which they mostly produce and source their own Poole merchandise and memorabilia to sell on these premises. Not only does this enable the club to ensure that they control the quality of the products but that they always manage to maximise the revenues and profits from these activities. An example of this strategy of control and ownership, would be the recent set up of their company, Pirate Videos, to produce their own videos, and latterly DVDs, of all the speedway fixtures run under their auspices at Wimborne Road. Given the importance and popularity of the club within the local area, their aim to retain these revenues and profits is to be admired as sensible business practice and, in the context of the spiralling expenses that afflict the sport generally, makes strategic sense. Particularly so, at a successful club like Poole, with its back-to-back League Championship and Cup victories, because these regular triumphs will have boosted its already healthy weekly attendances and further increased the demand for its Pirates branded merchandise.

Nonetheless, they don't rest on their laurels at Poole Speedway, so they also have a very proactive relationship with the local media and go to great lengths to ensure that the radio, television and newspapers have all the information they require. This is managed and coordinated by Gordie, to ensure the national and regional media has the appropriate level of access to the riders, management and other club officials. This thereby enables the print and broadcast media to create interesting news pieces or to provide regular insightful comment for their readers, listeners or viewers. It's a very well-oiled and efficient PR machine, which Gordie professes himself happy with, since it generates a level of coverage that befits its importance and its own view of itself, within the local region and, to a lesser extent, nationally. Not that as a truly professional PR man Gordie ever really rests from his continual search for more avenues and new ways to make Poole Speedway appear fresh and all the more thrilling to his extensive network of contacts. I watch Gordie efficiently carry out many last-minute tasks in the blazing hot sunshine as we rush around the grounds of the stadium, while his pride in the club shines through in the wealth of anecdotes and snippets about Poole speedway that continue to pepper his conversation. Speedway is a very broad church and he's been privileged enough to have met and known a wide variety of its many unique characters, from riders, too numerous to mention, as well as many others that form the great and the good of the sport. Whatever the capacity of their involvement, within Poole Speedway or at other speedway clubs, whether they're promoters, reporters, fans, mechanics or from the back office staff; at some juncture, Gordie's path has inevitably crossed with them. Consequently, Gordie has a rich network of people, met throughout the years that he'd consider friends as well as an extensive catalogue of incidents, events and memories to fondly remember or endeavour to recall. Sadly diplomacy and discretion, never mind his job position, dictate that these stories remain confidential!

Whether he talks about notable individuals off the track – from Dave Lanning to Ian Wooldridge ("who lost his hair banging his head on the wooden roof of the old stand") – or on the track, you really could listen to Gordie for hours. You can readily believe him when he says "I still feel like a little lad when I walk into Poole stadium, particularly as so many of my heroes have ridden here!" Doing the public relations work that he does for the speedway club is "an ideal job that just knocked on my door, one day" and , he modestly claims, only involves the simple proposition of "getting them interested and keeping them interested". All jobs and sports have their irritations or faults and for Gordie these are the frequent "rule changes" and the existence of "guest riders". Another slight bugbear is that he wishes some other speedway promotions, and their press officers would "take the sport more seriously" (like he does and the Poole promotion does) but, ultimately, he only really feels any anger towards some of the ill-informed "idiots that go on the Internet". These anonymous people anger him, particularly those whose opinions cause unnecessary damage or who are erroneously given undue importance by others, even when they are not in full possession of the true facts or the complete picture. Gordie prides himself that he goes out of his way to always listen to any of the "7,000 people who come here every fortnight". He is adamant that he will speak with absolutely anyone who wants to come up and talk about what's on their mind as well as what concerns, troubles or delights them about the Poole club.

Gordie has seen so much over the years and so believes that, despite the inevitable changes in popularity, personalities and equipment, speedway remains a "macho sport" with the ever-present danger of injury for any of the riders involved. The example that immediately springs to his mind concerns former rider John Davis, whose horrific scars from his career includes the 250 stitches he required after an accident on the track; he then concedes it's "part and parcel" of the work, "they fall off and get hurt". Although Gordie is of the school of thought that the riders shouldn't sit around too long after they've claimed on "their insurance" but should always remember "that it's best to come back quickly", particularly before the understandable "doubts set in" the riders' minds about the possible dangers or long-term advisability of regular competition in the sport. Most riders do rush back extremely quickly, get back on their bikes and start to race again after an accident, often too early and without proper time for recovery so, to judge them by their actions, it's an opinion shared by

The riders laugh before the parade. © Jeff Scott

Adam Shields models his golden glitter helmet cover. © Jeff Scott

Floppy studies the track. © Jeff Scott

the majority of modern speedway riders. Ultimately in Gordie's opinion, when it comes to the speeds generated or the combustible and potentially lethal combination of men and machines "there's no such thing as a safe safety fence!"

Unable to resolve the scoreboard problem without the laptop, we stroll back out into the bright sunlight. The "weather's too good for speedway", Gordie jokingly concedes, before he banters with the catering staff as to whether the club would be better served by an outdoor barbeque tonight, "just imagine it now with the aroma of roasting prawns and meat drifting across the stadium". After we retreat back to the cool shade of the reception area, Poole co-promoter Mike Golding talks animatedly with Gordie about the match programme for tonight's fixture, which he was studying intently when we arrived. I'm impressed at the intensity of his interest in this document and the level of attention that he gives to the small but important details that make up its content. He's not happy with the quality of the photographs that have been included, "they look really anaemic inside this week", and though his critical comments were a softly spoken aside I'm sure that they'll be promptly acted upon, but is precisely the sort of detail that would probably rule the club out of contention for the coveted annual *Speedway Star* programme awards. This further demonstrates that the professionalism exhibited throughout this speedway organisation starts at the top of the club, continues throughout, and doesn't happen by accident. Their brief conversation is bizarrely interrupted by the arrival of a courier with surprise gifts for Mike, "for all your help at the [Cardiff] GP". These tokens of esteem are a gift-wrapped bottle of some sort along with an incongruously large bunch of flowers, which Mike quickly puts down as though not to be seen with them. Gordie and I then head off through the large, spacious and glass-fronted home-straight grandstand to investigate the situation in the pits among the Poole riders and mechanics.

Gordie has a word for everyone in the pits, with all the Pirates' and the Eagles' riders, staff and mechanics, as this area gradually crowds out with people as they prepare for the rapidly approaching start time. Gordie's role with his riders appears to be to adopt the role of a benevolent uncle for his charges. In this capacity, he spends considerable time with Poole's young Polish star rider and heat leader with the very bright dyed blond hair, Krzysztof Kasprzak (KK), mostly to offer reassurances about the accommodation difficulties he experiences when he rides in England. These problems inevitably result from the logistical demands that a gifted riders' travel schedule will place upon them, their machines and mechanics throughout the period of their career when they ride in the Polish, Swedish and British Leagues as well as the Grand Prix. Krzysztof carries on his family dynasty and destiny, since he has followed in his father Zenon's footsteps to become a successful rider, albeit in a slightly more complicated era of frequent inter-country air travel that is required in order to fulfil complex race commitments. KK's schedule for the week has already seen him ride in Poland on Sunday, Coventry on Monday and Sweden on Tuesday before recently arriving this afternoon in Poole. The next week will find him with yet another demanding schedule that involves Poland, England, Sweden, England (for two nights, hurrah), the Czech Republic, Poland and England again. This type of schedule is not at all uncommon for a select cadre of Elite riders throughout the summer months at the height of the season. It's also something for which they are well rewarded by their various clubs and sponsors as well as being personally cosseted throughout, as much as possible, by all parties who keenly try to protect their investment.

From Poole's perspective, it's vital to ensure that they've considered every possible aspect of all their riders' schedules and, in this instance, to ensure that KK arrives on time and as refreshed as possible for every Poole meeting that they expect him to compete in for them. Thereby, with the potential distraction of all these details taken care of, the team will, hopefully, perform to its best abilities without incurring the irksome and unnecessary fines that are inevitably levied when some riders don't turn up. This is a far from simple task, one that is already fraught with difficulty and anxiety when it applies to just one member of your team but, exponentially much more complicated, when it also applies to three other gifted riders within your team like it does for Poole Speedway. Ryan Sullivan, Bjarne Pedersen and Antonio Lindback all operate in this frequent-flyer realm of demanding inter-country travel schedules and also remain of vital importance to Poole's chances of success on the track. It's the type of challenge that other tracks, with less prestigious rosters, would relish. Though it's no surprise to Gordie that Poole have such a roster of star riders since "everyone wants to ride for Poole" and he knows the club can attract riders with this high level of ability because "it's easy with the crowds we get". The present appeal of Poole has been gained under the "shrewd" stewardship of promoters Mike Golding and Matt Ford but another strong influence is the appeal of the chance to work under the expert guidance and tutelage of the England (Team GB) and Poole team manager, Neil 'Middlo' Middleditch. Gordie believes that if the club management and facilities are "good enough for the five times world champion Tony Rickardsson", then they should be even more acceptable for anyone else of lesser abilities!

Back in the realm of the practical realities of speedway life for its riders, Krzysztof finds himself at work in the home side of the pits with his uncle Darek, who is hired by KK to work with him in England. Primarily his role is to be a mechanic, but, also, to be a familiar face and someone with whom KK can speak in Polish without the further difficulties that attempts to communicate in your second or third language can cause on a day-to-day basis. It's a very sensible approach for the rider's own mental equilibrium and it definitely benefits Poole, as a team, to have a gifted and contented rider. However, there are still some outstanding logistical concerns about the locally rented house that will be used on the nights that KK intermittently stays in the Poole area. Gordie is taciturn with KK who manages to combine an interesting mix of polite and excitable, along with his broken English, when he outlines the problem. In contrast, Gordie exudes a confident calm as he reassures him that it'll be easily sorted and that, instead, he should just concentrate on what he does best – his riding. After we walk on, it's noticeable that KK resumes the impressive display of warm up callisthenics we originally interrupted. This involves sprints up and down the length of the home pits lane before he again continues with his various athletic stretches and bends.

Further down the pit lane Poole's polite, perfect English speaker and intelligent Swedish reserve, Tobias Johansson, isn't plagued with such a difficult travel schedule but, instead, has had some problems to adapt to the particular demands that racing on the sheer variety of UK tracks requires. In comparison to Sweden, it really doesn't help that the tracks in the UK are mostly completely different from each other, "it's a different structure in the UK with tight corners". The fact that our tracks bear little similarity to the type and shape of the tracks Tobias has grown up with, and learnt to ride on, is a major problem that continues to affect his mental approach and confidence. Consequently, he's failed to achieve the level of form that he exhibits in Sweden. It's a situation that worries both him and the club. Even more mystifyingly to Tobias, when he thought about and investigated possible explanations for his lacklustre form, are the comparisons he can make with other riders that he regularly beats in Sweden. For example, included in tonight's opposition for Eastbourne is David Norris, who is a "successful rider in England" but in the Swedish League "he struggles as a reserve with only a three or four point average". But, for Tobias, the situation is reversed. We leave Tobias to ponder the mystery of it all, just as the flame-haired Poole team manager, Neil 'Middlo' Middleditch, arrives to motivate, counsel and manage those of his riders who are already in the pits to prepare their equipment.

Excitingly I then get to walk round the freshly watered and newly prepared surface of the Poole track in the blazing sunshine with Gordie as he patiently outlines to me that, for most local fans, the Middleditch family represent a "dynasty at Poole". Neil's father "rode from 1950 to 1962" before he then went on to manage the team but, throughout, still remained "an absolute gentleman". Neil also rode for the club that he now manages and is "Poole Speedway through and through". Gordie would be only too happy to introduce me to Neil later, for a brief word, if there happens to be a temporary and convenient respite in his managerial duties[1]. Gordie patiently explains the weekly difficulty that the management of the racing surface of the Poole track creates because of the different drying times that various sections of the track exhibit. The vagaries of the weather and its basic layout regularly combine to ensure that some areas are more difficult to prepare and subsequently ride than other apparently similar sections. This particularly affects those parts of the track prone to shade, such as the third bend where, as we walk round, it's evidently the wettest. Overall, the Elite League "mostly has good racing surfaces" so, usually, it's a negligible factor in the perception that speedway is "a hard game" or one that "people pretend to be hard". Gordie immediately corrects himself, "the job is hard, there's no need for pretence" since it's a sport that's "often raced high on adrenalin", with riders often getting "uppity, when they stand and shout and scream" but away from all the action, he believes, "really they're all pussycats".

After Middlo has finished handing out match programmes and various soft drinks to his riders, he kindly finds the time for a brief conversation about his work for British speedway and for Poole. As England manager, "young rider development" is a topic he's passionate about and he's pleased to have recently organised a "test match with the kids" against Australia at Wimborne Road. On the night, the "Aussies were the best team" but then the aim behind the meeting was to give our young riders confidence and test match experience, so the "fact we'd lost didn't enter people's heads". Whether for club or country, Middlo is a staunch advocate of the need to take the long view on youth rider development, though it's a perspective not necessarily shared by other UK promoters or the Poole club (!) in the quest to see instant results. Middlo believes that it's detrimental to their own potential for long-term success when many young English riders prefer to continue to excel in the Conference and Premier Leagues but shy away from natural progression and the chance to regularly test themselves at the highest level. He believes the 'big fish in a small pond' syndrome is a key factor that stymies our chances of international success or to find a future British World Champion. However, the motivation for this disinclination to risk failure is primarily economic since the points are easier to come by in other leagues than in the Elite League and, because the number of potential meetings in a season is far greater, your short-term earnings are thereby much higher. For Middlo, this represents a worrying "lack of ambition" that he doesn't see exhibited by foreign riders of a similar age; though he does admit that there are "less meetings" and, due to the initial difficulty of competing successfully, in reality it's often "half the money, if you're lucky". Nonetheless, Middlo would welcome the chance to "talk to the fathers" to reassure and persuade them that he and the clubs involved would exhibit the appropriate duty of care to "look after their sons properly".

All this has to be balanced with the fact that Poole are "running a business" and "you don't win a league on sentiment". Nonetheless, while "people want to come and watch you when you're winning, not getting your arse kicked", he believes there is still a place for the development of the talents of our young riders within the context of the pursuit of success. As a case in point, the British Under-21 Champion Edward Kennett rides intermittently for the Pirates this season and his skills and technique have improved with the benefit of regular competition at a higher level. Middlo considers himself fortunate to have worked with World Champion Tony Rickardsson when he rode at Poole Speedway, and "Tony lived with me for

[1] The Poole track surrounds a large centre green with its historic football pitch. It is hallowed turf upon which the famous Middlesbrough footballer and hero, Wilf Mannion, actually played on for Poole Town in 1948. Gordie often delighted ex-World Champion, former Poole rider and committed Middlesbrough fan, Gary Havelock, when he reminded him of this fact.

years". He got to witness first hand his "professional" approach to everything he does in connection with his involvement with the sport, though Middlo is quick to admit, "there's only one of him"; nevertheless the "diet and the training", the "culture of fitness regimes, psychologists and personal trainers" are all part and parcel of the Rickardsson package and should be universally emulated. Like Gordie, he doesn't deny that the speedway world is a "tough world" with a need for exceptional ability and dedication but until you've done it yourself or worked with riders like Rickardsson and Leigh Adams that have "been there and done that", you really can't properly comprehend what is really required to "really excel and win respect".

Middlo also speaks very highly of the culture and environment provided by the promoters Matt and Mike at Poole Speedway club. They run the club in a "very slick" fashion and both are "very passionate about the club and have a huge desire for success". Middlo gets to experience Matt's fanaticism firsthand as they often "travel together" and believes he's only "happy when winning". Victory is something that Matt has experienced a lot over the past few successful years with repeated accomplishments in the League and the KO Cup, though it's something, as a manager, Neil relishes but claims he doesn't take for granted. In Middlo's opinion "everyone loves Poole speedway"; the track is the "FIM shape with a fairly good surface and not just one racing line" which, when allied to success and overall professionalism of the organisation, makes a complete package. "Our corporate entertainment is second to none" within the sport and the club prides itself on the fact that it looks after its many large sponsors very well. This is in addition to the fact that the sponsors have all benefited from a raised national and regional profile as a result of Poole's trophy successes and regular television appearances that inevitably result. This applies as much to the Pirates' number two sponsor, the local company Poole Bay Freight, who've welcomed the increased profile and visibility but also to the number one sponsor, particularly as Middlo has started to "notice the RIAS name everywhere". This is excellent news for all their sponsors, but particularly for RIAS who specialise in insurance for the over-50s, a target group for which speedway fans are, arguably, their ideal demographic grouping! Middlo is also pleased with the extra attention that all the media coverage has generated for the town of Poole itself, so much so, that the Poole Tourism Office have decided to sponsor him. He always makes a point to wear their "hats and caps" wherever possible, particularly during television interviews, since he genuinely believes in the importance of "looking after your sponsors".

There's greater media awareness across the whole of the sport since the advent of regular coverage on Sky Sports and Middlo has even just been on a "media training course at the BSPA"; though he was already "very aware" of the importance of appearances and the need for "articulacy and eloquence". But then, he benefits from the harshest, most difficult-to-please critics imaginable, "my father and my family", who closely monitor his every appearance on the television and provide frank feedback. This attention to appearance and detail extends to his own family involvement at Poole where Middlo's daughter, Gemma, works at the track as one of the four extremely glamorous and elegant young women who appear as the "start girls". They all wear "specially designed race suits", made to an exacting specification provided by his daughter Gemma. The look of these uniforms exactly match the kevlars worn by the team itself, except for the bare midriffs that the riders themselves appear not to favour. The start girls all really look the part; they stylishly imitate the glamorous style of the Grand Prix motor racing circuit staff and they're all very professionally choreographed in what they do on a race night. In addition, Middlo proudly notes, "there's no ugly ones!"

Another man in the pit lane who is extremely proud of his daughter is, the club's pit and environmental marshal, Roy Perry. He first came to Poole in 1948 and has been "hooked" ever since then although, in his experience, the sport rarely inspires indifference as "you're hooked or you're not" with nothing in between. Roy started work in the pits in the 1960s and hasn't looked back since, but can still vividly recall, "in 1969, when we won the league, me and the missus never missed a meeting!" Just to speak with him for a few minutes, you immediately sense that he's one of life's true gentlemen who, throughout the evening when I watched him, spent as much time on "the visitors' side making sure everything's alright" as he did on his own. Roy's daughter Louise also attends regularly and watches from the fenced area in front of the pits, not far from where her father works patiently. She's is extremely knowledgeable and fanatical about all things Poole speedway, studies the events on the track throughout the meeting with a touching intensity and, you quickly gather, shares her father's easy charm, warmth and sincerity. They share a love of Poole Speedway and they're clearly very close, since her father brought her up on his own "from a few months old" and also quickly indoctrinated her into a lifetime love of speedway. Earlier in the evening, Roy had spoken with great pride about Poole but equally so about his daughter – both her work as a nanny as well as her prowess on the football pitch which included regular accomplished and skilful performances for Ashdown Rovers. They both typify the speedway culture in this country, since they're charming people and great company.

If the hills are alive with the sound of music, then the Poole pits is completely packed with interesting but fanatical fans of the club as well as Krzysztof Kasprzak as he conducts more of his elaborate warm-up exercises. Another such character is Glynn Shailes who, along with the eponymous speedway author Robert Bamforth, shared his considerable knowledge of all things Poole Speedway with the world in *Poole Pirates – 50 Greats* (as well as working again with Robert on *Swindon Speedway – 50 Greats*). Glynn is far and away the most dapperly dressed person in the pits with his hat and smart jacket, so looks for all the world as if he's just come from a wedding reception or formal garden party. He's been a regular at the club "since the place opened" in 1948 although he no longer observes the racing from the open terraces. Now he prefers the luxury and comfort of the impressive grandstand, where he joins friends over a bottle of wine, "watching the civilised way", which thereby enables him to enjoy the spectacle of the racing while also "putting the world to rights". Although he's a Poole fanatic, Glynn's first-ever meeting had been in 1947 when he went to watch Bristol versus Wigan at Knowle Stadium. He was in Bristol to perform at the cathedral – as a choirboy and local church organist – and just went along to the meeting to pass the time. He vividly recalls the huge, packed car park – filled with cars and large numbers of buses – before he bustled along to the packed terraces. Laurel and Hardy made a personal appearance and the first event was a special "one lap track record" contest won by Fred Tuck. The vibrancy of the whole event and the atmosphere of the meeting, with its smell and the noise of the "revving" and the crowd made an indelible impression on Glynn. "I'd never seen anything like it" and he was soon able to persuade his father ("a very good and patient man") to take him along to the first-ever Poole meeting.

His eyes sparkle as he recalls races "on the cinder track", all those years ago when he joined a "packed crowd of 8,000" to watch the first ever Poole meeting against Yarmouth. He's come to watch them race ever since, though sometimes he could only attend on "high days and holidays". As a fan and author, Mr Shailes has an incredibly detailed recollection – "there's so much history" – of the various riders, promotions and events that have captured his imagination or delighted him ever since his first time at Wimborne Road, all those years ago in 1948. For the next 15 intense minutes or so, Glynn recalls and catalogues practically every single one of the many League and Cup triumphs he's witnessed at Poole along with the impressively colourful characters who've been involved as riders or the promoters of the club. He speaks with intensity and a genuine reverence towards the people and the events of the 1950s and 1960s, as if they were common knowledge and had only happened yesterday.

Poole's history has so many trophies, but also includes the closure of the club in 1956, which led to many intricate machinations to stage open meetings or, later, the necessity of "riding black" outside the auspices of the sports governing body "the Control Board". The thrill of the events he recalls and the vibrant history of the track comes across vividly in the force and flow of his animated descriptions. Most of all Glynn is "amazed at these Poole supporters" for their open attitude towards and appreciation of the skill of all riders, irrespective of the team they ride for. "We've always cheered the opposition here" and it's this fact "that everyone's so wonderful and friendly" that delights Glynn the most about Poole and the sport in general throughout the country. Absorbed in his memories, Glynn meanders off to settle himself in the comfort of the main grandstand in anticipation of another closely fought local derby meeting with their rivals Eastbourne.

By now, all the riders have arrived and changed into their race gear, while their mechanics warm up the bikes or make vital last-minute adjustments to the equipment. Roy Perry is in his element and already dashes about hither and thither, in anticipation of the order he'll try to impose on the mêlée of men and machines to be found in any pits. He's ably assisted by his assistant pit marshal, Lee Dean, who looks the height of efficiency as he wears the sort of headphones with a mouthpiece that you usually see in call centres or NASA Mission Control. I hesitate to even speak to him as he's way too involved in his work, though earlier, I'd learnt that after his career as a rider wasn't the success he'd hoped it might be ("Crumpie was nice to me when I rode"), Lee jumped at the chance to still be involved in speedway. It was in 1995, when he seized with alacrity the opportunity to serve an apprenticeship in the Poole pits and he hasn't looked back since. His ultimate ambition is to, eventually, become clerk of the course but before then Lee realises that he'll have to continue to learn everything he can, but still plans to enjoy himself in the process. Throughout the evening he rushes about in his headphones like a man possessed, with a broad smile never far away.

As a guest of the club, I'm incredibly fortunate to be able to watch proceedings through the fence, on the second bend, from an area adjacent to the pits with a great view of the entire track. I can also watch what happens on the home side of the pits, which includes Krzysztof Kasprzak as he still continues with more of his elaborate warm-up exercises! During each race, I'm joined by the fence by the riders, mechanics and managers of both teams, along with other guests, and we all intently study the events on the track. And what action it is both on and off the track! Most noticeable is the incredible team spirit of the Poole riders who work together to help each other throughout in their section of the pits. It's always frenetic in the pits at every track, given the usual intensity and fast pace of a meeting with its brief time between the races. Poole's young, gifted and Brazilian-born Swede wins heat 1 impressively but is practically no sooner off his bike than he's advising others on track conditions and starts to enthusiastically help out the riders who will be involved in the next race with their bikes. Gordie isn't at all surprised at Antonio's behaviour "once you wear the skull and crossbones, there's no distinctions or pretension, it's just a 'that's my team, you're riding for me' attitude". If the help and advice doesn't come from your fellow riders, you'll also get help from the "long-serving backroom boys, the pits and gate staff". Despite, or perhaps because of, the fact that they were already the champions for the last couple of years, there's a palpable desire or intensity in the hunger for success throughout the club. However, it's initially a night of frustration for the home team since local rivals Eastbourne have established a small lead from heat 3 which isn't finally clawed back until heat 7. At this point, having just fought their way back to be on level terms, Lindback falls and is excluded in the very next race. As he comes back towards the pits he wears his frustrations on his sleeve, when he angrily shouts and screams Swedish words I don't understand but need no translation to gather the meaning of, as he slowly trudges back from the track.

The turning point of the match is heat 9, when things really kick off right in front of me on the track and subsequently very close by to me off the track. Nicki Pedersen, Eastbourne's ex-World Champion and their outstanding superstar rider, appears to accidentally or, maybe, deliberately take off Poole's Matej Ferjan, who painfully flies into the fence at some speed and ends in a crumpled heap of man and machine on the second bend. The Poole track staff and riders are incensed and have absolutely no doubt that Pedersen did this with some premeditation or malice aforethought. Though it happened right in front of me, it would be difficult to know what exact conclusion to draw, other than it looked an aggressive intervention that wouldn't meet the generally accepted concept of studiously 'fair riding'. Although, then again, where Nicki is concerned, his reputation for being a hard, 'take no prisoners' and combative rider – who often as not really doesn't given the expected inch to his fellow riders – has gone before him and, inevitably, everyone is always quick to judge his actions harshly. None more so than Poole's captain, the diminutive Australian Ryan Sullivan, who angrily sprints from next to me, as do most of the Poole pits team, track staff and riders along with many of Eastbourne staff, to angrily confront Pedersen on the track. In fact, Ryan is a man immediately enraged to boiling point, who vehemently shouts, gestures and screams at Nicki. Ryan makes a point to stress "I'll freaking have you anytime", which is an offer Pedersen affects to ignore as he ambles back to the Eastbourne side of the pits. Sullivan is told, in polite but firm terms, to calm down by fellow Australian, Davey Watt. It's a suggestion that only serves to enrage Ryan further, who thereby switches his attention from a confrontation with Nicki to angrily gesticulate and shout at the hardier Davey instead. Meanwhile, the cause of his volcanic anger, Nicki, is sat calmly by his bike for all the world as if nothing untoward has happened.

The crowd of spectators by the public side of the pits fence swells considerably; with a larger number of Poole fans similarly enraged by Nicki and then further stoked up by Ryan's subsequent violent reaction. With tempers immediately arriving at boiling point, they are quick to share their thoughts and opprobrium directly with Nicki and other members of Eastbourne staff close enough to the fence that separates the enraged Poole fans from the Eastbourne side of the pits. Jon Cook, the Eagles' team manager, exchanges a few curt words with the most vociferous and heated members of the crowd. The most notable of whom is a very soberly dressed chap in his mid 50s, who wears his office attire of a shirt, jacket and tie, who screams a steady stream of colourful obscenities and explicit threats with some passion. You definitely get a better dressed fan threaten you at Wimborne Road and he appears to be in ignorance of the tolerant and appreciative approach usually taken by most genuine Poole fans towards visitors. This angry man is barely able to suppress his anger and voices his strong doubts as to the lineage and parentage of everyone in the vicinity whom he assumes to be involved with the Eastbourne team. He also has some colourful, inflammatory and unsubstantiated claims regarding an unconventional attitude towards relationships formed by Eastbourne-based people with their own siblings. Away from these shenanigans off the track, after the capable ministrations of the St John Ambulance team, Matej groggily rises to his feet and is helped back to the pits. As a member of the speedway riding fraternity, Matej inevitably dusts himself down and, it never ceases to still amaze me, recovers enough from his bad crash cum very heavy fall to immediately take his place in the re-run of the heat. He comes second in that race and, despite the shock to his system, even manages to win his final race a few heats later. I was too distracted by the running altercations among the riders to have noticed Poole's state-of-the-art scoreboard software had, reportedly, enabled the operator to post his own inflammatory impressions ("dirty bastard") about Nicki Pedersen's deserved exclusion.

From this point onwards the result is never in doubt as the Poole team wakes from their early torpor to power to an easy and deserved victory on the night. It is quite clear that the charged atmosphere among the riders, and the Poole fans for that matter, has continued to their benefit throughout the remainder of the meeting. Sullivan remains arguing heatedly with Pedersen, close by me, at every opportunity for the rest of the meeting but, at the end of the day, the Poole team have used the shock and outrage of the incident to buck up their performance and stir up their collective resilience to their own subsequent advantage.

Not that the Eastbourne team aren't similarly fired up by events, but they just aren't able to meaningfully channel this aggression into their riding on the track. Instead they dissipate it in some fractiousness off the track. Most notably prior to a vital heat 13, when David 'Floppy' Norris has a manically heated, but strangely pointless, helmet-to-head confrontation with a red-overalled member of the Poole pit gate and centre green staff; who quite correctly refuses to open the pit gate for Norris, and thereby prevents him from going onto the track while it undergoes a thorough track grade. In considerable ire, Floppy turns round and storms off on his bike huffily, noticeably at huge speed and somewhat dangerously given the confined size of the pits area, before when he finally makes it onto the track he finishes a disappointing last in the subsequent race. He also has a heated exchange with the Poole fans, who goad and bay at him from behind the pits fence. Floppy was, allegedly, also subject to some unsavoury spitting from these fans. Whether he was or wasn't I'm in no position to exactly comment, though it was very apparent that he was highly displeased with the situation and struggled to contain his annoyance with events, officials, Poole fans but typically, most of all, with himself. The Poole fans delight in his misfortune and ostentacious downcastness, and that of the Eagles generally, as they go wild with ecstatic celebrations by the fence, in the grandstand and on the bends, as an eventually surprisingly easy victory becomes assured. Gordie Day shrugs his shoulders as he passes by, apparently oblivious to the heightened tension all around him, and then waves his arm in the general direction of the fans, before he says enigmatically in the style of a Zen master "look around you, this is Poole, this is speedway!"

Everyone connected with Poole Speedway club, from the riders to the fans, appears visibly delighted with their victory. Jon Cook takes a few moments to unsuccessfully try to reason with his most vociferous and loudest tormentor, who still sports his tie, and thereby confirms that you really do get a better class of hooligan element on this part of the South coast. Jon's voice of calm and reason doesn't mollify him; in fact this irate man doesn't listen to any reassurance or reason but instead prefers to continue with his limited repertoire of more verbal torment and vitriolic abuse. During this contretemps, the majority of the Eastbourne team quickly pack up their gear and equipment with almost indecent haste before they load it all into their wall of parked white transit vans. You can almost hear the engines of the vans revving highly before they leave together en masse to run a by now sizeable gauntlet of angry Poole fans, who have gathered by the exit gate, still keen to share more of their predictable opinions with the team in general and Nicki Pedersen in particular. The ever-sociable and Eastbourne party animal, Dean 'Deano' Barker doesn't leave with the team but promptly makes his way to the loud music and flashing lights of the disco that takes place after the fixture in the grandstand bar. No doubt, his off-track reputation would have you believe, in search of some liquid consolation and some well-deserved companionship.

The Poole riders are also pretty much packed up and gone from the pits. Except for Ryan Sullivan who painstakingly packs his equipment away, with his tall and elegant girlfriend stood by his side, while he still continues to loudly hold forth to all and sundry about Pedersen's dangerous tactics on the track. It's no secret that Ryan believes that Nicki deliberately tries to injure fellow riders and should, therefore, be severely punished accordingly by the sports authorities. Gordie Day, ever the perfect host (and PR man) kindly arranges for me to grab Ryan for a few words. Ryan has, patently, had a few bad interview experiences so he sensibly starts our chat with his own question "this will be brief won't it?" And it is a brief, courteous but mostly anodyne three minutes together before the demands of a successful speedway riders schedule kicks in once more. Ryan's delighted that "we hung together as a team", having "dug deep" with the most important contributory factor identified as "not individual scores but the team score". Ryan believes that the "importance of captaincy" is to get the best out of people, which for him at Poole, is aided by the fact that "we've a lot of good riders who go well here but our team spirit showed through". Your background and nationality is apparently "irrelevant in this team" provided that you remain committed to a Poole victory. Although he's keen to stress that, with quite a few riders who also compete regularly in Poland and Sweden, it's worth each rider remembering "to try to have an affinity with everywhere you ride". The only dark cloud for Ryan, on the evening and on the horizon, was the high level of aggression shown by Nicki Pedersen during the meeting, "we expected it to be tough but not so 'hard', it's part and parcel of the sport but we're lucky that no-one got injured". I thank Ryan for his time and with that he walks off into the distance arm in arm with his girlfriend, Sophie Aal. I shake hands with Middlo who also leaves the pits, after a successful night's work, to head off to the bar to chat animatedly with the home supporters and to put his arm around the shoulders of the affable 'Deano'. The grandstand bar is packed, the disco music blares and the coloured lights flicker brightly as I make my way to the large, gradually emptying car park[2].

22nd June Poole v. Eastbourne (Elite League B) 50-40

[2] I rang Gordie the next afternoon to thank him for his time and hospitality as well as his help with the research for my book. He hopes that I avoid the pitfalls that have befallen other books "as so many speedway books don't manage to live off the page". Surprisingly, Gordie's mood is downbeat compared to his optimistic public persona from the night before and his assessment of the present Poole team, as well as its prospects for the season ahead, are similarly sombre. It's a shock after his earlier easy enthusiasm and ebullience the previous night to hear him frankly doubt whether Poole will even manage to retain any of their titles. He's very concerned about the "inconsistency" of "Matty and Antonio" but most of all is extremely worried about Ryan Sullivan's increasingly erratic and often downright poor performances. Though Ryan was originally brought in to replace (a difficult task if ever there was one!) Tony Rickardsson, and has had enough time to settle but nonetheless "he remains the worst number 1 in the league and, sometimes, he's not even a number 2". Added to the problem of Ryan's inconsistency is a continued and worrying weakness in the reserve positions at Poole, which "is where we'll lose the championship". Gordie resists all my attempts to emphatically disagree before he mutters the unthinkable, "we might not even make the play-off finals".

Dean and Nicki put the world to rights. © Jeff Scott

Poole riders congregate angrily. © Jeff Scott

Antonio studies the action. © Jeff Scott

Chapter 14: Showtime at the Showground
29th June Peterborough v. Eastbourne

"This is the true way, to give 'em a chance, this is racing" Sam Ermolenko (on putting all 4 back without an exclusion after some hard riding not by Nicki Pedersen)

"He's broken more bones than the bionic man" David Norris (on Sam Ermolenko)

18.1.4.4. iv) A PL rider is restricted to a maximum of 6 (in total) Guest appearances per season, NB. Appearances as a declared number 8 do not count towards this total

---

The East of England Showground (EOES), the home of the Peterborough Panthers is conveniently sited a mile or so away from the A1(M) with a network of roads that link it easily to many other towns throughout the Midlands. Their fans are drawn from towns that dot the region – "from Northampton and Corby way" according to team manager Trevor Swales – although in recent months there has been a resurgence of interest from people based in the town itself. Peterborough is one of England's many cathedral cities and has recently attracted national newspaper attention to its Cathedral Square. Primarily because it's the Saturday night location for stand-offs between large gangs of marauding Goths and Chavs that throng there. Although less volatile than the Mods and Rockers of the 1960s and because of their contemporary pre-occupation with style over character, the groups usually do nothing more than strike poses and glower at each other with fashion model menace. Still, this is enough to frighten ordinary members of the public who insist on their right to shop and eat in the town square whenever they choose. Given speedway's deserved reputation, as an inclusive and community orientated sport, the local council ought to send these recalcitrant youths along to get their kicks from speedway instead.

Sadly not so enlightened, the council has chosen to spend local taxpayers' money on an innovative ruse to reform the youths' restfulness with some much-needed paintballing.

The scheme has inspired great apathy, among the Chavs in particular, and for this age group speedway has proved similarly blessed, since when I arrive at the Showground on American Independence Day there isn't a Chav or a Goth anywhere. If fact, hardly anybody is there since it's many hours before the scheduled start time. The vast expanse of the grounds themselves are increasingly edged with newly built estates of Persimmon executive houses, bordered by the shouty roadside signs that proclaim the superior design and interior delights of their display homes. The sky is black and the clouds above the speedway track and stadium buildings, which stand imperious and isolated in the centre of the Showground, threaten imminent rain. Track curator Julian Pettican has been hard at work for many hours already and presently he's circling the track repeatedly in his tractor, as he grades the surface in preparation for tonight's fixture with visitors Eastbourne.

Julian has a varied background in the sport; he progressed to become a machine examiner after he had previously been a mechanic for Brett Woodifield. This year he has officially become the Peterborough track curator, "I was volunteered into it", and delights in the opportunity to practise this "black art". It's a job that requires skill and patience and usually takes around two full days to prepare the track to the standard required for an enjoyable evening's racing. Julian loves the fact that he works for his local team and can play his own part in the excitement it generates in the area, especially now the track wins plaudits from the riders themselves. This has reached such a level of approval, that not only has he been praised in the local papers for his preparation skills, but also the riders clubbed together to signal their appreciation of his efforts with a case of beer. They all enjoy mutual respect ("they're good lads") and Julian is always keen to find out what they want or what they suggest for the track. Consequently, he spends the majority of his time to ensure that he's prepared "the track just how the riders want it". At Peterborough this usually involves using the flat grader to take the ruts off the surface, before Julian applies lots of new loose shale – especially to the outside – and then he spends time "blading it all back in". By the time I arrive the track looks incredibly thick with dark-hued shale throughout its circumference. The Panthers have a track renowned for the speed and exhilaration of its racing, mostly due to its length and distinct oval shape, which encourages a flat-out racing style and approach among the riders. Julian expects the track length and surface to massively favour the home riders rather than Eastbourne's squad of small-track specialists.

I wander round to the impressively substantial main grandstand that overlooks the start gate and home straight, outside of which the caterers have begun their food preparations and have already hoisted the awning over their van. The preparations at the track shop are also well underway as Nick Barber and his brother Jon lay out an array of goodies, merchandise and memorabilia in their glass-fronted outlet that occupies a prime position for passing trade in the main grandstand. It's one of the most attractive sites they use within their extensive network of track shops at speedway clubs throughout the country. The Barbers perpetually travel during the speedway season but, despite it being their job, they remain real enthusiasts for the sport (and its merchandise!) and are always a friendly mine of information on the latest gossip, opinion and team news, particularly about the tracks they service. Tonight, rather gloomily, they don't expect a close contest or, most likely, even a contest at all because of the weather forecast.

Outside the shop, I find the avuncular Peterborough co-promoter and club administrator Neil Watson in typically cheerful yet thoughtful mood. Neil enjoys many responsibilities simultaneously and works long hours at Peterborough and also with Conference League Mildenhall, where he is club chairman. In common with all but the lucky few, Neil pursues a full-time job away from the speedway and somehow finds the time to run his own busy letting agency business. The name of his agency is Renaissance and the club too has started to experience an about-to-be-born-rebirth, ever since Colin Horton took over as owner from his brother Mick. With unsubstantiated but frequent rumours of financial trouble and unpaid debts, there was an urgent need for considerable financial investment in the Panthers, without which there was every likelihood that the club might have gone out of existence. Not that these worries appear to occupy Neil in the slightest during his ruminations upon the sport of speedway.

Neil's major concern is the lack of talented English riders who are presently coming up through the ranks within contemporary British speedway. The old certain certainties of progression and graduation from an apprenticeship, from what used to be called Division 2, after they had developed the appropriate level of skills required to succeed, into the rarefied atmosphere of Division 1 have long since disappeared. If you listen to Neil, the Elite League is full of "overseas riders" and suffers from a comparative lack of loyalty to its riding staff, because promoters and team managers continually search for the ideal team formation in the quest for the financial rewards to be gained through instant success on the track. This is a worrying but long-term trend that has recently been exacerbated and intensified by the oxygen of publicity provided by regular national television coverage on Sky Sports, which has ensured that track success is often rewarded with increased and lucrative sponsorship. Along with every other Elite and Premier League team, Peterborough have chased success at all costs and have thereby contributed to the reduction in opportunities for career progression of young British riders with potential. There is a dearth of home-grown talent, though Neil names his own list of the next generation of talented Englishmen that includes, "cracking riders like Chris Harris, Simon Stead, Oliver Allen and David Howe with a small gap to James Wright". Apart from these exciting young prospects, the future looks bleak, since while you can still watch many talented young men race in Britain, they inevitably come from overseas. Peterborough themselves have had to frequently change their team around in the hunt for success today rather than exhibit perseverance until tomorrow. But, in mitigation Neil points out, that often this has been thrust upon them by circumstances rather than by design.

Just like the poor are always with us, so it is in speedway with injuries to riders. It is accepted that there are always the inevitable and unenviable broken bones, wounds, abrasions and mental distress, of varying severity, thrown up by participation in the sport. Neil mentions Joel Parsons, a promising young rider, who when he recently competed against Mildenhall has "just had his leg smashed to smithereens". Already this season Peterborough have replaced Paul Lee after a "particularly bad crash", though he was unlucky "as after the really bad crashes they often just get up and walk away, whereas it's the silly little ones often cause more damage". Neil has "huge admiration" for all riders, especially because it's a "rough and tough old sport and they say the riders often leave their brains in their toolbox". Team changes can often be a result of injuries or loss of form but sometimes it's surprisingly thrust upon the clubs by circumstance. Neil starts to speak about "the decision made by that Judas, Joonas Kylmakorpi, to withhold his services" before he changes his mind and decides, "it's best I keep my thoughts to myself!" Which is a shame, as there's definitely an interesting story there (!), but to

get a fully accurate picture I should also speak with Joonas for his version of events.

Neil believes, if there is any secret to success in this division, it's the old truism that you have to have a strong combination of riders throughout the team. While the crowd remains almost totally home grown the riders that grace the track are mostly drawn from overseas and, as Neil delicately puts it, " they're no longer predominantly English". Strong riders in the reserve positions can also help a team overcome the "restricted tactical options" provided by the current version of the rulebook. Fortunately the Panthers have the rejuvenated Lukas Dryml, who rides in the key position of reserve. Lukas can ride like a world-beater on his day but, until the recent faith shown in him by the present management paid off, tended to ride like a novice. As we speak, Lukas has just arrived at the stadium having flown into the airport a short time ago and, while he dashes past us to the bathroom, he gloomily reports heavy rain only 10 minutes away from the track.

A short walk away, over on the Eastbourne side of the pits, the threat of rain is the least of promoter Jon Cook and team manager Trevor Geer's problems. They're both decidedly chary about their team's prospects tonight in this fixture against the Panthers, Jon nods towards the fence and notes, "there's a hell of a lot of dirt on the track like tonight!" Even if you ignore the huge disparity in track sizes between the two clubs, he feels it'll be "very fast and totally different to Eastbourne, though in fairness we never go well here". For Trevor, success in the sport boils down to "a confidence thing as it's all in the mind" and he expects the Eastbourne riders will closely watch the demeanour of the opposition, just like he "used to look around at the other riders" to try to gauge his own likely performance during the evening ahead. But then during his own career, Trevor admits he "used to let things go" rather than concentrate on his own ability to influence events, this continued until he realised it was an attitude that had cost him money. He now knows "if you believe in yourself things come together, I know when I rode it was". However for Steen Jensen, who rides at reserve for the Eagles, things still aren't really coming together at Eastbourne. Though he has the ability, Steen has lacked the confidence and consistency. As a case in point, Trevor emphasises Steen's recent victory against the ex-World Champion Gary Havelock at his home track at Arena Essex[1]. Trevor has tried to boost Jensen's confidence wherever possible, "afterwards I congratulated him saying 'you've really cracked it' and then he went out there and won a race and span in another when leading". Mostly though it's been a season of frustration with Steen for Eastbourne. Whenever he's ridden for the Isle of Wight in the Premier League, Trevor always

[1] This might have been almost accidental as Trevor immediately notes, " although to be fair, Havelock couldn't get past him as he was all over the place and he didn't know which way Steen was going to go!"

keeps a close eye on his progress and scores, as he does with all his riders, before he turns to Jon to say, "and he had another interesting score of zero last night, even when he gets eight he beats no one of note". Jon Cook shrugs before he wryly notes, "Steen's been a big disappointment to himself and us though, luckily, he declared himself unfit otherwise I'd have had to!" It's also been a season of bad luck with injuries for the Eagles. They've particularly missed David Norris as a result of his protracted recovery from injury and, to compound that, have just endured a surprise but comprehensive home defeat at the hands of Coventry. With gallows humour, Jon claims, "we're falling so fast we could soon disappear out of the bottom of the league". After being so candid, Jon reverts to the more guarded comments expected of Elite League promoters when he observes, "because of the play-off system every point is vital, so only a few points will make a big difference" to the relative league position of your team at the end of the season. He remains confident that "once we get David back we'll definitely start flying again". There's still time for Trevor and Jon to meander back to their side of the pits to chivvy their team along for the task ahead against Peterborough, though with jet-black skies overhead the forecast rain looks increasingly likely.

On the Peterborough side of the pits it's (as Top Cat might suggest it should be) busy, busy, busy even as their experienced captain Peter Karlsson drives in with his mechanic and begins to efficiently unload his equipment, before he starts to prepare for the racing ahead with some speed. Peter Clarke, tonight's affable referee from Doncaster, arrives with his smart black briefcase in hand. His verdict on weather conditions in the nearby area doesn't inspire the hope that the meeting will even go ahead, "it was fine all the way down until Stamford, from there it's been a heavy downpour". Trevor Swales, the plainly spoken but avuncular Peterborough team manager, listens intently and shrugs. But then Trevor quickly strikes you as the kind of man that would shrug in the face of most setbacks he encountered. They chat together amiably about the disputes that often arise between referees and managers, Trevor recalls, "Ackroyd and Oakes didn't speak for years" while Peter's work as an SCB official means that he often encounters an unidentified team manager, "who regularly just walks off the other way". Peter and Trevor get on well enough for Trevor to comment, "you must be one of the oldest refs nowadays?" before he walks off to resume the marshalling of his team and staff in his section of the pits. Team management is a job he appears to bring an easy, down-to-earth manner and matter-of-fact calmness to, if judged by this evening and when he is interviewed live on national television. I watch him closely at work tonight in the flesh, so it quickly appears that he knows everyone around him and takes the time to have a word with them all, in his own inimitable jovial, hale and hearty kind of way.

Trevor has always been reasonably local to the Peterborough area, and comes from the village of Holywell-cum-Needingworth near St Ives in Cambridgeshire. This region is his part of the world and he's so attached to the area that he still lives on the road where he was born. From an early age he had a complete fascination with bikes and it was an enthusiasm that led him to progress into riding speedway professionally in the 1970s at Peterborough. After he "packed the sport in to ride motor cross", he eventually found himself back in speedway team management because it is, "as close as you can get without riding". Like many people active in the sport, "once you get the bug you never get rid of it, as it's inbred in you". He particularly loves the fact that you can be "great rivals on the track and best of mates" off it.

It's definitely a family affair at Peterborough Speedway for the Swales family, since his son Wayne helps out as an assistant manager to Trevor, while the clerk of the course is his brother Dick Swales. Wayne, until recently, had been very proud to be "the youngest team manager in the country" at Mildenhall Speedway, where again he worked with his dad, this time under the auspices of the Fen Tigers owner Mick Horton. Complicatedly, the present owner of Peterborough Speedway, and its reputed saviour, Colin Horton, bought his interest in the club from his brother Mick. Wayne and Trevor now both find themselves at Peterborough, and work for Colin, after they severed their connections with Mick Horton at Mildenhall. Perhaps, we should draw our own conclusions; or then again not, since Trevor indicated very strongly that he would prefer not to talk about it at all. Instead he pointedly praises Peter Oakes for "having taught me all I know about speedway management". These are lessons that Trevor still strongly believes in and adheres to; most notably, "never tell a lie [slight pause], knowingly; and [another slight pause] never promise what you can't deliver!" He believes that these are proven

approaches as to how to conduct yourself that apply equally to life as much as they do to speedway. Though Trevor is keen to stress that involvement in the sport is as much a calling as it is a job, "we do it for love not money, as what we make isn't really worth talking about". Away from speedway, Trevor runs a motor repair business, "as we're all normal people and all have other jobs". His speedway duties are basically a "part-time hobby or job" with lots of really necessary but remarkably unglamorous tasks, "if something has to be done, you just do it; whether it's washing the fence or doing white lines, you just get on with it".

Trevor is keen to emphasise that within the sport, "genuinely we're one big happy family although we're not friends at the start of the meeting with the opposition". This is all part of the appeal for him and he relishes the chance to employ a bit of "psychology", in fact, I'd say he loves this aspect of speedway, particularly as he freely admits he always "loathes being beaten". With the referees, he views it as part of his role as a manager to "constantly question their decisions", often as a form of gamesmanship, particularly "after you've noticed they've made a mistake". He believes that you should also question their decisions even if they haven't actually made a mistake, just to keep them on their toes. Generally Trevor is keen to get the official's attention during any meeting, just in case it has a minor influence on their present or future decision-making. Not that he fails to appreciate the referee's value to the sport, "we have a really nice bunch of refs; though some of them are ageing a bit so we're having a bit of a transition to younger ones, and we've even got some women referees nowadays which wouldn't have happened in the past". He appreciates them as people and for the responsibilities they fulfil. Always mischievous, Trevor then affectionately mentions Tony Steele, by common consent the best speedway referee of his generation and still a comparatively youthful 49 (at that point), "I bet you didn't know that he used to be a start marshal here!" I think we all know that this previous employment at Peterborough wouldn't ever affect Tony's impartiality as a match official.

If Trevor enjoys the psychological banter with referees he enjoys it even more with the riders, particularly those from the opposition. Eastbourne's experienced Dean 'Deano' Barker bounds over to where we're stood by the track safety fence, in order to theatrically gesture at the track, before he asks in a mock outraged but distinctive London accent, "as a captain I have to ask – what is that out there?" Trevor smiles broadly and delivers another trademark shrug, while Dean warms to his theme and continues with "I'll need a moto-cross bike out there". Trevor laughs some more and offers to lend him one "from the truck".

Dean is also keen to indulge in a bit of pre-meeting psychology himself, and so nods over to the veteran Sam Ermolenko who has just climbed from his van and loudly calls out, "how's yer eyes, then?" It's a none-too-subtle reference to the recent injury sustained by David Howe at Peterborough, who was controversially, if you believe some accounts, rather hypocritically and deliberately taken off by Sam[2]. Sam either doesn't hear Deano or deliberately ignores him but Trevor will not let this slight or the implication of hypocrisy against his rider rest for a moment, and he staunchly defends Sam with a lengthy and believable explanation of "the incident" in question. At the outset of his explanation, Trevor shrewdly appeals to Deano's longevity in the sport when he highlights, "Sam has years of experience, you know what he's like to race against Dean, and how he leaves room". He follows this introduction with a lengthy and detailed description of the build up to the incident, before he closes his explanation with an almost lawyerly and clever rhetorical flourish that again appeals to Dean's own experience, "he went on the outside, you know you can't do that, and then hit the fence". The very confident and chatty Dean then leaves, after having agreed with Trevor that he'd suffered a misapprehension of events based on inaccurately reported comments. If Trevor's happy to have put the record straight on behalf of Sam ("always a pleasure to deal with and a gentleman") he's even happier with his "earlier bit of psychology with Deano". Trevor smiles broadly at his own cunning and laughingly notes that his 'blokes together discussing the world' mateyness with Deano about tonight's track conditions has ensured, and laughingly notes, " that the track'll definitely have him beaten now!"

Something Trevor does have the odd quibble with is the present version of the regulations that appear in the latest SCB rulebook, which "are so complex nowadays that no one understands them, that's God's honest truth" before, he slightly contradicts himself, when he notes that the regulations are "there for the safety of the sport". An improvement that Trevor massively favours is the air safety fence, "it's a godsend as it cushions the impact" though he worries that, in some of the riders, it "inspires a false sense of security". He believes it should be mandatory equipment in all the leagues but this is unlikely to happen on account of the sheer cost. At Peterborough the price came in at close to £50,000. The size of this figure is partly because the EOES has such a large track, and its circumference thereby requires a large amount of pipes and connectors, but also because the costs are inflated (no pun intended) by the maintenance it requires each week. In total it takes six hours to put up, inflate and secure the air fence and another six hours to take down again after every meeting, which is a huge amount of additional faff and hassle that many tracks cannot afford.

Trevor is confident that his riders have started to gel together well as a team and, with the improved results, they have noticed the impact at the Showground where "crowds are slowly on the increase with returnees and new people". This renewed interest leads him to be, "optimistic that the sport is on the up, with Sky Sports helping big time" to draw speedway to the attention of a "wider audience". Also when Trevor's out and about his increased notoriety through the television coverage has the unexpected benefit that people stop him in the street to discuss recent meetings or the sport in general. Though he claims that this increased attention "just goes with the territory", I suspect it's something that he secretly really enjoys. He's quick to praise the professionalism of "the Sky people" and makes no attempt to conceal that he's delighted that his duties include interviews with the attractive Sky Sports presenter, Sophie Blake. Though Trevor admits his admiration for Sophie can be a bit of a distraction sometimes, especially on live television as he, "can't help but stare".

This increased television exposure has inadvertently given Trevor an insight into the demands of live broadcasts but has also made him an authority on the ways and presentational techniques of the tabloid print media. Since I honestly answered "no" to his enquiry, "did you see her [Sophie Blake] with her kit off in *Nuts*?" I had to rely on his superior insight into the photos themselves because, according to Trevor, "they'd definitely been airbrushed" by the *Nuts* magazine staff since Sophie "didn't have the mole on her breast you can see when she's interviewing you"[3]. Moles aside, which Trevor would apparently recognise anywhere, the semi-naked photos of Sophie had caused quite a stir in speedway circles,

---

[2] I believe Deano refers to the fact that Sam is an evangelical and repeated advocate of the necessity of "fair riding" in speedway races, both in the press and on television. He is often keen and particularly prone to identify Eastbourne's combative Nicki Pedersen as the specific object of his criticism and frequently leaves the viewer/reader in no doubt that he views Nicki as the most unacceptably 'dirty' rider of his generation. However, when other riders execute similar 'hard' riding manoeuvres, Sam is, in these instances, often silent, muted or less trenchant, and prefers to characterise these incidents as 'old-fashioned hard riding'.

particularly when their publication coincided with the 2005 British Grand Prix round in Cardiff ("she's got her head screwed on, that girl"). We couldn't stand around talking moles, breasts and attractive naked women any longer, as Trevor had a team to get off and manage his team! Albeit one that was highly unlikely to ride that evening, since the first heavy drops of a torrential downpour had just started to fall.

Everyone immediately rushed to shelter under the covered riders' area in the pits, and thereby caused an instant crush around the tea urn where Neil Watson loudly lamented the "big, big hit" that the cancellation of this fixture would financially cause the club. "It's a disaster," Neil grumbled before he paused to add, "what with all the variable costs such as wages and the like that kill you once it gets to this stage". I'm able to stop my intrusion into his financial grief after he kindly breaks off from his chagrin to take the time to introduce me to "one of speedway's unique figures" the Peterborough Panthers resident club chaplain, the Reverend Michael Whawell. My own ignorance aside, Michael very politely coped with my evident surprise at such an encounter with a man of the cloth outside of church and at work in a formal capacity at a speedway meeting. I quickly learn that many sports have active sports chaplains, even my beloved Sunderland Association Football Club, and in speedway a number of clubs call on the services of the Almighty's spokespeople on a regular or ad-hoc basis at their meetings. Oxford has a chaplain and on the basis of this season's frequent team changes, God must have a wicked sense of humour. Though, admittedly, the Oxford chaplain is one of the few staff at the club not to have been given a run out on the track this season in their season of continuous team changes. Back in the pits at Peterborough, Michael had an easy charm, was very humane and engaging company with a real, infectious love of the sport – that began for him when his grandfather took him to watch Poole in 1950. If he can ever be accused of a partisan outlook or bias at all, Michael admits that he always loves the track that is nearest to wherever his home happens to be at the time, particularly since he has often travelled around the country with his work. Michael has always relished the thrill, excitement and gladiatorial nature of the sport, "speedway has simplicity and even a purity of format which is not found elsewhere in contemporary sport". Most of all though he appreciates the "great characters – riders, promoters, staff, fans and journalists – that I have been privileged to meet, few sports can present such variety and richness of characters". Away from his work, where he ministers and preaches to parishioners or offers pastoral care, Michael is a lover of life, literature and marathon running, 12 so far; plus, he's also Chaplain to the Veteran Speedway Riders Association.[4]

By now the rain falls heavily around us as we talk, already most of the Eastbourne and Peterborough riders have left, and the pits area has emptied of men and machines as quickly as it filled up earlier. Sam Ermolenko's mechanic slowly loads his van while Sam remains under cover to hold court. He noticeably counterpoints his flow of words in a welter of smiles and expressive gestures with a gaggle of young female admirers gathered around him, one of whom rather adoringly sits on his legs while clasped, limpet like, around his neck and shoulders. Perhaps not the best time to introduce myself although Sam is extremely friendly and jovial, he introduces the young woman as his daughter before he retracts that straightaway to loud laughter from them both. Sam listens interestedly, we chat about his autobiography (which I enjoyed), he asks some perceptive questions and says he'd only be too happy to meet with me another time provided that my book "isn't being negative about the sport". He's courteous and, speaking as you find, a fantastic ambassador for the sport as

[3] Solely in the interests of research, later in the year I bought the 'biggest ever issue' Nuts Special Edition to check for moles in the '100 Sexiest British Babes!' feature. Sophie was placed at 87. As if to confirm how media savvy Sophie is (or how good the Sky Sports publicist is), she appeared much more modestly, albeit almost topless, 13 days before the 2006 Cardiff GP in the News of the World. I'm not sure if Trevor caught up with this more sophisticated photo, which was headlined 'What a Sky-ful! Speedway Girl Sophie shows her tight bends'. We learnt that she is single, aged 33, her love life is "stalled" but she remains on the lookout for a "cute guy". However, she does have a 5 year contract to present the speedway. That weekend The Observer published an action shot from the 1981 Wembley World Championship Final entitled 'Speedway's final flourish', which is part of their intermittent feature 'Parting Shot: moments in sport that signalled the end - not the beginning'. May be the ongoing BSI Speedway GP success story has yet to properly percolate through to this sports department yet?

[4] In this capacity he delivered an incredibly moving memorial address, to a congregation formed of family, friends and attendees from the V.S.R.A. It was 'A Service of Thanksgiving' on the occasion of the 40th anniversary of the death of Peter Craven held at Liverpool Cathedral in 2003. It is a sermon that any summary I attempt could not begin to do justice to Michael's elegant, moving and evocative use of language in memory of Peter Craven. I remain hopeful that I can, with others, persuade Michael to overcome his characteristic modesty to actually publish it and make it available for a wider audience to be provoked and moved by. It is a work that simultaneously offers subtle insight into what makes speedway so great as a sport but also how it resonantly echoes with life in all its variations and, of course, its essential connection to the work of the Lord.

you could possibly hope to meet. He kindly invites me to come over to "meet at my workshop, you can try my atmosphere and see my environment" while he remains curious and apparently sincere throughout our conversation. Sam's interest and charm are a credit to his parents, his country and the sport. I leave the EOES in heavy rain; delighted with the warmth of reception I received from everyone and especially chuffed to have just met Sam, an ex-world champion in this great sport who repeatedly called me, as I imagine he does with everyone, "buddy". I can't wait to take up Neil Watson's kind invitation to return "at any time you like in the future to Peterborough" and, when I eventually do, if the racing is anything like the people it'll definitely be something to remember.

29th June Peterborough v. Eastbourne (Elite League A) postponed rain

Chapter 15: Down Memory Lane at Smallmead

11th July Reading v. Edinburgh

SKY CHATTER

"He's got Nicki Pedersen – the most ruthless rider on the planet – behind him" David Norris

RANDOM SCB RULES

14.9.2 [Referee's during the meeting can] refuse access, either in person or by telephone from any Competitor or Official, subject to reasonable communication being granted to the Clerk of the Course and Team Managers

The postal address of the Reading Racers' track – Smallmead Stadium, their home base since 1975 – is nowadays given as the A33 Relief Road, Reading, Berks RG3 0JL. It's a peculiar address since, I believe, it always used to be known as Bennett Road, Smallmead, Reading. Nonetheless, it's an address that reflects the slightly forgotten atmosphere and position of the stadium itself in this part of Reading. It is, arguably, the most emblematic of all the active British tracks if viewed as a manifestation of the many changes that have affected perceptions of speedway in recent decades. There have, of course, been on-off plans for quite a few years to relocate the stadium to another council-designated site just down the road from its present location. The latest iteration of these intentions has the team scheduled to move into their new facilities in 2007. The council, like the promoter Pat Bliss, are keen to get on with the move provided it doesn't disrupt any fixtures during the season. In the meantime, the stadium lingers in regal decline since it mainly stages Greyhound Racing although Monday night speedway for the Reading Racers still remains, to my mind, its true activity.

You can't help but think like this if you started to watch speedway, like I did, around the same time that Smallmead was built and opened with some fanfare as the brand new stadium and home of the Reading Racers. To step through the gates is to see it almost exactly as it was then, only older and shabbier like a close friend who's taken to drink, let themselves go a bit but still affects to have the beauty and confidence of their youth. Apart from the back-straight stand that has been closed for a while now due to safety reasons, the stadium (dare I say it) looks a bit flasher than it did only a few years ago. Particularly since it has benefited from some basic maintenance, redecoration and work to ensure that the majority of floodlights do actually work, so that the action on the track, during the dark evenings, remains a spectacle for the fans that you can actually make out rather than almost make out in the gloom. The track itself isn't quite as I remember it – well its shape and location appears roughly the same and it is still separated from the fans since it runs inside the dog track. However, there's the bend 1 dip that I honestly don't recall from 1975 and, most importantly, there is a basic lack of the shale I vividly remember getting sprayed by on the second bend every week (in an age before dirt deflectors). If you ignore the deterioration of the fabric of the stadium and the decrepit interior layout nonetheless, every time I visit, I continue to find these environs reassuringly comfortable – in a way that always makes it feel like the only proper speedway track in existence and always like I've come 'home'. The whole place now appears to come from a bygone era and a time of greater simplicity. It's reassuringly mostly all still there, just as it was, just a bit more careworn as it definitely shows its age. The lengthy home-straight stand with its covered outdoor terraced seats, the bar/refreshment area with inside seats at Formica tables by the windows is all as it once was. Only shabbier. You can still stand on the grass banks of the bends, above the cinder path by the low perimeter wall of the greyhound track, or wander round to your own ideal viewing position or rest against the breeze blocks which form the painted wall that mark the boundary of the stadium. You can even still spend the evening by the fence that overlooks the pits close by to where the riders arrive through the pit gates onto the track. All that is closed is the back-straight grandstand, which looms large like a darkened and decayed memorial to a more glorious era of Reading Racers' speedway.

After your vision, they say your smell and hearing are the last senses to go when you die; in which case, God must be a speedway fan as these are the key senses you engage at each and every meeting. There's the throaty roar of the bikes allied to the exhilaration, speed and spectacle of the racing itself as well as, inevitably, the distinctive bouquet and aroma of the methanol that fuels these powerful machines. Everyone I quizzed about their earliest memories of the sport and its appeal to them will, usually, emphasise the thrill of the racing but also then quickly mention how evocative they find the smell and the noise. Someone has even confessed to me (or is that gave me the business opportunity of a lifetime?), "I know it sounds weird but if they could only bottle that smell as a perfume or eau de cologne, I'd definitely buy it." Reading Speedway, like tracks everywhere, has always had these smells but, also, had the added bonus of the strong scent of hops from the fermentation processes of the nearby Courage brewery as well as the distinctive wafts that emanate from the adjacent sewage works.

I still find all these smells as an evocative and significant part of the track's particular history and heritage. Especially its light industrial heritage since it was definitely a development of its time. The social engineering project that dictated Reading Borough Council policy of that era ensured that the stadium was rebuilt in an industrial estate, on the site of a council refuse tip in fact, when it moved from its previous home in the increasingly residential area of Tilehurst. Inevitably, Smallmead looks an archetypal stadium of its time and was quickly built with the materials of its era, most notably the concrete blocks that form the perimeter wall. It took its place as another new facility in an area already dominated with a variety of other red-brick factories and factory offices that housed local firms and multinational manufacturing businesses like Gillette. It was a stadium deliberately located in an area that was designed to constantly change and gradually renew itself, particularly through the wholehearted embrace given to the new materials of prefabrication along with the new fangled modern practices of manufacture and management. It also existed in a more innocent period before the dramatic impact of the 'Thatcher Revolution', with its savage labour law changes and the rapid decline of the trade union movement. The whole area, both the industrial estate and the Berkshire County town that was Reading itself, had yet to develop in a way that denied its past and gave full reign to its material aspirations and pretensions. The arrival of the speedway in a new stadium in this part of the city was a palpable and instant success with the crowds, drawn from the local area and beyond, which indicated an optimism in the future of the sport and society as well as limited entertainment options, that was in its enthusiasm oblivious to being precariously balanced on the cusp of the many cataclysmic and cultural changes that would dramatically reshape the fabric of our society.

The city of Reading itself was one of many nearby towns, along with Bracknell, Newbury and Wokingham among others in the area, which benefited from their comparative proximity to the burgeoning expansion of Heathrow Airport and the M4 motorway. The visible consequences of this proximity were the acres of nearby offices and myriad industrial estates that rapidly sprang up. Modern businesses – like technology, banking and communications companies – were typically the type of 'new industries' attracted to locate their offices in this part of the Thames Valley, so much so that this part of the M4 corridor soon became dubbed the UK's 'silicon valley'. These rapid changes, allied to a general gentrification of the town and the surrounding countryside, realised huge pent-up demand for work and leisure activities, which historically could not be satisfied by Reading Football Club's traditional struggles or Berkshire's involvement in minor county cricket. Ultimately the modern demand for innovation, excitement and engagement in the leisure pursuits we choose to spend our valuable but limited leisure time on sadly passed Reading Speedway by, along with the rest of the speedway in this country. The surge in demand for varied entertainment and the rise of the affluent but discriminating consumer is reflected in the complete redesign of the roads and area that surrounds Smallmead over recent years. The stadium now looks forlorn, out of place and totally incongruous in relation to all the other buildings in its neighbourhood. Though, personally, I find this part of its charm and appeal, there's no doubt that most modern consumers will invariably be put off by its appearance.

In Reading, we now have a preponderance of out of town shopping malls for the more affluent inhabitants who, no doubt, work at the many nearby 'big-box' developments or the modern state-of-the-art buildings that surround Smallmead. Another long-time business resident of the area – Courage's Brewery – has grown and moved with the times to the extent that they have built futuristic silver silos, which are easily visible from the stadium and the motorway. Even the notoriously down-at-heel and under-achieving Reading Football Club has reinvented itself for the 21st century with the club's

---

[1] Admittedly, this is really only due to the drive, ambition and strategic vision of John Madejski, Reading FC's millionaire fan and benefactor. He is an immigrant businessman who, ironically, made his considerable fortune through his management of a newspaper business with a practical, almost speedway, ethos. It was an empire that included *Auto Trader* magazine along with many other comparatively unknown but very lucrative and profitable brands.

relocation to the hotel, conference and dual-use entertainment complex of the very contemporary Madejski Stadium[1]. This development has, arguably, had the biggest impact on the Smallmead Stadium owners. Since it visibly heightens the sharp contrast between wealth of the new-found fervent Royals supporters and season ticket holders who regularly attend the football in comparison to the loyal but dwindling band of fans enticed by the lure of the greyhounds or the speedway. The status of Smallmead as the poor relation of the neighbourhood is magnified every match day throughout the soccer season, when the open but derelict space of the wasteland like car park outside the stadium attracts 3,500 prepared to pay £5 each to use these extremely basic facilities. These temporary customers, who don't even enter the stadium, generate considerable revenues in comparison to that raised when the stadium owners stage any greyhound meeting, never mind what they can expect to raise through the turnstiles nowadays from a Monday night speedway fixture. Sadly, this is closest the speedway club any longer gets to attracting the average gate of 6,000 people that once swarmed to the club in its heyday. In the late 1970s, it was even necessary to arrive an hour early to try to reserve your usual place from which to worship at this hallowed temple of speedway.

While the speedway club doesn't have a Madejski-style benefactor, it still continues a family tradition that arguably typifies the sport of speedway and its traditional values. In point of fact, the Racers are part of a family dynasty that has passed on the joy and the burden of club promotion at Reading from her late father, the pipe-smoking Bill Dore, to his daughter Pat Bliss. She has been a promoter at the club for nearly 26 years, which, Pat informs me, is presently "longer than any other British promoter at a single track."

It's a scorching hot day when I arrive at the stadium, a few hours before the official start time for that night's encounter with the Edinburgh Monarchs. Pat has kindly agreed to meet with me to briefly discuss all things Reading Speedway. Unfortunately, upon my arrival she's slightly delayed by news, from a very hot and harassed member of the track staff, who reports that the "water's packed up" which he suggests, in colourful language, is due to lack of care for the stadium bowser. It's all part and parcel of the multiple details and pressure on your time that defines the often thankless task and art of speedway promotion. We have to put our planned chat on hold for a few minutes, while Pat resolves what she politely but euphemistically calls, "a bit of problem". Given its later impact on the meeting this is something of an understatement. Regardless of the water problem, in the blistering late afternoon summer sunshine the tractor is busily doing its rounds as it grades the dry track and it even has a brief but soon unsuccessful attempt to use the faulty bowser to douse the track. The only tank of water that remained available to the club for tonight is quickly dispersed before the tractor retreats to the pits to leave me to contemplate the scene in silence (except for the nearby passing traffic which quickly builds up to its usual congested rush-hour volume). This slight delay provides a unique chance to observe the stadium I know so well, while it's completely empty of the usual crowded bustle of staff, riders and fans. It looks a weird combination of forlorn but to my eyes, proudly resplendent when empty allbeit in a magnificently decrepit seen-much-better-times kind of way.

Mrs Bliss joins me a few minutes later by bend 4, fresh and apparently unfazed from an unsuccessful call for water to St Swithin. Some additional water supplies are still urgently needed, for tonight's fixture and the greyhound meetings throughout the week, but Pat is happy to chat amiably while others panic or, perhaps, find a much-needed solution to the problem. She says she began to help out for the club behind the bar on a Monday night many years ago before she gradually undertook a few more jobs that were required around the place, "I did every job that was on offer, everything short of actually doing some riding". She demonstrated skill and capability at these many and various tasks. The expertise she gained gradually resulted in her increased indispensability to the club and she slowly become drawn to perform more and more tasks at Reading Speedway without ever really having a conscious intention to do so. Similarly, in almost parallel fashion, Pat fell into the world of greyhounds at the stadium, and progressed through the ranks from paddock steward to announcer and, eventually in another example of mission creep, to manager of the whole thing. Despite this power and authority, Pat is very easy to talk with and appears, as with the majority of people in the sport, to be without unnecessary airs and graces. Her voice has the soft but pronounced burr of a regional rural accent, difficult to place, but most likely from her native Oxfordshire, albeit slightly altered after many years in Wiltshire.

She observes that there have been "too many changes in my time in speedway" for her to remember let alone try to mention. However, Pat requires no second invitation to fondly recall a litany of riders – from the brilliant to the loyal ("the riders we had at Reading were an incredibly loyal band, only a couple of them ever asked to leave and then usually wanted to come back!") – that will forever be fondly associated with her vivid memories of the speedway club. She name checks all the usual Reading favourites throughout the recent years and she spontaneously recalls: Bobby Schwartz, Mick Bell, John Davis, Dave Mullet, Per Jonsson, Jeremy Doncaster, and wickedly recalls how an "eminent promoter" once questioned why she continued to persevere with a very young and inexperienced Lee Richardson. This was during a time when "Lee spent more time lying on the track than riding on his bike"; Pat is delighted that his subsequent improvement and development has proved all the doubters foolish and completely wrong[2].

Pat furrows her brow anxiously as she worries about the present dearth of "young Brits" rising up through the ranks in comparison to the quantity that comes through, for example, from our traditional speedway rival nations of Denmark, Poland and Sweden. There are a number of factors that exacerbate this situation but Pat has the most concern about the lack of what, for the want of a better term, could be viewed as the present lack of a 'speedway apprenticeship'. The idea that you take your time to learn your craft and embark on a gradual progression – from the Conference League to eventually establish yourself in the Premier League before, in turn, you move onto the Elite League – which is now completely unfashionable and almost no longer happens in this country. There's a greater tendency throughout all the leagues, but especially the Elite League, for riders and promoters to chase the holy grail of quick results and instant success. The substantial financial rewards that this kind of approach can bring to the fortunate few, in terms of attracting lucrative team sponsorship, increased crowd levels and further talented riders, doesn't leave much room to nurture young, inconsistent but possibly talented riders. Inevitably, there's less patience among promoters or any real desire to persevere with the slower development of young British riders. It's invariably easier to sign, albeit often more expensive, a promising overseas prospect than grow your own. Young riders, of all nationalities, are often quickly and capriciously discarded by promoters in all the contemporary British leagues without appropriate levels of patience being shown. Not that Pat, as she admits, is exactly blameless in this respect herself. She has serially committed the cardinal sin of foreign rider recruitment and

[2] Although a great British talent, one of our few world class riders, for the early part of the 2005 season Lee spent considerable time with his many engines at the tuners and frequently complained about the impact of the lack of availability of skilled tuners instead of riding to his full potential in the Elite League or during the Grand Prix series.

frequent results-driven team changes that she complains of, which for the Racers has been compounded by the complete failure to nurture British talent by running her own Conference League team at Smallmead. She is keen to note that some promoters are much more cavalier and short term in their outlook than even herself[3]. Without these important but early slow stages of development, ambition plus the understandable pursuit of fame and fortune leads some inexperienced riders to advance beyond their limited abilities far too quickly. It can quickly dishearten the rider with inflated ambitions, as they're often woefully unprepared to consistently succeed, never mind excel, at the Elite League level. Pat stresses that this attitude also devalues the speedway product that the Elite League promoters offer to the public, "at least in Premier League we often have races where all four riders could actually win the race rather than just make up the numbers". All in all, without some substantial changes in rider development, Pat is sure that we're not going to have the structure or the patience to produce any future British World Champions. This gloomy prognosis also ignores her own personal preference for the days of the one-off final, "the way it should be done", where you won "on the night". Pat appears simultaneously sad at the lack of world-class British speedway talent and quite genuinely misty-eyed when she recollects the "on the night wins for Bruce Penhall at Wembley or Per Jonsson at Odsal". Both will always still stand out to her as, "something else, really fantastic and special."

Not that these are the only strategic concerns on the horizon for Pat. Central among her other major bugbears are the frequent changes to the SCB rulebook, during the close season and frequently after, for often spurious reasons, which exasperates her since she finds it a definite barrier for her to present the sport in the most attractive light to possible newcomers. This perpetual tinkering and regular "moving of the goalposts" along with indulgence in some unique case-by-case, often self-satisfied, decision-making often leaves you, "not knowing where you are". The sharp contrast with the dogs couldn't be more marked where, Pat notes, the rules are the rules, but then they also benefit from simplicity and total compliance from the outset; rather than the speedway equivalent of ad-hoc and piecemeal changes driven through without proper consultation by the sports governing body. Pat despairs when I recall my personal favourite example from this season – the adjudication that saw Belle Vue's Ian Thomas lose an appeal against an unwritten rule that didn't appear in the official rulebook or the subsequent amendments. Before she continues her hunt for vital supplies of water for the track in time for tonight's meeting, Pat's final concern is Sky's regular weekly televised speedway coverage of Elite

[3] As an example of the rider-development model she advocates, albeit he's not a British rider, she points to the talented Matej Zagar as someone who's been prepared to bide their time and serve their apprenticeship and stay for that vital extra season of development at Premier level to the benefit of the league, the rider himself and the chances for his potential long-term success.

League fixtures, predominantly on a Monday night. Even if you ignore the often overwhelming tendentious and completely self-interested promotion by Sky Sports television, as the exclusive British holder to the live televisual rights, of the Grand Prix Series as the so-called pinnacle of achievement within the sport. Pat still despairs that the live televised coverage of league racing is "killing the sport of speedway in this country". She notes that Premier League crowds continue on a general downward trend while, as a long-time Monday night track in existence long before the contract negotiated by Terry Russell, Reading also suffers from a fall in crowd numbers. It's a trend, which is especially pronounced if there's an attractive televised fixture or, if the often unsettled weather of a British summer, means that people will prefer certainty and stay in, rather than risk the potentially wasted journey to the track. You can easily understand why this state of affairs might irk her and frost Pat's Friday.

It's still really baking and the fans have begun to fill up some parts of the stadium, these fans include 39 from my favourite supporters' club, that of the Edinburgh Monarchs, who have already made themselves at home in their traditional place by the pits on the third bend. They're mid-way on their 'Southern Tour' happily ensconced, as for many years, at the Blunsden Hotel in Swindon. The hotel has been the regular touring base for the itinerant Monarchs' fans for so long that they get a special rate on their annual group booking. They appreciate the high standard of the facilities, because it provides a slightly luxurious home away from home for them. According to the amiable Mike Hunter, one of the directors of the club and long-standing home-meeting reporter for the Monarchs in the *Speedway Star*, "it's very comfortable and they look after us well". From the relative shade of the bar, the ever-affable and incredibly well-informed Mike bemoans the Monarchs' team's weakness, since they have recently been "decimated by injury" with Kristian Lund ("not a good choice") brought in to replace the popular Ross Brady. Apparently much will depend on the performance of Cameron Woodward, who "can be very inconsistent." Ever the pessimist, Mike talked down the visitor's chances of an away victory, despite the continued absence through injury of the talented Danny Bird from the Racers' line up, and was keen to highlight to me that, "we'll be seeing our tacky subs this evening."

The 'Southern Tour', so far, has already taken in the meetings at Stoke and Oxford and tonight's fixture with Reading will be followed by visits to the Isle of Wight as well as Poole (by a narrow vote instead of the alternative but much less popular choice of Wimbledon v Armadale). Later the personable Gary Lough, one of the many knowledgeable Monarchs' fans on this trip, informs me that he only pays a bargain rate of £250 for all his travel and accommodation, when he shares a room, for the whole week. For most of the pre-race build up, since he suffers from extreme sensitivity to the sun's rays (even in Scotland!) he's slavered in sun cream and shelters in the sauna-like shade of the main grandstand. Temporarily without their esteemed author in their midst[4], the remainder of the Edinburgh supporters are a happy bunch who relentlessly banter with each other while they display a selection of apparently home-made flags, hung nearby on the pits fence and adjacent wall to let the Reading fans around them know that they're there. Not that it's exactly easy to miss a large group of pale-skinned strangers at Smallmead who speak in, to the untrained ear, broad Scots accents! It's fun to sit on this bend, glance in the pits, while you casually listen to the visitors' many impressions of Smallmead and how the evening might unfold. The fans include Ella MacDonald[5] who first watched Edinburgh in 1963, when she was a teenager at a "loose end one evening", so for fun she went along to the speedway with friends and has been hooked ever since. She stands close to Dennis Darling ("what he doesn't know about speedway isn't worth knowing") who's attended since 1949, when he was aged two and a half. Not that he remembers it, though his earliest memory is from two years later 1951. When he vividly recalls an image of Jack Young circling Meadowbank Stadium on a carriage pulled by a pair of horses, as he held the World Championship trophy aloft. He further illustrates his deserved reputation for an encyclopaedic knowledge of speedway, when he casually mentions that Jack Young "is the only Division 2 rider to ever win it!" He then playfully grabs Ella's shoulders and says, "and this is the original track spare, make sure you put that in your book", before he quickly retreats to avoid being thumped by Ella.

[4] Gary's book is an enjoyable account of Edinburgh's victorious 2003 Premier League championship season called *10th yer baws!*

[5] Who organises the supporters' club coach trips to home meetings and some selected away fixtures but who doesn't actually organise the 'Southern Tour' coach trip.

The track staff admire the handiwork of the firemen. © Jeff Scott

A rare sighting a fire engine at speedway. © Jeff Scott

Tractor at dusk and at speed. © Jeff Scott

A voice on the tannoy announces that, "there will be a short delay to the start of the meeting", due to the need to water the track, which it's stressed is primarily because of concerns for "rider safety". A few moments later we're treated to the rather unusual sight, at a speedway fixture, of the rather tentative arrival on the track of the second emergency service (along with the ambulance already in situ) to visit the stadium this evening, namely the local Fire Brigade. It's a sight greeted with disdain and derision by the Monarchs' fans as well as an "Ooh, look Ella, men in uniform!" By now, the track area has become impressively crowded with an array of vehicles that include speedway bikes, a tractor, an ambulance and, now, a fire engine. To sarcastic applause and ironic cheers, the fireman begin to painstakingly water the whole track for which they use their rather less than impressive hose. On a normal summer's day, most tracks will inevitably drink up the water as quickly as blotting paper absorbs ink but, after the sweltering day we've had, prospects look even less promising for the fireman, other than for cosmetic effect. After this probably pointless task is slowly and thoroughly completed, we're then treated to the reappearance of the meeting referee. The official in charge of this fixture is the quixotic but experienced Frank Ebdon – notoriously, he of the 'lightning finger' when it comes to the swift running of any meeting – who diligently inspects the Fire Brigade's handiwork. Dressed immaculately in jacket, shirt and tie set off with smart black shoes but without the what Frank calls his trademark "modest, slim handle-less document case (£4.99)" he favoured for his initial inspection. It's a look that has gradually fallen from general favour in our modern casual-wear society, never mind in the messier environment inevitably found at speedway stadiums on the track or in the pits area. The Edinburgh fans loudly question the age and provenance of his attire. He studiously ignores their claims that he's never changed his clothes in all his years as a referee and, despite their jeers, he still manages to deport himself with a confident almost aloof demeanour, while he apparently wears the loss adjuster look just as it was once frequently portrayed in the 1970s throughout the Kay's catalogue. Frank amuses the crowd as he gingerly picks his way from dry patch to wet patch on the track, which he theatrically prods every few yards with a delicate scrunching motion from his right foot. All the while he looks visibly irked and annoyed, it's an irritation that manifests itself in a Kenneth Williamsesque manner that appears to mix part mime and part pantomime. In an elegant fashion, he displays those smart dress shoes that he appears to favour as his footwear of choice at speedway meetings, while he slowly continues up the back straight and grinds the surface in a studious but desultory manner. Finally satisfied with track conditions, Frank then rapidly retreats with short, quick steps to the referee's box, perched above the slightly dilapidated home-straight grandstand, no doubt to be reunited with his executive briefcase. His demeanour throughout this performance definitely communicates a slightly authoritarian and rather bank managerly approach to interpersonal relations of the 'don't speak unless you're spoken to' school of thought.

The bored but boisterous Monarchs' fans indulge in yet another quick burst of "why are we waiting?" accompanied by some ostentatious consultation of their watches, just before the sound of the first two-minute warning of the meeting, finally summons the riders for the first race to take to the track at around 8 p.m. In a bizarre moment, totally in keeping with the fixture so far, the tractor also takes to the track for a brief spot of very last-minute grading, only to finally stop with this task half completed when wilfully obstructed by the riders already at the line. Inevitably after all this prevarication and delay, the lifting mechanism of the start tapes is on the blink, and thereby causes the tapes to rise in an incorrect and uneven manner. Attempts at repair of said equipment are quickly made without any real sign of success. After much fiddling about and a collective scratch of puzzled brows by the track staff, the referee bows to the logic of unforeseen circumstance that apparently dictates tonight's meeting, when he decides to use 'green light start system' throughout to resolve the situation. The meeting then starts again, 45 minutes late, but Edinburgh riders adapt to the delays, and the enforced change to start procedures, with equanimity and some aplomb when they quickly storm into the lead. By heat 6, they're already 12 points ahead, though they have benefited from Reading tracking Jamie Westacott as a replacement rider for Bird at Number 1. The Edinburgh riders have also shown a much greater facility from the 'green light' starts, albeit a bit suspiciously at times, which Frank – the notoriously pernickety referee – strangely doesn't initially query. However, in a pleasantly surreal turn of events, the Racers' 'Sam' Simota is then excluded when he is deemed to have touched the tapes. It has to be remembered that these are tapes that no longer exist in the usual corporeal sense because, physically, they are already absent. Nonetheless, Simota has to start his race with the addition of a 15-metre handicap, for his tapes exclusion, in what turns out to be the pivotal race of the meeting (heat 6), after which Edinburgh never relinquish their lead.

The Monarchs' fans are well used to defeat being snatched from the jaws of victory on away trips (most recently at Newcastle, Stoke and Sheffield), so show little premature excitement at this positive turn of events. Except, of course, for the traditional exhortations of "go on Daniel" and, to illustrate the impact technology has on the contemporary era, the silent earnest, Morse code like, frequent taps of text message updates of the score to the Monarchs' online results service. An unintended bonus of Reading's poor home meeting form this century has, from the totally disinterested speedway spectator's point of view, been the opportunity to witness a large number of very closely contested meetings. This propensity for close meetings was especially pronounced during the extended anni horribili of 2000 and 2001. Tonight's fixture is another fine example of the genre, since the Reading Racers' team indulge in a fight back that, you just know as a long-suffering Racers' fan, is never quite going to succeed. Not that you completely know that this is definitely another defeat until the final heat has been raced. The Reading Racers are a team that often keep you in a state of prolonged and heightened uncertainty, since you always optimistically anticipate an unlikely but successful recovery, before they finally dash these hopes.

The *Evening Post* mascot – a lion that supports the Racers – clearly isn't happy or impressed at the turn of events on the track. It's quite an achievement to communicate this level of displeasure when ostensibly you are officially employed to delight the children with frequent gift showers of violently flung sweets. Except tonight, the mascot doesn't wear his habitual Monday evening attire of a lion suit but instead wears a glum face. Hopefully it's a sensible and maturely taken decision brought on by tonight's sauna-like conditions but, then again, definitely not if it's another minor example of how the encroaching mania for health and safety regulations have slowly killed off quirky but vital facets of traditional British life. In this case, the freedom to dress up in American-style mascot uniforms! The costumeless Lion happily shares the sweets with the Monarchs' fans, while he morosely remarks sotto voce, "John Cleese couldn't have scripted this farce tonight any better!"

The band of Monarchs' fans become more loudly ecstatic with each passing race, though they're completely surrounded by quiet Racers' fans who go about their defeat stoically albeit with scowls; in that friendly, live-and-let-live manner that characterises all speedway crowds. The Monarchs' fans amuse themselves and signal their derision, at some lax interpretations of the two-minute time allowance rule – to the repeated benefit of the home side – by pointedly counting down the arrival of each missing Reading rider onto the track. The 'extra' time is all to no avail and the delight of the Monarchs' fans is infectious and communicates itself to their riders. Lund shakes his fist in celebration as he passes the gaggle of celebrating Monarchs' fans after he wins heat 11. Only to immediately have an engine failure, as his celebration lap continues, which results in a long trudge back to the pits while cries of "Kristian, Kristian, give us a wave" greet his return. When the Edinburgh fans again helpfully conduct a loud countdown of the two-minute time allowance to zero in heat 12, the announcer is moved to react and he intones, incorrectly, "10 seconds left". The fixture ends with an array of giddy and peculiar dances from the Edinburgh fans to the musical theme of 'Is this the way to Amarillo?' They then accompany this with chants of "2-4-6-8 who do we appreciate? M-O-N-A-R-C-H-S", which they loudly use throughout to rather ebulliently greet the Edinburgh riders' very enthusiastically celebrated victory parade. Afterwards, in the bar again, a now cheery Mike Hunter claims, "you brought us luck" before he adds, "there were so many fiascos tonight it would be difficult to list them". Despite these hiccups and the home defeat the faithful Racers' fans will return next week for another evening's rich entertainment at the lovely, dilapidated but always wonderfully special Smallmead!

11th July Reading v. Edinburgh (Premier League) 46-47

Chapter 16: Big Track on a Small Island
12th July Isle of Wight v. Edinburgh

"You could write a book of antidotes" Kelvin Tatum

RANDOM SCB RULES

7.4.2 A rider having been the subject of a Transfer (except where it is requested by the Rider) shall receive a proportion of the transfer fee, subject to being under agreement to the transferring Promotion for a minimum of 8 months, of 10% plus 2.5% for each previous 8 months of continuous service

The trip to the Isle of Wight, by ferry from Portsmouth, has to be one of the most exotic journeys you can go on to watch British speedway. There's a real sense of departure coupled with an atmosphere of promise and excitement as the boat leaves the mainland for the Island. This atmosphere is enhanced by the superb mid-afternoon sunshine that shimmers on the water as the ferry heads away from the shore. There's a choice of Wightlink ferries – either the modern FastCat or the slightly more sedate but surprisingly luxurious car ferry. I've met up with Dave Pavitt, co-promoter of Isle of Wight speedway for the journey over to the stadium. Dave is a straightforward, plainly spoken Londoner who's been involved in speedway in some capacity for as long as he can remember, which includes the last 24 years as a promoter. The ferry journey is something he's done hundreds of times to the Island but is clearly something he takes pride in and still relishes, "but for Portsmouth on the coastline, on a sunny day like today you wouldn't know you weren't in the Caribbean!" says Dave as he gestures expansively at the glittering sea view.

I've eagerly anticipated my trip, especially the chance to experience some speedway action on the Island, particularly as it's the second longest track in the country (three yards shorter than Exeter) and where the racing has a reputation as full on and full throttle.

On the journey I hope to learn more about the organisation of this unique club from Dave. It is different from the normal run-of-the-mill speedway set up, since it has a distinctive management structure that results from its public ownership by 120 different shareholders, that trades under the name 'Island Speedway (IOW) Limited'. The collective approach taken to ownership and decision making means that many of the investors-cum-fans have a much closer relationship and direct input into the policies and practices of the organisation. Their responsibilities include the election of the five-person board that supervises the practical running of the speedway club on a day-to-day basis. Not that the club finds it any easier to survive or adapt to the challenge of the present economic climate with contemporary British speedway. The attendances at the club vary dramatically from the 'hard core' of around 300 to "double, treble, quadruple that" at the height of the summer or during half term when they can attract large numbers of 'casual' visitors to the track. People notice the adverts for the speedway placed in popular tourist locations and, according to Dave, come along, "because they're stuck on the Island and there's not a lot else going on here, on a Tuesday night". Throughout the year the club also have attractive promotions for kids and pride themselves on their friendly welcome and the family atmosphere.

Dave has been at the club since he was approached to run it in 1998; it was a time when they had a big need for an "experienced licensed speedway promoter". Nowadays, along with co-promoter Martin 'Mad Dog' Newnham, they stage a whole variety of events at Smallbrook Stadium to ensure that the speedway club survives. These range from motorcycle rallies that feature other types of bikes and sidecars to the use of the club buildings and facilities for birthday celebrations. There's also a gym at the stadium as well as a cricket pitch (although I doubt that this feature exactly raises much money) plus some accommodation facilities for their riders. I discover that Steen Jensen, Tomas Suchanek and Jason Doyle all actually live at the stadium in good-sized caravans and also have use of the onsite workshop amenities. The track is run "for the people, by the people" in Dave's eyes and there's "respect for the riders and everyone else involved at the club". Work is undertaken on the track all year round with most of the off-season winter labour focused on the enhancement of features on or around the circuit, which recently includes the track banking and the fencing. It's a full-time job for those employed by the club along with their band of hardy volunteers. This collegiate structure is a benefit since it allows the club increased flexibility to overcome problems or find solutions to unforeseen circumstances, such as the financial crisis brought on by a summer of bad weather in 2004. In that instance, an appeal to the shareholders was able to raise the £11,000 necessary to ensure the club's survival over the previous winter by issuing 'gold bonds' or through "donations in other ways". This all-hands-to-the-pump approach isn't always possible at other more commercially oriented tracks where they have a different ownership structure nor are they able to subsidise the speedway activities with non-speedway income as is so often required at the Isle of Wight. Unfortunately, it also means that the Islanders can't directly pay their team as much as they can and do at other rival tracks. However, apart from the possibilities of using the facilities or living in a mobile home at the stadium, they "help riders privately" in other ways, which can be of overall benefit to the riders if they properly consider the complete package of accommodation, workshop facilities and actual pay. I'm sure that Dave always stresses this is the way to look at it to them!

The club also attempts to remain loyal to all their riding "assets" and each season's racing staff, despite Dave's opinion that in general "riders are very difficult" as a species to deal with. The wider needs of motorcycle sport and community are addressed through their major fundraising activity, the annual 'Smallbrook Spectacular' which is staged to generate contributions for the ACU Benevolent Fund. Their donation of all the gate receipts from this meeting makes the club, along with Len Silver's Rye House, one of the largest contributors to the fund. Dave immediately then excuses the comparatively lesser fundraising efforts on behalf of the ACU undertaken by other commercially owned speedway tracks, when he again points to the unique shareholder structure and freehold ownership on the Island that ensures their flexibility and generosity, "it's fine to do, if you own your own bars and catering".

Everyone at the club is proud to be part of the Island community, particularly since it's the biggest spectator sport on the Isle of Wight. It's a status that thereby ensures good coverage in the local press for the club, whether in the papers or on the TV and radio, which is aided by the fact that the club endeavours to work closely with the local council. This policy of active engagement and consultation worked exceptionally well when the council granted the club a 50-year lease to run on its present site, which has provided excellent stability for future plans and investment. Though the relationship is not without its frustrations, most notably when it comes to the protracted campaign to get permission for the new on-site sewage plant ("they're so slow" is the kind summary without expletives of the six-year campaign and process so far) or, another of Dave's bêtes noires, the failure of the council to erect the distinctive brown traffic signs that advise drivers of local tourist attractions.

While it's the case that the management and the team enjoy the fun and camaraderie of their away tours to other tracks in the Premier League – particular favourites being the northern outposts of Workington ("a lawless outpost"), Sheffield ("a pleasure") and Glasgow ("nice people and a nice little set up") – they invariably don't take many fans with them when they journey away from home. Dave believes that this is mostly due to the tricky logistics of transport to and from the Island, particularly the severe difficulty to get back over the water onto the Island after an evening's travel away. This reluctance to travel elsewhere is generally held by the whole community throughout the Isle of Wight. It is reflected in an atmosphere of quaintness that infects the whole place and contributes to the lingering sense that things are still a little old fashioned here, if not almost completely stuck in the past of 20 years ago. For Dave, who resides on the mainland, this is most noticeable in the slightly retro clothes still worn by fans to meetings – "there's brothel creepers, the works, jackets covered in badges", which he playfully judges to belong to a similar era as referee Frank Edbon's usual attire, "since he's still wearing the same pullover from years ago!"

However, Dave's equanimity and general bonhomie, along with his abiding affection for the Island, the Islanders and the vast majority of the loyal, hard core support of Isle of Wight speedway fans can be severely tested at times. Mostly by a "small minority" who post critical, ill-informed or intemperate comments on "the freaking Internet" who regularly undertake this test of his temper. He's happy to speak with anyone face to face who has comments, suggestions or criticisms but vehemently dislikes the bravado that the anonymity of the web brings to the opinionated, "I never read it," adds Dave unconvincingly, given how annoyed it appears to make him. In an ideal world, he would like to "lock 'em all out so they

can hear everything running smoothly but not see it". Sadly, for pragmatic and commercial reasons, Dave regrets that this is not possible. The time and energy expended in idle criticism never ceases to amaze him; recently some fans had even questioned "why there's fireworks at the end of meetings when we have no money". He shakes his head in disbelief, "it's amazing what small things they think of to get bothered about!"

After a brief journey from the port to the stadium, we arrive in Dave's air-conditioned car a very long while before the tapes go up and I'm told I can go anywhere I like or chat to anyone I like without restriction. He suggests I find him later to get a pits pass and recommends that I watch some of tonight's fixture from the centre green which gives a unique perspective on the actual races that very few people get to experience anywhere, let alone at an exceptionally fast track like Smallbrook. Dave proudly gives me a brief tour of the major facilities of the site. The guided tour starts off in the reasonably smart and modern looking main building, where we drop off his things in the administrative nerve centre of operations – his cosy office handily located right next to the large bar area. We have a brief look at the slightly spartan gym and its adjacent empty cricket pitch before we head out through the car park, past the large caravan from which Jason Doyle emerges, to the rider's workshops. I'm introduced to the riders who are already there – Steen Jensen who works on his bike, the friendly Krister Marsh who I had already met on the ferry over and Tomas, the young star for the future from the Czech Republic ("speak to him all you like as he hasn't much English yet"). We then prowl off towards the track where we meet Kia whom Dave interrogates on recent track maintenance and progress. Kia has returned to this country from Denmark to again work with Steen Jensen, both as his mechanic and as his personal mentor. He will also help out Brian Morris with the track itself as a temporary "track curator". He informs Dave that he has made considerable progress on the track since his arrival on the Island and is keen to update him fully with many intricate details, which leave both convinced that the surface will now markedly improve through the combination of Brian and Kia's skilled and conscientious curatorial efforts. Dave is pleasantly avuncular with everyone he meets, but has become more distracted since he arrived at the stadium and, shortly afterwards, leaves for his office to get on with some urgent pre-meeting preparations, though apparently well satisfied with reported progress.

Dave's departure is taken as the sign that everyone can immediately start to do their own thing once again now the boss has gone. Tomas wanders off after a few minutes and Krister zooms around the car park on some sort of mini bike while Kia, Steen and myself retreat from the bright sunshine to the comparative cool of the shade of Steen's workshop. Since I'm researching a book on speedway, Steen is instantly under the misapprehension that I'm Peter Oakes "are you the chap that I'd never heard of, who rang me up in the winter and asked lots of questions for his book and never rang back?" Unconvinced by my denial Steen checks again within five minutes whether I'm definitely not the Peter Oakes who called him, though he still appears philosophically unable to accept that it's definitely a case of mistaken identity. Kia, a long-time friend of Steen and a fellow countryman from Denmark, is in the country to help him. It's already his second visit to Britain this season, though this time he has arrived with his son, who is here to recuperate from three broken vertebrae in his back and will take the time to rest on the Island for six weeks in one of the club's caravans. A father's natural pride in his son's achievements dictates that Kia shows me some graphic photos of the impressively mangled bike his son rode when the accident happened and, as if to illustrate the relative nature of these things, Kia sincerely claims that the injury was a "lucky one". When he's at home in Denmark, Kia is usually based at Hans Nielsen's old track (Brovst) but is convinced that now he's returned to England once more, that his friend and protégé Steen will once again start to live up to his full potential as a speedway rider under his support, guidance and tutelage.

It's widely acknowledged that speedway is a sport built on confidence. With Kia's return to attend to the mechanical and mental aspects of things, Steen will be able to rest more thoroughly, go to the gym to build up his upper body strength and concentrate on the most significant aspect of his work – his performances on the track. The isolated routine of the extensive travel, the preparation of his bike for two different leagues had taken its cumulative mental and emotional toll on Steen, which was then reflected in his results. Kia hopes to build up Steen's confidence again, particularly as he has been around him "ever since his first 500cc ride". Unlike some overexcited fans on the Eastbourne Internet forum, Kia doesn't see himself as "a miracle worker" but as here to re-energise Steen's self-belief in his own skills and to rebuild his esteem. He's keen to help Steen conquer his sensitivity to and awareness of the proximity of other riders racing alongside him; it's apparently this hypersensitivity to others that enables competitors to easily defeat him, even when he has the lead. To resolve just this important aspect of his outlook would pay considerable dividends during his UK apprenticeship and should, if it works, immediately improve his performance on various tracks throughout the country. Steen goes out of his way to stress the contribution that the poor standard and preparation of the tracks he's mostly encountered so far on his travels in the Premier League, have had as a significant factor in his dramatic loss of form. Kia listens patiently but shrugs in disbelief, though he already has plans to prepare a track surface at Smallbrook that will be ideally suited to Steen's riding style. Apparently buoyed up by what he's heard, Steen heads off to the pits while Kia retreats back to the caravans to check on the recuperation of his son[1].

Around the corner from the riders' workshop area, just inside the entrance gate, is the shady but compact track shop where I find its manager, Dudley, stacking boxes with his arm in a sling due to his 'tennis elbow'. He is one of the many local shareholders in the club, a long-time fan and the club's track-shop manager, albeit his natural approach to his work is presently a little cramped by his injury. Away from the track, he works in the upholstery business and his company sponsors heat 5, which later earns him the affectionate sobriquet "cuddly Dudley" from Bryn Williams the announcer. He's had a lifelong fascination with speed, whether at the speedway track, the Grand Prix circuit through his work for McLaren or as a part-time flying instructor. This afternoon Dudley has made the journey across the water from Gosport on the car ferry, a much humbler, more sedate and much less glamorous mode of transport in comparison to those he usually enjoys in aviation or motor racing.

In Dudley's opinion, the club thrives with crowds boosted by summer visitors though the shop does well throughout the season since it sells Isle of Wight branded merchandise – such as coats, boards, badges and model riders – to the hardcore of supporters. Dudley is a big advocate of the need to inject some more razzmatazz into the presentation and spectacle of speedway in general because the casual but observant spectator can't help but notice that the sport remains

[1] In his 2005 season review, the Isle of Wight team manager Dave Croucher said of Steen, "he took time to settle, produced some of the more erratic performances of the season, but when he got it right, boy, did he do it in style".

Monarchs on parades. © Jeff Scott

Kai walks past the Islanders on parade. © Jeff Scott

Away from the tapes. © Jeff Scott

resolutely stuck in the slow lane when it comes to entertainment. He remains convinced that once people have been enticed through the turnstiles into the various stadiums dotted throughout the country that they will definitely then return, since the spectacle of the racing itself has all the speed, thrills and excitement required to tempt punters back for more. However, since the sport as a spectacle or entertainment now competes for the money and attention of an audience schooled to expect that all attractions would market and present themselves with far greater élan or pizzazz than is traditional at speedway. Dudley views the promotional efforts of the indoor Brighton Bonanza and the Cardiff Grand Prix meetings as the exceptions to this rule and as the role model for the future. Dudley stresses that as a traditionalist "I wouldn't have much time for it myself" but then he believes that the best interests of the sport allied to the need to ensure its progression and longevity definitely won't be served by appeals to the converted. After he has outlined his vision for the future, with the recent excellent weather, Dudley expects the club to attract a large crowd tonight and so has to return to busy himself with the organisation of the piles of merchandise in the track shop.

I decide to take full advantage of my licence to roam throughout the club in the hot sunshine, which gives me the chance to catch up with the friendly Dave Croucher, the club's away-team manager, while he methodically waters the track by hand with a hosepipe. Dave has extensive speedway experience gained over the many years he's been involved and his love of the sport still burns brightly within him. Prior to his involvement with Dave Pavitt on the Island, he had been instrumental in the reintroduction of speedway to London in 2001 when the Wimbledon Dons returned to Plough Lane to compete in the Conference League. This achievement particularly pleases him because the Wimbledon club name has strongly resonated within the sport as a brand, ever since speedway was introduced into this country in 1929, and Plough Lane was historically one of its most important and magnificent venues. Dave subsequently left the Dons to become an important part of the set-up at the Isle of Wight but remains proud of the work he'd done in the Capital, which subsequently, "has been carried on brilliantly by the PLC Chairman, Ian Perkin".

Our talk of Wimbledon's success at reopening leads him to quickly lament recent experiences within the sport where "more tracks seem to get closed nowadays rather than open". It's trend closely linked to precarious finances and rise of his own personal twin bêtes noires of rampant NIMBYism and the intrusion of stifling legislation. In Dave's opinion, we live in a modern world where pretty well all risk taking is slowly being eliminated or has been curtailed by a raft of often pointless rules and regulations. He believes that the modern preoccupation with health and safety has placed many traditional activities, such as speedway, increasingly under real threat. More often than not, the authorities usually "consider speedway anti-social" because of a variety of environmental factors that enraptures the true fan – whether it's the noise, the speed or the smell – but simultaneously alienates its worried neighbours. In recent years, a whole myriad of legislation changes have been introduced and these include those governing silencers, the ban on 'total loss' engines and many post-Bradford crowd safety measures to briefly name but a few of them that immediately spring into Dave's mind. It's a tightening legal and regulatory straitjacket that is increasingly unavoidable though, Dave notes, the Isle of Wight speedway club is much more fortunate than many other tracks because of its comparatively isolated location and the length of its lease. However, it's a good fortune that isn't evident elsewhere in the league, for example at Exeter and Edinburgh, where you can see the continued "low investment", a pragmatic decision in the context of increased residential demands for land or pending possible future noise complaints. In Dave's vision, the cumulative impact of a lack of finance and troubling environmental factors are a possible killer combination for the future survival and stability of the sport in this country.

The motivation behind his own concerted efforts into speedway on the Island is part of his keen desire to leave a "legacy"; it's an ideal choice since not only is it "something permanent" but it also gives a lot of pleasure to him and others. He's quick to point out that it has one additional benefit, notably "I've got my speedway to watch for as long as I want to". However, in Dave's view, not only do you get back what you put in but you're always part of that wider speedway community, "I wouldn't be standing here watering the track if I was just in it for the money!" Dave goes out of his way to celebrate and describe the many friendly people he's encountered within the speedway world. These include the genuine warmth and camaraderie generated by "the old timers involved in the Veteran Speedway Riders Association" or, the brilliance and experience of many of the people involved behind the scenes, like Alan 'Doc' Bridgett with his renowned track preparation skills ("he's a bit of a hero of mine"). It's a rich legacy that stretches throughout the country, whether it's the "smashing" people at Hull or the welcome you always get from the pits marshal at Sheffield who's worked there over 50 years; everyone plays a part! Justifiably to his mind, British speedway is renowned the world over, "if you really want to make it, you come here". When riders learn their trade in this country – as opposed to Sweden, Poland, the US or Australia – they gain unparalleled experience through the "sheer intensity of the racing season here" which thereby enables them "to get lots of riding in, on many tracks and experience a proper volume of competitive racing".

Dave's upbeat mood and assessment instantly darkens when we turn to the vexed issue of the World Wide Web, especially since the local Internet message boards about the Isle of Wight speedway and he angrily notes "it does my swede in". However, he has coined a brilliant term of disparagement when he describes these people as "keyboard commanders", a similar but harsher version of the derogatory term from American Football of 'Monday morning quarterback' used to describe armchair critics and experts. He has no time for these "embittered anoraks" that are nameless and faceless though they are nonetheless clearly a major cloud on his horizon. Dave does grudgingly concede that these people pay their admission money, that he still wants them to attend every week and are therefore ultimately more than entitled to their misguided opinions. However, while one minute he claims "I can't be bothered with them", the next his grievance results in slightly forced comparisons like, "when I pay to go and see an Andrew Lloyd Webber play I don't feel that I have the expertise so that I can tell him how to run it!" Dave finally marches off to find something other than a small hose with which to water the track some more, since its so far soaked up all the water like a sponge. I can't help but feel that these anonymous fans who moan and complain are quite well advised to continue to hide their identities from this passionate man (or from co-promoter Dave Pavitt for that matter) unless they're prepared to contribute their own time, effort and money to the continuation of this speedway club on the Isle of Wight.

On the way to the pits I clamber up the wooden stairs to the gantry-cum-viewing-platform constructed from scaffolding poles and planks that gives Ken Burnett the panoramic view he requires to film each week's action at the track. Ken is part of the funiture at Eastbourne, as a long-time supporter and archivist who also films at Arlington and at other tracks, like the Island, for his TVT2 Company. He's accompanied by his friendly and knowledgeable wife Jackie who forms the vital other half of the capable and professional team that's needed to capture each fixture on film. You often see Jackie or Ken, on his crutches, at Arlington as they rush here, there and everywhere to get that vital interview or camera angle. No matter what the weather or temperature, Jackie is a fixture as she crouches by the start line on the centre green with her film camera pointed at the riders or when she stands in all weathers on the roof of the referees box. Since he has watched and covered the sport for many years, Ken is an authority on speedway, particularly Eastbourne speedway[2]. It's an expertise that has been consolidated by his modern-day video and film work, but also from his work with fans stock of old 8 mm cine footage which he has used to compile compelling archive material from defunct (and some continuing) tracks for the Days Gone By films, which feature the racing of the 1970s and 1980s. On all these films of past and present Ken commentates in his own distinctive but inimitable manner. It's a style that caused Tony McDonald of *Backtrack* magazine to affectionately note in print, "though Ken himself might not be speedway's answer to John Motson" before he went on to stress that he makes up for this perceived presentational deficiency with boundless enthusiasm[3]. Today, however, with all the preparations required, the camera angles to adjust and given it's our first-ever proper encounter, Ken doesn't really have the time or the inclination to talk speedway since there's too much other work to be done.

After I gingerly negotiate the climb back down the steep steps from the gantry safely, it's a very short walk to the fenced-off section that forms the pits area behind the main grandstand. There's a gaggle of fans that watch from behind the fence, since by now the Monarchs' team and mechanics have arrived to begin work on their bikes and equipment, as have all the other home team's riders who aren't resident at the track. The scene the fans watch is the usual pre-meeting industrious hive of activity as everyone swings into action and bustles about to ensure everything, hopefully, goes to plan. Sadly I have missed the SCB referee, Margaret Vardy, who has already conducted her mandatory pits inspection. Independently of each other, both Daves have suggested with some pride that I watch the meeting from the centre green, particularly as it's an out-of-the-ordinary experience for any typical speedway fan. Dave Pavitt notes, "you think it looks quick from the terraces, but not many people get to see how quick it really is!" Before I can enjoy this privilege I need to "sign on" for insurance purposes with the marshal, a friendly older gentleman who kindly mentions "now you're insured, but do look out for the bikes as we don't want to make a claim or clear up the mess". Everyone who works in the pits has to be insured, as do all riders who compete in the Elite and Premier Leagues (but not the Conference League riders). Each rider has to take out a compulsory £4.50 per race insurance for every single ride they have, though it's common practice for the riders to also take out their own private insurance against 'loss of earnings' through injury. Although, if this is the case, I'm at a complete loss to understand why so many riders throughout all the Leagues rush back onto the track when, by almost any standard, they're not fully recovered from injury, unless the insurance payments are very small or they are anxious they will lose their team place if they do not quickly compete again. A case in point at tonight's meeting is the Monarchs' rider, Robert Ksiezak, about whom Krister Marsh pointedly noted, with raised eyebrows, that he had so little mobility last night at Reading that Ksiezak still needed crutches just to move around the pits. Ignoring the possible long-term damage from an early return to racing – since all riders, as a matter of professional pride, recklessly do! – Ksiezak could still ride a bike but only managed to score zero points from these six rides at Reading and the Isle of Wight. So, in the cold light of day, any level of insurance payments, if he were entitled to them, would in comparison surely have been to his financial benefit.

The pits marshal recommends that I stand on the weed and thistle covered scrubland that rises above the banked bend of turns 3 and 4. He tells me that it's the "best view in British speedway" and when I stand there I quickly realise that the banking on the final bend looks like a miniature wall of death when viewed from above. I then climb down and head back into the pits area. As I do so I finally notice the large sign attached to the fence that advertises "Dave Death Motorcycles". What a name for a company! But not the ideal psychological phrase for the riders to pass every single time they head out onto the track to race. Doubling back past this amazing advert, I cautiously pick my way across the very well watered track

---

[2] I'm very keen to read Ken's forthcoming *75 Years of Eastbourne Speedway* which is due to be published in 2006. It's been a labour of love for Ken and the collation of all the records and associated statistics has occupied many hours of research but will be an essential purchase for all keen Eagles' fans.

[3] Jon Cook suggested to me when I started my research that I would do well to speak with Ken, especially if I was particularly interested in events at Arlington ("he's really 'Mr Eastbourne', much more than me, when it comes to the history of the club").

but take good care to avoid the tractor as it passes or the mechanics as they wheel out the bikes. I stand right in the middle of the centre green, so I'm in prime position in the still warm late evening sunshine to watch the home riders pose for a team photo on the centre green, before they return to the pits to be immediately called out one-by-one to take part in the introductions and the parade of both teams by the start gate.

The whole spectacle already feels completely out of the ordinary as this perspective enables me to watch all the riders from behind as they wave to the boisterous fans in the crowded main grandstand. My sense of dislocation is instantly magnified as soon as the riders take to their bikes for some quick pre-meeting practice laps round the circuit. The length of the track itself disorientates me as I watch and, in combination with the effect of the last-bend banking, I'm tremendously excited, almost breathless, at the exhilerating beauty of the spectacle as the riders flash past at great speed. Almost immediately the riders vacate the track and retreat to the pits for some final adjustments, which gives me time to carefully choose the exact spot on the centre green from which to watch the fixture. I elect that I'll stand just behind the photographer, when he crouches down at the point the straight enters the first turn of Bend 1. From the very first race and throughout the evening, the sheer speed and power of the bikes along with the palpable determination of the riders to hit the bend first from the start gate is truly exhilarating. It's simultaneously hypnotic, fantastic and addictive. What looks congested and combative from the terraces is almost gladiatorial when viewed from this perspective inside the racetrack. The speed as they fly past me is so awesome although, it has to be noted, my attempt to watch the riders as they shoot around the track quickly leads to actual levels of dizziness that I've never previously experienced, except at the funfair, when I usually watch from a 'fixed' perspective on the terraces.

Even after just one heat, I mentally resolve that I'm going to try to become a speedway photographer if it means I'll regularly get the supreme privilege of being able to watch every meeting from this or other equally unique vantage points! Unfortunately, these dreams are almost instantly shattered as I've ignored the fact that there are already many skilful exponents of this art, who've successfully managed to keep it to themselves how great the racing looks when viewed from the centre green. Between races, when I chat to the friendly David Valentine, the official Isle of Wight photographer, I'm disillusioned to learn that the 'golden age' of speedway photography has also probably already passed. This isn't, as you'd expect, due to advances in digital technology, which has helped their work immeasurably, but due to the increased reluctance of many Elite and Premier League tracks nowadays to countenance the presence of visiting photographers unless they're officially with the rival team. Previously, as an 'Official Speedway Photographer' you could without question gain access to every track in the country irrespective of whoever raced. Unfortunately, David puts the reason for this recent change down as another example of the relentless pursuit of "money" within modern speedway. In David's opinion, the desire for profit at all costs drives yet another nail into the coffin of the charmingly old-fashioned values that used to characterise the sport. It's another change in the prevailing attitude that again confirms, "it's not the speedway of old".

To satisfy my desire for centre green access and to overcome the difficulty of no photographer vacancies, I immediately opt to instead volunteer to join the St John Ambulance service, since no speedway meeting can go ahead without the benefit of the first aid and diagnostic skills of their trained staff, who legally have to be in attendance at every meeting in the country. The St John's staff, who also stand close by my vantage point, then kindly remind me that extensive training and practice is required to master the skills that are a prerequisite for their work. This is before you even get invited along to help out at any speedway meeting, never mind that you have to be available every week for all manner of other more mundane events and not just the glamorous occasions. Again I've overlooked that there would already be many other committed fans who would have already taken steps to ensure that they could always watch their speedway meetings from such a prime position. It would also ensure that they got the occasional chance to get up close and personal with the riders during the racing and, for once, the riders would almost be pleased to interact with them! The Isle of Wight St John Ambulance man I manage to speak with had figured out the basic facts of the situation some considerable time ago and long before it had ever occurred to me. The idea came easily and obviously to him, particularly because he has had a lifelong affection for bikes and biking, but also because he had enjoyed his own participation as a competitor, mechanic, spectator and it was only logical for him to carry on but instead attend with bandages and breathing salts. I suddenly remember that at Eastbourne we recently celebrated the 50th year of voluntary work by one member of the St John Ambulance staff, so it's unlikely that they'll be any call for me to hold the plasters or unwrap the bandages in the near future at any speedway track.

Luckily, I'll just have to appreciate and savour these moments of my fantastic good fortune, so kindly granted by Isle of Wight speedway management, and drink in the thrilling atmosphere that is immeasurably improved when you stand so close to the action. If viewed from here, even the dullest meeting would boggle the mind, though again I was fortunate enough to be able to witness a keenly contested fixture between two competitive sides. What a fantastically exhilarating spectacle it all was, despite the comprehensive nature of the Islanders' ultimate margin of victory. I made a point to follow the advice I'd been given, by Dave Croucher, to watch for the increase in passing on the outside because, as the meeting progresses, the "dirt line always moves out". His forecast that the overtakes and passes by the home riders, on the banked bend, would be something for me to savour throughout the night proved accurate, except for "Glen Phillips who gets a nose bleed when he goes on the banking". The practised familiarity of the home riders with the strange topography of the track was hard to ignore since it happened so regularly. Though, naïvely, I felt that the Edinburgh riders might eventually cotton on to what kept happening and so gradually learn to expect these passing manoeuvres before they happened and thereby adjust their tactics and riding lines accordingly. However, this adjustment didn't happen (to much frustration among the visiting Monarchs' fans, I gathered later on the ferry back across the water to the mainland) apart from the first ride from their guest Michel Makovsky, who was theoretically already extremely capable at exploiting steeply banked circuits since he rides each week on a similarly contoured circuit with his home club Berwick. According to Krister Marsh, who claimed in the pits afterwards that he "didn't do so well tonight" (which ignores his brilliant pass to win heat 12 on his way to seven, paid eight), "there wasn't much dirt on the bends". To illustrate his point, he drew my attention to the remarkably clean advertising hoardings that lined the Smallbrook circuit tonight on which, ordinarily, it would be impossible to still clearly read the advertisers' names because the shale the bikes throw up "usually sticks to the boards".

Whatever the result or the behaviour of the dirt, the whole event was a great thrill and the racing spectacularly quick all evening when viewed from my position on the centre green. It was so awesome it was as though I'd never been to a meeting before, in terms of the exhilaration, the thrill of the incredible speed and the sheer visual impact of the racing. The whole experience was magnified and enhanced so that it was almost magical and even more thrilling than usual. Some of the manoeuvres executed by the home riders on the steeply banked bends were worth the admission money alone and, when viewed from a raised vantage point on the last bend, looked even more brilliantly skilful. The track announcer Bryn Williams also justified his reputation as an informed and witty commentator on the track action. At the outset of the fixture he warmly welcomed the visiting fans to the Island, noted the attendance of speedway doyen Mike Hunter and then immediately gloried in Edinburgh's last night win against "Auntie Pat's" Reading. Bryn set the tone for his subsequent light-hearted observations during the riders' introductory parade when, after he heard the audible cheers for the Monarchs' guest Michel Makovsky, he wryly observed, "did I hear an Edinburgh fan cheering for a Berwick rider? That's a rarity!" No one was spared his rather caustic asides and comments, even absent people and places, such as when he looked forward to future Islanders' fixtures in the North of England and cuttingly described Newcastle's track as, " Brough Park or Rough Park as it's commonly known". Though Bryn did also make a point to compliment any good racing whenever he witnessed it throughout the evening. Heat 11 particularly drew his warm approval after the tensely exciting four-lap contest between "those two youngsters Doyle and Lawson". The soundman added to the professionalism of the presentational experience in heat 3 when he played 'Waltzing Matilda' the first time the diminutive Islanders' captain, Number 1 and always patriotic Australian team manager Craig Boyce won a race. Only to follow his choice of musical accompaniment up with a quick burst of 'Tie Me Kangaroo Down Sport' after Boyce won heat 6. The heat time in this race was only 0.1 seconds outside the official track record but all the races when viewed from the fantastic location of the centre green meant that every heat appeared to be raced at a speed that would have had the riders set a new track record each and every time they took to the track. When the fixture was finally over, all I could do was reflect upon my good luck and realise that it was a crying shame to have to return to the mainland after such a fantastic night's racing on a unique track at a special club owned by a set of enthusiastic and committed shareholders-cum-supporters! If only everywhere was like this or how attendances would rise even if only everyone could have the occasional opportunity to watch their speedway meetings from inside the track.

"Speedway riders like a little moan... now even the sun's against us" David Norris

17.4.4 A BSPA MC Member will adjudicate in the event of a dispute up to 30 minutes prior to the start of a Meeting concerning a Team Line-Up (see SR 14.9.1)

There are very few roads that lead to Weymouth and, the few that there are, were being fully used by eager visitors and residents on the afternoon of my visit. I decided that I had severely underestimated the appeal of the town's glorious sandy beach, its promenade or the rival attraction of a visit to the Isle of Portland, though it isn't technically an island, to inspect its renowned stone. Portland stone is famous for its strength and colour so has found itself used as a high quality material for impressive buildings throughout the country including St Paul's cathedral.

Whatever the reason for the slowly grinding queues of nose-to-tail vehicles, traffic congestion is increasingly the bane of the modern road experience, almost irrespective of the time of travel. If the queues I encountered are anything to go by, I fully sympathise with any speedway riders who have to journey regularly to the Wessex Stadium from any distance away from Dorset. The windy downhill road into Weymouth affords a spectacular view, as the countryside opens up to provide a panoramic aspect over the town and bay which, this afternoon, is laid out before us and attractively glistens in the distance.

The place itself is a pretty and underestimated little Georgian seaside town that historically saw Weymouth dubbed "The First Resort" as, some 200 years ago, it had regular royal patronage in the form of King George III and his family. While times have changed dramatically from this period, even today, the headgear of choice is much more the straw boater beloved of Broadstairs or Bournemouth than the kiss-me-quick hat say, perhaps, closely associated with Blackpool or Skegness[1]. However, among the riders and mechanics in the pits at the Wessex stadium, the de rigueur headgear of choice is more baseball cap, with mandatory three-quarter length baggy shorts; before work only, as their employment later dictates that these get swapped for kevlars and crash helmets. Although, bathed in the warm late afternoon sunshine, in the highly unlikely event that the fans were inclined to sport them on the terraces at Wessex Stadium, the ostentatious wearing of boaters would have brought a certain rather distinctive elegance to the place. But, along with many other things since its heyday, like the bumper crowds, the wearing of hats at speedway meetings has sadly shown a dramatic decline.

The Wessex Stadium is built on land adjacent to Weymouth Football Club ground and it is the football club who are the Wildcats' landlords. The present speedway track is built on the same site as the former Radipole Lane track, which closed in 1984, albeit with a 90-degree turn from the original layout. While I arrive later than I expected, at least I've bothered to turn up, which is much more than can be said for the Newport team who were, according to the BSPA fixture list, supposed to provide the opposition for tonight's fixture. The Mavericks have, earlier in the week, unexpectedly cried off from this eagerly anticipated Conference League clash. It's a last minute turn of events that gives the Weymouth promoter, a considerably angered Brian White, very late notice to scramble together some sort of a meeting for the fans. More importantly, given the precarious finances that afflict the sports at all levels, its essential that a meeting takes place this evening as the local branch of Travis Perkins have sponsored the event and have also invited 165 people to witness a night of exciting racing. It's all part of the trials and tribulations that beset those employed as speedway promoters and, with his network of contacts, Brian has quickly managed to organise a replacement meeting. It's billed as a Conference Challenge between the Weymouth 'Carpets Galore' Wildcats and a Travis Perkins Conference League Select. It doesn't exactly trip off the tongue but has had the desired effect as, waiting patiently with their cars outside the stadium, is a reasonable crowd of expectant people keen to gain admission.

This season is the Wildcats' third since they re-opened in 2002, after

[1] Weymouth still appears to have some residual airs and graces, at least it does when it comes to the wearing of inappropriate T-shirts. Shortly after my visit, a young man wearing a Cradle of Filth T-shirt that showed a nun in a pornographic pose, and betrayed his Goth predilections, was awarded 80 hours' community service for his crime against public taste and decency in the town.

many years break from the staging of speedway in Weymouth since the closure of the previous incarnation of the club in 1984. There's still a strong local interest in speedway locally among the die-hard fans as well as from new supporters enticed along to watch the racing. The layout of the stadium itself has a slightly temporary feel with a large pits area parallel to the home straight, close to a rather cute tiered temporary wooden stand along with two nearby white portacabins rather dramatically but carefully laid on top of each other. The downstairs container serves as the club shop, while the one above it provides a dual purpose of referee's-cum-announcer's box, accessed via some stairs at the back. At the top of the stairs, there's a small wooden platform from which you get a commanding view of the whole pits area, the car park and the buildings of the nearby football ground. Chris Durno, tonight's Speedway Control Bureau official for the fixture, later mentioned that it's his "favourite track to officiate at" precisely because, at any time, the position and layout of the box allows him to briefly pop out to view for himself exactly what the activity is in the pits. For Chris, it's a refreshing change from many other tracks as, "you can see if they're being honest about bike trouble and you can chat to the riders, well shout to them actually, during the meeting".

The track circuit itself is situated in the dip of a natural bowl, which affords the majority of the spectators the pleasure of watching from a height of approximately two metres, and thereby provides an ideal vantage point from which to view events on the track. As you look away from the referee's box, where the last bend merges into the home straight, you can climb the steep slope to the refreshment kiosk or, right next to it, there is another brown-coloured converted portacabin. This box structure with windows and a door serves as the popular 'Bar on the Corner' for the club, a facility that is very much in demand tonight as it's a delightfully warm and sunny summer's night. You can actually watch the racing from the bar if you so choose or, as most people prefer to do in this weather, from the raised banking of the final bend and throughout the length of the back straight.

By the time I eventually manage to catch up with promoter Brian White on bend 4, later than planned, he's in mid-struggle with some extremely long hoses. They're heavy, recalcitrant and resist him when he yanks them, he's thereby brought to a temporarily halt from otherwise rushing about the place like a man possessed in an attempt to personally do all those crucial last-minute tasks before tapes up. It's not an ideal time for me to arrive, let alone try to conduct an interview with Brian, especially as the tractor has still to go round the dusty track with the bowser. Even if he could ignore the stress of all the last-minute rearrangements brought on by the fixture change, which he can't, or the numerous tasks still to be done, my late arrival causes Brian to react angrily as if he's never heard of traffic delays on the roads to Weymouth. I cringe at his sharp tongue and temper loss, since it's understandably a bad time for my late arrival, though Brian quickly calms down slightly to grumble, "I've got tons to do, with lots of water butts to fill, the burger van to sort and I haven't even got changed yet!" With that, my audience is over! Brian stomps off purposefully towards the burger van while he loudly shouts instructions and advice at a member of his track staff.

Shortly afterwards I find myself in conversation with an affable, long-time Weymouth speedway fan Trevor Davey. He's lost in his own world, oblivious to the stress close by to him, while he studies the match programme. He is in sole charge of issuing the tickets, at a bargain price of the £1 that adults are charged to avail themselves of the pleasure of being able to sit in the start-line stand. While most of the early arrivals ignore this opportunity and decide instead to cluster by the wire fence and look into the pits to watch the riders prepare, Trevor can still relax, as he waits for those who will eventually decide to reserve their place on the wooden grandstand. He volunteered to supervise admissions to this stand every week on race night and it's a task that mainly requires vigilance, some standing around, the opportunity to wear the yellow sleeveless jacket of officialdom, and generally issue tickets and be affable with the people who take their places on the wooden platform. Friendly is Trevor's default setting and traditional approach to life, you quickly gather after only a few minutes in his company. He pays close attention to everyone who arrives, quietly asks for the £1 each from the adults keen to enjoy the pleasure of the start-line stand and he genuinely delights in the bargain of "free admission for accompanied children".

Later, by the time the meeting starts, the stand is almost full and the white cloth cash bag that sits on Trevor's small round table overflows, while he stands by with a benign but satisfied air of authority.

Trevor has come continuously to watch the speedway in Weymouth since he was six years old. He carried on going until the last sad closure of the track in the early 80s. When he began the club were known as the "Scorchers in those days" before they underwent a number of name changes that saw them transform "from the Eagles to the Royals, which includes a time when we had Len Silver promoting down here; then we had the lost years, 19 of them, before we became the Wizards and finally the Wildcats". Also a modest man, Trevor grabs the passing Ray Collins, the official club historian, for some additional insight into his own living memory of Weymouth speedway history. Ray has followed all things Weymouth "for 40-plus years" and is another member of that capable army of volunteers that the club needs to run smoothly each week. Ray didn't enjoy the long enforced break without speedway in Weymouth, though he did continue to watch for a couple of years at Poole "but it wasn't the same and I gradually lost interest". Nowadays, his ardour and love of the sport has completely returned with new vigour. He definitely needs this energy, because not only does he write a column in each programme but he also provides a weekly report for the *Speedway Star* along with the occasional piece for the local press. Though he's keen to stress to me that the *Dorset Echo* is a big supporter of the club and already covers it very well. Trevor has spent most of the afternoon with the latest version of the in-house produced match programme, which he collated, folded and stapled just in time for it to go on sale tonight.

We stand there and watch while the home riders, all still casually dressed, pass by as they slowly inspect the track. The young prospective star of the future, Edward Kennett, who rides at Premier League Rye House, wears oversized blue shorts that are probably fashionable but look slightly peculiar to people from a different generation. Trevor and Ray explain that Edward, as usual, isn't here to ride but is frequently in attendance as part of the "Eastbourne mafia"[2] to help out and hang out with his mates and contemporaries in the Weymouth team – notably riders Danny Betson, Dan Giffard and the 15-year-old prodigy Lewis Bridger along with Chris 'Geernob' Geer who mechanics at Weymouth among many other places.

After I quickly scan the extremely limited almost pitiful display of merchandise, nothing in the track shop takes my fancy and as I leave I stumble across tonight's SCB official, Chris Durno. He kindly invites me to survey the track from the perspective the referee enjoys during the meeting in his raised portacabin. It's a surprisingly large space that

[2] They've all taken their first steps in speedway on the small training track at Arlington, or the one at Sittingbourne, and all still live in East Sussex.

provides a great view of the track (and the pits) that he shares throughout the meeting with the timekeeper and the announcer. He's as surprised, as I was, to learn on his arrival that the Newport Mavericks wouldn't be in town to race this evening. It's a decision Chris views as particularly disappointing during the "height of the summer" ignoring that, in these financially straitened times, Brian has fortunately managed to arrange "loads of sponsorship for the meeting, including a big new local sponsor Travis Perkins". Instead of the excitement of a Conference League encounter, we're to be treated to "some ponce meeting". Chris is still "expecting some good racing" on a track he rates highly, even though sometimes it "gets a lot of unfair criticism for the ruts and bumps on bend 3". Chris will be the SCB referee at Newport in two days' time so he's keen to hear the other side of events from the promoter there, Tim Stone, about the real reasons behind tonight's postponed fixture.

After I leave Chris perched in his eyrie to concentrate on his many pre-meeting duties, I bump into the official Weymouth track photographer, Julie Martin, deep in conversation by the wooden stand with Trevor. She has followed in her father's footsteps as a photographer and covers many of the local teams.[3] Jules specialises in sports photography – mostly the local football, speedway and rugby teams – but has a real enthusiasm, bordering on a burgeoning obsession, for Weymouth Speedway in general and the gifted Lewis Bridger in particular. She'd spoken highly of the people, the track and the entertainment provided at Weymouth when we'd met at Poole. But had also spoken even more enthusiastically of Lewis and, given his precocious talent, she confidently expects he might be "a future World Champion and a huge success in the sport". Confidence in general is high among the riders, volunteer staff, fans and officials at Weymouth Speedway, Jules notes, "there's no reason, with a bit of luck and barring injuries, with the riders we've got that we can't win all three remaining trophies – the League, the Cup and the Pairs!"

While they mull over the characters and characteristics of their local speedway club, Trevor and Jules highlight the many positives about speedway at Weymouth and both have particular praise for and pride in the impact the regular Friday "Winter Training School" has on the development of their locally based young riders. They both agree that, "you can see them improving right in front of your eyes". The course is often run, with great patience and insight, by Steve Piper although they have had one special evening under the expert tutelage of that experienced, relatively young but patriotic Welshman Phil Morris.[4]

Since the meeting is just about to get underway, Jules departs for the centre green to fulfil her duties as official club photographer. She publishes her photographs in the match programme every week, occasionally in the *Speedway Star* and sells them to speedway fans via her own website. Her spectacular photography of Lewis Bridger riding, particularly his trademark celebration wheelies, appears very prominently on both Jules's and Lewis's websites. Jules is a friendly, genuine and down to earth person who has gradually made her way in her chosen profession of sports photography. Speedway, never mind other team sports, isn't exactly over-run with skilful lady photographers but Jules clearly has the commitment and ability to succeed. She's definitely different from those photography legends of our sport Alf Weedon and Mike Patrick who are not usually, to my knowledge, seen wearing purple nail polish.

Jules is extremely modest about her work, "it's a bit like everything else really, the more you do it the better you get; I'd like to say I don't compare mine to other photographers – but, of course, I do!" Always after the perfect action shot, she is a bit

---

[3] I'd recently met the talented and vivacious Jules at Poole, where she'd patiently waited around the pits all evening for their home fixture versus Eastbourne to end. She was there to capture a keen 13-year-old Poole lad, Brendan Johnson, flying round the circuit after the match. He's one of the many young lads showing promise at the regular training sessions run by Steve Piper, father of the Wildcats' mascot George, at the Weymouth track during the winter. Although sadly, to sarcastic cheers from the Poole crowd and the chagrin of his anxiously watching father Dave, that night Brendan scuppered his initial chance at immortality on film with an unfortunate fall on his very first lap of the Wimborne Road circuit.

[4] They speak highly of Phil's impact on the youngsters – paid for by a father of one of the young riders – in combination with Steve's regular dedication, advice and skill throughout the winter. Attendance at the school involves tuition in track craft, basic skills and sometimes involves the use of Phil Morris's favourite teaching aide – a series of bollards arranged in complex but educational fashion. On the subject of fashion, they are surprised to learn that, a few years ago, Phil Morris was an erstwhile male model (!) with an appearance in the official Liverpool Football Club merchandise catalogue.

View from the third bend. © Jeff Scott

At the start line © Jeff Scott

Bike problems. © Jeff Scott

of a perfectionist and admits, "I tend to be very critical of mine but then I think most people are of their own work". Many speedway fans would give their right arm to regularly have access to the centre green like (or with) Jules but as we all know it gets pretty cold out there some nights and the racing isn't always what it could be. She ruefully admits that "sometimes if it's a very one-sided meeting with no real racing to speak of, I get a bit bored and frustrated and start playing around with shutter speeds and things like that and seeing how slow a shutter speed I can use and still keep the photos sharp – God, that sounds very anorakish!"

Later Jules notes, "some riders are better to take photos of than others, I have my favourites but, as I am new to the sport, I take it as it comes, so it's been a big learning curve!" With some experience and practice she finds, "watching the way the riders position themselves on the bikes when they are going round the corners and just small things like that can make it much easier to get good photos". It's also made a lot easier, "when you watch the same team each week you can predict what they are going to do, like Lewis and his wheelies, and Dan Giffard has started doing very strange things with his legs when coming out of bends". It's obviously a thoroughly male-dominated profession and preserve at speedway, plus practically every other sport you care to name, "I'm not sure I look for different things than male photographers, the only thing that may be different is the amount of photos I have of Tom Brown with his shirt off!" Often though it's all a matter of luck and timing as much as skill. Jules happily admits "sometimes you know that you have a good shot as soon as you press the shutter, but I also find in all aspects of photography that the photo you take when not really concentrating or even thinking about it is the one that captures the moment.[5] When you listen to Jules you just want to get out there yourself with a camera, since it all sounds so easy and spontaneous but, given the quality of her work, she is characteristically modest, "just happening to be in the right place at the right time always helps"[6]. As she scoots off to the centre green, Trevor's mind has been elsewhere, rather than absorbed in the master class in speedway photography, since he observes apropos of nothing at all that, given how sunny it's been, it looks as if there's "not enough water on" the track.

Just before the riders troop out to their bikes for the parade and introduction to the assembled crowd, the queues at the snack bar have

[5] After the season Jules recalls "for instance I was sat on the tractor at Weymouth when Lewis was breaking the track record and Dan Giffard was standing watching and I happened to take a photo of him looking really grumpy which was sandwiched between the photos of Lewis flying round the track and afterwards Brian, the promoter, congratulating him on breaking the track record".

[6] There is no denying that she is a huge Lewis Bridger fan, arguably his number-one fan outside of his close family, who constantly praises and delights in his riding ability. It's an enthusiasm based on his track performances but also through having got to know Lewis and "granddad, Tony" really well as people during her frequent travels this season to watch Weymouth compete away or Lewis perform in all his various Championship meetings. She's almost become a surrogate member of the family, like a protective elder sister. Not that this level of interest is without its complications, "it's got to the point where I can't watch him any more, not very good when you're supposed to be taking photos of him". Judged by the impressive array of action shots on Lewis's own website supplied by Ms Martin and the greater number of Lewis on her own site, her professionalism always takes over when it matters the most!

already grown too long to join. Nonetheless, I have a word with Laura Filmer, who's working hard behind the counter; she's someone I'd accidentally met previously at the British Under-21 Championship at Rye House and later at Mildenhall. She's definitely keen on her speedway – well, more specifically, she has a keen personal interest in a particular Weymouth rider, namely the recently resurgent Dan Giffard. Nicola is very dedicated to him and his career so she travels to all of Dan's meetings throughout the country. Her dedication is to such an extent, that she's even got this job every week in the snack bar at Weymouth, and thereby earns some extra money while Dan rides for the team. She's also a passionately committed girlfriend, if her shouts and screams of encouragement for Dan when he raced in the Under-21 British Championship at Rye House, are anything to judge by. Nicola has another strong personal speedway racing connection; she's the sister of Adam Filmer who rides tonight at reserve for the Travis Perkins Select. Should the queues ever subside, the van would provide an ideal vantage point, as it looks right across the track, from which to watch the fixture. Sadly, none of tonight's races are scheduled to feature her boyfriend and her brother in the same race, probably just as well given the large gulf between their relative experience and abilities.

The talk among the crowd, as the riders limp out for the parade to the sound of the seventies in the form of ELP's 'Fanfare for the Common Man', is of Newport's non-arrival. The crowd consensus is that Newport were "scared" to compete against an in-form team, whom many keenly anticipate will achieve success in all the various Conference level competitions that remain this season. I gather from the introductions over the tannoy that a few of the riders in the Select team might be quite motivated to perform well, though it's only supposedly a friendly meeting, since some of them have something to prove to both the local management and the fans. Most notably Gary Phelps, who was released from the team in preference to Weymouth captain Dave Mason, and Paul Candy who has just been cut from the team in favour of Danny Hughes. Added to the equation, this promises to add a bit of spice to an otherwise 'friendly' encounter though many riders, once they put on a helmet and get out on the track, invariably forget anything but the idea of victory over their opponents, completely irrespective of the status of the prize to be won.

However, almost as soon as the meeting starts, it stops again for safety reasons, "due to sunshine affecting the riders' vision". In a manner that befits the sport of speedway, practical considerations always play a large part and the crowd settles back down quietly to enjoy an exceptionally early interval break while we watch the sun start to sink below the horizon. Or, at least, sink below the riders' line of vision.

When it restarts, the racing is full on throughout and the riders approach the task in hand with a gusto that would indicate a very strong desire to win or impress and succeed. It's also noticeable that there's a strong camaraderie among all the riders. Particularly those of a certain age, who prepare, ride, travel and party together as well as generally help each other out. For example, in the pits and on the track, we've got Edward Kennett working with James Clement on his bike, while David Norris's mechanic, Chris 'Geernob' Geer, helps and supports Danny Betson. The races pass in a quick rhythm, while it's very noticeable that every time Chris Durno sounds the two-minute warning, he immediately takes advantage of the intimacy of his surroundings to look out of the backdoor of the referee's box to check on the frenetic activity in the pits. Just as Jules expected and predicted, Lewis Bridger displays great composure and style, especially for one so young, when he comfortably races to four straight wins. Each win is celebrated afterwards with some exuberantly executed post race wheelies along the length of each straight, which the crowd lap up appreciatively, and Jules religiously captures for posterity.

By the time the meeting draws to a close, she is perched on the red tractor roof parked close by the pits bend rather than stood by the notorious bump in the track where the unaware riders often fall, to try to capture those special racing moments from the meeting. Absorbed in her work, apparently oblivious to the fact that all around the tractor, nonchalantly stripped to their waists, riders also congregate to view the action. Never one to miss ever really these things, Jules later rather coyly notes, "they were all showing their six-packs". The arrival of heat 15 finds friends, erstwhile teammates and not so secret rivals, Dan Giffard and Lewis Bridger, both undefeated. Notionally they'll race together for their team but nonetheless, in reality they will unofficially race each other for pride and bragging rights[7]. Their rivalry needs little further encouragement if the intensity of these compelling last four laps of the meeting is anything to judge things by. So much so that Chris, the referee, asks promoter and team manager Brian White to have a quiet but instructional word with both riders afterwards about racing safely together, if only in due consideration of their fellow riders.

For a meeting put on with riders who were only available at the last minute, Brian professes himself very well pleased with how things eventually turned out. The crowd was vocal and, I thought, very sizeable but, then again, it was a wonderful summer's evening and Weymouth presently have a successful team racing at a great venue for the local or interested spectator. Mark, the local sponsor from the Travis Perkins depot just about located within sight of the track itself, has had "a great night out" and thinks that the 165 customers of his that were invited to the event will have definitely had an evening to remember and talk about. From his point of view, staging a sponsored event has had a "big impact" since it raises awareness of the business, but also he's pleased to have taken the opportunity to "spend national money, locally". Mark confesses that he hasn't been to a speedway meeting since it last shut down in 1984 and will, having been bitten by the bug once again, start to attend again in future. Though he'll be back shortly, the racing he witnessed has left him shaking his head and in no doubt, "that they must be completely mad to do that once, let alone every night!"

15th July Weymouth v. Travis Perkins Select (Challenge) 51-41

---

[7] Back where they live in East Sussex, in preference to study, when he's not racing or supervising granddad maintain his bikes, Lewis is often hangs out at Dan's father's moto-cross shop. Inevitably Dan and Lewis get a regular chance to compare notes and verbally stoke up the rivalry among themselves, often goaded on by Dan's brother Jon.

Chapter 18: Professional Motorsport in the Heart of the City of Sheffield

28th July Sheffield v. Berwick

"Wow – what a race, we're seeing the best from the best"

Nigel Pearson

9.2.1 [A track] must be formed by two straights and two bends

---

A long drive in the often torrential but mostly pouring rain isn't the best preparation for a late July evening's speedway at one of the fastest racetracks in the country, Owlerton Stadium in Sheffield. An even less pleasant end to the journey is to learn, upon arrival, that the meeting was abandoned just around the time you originally set off, some seven hours beforehand. In prospect, there was a combative meeting between a recently resurgent home team and the season's surprise league leaders the highflying Berwick Bandits. It had all the ingredients to potentially be an entertaining night of full-throttle action on a notoriously thrilling and exhilaratingly fast track.

Not that the tanned promoter Neil R. Machin, sat with legs up on the desk in his speedway office when I arrive, feels at all happy about the cancellation of the meeting either. As I enter the office I hear him say on the phone, for the first of many times in the next few hours, "we're absolutely under water here, we had nothing to work with so we cancelled early today – yes, I hate rain-offs, you just keep calling me". It's the second rain off of the year, so far, but was an easy decision to make

---

that morning given the condition of the track and the weather forecast of continuous rain throughout the day. For once, the meteorological office had been completely accurate and the track, along with many roads in the city, struggled to cope with the deluge of water. While it might be good for the garden, the waterlogged track soon doubled as a large paddling pool beyond any attempt at last minute remedial work, no matter how conscientious or skilful. That doesn't stop the phone from ringing constantly in the trophy-filled Sheffield Speedway office, especially when the programmed race time nears, with last-minute hopeful enquiries from optimistic souls dotted throughout the region.

Neil explains to me that the area around the stadium is prone, due to the topography of the hills and valleys as well as the prevailing winds, to a whole series of micro climates that can see it raining a few miles away in West Yorkshire but sunny in Sheffield in the south. Or vice versa tonight it appears. He welcomes the chance for a dialogue with his valued customers and throughout is unfailingly polite to all callers. Despite having roughly the same conversation over and over again, he sounds genuinely delighted to answer these queries. This charm and courteousness very much belies his reputation for bluntness and contradicts the jealous suggestions of his many rivals that he's the speedway equivalent of Sheffield United's Neil Warnock, particularly when it comes to tact and diplomacy. The comparison has some relevance in that they're both successful and experienced managers with a streak of obstinacy mixed in with their strong opinions. Not that this reputed will to stubbornness is at all apparent to the casual listener when Neil politely thanks all enquirers for making the effort to call. He naturally adheres to the advice on how to run a successful business that you find in management textbooks when he sincerely commiserates with their disappointment before he reminds all of them to come along to next Thursday's meeting when Stoke will be in town attempting to dent Sheffield's 100 percent home record in the league (though he omits to mention that they're highly unlikely to succeed). The decision to call the fixture off as early as possible in the day is shrewd business, since you get the added marginal benefit of a slight reduction on all the inevitable fixed costs involved when you stage a speedway meeting. The later the decision to cancel is left, the greater the level of the expenses you incur (travel money, staff pay etc.) without, of course, the ultimate benefit of the admission monies to cover these costs.

Between the barrage of calls that wouldn't disgrace a call centre, I'm fortunate to get the chance to spend some time in conversation with one of the current generation of speedway's most passionate and colourful promoters. I'm treated to a master class in how to be a speedway promoter from a man who has also been elected as a member of the British Speedway Promoters' Association and its small but perfectly formed management team. It's a position that undoubtedly makes Neil privy to the background, discussions, people and characters that influence the strategic direction of the sport in Britain. These particular insights remain confidential throughout our conversation though, since we discuss his work at Sheffield and some of the many issues plaguing the speedway industry, it's possible to glean your own perspective on some of the sport's important people. When you listen to Neil speak with the callers, you quickly form an impression that he is a man obsessed with Sheffield speedway, the sport in general and proud to be in Yorkshire (albeit he winters in Australia). You could also guess at his Yorkshire roots from his pugnacious attitude. As the old saying goes, unfairly to some people's mind or accurately to others, 'you can always tell a Yorkshire man, but not much'. Nonetheless, you can't help but recognise the Sheffield leanings of his Yorkshire roots; though, anyone would be hard-pressed to realise this from his accent that has somehow, accidentally on purpose, been lost along the way. Both as a result of the discrimination he suffered when he spent time in his early 20s in Lincoln, you quickly become accentually neutered when you're berated as a "Yorkshire pudding", as well as from his winters spent away from Yorkshire in the warmth and freedom of an Australian summer.

Neil has been at Owlerton for 13 years and the speedway business is run on behalf of Class Trend Ltd with his partner Malcolm Wright; who is a very experienced speedway man from his involvement in promotions at many tracks that include Middlesbrough and Hull before latterly he took on the challenge of Sheffield. When Neil first came to the stadium in the "bad old days of mid 1992" his partner was Tim Lucking who is still sadly, Neil took one of his rare (pregnant) pauses at this moment, missed though he died nine years ago the next week, in 1996. Neil speaks highly of Tim for his "fresh, intellectual perspective", which was an outlook he gained through his university background and his personal interest in politics, journalism and history. Neil praises Tim as a "great public speaker and front man", he needed to be as when they took over at the club, it was close to bankruptcy, "haemorrhaging money" with poor crowds and effectively had no "rider assets" to speak of. It was a hard but instructive period when they were "continually struggling to stay afloat as a business" while they put up with performances that were usually execrable away from Sheffield and were often subject to "being bloody slaughtered" at home. However, Neil proudly notes, "we grafted and stuck at" and they made the most of a number of factors that were to contribute strongly to their good fortune. This mostly revolved around "accessing the media and the outside world, not just the people in the stadium" through local TV, radio and paper ("the Star has always been very supportive") and through their strategic focus to acquire "a proper sponsor whom you work with closely to ensure you develop their reputation in the right, high profile, positive way".

They were also fortunate to have "good commercial long-term support" from the stadium owners who were delighted to have Sheffield speedway run along with their five regular greyhound meetings – held weekly on three packed evenings and two busy lunchtimes. The landlords' basic business strategy is to 'invest for success' in all their (predominantly) leisure and gambling businesses, which has resulted in £10 million being spent on Owlerton in the last decade. Operating speedway at Owlerton is not a recent or accidental circumstance. The club has a rich tradition and history that has seen Sheffield compete as a speedway club since 1929 on the very circuit still used in 2005, which is sadly waterlogged this evening. It's an enviable story of continuity and tradition that Neil, with Malcolm, is proud to continue, "I only see myself as a custodian of this place at this moment in time – this [club] will definitely outlast us all".

Even while being a conscientious custodian of the club for the benefit of future generations of Sheffield fans, Neil is adamant about the need and importance to continually strive for success which, "never stops, you just keep trying to build it up". One of the key factors in the club's recent success is the mix of experience and commitment provided by the people it employs. This might sound like just the usual business cliché that is trotted out across the country daily at every staff meeting, appraisal and shareholders annual conference on a cynical and ad nauseam basis. However, a casual run through the roster of staff and officials at the track quickly adds considerable weight to his claim and a brief glance at the programme confirms the importance at Sheffield of the fundamental value of continuity, knowledge and commitment. There's John Whitaker who became clerk of the course after his retirement as a domestic and international referee in 1993, and who has been a licensed official of the S.C.B. for 65 years (!) While the track curator Graham Trollope – "pronounced

'Tree-Lope-Pee', it's really Trollop with an 'E' but he hates that" – served his apprenticeship with Frank Varey and has worked at Sheffield for 30 years. The start marshal Lou Charlesworth has "done 30-plus years" – "he's the most famous man in Sheffield as he's in every photo and every bit of film footage at the start line" – while Michael Beck "our time keeper has done 30 or 40 years". The Sheffield legend Reg Wilson is the club's team manager and, to Neil's mind, typifies the ethos of stability that is the hallmark of the club, since he's been there as "man and boy" as a fan, a rider and, now, the team manager.

Neil loves to watch how the older generation of fans still hold Reg in deep affection and admiration, especially when they travel to the away meetings, where Reg "loves to have a yarn with the old timers". These supporters all remember and still talk about his riding days when he "used to bang in all those maximums wearing the blue and gold". Although he's heard it hundreds of times he still laughs at Ray's "Sheffield joke" which rather amusingly goes "I come from the city of Iron and Steel – me mum used to iron and me dad used to steal"[1]. Comparatively, the really new kid on the block is press officer Nigel Pearson who's only been at the club for 10 years. Neil had first seen Nigel around 1994 at the late lamented Cradley Heath track where he noticed the "guy with the roving mike really knew his stuff and up to date content". He's come a long way since then and has "developed his own one-man industry within speedway"[2] All in all at Sheffield, along with Betty who's managed the office on race night for around 25 years, plus Roy who has run the training school[3] for a similar time, this wealth of talent and expertise on the Sheffield Speedway staff combines to provide Neil with a "dream team" to work with, "they're the best in the industry, to my mind!"

[1] Neil failed to mention another unique claim to fame for Reg – namely that he was once sponsored by Freddie Starr, as noted by Ian Thomas in his recent book Wheels and Deals

[2] Nigel 'Scoop' Pearson is British speedway's premier communications specialist and, naturally, is involved across every media medium – whether print, broadcast or online. He provides web articles and programme content for some tracks but has also specialised in live commentary duties – speedway for Sky Sports and football among other things for his other major employer TalkSPORT. He approaches his commentating with considerable research and some gusto in his own inimitable, sometimes slightly histrionic, style. Nigel fulfils all these commitments and still manages to keep in touch with numerous incidents, the latest news and views as well as the promoters and riders in his capacity of official press spokesman for the BSPA. Never mind all the relentless networking with important figures throughout the industry that his work necessarily involves – he regularly speaks or lunches with influential speedway people like John Postlethwaite, Terry Russell, Philip Rising, Matt Ford, Tony Mole, Peter Oakes and the like.

[3] Chris Durno commented afterwards: "one of the main advantages at Owlerton is the mini-training track situated behind the back-straight second bend terraces. This facility has enabled Machin to fulfil the dream of operating with an all-English team, since he has been able to catch aspiring wobblers ahead of other promotions and nurture them through to be capable of taking a first-team place within a couple of seasons. This has been the successful path that trapped and rewarded the Tigers with such riders as Andrew Moore, Ricky Ashworth, Ben Wilson and Paul Cooper. Sheffield seems to be able to find at least one new British rider each season." Sadly, it has just been announced that this training track will close after SCB inspector Colin Meredith condemned the safety fence. Neil Machin commented, " The fence was condemned despite the fact that we are licensed as a training track and not a racing track. In my opinion, the fence is adequate to accommodate such a small track with proportionately slower incidents. The track was all about technique rather than speed... it was the last of a string of problems...There have been additional running costs imposed by the SCB within the last 3 years. We have had to have a fully equipped ambulance on stand-by, replacing our regular first aid staff, while there has also had to be public liability insurance for every session. On top of that, parking has been restricted because double yellow lines have been painted outside the stadium because of the new college annexe across the road...Our thanks go to all the people who have spent countless hours to keep the wheels turning, especially training manager Roy Wilson and Peter Brown, Sandra Brown, Ron Haglington, Graham Smith, Graham Trollope and John Priestly".

For the Sheffield promoters and staff, there were many periods of struggle before the youth development policy finally started to show some real recognisable results on the track. In fact, it took just over seven years before it all came together for the club – in one "great big year, 1999". That time of achievement was the ultimate triumph, "our first real success" and fortunately came along hand in hand with the club's 70th anniversary commemorative celebrations. They'd taken the rough with the smooth ("we all like the smooth") before the Sheffield rider-training programme had finally paid dividends through the development of young, mostly local, riders for an "all-English team" that swept all before it. Neil proudly notes, "we were dominant across the season" and this superiority was illustrated by the results when Sheffield won "the treble" of all three major trophies in the 1999 season.

Though the club enjoyed its greatest and most triumphant season with a team comprised of British riders, Neil is quick to stress that he "doesn't have any problem with [employing] foreigners". In fact, in the past he's been unafraid to experiment with a whole slew of men from "every part of the world where riders with talent on a speedway bike are found". Sadly this approach hasn't brought the expected results on the track or, more importantly, off the track in terms of publicity coverage. With English riders "there's always a story you can cover, invent or regurgitate". Subsequently Neil has made a virtue of necessity, this patriotism at Sheffield "has become our hallmark, an all-English team is the way we go and the way we want to go". There are other advantages to be gained from this strategy, especially since it's logistically easier and much, much cheaper too for the cost-conscious promoter, who with a predominantly British team doesn't have "to pay for all those flights, hotels and taxis when you fly riders in and out of the country".

You only have to spend a short time in his company to form the impression that Neil is a man unafraid to consider new ideas, bluntly state opinions and to avoid any inclination to rest on his laurels. To ensure that the grass doesn't grow idly under his feet, I gather Neil's default setting is to constantly question the how and why of everything within his own club and the rest of the industry. He fondly recalls the massive crowd levels of yesteryear; it was a period when he stood on the terraces as a 12 year old during the "halcyon days our forefathers enjoyed in the 1960s". While Neil vividly recollects the many impressions he formed during his time on the terraces – the potent and unforgettable combination of the "smell, the birds, the speed, the noise and the atmosphere" are fondly remembered. Rather than romanticise the past, he is well aware it was during this period of burgeoning crowd numbers that speedway started to sow the seeds that has led to its gradual decline as a spectator sport.

Investment and sensible strategic planning by the promoters and speedway authorities involved during that time didn't match their easily gained short-term success. Neil notes, "the people then presided over the decline of the sport" since they singularly failed to invest the considerable revenues they gained through the "sheer strength of the crowds". These riches were extracted or effectively frittered away without being properly channelled into any really effective long-term marketing projects for the sport or any concerted efforts to ensure the continuation of British success through a systematic youth-development policy. To try to arrest this decline in support and to generally live with the consequences of this tragically squandered legacy is the task and responsibility that faces the contemporary speedway industry as a whole, and in its ongoing struggle to "lift it back up to those levels of support".

In recent years, the event with the biggest potential impact on speedway has been securing the contract to ensure valuable coverage of the sport on Sky Sports TV. Though, sadly, this relationship has had a much greater impact on the income of the Elite League tracks, who are in the minority within speedway, rather than the whole sport within Britain. This development has been the biggest news in town and I could fill a separate book with Neil's thorough examination of the present situation and his considered but often controversial thoughts for its possible future improvement[4].

However, the issue of the correct format for the most effective presentation of speedway on the television is a sideshow compared to some of the other issues that presently impact the industry. There's the continued but vexed issue of the individual tracks' profitability and finance. At many UK venues it continues to be the case that it's a fairly hand-to-mouth

existence with the financial support of generous local sponsors being a vital contributory factor to many clubs' survival. While, to a great extent, you have your destiny in your own hands when it comes to the financial control of your own particular situation, the opportunity to maximise revenues of your business has to take place within the competitive environment in which you find yourself. This landscape has been dramatically affected by a significant external factor – and particularly impacts the health of the sport in the lower leagues – namely, the increased tendency towards track closures, rather than openings, in recent and, most likely, future years.

A big factor in these closures, apart from finance, has been the rise of environmental disturbance issues, which have found a greater voice or a receptive ear in local government. Neil is worried, "we can't just stay still, we desperately need new venues; they don't have to be on my doorstep, they can be anywhere in the country". The Yorkshire-Lincolnshire border has bucked the trend and recently seen the construction of a purpose-built new track in Scunthorpe. It's an exciting development and one that Neil has endeavoured to support to the full from the outset. They've had to build their own facilities from scratch ("literally started from grassroots"). Neil believes the arrival of Scunthorpe "is brilliant news", since any promoter at Owlerton will always benefit from more teams in the local area, "Hull on a Wednesday, Sheffield on a Thursday, and now Scunthorpe – it's not rocket science is it?"

However, Scunthorpe is the exception that proves the rule, because the national trend is for tracks to close (or teeter on the edge of extinction). A recent example was the arrival but swift demise of the speedway track at Trelawny; a venue where "with those dramatic surroundings, it was like speedway on the moon". The location gave Neil a "great feeling" and he mourns its demise as a "sad loss", but it typifies the current direction of the industry. If the industry has suffered death by a thousand cuts then the deepest cut of all was the closure of the Shay Stadium in Halifax. For Neil, it was always a wonderful night out – "Halifax versus whoever" – mostly because its "fantastic banking", along with the "gradient into the turns that easily made it the most dramatic and exciting venue on the planet!" The thrill of his reminiscence about this

---

[4] In essence, Neil worries that the natural trajectory of Sky's broadcasting "live approach" inevitably leads to long gaps in the on-screen action between heats or as a result of delays through crashes, re-starts etc. He's concerned that these longueurs during a live broadcast might not be the best way to control or reposition the sports image, especially while it attempts to find and appeal to possible new audiences. This is particularly true for young consumers who have repeatedly been identified as the key generation that speedway needs to attract. They are a very fickle but sophisticated consumer group that advertisers widely acknowledge to be characterised by their high disposable income, short attention spans but who require frequent stimulation and excitement to ensure they persevere and remain interested. I'm sure it's not contractually possible, within the agreement negotiated between Terry Russell, the BSPA and Sky Sports television, but Neil's enlightened suggestion of a weekly package of thrilling highlights drawn from across all the leagues racing would have real potential! It addresses the needs of new and existing consumers – plus it would also allow much greater editorial control – so that the home viewer would always be guaranteed to avoid the dull bits but instead see the most exciting action and interviews. Neil believes that the opportunity to watch speedway live has already been proven not to attract a contemporary audience, so replicating this on television, as Sky Sports does at present, doesn't overcome this structural impediment to audience growth. Rather than allow the capriciousness of the weather, the format of the sport or sheer bad luck to intervene to frustrate the viewing experience; the chance to watch a package of the best races, finishes, passes or crashes would be a much more compelling proposition.

great track quickly transports Neil beyond the earth's atmosphere but, closer to home, particularly in city-centre locations, anxiety is never far away for most promoters. Particularly where you have the "constant worry of wondering when the developers are moving in". Exeter is to shut at the end of the season with its track to, eventually, be replaced by more houses. It's a fate that will also probably befall Edinburgh Speedway in Armadale, sooner rather than later, despite its location on the periphery of the local town, because "houses are being built up right to the edge of the stadium".

The appetite and demand for new housing developments is inexorable across the whole country and is government policy. Most newly arrived neighbours usually aren't enamoured to find that their commercial neighbours have the temerity to run what's perceived as a disruptively noisy and dirty sport on a speedway track in their backyard. Clubs rarely have to wait long before the complaints start to wing their way towards the local council. Even at the East of England Showground, where Peterborough's track is based, Neil remembers, "for years and years, it was fields forever and now I worry about the show houses". It's a trend that just won't go away if you ignore it, and that's before you even consider noise and environmental considerations. It's clear that a large number of existing British speedway tracks are presently located near housing or are based in areas suitable for housing development.

In addition to all these external factors, Neil notes, "different competitors have different commercial priorities". At Sheffield the priority is "the buzz of discovering riders and watching them grow and develop in the system". It's an approach that requires patience, something that's in short supply with some other promoters who "bring in the riders ready made, often from abroad; whereas my priority is youth, rather than flying Swedes and Poles in and out all the time". Everyone has a different approach in their attempt to find success on the track with the aim to, hopefully, bring in the bigger crowds. Whatever your approach, the aim is to get "job satisfaction" and carry on "paying your bills" despite all the issues and problems that beset the industry, "it's not hard to figure out, if you don't pay your bills you're out of here!"

For Neil, the approach in the Premier League is generally more collegiate than the cut and commercial thrust of the Elite League, and operates with a general attitude that is based on trying to understand each others needs and accommodate any problems, "Christ, we have big bloody arguments but usually we always get on". The Premier League level promoters operate with the tacit understanding that, "our competitors are our competitors but also our business partners". There are still some difficulties, and no room for the faint hearted or the naïve; but equally, unlike elsewhere, "we're all not bloody savages at each other throats all the time". But then Premier promoters have an advantage compared to their Elite League counterparts, "as we don't have to deal with the greater attention – the TV coverage which brings bigger numbers and the money issues". Neil pauses to consider his lot, and that of his fellow promoters, before he ponders aloud, "maybe that's when you lose that respect for each other?"

Whatever the real or imagined differences in ethos and attitudes between the various leagues, all speedway clubs share the same need: to attract new or lapsed customers to their tracks on a regular basis. The key word in this equation is regular. Many attempts to solve the frequency problem have, ultimately, proved to be fruitless and Neil believes speedway "is the hardest product I've ever sold!" The job at hand for any promoter is to ensure that everything about each evening is run professionally and in a manner that generates excitement in the fans and so makes them want to return. All the major ingredients fall within the control of any competent promoter, since the structure of all team fixtures necessarily leads to the climax of the "grand finale of heat 15". Hopefully, it is a climactic race that caps off an evening of great excitement and entertainment.

Neil believes the aim of any speedway promoter who stages a meeting is "to send them across the car park having had a good value evening of the best entertainment". If that is what actually happens, then commercial success should follow through the word of mouth it generates, "our patrons are our best sales force". However, it's no longer enough to preach to the converted: there is a necessity to market the sport differently. To market and sell it in such a manner that nationally and, most importantly, locally it attracts the curious punter. The quest to convert these casual attendees into stalwart supporters requires, in the first instance, enticing them through the turnstiles but, afterwards, needs them to return again. The importance of "selling it to them twice" is particularly crucial to long-term success, since you want these customers to leave with enough curiosity, motivation or excitement to want to come back again. It is on subsequent trips to speedway that they can start to get to grips with the arcana of the sport – the funny rules and behaviours, the acronyms, the team structure and the "basic procedures" – in order that they can build a better understanding of what they actually witness. And, hopefully, they will then develop a love and appreciation for what is, in all reality, a complicated beast of a thing to grasp and follow!

As often in business life, it's a Catch 22 situation where you need the crowds in order to have the finances to invest in the fabric and, crucially, the marketing of the sport. As Neil succinctly identifies, "if you don't generate the capital you can't invest in the marketing to create the profile". This though is, ultimately, half the battle, as the sport must grow beyond its core audience to speak to the younger generation in its own language. It has to compete with a variety of other entertainment outlets that have a much more ruthless approach to gain or maintain their share of the available discretionary spending power of the "teenage element". In a nutshell, for speedway to survive it has "got to become trendy". At Sheffield, the promotion has set out its stall "we aim ourselves at the family unit" and Neil wants these families to "recognise the perceived value of their spend at Owlerton and, hopefully, recognise the entertainment that we regularly provide for them as a sport".

Neil has extremely high hopes for the market research campaign, just being undertaken on behalf of the BSPA, which aims to discover the demographics and predilections of the current audience that the sport attracts. The ability to be able to explain your target demographic, all the business books assure us, is the vital element when it comes to being "able to draw in sponsors". Neil feels everyone in the sport should understand the "division between what we do" and the real dynamics of the demographic "whom they entertain". This survey is a small step but an important mark of the industry's determination to start to get professional guidelines through which to understand and interpret their audience for interested advertisers. I certainly hope that his faith in this survey is well founded[5] as a large number of questions about the future of this great sport still remain unanswered. Quite who can answer these outstanding issues, debate them successfully or plot a sensible future strategy for the sport is uncertain. One thing is for sure, these discussions would always benefit from including Neil Machin in the debate.

28th July Sheffield v. Berwick (Premier League) – postponed rain

---

[5] Although having seen its questions and noticed the questionnaire run out rapidly when circulated at a number of tracks, I have my doubts about the weight of the statistical relevancy of the sample to be within meaningful significance limits. Or, that the information will prove compelling to waivering potential sponsors.

Chapter 19: A Night with the Comets
29th July Workington v. Stoke

SKY CHATTER

"I've never seen as big a crowd as this" Kevin Tatum

RANDOM SCB RULES

10.5 All motorcycles will have the Riders name displayed on the rear of the seat or on the rear mudguard.

If all roads lead to the charms of Wigan Pier, they should by rights really lead to the coastal town of Workington in Cumbria. The journey there is through the magnificent countryside of the Lake District with its steep hills, lakes, and the lush though often desolate landscape that surrounds you. You pass close by to the villages of Keswick and Grasmere with the famous attraction of Dove Cottage, where Wordsworth composed so much of his inspirational poetry. For the length of my journey to the town, the panoramic hills are shrouded in huge angry rain clouds arrayed in such large groups that today they'd struggle to wander around lonely as the proverbial ones William wrote about. When you travel to the end of the most beautiful cul-de-sac in Britain you eventually arrive in Workington where I'm to spend the night after I watch the Comets race against the Stoke Potters at their home of Derwent Park.

The town itself is an ancient market and industrial town at the mouth of the River Derwent. Some parts of Workington date back to Roman times. Historically though, it's more famous for the area's iron ore and coal pits, which resulted in the

town's expansion to become, at one point, a major industrial town and port. It's even the place that Henry Bessemer invented his revolutionary steel-making process, the Bessemer converter. It also became renowned as Britain's third port and, like its southerly neighbour Whitehaven, it once swapped coal for slaves and rum as well as decking itself out in splendid Georgian architecture. While many of the buildings remain, sadly this rich industrial heritage has sharply declined and the only steel you encounter is the steeliness behind the friendly determination of the town and the people to survive the decline of its key industries. The port still works and the marina is littered with boats, while a cluster of wind turbines, in the near distance on the shoreline horizon, dominates the skyline. It's a breezy day and they turn at quite a pace even though it's late July. At certain points in the perennially unpredictable weather event of ours that's known as a British summer, you're bound to spend quite some time under threatening rain clouds. A blackened sky isn't what the doctor ordered for cricket and is equally hazardous to the running of speedway meetings. Since I've travelled around to all the British tracks scattered throughout the country, I'm realising that the essential skills I require are navigational and meteorological. Our robust British tradition of talking about the weather – what's here or what might be about to arrive – translates for me into a rather compulsive obsession with radio and newspaper forecasts. After I suffered a torrential rain off the night before in Sheffield and, since I'm a considerable distance from my usual base in Brighton, the intermittent rain and lowering sky that I encounter while I drive through the stunning wilds of the North West of England landscape certainly doesn't bode well for the prospect of an enjoyable evening's entertainment.

I head straight to the stadium, while the track receives its thorough pre-meeting preparation and attention at the hands of the legendary track man Tony Swales and his staff. Well, it just has received it but since I've arrived six hours prior to the meeting, they're about to have a brief break for a sandwich. I leap from the car and rush over to Tony to check on his version of tonight's weather prospects and an in depth discussion of what this might mean for the track. He kindly explains that the locals always say that when the tide comes in quickly the rain clouds (and seagulls) usually also rush in too. I dutifully ask, "when is the tide coming in tonight?" only to learn that Tony actually lives in the beautiful country side of North Yorkshire. So, sadly, he himself doesn't have the actual times of the tides for this area and, though he knows the saying, he can't use this local weather lore for today's preparations. Despite the previous day's heavy downpour, he's confident with no more heavy rain that the meeting will have absolutely no problem to go ahead as planned. He informs me that the natural bevel of the banked shape of the circuit, which surrounds the Rugby League pitch, naturally lends itself to exciting racing and has the additional benefit that it helps provide excellent drainage.

I'm delayed on my return to the stadium from the town centre by a huge traffic jam, which is surprising for such a small place, until I arrive at the complex network of roads around the mini-roundabout by the railway station. The roundabout is surrounded by police cars, with their lights flashing, and at its centre completely covered in shattered windscreen is a high performance but crumpled motorcycle crushed beneath the wheels of an ageing blue Mini-Metro or similar. There's no sign of either occupant but there is no doubt that the motorcycle has been horrendously damaged. Not that I needed any reminder of how dangerous powerful motorbikes can be, on the road or on the speedway track, but I get it nonetheless. When I return to the stadium later the wind is still strong and the low, dark clouds still hover menacingly. There's slightly more activity in the pits and there are many more staff in attendance to get the stadium ready for the turnstiles to be opened and the arrival of the fans. The stadium has a large old-fashioned seated grandstand that overlooks the start line on the home straight, and it provides an excellent vantage point to watch the speedway and, at other times, rugby matches. There are open terraces for tonight's hardier fans on the first bends with a low covered terraced area the length of the back straight. It's a pretty long track, since it surrounds the pitch in an elongated oval shape, which is particularly distinguished by its generous banking on the final bends which promise exciting passing possibilities for the riders as they run down to the finish line.

Away on the skyline in one direction there are the wind turbines from the modern era and in the other direction the prominent landmark of the parish church of St Michael's from another. There has been a church on that site since the 7th century. The version we see dates from 1770 when it replaced the 12th century Norman church. The Comets attract larger numbers to the stadium nowadays than the church does, plus there's a fervour and devotion to the club's fans up here in Workington that borders on the messianic or, at least, the very religious.

Inside the stadium the bikes already there remain resolutely silent, but glisten and ready for action on both sides of the pits. While I've been away, work on the track has carried on apace and Tony kindly suggests that I walk around the track circuit to accompany him as he inspects the results of his handiwork. It's a walk that I consider I should do in the quizzical style beloved of visiting riders to any track; I could ponder the shale depth with a few seemingly random but expertly aimed kicks to the track's surface or, if really keen, stop to examine the relative security of the fixtures and fittings that hold up the track safety fence. It's a pre-meeting ritual that is the same everywhere when it comes to kicking the track; but a thorough examination of the fence prevails much more at the Premier and Conference League levels where there are no air fences and so possible encounters with the fence (or steel wall at Exeter) are potentially going to be much harsher. Since my last visit to the stadium to watch the Comets ride, I notice that the Derwent Park track has been considerably widened on the exit from bend 2 and so creates a much wider and smoother access route to the lengthy straight itself. This is an extremely important safety adjustment on a fast track such as this one, particularly when the previous 'bottleneck' resulted in a higher frequency of 'comings together' from the riders. It's something that a hugely experienced and extremely capable groundsman like Tony is justifiably proud to have achieved, especially in the face of frequent harassment in the form of regular visits from the local council's Health and Safety team. Give a man a clipboard and tape measure as well as an inflated sense of the importance of their power (which is important, but it goes to their heads in many respects) and you usually have a recipe for disaster or, at least, considerable delay. So it proved in this instance. Tony is very proud of his handiwork, but it was achieved at the cost of innumerable consultations and discussions. I naïvely thought that this would have meant frequent track inspections but apparently during these visits the council officials "don't bother about the riders only the public". So, the track widening was the easy part of the process; whereas their inflated concern to protect the safety of the public has had the result that the available area of the back straight covered terrace has shrunk. Mostly to accommodate both a six-foot wall and a four-foot protective gap that now separates the track fence from the endangered fan. Not that Tony underestimates the importance of rider safety; the *raison d'être* of a brilliant racing surface is to maximise the thrills and exhilaration for the participants and spectators, but in a predictably safe manner on a smooth as possible surface. The numerous gradings and scrapings that Tony orchestrates right up until the end of the meeting continues to ensure this as well as demonstrate his pride, craftsmanship and skill in his track preparation.

The thorough attention to the track condition has added piquancy this season for the Comets who've been plagued with a horrendous run of luck with their crashes and injuries. The whole team has suffered mishaps at home or on their travels. Their frequent departures from the bike at speed have resulted in an impressive array of broken bones and, often, medically complicated injuries that require time on the sidelines to recuperate for part or, in some cases, all of the season. The previous week's meeting continued the abominable run of bad luck and involved Jamie Courtney's thorough test of the safety furniture with his journey over the fence at a speed talked of as around 70 m.p.h.; but the resulting painful damage to his coccyx hasn't kept him from his place in the team for this week's fixture. While the crash suffered by Carl 'Stoney' Stonehewer (a Mancunian but adopted first son and legendary talisman of the Workington faithful) ended his season prematurely. It's an incident, which Tony euphemistically describes as a "clash with Boyce on bend 4 in heat 15". Stoney sustained injuries that were severely complicated when he got his "arm trapped between the wheel and the mudguard" and so suffered "burns that require a skin graft". Given that speedway is a risky sport, where injuries occur on a weekly basis at tracks around the country, it's an incident that still provoked strong emotions on the night and frequent subsequent discussions in practically every possible medium. The phone lines and Internet forums have hummed with theories, various accounts and updates; while everyone I spoke to at any length, or overheard in conversation with others, brought up the injury or the events that surrounded it throughout the evening. Well, with the notable exception of my brief meeting with Graham Drury, the Workington team manager, who only mentioned it in his weekly notes in the match programme.

On any normal race day at Workington, Carl Stonehewer would be a larger-than-life character in the pits, just as he is throughout the sport. Only a few seasons ago, he was the only Premier League level rider who competed in the media circus that is the present Speedway Grand Prix series, and it was an event that was always enlivened by his distinctive dulcet tones in the pits. He often took a huge contingent of Comets' fans that loyally followed him throughout Europe for the Grand Prix with noisy abandon. Though he comes from Manchester, he has become inextricably linked in the public imagination with Workington Speedway Club. His down-to-earth and plainly spoken approach has endeared him to many fans and he has been widely seen throughout the sport as a 'rider of the people'. His natural ability to come across refreshingly in interviews and in person, along with his give-it-a-go and get-on-with-it attitude, has enabled Stoney to stand out both as a rider and as a man. He appears to have come from a different, less complicated, era of competition and expression. Carl is a man who will not dress it up politely in interviews and finds the time to say "hello" or pass on his love to his fiancée Juliet (nowadays his wife), on live television. He is a man you can particularly admire for his honesty and straightforwardness in a sport that invariably prides itself on its straightforwardness.

However, at Workington Speedway, with the enforced absence of Stoney things definitely did not hold out so much promise for the remainder of the season. Although you wouldn't guess this from the extremely positive outlook of Graham Drury who, along with his wife Denise, has just taken up the promotional reigns at the club this season. Denise is unavailable tonight because she's away at a funeral but Graham is happy to speak with me for a few minutes before he tries to get the best out of his depleted team. Graham and Denise had jumped at the opportunity to become the promoters at Workington following three successful years in the Conference League at Mildenhall[1]. When offered the possibility by the club's owner, Tony Mole, of the chance to test their abilities at a higher level by advancing a league, as well as the opportunity to work in one of the speedway world's hotbeds of support, it was too much of a temptation for them both to resist. Graham speaks in a soft Welsh accent and has a patrician demeanour, which belies his reputation for often strongly worded and passionate interactions with his riders; though this ease and familiarity undoubtedly comes from his extensive experience as a rider from 1968 to 1984 for Mildenhall, Long Eaton and Stoke. He recalls that time fondly "as a fantastic way to earn a living" and to get to "travel the world". He suggests that the contemporary rider is much more professional and career focused compared to those in Graham's riding days, especially since they're no longer "in the bar after the meeting, going to parties and rolling up home at 8 a.m." Graham finds it "advantageous" to have the "authority with the riders" that is conferred on any team manager, if they are an ex-rider. However, just as in his day, there's a common misperception among the riders about what doing the job of a promoter "properly and professionally" actually means. Graham immediately strikes you as a man used to formulating plans and acting upon them thoughtfully; so it's no surprise to learn that he's accurately accounted for, with a stopwatch, the "85 hours" he spends each week on his work as a speedway promoter. Most people "don't realise what's involved", particularly the riders who think the promoter simply "pockets the money and goes home". The reality is much more complicated and, on any Monday for example, you would typically find Graham and Denise involved in a series of necessary but important administrative tasks. These tasks require analysis and paperwork and includes some study of the referee's report, the preparation of the riders' home and away pay sheets, analysis of the attendance figures, and organising staff availability for the week ahead, even before they've started to consider anything to do with team selection! It is all remarkably complicated and tedious, never mind it appears a million miles from the glamorous and widely held popular conception of what the job is actually supposed to involve. And all this activity is before they've even begun to contact and work with fellow promoters. Everyone tries to co-operate, but sometimes that can be "difficult" as understandably the competitive structure of the sport is such that "naturally everyone wants what's best for their own team". Graham has a lot of time and "respect" for some other promoters – such as John Louis or Len Silver – while "some I don't rate at all, but then it's their money!"

Expectations run high in the town and the Drurys have the enviable position that they manage the team with the "highest attendances in the [Premier] League" with an average gate in excess of 1500. It's a "prestigious" position that, given the raised expectations, "brings its own pressure"; particularly since the speedway team "attracts better crowds than the football and rugby teams added together". The "whole town buzzes" with all things speedway. It's extremely important to a lot of local people and the Drurys are "desperately keen to bring success on and off the track", especially with the current and "prospective sponsors". They're also very keen to land some trophies to repay the faith that Tony Mole has shown in them, but also because it would be appropriate to the importance of the speedway club to the people of Workington. While there has been some limited success in 2001 and 2004 in the Four Team trophy, success in the League and Cup has consistently eluded the club. You hesitate to think of the crowd levels that would be generated by a triumphant campaign in the League or the Cup. With their performances so far this season in the KO Cup, maybe this will finally be the year that they gain some more silverware to reflect the strength and passion of the supporters. Graham desperately wants to have

[1] Graham had previously been a promoter at Long Eaton and, along with co-promoter Ian Thomas, has for two decades run the acclaimed World Indoor Ice Speedway British Open Championship meeting at Telford during the winter close season. Though, with competitive ice speedway meetings held throughout continental Europe, especially Poland and Germany, it's a 'world' event in the same sense that the 'World Series' of baseball only includes teams from North America.

something to show for the team's efforts every season, but particularly in his first season as promoter, since "Workington, and maybe also King's Lynn, are both remote but inspire great loyalty and fanaticism among the fans." My time is up and Graham leaves to supervise the team, rain clouds permitting, in their preparations for the fixture against tonight's visitors Stoke. He hopes that I enjoy the evening and you sense he's sincere with his parting words: "I'm very lucky to be doing this job".

I leave the manager's office cum steel container and pass through the busy pits and exchange it for the almost sepulchral calm of the stand terracing to eat my sandwiches. It's en route from the riders' changing rooms and there I snatch a brief chat with the down-to-earth and extremely affable Stoke rider Paul Clews (and get his autograph) as he wanders back from the changing room in his kevlars. I'd followed Paul's progress from his early days on the track at Reading, where he'd progressed from keen novice to become a much more accomplished and consistent performer with a marked tendency to attempt or indulge in thrilling overtakes around the outside, extremely close to the fence. I was very disappointed when he moved onto Stoke, since I knew that I'd be deprived of all the excitement and entertainment that almost invariably resulted whenever he came out to race in his heats. Apart from the professional changes brought on by the move to Stoke, there have been great changes away from the track since Paul got married two years ago and he and his wife's first baby is due next week. Paul's very excited ("the little one will make a big difference") and jokes that "I'll be pleased to get in the garage or on the track". At Loomer Road, Paul enjoys the warmth and friendliness of the people as well as the track: "it's a similar track to Reading but with proper red shale". Although he's keen not to appear to disparage Reading in anyway, he nonetheless still observes "Reading has changed totally in the few years since I left, it's even slicker". Under heavy skies, I'd noticed Paul intently study the track surface on his walk with the rest of the Stoke team a short time earlier and his verdict is that it's "slick here tonight so we probably won't see much passing". Paul believes that this is in marked contrast to Stoke, which is a "great track with lots of passing". I hope his prediction for tonight isn't accurate since Derwent Park is usually a great track at which to watch racing and passing, particularly with the added excitement provided by the banked final bends. Paul glances at the sky as he heads off to attend to his bike in the pits but notes, "we want to get this meeting done, as it's a long way to come". I'll watch the return fixture at Stoke the next evening too, and, ever polite, Paul says the forecast doesn't look good for tomorrow night, "so I hope you get to see it properly".

I wander over and hang around the pit gate and listen to David Hoggart, one of the announcers at Workington (along with the ebullient and colourful Michael Max) record updated information about tonight's meeting for the supporters' call line on Club Call. These recorded messages usually include information about prospects for the fixture that takes place that evening in light of the anticipated weather, the team line-ups for both sides from riders 1 to 7 as well as any other team news. Often these recorded items also include interviews, when possible. David records all this information easily and very professionally in just one take, which reflects his 30 years experience as an announcer and disc jockey. He started in the business "with Essex Radio" and he records these messages in a measured style that he characterises as "clinical, official and by the book". It exactly mirrors the role he'll play all night when he announces the results and times, which will contrast to the presentational style of his co-presenter, Michael Max, who will be altogether more colourful while he roves amongst all the action from his location in the centre green. David informs me that the Club Call organisation has "correspondents" in each area throughout the country, that report on every sport imaginable with the goal to "provide sufficient information for fans to ring in and want to listen". David stresses that it's "only 60p per minute, for a maximum of three minutes but often less" and he believes isn't charged at " rip-off prices". He will continually update the information throughout the evening, so it's a service popular among the home fans not at the meeting and with "away fans that will see how their teams are doing".

David has gone along to speedway since he was six, when he went with his dad, and has been seriously involved in the sport ever since "it's like a disease: it's in the blood". He had a spell as a rider in the late 1960s and early 1970s. It was a six-year career that saw him ride for Rayleigh, Canterbury and Hackney. After he retired he went into the motor industry since he'd sensibly also simultaneously served his apprenticeship as a technician while he competed as a rider. Today he lives in Wakefield – the UK's centre of excellence for abattoirs – and is fortunate enough to be able to combine running the local Ford dealership with his various other work at sports stadiums. In the world of speedway he's regularly involved at Sheffield and Workington.

The diminutive and hardy Sean Wilson who will guest that night for Workington in place of Stoney interrupts us. Sean has just returned from a relaxing holiday in the South of France with "the wife and three kids", where he rather pointedly notes it was 37 °C and in marked contrast to the fresh cool wind and dark clouds that presently sweep across him and Derwent Park. He's keen to find out any news he's missed while he was away from Dave; particularly the latest on Stoney's outlook and the progress he'd made after the incident with 'Boycie' the previous Friday. David recounts the events that led to Stoney's injury in matter of fact but graphic detail and then explains that Stoney has just had a skin graft operation that very day. Sean and David both have some familiarity with these operations, so they both already know it usually takes five days to establish if it's even been successful. Though David has no answer for Sean's quick fire but concerned question of "what about the nerve damage though?" which invariably will be horrendously and excruciatingly painful. He does report that apparently "Carl is upset" because he'd taken the incident to be a "racing accident" since he always considered and thought that he was friends with Boycie. But "as Boycie hasn't rung up" to enquire about his condition, he's now not so sure. After he mentioned this fact, David searches for some extenuating factor and then rhetorically suggests to Sean that "it's just an oversight?" who pointedly offers no comment. Equally Sean has also made no mention of or comparison with the horrific experiences he's had with the serious injuries that he's suffered, and recovered from, in the past few years. Just as he leaves to get changed, Sean wishes Stoney well but notes that speedway injuries are always unpredictable in their arrival and effects but "are part of the job we do". Until he broke his neck "I'd never had a freaking thing, except a small shoulder injury, in eight years then boom, boom, boom!"

After Sean has left to get changed for the meeting, David mentions that he believes that Stoney has a strong "instinct to race" and his preference is always to ride "fast and hard" to try to beat his opponents fairly. Even when he rides in the World Championship, where mental and physical toughness is paramount, he "won't nail them even though he's had it done to him lots of times, but won't do it back to them". In order to become World Champion, it's widely acknowledged that you must be "totally focused on that objective", almost to the exclusion of everything else in your life. Friends, family and especially other riders have to become secondary to your ambitions. You also need to exhibit a strong will to win that allows you deliberately push others aside and sometimes put other riders into the fence with equanimity. You may be the most easy-going and friendliest chap off the track, but on it you've got to be a "Jekyll and Hyde figure" and "change your personality" to really succeed. For David "every era has its ultimate professional" – he names Ivan Mauger, Ole Olsen, Hans Nielsen and Tony Rickardsson as examples – where it's "ability that has got them on the ladder, but focus and dedication got them to the next level". After his many years involvement in British speedway he sadly concludes that the "English riders don't have the commitment to produce that little bit extra". Not that the English riders "can't ride well on a given day and with a bit of luck succeed" but they can't consistently compete like some of the more dedicated professionals. Many of these great riders establish their greatness by ensuring all aspects of their life are "focused on their objectives" and have strict regimes that include "coaching and mentoring, diet and training" to enhance their ability and, obviously, compliment their top-notch equipment. Success lies not only in the preparation and approach, but also "none of these are getting distracted by the social side – the drinking, the girls and the like". After he has painted this slightly gloomy picture, David goes on to see some positives on the British horizon. Although we have had a "raft of good guys coming down the rankings", we have still possibilities for English success in the Grand Prix with Scott Nicholls and Lee Richardson. He also believes that "it will come again, after a bit of a hiatus" since we have young riders with promise like Chris Neath, Chris Harris and Simon Stead who've "got the opportunity if they can sustain it". On this positive note for England's future on the world stage, David heads off to join the referee in his box for his final preparations for his announcer's duties for this evening's fixture. He might quickly return since his regular verbal partner in crime, Michael Max, has left it right until the very last minute to arrive this evening for his duties on the centre green. After I saw Michael whip the crowd up at Glasgow Speedway in an extremely partisan fashion, I'm surprised and mystified that his pro-Scots, pro-Glasgow allegiances aren't obvious to the Workington faithful. David reassures me that "Michael is the ultimate professional, you'd never know about his allegiance to Glasgow" or how partisan he is against Edinburgh "always calling them scum but that's how they like it in Glasgow".

Just as the riders come out for their introductory parade, Michael finally arrives in time to join them before he seamlessly but confidently and wittily launches into his introductions of them all to the crowd. Michael is a larger-than-life figure – in his distinctive Joe 90 cum Harry Worth type glasses – with a larger-than-life presentational style which he intersperses throughout with wry, sardonic comments and asides. In the main grandstand it appears most of the seats are already taken and there's also a good crowd scattered throughout the rest of Derwent Park. That said, the crowd definitely doesn't appear as large as I remember it on my other visits, although the cold wind and black clouds throughout the day can't have exactly helped boost the overall attendance. There are a noticeably large number of women in the crowd, of all ages, and many people wear a variety of blue items that proclaim their loyalty to all things Workington Speedway. Michael does his bit for the future of the sport when he urges the crowd to give the BSPA questionnaire and survey their full attention tonight, since it will hopefully provide some vital "demographic data" to benefit the understanding of contemporary British speedway.

The Comets lead after the first race before a bizarre heat 2 sees both of the home sides reserves painfully collide with each other after, as they often say, James Courtney "lost shape" (after his chain snapped) in the corner and was then avoided by Barrie Evans but the following Aidan Collins had no choice but to crash into his stricken Comets' team-mate. The ambulance is called onto the track and there's a long delay to minister to the fallen riders, which finally includes a short trip on board said vehicle back to the pits. Despite the crash, both riders carry on with the rest of the meeting in that resilient fashion for which speedway riders are justifiably renowned. Though in the re-run of the race, without the excluded Courtney, Stoke ease to an uncontested 5-0 after Collins unfortunately retires at the outset feeling the after effects of his injured ankle. Michael tries to rouse the crowd and inject some fervour, when he asks for a shout of " W" and a series of other letters that ultimately and rather mutedly spells "Workington". The next few races go against the home riders and their supporters fidget listlessly in their seats. Michael takes the opportunity of a gap in proceedings, while they attempt to grade some problematic first bend bumps from the track, to thrust his roving microphone under the nose of Comets captain Shaun Tacey for his thoughts on the season so far. He notes that overall for the team "it's been a really bad year for injuries" for which there's no real explanation except bad luck and circumstance. Shaun rejects Michael's suggestion that the improved performance of the modern speedway bikes might be a contributory factor in some of these accidents, "the bikes aren't quicker for four laps, but the engines rev quicker, making the back wheel go faster, so when you do hit a bump you really take off". He's also quick to stress that injuries to visitors often come from "riders who don't know the track, who don't treat it with enough respect".

A rider that treats the track with respect and rides it with considerable aplomb is Workington's young and rising star rider, James Wright. A thrilling heat 5 sees Stoke's Robbie Kessler power past Scott Robson on lap 2 before James Wright then tracks him for the next two laps before he swoops up the banking of the final bend to spectacularly overtake Kessler on the line for a win by a hairs breadth. The excitement overcomes Michael Max sufficiently for him to temporarily become a Zen philosopher, albeit one with a marked Scots accent, when he remarks, all knowingly, that "on such moments do seasons and matches turn". The chorus of the music played over the tannoy echoes these sentiments with a quick burst of "if you're going to do it, do it right". Heat 7 sees Stoke's rejuvenated and very experienced rider, Alan 'Moggo' Mogridge, add a second place to go with his first race win. Moggo's whole body language, demeanour and riding style throughout the evening suggests great confidence, skill and the certainty of knowledge gained through years of speedway endeavour, which he also capably allies with visible determination. It's as if he's casually "just riding a sofa" the man behind me in the crowd noted. After he rode a sublime racing line throughout the heat, Moggo just lost out to Nieminen who dramatically 'cut him off' when he swooped round the last bend. It's an action that definitely isn't appreciated by Moggo and which immediately results in an angry helmet-to-helmet confrontation between them afterwards. Michael Max, still in Zen mode, euphemistically alludes to this confrontation as merely "words being exchanged". In fact, the season has seen Moggo consistently ride with verve and panache but, also, have a large number of confrontations[2]. At least someone's definitely feeling hot on what has turned out to be a pretty cold evening in Workington.

While he banters with the crowd, Michael galumphs about the centre green throughout like a territorial mastodon. He tries to crank up the tempo when he attempts to lead us in a chant with loud requests to "give us a C, give us an O" all the way to "Comets!" The veritable cornucopia of extremely varied Comets' sponsors mentioned in the programme get name-checked before and after each heat, almost seamlessly, throughout the evening. Michael deliberately encourages us to bear in mind their valued support, for example, when we choose our kitchens and bedrooms, identify our landscaping needs, decide to hire cars or buy them already used and even when we wish to sample the luxury of someone else doing your laundry. Many of these announcements happen as Michael stands next to the large centre green sign that advertises the Waverley Hotel (where I'm staying at the bargain rate of £28 for B&B) as it has "special rates for speedway fans".

The start-line girls don't appear at all interested in the possibility of bargain rates, no doubt because they already live in the area, or at all bothered by the freezing cold wind that blows through the stadium when they nonchalantly sit down to fill out their match programmes, with noticeable absorption, after every race. I can't say that I've noticed the start-line girls do this quite so earnestly at other tracks, well I noticed them everywhere, but not so conscientiously and assiduously filling out their programmes as they do here. They're also unmoved by the frenzy that Michael Max regularly tries to stoke up in the extremely almost catatonically quiet and largely apathetic crowd. Michael amuses himself with comments upon the standard of the racing fare served up for the punters by the Workington riders tonight. A win for Nieminen in heat 13 has him ecstatically claim, "I'm convinced that there aren't many more exciting sights than a rider going high and wide to overtake an opponent". This might not be everyone's universal first choice, but it's enough for Michael and there's very few in the crowd that will gainsay him. Not that there's still any real reaction from the assembled crowd, until they finally stir themselves sufficiently to loudly dispute the referee's decision to order a re-run of heat 14, after what Michael rather neutrally describes as "movement at the start gate". From the home crowd's perspective, justice is seen to be done in the

---

[2] Neil Machin, after Moggo and Sheffield's Andre Compton had a contretemps, refers to these spontaneous confrontations generically as "an example of the over-35-year-old speedway rider syndrome". Suddenly racing incidents that you'd have ignored in your youth become seen, by the older rider, as personal slights that require physical confrontation. Neil worries that this attitude of increased hypersensitivity and the aggressive behaviour that results could lead older, more experienced riders like Moggo onto a slippery slope, since the stronger and more combustible of these younger lads might instead get provoked and "really twat him one day". Neil also, I assume, half-jokingly suggests that all riders should be compulsorily retired when they reach 35.

The Workington 'Brolly Dollies'. © Jeff Scott

re-run of the heat when the young Workington riders, Courtney and Wright, race to the chequered flag ahead of their opponents to record a 5-1 heat victory that takes Workington into the lead for the first time this evening. It's only a narrow one-point lead, but the crowd moves easily from catatonic torpor to ecstatically wild scenes of celebration in a blink of an eye. They hop around deliriously as everyone, young and old alike, appears to have leapt, as one, to their feet to celebrate the race win.

Since everything depends on the result of the last race, Michael stokes up the atmosphere further with a few well-chosen phrases that repeatedly emphasise the potential thrill of this dénouement that will, he predicts, most likely feature a Workington victory. The crowd bubbles at the prospect of an exciting finale but in the end, it's anti-climactic. An engine failure for Ashworth near the start line guarantees a narrow Workington victory, of 45-44, when the subsequent three rider race results in a drawn heat. The crowd, as one, wave their programme boards and fill out their programmes, including the four start-line girls who did so rather than immediately rush to the warmth of the changing rooms. To my mind that not only demonstrates their love and dedication to the speedway but also shows where their true priorities lie. The loud cheers that greet the rider parade — as if there's been a vital, closely fought victory in a World Cup Final or a Third World country that has just won its independence — is extremely animated among the crowd and the riders. The riders smile broadly, joined as they are by a delighted Michael Max, who waves to all and sundry with a gusto that would never betray his Glasgow loyalties or Scottish roots. By the time he returns to the pits, Michael is happy to chat for a few minutes but is also anxious to set off on the journey back to Glasgow that he's done at high speed many, many times before. The meeting has inexplicably finished later than usual, so if he doesn't leave soon he'll miss his regular treat of a late night snack at McDonald's along the way home.

Off to eat and drink elsewhere, the crowd swarms from the stadium in a hubbub of chatter about the evening's racing in the way that you get in proper speedway towns; where it's *the* sport for the local people and something that's regularly discussed within the community. The sort of cool town where even all the girls know everything there is to know about the speedway and appreciate its many fine, often complicated, intricacies. It's cold, but I think that maybe I should hang around for a little while longer in case I'm lucky enough to bump into one of those keen and well informed start-line girls. The riders and mechanics pack away their tools and efficiently load their vans. In contrast to the week before, the visiting riders will have no need for a police escort out of town, nor does it look remotely possible that anyone will have their van

[3] The start-line girls were known as the Workington "Start Tarts" until Graham and Denise Drury arrived as the promoters at the club. They are now more sophisticatedly known as the Workington "Brolly Dollies". They are by brolly colour – Red: Catherine McEuan; Blue: Charlotte Hayton; Green: Adele Rodgers and Yellow: Kayleigh Boag.

window broken, like Boycie did, since the meeting has passed without injury and almost completely without rancour. Though, if there had to be a candidate for collective mob violence, the smart money would probably identify Moggo as the likeliest target. To my great disappointment, it has begun to look more likely that I'll be invited to ride for Workington the next night, than I will have a chance encounter with the start-line girls[3]. Though, maybe I just haven't recognised them now they have changed their clothes. Either way, I leave to join the throng in the car park to for the short trip back to a warm speedway welcome at the Waverley Hotel. Hopefully there will be lots of animated speedway chat there and, maybe, not too many coins already lined up on the pool table when I arrive.

29th July Workington v. Stoke (Premier League) 45-44

SKY CHATTER

"I think he's got the bike made out of elastic bands, it takes him a lap to get it wound up" David Norris (on Scott Nicholls)

RANDOM SCB RULES

12.2.1 In the event of accident resulting in a Competitor being taken to Hospital, the Helmet should accompany the Competitor.

I start the day of the return meeting between the Stoke Potters and the Workington Comets in the Waverley Hotel located in down town Workington. It's an establishment recommended by the club and even advertises its services on the Comets' centre green. This sign boasts of 'special rates' for fans and is conveniently located five minutes away from the track in the town itself. It's a comfortable and popular hotel with fans and riders alike as well as being frequently used by the Comets' owner Tony Mole and his family. Over the years the hotel has returned the gesture of support, since it has regularly sponsored many Comets' riders over the seasons. They say the most important meal of the day is breakfast and the Waverley Hotel serves a meal that, if not fit for a king, is definitely fit for most speedway riders, judged by the gusto with which they clear their plates the morning I'm there. Breakfast consists of a self-service buffet, which offers a selection of hot and cold items, but sadly doesn't include Cocopops, though there is the chance to use one of those nifty industrial-sized continuous toasters. It's popular with the riders who've stayed there and last night these included Sunderland born Scott Robson, unusually minus his brother since it appeared for years you couldn't see one without the other, and

Too early to enter. © Jeff Scott

The entrance team before the rush. © Jeff Scott

Shaun Tacey by pits access way and mascot.
© Jeff Scott

Norwich-born Shaun Tacey. He is dressed in that off-duty speedway rider uniform of jeans, T-shirt and fashionable trainers (brown in this instance) and Shaun is accompanied by his rather cute three year-old son, called Vans O'Neil Tacey, from which we can probably surmise some degree of interest in the world of surfing exists within the family. Shaun is a very attentive daddy; he constantly chats with and reassures his son ("I love you") in an easy manner, throughout breakfast while he makes sure that his son is happy with his selection from the wide variety of possible choices that the buffet has to offer.

It's also a breakfast fit for a speedway owner, since we're joined in the breakfast room by "Kidderminster based businessman Tony Mole" (as Nigel Pearson in the *Speedway Star* invariably describes him), along with his partner Zanna and their attractive daughter Emily, who closely clutches her ubiquitous dolly. Emily is a sweet and wilful three and a half year old child, who appears totally disinterested in breakfast or even remaining still for any short period. She'd much rather explore the room, establish her boundaries and get to know the other residents in the dining room. She's particularly enamoured with how close she can get to the two riders who breakfast in front of me, and stands fascinated on a raised walkway that's just right for someone of her reduced stature, captivated by their every movement. She studies them closely before she makes an unexpected move to playfully grab one of them round the neck from behind. She's resisted Tony's increasingly loud and hectoring instructions to come back and away from the other guests. When she tries to embrace the riders, Tony calls, "come away from them – they're not interested in women". It's an accidental double entendre that has the whole room laughing and the two riders, suddenly with everyone looking at them dining together, struggle to find a reply, since they appear to all the world as a gay couple. When the laughter dies away, Tony sheepishly explains to the room, "I didn't mean it that way, I meant it's great when a strange woman puts her arms around your neck from behind but disappointing if she's only three".

Outside the hotel after breakfast, Shaun loads things into his blue van which has a drivers cab that shows all the usual signs associated with a long distance driver. There's a proper mug rather than a disposable one, the scattered papers and wrappers from various food items along with the essential trusty map for all those diversions undertaken by the knowledgeable driver in an attempt to avoid the inevitable but unpredictable traffic jams. I tell Shaun that when I saw Vans dressed in his replica mini-kevlars in the Workington pits last night, he looked "very cute" and really looked the part, in miniature, when he stood next to his father's speedway bike. Vans looks at me quizzically so I reassure him he "looked very grown up, when standing with daddy". Shaun, as a super proud father, informs me that at three years Vans already rides a motorbike with some skill and real aptitude. I quiz Vans with "are you going to grow up like your daddy?" to which, quick as flash, Shaun replies, "I hope not!" We would have chatted for longer but Shaun is delighted to see an old friend pull up in a car alongside his van, smartly dressed in snappy suit with a flower ostentatiously pinned in the lapel for the wedding he's going to later. They both appear delighted to have coincidentally met again and they immediately start to excitedly catch up on gossip, mutual friends and old times. Shaun waves goodbye to me saying, "drive safely; I'll see you later at Stoke".

The journey out of Workington is mostly on a beautifully scenic road that is, inevitably at this time of the year, crowded with convoys of cars with caravans or battered camper vans that slowly crawl through the spectacular beauty of the mountains, hills and lakes of the Lake District towards the M6. Once I get there I will have easy access south to the Stoke and the Potteries or, if the fancy took me, north to the Scottish Borders. However, since the road is jammed with slow vehicles, I get another chance to appreciate the rugged appeal of the beautiful landscape, adjacent to the Lake District towns of Keswick and Windermere. There are still many large black rain clouds, that scud across the sky extremely quickly, and the contrast in colours highlights the magnificence of the scenery. The empty road, back towards Workington, has a phalanx of vintage Rolls-Royces and Bentleys decked out for the many weddings that they'll be an essential romantic part of later in the day. It makes you think that Romance and Workington must really go together; maybe it's something in the air or the water to make the demand for commitment so high among these affectionate couples?

Once we've all wended our way through the amazing vistas of the countryside and hills, there's the additional pleasure of the lengthy traffic jam that forms just before you reach the motorway junction roundabout. Still, it gives us the chance to look at the stationary queue of cars that vainly attempt to leave the very popular Saturday morning car boot sale or, with a large number of broken down vehicles unable to negotiate any more steep undulations, admire the earnest but pointless attempts of their owners who struggle to cool their steaming, overheated engines.

The open road of the southbound motorway is a relief to experience after the tortuous drive out of the environs of the Lake District you invariably encounter at the height of the holiday season. It's a joy that's short lived because, just beyond Manchester, I join a huge tailback of traffic queued back for eight miles before the first available exit junction for Stoke. A considerable time later, after I've slowly inched my way through this unexpected but huge M6 traffic jam, I find myself near the end of my journey to the Potteries.

Unfortunately, the speedway club's advice about a bed and breakfast they'd recommend to visitors leaves something to be desired. It is spartan and reasonably comfortable, though my room is continually heated to sauna-like temperatures and has sealed double-glazed windows. Most likely to dull the noise of the nearby motorway traffic, when it actually moves quickly enough to create a noise, since the hotel is located practically on the traffic island that leads off from the motorway junction. Still armed with directions from my friendly landlady and an ill-fitting key for when I return in the pitch darkness much later, I head off in search of Loomer Road Stadium, the home of the Stoke 'Easy Rider' Potters Speedway Club.

Stoke is habitually referred to by non-residents of the area as a city; whereas it's really made up of a loose association of five towns, all located in roughly the same locale and helpfully known to outsiders as Stoke. As if to illustrate this very fact, the home of the Stoke Easy Rider Potters is based on the Loomer Industrial Estate in the Chesterton area of Newcastle-under-Lyme. When I arrive, though I passed through torrential downpours only ten miles away, it's a bright but very cloudy day with thick black clouds that threaten in the near distance. It's the sort of day that hampers track preparation and reduces crowd numbers, since they stay away in the full expectation of later rain that will force the postponement or possible abandonment of the fixture. Although the meeting is due to start in less than three hours the large car park is barred by a locked barrier at its entrance with the stadium off to the right in the distance. I wait for a while outside which gives me the chance to study the nearby surroundings. There is countryside and hills in the distance while Loomer Road itself is made up of many industrial buildings on one side of the road with a small estate of houses on the other side of the street. Which, with my town planners hat on, makes this a mixed use light industrial area and the warehouse buildings

noticeably appear to be of a much older vintage than the more recently arrived residential dwellings. I'm sure that this won't obviate the traditional noise and dirt objections that all tracks attract but, as it's clearly an area of business use, it might mitigate the power that any such complaints enjoy with the local council officers.

I duck under the barrier and wander off to the apparently deserted stadium. In fact, while nothing stirs on the impressive but desolate standing terraces and there's absolutely zero signs of movement in the darkened interior of the stadium grandstand, there are a couple of men in overalls industriously at work on the track, who alternate their turns to drive the tractor around the circuit to grade the track surface. From the terraces of the covered home-straight grandstand, I watch them work feverishly, while I stand just in front of a glass-fronted and presently darkened bar that signals the back edge of the terraces. After some time spent in silent contemplation of the scene around me, I wander to the perimeter fence of the track and loudly call over, above the engine noise of the tractor and the grinding sound of the grader, to the shorter tanned man with hair that's lightly thin on top. He's dressed in well-used overalls and watches completely absorbed as the tractor slowly completes another circuit. After I shout, "I'm looking for Dave Tattum" a couple of times without response, he eventually says, "That's me!" as though this has surprised him. Not that he's called Dave Tattum, but that someone bothers to look for him at this time of the afternoon on a race day. It's not long before I realise that Dave is one of those preternaturally frenetic men, though ideally suited to be the energetic, hands-on promoter of the Stoke Potters club. Dave multitasks relentlessly throughout the evening without any noticeable diminution in his very high energy levels or any drop in his enthusiasm. He is more than happy to chat amiably about the club and his vision of the future for the few minutes he can just about spare, before he has to again crack on with the many tasks that form his many responsibilities as the promoter. Throughout all the time we stand talking about life and his speedway philosophy, until Dave finally rejoins him, the other man in overalls continues to work industriously on the track preparations. This diligent worker turns out to be Nigel Crabtree, a former rider at the Club, but currently the Track Curator as well as the manager of the Stoke Premier League team.

Dave has been promoter at the club, this time round, since 1998 along with his wife Caroline, though he's quick to inform me that they're separated with "new partners" but they continue to work successfully together "we work well at the speedway just not away from it". The programme lists Dave as Promoter and Caroline as Finance Director, "she's very much involved in finance and fixtures", by extension, this leaves him in charge of the traditional responsibilities of a promoter – such as the recruitment and selection of a winning team that attracts fans to watch the club race regularly. They have a long lease at the stadium and it's "all under our control", not just the speedway but also the "bars, football and dogs" and, wherever possible, they try to "maximise the use of the stadium"; especially the track, on which they run 'short track' and bantam grass track meetings, sidecar championships as well as the speedway. They also run "loads of training days, one or two a week if possible" which I gather involves Dave in some "personal tuition" along with Nigel Crabtree. Although, unlike Nigel, he was never a rider he "understands riding" and "can put three decent laps together". Not only do the training schools ensure the track is regularly used, it also gives them the early chance to spot potentially talented young British riders. The Conference team already has two successful products from this approach to rider development in the shape of Kriss Irving and Jack Hargreaves, who have already impressed and progressed sufficiently to regularly ride at reserve for the senior team at the club in the Premier League. It's these sorts of dividends from his hard work that Dave particularly relishes.

Dave is unequivocal that speedway has always been "my sport" which he has "followed for many years". Both Caroline and Dave are local and consider Stoke as their "own town" though, to be exact, in Dave's case it's "Hanley really". He's followed Stoke from their early incarnation, when they raced at the Sun Street track located at the bottom of Hanley. Sometimes he still can't believe that he has been lucky enough to have managed to find a way to apply his own "knowledge and talent" into a sport he loves. Not that you're born with these abilities as Dave notes he has "learnt off other people, you never stop learning". A roll call of many influential teachers slips easily off his tongue including the "riders of their time in the 1980s Eric Monaghan and Nigel Crabtree"; Peter Jarman who "rode here many moons ago"; along with the influence of John Dews, "if you could follow John successfully – especially in track preparation – you wouldn't go far wrong" and he "mixed a lot" with Dave Parry, the former rider, team manager and now main sponsor at Wolves.

The speedway at Stoke is a "family run show, a good clean sport" run for "complete families, which you can see for yourself as there are always loads of little kids running about the place". Dave proudly states the "racing here is absolutely superb" and claims that visiting teams "like coming here". However, for Dave, the overall success of the club and the atmosphere on race night is down to a coordinated team effort with a "huge circle of people who make it happen on the night". He "wouldn't like to single anyone out in case I miss one out!" but is keen to stress that he doesn't lose sight of the fact that "we're putting a show on with Nigel and I playing to the crowd". Dave emphasises that they've "all got a will to win" at the club but the "rivalry with other clubs is very good, not naughty and nasty at all". Though, it is also fair to say, that this is not an opinion necessarily shared by some of the other clubs who visit Stoke. He also places great importance on the clubs relationship with their loyal fans, "I'm a hands-on person; very protective of the supporters – I need to understand and take on board their frustrations, thinking and expectations." Generally the knowledgeable Stoke crowd has a good understanding and tolerance of the trials and tribulations that ordinarily impact upon a promoter's life during the season – no matter whether it's guests, averages or the weather. The proof is definitely in the pudding since speedway at Stoke bucks the national trend with "crowds going up last year and maintaining this year, although you always want more". Though, despite this success through the turnstiles, it's still impossible for them to survive solely on their attendances alone, so their vital relationship with the "very good sponsors Easy Rider is essential", particularly since it would be "very hard to improve without their help". They continue to gratefully enjoy the assistance "year after year" from Cyril Chell and his motorcycle companies based in Stafford, and it's a level of support that enhances his already well-deserved reputation in the road racing community[1].

When asked to describe what he loves about the sport, Dave immediately calls, "everything – I wouldn't single out just one thing" as he heads back onto the track to help Nigel with last minute ministrations to the surface for tonight's clash with Workington. By now signs of life stir elsewhere in the stadium, many staff arrive and even a few fans that immediately claim their favoured place on the terraces adjacent to the pits area. From this activity, I gather that the gate has finally

---

[1] The 2006 season has seen Stoke become the first Premier League side to introduce an air safety fence. Dave noted about this development, "I have to admit that it is something we are very proud to be associated with, though the credit goes to Cyril Chell of Easy Rider who was the driving force behind it all". It's also a financial boon since it has increased the level and number of sponsors the club can attract to advertise on the fence itself.

opened at the entrance to the stadium car park and I can see a small queue of keen punters start to filter into the grounds early, in eager anticipation of the evening ahead. In charge of the gate operation and numerous other behind the scenes functions at the speedway club is the charming, practical and very plainspoken Mrs Caroline Tattum. It's very much a family affair on the gate as her young cousins Torty and Gabrielle Goring also help out. They're both very capable and superbly well informed about their work – since they have worked with Caroline for two and four years respectively – as well as all things to do with speedway in general and the club in particular. After they've helped out with the rush of fans at the gate, they'll both head off for their next duties of the evening as the club's rather glamorous start-line girls. Torty has taken her interest in speedway even further than her race night responsibilities, since she is also the girlfriend of Stoke's potential star rider of the future, the young Jack Hargreaves. It was a case of romance across the bikes in the pits; they met when she was 15 and have been going out ever since. It also enables Torty to keep a really close eye on Jack's progress and professional development from the vantage point of the start line, when she's sat on the centre green between the heats or slightly less so when she snogs with him enthusiastically in the pits after the meeting.

It's very noticeable that Caroline, Gabrielle and Torty appear to know absolutely everyone by sight or name as they arrive, whether they're fans or riders. Caroline has a kind word, sarcastic comment or solicitous enquiry for everybody that passes. Her engaging, albeit very direct manner, comes naturally to her and her ability to easily get on with people, to know their individual foibles and idiosyncrasies, is vital to ensure that everything at the club runs as smoothly as possible. All her staff throughout the stadium – whether Gina in the kitchen, the other kitchen girls, Pam in the bar and anyone else – work as a "very tight team, we're friends really but we're all quite professional". You only have to spend a few minutes in Caroline's company to realise that she'll miss very little that's going on around her, and it's a skill that's helped by her work on the gate as, "you can hear what people are really saying". I'm captivated with her knowledge and company; the combination of her strong opinions and blunt indiscretion make for a delightfully enjoyable hour with her and all the staff on the gate. Caroline's mother, June, arrives to work on the turnstiles and, shortly afterwards, we're also joined by her "partner in crime" the bubbly and friendly Gaynor who is usually a company rep for a stationary company but on race night works the cars at the gate with the rest of the girls[2]. Caroline is justifiably very proud of the whole team of her staff that work on race nights "the girls are all brilliant, they never put a foot wrong". Caroline proudly claims that when you visit Stoke Speedway, it's always memorable "it's a good evening – though the racing is everything, the bar is good afterwards and the atmosphere's loads better than lots of other places!"[3] Not that the management of the club hasn't been without its struggles, particularly since the whole Potteries area has suffered economically over the past decade with the closure of the areas traditional industries (" particularly where they've shut the pots"), which has drastically reduced the spending power available for discretionary activities like entertainment. While there has been a recent upsurge in major companies who have located their distribution centres in the area — mostly due to its easy access to the vast network of motorways and the ready supply of cheap, hard working labour — the majority of local people are still careful with their money, unless they know that they'll be properly entertained. It's a situation that's compounded by the Stoke people's traditional attitude to speedway, since they notoriously look down on it ("they all frown about it") as beneath them, due to it's long standing reputation for being common and dirty. It's a perception not helped by the fact that "this place has a terrible name for shutting down, even Dave had it in 91 and it went under!" However, the Tattums along with everyone else involved at the club have slowly built the club back up. The general improvement has been reflected in the increased crowd numbers as, "people appreciate the entertainment with good racing and riders giving their all!" According to Caroline, this is particularly true of the racing witnessed in the Conference League. The campaign to convince local people, across a wide catchment area, of the value of a night out at the speedway has been a long haul from when they began in 1998, but has now just started to show demonstrable results. If you listen to Caroline speak passionately, and I believe her, "what we're doing and achieving must be working as our gates have steadily risen; we've held onto last years promising increase so far in 2005 while throughout the industry many other teams have seen a bit of a drop". Like speedway everywhere, the sport has the advantage of "being a good, clean family sport also here, not like some places, it's friendly and not at all cliquey!" Caroline is down to earth about all her justifiable claims of staff commitment, family atmosphere and her careful management because, ultimately, the only criteria that counts are the attendances, "all I know is how many people come in or not".

The overall success in improved attendances Caroline ascribes to "team work" with her close-knit group of capable staff in combination with "Dave's work on the speedway side", particularly the motivated and very committed riders that Stoke have in their various teams ("I pay them when they come in"). This success has come at severe cost, in terms of sickening injuries to key riders including "Pickers" [Paul Pickering] who's "sorely missed" with his "arm really bad all full of pins" along with "Jan [Staechmann] who would give his all for Stoke and go through a brick wall for us". Caroline appears genuinely upset when she speaks about these injured riders to me; the club has, obviously, to carry on but it's not without pause or consideration for the personal implications for the people that have become injured.

I can't speak highly enough of how impressed I was with the smooth operation of all the staff on the entrance gate of the Loomer Road Stadium. In another life, it would be great fun to get a job there but, sadly, even if there was a vacancy I'm not sure that I'd be good enough to join the team! The work is intense and the Saturday race night is extremely popular, if the crowds I saw are anything to judge things by. Throughout the evening, all the gate staff banter with themselves and everyone who passes the gates — the riders, mechanics and fans. They work together smoothly as a team, get the job done and let everyone through with an easy familiarity and confidence backed up with a friendly word or jovial comment. Whenever there's a brief slack moment, which are few and far between, they dance around or chat in desultory fashion among themselves. They're perceptive people and can also be quite cutting. I've hardly been there any time before Caroline rhetorically but with faux innocence asks, "are you a bit of an anorak yourself, Jeff?"

---

[2] Caroline and Gaynor are an inseparable duo — they're friends away from the track, they work at all the home meetings and travel to away fixtures together. They're a pleasant but slightly frightening combination of women, with diametrically opposed approaches to life's inevitable little crises. Caroline is the 'Weight Loss Queen' of the pair and has previously "lost ten stone, put it all back on and then lost seven stone again". However, they've been nicknamed Britney Tears and Christina Aggravation on account of when there's "trouble" Gaynor gets "tearful" and Caroline gets "fired up". They have numerous stories, though only very few of them are repeatable! Their travel together to away meetings is always fraught with difficulties, despite Gaynor being a "calm, brilliant driver", mostly due to Caroline's legendarily poor navigational skills. Already this season they have had a marathon 13-hour return journey to a rained-off meeting in Berwick "where we never saw a wheel turn" before they got marooned in thick fog on the Buxton Hills, after they initially got lost somewhere around Sheffield. On another occasion, they got severely lost on a Conference League trip to Mildenhall, mostly due to a route "plotted after half a bottle of wine the night before" which took them to Mildenhall in Wiltshire not Suffolk as required.

[3] Prior to the Tattums' rule, Neil Machin had informed Caroline that "there used to be a lot of 'game' girls at Stoke". This is no longer the case and Caroline has even had to confront Gaynor about the persistent allegations about her previous wilder incarnation at the club, which she denies.

Caroline provides great entertainment and good value when it comes to her observations on the people and characters that regularly attend the speedway at Stoke as well as many others within the sport. You definitely known where you stand with her, while she has a refreshingly blunt attitude to her own life and the people she encounters. She definitely has a long list of favourites – whether riders, officials, rival promoters or fans – and a shorter list of people for whom she lacks respect or, worse still, harbours antipathy. One of the first of her favourites to arrive is the experienced Stoke rider Alan 'Moggo' Mogridge. By contemporary standards he'd be classed as a veteran, though his recent form has undergone a bit of a renaissance this season with some consistently high scoring. Moggo greets them with a smiling, jovial "good evening people" before he swiftly heads off to the pits, Caroline notes, "unlike some moodier riders he's always happy and easy to get on with". She particularly approves of the referee's "you can have a laugh with" – she names Flint, Ackroyd and Dowling as well as her good friend Dave Peet, who's now gone over to "the other side" when he became co-promoter at Hull[4]. She speaks very highly of many of her speedway colleagues at other clubs. Her list includes Alan Dick at Glasgow "he's wonderful and will move heaven and earth to help you" and she holds the Glasgow supporters in equally high regard. She also "loves" George English, particularly because he'll change fixtures to accommodate you and has been extremely flexible in the past, for which Caroline is sincerely and vocally most grateful. While Neil Machin is the authority figure for her in the sport and "is the first one you consult about anything you're not sure of!" She gets on well with Peter Waite from Berwick and the Stoke club prides itself that it enjoys a jovial and bantering relationship with him. Caroline isn't ever afraid to chase for outstanding payments from any promoter, but knows from experience that humour works best with Peter. A few references to his exotic foreign holidays, big car or ready sympathy "I know he's struggling, we're all struggling but he always laughs with me" always works wonders[5].

She stresses to me that she respects many promoters that she doesn't know so well, such as Newport's Tim Stone and Workington's Graham Drury, who'll shortly arrive with his wife Denise ("they're a very nice couple, I can't wait for them to arrive"). Some of the rider's girlfriends have earlier made allegations of aggression, temper loss and bad language towards them by Graham before last night's meeting. Caroline summarily dismisses these allegations as tittle-tattle and absolutely nothing to do with her relationship with the Drurys, whom she has very little to do with never mind that "I don't really speak to them". These rather lurid accounts of swearing, extreme anger and temper loss in public also contrast sharply to my own experience last night, when Graham was very busy but nonetheless hospitable and polite. Nor does it sound like the sort of behaviour you'd expect of someone who, away from speedway, reputedly works as a magistrate.

However, there are also a number of *bêtes noires* for Caroline within speedway about whom she's either brutally cutting or pointedly vociferous, when their names arise. Not that I need to raise any names since, once started, Caroline has strong, spontaneous opinions. The Oxford promoter Nigel Wagstaff is someone she mentions strongly in dispatches; mostly for a dispute that involved a surprise birthday cake for Jack Hargreaves, which he, allegedly, refused to allow to be brought into the pits. This incident happened after Oxford had just lost a Conference League fixture to Stoke, so was seen by most people there as sour grapes before some semblance of common sense finally prevailed. "Make sure you put in about that freaking man, he hates us anyway and he really fancies himself with his two pound Oxfam suits and his terrible black roots". Gaynor nods in agreement at this tale and calls Waggy a "tosspot", which then causes Caroline to take the moral high ground, "I can't comment on other promoters". Overall, according to Caroline, the best rule of thumb about the quirks, foibles and personalities of other promoters is ultimately "whoever Dave likes is not a good sign"[6].

[4] Caroline jokingly answers all calls from Dave Peet, when his name appears as the caller on her mobile, with "sorry I'm still not sleeping with you".

[5] After my visit, Caroline is subsequently keen to stress the strength of her relationship with Peter and to emphasise my misapprehension when I thought she fulminated about a disputed loan fee for Joachim Kugelmann, unpaid travel expenses or any consideration of the use of the ultimate sanction of the involvement of the BSPA to resolve the situation.

[6] Caroline is not the only blunt and plainly spoken woman at the Stoke entrance gate since her friend, Gaynor, is also not averse to giving people the sharp side if her tongue, if the situation merits. She particularly recalls a coach load of Edinburgh fans in 2003, many of whom insisted that they didn't want to pay their entrance fee because they were going to remain on their coach throughout the meeting. A stand off ensued, as Gaynor suspected that they would still watch the meeting from the comfort of the coach, but without payment. As there are two sides to every story, it was an experience that made a strong enough impression on Gary Lough for it to appear in his book *10th yer baws!*

Back at the entrance the young Wright brothers arrive, James and Charles, with their granddad and ex-Belle Vue rider Jim Yacoby, who drives the van. Caroline characteristically greets them with some pointed observations regarding the mystery of hereditary genes between Jim and his grandson James, "when the granddad is as ugly as this, how come he's as handsome as he is with the blond hair?" Before she immediately asks James, in the same breath, "is your Dad sneaking in the back?" After they've laughed, shared some jokes and driven off Caroline very approvingly notes the gifted talents of both "young lads" and even admires that their mum Lynn's "dog won Crufts"[7].

The arrival of the club's security man Phil Farrelly provokes great hilarity among all the girls on the gate; mostly it appears for his previous attempts to "try to impress everyone with his muscles and fake tan". The fact that he's a figure of fun to these women seems to have passed Phil by, not that Caroline is surprised "as he's got the brains of a gnat". He appears oblivious to their loud teasing or unkind comments from any of the girls on the gate, Gaynor loudly claims, "he's like Bo Selecta, so ugly he shouldn't be allowed out". His reputation is such that the girls have also teased Robbie Kessler that he's Phil's twin, which Robbie didn't see the funny side of when they brought it up. After the break up of Dave and Caroline's marriage, Phil even took it upon himself to pose close by to Caroline in the freezing cold in skimpy tee shirts, without success, blissfully unaware that she often wondered about his level of activity upstairs. Not that these girls actually need any protection from unwanted male advances, though they put the fact that many people "don't take liberties" down to their approach to "try and work with everyone". Caroline counts her good fortune at the club, "we don't get trouble at speedway" although they feel Phil is somewhat ornamental in his role because "he's supposed to be security yet we have to tell him who to keep out!" Despite the apparent ferocity of the badinage, they're all (in my opinion) lovely caring people really with a soft side they deliberately keep hidden in case it disrupts their façade[8].

By now the queues of cars and riders vans have built up into a long double line but are still processed very swiftly, with a pleasantry or comment here and there, by the entrance gate ladies. Caroline, Gaynor, Gabrielle and Torty make a brilliantly effective unit; they move people through then, once they're through the gates, they marshal them enough for them to park carefully to fully utilise the limited parking space available in front of the stadium. They all aim to ensure that everyone pays the appropriate admission charge, buys a programme and, hopefully, also purchase a "lucky raffle ticket". Torty deliberately slightly hangs back before she then pounces to offer the occupants of the car or van the chance to buy a raffle ticket from her. Whether it's sheer charm, politeness or just the way she asks the question of people, Torty is remarkably persuasive. Caroline watches her work with approval, "this little thing is brilliant with the raffle, none of them can resist a pretty face or the way she sweetly asks them, not knowing she really knows what she's doing with them". The endless meeting and greeting, where everyone is (or feels they are) a valued friend of the club and who's attendance is warmly received; also includes especially warm welcomes for the two guests riders for tonight's meeting. The Workington guest is greeted with a muted squeal from Caroline of, "Ooh, look, it's Trent Leverington!" which appears to tie his tongue comprehensively since he can only respond with a shrug and a sheepish grin. Or, in the case of Stoke's guest, there's a screechingly ecstatic squeal of, "Ooh, look it's Phil Morris AND his dad". These greetings appear to slip easily and genuinely off Caroline's tongue, I imagine that it must be great to have your arrival create such a stir when you arrive at, what is after all, your place of work (albeit only for the evening).

However, not every young man can cope with the banter and attentions of these greetings; indeed, Stoke's young looking

[7] The dog, Didi, won 'Best in Show' at Crufts and briefly had promoter Ian Thomas working on its behalf as the dog's agent, according to his autobiography *Wheels and Deals*.

[8] They also affectionately disparage the odd job man "Tracklight Dave, only he likes to call himself 'Speedway Dave', but we all call him 'Tracklight' 'cause he can see the track lights from his bedroom". Away from his voluntary tasks at the track, Dave suffers from a condition; but, when there, he loves his work and appears to particularly enjoy the fulfilment, socialisation and camaraderie he finds at the club. I gather, though they don't say it, that they take a quiet satisfaction in the fact that working at the club makes him feel good about himself. Caroline affects to be amazed at how petty minded some people can be though, since "some freaking bastard reported him to the social" in an attempt to deprive him of his state benefits unaware that he's "not paid so they were wrong and it's okay for him to do this, plus it really helps him mentally". You could miss the sensitivity and concern that Caroline has towards other people if you only took account of her words and not her actions.

Conference League rider Kriss Irving, very touchingly blushes a deep red colour upon arrival when Caroline welcomes him with, " my – he's a handsome lad". Coincidentally enough, given tonight's visitors, he's also just driven down from Workington though the consensus on the gate is that, "he's sweet – when we visited him in hospital I said 'can I get into bed too?' and he didn't hesitate to pull back the covers".

Caroline and her team remain energetically friendly, in control but canny throughout the night. For example, during this season Stoke have had to have a different guest every week, so when any of the faithful Stoke fans actually enquire, "who tonight's guest is?" They deliberately make a point of talking that person up. Caroline thinks very highly of George Stancl and Magnus Karlsson, so it comes easily and is mostly genuinely felt and always good business sense. They speak highly of Phil Morris, though Gaynor tartly notes, "Phil rode like a freaking tosspot for six or so the last time he was here four weeks ago and we don't want to put them off by mentioning that".

By now the cars stretch an impressively long way back way down the street in double file, although I'm impressed no-one else is and I'm quickly told "this is nothing compared to the time in 2003 when the cars were backed up so far back it even affected the traffic on the A50!"

I decide to leave them to it and go to savour the atmosphere build up further from the pits area. The car park looks very crowded, as are the terraces, when I head over to the pits, a short while before the scheduled start time, it's almost a case study of the usual pre-meeting hive of activity you'd typically find everywhere throughout the country. There are mechanics everywhere with bikes in pieces and half put together, tyres being inflated and engines being fiddled with, as the riders from both teams intermittently filter back from the changing rooms in their racing gear. The home teams area of the pits looks out onto the track while the away team are hidden away round the corner; all the riders have to funnel onto the track via a sloped slip way, which itself joins the track at the fourth bend of the circuit. You can imagine that as the away riders always have to pick their way past the line of bikes in front of the home section of the pits, that it might be possible to 'accidentally' delay the odd tardy away rider and thereby, through this additional delay, occasionally earn them an unwanted time exclusion. Adjacent to the home pits, there's also a raised standing area for interested riders, promoters, mechanics and their guests to watch the racing from should they choose or have the time to do so. From this vantage point I can comfortably watch all that happens in the pits and on the track. Most noticeable, throughout the whole evening, is the manic activity of Dave Tattum and Nigel Crabtree who are absolutely everywhere for the duration of the racing. They cajole and encourage the riders, staff and each other repeatedly, one minute they're trackside on the centre green, the next moment they bark out orders in the pits or offer words of advice to the riders individually. They're passionate men who are completely absorbed in the tasks in hand. Out of the two apparently equally manic men, Nigel appears to be more prone to shortness of temper when events transpire against him. The Comet's co-promoters, Denise and Graham Drury, take a more measured and much less demonstrative approach to their interventions during this fixture.

Although, since they often stand right next to me to watch the racing, to judge by the wide range of their frequently changing facial expressions as well as Denise's frequent shouts and bellows of loud encouragement, they're no less as keenly involved in each race. Like many people I've observed on my travels, those with responsibility for the management of any speedway team, who don't actually ride, tend to spend the meeting living on their nerves and mentally ride every inch of the track themselves, albeit from a stationary position. The Drurys are no different and they issue frequent instructions, often with some impatience in Graham's case, or rush to advise on some nuance or other during a bout of frenetic pits work on the bikes between the races. As a couple they don't indulge in the frequent running about, in Dave's case he often actually sprints in his tightly fastened red and white Stoke anorak, that the Potters' managers appear to favour. Nonetheless for a last minute emergency or crisis, Graham shows a remarkable turn of speed. It's easy to form the impression that if Graham tells you something, particularly when he's in high dudgeon, you remain very much told.

Just as the meeting is about to get underway, I manage to snatch a brief word with the always friendly rider Shaun Tacey.

Apart from, obviously, hoping to ride well himself tonight Shaun has the additional responsibility of his position as Workington club captain to fulfil. Apparently, they're a relatively easy going bunch of riders so the major part of his job is to check that everyone is sufficiently motivated (something Graham makes it his business to ensure as well!) and rally the team round to help any rider in need of assistance during the always intense period of activity that is any pits area for the duration of any speedway fixture. We also chat about some of the recent topical incidents and controversies, which include, among others, Stoney's recent burn injury at Derwent Park from Craig Boyce's spinning wheel. Shaun refuses to be drawn into any real comment, merely settling for the hope that Stoney will quickly recover[9] and prefers instead to just observe, "we're a really small community, everyone knows everyone else, if there's any bad apples they soon really stand out". Minutes later, as if to emphasise the community nature of the sport of speedway in general, never mind just among the riders, there's a loud collective cheer from the crowd as the announcer congratulates the injured Paul Pickering and his wife Rachael on the birth of their baby daughter the night before. Mother and baby are reported to be doing just fine. The announcer then moves onto the business in hand between tonight's two teams and ends with the rhetorical flourish when he promises an evening of "top class speedway with no quarter asked and no quarter given".

Also stood in the crowded pen by the pits along with me and many others is the genial co-promoter of Newcastle Diamonds speedway, George English, who would usually just be an interested observer here to watch some of his Premier League rivals compete with each other. Though he is still here to watch that encounter but self-interest dictates that he's really here to watch the pair of his key riders who will both guest at Loomer Road tonight. For the home team Stoke, there's Phil Morris and the guest for Workington is the fiery and diminutive James Grieves. George is extremely anxious about the possibility of either rider sustaining any form of injury tonight, particularly since he has a vitally important race meeting at Newcastle the next night versus league leaders and local rivals Berwick. Throughout proceedings George will keep a keen weather eye on each and every race they participate in, and some of these will be against each other, while all the while he hopes for an incident free evening for both of them. George's very friendly and well-informed mother, Joan, is also at the meeting but she's away off in the crowd so I don't get to see her (or hear her) until much later in the evening, after the meeting has concluded.

During the initial heats the Stoke team appear to be a very much more confident group of riders, at least when they race round their own circuit and much more than they had been only 24 hours previously at Derwent Park. In both contests, they quickly establish an early lead in the match score but here at Loomer Road, this was due to some spectacularly effective riding rather than through misfortune for their opponents. Though that said, Trent Leverington did suffer an engine failure when he led the first race only for Adam Allott and Robbie Kessler to pass him for an opening 5-1 score. The slight improvement of a second place for Leverington on his repaired equipment, sandwiched by Evans in front and Hargreaves to the rear, was a brief respite. To say that Graham Drury looked displeased while he watched his riders perform poorly would be an understatement and his face became even more of a picture, when Paul Clews and Mogridge both easily overhauled the initial leader Scott Robson during the course of heat 3. This stretched the overall totals on the night to 14 points to 4. The next race has George English anxiously swap his weight from foot to foot throughout its duration as the Newcastle pair appear for the first time for their respective teams and then indulge themselves in their first head to head encounter of the night. The honours go to Phil Morris who defies his earlier "tosspot" moniker to win from the promising Leverington, who has already had a very busy time of it appearing in three of the first four races and, would surely have racked up more points, but for his engine problems. Or, indeed, he might have had more points money already with greater support from his team-mates. Grieves finishes third and both Diamonds riders safely negotiate the initial skirmishes, though Stoke remain comfortably in the lead.

Heat 5 results in a surprising last place for the talented James Wright who, like many in his team, appears to be in a psychological struggle to come to terms with the Loomer Road circuit. The points deficit is already so great in this contest

---

[9] It remains unspoken that we both know that he won't recover quickly.

that, by heat 6, Workington are able to call on the services of James Grieves, who wears the black and white helmet colour that signifies the use of a tactical ride. It's a necessary but inspired choice by the Drurys, since Grieves wins comprehensively to provide the Comets with their first race winner of the evening and, more importantly, reduces the deficit to 24-15. Neither of the Drurys are at all prone to Latin style displays of spontaneous elation; though Graham does permit himself a small arm gesture of celebration in the form of a brief, almost hidden, clench of the fist. I'm well-positioned to watch how much this race victory means to him, since I'm stood directly behind him. Dave Tattum contents himself with scuttling about the pits purposefully, whereas a scowling Nigel Crabtree looks a long way from contented. George English looks just plain relieved and, apart from when his riders appear on the track, he affects a supreme level of detachment.

The interpersonal dynamics of the Drurys fascinate me throughout the contest and, in my personal opinion, anyone who underestimates the contribution of Denise to their work partnership is seriously misguided. She doesn't have any outbursts, like Graham does, but this aside, she is a keen student of speedway and frequently comments to her husband on some comparatively small details that he might otherwise not have had time to appreciate. They are quite a combination with Denise who stands apparently emotionless and watches, apart from when she fills out the scorecard in her programme quickly and meticulously; while Graham either issues instructions in the calm manner of a country parson that his dress sense strongly suggests or, instead, barks them out with some ferocity.

The Grieves win is the start of a run of three successive heat victories for the Comets. The next win features a stylish victory for James Wright that included a truly exhilarating piece of riding skill to pass the experienced Phil Morris on the inside. Tacey then demonstrates superior technique to catch up with and eventually overhaul young Jack Hargreaves in heat 8 and that man Leverington occupies the minor placing, after a comparatively long four heat rest period in the pits. The match score has dramatically reduced to 28-23 and that fact is enough to bring the hint of a glimmer of a fractional show of reaction to the faces of the Drurys. There is much ostentatious stomping around by a positively glowering Nigel Crabtree, accompanied closely by Dave Tattum who generally paces about. Though to be accurate, from this race onwards Denise Drury, who until then has been a model of demure detachment, suddenly dramatically switches demeanour and instead frequently indulges herself with passionate and loud shouts of "go on lads, come on lads" throughout the subsequent races.

Strong words from Nigel Crabtree or a spontaneously inspired ride from Alan 'Moggo' Mogridge enables the Potters to pick themselves back up and slightly extend their lead. Though it took a fantastic battling performance from Moggo to just about stay in the lead from James Grieves who, on the basis of this level of effort and his overall commitment, would be anybody's ideal choice of guest. He rode with an intensity throughout the race that would lead you to think that he rode for Workington and something much more important than a Premier League meeting race was at stake. Not that this is any consolation to a nervous looking George English who watches his star rider compete with bravado, gusto and aggression. The relief for the boisterous Stoke crowd is short lived as heat 10 showcases a superb example of team riding from Scott Robson, recovered from his early morning encounter with Tony Mole's daughter Emily, and a resurgent James Wright who rides with a skill and maturity that belies his years to magnificently hold the experienced Robbie Kessler back in third place. The Workington riders are loudly implored round the four laps of the circuit by Denise Drury and Graham who immediately rush to the pit lane to joyfully congratulate the returning riders as the scores narrow further to 33-30.

As a contest it is now delicately poised and both sides demonstrate a real determination to win and, for the neutral, you really couldn't ask for a more compelling encounter. The arrival of heat 11 isn't anything like so exciting for George English who finds "his Newcastle riders" once again pitted against each other, while he can only nervously pace about the enclosure pen in the pits. Also featured in the race is the experienced Shaun Tacey and Stoke's much improved reserve this season, Barrie Evans. All four riders competed for that vital inch of space and the lead over the first lap before the race order settled down into an enthralling contest with Tacey holding the lead from Morris. Grieves proceeded to size up

Morris and found the line and the speed to almost but not quite surge round his team-mate and thereby ideally place the Workington pair to try to extract maximum points from the heat; though, like most riders, he'll have probably lost sight of this outcome in the heat of the racing moment. Welshman Phil Morris wasn't going to allow himself to be bested so easily by his Scottish colleague Grieves and, having also found sufficient additional drive and speed from somewhere, thereby enables himself to retain his lead by the end of the back straight by a mere fraction. Always a fierce competitor, Grieves then tried to cut back under Morris as they entered the bend together albeit with the Welsh rider still fractionally ahead by a 'short head' as they'd say in horse racing or a handle bar grip as we might say in speedway. It was a typically aggressive manoeuvre by Grieves that was sadly misjudged at this speed because, with the additional momentum he generated on the straight, there was a spectacular collision of men and machines. This encounter resulted in them both taking off tangled together to violently slam into the safety fence with tremendous velocity. It was a crash that everyone in the home pits and pits enclosure was supremely well placed to study in close up detail, since it happened almost exactly in front of our raised viewing position. George English is immediately off and running with an alacrity that would please Ben Johnson in a hundred metre sprint, down the slope of the pits lane, through the gate and over to the heap of stricken riders so quickly that he almost outpaces the medical staff of the St John Ambulance crew, who had the advantage to start from the centre green. It's the sort of spectacular but strangely ugly crash that you suspect will inflict severe injuries on both riders, if judged from the velocity of the impact in combination with the awkward tangle of the riders and equipment.

Stoke's down to earth and friendly rider, Paul Clews coincidentally watches the whole incident stood next to me and he calmly notes, with a magnificent level of understatement typical of speedway riders when they comment on injuries and crashes, "both of them went in a bit heavy, the two just locked up and went in together". From my viewpoint, it appeared that Grieves went in strongly under Morris without sufficient control just before the instant before the crash. The referee takes a similar view and excludes Grieves as the cause of the crash. Not that this is any consolation to either of the stricken riders still laid out on the track, who receive the ministrations of the medical team. The management from three teams – Stoke, Workington and Newcastle – impotently stand close together, look disconsolate and vaguely supervisory. While the carnage of equipment that was once a couple of pristine bikes are disentangled and slowly carried-cum-wheeled back to the pits by various mechanics. After considerable delay, Grieves immediately withdraws with a suspected broken thumb surprisingly, though it confirms his reputation as a very tough and hardy rider, Morris manages to take his place in the subsequent re-run of the race. It's a decision clearly taken just on adrenaline rather than sensible consideration of his injuries, since he trails round disconsolately in a far away third place before he then withdraws from the rest of the meeting. All George English's worst fears have been realised and he disappears from the pits for the rest of the meeting to stand like an expectant father outside the door of the close by medical room[10]. George commiserates with his anxious mother Joan and he confirms, "Phil's definitely out [of the Berwick meeting] with injuries to his hip, thumb and head". It's a catalogue of pain for Phil Morris and a big question mark also remains, until a further examination the next morning, over the possible participation of James Grieves in that important meeting for the Newcastle team. The lot of the speedway promoter, with its trials and tribulations even when their teams don't actually race, remains a complicated and difficult path to follow. It's a path that has left George English frustrated and wretched this evening.

Heat 12 allows Stoke to re-establish some semblance of an overall and aggregate lead although Denise Drury isn't at all happy with Jack Hargreaves contact with Trent Leverington which thereby secures a vital third place, "there's hard riding and then there's taking his leg". By heat 13 the threatening clouds have finally resulted in a few spots of rain and, just before the tapes rise, we witness Workington's owner Tony Mole rescue his independent minded and rather delightful daughter Emily (and her dolly), after Denise points her dangerous location out to him. She has strayed off and chosen to

---

[10] By the close of the meeting, Phil Morris is still inside being treated in the track emergency room. In part this is due to his injuries but also because of his reluctance to visit the hospital in Stoke, rather than the one nearby to his home in Wales since, for health insurance purposes, he would frequently have to travel inconveniently long distances back to Stoke for his subsequent treatment and examinations. Phil is apparently unaware that the knowledgeable Stoke paramedic, Steve Walker, has an excellent relationship with the local hospital, which ensures the hospital is already forewarned and waits for the arrival of any riders injured at Stoke. Though it's only four minutes away, Caroline describes the club as having "the Manchester United of ambulance services".

play obliviously on the rider's access lane to the track, arguably the most dangerous spot in the stadium other than the track itself, since bikes hurtle up and down this slope without warning and at speed. Particularly since the two minute warning has been sounded by the referee to summon the riders to the start line and, therefore, is the period with the most intense activity for this access way. In her short life so far, Emily has grown up completely in and around speedway tracks, so is completely at home with the noise, clamour and atmosphere of a speedway meeting and pits area. True to form, she appears completely unconcerned, though Tony Mole looks extremely relieved. On the track Kessler wins from Tacey, while the immediate re-match of Hargreaves and Leverington (who replace the injured heat leaders Morris and Grieves respectively) enables the Australian to extract some small measure of revenge. Leverington is out again to ride his third successive race and, while he manages to secure another third place, this penultimate heat is notable for the superbly executed pass ridden by Mogridge to simultaneously overtake both Wright and his partner. It's a brave but skilful manoeuvre that ensures, with a race to go, Stoke have victory on the night but not before we witness a thrilling almost four lap duel between the experienced Mogridge and the young dashing but extremely determined James Wright.

Before the final race, stood in front of me with Tony Mole, Denise Drury gets her excuses in early with the Comets' owner when she notes, "they don't have as many injuries as we have". Tony just nods in acceptance but, as a keen student of the sport, I'm sure that he realises that it's not strictly an accurate claim. Workington have, indeed, suffered without the inspirational and talismanic Stoney but then equally Stoke have remained without both Paul Pickering and Jan Staechmann for all the season. When the final race gets underway, we're treated to another superb encounter – this time between Wright and Kessler that's arguably nearly as an exciting encounter as the previous Wright/Mogridge dual and, again on its own, would be worth the cost of admission, even if only we got to view this final nominated heat 15. Once again, after making a good start with Kessler, Moggo uses all his knowledge, experience and track craft to surge victoriously to the finish line. Behind him, though the aggregate result is now no longer in any doubt, a determined Wright tries for nearly four laps to find a way past Kessler before he manages to do so on the final bend of the race with a brave and cleverly executed piece of skill.

As the riders and mechanics from both teams begin to pack up their bikes and equipment, during which a delighted Dave Tattum scoots about the general area going excitedly hither and thither, I witness a touching scene. Without the kindness of the Stoke promoter Dave to provide this access, I wouldn't have been aware or overheard that Moggo immediately went out of his way to take the time to seek out James Wright to praise, encourage and motivate his diffident, young opponent. It's a surprisingly touching scene, as the older, wiser gnarled professional – in the (recently reinvigorated) twilight years of his career – passes on some tips and advice before he deliberately emphasises that, in his view, James will achieve his ambition to reach the pinnacle of the sport. Moggo stresses that if he applies his talent and skill, while he continues to strives to develop it further, then James will get to the top of speedway, just like the contemporary Grand Prix riders he aspires to emulate and study, "keep doing the same as you're doing and you'll be doing the same, keep it up!" James already has a reputation, as an eager pupil and an attentive listener as well as a gifted young rider, so he concentrates fully on Moggo's advice. With some smiles and a handshake they part and I'm left to reflect that it's the type of scene that confirms your belief in human nature, let alone just the loose camaraderie of the speedway fraternity.

Afterwards, in the heavily crowded bar, the Stoke fans exuberantly celebrate their success while the track shop merchandise is in the process of being packed away into some easily transportable containers. The supporters of both clubs mix easily with the riders over a relaxing shandy or alcoholic beverage. By the windows that overlook the home straight of the track, the lady photographer in the Wolverhampton jacket, who I take to be Claire Perkins, earnestly reviews her handiwork on the computer. Caroline Tattum very capably works the room, as she meets and greets numerous people in her very personable manner, while she slowly threads her way through the crowded bar area[11]. Paul Clews breaks away

---

[11] Caroline stresses that she's away busy behind the scenes on race night, "Dave and Nigel look after everything to do with the speedway, I just do the admin". Except when she ventures onto the centre green during the interval each week to do the prize draw, "so I never see any of the fights, if we have them, I just hear about them in the bar afterwards; so they're all just allegations to me".

from a group of his friends to chat amiably to me about the meeting. He's quick to modestly shrug off my praise for his two exciting race wins, achieved with typical Clews style brave passing manoeuvres in the thick dirt of the outside line perilously close to the safety fence. Paul is in huge demand from well-wishers and friends but still finds the time to be genuinely concerned as to whether I'd enjoyed both nights' meetings. He also checks that I now understood what he meant about the exciting racing regularly served up for the fans at Loomer Road, "I love it here, everyone's so friendly and welcoming. I used to go to the bar after meetings at Reading and often stand on my own but here it's been a real contrast; I've been welcomed with open arms from the outset which makes a real difference to me and to my family". After a fantastic fixture packed with incidents galore and, after the genuine pleasure of briefly getting to meet the key people who work behind the scenes for the Potters, there's not much more I could think to add in reply to Paul's summary of the club's outlook and ethos. I contentedly head away into the emptying car park, as Paul's best wishes for my book echo in my ears, and I leave to get massively lost around the five towns – Burslem, Hanley, Stoke, Longton and Tunstall – that supposedly constitute the conurbation that is the "Loyal and Ancient Borough of Newcastle under Lyme".

30th July Stoke v. Workington (Premier League) 50-43

Showered in Shale

Chapter 21: Sunday in Scunny and the Marmite Question

31st July Scunthorpe v. Hull Angels

SKY CHATTER

"Respect – it's a small word but a big thing" Gary Havelock

RANDOM SCB RULES
9.5.2 In the Pits there shall be (signage must be used to signify their position)
d) At least 3 buckets of dry sand
f) Toilet facilities, adequately lit and heated Changing Rooms, sufficient for 20 Competitors including showers or baths with hot and cold controllable water supply. (These may be positioned in the Pits or within the confines of the Stadium.)

All roads don't automatically lead to Scunthorpe, but when you arrive on the outskirts of the town you realise just how remarkably handy it is for the motorway. Especially when you consider that it's in North Lincolnshire, a part of the country that you always sense you'd have difficulty to readily identify on a map of England or even get to. The facts I have about the town are severely limited, though I do know that the locals call it Scunny and that Ian Botham briefly played for the professional football team in the town. Another useless fact that springs to mind is that the football team are known as The Irons, which is a reference to the traditional industries of the town (iron and steel) rather than cockney slang aspersions about their sexual orientation. Although on the subject of sex, a word that does not usually bring Scunthorpe to mind, the town does have some notoriety from the mid 1990s, around the time of the advent of Internet search engines. If you had been keen to visit the town or find out some further information on the local cat protection society, the Conservative club or wanted to sign up for the local choral group (all of which immediately came up on my Internet search), you would have been completely out of luck; since the town just didn't exist through the ether of the Internet due to some rather stringent and bonkersly inefficient obscenity filters. Pretty ironic when the Internet's usage has exploded, primarily on the back of an exponential increase in the amount of available salacious and pornographic material people wish to view. But, there you have it, those programmers at AOL, motoring organisations and Google just couldn't be too careful or sensitive enough about what material and 'rude' words they tried to filter out or disallow you access to in the privacy of your own home.

While search engines in most parts of the world have advanced sufficiently to no longer deny the existence of the town [Scunthorpe], I discovered it was still difficult to try to get online directions to the town, from either the route planners provided by the RAC or the AA, unless you had an exact postcode to go along with the name of the town. It appears that it's still very tricky to travel to Scunthorpe without your enquiry being interpreted in a vulgar way. Although this probably says a lot about the proclivities and mindset these motoring organisations infer among their members who want to access directions online, it can't exactly help promote tourism or the growth of the local businesses in this part of North Lincolnshire. Luckily help was at hand with the directions the *Speedway Star* handily provided for all the UK's speedway tracks.

When you head to the Normanby Road track from the Stoke area you can try out a great selection of different English motorways – the M's 1, 18, 180, 181 and 6 in my case, after I made an initial wrong decision – all in one short journey. As you exit from the carriageway onto a substantial roundabout, you find yourself confronted by another identikit 'out-of-town shopping area' which I think we can guess will eventually drive the few longstanding local traders that remain in the town itself to the wall. Scunthorpe, like towns throughout the country, is similarly blessed with an apparently thriving out-of-town shopping area where the consumer is spoilt with a wide choice of superstores and warehouses[1] After all, this is what the older generations fought a couple of world wars for in the pursuit of freedom, democracy and the chance of a better future. This sacrifice hasn't really percolated through to the people in the queue ahead of me at the Tesco Express or Tesco Something, whatever they call the bigger ones that sell you TVs as well as tampons and food. It's the last convenient place to stop off to purchase a range of refreshments before you arrive at Scunthorpe speedway. As a result of my research and travel for this book, and not that I've consciously taken note, but I reckon it could be the third closest Tesco to any speedway track, after the closest in Oxford and the one near Newport's stadium. Though, I

[1] A striking feature of modern consumer society is that as we have generally got more affluent, we've gradually migrated to 'big box' shopping complexes and superstores. As though our modernity and our identity as an affluent consumer was founded upon a deliberate move away from the variety of a local shopping experience and more tailored personal service. The prevailing attitude continues to be 'who needs personal service and the added inconvenience of people who know you or your family' when you can shop for everything you need all in one handy place. The price advantages that lured us there have long gone, customer service disappeared many moons ago and the 'Tescoisation' of our shopping habits has sucked the vibrancy and life out of practically every town and village in the country.

stand to be corrected and, as speedway has declined in popularity while Tesco has massively increased, they spring up at a great enough rate throughout the country that another has probably been built near a speedway track since my visit.

Before my paranoia can fully overwhelm me, and after I have 'gained' some more Tesco Clubcard points, I head straight off back to the roundabout to use the correct exit to the speedway stadium and ignore signs that direct me to the town's renowned football club. When I drive along this road, I'm immediately struck by how closely the surrounding rural area here strongly reflects its own recent history. The area is essentially farmland converted for commercial purposes for new businesses eager to locate here and take advantage of Britain's excellent regional communication systems. Consequently, this spelt big trouble for the remaining farmers and homeowners who had previously enjoyed gazing upon splendidly bucolic and beautifully unblemished Lincolnshire countryside. And now, instead find their carefully chosen rural prospects sadly and rapidly despoiled through the misfortune of poor timing; particularly those unlucky enough to have chosen to live here just before the motorway, with all its attendant possibilities and variety of traffic connections, further stimulated the construction of yet more buildings. Indeed, the local council has declared the area a 'vital development zone', which had the unexpected benefit that it enabled speedway to finally return to the town of Scunthorpe.

In fact, it's at the outer edges of these trading estates that England's newest speedway track and promotion has found itself also growing like billy-oh, in a town that's had a history of lost speedway teams. The original version opened in 1972 at the flat and bumpy Quibell Park circuit with its cycle track round the perimeter, in a stadium that was also used for athletics meetings. There was then a brief move to Ashby Ville for nine National League matches in 1985 before poor crowds saw the club go the way of all flesh. Then nothing at all, until this season's rebirth, after nearly 20 years since a speedway club last properly operated anywhere in the town. I pull up in a car park of sorts adjacent to the Normanby Road Speedway Stadium, which is a strong way to say that there's basically a track in a field surrounded by neat fencing; also with a fully functioning pits area and a couple of portacabins by the start line that serve as the bar, the track shop and referee's box. Did I mention that there's another portacabin that houses the toilet blocks? The track looks in superb condition and has a similar shape to Sheffield's one, only smaller. It has been laid down under the expert guidance and direction of the UK's track guru Colin Meredith, while on the management side the promoters have benefited from much help, which includes local Sheffield speedway promoter Neil Machin's advice. To establish a fully functioning speedway club in such a short time, after approval was given, is a marvellous achievement. It visibly signals the determination and commitment promoters Norman Beeney and Robert Godfrey as well as their army of helpers, though it took a lot of paperwork and tussles with the council to realise their dream to bring speedway back to the town.

Norman, middle-aged, balding and dressed in a fluorescent yellow jacket is hard at work with the many chores, routines and various preparations necessary to ensure that everything is ready for that afternoon's hastily organised friendly challenge with the Hull Angels. Against whom they will compete for the newly created 'Humberside Trophy'. It will be the first ever fixture for the Hull Angels team, but given the brisk cold and very real threat of rain, it looks highly unlikely that the meeting will start at all, as Norman and I wander round the facilities three hours before race time. Norman works with Rob in the motor trade – as an MOT inspector – and moved to Scunny in 1984 from the pretty Georgian town of Hastings in Sussex. He had neither ambitions to own sports facilities nor had any original local connections, but it was Rob's initial enthusiasm and general talk about speedway that led to the truly eccentric idea that they start their own track. Rob's love of and evangelism for the sport were the factors that finally fatally infected Norman. Though, as they began to search for suitable venues, they found a number of sites but then suffered numerous frustrations at the hands of council officials. Particularly so after they directly approached Scunthorpe Council with their idea to build a new speedway stadium from scratch. There were many obstacles to be overcome with regard to noise permissions, environmental regulations and to obtain the necessary planning consents. After a number of false starts they were eventually tipped off by a sympathetic local official that the area we now stand on had already been "specifically designated for disruptive motor sport" by the council. Curiously, in its zeal to nod through the sprawling nearby factories and shopping developments, the council had strangely omitted to pass on this vital piece of information. After they had coped with these knockbacks, the promoters set

about the construction of the stadium and its facilities with considerable gusto. Without the handicap of previous experience or the realisation of the many difficulties that potentially lay ahead of them, they attacked the complex task of building a speedway club. In point of fact, Norman and Rob have built everything I see around me.

Norman introduces me to the club's security staff, Dean and Trish, some of the few people who have so far ventured out to arrive at the track on this cold Sunday morning. Norman professes delight to have such "professional people on duty", especially as they have monitored the site from the outset to ensure that the grounds weren't commandeered by the local gypsies as a temporary campsite. With the commitment of a guaranteed 21-year lease, they excavated the track and then laid it themselves. They put up all the perimeter fencing – "we're very proud of that" – installed all the plumbing and majority of the electrics themselves, although they have needed to occasionally call upon the services of various skilled and qualified tradesmen. They've kept a sharp eye on budgets throughout; and initially preferred to buy a second-hand Rolls-Royce generator for £1800, plus £200 shipping, rather than pay the £14,000 charge for a mains connection. They have a five-year strategic business plan with a set of milestones for each year that, in their zeal, they've already started to exceed. Some of their future goals, such as the installation of floodlights and raised columns for a covered standing area, have already been completed. This is important since the erection of permanent buildings is a significant condition of their lease with the town council. Given that the club has only had 17 meetings, which includes the Grand Opening inaugural meeting on March 27th, the progress made has been substantial and continues. The crowds are also considerable as well as the praise for the club and the track that they've garnered from the speedway pundits, fans, riders and officials.

Rob and Norman had both worried about their ability to attract enough high calibre riders, but the opposite has been the case, since they've been "drowning in young, talented riders" who appeared from everywhere. Rob arrives and immediately goes off to drive the tractor round to prepare and grade the wet but smooth looking track surface, and this leaves Norman to continue to enthuse about the riders. He's especially pleased with the future potential of Benji Compton and 16-year-old Richie Dennis who has a trials riding background but is "a natural speedway rider". Norman is keen to stress that both promoters believe that they've "never had a bad days racing" and, as a consequence, have been able to attract approximately one thousand fans to regularly come and watch the club. They're very pleased with the level of their away support too; they reputedly attracted five hundred Scunny fans to Buxton and even 60 or so diehards recently made the long trip to Armadale in Scotland. However, it's likely that this afternoon's meeting will be a test of the fans loyalty because the weather doesn't look promising – though the club's fans do come from throughout the Lincolnshire and Yorkshire region rather than just this presently windy and cloudy corner of the country in Scunny – and because the fixture is a hastily arranged friendly challenge match against unknown opposition, albeit from local rival Hull.

Norman continues to chat, rootle about and work at the same time, though he clearly isn't happy with the level of support they receive from the local paper, *The Scunthorpe Telegraph*. I gather that, earlier in the year, there was a fiasco with regard to potential sponsorship that didn't materialise, a disappointment that was compounded by the "very unprofessional" attitude and actions of the paper's staff. In contrast, the discussions they've had with regard to possible team sponsorship with the Director of Communications at Lincs FM, the area's biggest local radio station, have progressed well. They'd love to be sponsored for the income and the airtime, so much so that Norman has already come up with a possible future team name, 'The Lincs FM Scunthorpe Scorpions'. The various iterations of speedway teams in Scunthorpe have several incarnations of different alliterative nicknames that range from 'The Saints' to 'The Stags' and now, in 2005, to 'The Scorpions'. Norman has even created an incredibly cheesy tag line for the radio adverts – "back with a sting in the tail" – a strap line which he appears to think is a linguistic masterstroke and it evidently delights him, in a Basil Brush kind of way, since he repeats it three times.

But aside from their climb up the steep learning curve of sponsorship, the level of support and help received by the club from all quarters has been tremendous. To illustrate his point, Norman gestures towards the nearby burger van run by Joanne and Colin. The catering outlet has been so successful from the outset that they've now bought a new van and Joanne's mum has given up her day job to handle and manage it. Norman is impressed with their food – "it's superb" – and so are the fans, which pleases him, since it's another aspect of their ongoing campaign to ensure that they achieve the correct overall experience for all their paying customers. It's an aspect of speedway promotion that Norman feels is often "underestimated but oh so important". He pointedly contrasts the high quality of the fare offered to patrons at Scunny in comparison to that elsewhere, particularly at King's Lynn where, in his experience, "you're better off eating before you go!"

They've enjoyed meeting the other promoters everywhere on their travels, if not the quality of the food, with the notable exception of Sittingbourne, which Norman describes with some feeling as "third world speedway". This opinion has arisen mainly because their rider Ashley Johnson's father was attacked in the pits by a member of the Sittingbourne track staff during their visit, so they now believe it's "not the friendliest club"[2]. They decided to avoid negative publicity and not press charges, primarily for the good of the League and the sport, but clearly events at Sittingbourne's Old Gun Site track have continued to leave a bitter taste. Norman wants to get beyond this quickly, especially as it's been the exception not the rule of their overall experiences during this first season at the Normanby Road stadium and when they have visited rival speedway clubs.

In order to even start to run a speedway club you need a lot of voluntary helpers and the understanding support of your family. Luckily, for Rob Godfrey, all of his family are actually involved at the club. These include his wife Gail who does a lot of the administration, especially on race days; his son Michael who occasionally rides for the team but mostly rides in the second halves at the club. Also his 19-year-old son Paul works at the track as the Machine Examiner and helps with many of the odd jobs that need to be done around the stadium. Paul is stood on the centre green when I meet him or, to be more accurate, he stands on the runway that cuts across the centre green of the track. He informs me that this was a runway built for the local aviation enthusiasts in the area, who used to spend a considerable amount of time flying their model planes off and then landing them again on this specially built miniature runway. The runway is marked up very authentically. Like pilots without planes, we both stand there on the landing apron and watch Rob drive the green tractor, with the bright blue bowser attached, and continue to heavily water the track, despite the threatening black clouds

---

[2] Later Rob Godfrey is equally vehement and describes them as "a bunch of Muppets!" My experience and impressions, when I visited Sittingbourne twice, was the diametric opposite.

overhead. Until his father was seized with the determination to run a speedway club, Paul had never really considered involvement with speedway. In fact he really didn't enjoy it at all to start with but, once you get properly inducted, it becomes addictive. He's pleased with the work and even happier as he's met a lot of "good people" through his involvement in the sport, particularly the "riders and that". However, standing around to chat isn't really the done thing on race day, so he's soon off to help his father continue to prepare the track.

I retire back to the bitter cold of the home side of the pits where Wayne Carter, the teams most experienced rider and 'old hand', already prepares his equipment ready for the meeting ahead. I also finally get to talk with Scunthorpe's official track photographer Steve Dixon and his partner Debbie. He's had a lifelong passion for the sport since he first went to the old Belle Vue track at Hyde Road in 1970. Those regular Saturday night meetings have left a huge impression on him ("it was a cracking race circuit – the best!") and over the last few years he's managed to find the ideal way to combine all the major loves of his life: speedway, photography and Debbie. Belle Vue and its many star riders from the 1970s generation – Peter Collins and Chris Morton – plus any other rider to pull on the red and black body colours, still hold a special place in his memory; as does the thrill of "jumping over the fence, running over the centre green to get to the fairground". They're very warm genuine people and Steve's extremely well informed and helpful. He explains that there's a real camaraderie among the 'official photographers' within the Conference League and, inevitably, they swap tales of fantastic photos taken in difficult conditions or exchange horror stories of over-officiousness or rudeness at some tracks in the country. It's a small select club without many members other than Julie Martin at Weymouth, Ian Charles at Buxton and Claire Perkins who works in an unofficial capacity at Elite League Wolverhampton but officially at Premier and Conference League Stoke.

Throughout the season I appear to bump into Steve and Debbie all over the country. They both always have a smile and Steve always has a bit of gossip, interesting information or some insight from his travels, which he effortlessly combines with an encyclopaedic knowledge of all things speedway. He always carries his large rucksack of photographic equipment and that essential tool of the trade, the small ladder, in his continued pursuit of the ultimate action shot from each fixture. When you look at his gallery on the Internet, where extensive photos from that day's fixture always magically appear only moments after the actual meeting in question ends, you appreciate his skill as a photographer as well as his innate understanding of the dynamics of the sport. How Steve manages to balance his work as a HGV delivery driver, with all that travel to speedway, from their home in Wellingborough is all a bit of a mystery. They're a really genuine couple and Debbie accompanies him everywhere, on their circuit of regularly visited clubs but modestly claims to be "still learning". Which may be true in comparison to Steve, but in three years Debbie already has been to more tracks and meetings than most usually manage. Apart from the pleasure of the activity itself and the opportunity to travel the country to watch speedway, the ultimate aim of this all is to get your work published, which, in speedway, means trying to appear in the *Speedway Star*. They pay £12.50 for an action shot or £7.50 for a portrait; so it's unlikely that Steve will be able to retire in the near future, not that I can ever imagine that he'd want to do so.

Before we can discuss things further Rob arrives in the pits area, since he's finished watering the track, with his wife Gail who clutches the teams' bright blue 'Scunthorpe Scorpions' race jackets. She then hands them to the riders, or places them carefully on the bench in preparation and easily available for the riders, when they finally arrive at their own individual section of the home pits area. While this happens, I take the opportunity to discuss how on earth Rob became so obsessed with the sport that he decided to establish and manage his own track! He laughingly recalls that he talked with Norman at the garage and they decided they should look into it, which "seemed a good idea at the time" and from then on it "just kept going". When you listen to Rob, it all sounds so easy and straightforward. After they spent an initial £5,000 or £6,000 on noise permissions and planning reports, the whole project "to develop the place" snowballed. The stand and the floodlights are budgeted and paid for, while there are plans in hand for a clubhouse and other modular buildings to bring facilities up to market expectations. Meanwhile, they both take great satisfaction that "we don't owe a penny and the future looks very bright". The team's goal is to achieve a top three or top five place in the league; though without indulging in a lot of "chopping and changing" of the riders, which other promotions seem to view as the necessary price for success. For Rob "all the riders are our mates and we have a good family like team"; consequently, the promoters "help out where we can" and try to "look after them all". Riders often stay over and the team has started to gel together extremely well. The promoters overall plan is to "hoe their own row" and they've found that they've been welcomed with open arms practically everywhere.

The decision to start to run a Conference League team has been an eye-opening experience and "in our short time the politics have been unbelievable". Rob believes that the Conference League urgently needs a management committee of three or four people who make all the decisions. He doesn't agree with how the league is currently run, "with one man, Peter Morrish, making all the decisions"; especially when he can, in Rob's opinion, sometimes be "so biased". Despite these dissatisfactions, the Scunthorpe promoters aren't tempted to have their team join the next rung on the ladder of the Premier League. Primarily this is a commercial decision mostly based on costs, specifically the cost of rider payments for points and travel. Apparently some Premier League riders can earn as much as what it costs to run a whole Conference League team. Also if you are a member of the Premier League, there is also the question of the bond you are obligated to pay to the BSPA in order to be able to actually stage meetings. This presently is ten times more than the £1,000 bond that you need to stage speedway in the Conference League. Rob would be happier if a few more teams joined the Conference League, particularly if these included some of those who presently struggle financially in the division above, to thereby form a "genuine division 3" that encourages the development of young, promising riders. He's also broadly "supportive of" the fledgling Under 15 Academy League but, as a result of short notice or miscommunication with its enthusiastic organiser Peter Oakes, they won't actually stage any Academy meeting at Scunny in 2005. The opportunity to help young riders is important for Rob and Norman, which is another reason why they're so involved in the sport. Particularly so when some of the promising young riders that they already have in the Scunny team have the potential to really succeed in the sport; riders such as Richie Dennis, whom Rob is confident is "going to go onto to be brilliant and do many better things".

We're interrupted by the arrival of Margaret Vardy, the match official for this afternoon's fixture who needs to have a few words with Rob before she leaves for the referee's box-cum-portacabin to start her pre-meeting preparations. I make my excuses and lurk around for a brief word with Margaret, while she bustles along to the box a few minutes later in her black Wulfsport jacket with the green trim, that is the "official" rather distinctive jacket that can only be worn by qualified SCB officials! In a sport populated with male competitors and officials, Margaret stands out as one of its few female representatives. It's not a surprise to learn that she's not only keen on the sport of speedway, almost evangelically so, but also that she has a number of strong opinions from her experiences as a fan and as an official. Although she's a keen fan of Walsall and Queen of the South, she's genuinely mystified by why more and more people go to football, especially when often they support teams that aren't their local team. "What's football got that speedway hasn't as a spectator sport?" she asks rhetorically. She always "loved it so much" and couldn't attend speedway enough. If there's any blame to be apportioned for the fall in popularity of the sport in general, as well as for the huge number of its lapsed supporters ("there are so many people who say that they used to go"), Margaret quickly identifies the promoters as the chief culprits. To her mind, it all "begins and ends with the promoters" and, given that so many people profess to like or have liked the sport, it must be that the organisation of speedway is "not correct".

In the match official's box, Margaret begins to check the race card in the match programme against a standard template that she has brought with her for this purpose. When asked how she views her role at any speedway meeting, she's very definite that "what you don't want is bad riders riding and you want everyone to walk away in one piece". In order for this to happen the match official has to be extremely vigilant throughout each race, watch for a whole range of "different things" and try to anticipate errors or "things that might happen" before they happen. This sounds a real challenge but luckily the section of the portacabin that houses the match officials, plus the announcer and music man, has a clear, unimpeded view of the entire track. From here you can see that away over the far side of the track and, since race time approaches, the pits quickly fill with mechanics and riders from both teams.

Over at the pits, the affable Richard Heasman now mans the crash barrier that separates the fans at trackside from the actual pit area. He's a friendly, balding grey haired man, aged around 60, who's dressed for the cold in jeans, lumberjack shirt and, to signal his official status, a sleeveless orange fluorescent top. Richard hails from the Sussex area where I live and fondly recalls that he first went to the Eastbourne track in 1952 with his father. He reels off a whole litany of names from his years following the sport – particularly Mike Broadbanks, Gordon Richards and Bob Dugard. Richard even used to work at the Eastbourne club, where he raked the track and quickly confirms Bob's superlative skill at track preparation that justifiably gives him the well-deserved reputation that he has gained for this throughout speedway. Richard also claims to have witnessed first hand Bob's desire to ensure, while his son Martin rode for the club, that his starting gate position was particularly well prepared and cared for to hopefully ensure his subsequent advantage. As my favourite all time rider, I made the point that Martin's natural ability meant that he could excel on any track whether or not his dad had had a hand in the preparation. Richard smiles and raises his eyebrows at my defensiveness and naïveté.

He's clearly delighted that the Scunny track has opened and that he gets to play a meaningful part in the proceedings at every home meeting. To his mind, the popularity of speedway has always had it's up and downs, and as a fan "you always end up having a break" though, equally inevitably, you return. Whether it's the smell, the racing or the atmosphere, once it gets in your blood, it's always addictive. Richard believes that there are strong connections that link the fascination with steam trains – the smoke and the steam are always evocative but most of all it's the "smell of a steam engine" – with a fascination with speedway. Here, too, there's a strong olfactory link with the pungent and nostalgic smell of "methanol in the wind".

It's a cold summers day and my lovely cup of hot tomato soup from the catering van hasn't quite warmed me up enough, so Richard kindly escorts me to the corner of the home pits that always serves hot beverages to the riders and the staff. It's looked after very capably, helpfully and charmingly by Cynthia Woofinden, who I'd been specifically told to look out for on my visit to Scunthorpe by Sheffield's promoter Neil Machin. She's very unassuming but clearly very popular and in demand throughout the entire afternoon. She began to go to speedway 27 years ago when her son Robert was 16 and started his career in the sport. Now she's very keen to talk with pride about her grandson, Tai, who at 15 has followed in his father's footsteps within the sport too; though Scunthorpe is a long way from his home in Perth, Australia. According to Cynthia, Tai hopes to ride for Scunthorpe when he gets old enough and skilled enough to hold his own at Conference

League level. She's known the Scunny co-promoter Rob Godfrey for years since he used to mechanic for her son. Indeed later I see Rob when he works on his own son's bikes in the pits – incongruously dressed in his smart promoters jacket with his tie worn, rebelliously, loosely – which confirms his wife Gail's earlier observation to me that "he's definitely not a shirt and tie man". Back at her kettle and coffee urn, Cynthia professes her unreserved love of the sport and, while she bustles about her work in the pits, you can see she's clearly in her element. Not that it has always been so easy to attend meetings and she recalls that she "used to hide in the toilets when Rob rode" since she couldn't stand the thought of his possible injury. She regards the speedway viewing public as lovely people in general, but she does "hate it when they sometimes cheer when a rider goes into the fence", since she can't ever forget that they're always somebody's husband or son.

Since the meeting parade is just about to begin, I wander off to the start line to enjoy the presentation of the riders to the fans. There's a pretty sizeable crowd to my eyes, particularly when you consider that it's only a friendly fixture which involves a newly created team of visitors and, of course, the weathers not been at all promising with the cold wind and threat of rain. Rob later moans that the crowd size is roughly only half what he'd expect to see at a similar Conference League fixture. However, in the true, perverse spirit of a British Summer, the sun starts to shine rather strongly through the gradually breaking clouds. The fans that there are – the usual speedway mix of generations and families – string themselves along the home straight or gather in a knot by the start line. There's a wide array of garden chairs and other seats along with the flasks, sandwiches and hot food from the catering van. A smattering of fans proudly wear Scunthorpe Scorpions memorabilia from the track shop. There's also a small girl with the most sensible invention of the season! She's brought along the discarded clear cover that you often see placed over computer screens, which allows her to watch the race and avoid the regular scatter of the flying shale, from what looks to be a very well prepared surface.

The riders enter the track for the introductory parade to the music of 'Fanfare for the Common Man' by Emerson, Lake and Palmer. It's a hardy and perennial tune, which has historically been played at many speedway tracks, and it seems doubly appropriate with its pleasing retro sound allied to its accurate description of the ethos of the sport. The announcer cum presenter Roger Westby stirs the crowd with his enthusiastic and knowledgeable introductions before he attempts to rally the riders with a cry of "come on lads!"

Once the racing gets underway, the thing that immediately strikes you, as a first time spectator at Scunthorpe, is the peculiar effect on the sound of the throaty roar of the speedway bikes that results from the lack of a grandstand or any permanent buildings. There's the usual noise of the bikes as they leave the start, but by the time they're over to the far side of the track there's an almost eerie noiselessness and silence. This isn't the sort of aural accompaniment that many years' attendance at speedway meetings has led me to anticipate. The track itself though is very conducive to fast, full throttle action. Heat 1 provides an almost textbook example of team riding with 'old hand' Wayne Carter using his skill and experience to chaperone the inexperienced Benji Compton round the four laps of the race for an easy opening 5-1 victory. Wayne demonstrates great track craft and anticipation to hold back the Hull pair who sporadically attempt to dash by him, often on either side, on the bends and along the straights. The sun starts to break through the clouds, warms the fans and takes the edge off the cold wind that gusts through the fields of the stadium.

I decide to accept the referee Margaret Vardy's kind invitation to join her in the box to see some of the racing from there, in order to gain a different perspective on the whole spectacle. Inside the portacabin there's quite a crowd with the man in charge of the musical interludes, the referee, and Roger Westby who smoothly conducts proceedings and keeps the crowd continuously informed and entertained. He's usually only the presenter, but he's pulling double duty today in the absence of the regular announcer, Shaun Leigh, who's away to conduct master of ceremony duties for the stock cars at the Belle Vue Stadium in Manchester. Roger also contributes an informative weekly column to the match programme, while his wit and deep love of the sport regularly comes across in his announcements. The result of the fixture is never in doubt from the off, but since the crowd are mostly Scorpions fans I'm sure that they enjoy the races and the capable exhibition of riding skill from many of the riders. It is informative to notice that Margaret appears to have a policy to allow five minutes between the finish of one race and the start of the next race. She times this from the moment the first rider crosses the line and, unless a rider will have two rides on the bounce, she presses the two-minute time buzzer exactly after a further three minutes have elapsed. This allows the meeting to hum along at a steady pace, and with a lower number of falls and crashes than you'd expect at this level, there aren't too many interruptions or delays. Between her duty to run the meeting or check and complete her paperwork, Margaret works as part of a team with the other people in her box. She's used to her fair share of abuse because she does this job, which she ignores but stresses, "some of them call me things you wouldn't call your worst enemy".

Scunny's exciting prospect Richie Dennis has a superb duel with Luke Priest in heat 4 that receives excited applause by the crowd as well as from all the officials inside their box. Co-promoter Rob appears to do practically every possible task he possibly can during the meeting. In the space of a few minutes, he drives the tractor round to grade the track, polishes the actual mechanism of the start tapes and urges his riders on in the races; and all the while wears his promoters 'smart' clothes of jacket and casually dishevelled tie. He greets each heat victory with a wave of delight or broad smile, lives his life to the full and enjoys the various moments of the afternoon. Later, when she visits the box, his friendly wife Gail agrees he's like a man possessed, "he does loads and loads of things on race day". Not that she's at all that surprised, as, after many years together, she's grown accustomed to his infectious enthusiasm and desire to be involved in the thick of the action.

An angry call from the pits to Roger, just before heat 7, curtly informs him that one of the Hull riders objects to Roger's use of his name. In all future announcements to the crowd, James Birkinshaw has requested that Roger refers to him as James not Jamie. Eyebrows are raised but no comment is required. A short while later when he announces Birkinshaw's tactical substitute ride Roger dryly notes "a rider in the next race has grown up today, Mr Birkinshaw is no longer 'Jamie' but is to be called James from now on". The increased formality, or perhaps anger over the lack of it, motivates Birkinshaw to win the race albeit under considerable pressure throughout by Scunny's precocious Richie Dennis. Margaret is clearly a fan of Richie's effort and resilience and admiringly remarks, "Ricky just doesn't give up, he'll always keep going right to the end". In a brief interlude Roger jokes that you have to be certified to be a referee or an announcer. Actually, you do have to be "certified" as an official "official" by the Speedway Control Bureau to occupy these positions and for the meeting to proceed. In fact, those old bugaboos of contemporary life, Health and Safety along with valid insurance cover, dictates that every man and his dog have to be legally certified at any speedway meeting. If there's no referee the meeting cannot proceed which also means that there will be no one to abuse or blame!

Heat 10 sees the riders clash on the first bend and fall in a heap of men and machines. Margaret orders a re-run, although she maybe could have excluded one of the riders as the cause of the crash. Not to ignore the fact that it's a friendly meeting, she's pragmatic in her decision making and reasons "that people come to watch four riders in a race" so you have to try to ensure that's what they get to see "as much as you can". Taking a stricter, more ruthless approach like some referees pride themselves on, she believes "just cheats the public". Margaret's quick to add the interesting insight that there is no specific rule in the SCB regulations that allow a re-run of a race for "first bend bunching", a justification that you frequently hear throughout the season all over the country.

I decide to watch the rest of the meeting back out in the sunshine, now that the sun has properly broken through and the clouds have disappeared. This dries the track out rapidly and the last few races all throw up clouds of fine dust, that slowly eddy away, as well as the more usual showerings of shale. Relishing his new-found James moniker, Birkinshaw offers the main opposition to the, never in any serious doubt, Scunny victory. He's undefeated throughout the meeting but only two other of his team-mates manage to effectively support his efforts. Not that he's shy to celebrate his triumphs, with a lengthy post-race celebration for his heat 12 victory that appears to require that he acknowledge every single member of the crowd during his victory laps – plural for once – so that he can gesticulate wildly and still get in a few extra victory wheelies.

Back over in the pits, lots of the riders quickly pack away their gear in preparation for a speedy exit from the stadium. Speedway riders usually have a tendency to be sized on the smaller side – in terms of weight if not of height – but the Hull number 7 seems to be on a one-man campaign to buck that trend. He's a tall, thick set man that appears to be more suited for rugby matches rather than speedway, which really must be an incredible disadvantage when he races away from the start line against some of the comparatively diminutive and feather light riders that he'll regularly get to compete against. Just like Barbara Streisand though, he can't help it if he's big boned. It's very noticeable that there appears to be just as many riders who get ready to compete in the second half practice races, as there are those who pack up to leave. Rob, still in jacket and tie, works frantically on his son Michael's bike just prior to his initial second half outing. He then stands there during the race totally absorbed as he watches Michael. Apart from when he finds the time to bellow instructions as to the racing line he believes that his son should take. It's not going to be heard but nonetheless Rob screeches his advice and lives every twist and turn of his son's race. It must be such a delight, when the meeting is on and you watch your son ride in the sunshine on your own speedway track, it certainly appears to make the long hours of work worthwhile for Rob. Michael returns and Rob straight away runs to him to immediately attend to the bike, before he carefully wheels it back into the pits. He's apparently oblivious to the oil on his hands and white shirt, while he tries to make those oh so vital last minute adjustments that will help his son race even quicker in the next heat.

Close by Paul Hodder, the Hull co-promoter, is happy to chat between races, while he stands on the bend to intently study the form of the young riders racing round the track. He professes himself pleased with the Hull Angels first ever meeting as a team, especially as it gives the youngsters some more practice on a different track. It's another step on the road to gain the experience required for the long apprenticeship to possible success, though he ruefully notes that the standard of the racing in the Conference League is at a "totally different level" to that of the Premier League. "They can look like World beaters here and yet not get a single point when they race at Premier Level, it's a huge, huge gap really!" I suppose this is all the more incentive for the young riders to practise and practise, whenever they possibly can. Margaret chats to a few of the fans that stand around with their families by the car park. Roger Westby is keen to find out more about the idea behind my book, and its actual title, so that he can mention it in his programme notes for the next week's fixture. Very kind of him, but then like lots of people I've met throughout my travels, he's got a love of the sport that manifests itself through an easy manner that's mixed with sincere interest in others. He believes speedway is a sport that inspires intense devotion or apathy in the general population, "it's like Marmite really – you either really love it or you don't". Personally I absolutely loathe the stuff, but while I'm definitely not a Marmite baby, it's strange to think that, if the analogy is correct, speedway could inspire an intense level of loathing and antipathy in many other people.

I leave with a lengthy queue of other fans in their cars for my long drive back to the South Coast in the balmy summer sunshine. I get the chance to savour the day and the sunshine, since I spend the next hour slowly crawling along behind an old-fashioned double-decker school bus. It's empty of pupils and without a school to go to, because it's the summer holidays, while it wends its way in leisurely fashion through the picturesque Lincolnshire countryside. It's not the traditional exit in a car that you usually get from a speedway meeting, since the exposure for a few hours to the buzz and exhilaration of the racing often infects fans with a desire to imitate their heroes by speeding in their cars like maniacs on the Queen's highways that surround our country's tracks. The slower pace allows me to think through Rob and Norman's marvellous achievement to manage to start up Scunthorpe Speedway once again in the town. It's a testament to the madness, dedication and vision of them both and the support of their families. But, also, somehow touching that in 2005 it's still possible to live your dreams, if only you dare to believe that you can succeed, or don't consider the obstacles. It's even more poignant for ageing fans everywhere, who'll never get to live out their fantasy to become a speedway rider, to know that we're just a pools or lottery win away from possibly being able to find an even more influential role in the sport – as a speedway promoter!

31st July Scunthorpe v. Hull Angels (Conference Challenge) 53-40

Showered in Shale

Chapter 22: Off with the Rousing Rebels
5th August Somerset v. Rye House

"The boy's not scared, he's still young!" David Norris

3.1.1 The SCB shall be the sole interpreter of these Regulations.

The home of the Somerset Rebels Speedway Club couldn't be more conveniently located by the M5 motorway, even if it were actually a service station. Come to think about it, the stadium is much more convenient than some service stations on the UK road network and, unlike them while there isn't the chance to join the AA, buy a mobile phone or play in the amusement arcade, there is the opportunity to watch the racing on one of the country's fairest racing circuits. However, in the very unlikely event that the evenings racing at the Oak Tree Arena doesn't sufficiently enthral you, there is always the added bonus that from the banked back straight of the Somerset speedway stadium you can watch lorries and caravans drive past the stadium. Apart from a spectacular view of the M5 motorway traffic, in both directions, as it passes Junction 22, the back straight banking also provides a panoramic view of the Cheddar Hills spread out in the distance. The purpose built track is actually situated in Edithmead on the outskirts of Highbridge, which is the type of small provincial town where it's definitely advisable to bring your own horse. However, Highbridge is a town famous for its very discriminating seagulls, if the prominent reports in the national press during the week I was to visit could be given credence. These reports made

Impressive Somerset Rebels van. © Jeff Scott

Queues to get in. © Jeff Scott

Large Crowd gathers by start line. © Jeff Scott

the delivery of the post sound as risky as some of the prominent scenes from Alfred Hitchcock's film, *The Birds*. It was claimed that the Highbridge seagulls persistently attacked uniformed postmen as they delivered letters in the town but completely failed to attack uniformed postwomen when they went about their work. With this fine example of reverse sex discrimination, it appears that political correctness has now even spread to the seagulls in this part of the world.

The Oak Tree Arena is reached with a journey down a short tarmac road adjacent to a large field, which serves as the car park on race night. I was unable to spot the oak trees in question or, luckily, any marauding gulls. Large signs by the entrance advise about the added attraction of the golf driving range and you're also informed that the site intermittently hosts markets and car boot sales. Since I noticed the speedway sign and turn off much too late, I accidentally shot past the stadium in the car (easily done since it's so unbelievably close to the motorway exit) and had a brief but unexpected tour of the surrounding area. On my return, I am immediately struck that the speedway stadium is remote from its closest neighbours, well except for three extremely important ones in the only nearby houses, one of which is occupied by the farmer landlord/owner of the stadium. These are the only permanent residents that the stadium has in close proximity before you encounter some more houses much farther down the road on the outskirts of the nearby town of Highbridge. The Cheddar Caves, Wookey Hole and the resort Burnham-On-Sea provide the area's main tourist attractions, so inevitably there's a large transitory population scattered throughout the surrounding countryside, who mostly stay in the various caravan parks and campsites the area boasts. This rich seam of potential casual speedway punters, who find themselves temporarily in the area on holiday, combines with the regular Somerset fans who journey from the near by Somerset towns or the city of Bristol. All of which thereby provides the club with a huge catchment area. Historically the nearest speedway club was the Bristol Bulldogs, who closed in 1978, but now Somerset finds itself in an extended geographic triangle of competitor tracks – Newport, Swindon and Exeter – from which it might also draw interested supporters to swell its weekly attendances. In the way of these things in British speedway, it's planned so that none of these rival speedway attractions also race on a Friday night.

Although it's two hours until the tapes fly up for the first race, there is already a healthy queue at the entrance gate and a good number of cars already stationary in the car park. Because I had been caught in the horrendous Friday afternoon rush hour and holiday traffic, as it slowly ground its way past Bristol, I'm half an hour late for my meeting with Peter Toogood who'll mainly wear his Somerset Rebels promoters' hat for our conversation. Apart from these duties, he is an influential figure within the sport since he is also presently the Chairman of the British

Speedway Promoters' Association, the overall governing body for speedway within the UK. The BSPA is, Peter informs me, run as an "association for the benefit of all of its members" in a democratic manner so that "every track has a vote" at the AGM where they decide, among other things, that season's "rules and regulations". Peter kindly explains that these rules, along with other legislation (such as health and safety, insurance etc.), are in turn governed by the Speedway Control Bureau who in their turn are responsible to the Auto Cycle Union. The ACU are apparently the governing body for all types of motor sport throughout the world. Peter is keen to stress speedway is left pretty much to its own devices when it comes to governance and administration ("luckily they don't interfere with the running of our sport"), mostly it transpires because the sport is viewed as a comparatively small and stagnant backwater in contrast to the other more exciting motorcycle disciplines the ACU has to govern[1]. However, a world away from all the complexity of these relationships, it's a work night at Highbridge with all the usual conflicting and simultaneous demands upon Peter's valuable time as the Somerset promoter, "there's always tons to do". My unavoidable but slightly later than agreed arrival isn't taken as at all helpful by Peter, particularly when there's a million and one other things for him and his staff to get done. Nonetheless, Peter quickly recovers his equanimity and then affably finds the additional time to take a temporary break from his many duties to escort me to "the sponsor's caravan", which is situated by the first bend terraces, for a private meeting in its modest but comfortable interior.

Peter has been involved with the sport for eleven years, after he initially broke into the sport in a joint promotional venture with former rider Martin Yeates. His previous promotion was located at Swindon Robins Speedway, a venue from which he's retained many of his key staff for this latest speedway venture at Somerset. Notably one of the stalwart riders of the current Rebels team, Paul Fry, along with the experienced team manager Mick Bell, one of my team-riding heroes from the Golden era of the Reading Racers in the early to mid 1970s, as well as his stepdaughter and co-promoter Jo Lawson. She very ably covers the many day-to-day administrative responsibilities involved in speedway promotion and they operate from the offices of the property development company that they run in Wiltshire. This support leaves Peter free to fulfil his BSPA duties, develop strategy as well as pursue his numerous other business interests and also to give Somerset his undivided attention on race nights. Peter's other business interests include Glastonbury Football Club, property development and an emergent interest in greyhound racing, though fully 50 percent of his valuable time is taken up with the various duties and obligations that his Chairmanship of the BSPA demands. He relishes the top job in British speedway, which has come about after his progression from the role of Vice-Chairman. This was an invaluable experience for him that served as a further part of his apprenticeship, along with his promotional duties, which has led him to occupy his present exalted position[2]. It is the possibility of his own influence and guidance upon the British version of the sport through this particular role that really currently excites him. Especially so given the impact that he feels, and makes a point to repeatedly stress, that the five-year contract for Sky Sports television coverage of the Elite League (and Grand Prix series) is having on the awareness of the sport nationally. Peter primarily bases his opinion on the criteria of the increased (from other years) national newspaper coverage before and after the Cardiff round of the Grand Prix series event. Which, Peter notes, can "only be helpful" after the comparative print and broadcast media doldrums that the sport has languished in during the majority of his previous eleven years close involvement in the sport[3]. When pressed to identify the direct benefits that actually accrue to tracks in the Premier League, where Somerset find themselves, or the Conference League as a direct result of the Sky television coverage Peter has very few specifics but instead requires we all take a collective leap of faith or optimism to justify his confidence. The safe and practised answer he provides is that "for tracks who have no nearby rivals there's bound to be an increase in interest". These are very carefully chosen words, almost lawyerly, and Peter uses a singularly narrow criteria by which to judge success. Speedway remains a sport that doesn't officially publish its attendance figures, so inevitably this claim is completely unquantifiable. It is widely acknowledged that empirically

---

[1] The world governing body of motorcycling is actually the Fédération Internationale de Motocyclisme (FIM)]

[2] In fact, my first dealings with Peter were in his capacity as Chairman of the BSPA. He helped the research for my book considerably by kindly contacting promoters around the UK about my quest to visit every track in the country. This was enormously useful and, subsequently, many promoters were able to be more accommodating than they otherwise might have been.

attendances fall, compared to normal, for any club that stages a live speedway fixture on any Sky Sports night and, anecdotally, so do the attendances of clubs that stage rival Monday night meetings (e.g., Wolverhampton, Reading and Exeter). However, all the Elite clubs have increased their levels of financial support through sponsorship and the impact on attendances in the lower League tiers of the sport should be limited for those clubs that don't have the misfortune to actually run meetings on the nights Sky's League or Grand Prix coverage is shown on the television.

Peter isn't, however, a man to rest on his laurels when it comes to the successful development his own businesses and their commercial interests, especially when it comes to the Rebels. After he'd overcome local regulatory obstacles to ensure the tracks continued existence, "it was difficult to get planning to start with", Peter hasn't hesitated to invest in the development and improvement of the facilities at the stadium. First in terms of the track itself, which tonight's official SCB referee Chris Durno praises for having matured from the "white line racing" that characterised it's early days of existence to its subsequent transformation into a much more exciting arena, with its increased racing lines and improved track conditions, from which to truly appreciate the sport. But also in terms of the general facilities, which inevitably include a variety of noise reduction techniques – notably earth banks and perimeter fences to control the noise and the strictly enforced 10 p.m. curfew, "people have accepted it and we only run 30 meetings a year" – in addition to improvements to the pits area and terraces. The stadium boasts a track shop, a popular catering outlet and, in the late evening Somerset sunshine, a tremendously popular and rather cute bar on the first bend. When Peter took over the club from Andy Hewlitt, he demolished the original bar on the fourth bend, since this had been built without planning permission and had perched precariously on brick pillar stilts. With other basic amenities and the hospitality caravan there's a very good basis for Peter and his family (his wife works on a race night at the entrance gate and his stepdaughter is fully involved in all aspects of the club in her capacity a co-promoter) to feel satisfaction with their many achievements at Somerset Speedway Club.

Tonight they expect the arrival of a very good-sized crowd for the visit of

[3] You would reasonably expect the British Round of the Grand Prix to garner column inches! National newspaper coverage of speedway generally still remains at pitiful levels, compared both to its heyday and to other 'minority' sports, and the much touted impact of the Sky Sports deal to increase either match attendances, sponsor revenues or national press coverage still remains a dog, which doesn't bark. Even the Murdoch press, which owns Sky Sports and usually rarely misses any chance for the blatant cross promotion of its commercial assets, in the main steadfastly, ignores speedway in sports reports. The *Sunday Times* in association with Sky Sports has produced an annual giveaway calendar for its readers, which lists every major sports event by month in 2005 without even deigning to include any of the speedway blue riband events. The same is true in the giveaway calendars produced by *The Guardian* and *The Observer*. There is a crying need for the BSPA Press Office to preach in a media-friendly and effective manner to the unconverted in the print and broadcast media within this country. Though, obviously, the Sky Sports exclusive rights to British speedway does massively preclude, editorially and contractually, any other significant national media interest, outside of the existing Channel 4 GP highlights package. Though, to be fair, Nigel Pearson at the BSPA is a media savvy publicist and press officer well versed in the ways and proclivities of the national media. *The Times* sports desk also confided to me that the "almost complete lack of coverage in the sports sections across the national press *isn't for lack of effort on behalf of the speedway authorities and its fans – it's just that for most sports editors it isn't that interesting or sexy!*" (My italics)

practically everyone's tip to be victors in this season's League campaign, Rye House. Peter is optimistic of a closely fought meeting with "Little Leaping Len's" all conquering team (as the match programme describes the diminutive doyen of speedway promotion at Rye House) although the omens aren't good as "they're on a high and winning away lots". The secret weapon for this important home fixture could have been the track itself because, "they don't like wet tracks but with the sunshine it'll be suiting them tonight". Even if you ignore the relative attractiveness of tonight's opposition for the informed fan, the club promotion has, as usual, "been aggressive on marketing the club locally". This takes many forms but includes the use of their rather attractive and snazzily decorated Rebels van along with the large roadside sign by the entrance, in addition to the local advertising campaigns which target casual visitors from the nearby caravan and camp sites. Peter rather pragmatically notes, "they're not going to come unless you let them know" especially when the general area isn't predominantly residential and therefore, "lacks chimney pots". When combined with speedway's perennial structural problem of a "lack of away fans" – mostly due to the distances involved and the resulting understandable economic reason of it being "difficult for people to travel" because of the "loss of a day in wages" – the need to attract healthy local audiences to attend on a weekly basis is absolutely essential for the club.

Our talk has flown by and my time is up, since Peter has to leave to attend to all the last minute tasks that beset him on race night, so he leaves me in the "sponsors' caravan" with his friendly and elegantly dressed stepdaughter Jo. Outside on the patio of the caravan last week's happy sponsors enthusiastically tuck into their burger and chips while Jo describes the importance of the work she does with the various sponsors at every meeting. There's an extensive range of possible sponsorships available every week, from the main meeting sponsor to the donations for such prizes as 'Rider of the Week' or 'Most Entertaining Rider'. She has graduated from her role as the Somerset Press Officer and now holds the reigns, along with Peter, in her capacity of co-promoter at the club. Jo enjoys her work since it generates the interest in the club and involves her getting on well with people generally, whether sponsors (after they finish their burgers and realise that she lurks close by inside the caravan, the sponsors from last week have returned quickly and are genuinely delighted to see her again) or the "regular fans". Even the girls from the local Tourist Information Office had had a thrilling evening when they recently visited for the first time. Jo began her involvement in the sport at the start of this century, "at the time I knew nothing", when her stepfather invited her to get more directly involved at Swindon. The 2000 season was a brilliant introduction, which involved a fantastic year of incredible and sustained success where the club won its first trophies for 33 years – the KO Cup and the Young Shield. Her work was initially restricted to the development of the website before she quickly expanded her responsibilities to include the compilation of the weekly online match reports – all of which required a dauntingly steep learning curve. However, she wholeheartedly threw herself into all things speedway and she quickly grasped the rules and intricacies involved, mostly through the help and guidance of Peter in combination with her knowledgeable group of "friends on the terraces". By her own admission, Jo's work as a co-promoter isn't just business but is generally "half a social thing". She loves the "atmosphere of the terrace", "going on the Northern Tour" or "taking a coach load of fans to an away meeting". Even last night's excursion, despite the poor result, to the Isle of Wight had confirmed to her once more, if it needed to be confirmed again, the variety of small but significant ways the basic friendliness of all involved in the speedway manifests itself, whether it involves the riders, track staff or fans[4].

If Jo is protective of all her charges – fans, sponsors, staff and riders – then it's particularly true of her relationship and attitude towards "her riders", particularly when she's got to "know them on the phone" and through having regularly "met them in the pits". Consequently "I know who's under the helmet" so when they crash it "hurts us much more than a fan, as we really know the person underneath". Knowledge of the man behind the mask and her own privileged insight means that Jo very much empathises with the anxieties that the riders girlfriends and wives go through as a result of their respective partners participation in the dangerous sport that is speedway. It's not something you really spend much time to properly consider as a fan, mostly because you just take it for granted. It's a different issue when it comes to the need to cope with

---

[4] Jo mentions that upon arrival at Smallbrook Stadium a couple of elderly Somerset supporters quickly required the toilets but were strangers to the place so couldn't find them. They were promptly shown the whereabouts of the facilities by a helpful and pleasant Australian young chap who turned out to be Jason Doyle, one of the up and coming riders on the Island.

watching your partner ride, and it's definitely a case of different strokes for different folks. Jo noticed, while she worked at Swindon, that Sue Mogridge was "fully concentrating on every spin of the wheel" and always wanted to analyse things afterwards. Whereas Elaine Fry, wife of Jo's personal hero Paul ("he's THE man"), doesn't watch him when he races. Whatever the approach, the partners delight in the triumphs but, when it comes to injuries, usually have to pick up the pieces afterwards.

There are many all too human aspects of the riders that remain effectively hidden from the fans, despite the stars of the track's apparent public accessibility in the pits or at the bar. Jo mentions that there are "so many times we've taken terminally ill people to meet them in the pits" which, she feels, they automatically appear to have a sixth sense about without ever having to be specifically told to be solicitous and courteous. The riders particularly fuss over these "special visitors, though we try to carry on like everything is normal", although afterwards some of the team admit, "it's really upsetting and they don't know what to say". Nonetheless it's very much its own reward to witness how much this contact often means to the ill person, their carers and their families. Jo had just received a very touching 'thank you' card from the family of David, a young boy with cancer, who'd been thrilled ("he's always speaking about it") to visit the pits and meet the riders on a trip with Chris, another Somerset fan and family friend. Such situations are incredibly tough and difficult to handle emotionally for all concerned, but more so if you know the person concerned very well[5].

The additional burden of close familiarity is very much the case with Jo's very ill close friend and fanatical speedway fan Barbara Blizzard, who is part of a close gang that's stood together for 20 years at Swindon but, sadly, only has weeks to live and is now much too weak to even speak or text, never mind attend, nowadays. You often make your friends hard and fast but keep them for many years in the speedway community. Though for Jo, Barbara is her truly special speedway and personal friend and her recent serious illness has thrown the importance and significance of their friendship into sharp relief. The situation is especially hard to cope with because Jo frequently and instantly recalls the type of person Barbara is, the laughs they've shared together and the many good times that they've enjoyed at speedway meetings throughout the country. Though she clearly tries hard not to be too emotional, she's unable to completely stop herself; after a few moments Jo breathes deeply and pulls herself together, then needlessly apologises for mentioning what

[5] In April 2006 Jo Lawson told me "the little lad is still with us but is on borrowed time. There has been times that the family have been told to expect the worst but he has battled on. We did not have a mascot (a new marketing thing at Somerset) for our first meeting this year and so I called up David's family and we treated him free of charge. Chris bought him a race jacket through us, as a surprise, and he put that straight on and we wheeled him round the pits and then out to the green for photos. Paul Fry said 'wait a minute I will just go and put my helmet in the pits' and I am like 'OH NO YOU WON'T' and offered David to hold onto it and of course his eyes lit up. Well I think they did, but I don't know as mine had filled up. Bless him. We were approached by the family of a down syndrome lad a week or so later, who asked if he could have a photo for his 18th birthday. Again, we were happy to let him be mascot one evening free of charge. It is so very rewarding seeing their faces!"

obviously strongly preys on her mind this evening. She shoots off with a million things still to do and calls back to me as she leaves towards the terraces near to the sponsor's caravan, "speedway nights are always manic!"

When I wander round the terraces there is a really pronounced atmosphere of excitement and anticipation about the night's racing ahead. In the track shop, brothers Jon and Nick Barber greet me warmly before going on to confidently assure me, "you'll really enjoy it here, you're in for a real treat!" They echo Peter's earlier comments that you can't ever understate the innate "appeal of the excitement and action in speedway racing". Tonight against Rye House, as with practically every race night, when I bump into him again, Peter expects to be enthralled by "15 lots of different action". The stadium is thronged with a broad mix of people and the size of the crowd reflects the warmth of the summers evening plus the additional appeal of the prospect to witness Somerset race against some high quality and challenging opposition. Before the tapes go up or the riders even come out on parade, the announcer apologises on behalf of the club for "underestimating the crowd size" since tonight's match programmes have already completely run out. I clutch my valuable programme and stand on the crowded grass bank by the referee's box, which overlooks the start line, with an excellent view of the large Oak Tree Arena circuit (and the tops of the passing lorries beyond that). There's lots of chatter – parents cajole their children who mostly ignore them as they either run wild or grouch tetchily in their pushchairs; people warmly greet each other and there's much animated discussion of the evenings prospects ahead – all, to my ears, in the strong but attractive regional accents peculiar to Bristol and this part of Somerset.

The opinions I overhear vary from "we haven't got a hope in hell" to the much more optimistic evaluations which concentrate on the particular skills and gifts of the Somerset riders, "I think Glenn'll like it tonight on the outside". Directly in front of me the Rebels' fan, with his large boisterous family in tow, wears a cap festooned with a magnificent array of predominantly retro metal badges that are strongly redolent of a different era of speedway fanaticism. It's a delight for me to spend the meeting looking closely at these distinctive metal blasts from the past and to reminisce about the era[6]. On the first bend both the food van and the bar do a roaring trade, while the children nearby repeatedly plead with their father for some chips. The ebullient and knowledgeable announcer David Lewis welcomes us all to "a glorious evening in Somerset at the UK's favourite track" before he proceeds with some insightful introductions of both teams. His house style is to effortlessly mix true insight and affectionate cliché in a relaxed conversational manner. During this presentation we learn that, "like red wine and cheese, Fryer gets better with age".

Under the vigilant gaze of the SCB official, Chris Durno, fresh from his traditional pre-meeting chill-out stroll along the front at Burnham-On-Sea, heat 1 starts with a pained shout of "is that our team at the back?" from the fan behind me before a brilliantly executed double passing ride by team captain 'Zorro' restores the crowds quickly lost faith. It's smiles all round already as Zorro passes with fists punching the air on his celebration lap of honour. The next heat is greeted with groans as the visitors dominate proceedings before heat 3 restores normality and features what the announcer terms a "first bend not for the faint hearted". The chatter I overhear between the Somerset fans behind me – which I later learn is mostly Paul Gallop, his brother and their friend – is also a treat throughout as they live almost every moment of the action on the track with great intensity, as it unfolds before our very eyes. Paul is an exiled supporter, from the late lamented but sadly defunct Bristol Bulldogs Speedway at Knowle Stadium, who's been only too pleased to adopt the Rebels as his local team in the last few years since they opened. They claim that over a quarter of the regular Somerset fans are from the Bristol area and are only too happy to make the journey up the M5 on a Friday night for another fix of speedway action. In that heat 3, supposedly ridden in a manner not for the faint hearted, Paul admires Ritchie Hawkins's skills when he avoids crashing into the fence: "How did he stay on his bike? I honestly thought he was gone there," before he loudly shouts, just as the riders flash across the finish line, "That's what we want! Go on you Rebels!"

---

[6] The badges on display included examples from numerous Test Series versus America from 1980-1982, the 'Lada Indoor International' at Wembley from December 2nd 1979, the 1980 'Inter-Continental Final' from White City and enough elegantly flagged Somerset Rebels badges to delight any homesick visiting Confederates who miss the sight of their distinctive flag.

The scores remain tied but the fans are far from satisfied as "we've been slow out of the gate, ain't it? In all three races." This remains true throughout the night's racing as the home side appears determined to gift the opposition a few bike lengths' head start, possibly so that the high quality of the track surface is repeatedly demonstrated and the excitement of the subsequent passes is even more rapturously received by the delighted Rebels' fans[7]. The re-run of heat 4 prompts Paul to exclaim, "they've already moved at the tapes before an'num!" In front of us I notice that while Peter Toogood casually wanders among the crowd for the length of the home straight, he often glances over the shoulders of the crowd at the racing or frequently stops to exchange the odd word with members of the throng of mostly Somerset fans who stop him. By heat 5 the announcer almost salivates at the race prospects for the rest of the evening, "this one has humdinger written all over it". The climax of the race causes Rye House rider, Edward Kennett, to show some petulance and temper with an obscene gesture to the referee as the race finishes to a loud and sarcastic collective "ah-ha" from the home crowd. Zorro wins heat 6 and celebrates with his trademark wild punches in the air cleverly executed while he stands astride his bike before his obligatory lap of celebration. Glenn Cunningham apparently responds to Paul's impassioned cry of, "he's windin' it up and he's gonna pass them!" with an outside swoop to get second place narrowly on the line. "He's never good from the inside", Paul sagely observes of Cunningham before he laments the Rebels' continued lack of firepower at reserve this season, just as the riders push out onto the track for the reserves race in heat 8. He needs no encouragement to warm to his theme, but nonetheless still notes, "we've had no decent reserves since we had Neil Collins and Jamie Smith at reserve last season". It's an observation that doesn't stop him loudly imploring: "Go on Jamie you can 'old 'im!" or make him contain his disgust: "For cryin' out, Millsie!"

After the bowser has been out to dowse the track surface to help the staff's frenetic ministrations and raking during the interval, Jamie Smith feels Paul's encouragement and support throughout, with a running commentary as Jamie trails into third place in heat 10, "come on sort it out Jamie. He'll 'ave 'im again, oh, uh, he's crap on the outside but brilliant on the inside". By heat 12 the announcer and Paul are both on top note for what is undoubtedly one of the races of the season so far (in my opinion) as the riders ride shoulder to shoulder throughout, passing and re-passing each other in a great exhibition of power and control. In the referee's box, announcer David pronounces the action as "tremendous speedway racing" but unlucky for the last-placed rider Chris Mills who, after he has battled and harried for all four laps, finds himself pipped on the line. The announcer can't resist unleashing a critical barb, for all the inevitably absent gainsayers of this sport of kings, when he sarcastically summarises the race as, "this dull, unexciting advert for speedway".

The crowd remains noisily expectant of a victory for the home team but not complacent enough to expect this result against a very strong Rye House. By heat 13 an early engine failure for Robson eases home supporters' nerves, while Paul predicts correctly, "once that Glenn's ahead on the outside it's hard to catch 'im!" Even by the final nominated riders' race, the result remains uncertain until continuing mechanical problems for Robson eases the pressure for Somerset. "I don't like injuries but enjoy engine problems for other teams," says Paul delightedly as he claps his hands gleefully together, just after Robson's engine expires on the start line. The final outcome is further delayed by the exclusion of Rye House's Oliver Allen, after his fall on the third lap. The race has to be re-run to the considerable ire of many home fans, who take the chance to gesture obscenely towards referee Chris Durno who watches impassively from the nearby sanctuary of the official's box. "You bloody idiot!" rants Paul, arguably the most polite of the objectors, before an easy win for the partnership of Zorro and Glenn. This is the excuse, if another were needed, for yet more elaborate post-race celebrations which involves Zorro waving his arms like windmills, he repeatedly shakes his fists in triumph and half-hearted attempts a strange performance of one of his renowned 'doughnuts'.

The crowd waits delightedly for all the riders to go out on a celebratory parade round the track, while Rye's Chris Neath makes a gentlemanly point of walking round on foot to thank personally, with many waves and handshakes, the visiting Rye fans who'd journeyed up from Hertfordshire for their continued loyal support. Afterwards, everyone I speak with is

[7] Mick Bell, the Somerset team manger, later informs me that what might have been exciting to watch was, in fact, the Somerset team's usual "lots of passing by necessity!"

unanimous in their praise for an exciting evening's racing that featured close, competitive duals throughout without any unnecessary rancour or any injuries. In the referee's box, Chris Durno enthusiastically praises the riders and the track[8] while the promoter Peter Toogood matter-of-factly notes, "I'm very pleased, it was a good advert".

Before I leave, I'm fortunate enough to briefly chat with one of my childhood heroes from the golden age of speedway in the early 1970s at the Reading Racers, current Somerset team manager Mick Bell. He wistfully pronounces the 1973 version of the Racers, "Reading's greatest team, we were all scummers together" while he takes the chance to remind Jo Lawson that he really was a "useful rider" once upon a time before he rather quizzically muses "where did those 32 years go?"

The announcer had already had the last word earlier as the fans trailed off into the night, after he had run through the final scorecard in detail, when he characterised the quality of the racing served up tonight as: "surely the most entertaining match here ever!"

5th August Somerset v. Rye House (Premier League) 48-42

---

[8] Chris officiated for both Rye House visits to Somerset in the 2005 season and he rated both meetings of sufficient quality to be included in his personal Top 5 for the season.

Showered in Shale

Chapter 23: The Club that Tim Built
7th August Newport v. King's Lynn + Newport v. Oxford

"Speedway can turn on its head so quickly" David Norris

4.3 SCB Courts
4.3.1 In exercising its jurisdiction all Courts acting under these Regulations shall be subject to the following:
b) Notice shall be sent by first class post to the last known address of the party for whom it is intended, in which case it shall be deemed to have been received in the course of delivery

When I speak to Newport Speedway's owner and promoter Tim Stone, a few days before my visit, he insists that I'll have to arrive at Hayley Stadium at 10 a.m. on the Sunday morning of the King's Lynn fixture, if he's to find any time to speak with me that day. As an extremely hands-on promoter who is unafraid to undertake menial tasks himself, Tim is always tremendously busy throughout the week but, on race day, he hardly has time to speak to anyone, let alone try to hold a sensible conversation. It's likely to be another long day at the track for the small but dedicated team who work there with him. There's a 2.30 p.m. start scheduled for the Premier League clash of the Newport Wasps versus the King's Lynn Stars directly followed by a Conference League encounter that features the Newport Mavericks racing against the Oxford Academy. I arrive early for my meeting with Tim, nearly five hours before the tapes are due to rise for the first race of the afternoon, only to find that Tim isn't expected to arrive until around 11 at the earliest. Let's be frank, you're not exactly spoilt for alternative sources of amusement on a Sunday morning on the industrial estate in that part of Newport, unless you fancy an early morning snack at McDonald's or a stroll down the aisles of the nearby Tesco superstore. The stadium

BAR

TOILET

WASPS NEST
—MENU—

CHEESE BURGER 1.80
BURGER 1.00
JUMBO HOTDOG 1.8
BACON ROLL 1.00

HOT DRINKS

address locates it in the Queensway Meadows area of the town that, to my mind, immediately conjures up rustic images of country walks by rivers lined by shady glades of flowers. The sad reality is that there's a complex network of roads and housing estates that surround this light industrial estate area. The closest thing that suggests country life or the hint of mud on your wellies is the Range Rover dealership nearby.

It's already a warm, sunny, cloudless summer's morning in South Wales, when I venture through the pits gate into the stadium. The sound of activity emerges from the storeroom cum cubbyhole at the base of the stadium's only grandstand, across from the presently completely deserted pits area. The stand appears incongruously out of place. It's a rather modern structure with many rows of seats located on the home straight that overlooks the start line and provides a perfect view of the whole track. The seats actually come from the demolished Newport County Football Club stadium at Somerton Park. Tim bought them in an auction and very sensibly stowed them until he could use them.

Already at work in the cool shadows of the cubbyhole are Andy Dean and Peter Brookes. They take a few moments to gather themselves as they chat amiably, in their soft South Wales accents, about the Speedway World Cup shown live on the television from Poland the previous night. They've already dated with a yellow marker the large mound of new tyres that are piled up in preparation for issue to the riders to use during that afternoon's fixtures. I enquire what they do at the track, dressed as they both are in telltale but impressively dirty and worn heavy-duty industrial shoes. Andy claims, "we do whatever needs doing," and Peter sighs but notes, "it's a labour of love". They've both helped at the track since it opened nine years ago. In the match programme quite a few people are listed as club officials, so they don't actually do 'everything'; however, they're officially listed as being in charge of track maintenance in Andy's case and race-day maintenance in Peter's. They're surrounded by an array of clutter throughout the cubbyhole with ropes, hoses and industrial pumps, an untidy workbench with an aged vice, a bench-fixed drill, spanners galore, numerous filing cabinets, fluorescent jackets and an umbrella almost fit for an office-bound gentleman. Did I mention all the discarded paint pots, plaster pots along with the obligatory scattering of large drums in different colours; all plastered with large signs that warn you about their uniquely hazardous contents? All in all, a place where a man can escape for a few reflective moments of quiet, a cuppa or a sandwich, away from the hurly burly of everything else at Hayley Stadium. It's a room that would also fascinate any child, because of all the interestingly shaped tools that are casually strewn throughout, that are just made to play and experiment with all day. I'm invited to make myself comfortable and patiently wait for Tim, so I pull up the remaining spare stool, that seems to have lost itself some while ago from an anonymous 1980s mock-Tudor lounge bar.

This season the club has been unluckily plagued by injuries, inconsistency and too many defeats to get the home supporters to flock along on a Sunday afternoon with a spring in their step. Andy and Peter are phlegmatically but stoically downcast, "we can't stand losing at home", but they return each week for more punishment. They're both dedicated to the club and are delighted to be involved behind the scenes, although they both admit that they "would prefer to be a rider any day of the week". They've retained the humour that defeat instils although they've developed a hatred for "yet another bloody double header". Not that the promise of double the usual number of heats presently proves much of a local draw for all but the most die-hard and long-suffering fans. Like everywhere else in the country, the casual supporter is attracted by success and the "need for a winning team". Not that this is a magic solution for the area, if the recent experience of Newport rugby is anything to go by – with success taking gates from 500 to a sell-out 11,500 before subsequent failures bring them back "to practically nothing again". Their gallows humour hasn't deserted them and Andy jokes, "first looking at you, I thought that you were a bloody millionaire come to buy the place!"

Their chat noticeably ignores Newport's prospects for the afternoon ahead but, instead, relives the drama of last night's World Cup meeting from Poland on the telly. They're agreed in their verdict that the Poles were "awesome last night" and they think the highlight was when "Gollob mounted Stead's back wheel from behind at 70 m.p.h., how he stayed on I don't know". I didn't watch the meeting but Britain were, apparently, a deservedly last with Joe Screen viewed as, "too old now, he's lard arse, no disrespect but he is – he needs two engines just to get him out of the gate!" They definitely don't enjoy the televised Grand Prix meetings on the box because of the majority of tracks prepared nowadays are "as slick as boards with no dirt to speak of". This isn't a surprise to them, since they have helped out regularly for a number of years with the track preparation for the Cardiff-staged British round of the GP series. It's always an intense effort at the Millennium Stadium to get the track laid properly and removed directly afterwards, and it usually involves working from Thursday through to Sunday. The organisers have stringent specifications for the track preparation though, inevitably, "it's always slick at Cardiff, as that's the way the Danes, well Ole Olsen, likes them". These conditions "favour the riders who're gaters rather than racers; if you have half a million behind you and your bikes, like Tony Rickardsson has, you just have to gate to win". Money, from earnings or from sponsors, is much harder to come by for the aspiring speedway stars of the future that have just begun their racing careers in South Wales. Peter tries to help in his own small way and do his bit, so he "sponsors Nealhie"[1] who's "got to get his consistency going, he must have rode shit last night as he hasn't rung me yet".

We leave the shade and comfort of the cubbyhole for the warm sunshine outside, just in time for our conversation to be interrupted by the eventual arrival of Tim Stone, in his small 'E' registration Mercedes, coloured in that popular grey cream from the early 1980s, probably known as 'pale panther mist' or something equally ridiculous. Tim already looks hot and bothered because he's so far behind his own self-imposed match day schedule. He leaps from his aged but executive car to issue some instructions to Peter Towersey, the team manager of the Newport Mavericks, who'll compete later in the Conference League. Peter is already on duty, since on match day he also supervises the pits gate entrance and paperwork. He kindly offers some practical advice to me, when he suggests that I "get signed in straightaway, so you're insured, in case you get killed". Tim has already switched his attention to check on the finer details of the progress with the track and its environs; immaculately prepared so far this morning, without his supervision, by Peter and Andy. David Dean, the equally jovial son of Andy, continues the family tradition at Newport and has just arrived to help with the ongoing track preparations. He's dressed in blue top and industrial shoes and looks like the spit out of his father's mouth, as my mother would say, albeit a taller version. Oblivious to discussions of the Dean family's association with Newport Speedway Club, Tim leaves and drives clockwise, the long way round the uncovered terraces, to the far end of the grandstand. There, unlike his counterparts in practically any other sport you could name, he will unload the boot of his Mercedes, which contains the club's stock of alcohol, soft drinks, Mars Bars and various delicious foodstuffs that he's brought along to replenish the grandstand bar and the outside catering caravan. This make do and mend attitude, that has everyone muck in together to

[1] Chris Neath who now rides for Rye House.

help run the club at Newport, is typified by the fact that not only has Tim 'done the shop' for this afternoon's stock for the bar and refreshment caravans but he unpacks it all too. Luckily he later has too many other more important matters to attend to; otherwise I'm sure that he'd help with the cooking and to serve the drinks in the bar.

David, exactly echoes his father, when he also claims to be "a general dogsbody" at the track, before he corrects himself to say, "I'm the apprentice of the family" before he then adds with a nod towards his father, "when he doesn't tell me off, that is!" He's keen to succeed in the long term and fulfil his curatorial ambitions, so has set his goals high "if it ends up I'm half as good as Bob Dugard at Eastbourne, I'd be delighted". There is nothing like the determination to set yourself difficult career goals that really stretch your skills though, perhaps, this target is too high. Nonetheless it's important to dream and have your aspirations, even if they're held back by the slightly less than ideal circumstances in which you find yourself as you learn your trade. Still, if you overcome obstacles, you'll arguably learn more during your apprenticeship.

Father and son both envy the track maintenance equipment that they saw available in Poland on the telly last night, when they watched four tractors and two water bowsers get involved in the preparations for just one speedway track, albeit a track that was to be used for a special occasion. The sheer amount of equipment ensured that the work involved in the preparation and subsequent grading of the track was much easier than is the traditional experience at Newport. Comparisons are invidious, but even the "dirt" on the track in Poland, which "hits the fence, drops and is even grippier" has impressed Andy, particularly in contrast to Newport dirt that, "hits the fence and sticks to the bloody fence like glue", and makes a notoriously slick track even slicker. I try to steer the conversation away from its current trajectory obsessing about tracks and track maintenance with a jovial "this'll be turning into a book about tractors soon"; the very idea of which suits Andy down to the ground, "that'd be right up my street". Andy started to watch the sport in 1949 at Knowle Stadium, the home of the Bristol Bulldogs[2] Throughout the 1950s he "never missed a meeting" when the Cardiff Dragons rode

[2] If John Postlethwaite, CEO of BSI, has any sense of speedway tradition, some people have argued that he would shy away from the 2006 name change of the Reading Racers to the Reading Bulldogs. The swap of a six letter word for a seven letter at this newly purchased BSI speedway club, albeit with the laudable aim to dramatically increase the crowds at Smallmead, has meant that the name Postlethwaite has sadly become a thirteen letter word to many genuine, long time Reading speedway fans. However this point of view ignores the huge strides elsewhere that Grand Prix series speedway has made under the auspices of BSI, both when it comes to garnering front page coverage for the sport in the world media (for example, in Sweden and Denmark) or to attracting major new blue-chip company sponsors to associate their brand names with speedway. These prestigious sponsors form a long list and include Pentel (Poland), ES (Sweden), Danksmetal (Denmark) and Fiat (UK). Many people hope that John Postlethwaite and BSI will bring the same success and expertise to the Elite League now that he owns the Bulldogs. There is no doubt that the challenge to run a speedway club in the same place every week at Reading will also give him a different perspective on the sport in comparison to running the 'prestige' events of the speedway calendar at a different location every fortnight, which has been his GP series experience to date. Ironically without the places available through the 'grace and favour' selection system I have commented upon there would presently be no English riders in the current GP Series. Or maybe the next! Obviously, the BSI needs the participation of British Riders given the importance of the UK sponsorship and advertising as well as the important UK television market. Nonetheless, the contemporary lack of top calibre talent is a worrying situation for the future of speedway in this country.

at Penarth Road, while he also found the time to follow Swindon on a regular basis. He seemed destined to follow the sport, particularly because his mother was a "big speedway supporter" and his earliest memories are of being one of seven boys in the back of a van driven by his brother-in-law to go to watch Cardiff. Another happy memory was when he joined the "speedway special train" every Friday, which started its journey in Cardiff, travelled via Newport before it finally arrived at Bristol Temple Meads station. It was a very popular trip with "at least twelve carriages that used to be packed with well over five hundred passengers. And you used to see the riders come with their bikes on the train, then take the bike from the guards van and push it from the station to the track". It was definitely a very different era in the "old days". The riders were then only paid "start money and points money", but he distinctly remembers a "top rider" who said that he could earn £600-£700 if he rode seven days a week; this was at a time when, in marked contrast to the present day, when in comparison a top soccer player only earned a fixed wage of £6 a week. Nonetheless, the majority of riders were "doing it for fun" and the overall ethos and atmosphere "was not as serious as it is now", although Andy quickly stresses "it was just as competitive though". After his loyalty to Cardiff went the way of all flesh, he then rarely missed a Newport meeting throughout the 1960s and 1970s when they raced at Somerton Park until the end of 1977, when they were thrown out by the football club and closed down. After the Somerton Park closure in 1977, Andy used to "watch Swindon in the intervening years" in order to carry on with his love of the racing. It's a love that's taken him to "16 World Finals at Wembley" and just too many other meetings "to recall them all". Fortunately, after a "20 year gap until 1997", the immanent reopening at Hayley Stadium, under Tim's auspices and whom they all knew from back then, enabled Andy to transplant himself back into the sport.

When he looks to the bright side of his obsession with the sport at such a wide variety of clubs, Andy is genuinely delighted but slightly surprised to recall that he even met his wife through going to watch speedway – in 1949! It was a much simpler time, "the biggest difference is that now so many other interests have developed", to the extent that speedway has now almost completely lost the competition for people's time and attention. When you combine this lack of popularity with the fact that it's "so expensive to travel and take the family", then Andy believes that it's an almost irretrievable situation. If you decide go to Somerset, the nearest track to Newport, Andy estimates that it will "cost you £50 before you buy any food, drink or the programmes". Not that, in his opinion, there is any real reason to travel anywhere else at all, other than to Newport, to get your weekly fix of speedway. He particularly resents the "most irritating outsiders saying it's boring at Newport 'cause it's first out of the gate" when in reality "we get some amazing racing here, as it's a small track it keeps everything together which causes all the excitement". Not that his work tending this small track isn't without its own difficulties, especially in the warm weather, since it requires "loads of water" to make it raceable and to attempt to keep the dust down to manageable levels. In order to continue to deliver the highest quality racing he can, Andy has completely soaked the surface "last night, this morning, then another time, with more shortly and maybe one more in the meeting".

Andy reckons "this season we had lots of safe riding, with riders giving room" but he especially praises "Stoney, Scott Robson and Mads Korneliusson"; though he doesn't approve of aggressive riders, like Nicki Pedersen, who is "a lovely feller off the track but on it the red mist comes down". He judges all riders against the standard set by Phil Crump when he rode in this country: "he always rode the outside line, but I never saw Crumpie take anyone out". Given his outline of the ideal way to ride at Newport, Andy definitely quickly bristles at my suggestion, which I'd repeatedly heard from others on my travels, that Newport lost their star rider Craig Watson, to serious injury early in the season, as a direct result of the parlous condition of the Newport track. Andy appears to be a calm man who would be slow to anger, but he belligerently notes, "everyone blames the track, though I'm not saying that the track is that good, but it's the same every week". In this specific instance, Watson was "sitting too far back, picks up grip which just shoots him off". He feels genuinely sorry for the injuries Watson sustained; notwithstanding the dramatic impact that it's had on Newport's fortunes this season without the expected and vital contribution of Craig's points, "because we've had such a poor side these last few years". He's also quick to point out that "there's lots of rougher tracks in the country, Oxford being one for example".

One of the keys to a club's success is the state of the track and so is the strength of the team, but another essential ingredient is promotion and publicity – particularly work to highlight its appeal to the uninitiated punters within the local community area. There's not much willingness to undertake this activity across the sport in general, especially now that its popularity has declined, and many contemporary promoters just prefer to preach to the converted; indeed, Andy believes, "a lot of promoters won't promote" or try to "go to schools and take the bikes or the riders". It's a frustration and is also something that Newport themselves could do, "but Tim just won't see it". It's a real pleasure to talk with someone who so sincerely cares about speedway and is so thoughtful. Sadly, Andy also has a job to do! With the thought of potentially more difficulties ahead that afternoon Andy – with his slightly discoloured cream top, Harry Worth style glasses and black cap – has a brief grumble as he hoists himself into his tractor with the dark blue bowser attached, to carry on to give the track the water and attention it again already requires in the bright sunshine.

I wander off and manage to briefly speak with the Pits Marshall, Raymond Evans, who began to watch Newport during their days at Somerton Park, where he "went as a nipper". Even at the tender age of eight years he'd started "doing odd jobs with track maintenance"; this stood him in good stead for "when Tim started all the old track staff, as they'd stayed in touch, all came back", sometimes just "to watch" but mostly to do the jobs that needed to be done to start the club to function properly. He's now been coming for "over 40 years" and can't imagine doing anything else.

By now the riders have slowly begun to arrive outside the gates in their vans, so it's definitely time to try to grab Tim and find out if he's free for a chat. Peter wanders by with the news that "later we'll get some milk and get you a drink" as I trot off, in search of Tim in the dark, deep bowels of the stadium itself. I'm also on another mission, an even more important one, my attempt to find the light switch for the loo in the pitch-black gloom. During my search I accidentally stumble across Tim while he replenishes the bar but, as a result, nearly don't get my interview after I give him a huge fright, when I suddenly speak after I unexpectedly arrive and loom out of the darkness. After he recovers his composure, he promises to meet me outside on the grandstand shortly for our chat.

Back outside in the already baking heat of the day, I stroll around the deserted stadium buildings and pass the catering caravan, the wittily named Wasps Nest. It has a reasonably varied menu of burgers, jumbo hot dogs and bacon rolls that serves to remind me that I'm pretty hungry. There are the turnstiles, close by what appears to be the track shop as well as a sign for the mysterious *High Octane Club S.W.A.R.M.*, which sounds like just the sort of curiously named organisation I should contemplate joining later. I wander some more and then lurk by the pits. They are no longer silent and conspicuously empty but, instead, slowly fill with a noisy trickle of riders and mechanics, who start to prepare their bikes and other essential equipment for the afternoon's fixtures. There is also an overspill area of the pits adjacent to the main pits area, which I gather serves as the staging point for visitors. Perched on the steps of the predominantly red coloured grandstand with its six rows of red seating, I shelter in its welcome shade and ponder the superb view it offers of the start gate, the home straight and, for that matter, the rest of the track. A short while later Tim passes by, with the slightly harassed look he has now definitely perfected. It's the look of a man concerned with the million and one complex details involved in "owning the stadium and running your own speedway club" as he has done for the "last nine years", though he has a lease to do so for 125 years! He's finally found sufficient 'spare' time on another busy day to talk with me, but is immediately preoccupied with thoughts of accidents in combination with the present weather conditions, particularly the warm sunshine and the slight breeze. He worries that "if there's a big accident" at the meeting they'll inevitably "lose the track for 15 or 20 minutes" and, with all the available bowsers temporarily stuck in the pits, the track conditions will quickly descend to such an extent that dust storms will be created, and thereby ruin things for the riders and the fans. Tim worries about many things to do with the speedway club, but this is one that could happen this afternoon, despite everyone's hard preparatory work earlier, since the track dries out so quickly when it's not regularly dowsed with water.

Tim is keen to stress that he always tries to do the best for the club and simultaneously fulfil his duties as the stadium owner and the club's promoter. However, this level of responsibility is a thankless task – and in recent years there has been even less praise than usual – that Tim has done now for some considerable time without complaint. This is, of course, the natural state of affairs and the usual experience of all promoters; but, in Tim's case, the situation has been exacerbated in the last few years by the continued poor results. Very few people understand, and even fewer ask, about the efforts that Tim regularly puts in on behalf of the club. Needless to say, when you meet Tim, you quickly realise his wholehearted commitment to the club is absolute, "my motivation is running Newport speedway, it's my business, I don't go anywhere else except when we visit other clubs". His strong, but thoughtful opinions go hand in hand with this undiminished enthusiasm. He echoes the overriding but universal theme at this club, and many other speedway clubs, that it's a "labour of love", throughout the season and "in the close season". Tim often goes to bed at the end of the week after he's "done 70 hours' work", which breaks the EU working time directive and is definitely a huge regular commitment on its own. However, since he spent "five years to find the land" he won't stint on the effort required to maintain the club successfully, particularly since it's "our buildings and everything". The winter months provide no real respite from his speedway commitments. He intends to continue to maximise[3] the use of the Hayley Stadium and its facilities; not only with his famous "only outdoor close season Winter speedway meeting" on the first Sunday of each New Year, but also the training schools as well as all the usual necessary maintenance and repairs. Throughout the summer, Tim regularly issues press releases to the media and, he believes, the club receives "good coverage" in the local papers, but not on the radio since "they never speak to me, unless I commit to advertising with them". He also notes that among the Premier League promoters there's a "far amount of camaraderie" but, overall, the continued survival of the club comes down to the hard work of Tim and his committed band of volunteers, a persistence that he views as a result of "desire not luck!" Rather modestly and incongruously, though, he still claims to be "learning the job".

Apart from the day-to-day stresses involved in the management of the speedway club and both its teams throughout the season, Tim takes considerable pride in what he views as his key developmental role within the sport. He conceives his essential function, as a promoter, is "to find riders and bring them on" and to "try to give them a chance". He achieves this by running Newport teams – the Wasps and the Mavericks – at the Premier and Conference League levels. It is the eighth

[3] There is a school of thought that Tim could also stage non-speedway activities at the stadium and, thereby, further maximise its usage. Though, obviously, this suggestion is made in ignorance of the restrictions that the local council may have contractually imposed upon the use of the stadium under the terms of Tim's lease, though it is already centrally located within an industrial area. The need for additional revenue streams is presently something that Tim is actively researching, particularly given that he owns a facility that is over seven acres in size.

season Newport have had a Conference League side and he endorses the belief that you "progress riders by riding them"; he doesn't run either club as a charity, particularly the junior side where there's "keen competition and not many wobblers". He notes with interest that most of the junior riders come from the local area but some come from as far a field as "Bristol or further". Always a Newport fan, Tim started going to Somerton Park in 1964 until it closed in 1977. During this time he worked as a mechanic to Phil Crump and Bob Coles besides "having a go at riding for a couple of years", mostly for the Exeter Juniors. He has a number of good memories of his time riding, most notably the old track at Mildenhall, but most of all he's pleased at the level of knowledge and understanding that his stint as a rider gave him and which he still brings to his job as a promoter. He was "hospitalised a couple of times" so has some personal insight into the difficulties and upset caused by the inevitable injuries that the sport inflicts on the riders. He also believes that until you've actually been on a speedway bike that "there's a void of understanding, [and] until you've tried to race one you have no idea of the real power of the beast". This lack of knowledge particularly prevails among the type of fan who complains about the lack of effort by the riders ("why didn't he wind it on?"). The solution for this, Tim feels, is that "everyone should have had a go on one" before they're entitled to criticise.

Tim's diagnosis of the present state of the sport is very economically based. He believes that "the sport has to reinvent itself every few years" and "just about manages to cope with every economic climate", although things have been "difficult" since "Black Monday" when everything "flattened out", and any talk of recovery is "all a lot of spin by the government". Admittedly Monday 19th October 1987 saw the largest ever fall in stock market values throughout the world but, if Tim is correct, the reverberations of these events continue to echo in this part of South Wales. Nearly 10 years later, Tim himself would demonstrate his own sign of economic optimism within the area when decided to re-open the speedway club. Suddenly, just like an urban bush tracker, he invites me to "just listen and tell me what you hear?" Before I can reply, he answers his own question, "you can only hear the tractor today, everywhere else is silent, whereas, three or four years ago, you'd see the activity and hear the sound of the steelworks". There'd be "lorries trundling up and down" but with the demise of this industry, "3,000 jobs have gone, plus 3,000 contractors". With all those jobs gone and the "severe impact on their families" it all adds up to a nightmare; particularly if you assume "with only three people per family, that's 18,000 people's spending power gone". Many people have gone hugely "in debt", and the continual television adverts for "various money services" constitutes an "indictment of the economic climate". It's "the way of the world for everything to be in competition with everything", particularly when it comes to "discretionary spending". Added to that is the competition from television where, "you have the world at your fingertips with two AA batteries and a remote control". This talk of television reminds Tim that Sky Sports has helped the sport become "far more glamorous" and the public's "impression of it is being changed". He enjoys watching the broadcasts with its "good production" values that highlight the intrinsic "gladiatorial" nature of the sport, "but it doesn't get any more people into *this* stadium". Tim feels that many tracks "suffer" from television's impact, while Newport suffers "twice" since many "shared events [in Britain] are now on a Sunday" and so directly compete with speedway staged in Newport. In this climate where "people are more choosy with their money" Tim still views the position of the club as "robust really, considering the situation". Another factor he believes is that very few clubs have the good fortune and control of their destiny afforded by the direct ownership of their facilities. "There's me, Coventry and Eastbourne who own our own stadiums plus King's Lynn, who're here today". But apart from that there's "no one, though I don't count Scunthorpe as – not being unkind – it's not a stadium, it's a track in a field". Luckily for the sport, there are a lot of volunteers to help keep costs down and, fortunately, there's no trouble "so speedway clubs don't have to employ police" at considerable additional cost for their crowd control. Tim shrugs and phlegmatically observes, "I'm not Manchester United though, am I?"

Over at the pit gate, Peter Towersey the Newport Conference team manager supervises the riders as they gradually arrive. We chat about Billy Legg's fall earlier in the season at Rye House[4] which was incorrectly diagnosed "luckily it wasn't broken, he was confident that he'd broken it, but hadn't". Peter started to work at Newport in 1999 but actually began to

---

[4] Where I heard one of the announcements of the season so far, "Legg has broken his leg"

watch the sport in 1956-57 at Wimbledon and has carried on ever since. Speedway appeals to him as a keen motorcyclist, since it's the "purest form of sport" and because it's all "throttle control and balance" while "massive technology doesn't really play a part". This contrasts with most other motor sports where advanced technology is paramount, plus most are unlike speedway where you can "see the whole of the track"; at many other motor sport events you "just don't know what happens half the time". Peter is delighted to be the team manager at Newport and to play his part to help to train the riders, improve their skills and help them to gain valuable experience. He's very aware that this progress is in the context of each league, particularly as each one of which is a "step up from the league before, another world, it's really hard". Consequently, progress for many riders can be "difficult" due to the "massive steps in skills and speed" required. Peter believes that definite improvements should be made in the assessment of rider's averages in the Conference League, but he's also pragmatic enough to realize that "promoters can't always go changing things as they have to bear in mind the finances", especially for Tim, since this is "his business and his livelihood". Peter has relished his involvement at Newport following his retirement as a driving instructor, "an easy job", and believes that he now works in the "most spectacular and viable" form [Conference League] of contemporary speedway. At the Mavericks they run training schools "so we pick the best of them" and, in Billy Legg and Sam Hurst, he's pleased to work with a "couple of 16 year olds coming on a treat". To Peter's great approval, Billy has improved so much that he "goes round like he's sitting in an armchair, he's rock solid nowadays".

As we talk, the riders and mechanics sign in at the gate and filter through with their equipment. There's a good deal of banter between all the riders with Peter and cricket is a regular topic of conversation with any of the Australians that pass. The most voluble and partisan is King's Lynn's Kevin Doolan. He's confident that Australia will continue their success and expects they'll easily retain the Ashes, despite the injury to McGrath, "he's our main strike bowler, mate". As he slowly pushes his bike off to the visitor's side of the pits, he says that "Warnie should be Prime Minister, I'd vote for him, I love 'im!" before he cockily adds, "I said England would win one Test". Currently there are more visitors and riders from King's Lynn in the pits than those from the home team. This is "normal" Peter says since the "visiting riders are always early as they come from such a distance". This is confirmed by the arrivals for Newport who so far only include Lee Dicken ("coming from Hull"), Tony Atkin ("from North Wales") and the sports oldest current rider Neil Collins ("from somewhere in the North"). While we stand there, some of the riders arrive not only with their bikes but also with huge additional quantities of tools and other equipment that I imagine must include everything and the kitchen sink. Peter laughs, "some of the lads turn up with enough stuff to build a bike from scrap". This contrasts sharply with Neil Collins who just arrives with a small domestic toolbox, since he's "always dead professional" and is convinced that you "only need three spanners".

Today's Conference League visitors are Oxford who have had a good run of form recently, but have also unfortunately been recently decimated by injuries to some of their key riders. They're without their up-and-coming stars of the future, Ben Barker and Craig Branney, who've joined Jamie Courtney on the injury list. Oxford are so short of riders that local rider Russell Barnett will guest for them in this afternoon's meeting. Peter says he's the "most consistent speedway rider ever, as he does the same speed everywhere!" Since he is an avid compiler of statistics and keen analyst of his own riders, Peter says that in the dry, Russell has a race time of 71 seconds and, when conditions are wet, he has an average race time of 71 seconds. Russell has a good bike and equipment generally, but "only rides a three-quarter pace". Peter frequently highlights this flaw and frequently counsels him to improve, "I say to him, Russell, you're losing it all on the straights, you'll have to open the throttle up; I often think, perhaps, he's on an economy drive with his fuel!" Worried that he's been too critical Peter mentions the caveat "though, to be fair to him, he'll go anywhere for a ride if you ask him". But then, according to Peter, Malcolm Holloway always said "everyone can ride a speedway bike but there are only a few who can race". Hywel Lloyd, the official club photographer, who has joined us, clearly agrees with this perspective but adds "it's best not to ask a member of the press to comment as we're supposed to be impartial". He's the official photographer at a number of speedway tracks – Newport, Exeter and Somerset – so he's keen to stress that he "doesn't have any favourites or support anyone". He's there to do a "professional job", which he's done successfully for 10 years, so he finds it best "to know what's happening but you don't follow what's going on, if you get my drift".

Over by the entrance gates, there's a hopeful bustle of activity among the staff in preparation for the hordes of fans that are going to be attracted to today's double-header meeting. Already at work are the husband and wife team of Sue and Gavin Morrison – he works as the track's incident recorder while she works on the gate. They met at teacher training in the town in 1972 and Sue still carries an excellent but nostalgic sepia photo of them together a few years later, taken in Newbridge around 1974. Gavin studied as a filmmaker and for a while worked at film school but, since it's the nature of our dreams to take us to unexpected places, now works for the Inland Revenue. Whereas Sue is the headteacher at Penllwyn primary school in the valleys, so her work at the speedway is "totally different" to her weekday job, since it markedly carries a lot less responsibility. Not that the schoolwork isn't rewarding especially the recent 50th anniversary celebration at the school, where they played the music of their famous ex-pupils, such as Tom Jones, which is not unusual, Catherine Jenkins and Shirley Bassey. Sue loves speedway, her work at the track and has known promoter Tim for 30 years since the old Somerton Park days. She relishes the fact that the speedway people are "very friendly, even when you go away".

Also by the entrance gate turnstiles is Dave, who came to his first speedway meeting in 1964 and has developed a love of statistics along with his abiding passion for the sport. This manifests itself in "his own programme grids" that he's specifically invented to record all the results of the club. He started doing this after the meeting versus Exeter on May 5th 1977 was abandoned after seven heats and, by now, has archived all of Newport's racing records since 1964 to the present day. He's travelled all round the country to follow his team and watch the sport; he speaks highly of the fans everywhere and even praises the Cornish pasties they serve at Exeter! Dave checks his culinary recommendation with Jayne and Janet on the adjacent S.W.A.R.M. desk, but they're too busy to have time to give opinions, since they have to concentrate on their preparations for the fixture ahead.

The S.W.A.R.M. club started in 1999 and is so successful at raising money that the Newport riders don't have to pay for their tyres, oil or fuel, either at home or at away meetings. This institutional saving scheme was unique to the club until, with imitation often best seen as the sincerest form of flattery, Sheffield copied the idea. Membership costs £7 per month and all the proceeds go to help the riders defray their costs. There's also the High Octane Club, which was started this season but already has 50 members who pay £10 per month. Fifty percent of these funds go directly to the riders and the remainder is used to fund the prizes for the draw that they stage to attract more donations. In addition they organise a 'Guess the Score' competition at every home meeting (at £1 a go) to try to raise even more funds. They're a keen and dedicated pair of ladies who know they're "well appreciated by the riders" but unselfishly praise the efforts of others, such as the "supporter who paid for all the race jackets for the Mavericks". All these fund-raising efforts strengthen the warm bond that Jayne and Janet share with "their riders". They're rather enamoured with Niels Kristian Iversen ('Puck' to them) although they despair about his lack of adventure, a fault they feel that originates in certain national characteristics, especially with the Swedes and the "dirty Danes" who are too prone "to rarely leaving the white line" on their forays onto the Newport track. Another favourite is Anders Hendriksson, who they warmly remember for when he finally won a race at the Exeter track he notoriously hated so much and, afterwards, embarked on celebrations of such vigour and jubilation that "you'd have thought he'd won the world championship". Overall, Jayne and Janet aren't pleased with this season's home performances by the team but, in part, they unusually put this down to the home riders allowing themselves to be "psyched out" by visitor's hearsay comments about the poor state of the Newport track! They wish that the Newport riders would follow Travis McGowan's sage advice, whether dealing with difficult tracks, hard riders or injuries, and "just get on with it!" [Jayne and Janet would like me to make clear that they unreservedly support Newport, the riders and have not criticised the track].

Close by the S.W.A.R.M. ladies is the doorway to the nerve centre of speedway operations at Newport, the Speedway Office, which is run by the very capable Ros Curtis. She's another returnee from the Somerton Park days, though she met Tim again years later and thereby returned to the sport. Ros enjoys her involvement with the office administration at the club because it has "opened up a whole new circle of friends" in contrast to her mysterious day job ("I'm a full-time civil servant, I'll just leave it at that"). She makes running a speedway club sound remarkably easy, when she characterises her work as the administration of "money coming in" – mostly from the gate, the shop, the car park and the bars – and "money going out". When I return to the pits area I bump into the friendly Paul Carrington, who is the referee for today's double-header meeting. He's already started his pre-meeting checks and inspections but finds the time to enquire "am I following you around everywhere or are you following me?"

If you were to judge from the numbers of people that arrive through the turnstiles, there's not going to be a huge amount of income raised for the club on this scorching hot Sunday afternoon. The small crowd particularly bothers the visiting King's Lynn promoter, the youngest in British speedway, Jonathan Chapman when we speak on the centre green after his team have posed for photos in their brand new team kevlars. He carefully studies the grandstand and the terraces for a moment, before he estimates the small crowd as "very poor". He matter of factly notes, "you're not going to get rich on a crowd like this" before he quickly identifies the major problem to his mind, which is "to run a meeting you have to promote it". "Why run at 2 p.m.?" he wonders, when you must compete for people's valuable leisure time and so inevitably find yourself losing attendance to people otherwise engaged at the shops or with their families over Sunday lunch. Soon at King's Lynn, they intend to try an experimental start time of Sunday at 6 p.m., to try to gauge comparative attendance levels at different times. Jonathan believes later in the day "would be a better time for Newport to run", but notes that this is highly unlikely, though, since "they don't have any floodlights". Whatever time of day or year the meeting is run, Jonathan remains extremely confident of victory, especially because "we won here earlier in the year when three of our riders didn't score".

As I walk over to the first bend to join Hywel as he prepares to capture the action on his impressive camera, I reflect that the way Jonathan has spoken about the prospects ahead this afternoon doesn't make it sound that appealing a fixture for me to decide watch at Newport. Hywel agrees, though it's okay for him since his work involves him watching each week's racing at Somerset, Exeter and Newport, and therefore he's spoilt for choice, never mind that he has many people "wondering why I do so many tracks". He's not exactly filled with joy about this afternoon either. Hywel doesn't offer specifics about the shortcomings he perceives in Newport's performance, particularly given that he watches them race week in week out, but instead errs on the side of, what I gather, is still diplomacy. In fact, despite Hywel's suggestion, I did not find this to be the worst track on my travels. Still it's almost traditional for visiting riders and fans to claim that the Newport track is definitely unique, albeit solely by dint of being the worst surface they race on during the season. Then again, the track shape and dimensions can also be a significant factor that determines the quality of the racing seen. Not that this is a problem at Newport, though it is at some other Conference League tracks. I don't have the expertise to gainsay this either way, but it does appear that everyone has so clearly made up their mind before they arrive, that it probably becomes a self-fulfilling prophecy. In extenuation, Hywel notes that the team has been beset by injuries and some personnel changes, which, along with the chronically unsuccessful operation of rider replacement, has led to Neil Collins frequently constituting a one-man opposition against all-comers. Neil is the "only one" to Hywel's mind that's tried to bring and preserve some vague level of respectability to some woeful score lines.

I'm delighted to have permission to watch the proceedings from anywhere on the centre green and decide to choose what I believe is the ideal location, just by the first bend, with an excellent view of the riders as they jostle for position, just as they make their initial first turns. This also luckily gives me the chance to study their various riding styles and the racing itself much more closely than a view from the terraces could permit. I've definitely acquired the taste to watch the action from the centre green and, after the seasons over, I resolve to embark on a campaign to become a track photographer or member of the track staff. Although, obviously, I realize that far cannier and far more dedicated and experienced people do these things already. But who could fault me for wanting the chance to bask in the sunshine and to watch, really close up, all the racing I want. By the end of heat 3, the score has already taken a desperate turn for the home side, as King's Lynn have already built a 12-6 lead. This then gives me the chance to closely observe the experienced and redoubtable Neil Collins, the oldest competitive rider still in the UK. He wears an old fashioned red bandana that flaps as he races, just like so many riders used to wear during my youth when I first started to watch the sport. He effortlessly exhibits the track craft and experience of his many years' track experience when he delicately avoids, at the last second, his suddenly fallen team-mate Jason King on the first lap. Neil then overcomes this unexpected delay to stalk and then draw close to Ashley Jones for the remainder of the race, before he judges his moment to easily slip by him, on a very well-watered and slippery surface, for his very hard-fought-for second place. In the sparse crowd, this exhibition of skill clearly enraptures the family in the home-straight stand who're all dressed in matching yellow T-shirts with some sort of message of support for the Wasps, that can't be easily read at this distance. They stand together on the terracing with five giant blown-up photographs of the individual Newport riders they support that they've brought to the meeting. As the race finishes, the children rush from the grandstand to the track fence, climb up it and then wave the giant photo of Neil Collins at Neil Collins in their own childish gesture of recognition and salute. I notice later that this family also have photos of Karlis Ezergalis and Lee Dicken as well as a couple of other Newport riders that I don't recognize as they aren't familiar to me but they might include their new rider, Henrik Vedel; someone that's unknown even to a well-informed consumer of the *Speedway Star* like myself. I had never heard of him until I'd opened today's match programme, although hopefully Henrik's exploits on the track for Newport will be just the tonic the club needs and will soon ensure that he's recognised throughout the country. Whether the other mysterious rider in the gigantic photo is Tony Atkin, Jason King or Mads Korneliussen I sadly never find out.

With Newport still to win a race, heat 6 features a nasty clash on the track that leaves Henrik Vedel and Oliver Allen in a crumpled heap of fallen bodies and machines. The crash has happened right by where Hywel stood poised with his camera until that very race, so he has to rush over from some distance away and quickly take a series of less inspired pictures of Oliver Allen. While he lies prostrate and motionless on the track, completely surrounded by the yellow-jacketed St John Ambulance staff keen to establish their diagnosis before they provide some much-needed attention. Oliver Allen's motionless condition is completely understandable since he landed extremely heavily on his back, at great speed after he'd been flung from his machine by the force of the impact. The ambulance drives onto the track and then Allen is gingerly stretchered into the back of it wearing breathing apparatus. The announcer then remarks, with masterly understatement, that he's "severely winded".

Hywel is pretty narked since he'd just missed the only drama of the meeting so far, "there would be an accident when I freaking moved, wouldn't there". He explains that the work of the local track photographer requires that he frequently gets good close action shots that will be of interest to local fans, which means that he mostly concentrates on the home team, since that's what the local papers inevitably want to give their readers to look at. Hywel is handicapped in this goal by this season's lack of race winners, which severely limits the opportunity for the action shots he can capture of the Newport riders as they lead, if not ultimately beat, rival riders in any closely fought races. Without many of these staple standard but often spectacular shots to be going on with, then it's crashes or fights that provide the next best chance of a publishable picture for any track photographer.

Some people allege that the condition of the Newport track is the cause of many of the ills that beset the team and depresses the already low number of spectators. This afternoon the tractor grade has exposed some stones below the surface on Bend 2. It's safe to say that the track is a perpetual topic of discussion that dominates the conversations of practically everyone who encounters it, except within Tim's hearing. He takes great umbrage at any real or perceived criticism on any topic, least of all the track condition. It's alleged that critics have been exiled or banished from the stadium including the local media, despite the club's need for regular coverage, and Hywel, who shrugs with nonchalant pride when he mentions, "anyone who's anyone has been banned from the track at some point!"[5] The tractor goes round and round in an attempt to grade the track surface, while there's a short delay for the medical team to perform miracles on Oliver Allen

[5] Tim later pointed out to me that their disagreement came after several discussions with Hywel, he'd eventually decided that while he had no objection to the sale of Newport Speedway photographs, taken at the stadium, to outside agencies like the local paper and the Speedway Star. However, Tim did object to paying what he viewed as an unfair price for a group of photos in which there were, in his opinion, very few of useable quality. There was also a period when the local paper chose not to report at the club for a year but that was their choice rather than an actual ban; which resulted from a contretemps about a report that appeared after one year's Winter Open, where the local reporter had spent most of the meeting in the bar. Hywel later dismissed these criticisms as "utter bollocks" and reiterated that it was "common knowledge that people had been banned by Tim".

back in the comparative comfort of the pits area. The track staff also water the track with a hose, which exasperates Hywel further as, to his mind, it will only serve to make the track "patchy". The track condition doesn't really bother him as much as the total lack of saleable photos so far. "All I need is one decent first bend photo. If I was the King's Lynn photographer, I'd be freaking laughing myself all the way to the bank".

With the track TLC temporarily at an end, the re-run of the race takes place without Oliver Allen. The announcer informs us that Oliver is to immediately withdraw from the fixture with concussion before he swiftly shifts to sing the praises of Tony Atkin as "Captain Fantastic here". Actually the Wasps' captain does come across an enthusiastic individual particularly when, a few heats later, he deliberately makes the effort to offer some words of encouragement to King's Lynn's young German reserve, Tommy Stange, after he had fallen just yards from the finish line through a mixture of youthful exuberance and inexperience, as he deservedly led Tony. By the interval break, which follows that race, the score heads towards cricket-like proportions. All that remains is for a Newport rider to win a race on their home track in a last-ditch attempt to salvage the last vestige of their pride. The music they play on the tannoy has, rather wittily, the chorus "everyday I love you less and less" while Hywel is much more direct in his comments, "this is freaking crap".

A brief rustle of excitement in the crowd ensues because the winning ticket in the prize draw is announced, with a rather magnificent £87.50 going to the lucky winner. So, at least, the low attendance has had the benefit that it has encouraged around 175 people to try to take advantage of the greater statistical odds, through the low number of attendees, which appear to be in their favour at this fixture. The brief interval break enables me to meet with one of the youngest start marshal's in British speedway, 20 year-old Craig Wright, who is already a veteran of three years' standing at Newport. Craig has also officiated at the UK's so-called prestige speedway event, the annual British round of the Grand Prix that is held nearby at the impressive Millennium Stadium in Cardiff[6]. Very efficient at his job, Craig spends most of the interval hard at work in the blistering sunshine, as he tends to the start-line area and then briefly relaxes in his seat to carefully study the match programme. He thinks that things haven't been going well on the track for Newport for a while, but is quick to rather exactly point out in extenuation that "we haven't had a full team since May 8th", before he goes on to catalogue the injuries for Watson and Korneliussen and the distraction of marital difficulties for Michael Coles.

The very next heat after the interval finally results in a race victory for a Newport rider and he is greeted with some delirium, at least by the four children with the gigantic photographs, who rush from the main stand to lean over the safety fence to exchange celebratory high five's with Neil Collins on his victory lap. On the first bend, two young girls also wait for a celebratory slap of hands from him, before Neil then attempts a half-hearted wheelie on the back straight. Though his heart's not really in it, I think that Neil does this more from the principle of fulfilling expectations and because it's the usual 'professional' thing to do, rather than from pure unalloyed joy. You can't help but sense, especially as a glance at the scores shows that this heat has just confirmed the home team's inevitable defeat. The music on the turntable that plays over the tannoy has another well-chosen chorus 'you're driving me to insanity'. The meeting swiftly runs to its conclusion but not before Matthew Tutton, a Newport rider from the Conference team, adds his own witty coda to the afternoon's events. Just before heat 15, he cycles out in full racing gear – kevlars, steel shoe, gloves, race bib and crash helmet – on a young child's bicycle that is much too small for him, lines up at the tapes and then, right after the tapes have gone up, exaggeratedly falls over just yards from the start. The crowd roars loudly in appreciation and the announcer adds "it's good to see that some things don't change whether there's an engine or not". The final score of 35-58 defines a massive home defeat, which is an especially poor performance given that one of the visitors' best riders, Oliver Allen, withdrew so early in the meeting. Hywel commiserates with me, "I pity you have to go to King's Lynn to watch that lot again". A member of the track staff adds "it's the worst performance I've ever seen for Newport speedway and I've been watching since 1966". Another member of the track maintenance crew, Robert Roderick, adds a much more measured judgment of events, "our

[6] The BSI, owners of the Grand Prix franchise, did have the business acumen and vision to decide to stage this event at a prestigious venue from the outset, when many gainsayers doubted their wisdom. It's the most magnificent location in which to stage a speedway meeting and is, undoubtedly, the best venue in Britain. However, though it's a temporary venue, rented for the night, it definitely adds lustre to an otherwise increasingly predictable event.

luck ran out weeks ago". Given that they all work here voluntarily you have to both admire their love and commitment as well as question their sanity.

One thing I've noticed in my travels is that once the meeting finishes or is very close to the end, the riders zealously pack away all their gear with a speed that wouldn't be out of place during a fire evacuation. A time-and-motion study in any post-meeting pits area would document some astonishingly fast times to completely empty an area of people and equipment. Maybe because you've just raced at exceptional speeds, you're caught up in doing everything quickly afterwards – whether it's just to shower and change, if there are showers, drink in the bar, sign autographs, pose for photos or to have a quick meaningless sexual encounter with the groupies. The exception to this feverish alacrity is Neil Collins, who remains in a deserted pits area to carefully attend to his bike in a languid, leisurely fashion and fully use the minimal amounts of equipment he's brought for the purpose. Outside by the line of parked riders' vans, the King's Lynn team must be on a promise or have an urgent party to attend, since there's a mad scramble of bikes, riders, spare parts and toolboxes as well as many girlfriends, while they all muck in together to quickly load up their vans with frequent clatters. The area they have just vacated on the visitor's side of the pits has already been taken by the visiting Oxford Conference League team with their own retinue of riders, mechanics and mad, keen, and perpetually advising proud fathers.

Between the meetings, the legendary Neil 'Bill' Street takes a lot of time and interest in my book and my research questions, while we sit in the welcome shade of the cubbyhole by the pits. He looks surprisingly cool in his trademark jumper, despite the intense heat of the day and the severity of the loss that he's just endured in his capacity as the Newport team manager. He has immense experience and an attitude to life that places him somewhere between Gandalf and Yoda in the speedway world.

Neil chats easily and animatedly about his great-grandchildren one minute or switches seamlessly to his grandson Jason Crump's progress in this season's Grand Prix – notably how difficult it is to be the defending champion, the strain of all the travel on a proud father of a young family, as well as his recent bout with chicken pox ("it's much worse when you get it as an adult"). Neil goes to practically all Jason's Grand Prix meetings to help out in his corner of the pits along with Jason's father and his son-in-law, Phil Crump. Neil travels much less nowadays, especially since he relinquished his responsibilities as the Australian team manager, "it was time to hand over to a younger man". Which it's fair to say, in comparison to Neil, Craig Boyce most definitely is; though as a rider he's already reached 'veteran' status. Neil has enjoyed the glory years of his management of the Aussie squad with great patriotism, particularly since he'd been so closely involved throughout the decade or so of their rise and dominance in team competitions. "We were so good they even had to change the rules to beat us," he says, but, sadly, in the way of all flesh, the team is ageing and, for Neil, has already passed their best until "hopefully the next generation comes through again". He chats affably with his eyes sparkling and alive but bristles immediately, at my reference to the common description of him as a "legendary figure" within the sport. The frequent repetition of this claim offends his modesty and frustrates him, "I'd like to dispense with all that bullshit about legends, as many people say this. I've done lots of things and made most of the things, as others would have done, I've been very fortunate". A brief run through his curriculum vitae would find that he followed on from his riding career in Britain to become a successful and very skilled team manager for both club and country, his beloved Australia. He has been particularly successful for his country, where he single-handedly has encouraged and shaped the development of many later generations of riders in the UK. Mostly through his avowed policy to bring over "hordes of blokes" from Australia to gain vital experience here. Neil has always been keen to develop a lot of young people's talents, which, inevitably, appears to involve "keeping them at my place in Exeter to get them settled in". There is also his widely acknowledged influence upon his son-in-law Phil Crump and his grandson Jason, the current reigning World Champion. And, of course, he revolutionised the equipment used in the sport through its adoption of his invention of the first 4-valve engine into speedway; the "Neil Street Conversion" as it was known, an innovation that he introduced in 1975. As he accurately but modestly notes, in a lifetime, "you do a lot of things!"

Neil came to this country in 1952, on March 2, from Melbourne on a one-way ticket that cost £25. He left behind a large family where, at an early age, he'd had to assume a lot of responsibility as the eldest child of nine who had a father who "was a drunkard". He grew up quickly "milking cows and the like" before he left for England at the age of 21 with no money to his name, to seek a different life. Upon arrival he was "very fortunate" to get to stay with Mrs Weekes in Exeter. The appreciation of good fortune really should be Neil's catch phrase (Neil "very fortunate" Street) since it peppers his conversation throughout and he always acknowledges it with wonder and such genuine sincerity. Mrs Weekes helped Neil find his feet "she looked after me as good as my mother", and eventually helped lead him to think about putting down permanent roots in this country. He was also helped to settle in England by Mrs Morgan, who he went to stay with after five years in the country, and he smiles when he notes, "I'm lucky enough to have had three mothers in my life!" When you speak with Neil, you recognize and feel his love of people and his essential humanity. He believes his journey to England was a great eye opener and formative experience for him. When Neil says, "it's been a wonderful life", you believe him since it somehow doesn't sound clichéd or trite. He arrived with no money "you learned to mix with people" with "lots of different nationalities" and through this process he gained a respect for common humanity. It's an experience he passionately believes that all young Australian men, who "luckily" (that word again) have talent for riding a speedway bike, should seek out. When they arrive in England and travel throughout Europe, they can "learn a broad outlook on human nature" and through "mixing with a variety of people" they can have experiences that teach them "to become more tolerant" of themselves and other people. He believes it "opens their eyes" and is "much better" than the formal education provided by University because it opens them up to experience life by transplanting them to the other side of the world away from the comfort of their "usual expectations".

Through Neil's eyes, people experience the same issues and concerns the world over, because there's an underlying, shared "common bond". He encourages every young rider he meets to gain this experience, as he "hates to see young people missing opportunities". Neil has intense pride in his family and also in his workmanship "I've built four houses, two in Victoria and two here, with my own hands". However, when push comes to shove you have absolutely no difficulty to believe that he's "not interested in material possessions" and that really "it's all about living". For Neil a little of the brotherhood of man goes a long way, "deep down everyone is just people and the best thing you can do is just experience life". He looks at it philosophically, if the young Aussies who come over to Britain "don't make it as a speedway rider, they've still really experienced something special in their life". It's definitely something that Neil encourages, since he says he encounters "more whingeing Aussies over here than Brits".

It's also a sad fact that many young men, of whatever nationality, who set out to be speedway riders just won't ever make the grade. In Neil's experience, "three quarters of the riders can't ride". It's a blunt analysis, but he believes way too many riders get obsessed with details that are ultimately irrelevant to their performance; "they get too complicated" and obsess about comparatively minor technical matters – such as clutches, gear ratios and ignitions – when really "it's all about throttle control!" In an ideal world they should ride their bikes "like a jockey, feeling everything through your backside – what the tyres are doing and the surface – and riding the bike using their throttle accordingly". This skill is beyond many riders ability and consequently hampers their performance. If Neil has any regrets about the sport, it's the impact of the necessary but inexorable rise of "professionalism" that you find throughout the sport in Poland, Sweden and England. It hasn't become "too stupid for words over money" like football but, Neil worries, that it's heading that way. Speedway was a "family concern that's now too professional", even the fans no longer mix with the riders in the bar afterwards, as they used to do in the past. The sport has definitely along the way lost this innate fraternity between the riders and the fans, probably inevitably so, with many riders' intense travel schedules that takes them throughout Europe for League racing and the Grand Prix's. "Speedway fans want to feel that they're part of the family" but "as money comes into it, they (the riders) lose identity with the fans", it's not as bad as football, but it still "makes me bloody mad"[7]. I could listen for hours to this kindly,

[7] Tim Stone is often quoted by Bob Radford saying "Streetie was my best EVER signing for the club, not just for speedway but for everything else he knows". Tim also always tells the riders, "listen to Streetie he's like a witch doctor".

informed and most humane of men but since he has already missed the first couple of races of the Conference League meeting, Neil just can't bear to miss the chance to watch the next generation of riders any longer. He heads off to the steps of the pits metal viewing platform, just like any other keen fan of the sport, to catch up on the detail of the races he's missed and complete his programme correctly with the help of another fan. Even after the first few heats Newport dominate the rather patched up and comparatively lacklustre Oxford Academy squad who feature 'Mr 71 Seconds' himself, Russell Barnett, as a guest heat leader. Along with many of the visitors, he completely fails to come to grips with the track conditions. Well, grip is probably the wrong word since, by this stage of the afternoon, the surface is a strange mix of dust in places, dirt in others, as well as the unique Newport track feature of a wide "blue line" throughout its circumference. The "blue line" has gradually appeared during the fixture and has been created after the shale surface had completely worn away to expose the tarmac underneath, in the centre of the track on the most popular riding line around the circuit. Even without this wear and tear, experienced riders would maybe struggle to master the track but for the visitors, who are here to learn their trade, it's horrendously hard (but good experience). The Oxford riders continually trail a considerable distance behind the home team riders, whose familiarity with the track makes light of these testing and difficult conditions.

The situation for Oxford isn't helped when their star rider, Chris Mills, crashes heavily into the first bend fence, after he careers off at great speed on his bucking, out of control bike. After some delay for medical treatment and for the demolished boards of the safety fence to be reassembled, Mills walks slowly and gingerly back to the pits area. He pauses to gesture rudely towards the referee's box, a clearly visible signal of his consternation at his exclusion from the race as the "primary cause of the stoppage". The pain of his injuries, along with his exclusion doesn't exactly add to the lightness of his mood. Nor does the announcers retort, in quick response to Mills' disgruntled gesture, that "if you can get up and walk away, you can stop and repair the boards". After another gesture, this time towards the announcer, Mills remonstrates loudly and at length about the danger he alleges is posed by the condition of the track with the referee Peter Clarke, who has come down to the pits. Along with the team managers, the trackman and basically anyone else within earshot at the pits entrance onto the track. Neil Street tries in vain to calm Mills and deflect attention away from the poor conditions, by the sincere and sage counsel that "you need to use throttle control when going from slick to rough". Mills has no time for this emollient voice of experience, or any other, as he repeatedly shouts, "I can freaking ride! I can freaking ride!" albeit with a few more swear words; or insistently repeats his demand that the meeting should be stopped in the interests of rider safety. His petulant histrionics do him no credit at all and completely undermine the limited influence or possible impact of his suggestions. To echo what they say in the Bond films, 'for you Mr Mills the evening is over'. Chris Mills then sensibly withdraws from the meeting due to injury and, with his withdrawal, the extremely slim chance of an Oxford recovery or triumph disappears. Oxford manage to continue to mirror the earlier performance of the Newport senior side, an unfortunate feat, since they had earlier only had one race winner in 15 heats; whereas the Oxford team wait until heat 14 before one of their riders finally manages to pass the chequered flag first. The match ends with another cricket type score of 67-26 with Russell Barnett roaring (at around 70 seconds per race) to a five ride 'minimum' score of zero as a guest rider for the visitors. If it had been a boxing match, the referee would have awarded the fight to save further unnecessary punishment[8].

The ease of the Conference teams victory hasn't lightened the mood on the terraces among the hard core of disgruntled Newport fans. Because I have an open notepad, spectator Roy Powell leans over from his seat, on the grandstands edge by the pits, to loudly share his thoughts with me, as he initially mistakes me for a reporter from the local paper, *The Argus*. When he learns that I do not represent that paper it doesn't surprise him because "they don't ask the supporters about their feelings, they just put in what Tim Stone wants them to say". Even though I'm not from the local paper, Roy is still delighted to seize the opportunity to vent off the steam that the afternoon's performance has generated in him. He's watched speedway since he was a boy, which is quite a while I gather, and hasn't missed a meeting at Newport since it reopened. However, now that he's endured the recent series of difficult seasons, today's abject performance appears to be the straw that's finally broken this particular camel's back. Roy is now determined to carry out his, often uttered, threat to never return to the club while promoter Tim Stone remains in charge. He's "not paying money to watch this effort" and he notes, "if they'd put the Mavericks on first we wouldn't have watched the senior side race". He lays the blame squarely on Tim's shoulders. Roy claims, "he puts on what he thinks he can get away with, it's not entertainment – at best it's mediocre, but really it's daylight robbery. Tim wants to be a one man band, with total control, ignoring that he's not the easiest promoter to get on with". Roy does praise the work of the many volunteers and Neil Street, whom he calls "Blinking Billy" because "he's an awkward sod who thought he was an aborigine" He then contradicts himself to praise Neil for the award of an Australian Gold Medal, for services to sport and Australia and, supposedly, though I never substantiate this, one of only seven medals ever awarded to notable Australian sportsmen or women. Roy then points out a few of the other regular, but not as disgruntled, faces in the crowd. I leave Roy to fulminate further and go in search of the reporter from *The Argus* to point him in Roy's direction. In fact *The Argus*'s reporter, Ray Parker, sits out of earshot only a few seats away, from where he closely monitors the action on the track, while he fills his notebook with careful shorthand written in a measured manner. He's absorbed in the racing and that's his sole concern and object of study, as it should be, for the remainder of the meeting. We agree to keep in touch in the future, when my book is published.

I ramble off and make a fruitless trip to find Tim before I leave, to thank him for the hospitality of everyone at the club, but not to pass on Roy's comments, since he should properly do this in person. The office is locked, though Tim is still somewhere on the site. Back near the pits, Neil Street has engaged in a lengthy conversation with disgruntled Roy and his friend. From what I can overhear, they both share their honest and frank opinions on the situation. It's also typical of Neil, just like he did with Chris Mills earlier, that he would take the time and trouble to respond to the point of view of another human being rather than ignore it. In the pits, Peter Brooks tidies some gear away into the storeroom and staff cubbyhole. He nods in Neil's direction and asks if I got to spend some time with him today. He observes, "he's unique, one of a kind really" before he makes it abundantly clear that the less said about the day is the better. Though Peter then notes, "there's no loyalty among the riders nowadays" before he stresses that everyone might have a strong opinion or think that they would run the club better but, in reality, most people would be stymied by the "politics between riders and the clubs" never mind that, as ordinary punters, "we just don't see or know the half of it". Nine hours after my arrival, as I ponder what I think I know about my half of it, I drive away from Hayley Stadium through the stillness of the Queensway Meadows light industrial estate in the very warm late evening summer sunshine.

[8] The first sentence of Jason Harrold's report of the meeting the next week in the *Speedway Star* notes that this was "NOT a meeting for the purists!"

7th August Newport v. King's Lynn (Premier League) 35-58
7th August Newport v. Oxford (Conference League) 67-26

SKY CHATTER

"Nowadays there's not a lot of riders who look for their team mate" Gary Havelock

RANDOM SCB RULES

9.2.4 An Approved Inflatable Fence may be placed on or against any type of fence and must be inflated at least 30 minutes before the start of the Meeting.

The city of Exeter has long been renowned as a seat of learning because of its famous and historic university. It's also legendary in the world of speedway for the longest racetrack in the country and has distinction as the only track with a steel perimeter fence. These famous sheets of steel originally came from the tops of the Second World War Morrison indoor air raid shelters. When the track reopened after the war in 1947, the make do and mend culture of privation and rations saw no objection to the material from the shelters being put to good use as the safety fence of the then promoters Bernard Slade and Frank Buckland. As if the stakes weren't already high enough for speedway riders – who risk life, limb and injury every time they ride their machines competitively – there's the nagging worry of the County Ground safety fence to contend with for all those who compete at this Premier League stadium.

But then again, with all other things being equal, they say that the key to success on a speedway bike is your psychological outlook as much as ability. Indeed, some visitors suffer from such a negative mental approach that they're effectively

Old fashioned turnstiles. © Jeff Scott

They like to water well at Exeter. © Jeff Scott

View from the third bend of the start line grandstand. © Jeff Scott

beaten before they even set a wheel on the track itself. To judge by the consistently high scores run up at home by Exeter in recent seasons, often in the high 50s and low 60s, this is definitely the case. Not that the Exeter team is always invincible when it rides at the County Ground since, like any other speedway team throughout a lengthy season, they suffer from injuries, various machine difficulties, arguable refereeing decisions and poor performances from individual riders.

Rumour has it that the track is very different this season compared with previous years, so the natural home advantage for the Falcon's riders on the rough, deep home track surface has significantly diminished. The chance to attend a speedway fixture at this stadium is, however, sadly a finite thing with its closure only weeks away at the time of my visit in early August 2005.

Indeed, the threat of the closure of its stadium has hung over Exeter Speedway for many years. The track is located within Exeter Rugby Club on a prime site for development close to the heart of the city centre and is quaintly surrounded by many streets of residential houses. It's been a protracted battle for survival that the local promoters finally lost, despite the best efforts of the late Colin Hill and the present incumbent David Short. The club intends to carry on the tradition of speedway in Exeter and, to that end, a number of alternative locations have been identified but the lengthy consultation process that surrounds any new track is inevitably fraught with difficulty. Sadly, at the time of writing, these plans have not yet come to fruition and the Falcon's will be without a home base for the foreseeable future.

Frustratingly, for all concerned whether promoters, riders or fans, there have been a number of false dawns. The most recent possible site, on commercial land conveniently located by the M5 motorway, has been dogged by a sustained campaign of hostility from tenacious local residents. All the usual reasons to disqualify the applications have been given a run round the block, most prominent of which inevitably is the usual suspect of environmental concerns. These disagreements will often include worries about the unholy triumvirate of noise, dirt and traffic congestion that besets every new speedway track application throughout the country. In the case of the latest site proposed by the club, possible noise objections have been to the fore of complaints, despite the ironic proximity of the site to Exeter Airport with it's unavoidable sustained noise pollution from the frequent take-offs and landings. The campaign of the protesters has, ultimately, led the landlord to reconsider his position and, for strategic and financial reasons, has reached the decision that Exeter Speedway Club wouldn't be the easiest choice of commercial tenants. This leaves Exeter well and truly back on the drawing board, but without the prospect of another unexpected reprieve on the stadium closure as happened in 2004. The County

Ground Stadium is definitively due for demolition, to make way for further houses, at the end of the 2005-2006 rugby season on May 1st 2006.

David Short confirms the incontrovertible fact of the Exeter track closure in his column in the match programme for tonight's fixture against the Edinburgh Monarchs. Even if this sad news wasn't enough, much more worryingly for the riders and supporters of the club than this news is the phrase in his column that reads, "I am quite hopeful that the Falcons will be able to race, if not in 2006 then the following year". David is to be applauded for his frankness and honesty to deliver this news and, when we speak, he explains that his future approach will be not to make any announcements about possible future site locations in the Exeter area before regulatory approval has been received. Mostly to avoid unnecessarily raised hopes, but also to reduce the opportunity that possible demonstrators will have to skilfully coordinate their campaigns of resistance to the club's proposals.

When I finally arrive at the pits gate on a very warm summers afternoon, it's clear that everyone connected with the club is determined to enjoy the final swansong of the last few weeks racing at this historic speedway stadium. I am welcomed at the stadium entrance by the club's 'Staff Co-ordinator' John Tombs, as he is listed in the programme (or "general dogs body" as he describes himself). John has been connected with the club for 43 years, ever since he began in his initial capacity as a track raker in 1962. He's an affable and avuncular moustachioed man with a veritable mine of information about the riders, the many characters and the people that are or have been connected with the club since that time. John exudes the easy attitude of a man who's very contented with his lot in life and confides that, as if I couldn't already guess from his demeanour, "there's nothing I don't like here". He particularly enjoys the opportunity to meet the sponsors, the children and the many carers that all find themselves at Exeter speedway during each season. Though he's been here as regular as clockwork on a Monday night for as long as anyone else can remember, John believes nothing can really beat the impact of watching the children's faces when they meet the riders or spend time in the pits.

When pushed to recall specific highlights of his career, John claims that there's been "just too many people, changes and memories" for him "to pick just one". Instead of a proper answer, he deflects attention from himself with introductions to everyone else around him and modestly claims they'd be much more interesting to chat to about Exeter Speedway than he would be. As if to try to prove his point, John points out a man of 75 on the far side of the pits who still rides grass track regularly before he guides me towards the home team part of the pits area to marvel at the beauty of the equipment owned by modern riders. John has an infectious love of life and gadgets, so it's only natural that he escorts me over to meet the parents of Exeter rider Lee Smethills; he's particularly keen that they demonstrate the practical aspects and built in luxuries that equip a contemporary riders van, which so fascinate him. The Smethills family tells me that they commute to Exeter every week from Manchester, so they decided to invest in a whole variety of additional creature comforts within their Mercedes (white) Transit van. Lee's Dad confidently expects, and his mum nods her approval, that the investment in Mercedes and its various comforts will more than repay itself over the 300,000 miles that they expect to drive in the van. John hovers by admiringly, while Lee's Dad demonstrates that the rear of the van has been customised with a variety of fittings to be able to comfortably store three bikes in the back and provide a sleeping area for Lee. The aim is to keep him fresh and rested for his racing during the many long distance journeys around the country that are part and parcel of a speedway rider's life in Britain. His Dad admits that Lee actually very rarely sleeps in the van but his girlfriend takes full advantage when she travels with them. Overall, the van has ample room for five adults and boasts the latest flat screen DVD player for any bored passengers. John is almost as delighted as the Smethills family with the van and he's not even going to ride in it!

Back by the gate, John matter of factly observes "times have changed" before he fondly recalls when the visiting riders used to wheel their bikes from St David's train station to the stadium in the 1950s and early 1960s. It was a long walk through the city centre, especially when you'd got your bike with its toolbox balanced on top. For him this era was the high point since, during the late 1950s or the early 1960s, unlike today, it was a time when most of the Exeter team still lived

locally or in and around the area. When they weren't racing or with you in the bar after a meeting for a drink or three, they were part of the everyday life of the local community and were people who'd often be seen "dancing and drinking around the town".

With casual recollections of these bygone times, we wander in warm sunshine round the perimeter terraces of the huge and heavily watered track towards the substantial main grandstand. The stadium was erected in 1898 but this imposing structure was a comparatively late addition to the County Ground when it was built in 1921 to replace the original stand, after it had been destroyed in a fire. Deep in the shadow of it's bulk, I meet with David Short who has been the promoter at Exeter for the last 15 months. He kindly breaks off his involvement in the frenetic last minute preparations required on race night for a brief conversation about all things Exeter Speedway. The facilities of the County Ground stadium are shared with the landlord (Exeter Rugby Club), which has its pitch with posts still erected on the centre green within the track perimeter. The whole picture before me has an air of dilapidation combined with an olde worlde charm, which communicates itself as a slightly nostalgic atmosphere from a different, more confident era. A casual glance around at the fabric of the buildings and the terraces reveals that the place has now apparently fallen on much harder times. The basic structure of the grandstand, with its ground level narrow, standing terraces and its upper tier of steeply banked seats, stands impressively beside the turnstiles. There's the long bar with windows that look out over half the length of the straight and various other offices, changing rooms and sheds dotted around the place in some of the adjacent buildings.

We leave the bustle of people and the associated hubbub behind, when we climb some steep wooden stairs to the small but perfectly appointed press box, set just to the side of the main grandstand. Its many windows give a spectacular and panoramic view of the track, rugby pitch and the nearby streets of closely packed, mostly terraced houses. David grew up in one of the terraces himself, in nearby Ferndale Road, from where he claims his bedroom window overlooked the pits. Though very compact, this press box would be the ideal spot to watch events unfold on the track or the pitch and also has, in the heat of this afternoon's summer sunshine, the atmosphere and musty smell of a room that's seen a thousand reports and reporters pass through its door. While we make ourselves comfortable, David quietly informs me that speedway was first raced here on 9th March 1929 and, smartly attired if slightly formal in his dark jacket with its prominent BSPA logo, as though prepared for the bowls club or a promenade on the cruise deck before cocktails, David appears to dress in a manner that echoes that era. Then again his formality of dress might just be the habit he gained through 30 years service as a Police Constable for the Metropolitan force[1].

David leans back in the Press Box completely at home and contentedly surveys the last dying days of his Exeter Speedway kingdom. He's good to speak with since he retains the eye and attitude of a newcomer, who's still prepared and able to analyse and question the status quo or the current orthodoxy of contemporary speedway mores. He's also used to researching and weighing the evidence. In common with many other promoters and fans, David strongly believes that the sport needs to attract new people to tracks around the country if it is to survive let alone thrive. "It certainly needs something, most likely the newer generation"; particularly if the sport is to ever sell itself beyond its regular audience and dwindling base of supporters. This task is handicapped by the "perception that it's a sport from the late 1940s or early 1950s" and very much stuck in its own time warp, "lots of people feel it hasn't moved on with the times, which is probably true, and that it's dirty, which is also probably true". Added to that there is the propensity for "many people to look at the sport through rose tinted glasses".

David is clear that the poor quality of the facilities at Exeter will not attract these new spectators, "I'll be honest the facilities are abysmal here". He's, obviously, been hamstrung by the protracted closure date and regulatory uncertainties that hang over the future location of the club. However, even if that hadn't been the case, David still views the sport as being fatally caught up in a "vicious circle" where the "comparatively low audiences" don't provide enough revenues "to invest or upgrade the facilities". Around the country it's a situation that is compounded by the majority of tracks having promoters who are only tenants within their stadiums rather than owners. To illustrate his realism and his roots as a supporter, David believes that a sad consequence of this situation of poorly managed decline is "in general we can't pay the riders what they deserve for the risks they take although occasionally we pay some riders more than we can afford, but usually not". Unlike many other clubs, Exeter have a tradition of loyalty towards the team they name at the start of the campaign and eschew the chance to chop and change throughout the season progresses and the riders averages change. This was something that was particularly important to the club's late lamented promoter Colin Hill and has, with one exception, been carried on by David since his sad premature death. This pragmatic approach acknowledges that it's in the nature of riders to be "out of form for a month or so" but frequent team changes often ignore that the same riders "might come back" to form shortly afterwards. The Exeter way is to show loyalty in the expectation that your faith will usually be repaid.

The main panacea and the magic solution to attract bigger crowds to speedway is frequently claimed to be the recent improved coverage of the sport through its regular transmission on Sky Sports television. Though it's often a dog that doesn't bark, David pauses thoughtfully, for a moment, to carefully consider its true impact. It would be fair to say that mention of the 'S word' rarely inspires indifference, but more usually strong feelings of support or antipathy. David weighs his words but still quietly praises the professionalism of their approach and anecdotally imagines it must attract a larger audience than when it started, since there are now more commercial breaks and a greater variety of advertisers. Nonetheless, he notes, "I can't get to the bottom of their impact on our attendances" and stresses that there has been no rigorous, scientific or conclusive research conducted by the BSPA into the real impact of the Sky broadcasts. Consequently there are no accurate figures upon which to base definitive conclusions with advocates and detractors alike only really relying on blind faith or assertions. However, David feels it's common sense that on a potentially wet night people might stay in the comfort of their own homes rather than venture out to the track, and, as a club that runs their fixtures on a Monday night, the Falcons unavoidably compete every week with Sky coverage. Nonetheless, he considers himself fortunate as he imagines the negative impact on his crowd at Exeter is "at most in double figures not treble figures"[2].

I quickly gather that David has many ideas and suggestions about how the sport could improve its present practice. If David attends the annual BSPA meeting in November, and it's a big if, since it's "definitely the last season at this venue",

[1] In fact he later informs me that for clubs with no team sponsor the "BSPA dress code is very strict – Blue blazer, SCB tie, white shirt, black trousers or skirt". Failure to adhere to these dress requirements can result in a fine for promoters who are improperly attired. There wasn't the remotest danger that David would be fined for this reason; though, luckily, I did catch him on a week he chose to wear trousers. :-)

Rider parade © Jeff Scott

Theo Pijper and Robert Ksiezak © Jeff Scott

Temporary respite between heats. © Jeff Scott

then he has a number of suggestions for his 24 other fellow and lady promoters. He checks that my book won't be published before that meeting before he decides to outline a few of his possible thoughts for the future. He believes that an external person should be hired, may be someone from outside the sport such as an experienced football referee, to look through the complex thicket of rules and regulations that govern the sport contained in the present rulebook. They should interrogate each regulation and ask pertinent questions, such as, "what does this mean? What is intended by this rule? Or, more fundamentally, is this clear?" David is strongly of the opinion that particular attention should be paid to some of the presently poorly conceived rules. These include the replacement facility for injured riders (his own favourite bugbear this season), and the unsatisfactory start. Also he believes that there is a definite need to tinker with the present double points tactical rules to ensure that they don't "defeat the object of cost cutting" which was their original justification.

Another point of exasperation is the (often late) start of season published fixture list "which bears no resemblance" to the order of the fixtures ultimately raced during the season. While David can and has fortunately managed to adhere, without alteration, to the home fixtures with in his control, "though hardly a week goes by without a promoter calling with reasons for altering the fixtures". Most of these requests are for perfectly legitimate reasons but is often extremely inconvenient for the majority of "working riders" who have to plan their precious time off around the original fixture list. Despite his reservations, overall David has found other promoters "extremely helpful, some wonderful quite frankly". However, apart from their fixtures together, the Premier League promoters only formally meet together, once a year, at the annual BSPA meeting[3].

As we leave the Press Box, David remains unsure about his expectations against tonight's opposition the Edinburgh Monarchs, "if you get a good night it's brilliant but we get some duff meetings here". The reputation of the track often goes before it – the high speeds, the steep banking and the solid steel perimeter fence all contribute to the "fear factor". At Exeter, since they have eschewed the latest innovation of the air fence or even a traditionally constructed safety fence, some first time visitors are almost beaten before they've unloaded their vans never mind set a wheel on the track. Recently David overheard a "well regarded visiting foreign

[2] The impact of Sky live coverage on attendances is very unclear. David has a rather confused and contradictory perspective himself. On the one hand, he imagines that the true fan will always choose to watch speedway live, if it's roughly within their local area, even if the televised alternative is shown on the same night. On the other, David then mentions his "personal theory" that the average wage earner "doesn't go out much" and subscriptions to satellite are so expensive that, if they subscribe, they'll stay in to get full value for their service. It's a confusing situation and often more heat than light is cast on the rare occasions it's debated. With regards to away fixtures, David is very definite that most people are "reluctant to travel any distance to watch their team".

[3] David believes that regular meetings would help the promoters to develop a coordinated youth development policy. However, because of his work as the Exeter promoter, David also admits that he himself hasn't watched any Conference League meeting so isn't practising what he preaches or placing him in the best position to comment.

rider" express astonishment at the narrowness of the bends "it looks too small for four riders, I'll pull out if other riders are level on the first bend". Like many riders before him, he was as good as his word later that evening. David anticipates that the Edinburgh team will be made of much sterner stuff.

As I stroll back towards the pits area I bump into Nicola Filmer who's at Exeter for the evening with her boyfriend, the rider Daniel Giffard, who will appear tonight as a guest for Exeter. I've met her many times already this season since she loyally follows Dan to his many meetings round the country. She's a very warm and approachable person who's clearly very dedicated to her boyfriend. Dan himself has managed to get his racing career roughly back to where it was, prior to some severe injuries he sustained, that otherwise had held his professional development back. With great fortitude, he's returned to the position from which he could fulfil his true potential. This evening is his first ever visit to ride at Exeter and, according to both his mechanic (Nicola's brother, Adam) and Nicola, he fully expects to give it a "proper go" later, despite the steel fence! Dan has scored for fun in the Conference League when he rides for Weymouth and has shown intermittent signs of promise in the Premier League for Hull. Consequently, he's buoyant and in confident mood, which is reflected in his full schedule of bookings that will see him ride somewhere in the country every single night for the next week or so. Nicola will, inevitably, accompany him on these long journeys from East Sussex. No matter how long the distance involved, afterwards Dan will return to his home base to try to recharge his batteries as well clean and maintain his equipment in preparation for the next meeting. Tonight he can share the drive with his mechanic Adam, who chats to me amiably in the bright sunshine by the steel fence of the track, while he wears a rather smart black shirt notable for its bright green "Giffard Racing" logo. After Adam departs to help Dan in the pits, I mention to Nicola that I'm sure that I've seen him ride quite well before in some second halves at Eastbourne. In that way that sisters have when they discuss their brothers she laughs, "probably, he's good when he can be bothered".

By now the pits area is a hive of activity and bikes are prepared, unloaded or checked on both sides of the pits. Mechanics and riders work calmly but quickly, with the occasional shout, as race time nears. The pits gate is now being well supervised by the bubbly, red-haired Jill Pike who's only worked at Exeter Speedway since the start of this season. It's a supervisory position that, fortunately for her and disappointingly for any erstwhile rival pits gate supervisors among the Exeter fans, she's managed to obtain this position through her grass-track contacts that had heard whispers of the vacancy. As always, the best and most desirable jobs aren't ever advertised. Once the meeting proper is underway, Jill moves from her back-entry gate duties and switches to her trackside pits-gate race-night supervision duties. Jill loves her work at Exeter; especially as it gives her chance to be in the thick of it, preferably "right in the action, in amongst it, the smell and the shale, plus all those men in leather!" Before Jill gets too carried away, I point out that modern speedway riders are actually dressed in kevlars since the age of leather has sadly passed from the sport, "you know what I meant," she laughs before she dismissively adds, "anyway, these are only boys not men". Before we can explore her outlook on men with bikes further, the demands of the job calls Jill away to sort something out with the machine examiner Sharon Lawry by the entry gate.

It's a gate through which tonight's referee Peter Clarke, dapperly dressed in jacket and shades with his modestly authoritative briefcase, has just arrived. Peter is very approachable, down to earth and friendly with a melodic accent of his that might be from Yorkshire or might be from Lancashire but you daren't ask. As with practically everyone else involved or interested in the sport of speedway, our conversation dwelt briefly on the weather before it moved onto the latest gossip. There's all the usual crashes, cock-ups, speculation or unprintable incidents to cover, on and off the track, along with the downright bizarre to the serious via the libellous and the funny. All the stuff which the life of the itinerant SCB referee, which is so intimately bound up in the warp and the woof of the incestuous speedway world, would inevitably expose you to. However, Peter is the model of professional discretion and confidentiality you'd expect of a dedicated fan and SCB referee, so I'm unable to fill this book with salacious material that he provides to rip the veil of secrecy from the sport!

We definitely stick to the safe topics, most notably the state of the track we'd both witnessed at Newport yesterday. Many teams that travel to Newport have not been pleased with track conditions and King's Lynn were no exception, though they did wryly claim that there was arguably more shale on the roads they'd driven on to get to Newport than on the track itself. All Peter could reasonably advise them was that, in his capacity as a referee, he was compulsorily obliged to compile a report about the meeting, of which track conditions was one important aspect. Any report or comments that they wished to formally pass to the speedway authorities after the meeting was their decision and responsibility. Discussion of one track inevitably leads to another, in this case the one we stood next to and its legendary steel fence. Peter joked that Stoney – Workington's Carl Stonehewer – isn't a fan of his annual trip to Exeter, "he hates it here, so he gets round it by always joking with the crowd saying that they should shut the place. And they laugh thinking how funny he is and what a great bloke he is, which he is, not knowing that he's really deadly serious"[4].

The meeting is just about to start with the riders about to go on their introductory parade so, as usual for this book, to get the full experience I decide to try to watch the action on the track from a number of different vantage points within the stadium. The main grandstand is as good a place as any to initially watch from and on my way there I meet some of the travelling army of extremely dedicated Edinburgh fans, Ella MacDonald and another fan called Joan. There are eight of them who've travelled together on this trip and they've made the most of the long journey to the south west with a mid-morning visit to the track ("they were watering it") and an enjoyable day out in the sunshine at Torquay. They both look bright red after a day spent at the coast but now, as they grasp their refreshing pints of lager, they remain hopeful but not exactly confident of a competent Monarchs' performance on a "tricky away track".

A few yards further round by the terraces, I bump into the delightful Neil Street who, despite the warmth of the evening, is again rather smartly dressed in a comfortable red pullover – he must really still feel the cold because of his Australian roots! Neil had already told me that he lived in the local area and that he came along to watch Exeter every meeting that he could, having done so for as long as he could remember together with another good friend. Neil chats affably in his usual modest, charming, interesting and informed manner about life and speedway. It's a measure of the man that he instantly remembered my name, greeted me as though he was pleased to spend some more time in my company, discover my opinions and, once again, appeared excited about my book plans. As if to confirm his notoriety, longevity and popularity within the sport, he is warmly greeted by practically everyone who passes in the last-minute rush of people who stream into the stadium. Sadly he won't be at King's Lynn later in the week, in his capacity as Newport team manager, since he has a 4 a.m. flight to Sweden to catch the next day. Neil will be part of the family team, along with his son Phil, that helps his grandson, reigning World Champion, Bristol-born Australian Jason Crump, in the pits during the latest Swedish round of the Grand Prix. Neil hopes that Jason has now fully recovered from the chicken pox he caught from his kids that caused him to withdraw at the last minute from the Australian World Team Cup side in Poland.

It's very crowded by the time I get to the standing terrace, so instead I decide to try upstairs in the seated section of the grandstand. The view of the track from the seats I discover, since it's really designed for watching the rugby, is extremely poor. The start gate and most of the home straight is partially obscured unless I stand up (which I notice later is what the locals do) so I decide to move elsewhere.

By now the parade has just ended and the riders have started to push off to do a few warm-up practice laps, just as I make my way past the windows of the home-straight bar towards the first corner. Though Neil Machin later advises "if you see a spinning back wheel always avoid it" nonetheless, unfortunately, as I walk towards the first bend this hasn't even crossed my mind. The next moment I'm conscious of a really strange but repeated sensation I can't quite put my finger on; only to discover that down my side I'm completely covered in thick, wet and sticky mud-like shale that has been sprayed remarkably quickly over me from head to toe without any chance to evade it. The sight of the arrival of a shale-splattered

---

[4] Stoney, according to Ian Thomas in his autobiography *Wheels and Deals*, actually said, in answer to a question on how speedway could be improved, "Drop a bomb on Exeter".

fool, and my obvious discomfort, causes great hilarity among the crowd of Exeter fans safely located a few yards further away round the bend.

I feel simultaneously stupid and irritated since I've managed, after 30 years' watching speedway, finally to get totally splattered in mud. The wet sticky shale is everywhere – all over my programme and interview notes, thickly splattering my glasses, hair and clothes as if painted on by some mad frenetic modernist artist. It also has the consistency of wallpaper glue when it's wet, and sticks to everything it has touched and is even thoroughly lodged in my ears. For the first time I properly appreciate how heavily the stuck shale must weigh on the kevlars of those riders you often watch get completely sprayed when they trail behind during a race. Even if you ignore its adhesive properties, it must really hurt when mixed with stones and other detritus when violently flung onto you at excessive speed. My picking at the wet gunk that thoroughly covers me is far from effective and the commonsense advice of an OAP who watches my pitiful efforts, with a smirk, is "let it dry first". The safe haven I've supposedly retreated to at the apex of the first turn provides no real respite from further random attacks of flying brown glue globules thrown up as the riders pass. The fans stationed there profess to relish the experience as they watch the racing every week in a hale of wet mud spray and try to reassure me that this effect quickly diminishes (they don't say stop) since the track dries remarkably effectively on a warm summer's evening.

I reflect that it's each to his own and that they definitely make them differently in this part of Devon when it comes to how to take their enjoyment, so I retreat to the pits, with my pit pass taped around my wrist, to the comparative sanctuary of the riders' viewing area. This spot is adjacent to both the terraces and the pits gate exit onto the racetrack. It's full already since it provides you with a great view of the pits, the pit lane, Jill on the gate and the entire racetrack. The initially wet track conditions, the ever-present danger of the steel fence plus the Falcons' riders' skill on the track, as they power along the straights and swoop round the banked bends, have enabled them to easily romp into an early 12 point lead over the Monarchs (that proves insurmountable for the rest of the meeting). Though I'm still not able to fully concentrate on the races, because I'm quite bedraggled and still continue to vainly try to scrape the thick layer of mud from myself. Any attempt to use my splattered, sodden programme to record the scores proves impossible.

By the next race, heat 4, Edinburgh get their first win in the form of the daring Australian rider, Russell 'Rusty' Harrison. Unlike some of his team-mates, he rides completely unfazed by the track or the rigidity of the steel safety fence. The next race features the enthusiastic, fast-gating but occasionally hard-riding Exeter captain Seemond Stephens; though he shows no apparent ill effects from his spectacular crash the previous week with the Isle of Wight's young Australian rider, Jason Doyle. Hywel Lloyd, proud Welshman and official photographer at the Newport, Somerset and Exeter tracks, fortunately captured the dramatic crash sequence on film. These significant moments are what track photographers aspire to take pictures of, and the sequence was so graphic that it was subsequently splashed, in almost pornographic detail, across the pages of the latest *Speedway Star*. Jason Doyle was also splashed, in his case into the fence, after he'd been effectively "speared" or "accidentally collected" (depending on the team you support) by Seemond's daring do on his machinery. The speed and impact of the crash was such that one of the bikes had also managed to concentrate the minds of nearby spectators when it flew at speed over the fence to crash land on the terraces!

Tonight we witness a much more restrained coming together between Seemond and Edinburgh's Dutch captain, Theo Pijper, which results in an awkward struggle with an out-of-control bike before a comparatively slow motion but painful looking fall for the Dutchman. The exclusion of Stephens by the referee, as the "prime cause of the stoppage" is greeted by a yelp of outrage by the men who stand next to me and clearly doesn't please Seemond very much. He rides back round to the start line to remonstrate with Peter Clarke in the referee's box; he then communicates his disapproval through a few direct but unmistakable gestures. I hesitate to ask the man next to me for his opinion, though I quickly learn that it was "just hard riding I'd call that" and, he claims that Seemond's remonstrations were an understandable reaction not at all unsportsmanlike, since they were due to his "surprise at discovering he'd been excluded when he got there". Nonetheless, it looked a fair decision to me so I remark, "you seem a big fan of Seemond's" to which the man next to me, who I then learn is Tony Stephens, replies, "I'm his dad".

When work permits, along with his mate Colin Brokenshire, Tony tries to see his son ride whenever he can. He travels up from Bodmin ("everywhere is North from Bodmin") for every home meeting and tries to get to as many of Seemond's away fixtures as possible, especially the 'Northern Tour' matches. They've always been a motorcycling family; Tony road-raced with sidecars whereas Seemond has tried a whole variety of motorcycle disciplines from motocross ("including the British Championship Rounds") to indoor speedway and even grass track. At around 30, Seemond came to try his hand at speedway comparatively late in life for any rider and, as luck would have it, was due to celebrate his 38th birthday the next day. Seemond ("it's a bit of a made-up name; it just came out") started his career at Eastbourne "when Gollub was there" and still remains their asset, though most of his riding has subsequently been spent at Exeter. According to his dad he's always been a fast gater, an advantage anywhere you race speedway, but especially so at Exeter with its long straights and steeply banked bends. Seemond's success is built on skill and enthusiasm but also, as his dad proudly notes, "he's very fit for his age". After the meeting Seemond claims, when he speaks with the same soft accent as his father, "age don't come into it, it's enthusiasm and up here [points to his head] not age, anyway most young riders have been riding speedway longer than I have". Seemond's spent most of his career at Exeter, "five years more or less, except for six months away at Trelawny". Seemond notes he came back from Trelawny to replace his "good friend Lol [Lawrence Hare] here [at Exeter]" after he tragically got badly injured, but is keen to stress that Lol is "doing well" and "coming to stay in September".

Now that I'm aware of the family connection, I notice the deep rapport that exists between the Stephenses. Their eyes always briefly meet, they exchange knowing glances, before each race while Seemond waits patiently in the pit lane on his bike to take to the track, and again afterwards. Seemond is a striking figure in his distinctively decorated kevlars; they're still immaculately clean since he's spent each race away from the spray of shale in the lead. Tony professes to love the thrill of it all, whether or not his son races, the "short sharp shock of each race keeps your interest" compared to the longueurs of any other motorcycle events. The "big old track here soon gets them tired out, especially as they tell me that they just about hold their breath all the way round with the nervous tension and concentration". Tony views the renowned steel fence as just part of the racing equation at this stadium though he's noticed that on bend 3 "there's more smack ups there, as it's more rutty!"

As the meeting draws to its foregone conclusion, the Edinburgh riders begin to adapt better to the track, which improves the entertainment with some close, exciting races in the final few heats. The large home crowd leaves happily or swarms down to the pits area to throng around the Exeter riders in the pits. Many photographs are posed for and numerous autographs patiently signed. Tony insists that I meet his son Seemond to let him know about my book and, while I wait, I overhear him explain his heat 5 exclusion, "I lifted and saved it, but probably took his line". This is as close to an admission of fault as you'll publicly hear from most speedway riders. Seemond is in great demand from a long queue of fans and is delighted with tonight's performance, "I aim to do that every week but it doesn't always work". He's especially pleased because he still carries the bruises from the infamous "metal fence that I had a good look at last week". This studious attitude of nonchalance hides Seemond's determination to succeed and belies the close attention to detail that underpins his approach to speedway. According to his father Tony, it's an attitude that's reflected in the meticulous records Seemond keeps of every speedway fixture that he's competed in throughout his career. If rigorous analysis of his bike, the set ups, track condition, times and results was good enough for Ivan Mauger, it's good enough for Seemond Stephens. The night's racing is over so, once again, father, son and friends pack away the bike and other equipment in an efficient, well-practised manner. Seemond then finds time to sign a few more autographs before he heads off across the centre green, with his kit bag swung over his shoulder, on his way to the showers.

John Campbell, the Edinburgh team manager, still remains in the quickly emptying pits and he professes himself delighted with the 53-42 defeat because "with Daniel not fit, our many injuries, and with Theo having holes all over him I didn't expect more than 30 points tonight. It was an incredible performance and we should beat them by 20 points at our place". Optimism is the stock in trade of speedway managers and promoters in general, John is no exception and he remains convinced that the Monarchs will have a late surge up the league table as "we've only two away meetings left and six or seven at home". Just as I leave the pits for the journey across the city to my university hall of residence, Exeter's Mark Lemon stops cleaning his bike for a moment to patiently pose for yet more photographs for his adoring fans. One keen snapper then asks, "Why are you the only one cleaning your bike?" Mark shrugs, pauses in mid polish, and then dolefully remarks, "my mechanic has fallen in love so has other things on his mind ..."

8th August Exeter v. Edinburgh (Premier League) 53-42

Chapter 25: The Jewel of Norfolk
10th August King's Lynn v. Newport

SKY CHATTER

"You know it never ceases to amaze me how tough speedway riders are" Jonathan Green (surprized again, to Kelvin Tatum)

RANDOM SCB RULES

12.6.3 All repairs to a riding suit must be of a "permanent" nature which provides protection to the same standard as the original garment.

The road to King's Lynn seems like it takes you to the end of the world or, at least, the road less travelled. Well, except for the fact that every time you drive to Lynn (as the locals call it in the same way that Hemel Hempstead is known as Hemel, except the other way round) you will inevitably spend a lot of time driving slowly behind lorries. Though it's never slowly behind the locals in their cars, since they appear to only overtake with alarming swerves past quite a few cars at a time. And always at the most unlikely places – blind corners or as you approach narrow bridges – they lull you into a false sense of complacency before they shoot past you, two other cars and a lorry. I assume this is due to their intimate local knowledge of the bends and chicanes of the road to Lynn, the A47, since they have driven it so many times before. The large number of fatal accidents on the road to Lynn doesn't statistically seem to bear out this theory, but there you are. I always relish the journey to Lynn, partly because I have relatives there but also for the real sense that you are driving through a 'proper' part of England and its countryside. I'm not sure how I'd quantify or truly identify 'proper', but you just know when it is. Maybe it's the way Ely Cathedral magnificently looms across the fields at you or the peculiar waterways

you pass parallel to the road but at a higher level. Whatever it is, you know that you are going somewhere special. You can't rush along these roads, not as a stranger anyhow, unless you're particularly suicidal, so you have to adjust your pace and take the time to appreciate the small villages, fields, tree-lined roads and estates. The lorry in front of me has a small sign on its back bumper that politely reads "if you can read this I can't see you, so I won't know that you're there when I brake. To know you're behind me, you have to be able to see both my wing mirrors. Pull back!" Then Lynn surprises you as you near it, because there's a rapid transition from countryside to town, almost unexpectedly so; but, nonetheless, it still leaves you with a strong sense that you've travelled a greater psychological distance than the actual miles covered to get there. Most visitors aren't aware of Lynn's age and historical importance until they arrive at the old town gate or, even more likely, the casual visitor will have absolutely no idea at all that it's a town located right by the sea.

In fact its location by the coast is the most significant part of its long history, since its success as a town is strongly steeped in its maritime past. For hundreds of years the water was more important than the roads for transport in England, and its location on the Wash and by the sea gave it significant access to the Scandinavian countries as well as Spain and Portugal[1].

In its own way King's Lynn speedway has a history steeped in tradition and family connections. The Maurice Littlechild Memorial Trophy 2005 sits proudly in one of the wooden cabins, the hospitality suite in fact, that lines the fourth bend of the Saddlebow Row stadium. Maurice was a great promoter at the club and is the grandfather of Cheryl Chapman wife of the present promoter Keith 'Buster' Chapman and is the great-grandfather of their son and co-promoter Jonathan Chapman. As I pull up and park my car in the car park, it's Jonathan that I can spy through the window of his office. I've been slightly delayed on the ring road, by what passes as the rush hour in these parts, as well as getting totally lost and taking an unexpected tour of downtown, where I had the opportunity to closely study the historic buildings around King Street,

[1] Originally called Bishops Lynn, meaning bishop's pool (probably because of the tidal pool on the Ouse), it was bordered by the Purfleet and Millfleet. It was so important a place that by 1101 it gained the right to hold a Saturday market, and annual fairs, while by the mid 12th century it had expanded to Newland north of the Purfleet (literally the Pur stream). The Tuesday market was founded on a site by the riverbank originally used for the landing of ships in mediaeval times, and it's close by this site that the still surviving St George's Guildhall was built, near King Street, in 1406, many years after fire decimated the town in 1337 and the Black Death had paid an unwelcome call in 1348-49 to kill half of the 6,000 inhabitants. The hall remains one of the oldest surviving medieval guildhalls in England. The plays performed there provide a rival source of entertainment to the speedway and stock cars for the modern 33,000 inhabitants of Lynn.

Many historians claim King's Lynn as one of the earliest original examples of a 'new town'. It became a settlement primarily due to the north-south road that connected the Saturday and Tuesday markets via the original bridge over the Purfleet. The town subsequently became famous for the various orders of friars in the local environs and by 1537 it became King's Lynn. By 1593 Shakespeare had reputedly staged a play at the guildhall, or at least the company of actors with whom he was strongly associated are said to have played the town. Initially known for its salt boiling as well as wool and grain exports, King's Lynn settled into its expertise in shipbuilding, plus the manufacture of ropes and sails. Lynn was a key port for the import of fish, pitch and iron before it became renowned for its imported wine from Spain and Portugal. By the 18th century Daniel Defoe described it as "beautiful, well built and well situated" which is high praise for the time, even if it sounds a little guarded or damned with faint praise to modern ears. The railway arrived in 1847, just in time for dinner, and the Second World War saw evacuees mistakenly brought to the town for safety before German bombing drove them away again. Less illustrious than its local neighbours Norwich and maybe Boston, nonetheless, Lynn is a key part of our English heritage.

the Guildhall and the railway station. I'd met Jonathan a few days previously in Newport when the King's Lynn 'Money Centre' Stars had thrashed the Newport Wasps. He'd struck me as a confident and ebullient young man in South Wales and, on his home turf, I expected that he'd be even more confident and forthright in his opinions.

I'm late and it's race night, so there's lots to be done before the fans start to flood into the stadium for tonight's return fixture against Newport. Not that Jonathan expects a flood; more like a trickle as Newport do not have a reputation as quality opponents among the knowledgeable support that typically indicates a loyal fan of Lynn speedway. Also he's extremely blunt in his assessment of their chances this evening, especially if Sunday's decisive result is anything to go by. Even though most home supporters like to see their team win, it's usually preferable for there to be at least a small degree of uncertainty about the result or the hope of some effective opposition from the visitors. Jonathan predicts that this will only be a night for the diehard fan to venture along to Saddlebow Road. Particularly because, in four days' time, Hull Speedway will provide the opposition for a much more potentially exciting and close-fought fixture. Like everywhere throughout the country, the ready constituency that most speedway teams draw their support from usually isn't able to lash their money around willy-nilly much more than once a week. This is especially so when there's the chance to see Boston ride here on a weekly basis in the Conference League every Friday, including this Friday, which will make it three home meetings in five days. I had been to Saddlebow Road about five years ago, when Lynn were still in the Elite League, for a meeting against Eastbourne. They thrashed the Eagles that night by about 60-30, 61-29 or some such score. It wasn't even close. It was a meeting that was also notorious for an unusual incident which involved the Eagles' rider, David Norris, who managed to fall down an open manhole or drain in the pits area and thereby injured himself or, at least, dented his pride.

Just a brief glance at the track and the stadium shows that it's undergone a massive transformation in the few years since I last visited. I almost don't recognise the stadium and track as the same venue! This metamorphosis is all the more surprising when you realise that Lynn have actually dropped down a league since my previous visit, so the usual expectation would be for the facilities to have declined. Under the guidance of Buster Chapman though, there has clearly been considerable investment throughout all the stadium facilities as well as close attention paid to detail in the remodelling or replacement of the fixtures and fittings. What I notice first is that the old riders' stand, and the main grandstand itself, are no longer situated, as they once were on the home straight. In fact, it's all very disorienting and it takes a few moments to try to get my bearings or understand the new layout. I quickly realise that the old large floodlight pylons have been replaced by more sleek and powerful modern ones along the straights; there's also a new small covered stand with a bar and toilets underneath, while by the pits area there is a new open-air all-seater raised grandstand. The skyline across from the stadium appears reasonably familiar, although I can't definitely say whether there has always been a large chicken coop type factory building just over the back of the fence on the second bend. I do recall, unless my memory has played tricks, that the tall, mysterious and unusually shaped building was there on my last visit, though I'm still unclear of its purpose. I continue to struggle to recognise familiar landmarks hampered by the high perimeter safety mesh fence that now surrounds the track. This fence is comparatively new, sturdy and built to a considerable height. It's another development specifically undertaken with the health and safety of the riders and the crowd in mind. Any rogue tyre that randomly escapes during the regular Demolition Derbies held here – along with the featured bangers, stock cars and free entry for the under 11s noted on the adverts – has no chance of causing havoc by careening into the crowd. However, it's a safety feature that didn't prevent the tragic death of the young rider David Nix, who was killed while he raced at the track on May 1st 2002, after he was flung over the safety fence and into the protective safety mesh fencing. But Health and Safety rules afterwards that the fencing did protect the public in attendance that evening from any further injuries[2].

It's a death that is remembered on the circuit with an annual memorial trophy awarded after the David Nix Memorial meeting is held at the Saddlebow Road track. David's dad presents the prizes and the sums of money raised on each

[2] Accounts of the incident vary with several people I meet during the evening who claim to have been present on the night. It is worth noting that the reality is that Health and Safety only concern themselves with the safety of the public as they believe that the riders by their choice to participate effectively place themselves outside their jurisdiction.

The various Saddlebow Road safety fences. © Jeff Scott

Fans study the pits activity © Jeff Scott

Pits staff supervise events. © Jeff Scott

evening go as donations to various children's hospices in the local area. So far over £4,000 has been raised through these events held in David's memory.

Whatever the circumstances or the reasons people claim influenced these safety infrastructure changes, the club has significantly invested in the crowd's safety as well as that of the riders, since the solid concrete stockcar track wall is now encased in wooden fencing for the entire circuit, with rows of go-kart tyres that line the gap between the fence and the wall, to also act as a basic cushion. Later in the year Buster would go on record with his doubts about the safety performance and efficacy of the sport's latest and biggest safety revolution – the air fence that's mandatory in the Elite League[3]. One thing's for sure, I won't any longer be able to watch the celebrations of the youngsters that so characterised my last visit. They would all hang over the fence with their arms outstretched to greet the riders as they rode past on their celebratory victory laps. There were a lot of these celebrations for the home riders that evening and the riders were always delighted to touch practically all of the eager, outstretched children's hands.

The track itself looks much better maintained than when I was last here, so much so that it now looks almost frightening smooth and extremely well prepared. On my last visit it was notable for its roughness and grit, which repeatedly showered the spectators in dust and shale on the bends when the riders roared past. Whatever my memories had mentally prepared me to find on my visit this evening, they have been overtaken by the considerable improvements that the Chapmans have wrought at the club. Jonathan is justifiably proud of the professionalism of the infrastructure that the promotion has brought to King's Lynn. He talks at a thousand words a minute, once he joins me again, in his office. I'm then escorted to look at the state-of-the-art electronic ticketing equipment that has been installed; it's the very same ticketing system that Manchester United apparently use and, it goes without saying, it is supposed to out-perform any rival system at any other British speedway club. Jonathan doesn't expect the ticketing system to fly to the moon this evening since he confidently estimates that the prospect of a fixture with Newport will only attract around 400 hardy spectators to the stadium. I'm then distracted by the arrival of his father, Buster, who is patently mystified by who I am and what I'm doing here. I explain my book to him and that the BSPA Chairman, Peter Toogood, would have faxed Buster in May about my intention to visit tonight. Buster bluntly says, "I

[3] Interestingly the air fences installed in the Elite League have yet to be tested and passed by the UK health and safety executive, nor has it received British Standards approval or similar kitemark. Two versions of the air fence are used within the sport. The Briggo version is used at Coventry, Arena and Stoke (these were crash tested with witness demonstrations) and the remainder of the Elite League tracks use the AirTek versions (I am in ignorance of how these were actually tested). It is also worth noting that while these fences have been an advance and have ameliorated the results of some crashes they have also inadvertently sometimes played a part in exacerbating the level of rider injury when riders have become trapped. However, safety considerations aside, the introduction of these air fences does have significant financial impact for the clubs that install them, since it enables them to gain additional sponsorship revenues, particularly relevant when clubs/sponsors embrace the oxygen of publicity that regular live televised appearances on Sky Sports necessarily generates.

know nothing about it but that doesn't surprise me with anything where the BSPA are concerned". You'd have to be an idiot not to quickly gather that he doesn't always hold the BSPA in the highest regard or affection when it comes to concrete help, "everything we do here we do ourselves," states Buster, "we expect nothing from the BSPA really, we need very little help and that's what we get!" When it comes to support from the Rugby office or, more specifically, from their press officer and spokesman, Nigel Pearson, Buster reckons that keeping the official BSPA website "updated with dates and start times is about the sum of it really". He's not really that keen to linger and speak with me, so he leaves that duty to Jonathan, since he has a contingent of sponsors to find and attend to that evening.

Jonathan and I then stroll to the fourth bend where, up some stairs, there's a terraced bank of wooden chalet-type buildings that wouldn't really be out of place in a continental ski resort and, I believe, were kindly supplied by buydirect.co.uk, a previous sponsor of the club. The interior of the chalets remind me of saunas; but placed in a row together they all look very new and smart, surrounded with wooden fencing, and they provide excellent views of the track. There's a corporate entertainment chalet that Jonathan takes me into to demonstrate its comfort and facilities. He takes the chance to introduce me to Lynn's young German reserve rider Tommy Stange who lives at the track when he rides in this country. Tommy is sat eating with his brother, who is over from Germany for a visit to Norfolk. The chalet next to the one we've hovered outside of has a sign that proudly advertises 'Roger Warnes Transport of Great Dunham', which is a sign that reflects the regionalism of their business, apparently 'bulk haulage' with 'sugar beet a specialty' and their pride in sponsorship of the club. Not that I can check out the Warnes-Lynn relationship since Jonathan has disappeared, after he rather optimistically says, "you can chat to Tommy for a few minutes for your book".

Tommy's English is much better than my German language abilities, which are strictly limited and can only extend as far as childish discussions of dirty kitchen utensils. We quickly exhaust our initial conversation in a few brief pleasantries and much general smiling, before the Stanges, once again, resume their interrupted conversation in quick, demotic German. The chalet that Tommy stays in with his brother has all the facilities that you would expect from an apartment: bedrooms, a kitchen, bathroom and toilet as well as a large lounge space that must serve as the hospitality area on race night. It's comfortably furnished with a large modern television; a sign on the wall has a few words of welcome from Buster and his wife, "Keith, Cheryl and all the Stars team would like to thank Money Centre for all their help in 2005, we hope you enjoy your evening". Close by to this sign is a small trophy engraved with the following: 'Maurice Littlechild Memorial Trophy 2005'. The race for this trophy opened the season for the club in March, with a special 'Stars' versus 'Knights' fixture. This was an appropriate fixture enough to honour Maurice's work and memory of the team he founded as the promoter at Saddlebow Road in the 1960s.

The evening hasn't started for Tommy and his brother Stefan, who both tuck in with gusto into some pre-meeting food while I interrupt them for a few minutes. Tommy comes from the Black Forest area of Germany, from Hoffenborg, which offers a big contrast to when he stays in King's Lynn. His hometown is renowned for the beauty of its forest and the challenging, hilly nature of the local terrain, whereas King's Lynn is located in a very flat area of the English countryside. Although, that said, Germany is such a large country that within its borders it has many contrasting areas with little or no similarity, other than a shared but complex language, between them. He plans to stay here for two months to learn more about his chosen craft, and vocation, speedway racing. Once they've finished eating, Tommy is happy to again try to bridge the language gap and he actually has very reasonable conversational English, despite his claims not to have any skill or capacity for our native tongue. While we speak his brother looks on attentively throughout, though he continuously fiddles with a blue crash helmet as if it's some sort of security blanket to help him meet peculiar foreigners. Tommy's gradually got used to riding at Saddlebow Road and finds the Premier League, in general, "quite hard"; with the Isle of Wight track particularly, "not so good for me". We now smile a lot and laugh, communicating easily with signs rather than language, while all the while the brothers murmur conspiratorially in German. Rather than unnecessarily prolong this strange talk with the Stanges, I leave them to the remainder of their tea and stroll outside onto the patio that overlooks the track. For all the facilities in the hospitality apartment, there clearly isn't a tumble dryer since Tommy's clothes are spread out along the

fence to dry. They already appear dry, which is handy, because he'll need to wear the majority of these items for his work tonight. Left out to dry are Tommy's kevlars, racing gloves along with a mixed assortment of T-shirts, boxers, socks and even his trainers.

Jonathan returns just as the large speaker next to us suddenly and very loudly blares out music, which thereby enables Jonathan to mention yet another recent investment at the stadium. I can now definitely confirm that the new sound system and speakers work efficiently. I mention the trophy I'd noticed to Jonathan, who then speaks fondly of his great-grandfather. King's Lynn speedway is in his blood since "I've been coming since I was born", which is over 25 years. Throughout his life he has been involved with speedway and has always been interested in it. Jonathan left school at 16 to do his "own thing", this involved work in advertising and promotions as well as casinos in London before he returned to work at the club. "My dad is happy to have me here with my finger on the pulse, studying facts and figures, doing competition analysis". Jonathan doesn't look at the sport through rose-tinted spectacles, he's hard-headedly commercial in his approach and analysis – just like his father he notes – and he places himself a considerable distance apart from the "amateur" or more romantically inclined school of speedway promotion. He runs a business that just happens to run a sports team, although he's keen to stress "you've got to be in it for the love of it and not the business [earnings]". In fact, he's very upfront that speedway in King's Lynn "isn't in a position to warrant its own stadium" but has had through necessity "became multi-purpose to support and invest in the facilities". The club is run as two separate businesses and "if you're lucky enough it [speedway] can pay for itself". In fact, the speedway "pays us a rent at the stadium" although the revenues generated are small. But there are revenues being earned, which bucks the general trend throughout speedway, where many other tracks bear their losses when they set these against the profits of another business also owned by the promoters. Jonathan claims that this is quite common in all of the speedway leagues but, ultimately, it's an unsound basis upon which to build a club, since you run the risk of eventual failure. He'd rather run a successful business and "pay tax at 40 percent" on the profits, rather than bear the ongoing losses against another business.

Around the club Jonathan has "made a lot of changes which doesn't fit with everyone". The changes to the infrastructure appear nothing short of stunning and have been all part of the process to bring the "team and the stadium into the 21st century". Changes to the track itself are singled out as significant by Jonathan because it's the primary focus for the entertainment values that all the other investments in equipment and buildings ultimately and, most visibly, support. The track now has the "right shape" for racing – its 340 odd metres can be covered in less than 60 seconds and, in Jonathan's opinion, it's the "smoothest, fastest, and best prepared with the best trackman". 'Huggy' the track curator works full time on the track with an impressive array of equipment that includes many tractors, a bowser, diggers, a crop sprayer, dumper trucks and all sorts of other stuff. He spends £20,000 a year on shale from which he manages to produce a track "without a speck of dust on a hot day" and one that can still have a good race on a wet day. Huggy provides all this care and maintenance of the speedway racing surface, while he also regularly runs stock-car meetings, both of which Jonathan proudly notes are located in "a proper stadium safeguarded with fencing".

Jonathan frankly admits that he's "upset a lot of people" in the process, but the Chapmans are very pleased with how things have progressed. They've brought in a lot of new staff, retrained others and have had some leave them. Overall, "it's not our main business so we don't want to make a million pounds, but we do want a sensible return" and the stadium is now, arguably, one of the best in the country. Jonathan claims that he doesn't want to make comparisons to other Premier league tracks, then he says "I'd like to think that we are the Premier League equivalent of Poole in terms of the set up, advertising, crowds and being professionally run". He rates the facilities at Poole Speedway as fantastic as well as for the fact that they are ambassadors for the sport, along with Coventry whom he also mentions favourably. He also claims that they're both profitable in contrast to, say, Oxford who are "losing money". I can't corroborate Jonathan's own impressions but, if the proof is in the pudding, at King's Lynn the "bottom line is that we'd look poor if we just ran the club for speedway".

His father has owned King's Lynn for the last 13 years since 1992. He hasn't always been the promoter, but he's always owned the team name "with other promoters paying my dad a rent to use the name". The most recent example was Nigel Wagstaff, who's now at Oxford, although Jonathan pointedly adds the caveat "whether he pays or not is completely another story". At 34 Nigel was the youngest promoter in the sport when he took over at King's Lynn, and now history repeats itself because Jonathan is "presently the youngest promoter" in the country. Before I'd ever met Jonathan he'd been spoken of disparagingly by other promoters who'd claimed that he knew all the answers but didn't know the questions. An elliptical but damning criticism; whereas I found him to be a thoughtful commentator on the sport in general and always keen to re-examine his role and responsibilities as a promoter at Lynn. He is also extremely well informed on the dynamics of his own operation and those of his competitors' businesses. If he were in business school, rather than the business school of life with his father, you'd have to say that he knows his onions. For example, my question of "what is your average crowd?" was greeted with a sharp retort that this was too general a question for someone who had analysed his business thoroughly. Jonathan's basic answer, based on his own segmented statistics, has the club median attendance in the Premier League at 1,000 adults, 300 children and 200 OAPs or concession admissions. He's very aware of his own audience for Lynn speedway and the interest it commands in the local area; consequently, he vehemently despairs of the inadequacy of the recent BSPA questionnaire that attempts to ascertain the demographics of the speedway audience throughout the country. The organisers of the survey, Impact Marketing, apparently have no background in market research and Jonathan is bewildered at how they ever gained the commission for this task from the BSPA. He also has methodological and statistical queries about the quality of the sampling, the inexact nature of the questions coupled with a complete lack of an adequate rating system, which will inevitably reduce the quality and usefulness of the data. However, Jonathan is content to control his own destiny when it comes to analysis so, ultimately, these perceived shortcomings aren't really his problem.

Jonathan identifies the club's business performance as driven by a "lot of pride in the town" in the speedway club, which is "the biggest sport here". There has been a perception problem to overcome over the last few years, particularly when the departure of Nigel Wagstaff coincided with King's Lynn reverting from the Elite League to the Premier League level. Understandably, this had a large number of loyal fans up in arms and many stated that they didn't want to watch speedway at this level of racing. Gradually the promotion has changed and become effective enough to alter their sincerely held opinions, and thereby gradually boost attendances. However, the "fact that our crowds have grown is not down to the support of the BSPA or Sky, it's all down to local efforts of talking and promoting within the area". I can confirm these promotional efforts, since I was passed, as I drove to the speedway tonight, by a car that pulled a mobile advert for the speedway on a trailer around the town. There are also signs that dot the roadsides throughout the local area as well as extensive coverage in the local papers and on the radio. The *Eastern Daily Press* newspaper dedicates considerable space to its coverage of speedway at King's Lynn. Buster and his son are sanguine about the appeal of a step back up to the Elite League, which they feel would require another 500-plus adults to attend each meeting in order to cover the significantly increased expenses of such a move. The need to attract this number of additional fans each meeting isn't something that Jonathan or Buster believes would be presently achievable.

Jonathan doesn't take the standard view of Premier League promoters that their level of racing is *de facto* a more exciting product to watch than Elite League racing. "I don't agree with PL racing being so exciting", mostly because it has the problem that many of the riders still have to learn their trade. While it's fine that the Premier League still, along with the Conference League, effectively finds and trains future talent, the rawness of the riders plus the limitation of only one visit a year to most tracks during each season, means that the home teams have an undue advantage over their visiting rivals. This is unlike the situation in the Elite League, where established riders in predominantly settled squads have great familiarity with each track they very regularly visit, so the gaps in knowledge and skill around a particular track aren't so great or significant to subsequent results. To illustrate his contention, Jonathan quickly reviews tonight's opposing riders' familiarity with the Saddlebow Road track, "Lee Dicken hasn't visited for years and Henrik Vedel and Karlis Ezergalis have never visited". While he acknowledges, "we're trying out Tommy so he can be hit and miss"; nonetheless, the odds still remain massively stacked in favour of a Lynn victory. Every visiting team will have its similarly easily identifiable 'weak links'[4]. It's not a perspective that I've ever considered before, but I have to admit that's it's a form of analysis that is both compelling and accurate.

Jonathan is supremely confident in his abilities and takes great pride in his knowledge of the contemporary speedway landscape: "I'm up on my riders". In his estimation there are only four Premier League riders who are real future Elite League prospects "in the whole world and I can name them[5]; a year ago it was 20 riders, but really the only way for success is to own your own assets and develop them. The only clubs who can afford to buy riders are the Elite League clubs, so the reality of the situation is that many clubs at our level are always looking for these types of riders". To compound the situation, the comparative lack of talented British riders means "everyone is determined to bring in foreign riders", especially Australian riders who are very talented, speak English and "they're never ill and you never hear them whinge" unlike some other nationalities he's encountered. This approach impoverishes British speedway, because it's a vicious circle, which ultimately restricts the number of places available for British riders. Overall, it's a "sad state of affairs for the future" but, to Jonathan's mind, isn't one for which the clubs could reasonably be blamed. He lays the blame squarely on the shoulders of both the government and the BSPA for not funding the structured provision of opportunities for young people at training academies that would, if available, provide a big influx of British riders[6].

Jonathan just can't see where the next British World Champion will come from. He concedes that Scott Nicholls is a "good racer and all round rider but he's hardly Tony Rickardsson". He's also not a fan of the present format of the Grand Prix series since "when I watch it I'm just so bored". It's a "great concept and run very professionally but it's lost it's edge and

---

[4] When I ask, for another example, this time about the Reading Racers, Jonathan points to Simota and Tressariou as potentially vulnerable riders through inexperience in comparison to the Lynn team.

[5] Though he then refuses to do so, since it's his own proprietary knowledge

[6] In an example of putting your money and effort where your mouth is when it comes to helping youngsters, March 2006 saw the club announce the formation of the 'King's Lynn Speedway Study Centre' as part of their participation in a nationwide government initiative called 'Playing for Success'. Basically, it's a scheme to encourage recalcitrant young learners to attend an out-of-school study-support centre through being based in an attractive local sports environment. Buster and Jonathan have to be admired for both their entrepreneurship but, more importantly, also their engagement with the local community. Though it's not going to provide more British speedway talent, it's definitely going to motivate the youngsters to learn English, mathematics and the information and communications technology that Jonathan utilises so well and by which he sets such great store.

cut-throat appeal". This is mainly because, "for whatever reason", the organisers abolished the ability for different riders to qualify for the competition ("it'll end up like Formula 1 going stale") while they simultaneously reduced the possibility of 'shock' results that the "old world final format" produced, in sharp contrast to the present cumulative system. All the television coverage hasn't attracted the new big sponsors it was supposed to automatically promise either, with the recent World Team Cup being another prime example since its main sponsor was ASL, a company owned by Colin Horton, who were already deeply involved in the sport.

My time is up and Jonathan has many fish to fry this evening, but wants to introduce me to one of the sports up-and-coming young riders of the future, Simon Lambert. Simon rides for Boston in the Conference League where his energetic and very affable dad, Stephen, is a key member of the management team of the club as well as its chairman. The younger Lambert doesn't ride through nepotism though, but rather through dedication, skill and ability. Also, he has managed to massively improve his racing average this season from an initial 3.469 to around 8.69[7]. Simon is a friendly and polite young man from Spalding in Lincolnshire who relishes being a speedway rider and all that it entails. "I love it," he says sincerely, and he relishes the opportunity to travel to other tracks where he can gain more experience and improve his overall abilities and technique. Jonathan adds the further details that Simon's own touching modesty omits. He attributes Simon's success to "hard work, dedication and fitness" allied with a willingness to spend many hours practising, and observing and questioning others to learn from them. His desire to understand and learn is voracious and sincerely held. Simon has begun to become familiar with the Lynn track and now performs so well at some other away venues that he recently top scored at Armadale with 12 points, despite an engine failure. When you speak with him, Simon definitely comes across just how you'd want your own son to come across to people, and I'd say he's certainly a credit to himself and to his parents.

I decide to tour the stadium's facilities and immediately find the always friendly Jon Barber in the track shop, which he describes as "our most salubrious track shop". It looks and feels like a sauna with all that wood throughout, which must be great in the spring but very hot in the summer. The shop has a natty range of rider clocks that I hadn't noticed elsewhere before. Some of these are predictable enough with photos of famous riders like David Norris, Tony Rickardsson and Gary Havelock but also, more obscurely, Jan Jaros the Lynn reserve rider. Jon recommends that I visit the 'Mad Hatter's Club' cabin cum shop on the fourth bend, which also has a wide range of speedway memorabilia for sale, with all proceeds donated to help the Lynn riders. Ever the source of insightful information, Jon surmises that rates of pay in the recent World Team Cup must have been "very poor" if you judge them from the standpoint of the actual effort expended by 'star riders' like Tony Rickardsson or Nicki Pedersen.

Race time is fast approaching so I quickly grab a soft drink in the spacious Pits Stop café under the covered grandstand before I leave for the pits area[8]. There I chat with machine examiner, Arthur Paske. He lives in Ely, used to road race and rode on grass when younger. He's also watched the sport since 1950 when he was part of the large crowds that regularly attended Norwich. He's nostalgic for the "olden days which were the best" but now looks back fondly on how King's Lynn has developed over the years. It was a "dirt track in a field when I first came" but since then "they've made a stadium of it". He approves of the recent but gradual development of the stadium under Buster's auspices, particularly as "there's not the money in speedway, so he's doing it as he goes along – with something new every year". Arthur would have to notice these things, since he's been the machine examiner here for 27 years. But he also stresses the generational nature of the sport among the riders and the fans. He remembers not only seeing his grandfather Trevor Harding ride, but his son Trevor and

---

[7] His final overall average for all Conference competitions in 2005 was 8.33, while his Saddlebow Road home average ended at 9.55. Extremely good when you consider his season was also held back by injuries. Simon also had two 'paid' maximums during the campaign and was praised for his commitment to help the riders and spirit of the Boston club. Sadly a badly broken arm sustained in may has ruled Simon out for the rest of the 2006 season.

[8] This is where the Chapmans, like Len Silver at Rye House, really make their money. In the past, Buster reputedly once claimed to have made £7,000 from the sale of burgers at a single stock-car meeting!

now his grandson Trevor – this family tree may be easier to recall than most – but also Neil Street, then Phil Crump and his son Jason. It's something that appeals and repeats itself when you've been involved as long as Arthur has. It also confirms his view that all those years ago were a golden age when a trio of gifted Australians arrived in this country together. There was Bob Leverunz who rode for Norwich, Jack Young who became World Champion and Trevor Harding whom he'd already mentioned. Arthur relishes his work and loves to watch close meetings, though he's pretty definite that tonight will not be one of those.

I climb the few steps of the riders' metal viewing platform to watch the evening's racing, surrounded by the riders and mechanics. It also has an ideal view of all the activity in the pits and on the track. In front of me is Colin Pratt, the co-team manager of Coventry, who has a long animated conversation with Buster punctuated with smiles and lots of expressive gestures with his arms. Tonight there is a guest announcer, the well-informed and informative Bryn Williams, who optimistically asks, "Is there anyone here from Newport?" without any audible response. However, there sounds to be plenty here to support Lynn, and to my untutored eye many more than Jonathan's pessimistic forecast of 400 people have actually turned up. They line the home-straight grandstands and all the bends, as well as queue in front of the snack bar by the pits. There's also quite a crowd of fans that peer over the crash barriers adjacent to the pits, and watch the frantic activity of the officials, riders and mechanics with curiosity.

Home supporters' hopes that Lynn will win every race with a maximum 5-1 ends immediately with the initial race, as Tommy Stange trails off at the back behind Tomas Topinka, Tony Atkin and Henrik Vedel, who looks comfortable during his first race round Saddlebow Road. The expected 'men against boys' nature of the fixture is then emphasised by three successive 5-1s for Lynn to take the cumulative score quickly to an impressive 18-6. The gulf in ability is so pronounced that the Newport riders appear unable to make any real impression on the home riders even if they, like Batchelor who sloppily runs very wide in heat 2, make unforced errors without punishment. By the end of heat 5, Lynn already have a convincing lead and one of the home team's many Australians, Ashley Jones, has decided to withdraw from the meeting. It was a decision forced upon him by his thunderous fall, while well positioned, and causes him to miss out on a potentially big night of points and pay. Bryn euphemistically notes that Jones "took a pearler on bend 3" which is certainly one way to describe it as he flew six feet in the air. Bryn then sympathises with Ashley on the pain caused by the aggravation of his recent shoulder dislocation, which we're told, "is very painful if you've ever done it". Ashley chats with Buster in the pits before he strongly relays his sentiments to the man in front of me: "I'm freaking pissed off, me throttle jammed and I've lost me freaking point money". Shortly we're told Ashley has withdrawn from the fixture with a concussion. Whatever the reason, it's one of the few glimmers of hope so far this evening for the beleaguered Newport visitors if they are to avoid an absolute thrashing, albeit through the misfortune of others.

While his father Buster bustles around in the pits, I've noticed that Jonathan has already watched a couple of heats among the crowds that line the home-straight fence, before he then moves onto the centre green for an interview. Over the new loudspeaker system, he relates his delight at the recent away victory at Newport and last night's meeting at the Isle of Wight; where he particularly enjoyed the daring do of Troy Batchelor "chasing Boycie's back wheel in heat 13 like you just wouldn't believe, I thought he'd overtake him". Stood in front of me, and for reasons that aren't exactly clear to me, Lynn rider Olly Allen remarks "what a tosser" to the man by his side as Jonathan, oblivious on the centre green, continues to talk away excitedly.

Tonight's clerk of the course, Andy Scotney, rushes about and marshals the pits area like a man possessed. Both teams seem to respond well to his cajoling and suggestions, but he has little time to talk during this important work. In the brief moments of conversation we have, he expresses great pride in all that has happened to develop the stadium over the last few years under Buster's guidance. There are already plans in hand for more stands to be built on the home straight and for another stand to be erected on the empty space on the apex of bend 3 and 4. Between the next few heats that all result in wins for the Lynn riders, we learn from the announcer Bryn that Buster will be 48 the next day, August 11th. My interview with the visiting Colin Pratt continues the theme of praise for the changes at the stadium. Colin is of the opinion that "it's improved here a lot over the last few years" and confirms the evidence of our own eyes that "Buster's running a good operation here".

Buster meanwhile takes the opportunity to motivate one of his star riders in the form of Troy Batchelor on the steps of the riders' stand. Troy has just raced to an easy 5-1 with his team-mate Olly Allen, but Buster counsels "you're not supposed to race your partner, you're supposed to guide them to a 5-1". Troy explains "we spoke before and he said don't clamp me down, then came through the inside so I went outside and past him so I thought 'freak it'". The disgruntled Troy wanders off and Buster notes to me, with the match score already at 35-13, "it's been hopeless against this lot for the last three years, though the crowd's better than I thought". Troy returns and the news that Buster has talked with Troy's father is ignored in favour of a rant about the state of his kevlars. I must say that they look very ragged and held in place by judiciously positoned tape. Troy gestures at them saying "look at this shit, I've been out injured and been trying to save up some money for spending on me bikes, so if anyone can help?" Buster calmly responds, "you only have to ask". Minutes later Troy is on the centre green for an interview about his view of his season so far. He mentions his return from injury and his good performances as well as his need for more sponsorship, if possible. The interviewer also appeals for any keen King's Lynn fan in the crowd with sufficient funds to sponsor Troy and help him with the purchase of some new kevlars. Appeal over, Troy jokes, after his large points tally, that "I've got a sore back from carrying the team at the Isle of Wight". When pressed by the interviewer on the contribution of the team manger to these performances, Troy specifically downplays Jonathan's role as a manager with a sardonic "he didn't do too much".

I wander anti-clockwise round the circuit of the track, past the bar and café on bend 2 and the covered terraces around to the first chalet hut to see the acclaimed Mad Hatter's Club shop. Everything that's for sale in the shop is contributed by the fans and is used to raise funds that are donated to the Lynn riders. There's no one in the shop when I enter as Mr Fuller, who runs the shop tonight, stands on the terracing while he savours his mug of tea in the cool evening air. The shop is crammed full of memorabilia and knick-knacks that would appeal to any speedway fan as well as the loyal King's Lynn fans. Mr Fuller followed Lynn "since it started 40 years ago" but actually started going to speedway "knee high to a grasshopper" 60 years ago at Norwich in 1945. The shop has been going for around 15 years and it has raised £32,035.54 during that time, as a sign behind him rather proudly and precisely displays. In 2004, the club raised £1,223.62. Everyone who works in the shop is a volunteer. Mr Fuller describes his role as one to "help out" but is very disappointed that the lady who started the club, Mrs Lake, isn't there to speak with me because she's away on a caravan holiday in Hunstanton this evening. Audrey rarely misses a meeting and founded the club with her husband the late Mr Neville Lake, who sadly passed away in 2003; nonetheless "she's still carrying on". Also missing tonight are the Sutton Bridge based, ageing Garwell twins, Bill and Don, "you can't miss them, they're only about four foot tall". They're also real enthusiasts for the sport and Mr Fuller is confident that they would have been delighted to meet me, never mind compare notes about the various travels involved for my book. They love their speedway and often travel with Mr Fuller in his car all over the country to watch it, "they'll go anywhere for speedway, them two will!"

A sign on the wall of the hut reminds all patrons that there is to be "no swearing", which corresponds with the tenor and ambience of the Mad Hatter's Club. But, Mr Fuller switches from benign to extremely heated in seconds when he recollects the behaviour of the number 1 rider in contemporary world speedway Tony Rickardsson. It all stems from when Tony won the 'Rider of the Year' trophy in 1999 during a time when he rode for the club. The award for this honour is a glass trophy that cost £300, which the winner holds for the year before it's then passed onto the next season's winner. The trophy has been renamed in memory of Audrey Lake's late husband, and is now known as the Neville Lake Memorial Trophy since he passed away in 2003. Whatever the name of the trophy, Mr Fuller believes it would be best if Tony Rickardsson could break away from his extremely lucrative riding schedule in order to return it to the club. Any fan can vote throughout the season for their favourite rider. A commemorative shield that lists the various winners remains on display in the Mad Hatter's Club chalet for all to see and marvel at throughout the year. Unfortunately, Tony has been a disrespectful custodian. "The bastard never returned it!" Mr Fuller angrily puts it, as he ignores the edict about foul language that hangs on the wall. Since he disappeared with the glassware all the subsequent winners – Leigh Adams, Jason Crump, Nicki Pedersen, Tomas Topinka and Adam Allott – have had to do without the trophy on their mantelpiece. Mr Fuller suspects that Rickardsson has probably lost it, particularly since they chased its return when they sent registered letters to him and the Poole promoter, without reply, when he rode at Poole in 2004. With perfect reasonableness they asked him to send the trophy back, provide the funds for a replacement, or substitute an unwanted equivalent trophy. Rickardsson's silence has deafened and severely disappointed, "he just doesn't care for the fans, for a World Champion to treat a club like this so badly when we give all the money to the riders is appalling". Luckily we can hear the sound of bikes as they take to the track for the next race after the interval, which saves Mr Fuller's blood pressure climbing any higher.

The rest of the meeting proceeds as before and the Lynn riders easily continue to dominate the fixture. Jonathan is energetically here, there and everywhere, while hundreds of moths repeatedly batter themselves onto the bulbs of the bright floodlights. Doolan and Batchelor win the final heat of the meeting before they celebrate exuberantly but as Bryn sagely notes, "it's an unusual celebration, but they *are* Australian". Batchelor is given the bumps by his team-mates, just as he dismounts from his bike at the pits gate, to celebrate his achievement at being undefeated throughout the fixture. The Lynn riders, along with an enthusiastic Jonathan, climb onto a waiting truck for a celebratory circuit of the track; by the time they return from this victory lap of honour the Newport side of the pits has almost completely emptied of riders and equipment. Buster is delighted with his riders' performance "especially as they're all our assets except Olly Allen". I raise the vexed question of the missing trophy with Buster, who is resignedly phlegmatic "that's Tony Rickardsson, that's how he is, he won't give it back". Tim Stone, the Newport promoter and team manager shrugs off the enormity of the 67-26 defeat, by far the biggest win for King's Lynn at their track this season, or the fact that none of his riders even won a single race. "All their riders are dialled in, we only really had Neil, and Vedel rode well, given it's the first time he's seen the track".

Soon afterwards, Neil Collins is the only rider to remain from either team in the rapidly emptied pits. He fusses over his bike, removes and cleans parts, adjusts others; and he generally just takes painstaking care to fastidiously maintain his own equipment. He's been the oldest rider here tonight, not many years younger than Buster, and has practically been a one-man opposition, as he has been throughout much of the season for Newport, home and away. He approaches his tasks with the experience of a craftsman – with patience, knowledge and control – while he works away in his bright red kevlars with his distinctive bandana tied round his neck and that ginger brown loose-permed or afro-knotted hairstyle he sports. As he works he chats to a woman in jeans with her pretty but distracted daughter in a purple skirt. They have an easy familiarity and comfort together that suggests they're in a relationship, or know each other well, and are apparently the only family together in the pits to go along with the many on the terraces.

Meanwhile, the second-half riders with their mechanics, sponsors and fathers busy themselves on the far side of the pits. Many of the crowd have stayed behind to watch the youngsters race and learn their trade with some practice heats. Colin Pratt is on the steps of the riders' stand and Buster hovers by the pits gate. Colin jovially calls over "Buster, you must have put that one on" as a rider crashes painfully in front of us, coming to a sudden unexpected halt when his chain came off. The stricken rider lies on the track for some considerable time before he gingerly gets to his feet to a relieved cry of "he's up" from the men that surround the riders who impatiently sit on their bikes, and wait to resume their racing. A short while later it's over when a fine drizzle starts to fall and I join the throng of the crowd as it exits the stadium into the dark Norfolk evening. I'm barely half a mile away when the heavens open and a torrential rain falls. My spirit is not dampened though, since I have enjoyed a thoroughly entertaining evening's racing at the renewed and invigorated Saddlebow Road that the Chapmans have proudly developed.

10th August King's Lynn v. Newport (Premier League) 67-26

SKY CHATTER

"He was as sharp as a bowling ball there" Chris Louis (on M. Ferjan's green light starting abilities)

RANDOM SCB RULES

3.4.3 No Protest or Appeal is permitted against a Referee's decision upon a question of fact or interpretation of the Speedway Regulations

The drive from King's Lynn to Ipswich takes you through some idyllic countryside villages, past verdant woods and lush fields. In the warm sunshine and intermittent shade, it has the look and atmosphere of an England from a slower, more respectful time. The sort of image of England that American tourists have in mind when they try to track down long-lost relatives from their complicated family tree. It would have been a lovely day for a slow meander between the two towns, or an ideal afternoon for a few trips to graveyards to establish your genealogy, but I was late, since I'd spent most of the day in a Volkswagen garage in Lynn. So I'd set off somewhat hassled from my family friend's house on the outskirts of that historic port town for my meeting with John 'Tiger' Louis, the Ipswich legendary rider and co-promoter. He'd been one of my childhood speedway rider heroes. When I was a teenager there were only two Tigers to speak of, the one in your tank and John, who rode in those leathers with the distinctively striped sleeves. He was not my all-time favourite but he was one of those excellent riders that you always noticed, especially since he was a vital and notable part of the hot bed of speedway action and clubs that was East Anglia in those days. I had never visited Foxhall Heath before, so I was excited by

the prospect and wondered what I'd find at a place that had fired my teenage imagination as such a potentially exotic destination. Like travel to all places with which you're not familiar you have to rely on the directions you glean from many different sources, although I felt reasonably confident having driven to Ipswich many times to see Sunderland play and, mostly, lose. I followed the directions from the helpful pre-season special edition of the *Speedway Star* earlier in the year that had listed information on every track in the country. They appeared to advise that I pass the town itself on the dual carriageway, which itself can be a bit of a trial since the roads around the town are always filled with huge numbers of aggressively driven lorries that rush about to pick up or deliver their cargoes. We cross the river Orwell and, closely following the directions, I find that I'm going back on myself, towards Ipswich, down a windy country road, however, I'm slightly reassured to have spotted a sign for the village of Foxhall Heath. The speedway club has placed 'Racing Tonight' signs on the verge, which indicates to all passers by that they're inordinately close to the proud home of the Ipswich 'Evening Star' Witches.

An unexpectedly sharp right turn finds my car bouncing down a tree-lined dirt-cum-sand driveway to the stadium. Unsurprisingly, the stadium stands alone in a large area of heathland – very sandy heathland – where I park the car, surrounded with trees in the distance. It's the sort of place that you could sensibly stage the film version of *King Lear*, particularly when he goes mad on the heath, provided that you kept the stadium out of shot. Over to the left there's already quite a collection of the distinctive white and other coloured vans that cry out 'speedway rider' to me nowadays. The stadium is famously shared, in this case with stock cars, just as it appears all contemporary speedway venues are shared with other more lucrative or frequently staged sports.

I've only just stepped from my car towards the open gates of the entrance when I hear a shout of "it's you again" in a broad Norfolk sounding accent, only to find myself warmly greeted with a "hello, my darling" by Shaun Tacey. We appear to follow each other around the speedway tracks of this country on an on-off basis. He appears politely impressed at my perseverance and enquires how the book research has progressed and is keen enough to be curious to establish which tracks in the country I've just recently visited. He nods at the mention of King's Lynn the previous night and sympathises at my future trip to Newcastle. He looks at these tracks with his speedway rider's hat on (should that be a helmet?); it's a perspective that leads Shaun to emphasise Newcastle's notable "narrow bends". Though he does speak very warmly of the co-promoter George and his mother, whom he considers "lovely people". This contrasts sharply to his opinion of the Newcastle crowd who, he believes, don't want to watch good racing but go because they "just want to see and cheer crashes". To Shaun's mind "you'll be pleased just to get out of there" whereas tonight at Foxhall, he notes that it'll be a completely different kettle of fish, with the ideal combination of a knowledgeable crowd and a well prepared track. Shaun used to ride here and is pleased at the short drive from his home in Norwich to take the guest booking he has for tonight's Elite League fixture with Poole. The Pirates have been shrewd enough to book Shaun, especially since he knows the track extremely well, will be keen to show his ex-employers a thing or two and will ride at reserve, from where Poole will be able to use him tactically in the meeting.

We would have talked for longer but at that point a rather smart luxury car (either a BMW or a Mercedes, I'm not so hot on actual car types although I know enough to notice that it's pretty smart) glides past us and enters the stadium through the entrance gates. Shaun nods and says, "that's John Louis, you'd best catch him", while the driver stops to unload some boxes of match programmes for the track shop from his boot. As you walk through the entrance gate, you emerge onto the first bend with the grandstand stand to your left and elsewhere inside I notice that there are tiers of standing terraces that surround and overlook the bowl of the track. A variety of buildings and catering vans also line the perimeter. John is in a hurry to get on with all the preparations regularly required on his biggest work night of the week, Ipswich's Thursday race night. He knew that I would arrive this afternoon for a research visit to the track for my book as well as to interview him. John has to hurry on and, since he will have to drive his car around to there, arranges to meet me shortly in his portacabin office adjacent to the pits.

Shaun by now chats to Nick and John in the track shop while a lady, whom I assume is their mum, has started to put out a table of badges and match programmes by the side of the shop, though only after she's checked that she should do so with her son Nick because of the dark, threatening rain clouds overhead. The brothers are friendly, welcoming people, who always have time for a chat and, since they are so closely involved with the sport, they have lots of interesting insights and snatches of gossip or intrigue. They run a successful network of track shops around the country so, pretty well any night of the week, you can find one or both of them as they set up, break down or run their shops at a variety of track outlets that include Peterborough, Mildenhall, Eastbourne and Ipswich. When I wonder aloud to Nick what he did in the winter without speedway tracks to attend, he proudly informs me that they research and source the basic materials that make up a track shop's merchandise from all round the world. There's a huge array of paraphernalia that requires many different sources and suppliers, particularly important when they have to ensure that each team accurately has its own logo on the branded merchandise. Just a brief glance in the Ipswich shop shows that the merchandise that they would have to source probably includes baseball caps, programme boards, badges, tracksuit tops, team-colour tops, anoraks, T-shirts, car stickers or fleeces to mention but a few of the items on display. Often these speedway garments come in many different styles, but I gather from Nick that they try to reduce their inventory to zero, if possible, by the time the season ends; particularly since each season they prefer to have the most contemporary look, colour, design or style to tempt the keenly devoted fans to part with more money for the very latest merchandise. My list of the goodies available in their shop ignores all the rider-specific merchandise that is also very noticeable here; every track has its own stars that the fans like to support with 'Team Hans Andersen', or whatever is locally appropriate, emblazoned on their jacket, cap or sweatshirt. And I haven't even begun to note the range of books, magazines, the ever-popular pens embossed with the team name and programme boards that are the staple accessories to be found at any track shop nationwide.

I leave this Aladdin's cave of possible impulse purchases and stroll back out to the car park, where I make my way past the phalanx of riders' vans. There, Poole's star rider, Ryan Sullivan, hangs out, and snogs enthusiastically with his very attractive girlfriend in the front seat of his state-of-the-art black soft-topped BMW. He obviously enjoys the visible symbols of his success, since he now travels in greater style and luxury than the majority of riders here tonight who will mostly arrive with their bikes in their van. Not that anyone will give this a second thought while he delivers the results on the track that his undoubted talent leads everyone to expect and take for granted, although some small doubts about this have started to creep in this season.

At the firmly closed entrance gate to the pits, through which all the riders must pass, there's a small crowd of fans. In this

case, it's Jerry and Dee Thompson who hope to pop in and see John Louis to catch up on old times. Not that these times are really that old, since Jerry first met John at a charity football match in 1995 before he got involved after that at Foxhall as "a dogsbody and track helper". Across the whole country, it's amazing how people compete to get the opportunity to be a track helper or a general dogsbody at a track. Because these valuable positions at speedway clubs are so well sought after, they're never advertised and, as with many things in life, it appears that you have to be acquainted with 'people in the know' to attain preferment.

The most noticeable thing about the work for Jerry is "how everyone made you feel at home". But after he had claimed that it was hard to describe, Jerry went on at extremely great length to stress the family orientation of the Ipswich club and repeatedly emphasised, "it's not just the racing side but it's the social side". I gathered it was something quite special – most likely drinking and talking speedway rather than wife swapping – but I luckily never quite found out since, at that moment, the pits gate was flung open for us for a few brief seconds. It quickly clanged shut again and, until 6 p.m., remained resolutely closed to the night's most important ingredient – the riders themselves. Although with all those bikes, general gear and equipment you can understand how they'd get under your feet and disrupt the orderly running of the pits area.

John fusses in the yard in front of his office but suddenly is surprisingly keen to escape with me to the sanctuary of his office for our interview, after a few minutes of hearty but convoluted reminiscences with the Thompson family. I now suddenly feel that John relishes and welcomes my visit, despite his rather guarded and taciturn demeanour earlier. It's a reticence that I'm later assured is his default setting rather than anything personal! Ensconced behind his desk with his briefcase open, in an office crammed with a photographic history on its walls, John slightly relaxes for a moment in the comfortable familiarity of his own environment. People pop by with last-minute questions and queries that require John's immediate attention, or linger to chitchat in, what to my ears sounds like, their strong Suffolk accents. It's all mostly about things to be done, that have been done or should be done. Straightaway John confides in me to say that we could have spoken with the Thompsons for a lot longer only we'd "never have got away" without the excuse of having to conduct our interview. The sport appears to be full of lots of lovely, knowledgeable fans but, John assures me, is also afflicted by others who go on at great length, "thinking that they know much more than they really do". I surmise that over the years as a rider and latterly as a promoter John has politely learnt how to keep his own counsel, nod sagely and then duck off as quickly as possible.

Our shared close shave and escape over, John immediately remembers to revert to caution in the company of strangers, particularly possibly prying strangers that have a long list of questions that they'd like to ask or who might wilfully misrepresent John and the club in the national press or in print. In fact I do have my usual list of research questions for my book but many times it has proven much easier to let the conversation flow naturally and ask some reasonably pertinent questions from the list, if the need or occasion arose. John's natural wariness means that our conversation stutters and stalls, particularly since he adopts a guarded manner of response that would have challenged the most skilled of PoW interrogators or easily frustrated the police should they have chosen to take him in to help with their enquiries. Throughout our interview, he is caught between the conscious need to remain polite and helpful, especially after that nice Mr Toogood from the BSPA had warned by fax of my track visit, and his much stronger desire to remain extremely vigilant in case of 'trick' questions or hidden agendas. John excels throughout the interview with his carefully considered approach and I'm sympathetic to the need to take care in the company of journalists and strangers, because so many people only like to accentuate the negative or write destructive accounts and stories that bear very little resemblance to the truth, especially on the Internet. But that is another story, albeit one that speaks very strongly to John, if his acerbic comments and strong reactions to what he occasionally calls my "misguided comments and opinions" are anything to go by.

For quite some time, each of my attempted questions elicits a question in response from John, rather than a direct answer; often in the manner of that old joke where one man says to another:"I hear you always answer a question with a question?" to which the other replies, "whoever told you that?"

In John's case, his stock responses to my rather gentle questions are "what did other people say?" or "what else have you heard? with some use of variants like "what answer are you looking for?" and "I'm sorry, I don't understand the question"[1]. If this is shadow boxing, I am mostly without a shadow, and definitely fail to land a punch. John would definitely represent a challenge to anyone who tried to conduct market research questions for any organisation, run a focus group, establish future voting intentions or try to find what food his cat prefers.

However, once John has warmed up to each of my questions with a parrying question or two of his own, which admittedly provides us both with plenty of additional thinking time, we start to develop a better understanding and gradually make some progress with his recollections on a sport he so evidently still loves. Towards the end of the 30 minutes (that John has assured me was all the time he could allot me for my questions) during which I sensed he often mentally checked his watch, he forgets himself and ceases to be so reticent in my company and no longer feels the need to slyly run down the clock. After he has cleverly avoided being unknowingly trapped in a snare that I haven't set, we manage to have a very instructional and honest conversation, albeit one in which John insists that he has to see my copy of afterwards; probably to check for inaccuracies or salacious *News of the World* type exposés that bear little or no relation to the reality of the topics we have discussed. I must honestly say that I felt privileged to meet John Louis, an idol of my teenage years, and I am even more grateful that he gave up his valuable time for my book. I see myself like David Carradine in *Kung Fu* with John as the 'master' figure, though we don't have any rice paper in his office to completely fulfil this image[2].

John replied to my question "what makes Ipswich different from other tracks?" with the simple answer, "there's nothing different", before he then provided a brief snapshot and history of the club. The speedway club emerged in 1950 but Foxhall Heath remained "predominantly a stock stadium" until "[John] Berry built another speedway track inside the stock track" in 1969, which appears to be the one that they still use today[3]. Attendances at the club vary tremendously nowadays

---

[1] To be strictly fair, the Wolves team manager Peter Adams also noted that some of my questions were unclear or needlessly inexact, so this reply from John might be the response of a sensible man.

[2] Later I gathered that John can deliberately shun public attention as evidenced by a letter of complaint to the *Speedway Star* a few weeks later. An Arena Essex fan who visited Foxhall Heath had written in to complain that John had knowingly hid in his office for an hour to deliberately evade discussions with, admittedly irate, fans when everyone outside knew he was already there, in the manner of Major Major Major Major from *Catch 22*. John totally refused to come out, basically to avoid a few querulous, angry but vocal critics, who were perturbed by their view of his management of that evening's events.

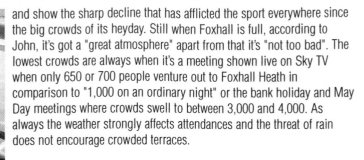

and show the sharp decline that has afflicted the sport everywhere since the big crowds of its heyday. Still when Foxhall is full, according to John, it's got a "great atmosphere" apart from that it's "not too bad". The lowest crowds are always when it's a meeting shown live on Sky TV when only 650 or 700 people venture out to Foxhall Heath in comparison to "1,000 on an ordinary night" or the bank holiday and May Day meetings where crowds swell to between 3,000 and 4,000. As always the weather strongly affects attendances and the threat of rain does not encourage crowded terraces.

A highlight of the recent past was the "jubilee thing" to celebrate the 50th anniversary of the club which attracted "lots of the old riders, veterans I suppose you'd call them" like Bert Edwards and Tich Reid to name but two. It was a "nice day, lovely". John is very modest about his own lengthy connection with the club since the name John Louis is so often synonymous with Ipswich Speedway Club. He concedes, as an aside almost, that his "whole life has been connected with the club". However at Ipswich speedway, like the Tom Jones song notes, this is "not unusual". The clerk of the course, Keith Barton, has been "here as long as I have although he started in a lesser job, then" so has the pits marshal, Richard Amott. There are "so many that haven't changed for years and years, even the same people make the tea as when I was a rider". If there's a secret to this longevity and sterling service, it's simply that "we're all very passionate about our speedway" and you know that "they'll all turn up on race night". The same is true of the spectators – the dedicated hardcore of whom, like the poor, are always with us – since John regularly sees "the same old fans I saw when I started". Even in the Ipswich track shop there's a form of continuity, as John mentions that Nick and John are from a speedway family since their father, Colin Barber, was a former promoter at Mildenhall and Birmingham. So at Ipswich, as at many clubs of all levels, it's still very much a family sport with many generations involved behind the scenes in the organisation of these clubs as well as on the terraces.

John has his own strong family ties here with both his Polish wife Magda and his son Chris, who are both famously involved in the promotion of the club. John himself switched to compete in speedway "late at 28" after he spent his formative years "scrambling, though they call it motocross now". From early childhood, he encouraged his son Chris to take an interest in the sport and he rode his first motorcycle at "three years, ten months" on the runway at Martelsham, on a monkey bike with additional supervision from John's "old mate Dave Gooderham". Under this expert guidance and tutelage, Chris was able to get a solid grounding and to develop the essential riding techniques,

---

[3] John omits to mention that he rode at Ipswich when John Berry was the promoter here and within the pages of the book *Confessions of a Speedway Promoter*, it thoroughly covers the Ipswich career of John 'Tiger' Louis in some detail along with many other notable characters that graced the club during that era.

which helped him progress through "schoolboys, grass track" before he embarked on his own glittering career in speedway. John rode in "many great seasons" and had a huge number of achievements; but fans always fondly recall 1975, when he raced to 24 maximums in only 50 matches. He is very casual with me about these considerable achievements; but, when John speaks of Chris, he ceases to be at all reserved and, instead, speaks with pride and enthusiasm that a father takes in his son's achievements, in this case on a speedway bike. The office is filled with photographs of Chris at the various stages in his sporting career. Whether it's the Under-21 World Championships, the Grand Prix, regularly riding for his country or at the highest level in the Elite League, you just know that John has been there throughout, as an extremely proud father, to watch his son compete. To confirm this, though it didn't need any confirmation, he has the full details of the story behind each and every framed photograph on the walls of his office, on the tip of his tongue[4].

When he looks back on his own career, John declares that he's always loved the "buzz of the sport", before he quickly notes that he's had a "good innings as a rider and promoter" since he's won trophies both on a bike and off it. He's keen to exactly distinguish each stage of his career. As a rider he identifies his role in Test Matches, especially when he was the England captain in the 1970s, and when they won World Team Cups. While latterly, as a promoter, he has presided over teams that have won the cup, the Craven Shield and, in 1998, the League. Although his work in the promotion of Ipswich is a "hard job" but he feels that "nine times out of ten" the fans leave the stadium happy after they have witnessed a good night's competitive racing. The dynamics of the sport and its economics have altered irrevocably since his riding days; but then again, when John first started, it was the British League that dominated the riding week with only the odd meeting abroad along with the occasional long track meeting in Germany. There were more Test Matches, which had greater importance then; so to represent and ride for your country was always something John "felt very passionate about". Overall, the sport has treated him well "it's been great for me, it's taken me all around the world, always meeting people". He's won plenty of trophies, but "I've got no medals", so he takes great pride in practical achievements, such as his involvement in the development of the first Weslake engine for speedway in the winter of 1974-75. He also values intangibles like "building the camaraderie of the thing" as England team captain and then again when he was England team manager.

Nonetheless, it's very noticeable that the top riders rarely only compete in England today in comparison to his riding days. Often as not, they also ride in the Polish and Swedish Leagues, plus the Grand Prix series and, recently, the World Team Cup. Not only does John strongly believe that "they ride too much, don't they?" but that all this "doing too much" is, ultimately, a significant contributory factor to the present lack of young British rider talent and development. Even the recent World Team Cup Final illustrates his point, since the British team "put their heart and soul into it and did their best", but still came last. While this performance wasn't helped by "Scottie's bike problems in the big races", John takes the view that some people are in denial about the problems that beset British speedway; people like Nigel Pearson who are guilty of exaggerating the presently modest achievements and "building the whole thing up and by still saying how well England have done". Outside the present team it's "unfortunate that the youngsters just aren't coming through",which worries John for the future for England (John isn't a man prone to use the more voguish moniker of Britain). As the Ipswich promoter, for him the club has a tradition of "excellent Polish connections" and he will find young riders there for the team and, if not, would "find our young riders in Sweden and Denmark". So it's quite a situation when an avowedly patriotic

[4] Though we don't get to talk about Chris's resilience during his lengthy recovery from his apparent career-ending back injuries. While these injuries finally ruled him out of the Grand Prix series, they had the happy benefit that they enabled him to once again to follow in his father's footsteps, when it kick-started the next stage in his career – his work in speedway promotion at Ipswich. Uniquely within British speedway Chris combines his work as a promoter with his work as a rider for the club. He also appears regularly as an analyst on Sky Sports, where you could easily argue that he's one of the most insightful and articulate commentators. Particularly since he's never afraid to be critical or opinionated – to articulate the "difficult words" – which bucks the trend when it comes to the usual surfeit of congratulatory or anodyne comment served up to the viewers. We also don't get to talk about Chris having one of the most elaborate (and as a spectator, annoying) pre-race preparation rituals. He's speedway's equivalent of what Brian Teacher used to be to pre-serve rituals in tennis. The Chris Louis pre-race ritual always involves that he thoroughly check, it appears, absolutely every wire, valve and washer on his machine just one yard from the start line before Chris will finally deign to join the others at the starting gate. You could almost run out of fuel waiting or maybe rebuild a bike quicker than the time it takes for this ritual to be completed before EVERY race. It's true that everyone has their little idiosyncrasies and foibles, but not usually played out at length in the public eye. One day I imagine we'll look back on these very distinctive habits, all misty eyed, as endearing.

Englishman like John Louis so bluntly acknowledges the dearth of British riding talent available to him as a promoter, when he has to try to compete against other promoters and run a successful Elite League club. Throughout, John skilfully keeps his comments and our conversation tied to specifics and steers things towards predominantly positive topics[5]. Though the club enjoys a "special agreement with the council" with regard to environmental noise, they're still only allowed "so many meetings a year". This limited number, agreed to because of the proximity of the "new housing estates, which are getting nearer and nearer", prohibits them from running "practice sessions, so we're snookered at that level". The decibel level is monitored regularly, plus there's an agreed curfew that ensures that the bikes can't start to warm up until 7 p.m. on race night and that every meeting has to finish by 10 p.m. A telephone caller briefly interrupts us to enquire about the weather, the likelihood of tonight's meeting going ahead and the start time. All of these questions John answers fully and patiently, while the caller remains unaware that he's just encountered the speedway equivalent of ringing Manchester United to find that the enquiry call is answered by Alex Ferguson. Then again, that's not at all unusual at speedway and all part of its continuing rather quaint, old-fashioned and unpretentious charm.

Despite it all, John still remains an enthusiast and evangelist for the sport of speedway. He never tires of the "thrill of the bikes at the start and racing to the first corner" although as the years have gone by his own appreciation has tended to favour the "technical side of riding". He prefers to analyse the approaches that different riders take to the steering and the corners, instead of just looking at the racing itself. He doesn't like to draw distinctions between the calibre of speedway in the past or in the present day since there's "lots the same, we still have four riders in a race". When drawn out, he expresses dismay that the modern rulebook increases in complexity every year, which is "so difficult and is creating more problems than I ever remember". These various interpretations of the rulebook itself have led to more arguments and greater emphasis upon the referees, which John believes necessarily diminishes the spectacle of the event. He believes a key example of the tendency towards yet more regulation, but with only detrimental impacts on the sport, is the change in the rules that govern the start. Out went the rolling starts and touching of the tapes – so skilfully and entertainingly exploited, to John's mind, by riders like Ivan Mauger – and in came stationary starts; which all adds up to mean that in the past "in some aspects there was a little more to watch". John believes the equipment has advanced through the silencers, the dirt deflectors, greater environmental awareness and regulation as well as the compulsory use of ear defenders (which John knows the "importance of through personal experience"). Though "some things have gone forever" like the total loss engines or the change in oil quality, which ended the use of the Castrol R oil – a vegetable-based oil that when "heated, hot or burned" gave the sport the distinctive smell that everyone still talks about as though it still exists. Overall though, John is pleased that you can still say that it remains a sport for all the family, just like it's always been with a mix of generations and with no crowd violence. He acknowledges that everyone at speedway isn't a saint and that there have "always been small incidents"; but usually nothing more than just the result of a heat of the moment dispute or flare up, no more comparatively than the incidents that you'd find in "normal life", whether at work or in town.

My time is up, since John has to press on with his various preparations for the evening ahead. He closes with a brief but illuminating guided tour of all the photographs that line the wall of his office. Suddenly he's much more engaged and alive, as he reviews each of the pictures of his son Chris in turn and tells the story behind it with a speedway rider's insight and a father's proprietorial pride. This brief but touching personal interlude and guided tour over, John picks up the phone to, once again, check the local area weather forecast and resumes the obligation of his promotional duties. He again stresses his suspicion of journalists in general though he's keen to point out that not all journalists are the same, since he enjoys his close work with those on the local Ipswich paper, *The Evening Star*. They're so in touch with events at the club that they're almost part of the club. John has been the sole promoter here since 1995 (though he started in 1989) and the paper has been a sponsor at Foxhall Heath Stadium for the last seven consecutive seasons and, John claims unverifiably, that they devote more pages to the coverage of speedway than any other newspaper in the country, whether locally or nationally.

[5] Earlier in the year he'd been in a more melancholy frame of mind when interviewed by Tony McDonald for the retro speedway magazine *Backtrack*. John had commented, "it's wonderful to watch a great speedway meeting ... but we seem hell bent on destroying it and I'm disillusioned with things now".

Each Ipswich match gets at least two full pages of coverage, while they also have sufficient space to devote to include various additional photos and comments. The local correspondent Elvin King, who sounds like he should be a fictional character from a folk tale but isn't, is a fanatical Witches fan. He writes in the match programme, reports on the home fixtures for the *Speedway Star* as well as writes at length for the paper. Like the profile of most of the sponsors of any speedway club, John notes that the "big sponsors tend to be big fans of the sport who just want to be involved". This also helps to ensure that there's never any really negative comment in the local paper, which is a situation that John wants to preserve. I'm also keen not to disturb the status quo that John values, so I decide not to quiz him further on his own recent enigmatic remark to *Backtrack* magazine, "there was a lot of underhand business that went on but then that's typical of speedway, isn't it?" Given how guarded he was at the outset of our interview when answering straightforward questions, John has already very much left me with the impression that any detailed or unduly "negative" questioning on my part, even about his own reported statements, wouldn't elicit any further meaningful information. They say the past is a foreign country and I'm happy that John has shared with me some of the memories he has of an era when his star shone brightly at Foxhall Heath, when he regularly conquered his opponents as a rider for Ipswich and for England.

Outside his office, I notice that the pits area now throngs with riders and mechanics, since the pit gates have opened to let the essential workers for the evening's entertainment have begun their preparations. Still waiting outside is Ipswich reserve rider, Kevin Doolan, who I've just seen ride for King's Lynn against Newport twice in the last week. Both of these fixtures, if they had been boxing matches, would have been stopped by the referee long before the end but, since they weren't, Newport were soundly thrashed on both occasions. As Kevin bluntly puts it to me, "they were there to be flogged, so we weren't going to take it easy on them". Words of insight and wisdom over, and since I've resisted any mention of the Ashes cricket series, Kevin quickly goes off to get changed into his work clothes in the single-storey building adjacent to the pits that houses the changing rooms. I see Shaun again, this time as he wheels his bike through to the pits, and he stops to briefly check on the economics of my travels "you're not paying for all this yourself, are you?" It's a question that's been on his mind but not previously asked. When it turns out I am, this only serves to confirm his opinion that I must be really mad since there's a huge amount of miles involved for us to have already met at all the tracks that we already have. With a shake of the head he heads off to finalise preparations for his own (paid) work.

I then wander to the pits area, to take advantage of my privileged author status to idle meaningfully on its perimeter. I easily fulfil my usual function on these occasions – absolutely none – with the aplomb of someone well used to the status of, as the saying goes, being as much use as a spare prick at a wedding. Just to review what I'm not during this time in the pits before a meeting: I'm officially not a rider, a mechanic, a team manager, a journalist, an official, a member of staff, a groupie, a girlfriend, a hanger on, a sponsor, a would-be sponsor, a physio, a confidant, a sports psychologist, an ex-rider, an announcer or even a friend of any of these people. I'm just here to linger and observe, neither vegetable nor mineral, and effectively invisible. However, I always lurk meaningfully and optimistically everywhere I go; but here, though I get rather too painfully close to Chris Louis, who works fastidiously and intently on his bike, in the hope that he might look up and chat. He did, to be fair, but only to look through me completely as though I weren't present and so, in a glance, he quickly establishes and confirms my 'untouchable' status. I had hoped to catch his eye and say casually that "I'm writing a book and I've just met your helpful and extremely proud father" or some similar authorly conversation stopper like that. However, the situation doesn't arise, and it doesn't take much sense to figure out that just before any rider starts work isn't the best time to try to speak to them; never mind to a rider with an invisible force field around them that appears to communicate "go away".

Since I have previously witnessed my fair share of pre-meeting preparations in the pits, there's nothing out of the usual to be seen here. I can predict that the riders of both sides will make a point to walk at least one complete circuit of the track, or maybe more, if they're particularly anxious about conditions. They will usually take "the track walk" together as a team and most often accompanied by the club's team manager. They always appear to be deep in conversation, though the increasing number of foreign riders might slightly restrict the conversational flow sometimes, and I imagine they discuss conditions, riding lines and tactics. But, then again, it could be a bit more normal and mundane with a lot of jokes at each other's expense, gossip, obligatory swearing and ribald humour about drinking, sexual prowess, pay rates, the weirdness of the home team's fans in comparison to the strange bunch you have at your track or, even heaven forefend, the relative comeliness of the groupies. Whatever it involves, it's a definite ritual, always to be undertaken in casual clothes – preferably with the bare minimum of warm clothing irrespective of weather conditions – and which will inevitably feature the latest fashionable shorts, some form of designer sunglasses that wouldn't look out of place on a member of the Aussie cricket team and the ubiquitous armless T-shirts. I will leave aside the complex issue of training shoe fashions as worn by the riders, since that would require a whole chapter unto itself. You will always see this ritualistic and almost invariable behaviour, as though it's a contractual obligation, at every track up and down the country; except, of course, on those rare occasions when the riders hope that the referee might be influenced to abandon the meeting before it starts, by the pitiful sight of them dressed in some form of wet weather clothing while they ostentatiously splash in puddles or kick muddy ruts. Along with the famed "track walk", it is incumbent upon the home team to smile a lot on their side of the pits, greet everyone heartily or glower menacingly at all and sundry (except for the 'extremely foreign' riders in the team with rudimentary or poor English who must speak Polish at all times with their cousin and/or mechanic). The away team is obligated to very much keep themselves to themselves, to mostly prepare their bikes in a fashion that could lead the casual observer to feel that they harbour some secret knowledge or weapon that they will unleash later on the track, but for now must disguise the existence of it at all opportunities. All this rigidly applies, except when they make a point to ostentatiously or surreptitiously check every other rider's equipment. Which, of course, can be combined with a brief chat of varying levels of bonhomie with friends on the rival team. And, since this is speedway, almost inevitably most riders have ridden with every other rider here or abroad at some stage, so there's no shortage of possible candidates for a hale and hearty chat. All home-track staff and officials must move quickly and purposefully or with studied casualness on all occasions, especially if they carry a clipboard or other token of authority, such as a rake or fire extinguisher.

I realise, yet again, that I can serve no useful purpose in the pits area so retreat to the main grandstand to find a spot to eat my salad and sandwiches. Already on the grandstand a lady sits on her own, in a carefully chosen place on the grandstand, around 90 minutes before the tapes fly up on the first race. There's also a young boy and girl who play boisterously on the railings at the edge of the grandstand closest to the track. They're absorbed in their playing but when they become just a little too adventurous, I take it upon myself to counsel them to be more careful. They stop and chat easily, in the way that children do, but especially in an environment they're confident of, which is clearly how they feel about the Foxhall Heath Stadium. Leon Armes is a friendly, bottle of pop who's full of information and long on opinion. He tells me that he, rather unusually but pleasantly childishly, supports Poole, Belle Vue and Ipswich. I learn that his favourite rider is Jason Crump "because he's world champion" and also informs me that he just "saw Hans Andersen bring in his toolbox". Then he boasts, "I know nearly all the stars and people's dads". Leon comes to the speedway often because his father, Julian Ames, works in the bar on the first bend while his mum, Teresa Reid, works in the third bend catering van. Leon says they're going to get married and Leon's granddad has died and "is in heaven". His playing partner is Rebecca June Hard, who tells me that she was born on August 15th and is already tremendously excited about her next birthday in a few days. She's here with her mummy Mandy, who's gone off to buy them burgers, and Nanny Cattermole (who I think is her grandparent but I can't tell) whom Rebecca points out to me, since she sits further along the grandstand and guards some bags. Rebecca tells me she supports Belle Vue but also "I like Poland", while on the rider front her favourites are "Scottie and Hans Andersen". Mandy has returned with the keenly anticipated burgers, so they fly off to get them while I lumber over to confess to my conversation with the kids and to having taken their photograph for my book. You can never be too careful with strangers or about strangers, after all.

Mandy, like Leon and Rebecca, is a huge fan of the Ipswich heat leader and star Hans Andersen – who is presently a bit of

[3] The start-line girls were known as the Workington "Start Tarts" until Graham and Denise Drury arrived as the promoters at the club. They are now more sophisticatedly known as the Workington "Brolly Dollies". They are by brolly colour – Red: Catherine McEuan; Blue: Charlotte Hayton; Green: Adele Rodgers and Yellow: Kayleigh Boag.

a *bête noire* to your average British fan. This widely held but unfair antipathy is mainly due to the perception that he cheated, and in the popular imagination was caught doing so, during last year's World Team Cup Final. All very silly and all a bit of a canard really, particularly as 'that's racing' and nothing can be proved. It could be argued that we lost due to the imaginary red light/Scott Nicholls incident and, I believe, that if the situation had been reversed and we'd won as a result of these 'alleged' actions, then nothing would ever have been said. To my mind, Hans is a young, gifted if slightly hard rider we'd praise to the heavens if he were English. Indeed, Mandy does praise him to the heavens for the next few minutes to the extent that I imagine he's only a short step away from beatification. According to Mandy he's "just a skilful, good all-round rider" who's "knowledgeable and can read a track". Although, she concedes, he still has a bit of a way to go before he rivals the world's ultimate rider and professional, Tony Rickardsson, who is "god, the master of speedway, the daddy". Mandy has come to the speedway at Ipswich for over 25 years and "there's nothing I don't like about it, well, except the races aren't long enough". She, like many others, especially "loves the smell of the methanol, that's speedway after all". She worries about the ever-present danger of rider injury, particularly through fatigue since "they often ride every night during the summer" and is even concerned enough to claim that they don't get paid enough for what they do. She believes that often financial success in speedway depends on what sponsorship you've got; though, luckily, her favourite Hans Andersen has "good sponsors". The kids have started to run amok once more, since they've now finished their burgers. Mandy wishes me luck and success with my book before she laughs and says wistfully "I'm gonna marry one, one day, in my dreams!" A rider that is, not a sponsor.

The stand has already got surprisingly full and, like Leon, I go off in search of tonight's match programme for the B fixture against the present Elite League Championship favourites, the Poole Pirates. It promises to be a close, hard-fought, exciting meeting and a considerable number of people have already taken up their favourite spot from which to watch from. I'm not sure where to stand just yet, so I decide to walk down towards the pits area again, via the pleasantly tree-lined path that passes behind the main grandstand. It's past the 7 p.m. curfew, so the pit gate proper is closed to all non-essential persons, while the mechanics warm up the bikes by revving them loudly. It's very crowded with expectant fans by the gate itself and also by the riders' changing room. I venture back into the sanctuary of the pits area, I vaguely glow with the self-importance of it all before I realise that I still serve no useful purpose and quickly leave; but not before Neil Middleditch, the England and Poole team manager, distractedly says "hello" and impresses me by actually remembering my name. Back outside the pits, if I can find a place to stand in this crowd, gives me a much better idea of and insight into the atmosphere and building excitement than feeling out of place in the pits. Indeed, it's quite fun to watch the riders, as they try to burst from the changing-room door and quickly negotiate their way to the sanctuary of the pits area. It's a brisk walk on which they also simultaneously attempt to sign as many autographs or pose for as many photos as humanly possible.

Though the Poole side is littered with stars, local fans at clubs everywhere inevitably clamour for the attentions of their hometown favourites. So quite a scrum and mêlée of adorers develops which interests me to watch, both in a Desmond Morris anthropological way and as a quick insight into the relative popularity of the assembled riders. It must be a relief for some of the riders to get back unscathed to the pits, from the crush of well-wishers and autograph bounty hunters, where they can then prepare for the comparative calm of just racing at high speed on a bike with no brakes with three other riders on a small track. The fans near to me are keen to have a word with John Louis when he comes out of his office; though the talk among them is of his serial reluctance to chat with the fans before a meeting. They put his greater recent reticence down to his heightened "sensitivity" because of the rain-off debacle with Arena Essex, but particularly the comparatively poor position of the club in the league, especially in comparison to the expectations your average Witches fan harbours about their 'rightful' league position. John Louis finally emerges from his office, in tie and his trademark Ipswich anorak to, as they say on the telly, answer questions. Well actually he doesn't, but just smiles and moves off to the pits area. Though he does stop and makes a point to chat to me to stress his view of the importance of the Premier League to British rider development in Britain, which he'd forgotten to do earlier when we spoke. He accurately observes, "many riders start their careers there, before moving up a league, and then they return". As an excellent example he cites Carl 'Stoney' Stonehewer who's "happy to ride at that level". He expansively gestures towards the assembled crowd with his hand and proudly points out "there's always plenty of fans keen to meet and watch the riders".

The notable exception to being thronged at the pits gate with admirers is tonight's match referee, Frank Ebdon. He slips anonymously by, strangely unnoticed for such a tall man and as the only one for miles to carry a modest, slim handle-less document case (though John has his in his office). He wears that famous but mandatory regulation BSPA issue dark jacket, which is delightfully set off tonight by a similarly mandatory bright green SCB issue tie. There's absolutely no doubt that he will live up to his well-deserved reputation and will run an extremely fast meeting; although, since the advent of close analysis and replays on Sky Sports television, his legendary status as a brilliant, omnipotent referee has slipped slightly to reveal his all too human failings unable to be disguised, as they were previously, through the force of his personality or the fact that the referee's word is always final.

I decide to take my place for the evening's racing on the crowded standing terraces that overlooks the first bend with the popular 'Garden Bar' behind me. There's quite a buzz of expectation among the Ipswich faithful unless, of course, there's a lot of Poole fans with Suffolk accents. The announcer greets the riders from each team individually, which includes the return of "former Witch" Shaun Tacey, whom he warmly welcomes back to Foxhall. The riders' parade itself is unusual, the first of its kind I've seen on my travels and appears to have been organised by Noah, since the riders circle round on the stock track in pairs that feature a home rider and his away equivalent. We see, for example, Hans Andersen ride round with his Danish fellow countryman Bjarne Pedersen because they both wear the number 1 race jacket for their respective teams. Another feature peculiar to Ipswich is that the riders don't have the usual *en masse* couple of warm-up laps and numerous practice starts that are the inevitable precursor to speedway meetings that you encounter everywhere else. Perhaps, this is a function of the agreement about noise control the club has with the council but, for once, it certainly makes it much more important than usual that the away team studied the track preparation with considerable care and attention on their earlier 'track walk'.

My own expectation of tonight's fixture is for a closely fought match where Poole's overall team strength eventually wins through. In front of me on the terraces there's a young woman, with a Kim Jansson T-shirt on, who enthusiastically cheers each Ipswich rider's name when it's announced. Sadly Shaun Tacey's return to Foxhall isn't all that he would want it to be, particularly since he breaks the tapes during the first attempt to run heat 2. He still manages to gain a point for third place, despite the fact that he starts the mandatory 15 metres back from the start line in the re-run. This is much more due to the ineptitude of his riding partner at reserve, Thomas Suchanek, Poole's recent late season Czech Republic signing from the Isle of Wight. In extenuation, it is Suchanek's first ever visit to the track and throughout the night he excels in finding even more new ways to get round the track four times in an even slower manner. Which is quite an achievement, given how painfully slowly he completes his first race of the night. The Ipswich fans salute their riders who've stormed into an early and deserved lead. The girl in front hoorays both Jansen and Louis for their second and third place finish in heat 3 before she queries with a loud "why?" the announcer's attempt at alliterative wit ("Kim Jansson known as Kim Handsome") when he broadcasts the result. Heat 4 has Tacey make a flying start from the start; once again he's attempted to 'get a flier' and predict when the tapes will rise, which this time he manages to anticipate without bursting through them. Though, with Frank Ebdon in charge of the buttons in the referee's box, it doesn't take great predictive powers to guess that he will let the tapes go up very quickly in each and every race. The race isn't called back, so it's left to Protesiewicz to easily outpace his fellow Pole but rival for Poole tonight, Krzyzstof Kasprzak; while Doolan is completely unable to make up the ground on Tacey's prompt departure from the tapes. The next race finds the young woman in front of me's ideal Ipswich pair of Louis and Jansson take to the track once again to the accompaniment of her ecstatic cheers and whoops of delight. These signals possibly encourage Louis to victory but sadly leave Jansson rooted at the back for the duration of the race.

I chat to the couple directly behind me on the terraces, which is all part of a peculiar vortex of coincidence. Garry had met me briefly in the gents earlier, while we washed our hands, when he'd asked a few questions about Frank 'Lightning Fingers' Ebdon, tonight's referee. He was also, it transpired, the chap who'd earlier rang John Louis with questions about tonight's meeting when I'd been in John's office listening. Unable to find evidence of the ley line or druidic circle I expected to find any second soon, I learnt more about Garry Turner and his 43-year-old wife Jan. It might be rude to ask a woman's age or even more so to print it, but I only do so as Jan replied "you look much older than me" when her descriptions and recollections of racing in the 1970s stupidly prompted my observation "oh, we must be about the same age then?" Jan came to Foxhall Heath very regularly as a child with her auntie from Kesgrave, which is "over the back" from the stadium. They'd park the car reasonably close by and then they used to walk through the trees to the stadium. She would always stand on the third bend, to watch her childhood idol John 'Tiger' Louis, who she's extremely chuffed to learn that Garry spoke with only a few hours earlier when he called about the weather. Her strongest and most abiding memories of her years watching the speedway at Foxhall are the smell ("cor yeah") as well as going home "absolutely filthy with all the shale in my hair". Garry is Norwich born and bred and has a lifelong fascination with motor sports "it doesn't matter whether it's bikes or cars". He's already been to the stadium many times, when he was a mechanic for Melly Cooke, twice world champion at National Hot Rods and Stock Rods. He remembers when Foxhall Heath didn't have the robust safety fence that now separates the fans from the speedway and stock car tracks. He believes that this strengthened fence has been there ever since a stray wheel killed a spectator. He's been keen to come for a while to watch the speedway at Foxhall, since he heard all about it from Jan and has seen it on the telly. His initial impression is that the speedway crowd is bigger (!) and "more civilised" than he expected, which he explains to mean that it's less boisterous, more well behaved and much "more family oriented" than he'd imagined. Since it has been a while since Jan attended any meeting, I take it up myself to try to explain events on the track from heat 10 onwards; but deliberately keep discussions of any of the many more complicated or arcane rules to a minimum, in order not to upset their new-found enthusiasm.

At the end of heat 10 Ipswich lead comfortably 36-24. This results in successive tactical rides for Pedersen in heat 11 and Sullivan in heat 12, which they both win. The highlight is Ryan Sullivan's win accompanied by a very determined ride for second place from Shaun Tacey, who finally marks his return to Foxhall by being fourth highest Poole scorer with four paid six points. Though I keep explanations to a minimum, Garry is still mystified how such a nonsensical rule – one that allows tactical riders to be used to score double points for the team that badly trails – can possibly exist if the sport is to have any credibility. Though now that the score has narrowed to 40-38 (a score which always reminds me of those famous speedway T-shirts that used to make the mysterious claim, for everyone who's never been to a speedway meeting, that 'Happiness is 40-38') Garry hopes, if those have to be the rules, that it will stir things up for a close finish. To his mind this evening's racing, so far, has tended to look much more processional when watched live than it does during the Sky Sports TV coverage that he's seen. An exciting exhibition of team riding by Louis and Stancl, in a drawn heat 14 that finally ensures victory for Ipswich, goes some way to restore Garry's enjoyment in live speedway as a spectacle. The final heat features another poor start by Chris Louis before he brilliantly cuts back and then uses all his skill and knowledge of the Foxhall track to remain in the lead. Garry enthuses that the final race was "worth the admission money on its own". I wouldn't disagree and neither do the Ipswich fans who wildly celebrate the 51-45 victory over the prospective Elite League champions elect in a manner that suggests that they'd just won the League and the Cup combined. The young woman in front of me cheers mentally for Louis while she dances round deliriously. The riders' victory parade around the circuit prompts more spontaneous outpourings of unrestrained joy among those fans that haven't rushed off to their cars for a swift getaway or to the pits area for further congratulation and celebrations with the riders.

The meeting has run very quickly and efficiently under the expert guidance and fast fingers of Frank Ebdon, while the forecast heavy rain has failed to materialise. The pits area has already emptied of practically all the disconsolate riders of the Poole team while their Ipswich counterparts bask in the praise and adulation of their fans. Yet more autographs are signed and photographs taken. I thank John Louis for his hospitality before I chat briefly to Shaun while he loads his van, just before he's delighted by the arrival of two old friends, whom he hasn't seen since his Ipswich years, who hug him excitedly.

A short wile later, as I cross the river Orwell on the A14, at the start of my drive back to Brighton, the dark night sky in the

near distance is lit up, almost as if it's daylight, by rapid flashes of forked lightning. The meeting has taken place without interruption, which is very fortunate since the promised torrential rainstorm is only a few short miles away. And what a storm it is! The ferocity of the deluge is such that I eventually have to pull over to allow the worst of it to pass, because the wipers can't cope and visibility has dropped to the length of my bonnet, even with the regular illumination of the flashes of lightning. The rain cloud itself is a huge beast and it lasts powerfully the entire distance of my drive down the A12 from Ipswich to the M25. The three or so hour drive home allows me to contemplate our mortality in the face of nature and emphasises to me once more the life of endless driving that a speedway rider endures throughout the season. They must continually cover huge distances, almost every night after they've raced at a meeting, only to have to rise early the next day in order to clean their bikes and prepare for their next engagement. During the season, even for the solely UK-based riders, this will involve many consecutive nights of travel all over the country. The traffic is the nightmare during the day that everyone experiences but, even in the dead of night, it's noticeable that there's always a high volume of traffic on the roads, especially lorries. Finally there's all those emergency road works and road maintenance gangs involved in vital work that only emerge after nightfall. It's definitely a trial for them and a hidden side of the regular life of a rider or a mechanic that I thought I knew about, but didn't really properly consider until I'd started my own regular journeys around Britain for this book. I eventually arrive home, after I've struggled to find a space in the parking nightmare that is central Brighton, for a refreshing cup of tea and I'm truly thankful that I don't have a bike to maintain and clean tonight, or any morning.

11th August Ipswich v. Poole (ELB) 51-45

Chapter 27: Speedway from an Eagles and Wolves Perspective

12th August Eastbourne v. Wolves

"I'm sure it will be seen as Nicki Pedersen getting a taste of his own medicine" Nigel Pearson "It was tough, it was hard, it was ruthless, that's GP speedway" Nigel Pearson (on a similar Jason Crump manoeuvre on Jarek Hampel)

7.6 Health & Safety
7.6.3 Stress the need for everyone to exercise a "Duty of Care"

They say that you often neglect those closest to you and so it's proved with all my travels round the country to visit every club, since I haven't caught Jon Cook the Eastbourne promoter on a race night at Arlington. However, I have caught up with him on a number of other occasions away from the track to try to get some insight into his views on the Eagles and on speedway in Britain.

Jon "began watching as a kid" at the age of 13 when he was taken to speedway by his dad. He fondly recalls going to Wimbledon ("the jewel in the crown"), along with Reading, Rye House and Cradley Heath, which he fondly recalls as "fantastic" and as a track located among the houses ("it wouldn't happen now"). Though he's now nearly 40, Jon remains as excited as ever at the prelude to any speedway meeting. He believes that the "build up is always as exciting as the first time you went or the previous time. It's a very intensive 15 minutes in two and a half hours; the fastest hours of the week, and the whole thing builds up during the evening. It's so different from other sports – there's the noise, the cranking up of

the bikes and the butterflies; the theatre of it all, plus it's very intensive in snippets. These feelings never lessen over time, so you don't ever think 'oh, here we go again'". If pushed, Jon feels that the only comparable sport is the dogs – "because it has a similar programme with bursts of action, though the difference is that between the races there's nothing to watch and just boredom, 'cause there's no cumulative build up".

Talk of the uniqueness of speedway sparks Jon's over-riding anxiety of a gradual decline in public interest, which he believes inevitably means, "there's unlikely to be 20 tracks existing in 10 years' time". The variety and number of speedway stadiums of his youth immediately remind him of the gradual death of the city-centre track within the sport, which he views as a result of "health and safety getting their claws in over noise, dust and danger" but also as indicative of part of a general trend away from the concept of community. "Speedway is treading a fine line and carries on okay until someone tries to stop it" and inevitably bring up concerns about noise, dust or spectator safety. The stadiums that he visited as a youth have become defunct or fallen into disrepair. The latest to go the way of all flesh is Wimbledon, "sadly they have to face the facts that the era of speedway in the area is over – like many places the area has changed completely and is no longer the white working-class place that it once was". There were high hopes among the Elite League promoters that Plough Lane could have become the neutral showpiece stadium for the whole sport, but sadly the reality is that the search for such a venue remains ongoing.

Jon supports the idea of my book and believes that it is a good one, especially if I can manage to capture something about the values of the people and country "through the eyes of sport – it's a good way to look at England through the perspective of speedway". For him speedway, like Englishness, is something to take pride in and to be protected; since both share the same values of uniqueness and, in some ways, both are bastions of a particular way of life under threat through the rapidly changing mores of a more disinterested and throwaway society. Jon is keen to stick up for speedway and he passionately believes that we should celebrate our "British values" and he worries that it's increasingly the case that there's "no respect left for the country and our history". He sincerely believes that we should strive to hang onto our values, local communities and traditions. Also that we should take pride in them rather than be apologetic, while we still endeavour to pass them on "down the generations" so that they too can grow up "safe, secure and happy".

Where Jon lives and where Jon works he views as a redoubt for an English way of life and an outlook on people and their communities that is under pressure within contemporary society by 'modernising' outside forces. His involvement in a speedway life is his way of escaping and protecting himself from these rapid changes elsewhere in society and the country ("I'm very fortunate to work in speedway to be able to escape from things in the country that really wind me up!"). He and his family have been part of the Shoreham Beach community for some time and consider themselves fortunate to be part of something that is comparatively cosseted from the dilution of the national values of our culture, as it happens throughout the rest of society. Locally he supports his local traders, schools and neighbours and he's concerned about the impact on the delicate local eco-system of his community that will be wreaked by the incoming people that the development of the nearby industrial units will attract. When he ventures around the local area in search of sponsorship for the Eagles he's shocked ("things have gone in such a short space of time") by the changes he notices in central Shoreham, Eastbourne and Brighton; which he already knew extremely well from when he ran a contract cleaning business, "I've seen all sides of it" from its glamour image to its seedy side.

Jon's strong desire to maintain and retain the vibrancy of his local community also finds clear expression in the make up and constituency of the Eastbourne Eagles club, which he characterises as unique, as having "an unorthodox look to our speedway", and a make up that "flies in the face of the average professional team". He views Eastbourne as the "team of the south-east" and as a club that is still strongly tied to and meaningful to the people within its local community. He believes that this is also aided and exemplified by the genuine and old-fashioned team spirit that's fostered by the predominantly English composition of the squad. Many modern Elite League teams consist of a heterogeneous group of riders who just fly in for the day of the meetings (and fly out again), but have little or no real connection to the place. Jon believes it's essential to have riders who are local born/based or are part of the community because they live and socialise there. Therefore, it's still possible for the fans and neighbours to get first-hand contact with the performers in everyday community life, particularly since the riders aren't closeted away in their huge houses with security fences. The heroes you admire at your local track are still part of "real life" and still part of your life. This is also carried on at the track before and after each event, since contact is still highly likely and easy to achieve every week. The Eagles 2005 squad has David Norris who is "really local whereas Dean isn't but appears to be". Though Deano lives in Lancing and is very much part of the area. Jon himself was born in Brighton and grew up in nearby Portslade; he believes that if "you can't have Brit riders then the next best thing are Aussies and New Zealanders" of which the Eagles have Adam Shields and Davey Watt. They both live with their partners in Poole ("which is unfortunate"), while Steen Jensen has a Scottish mother and has often shown himself to be "totally besotted with the Eastbourne scene when he goes down town, where's he's loud and proud to be an Eastbourne speedway rider". Nicki Pedersen is the only real superstar and foreigner with a demanding travel itinerary to match ("wherever he puts his head down during the season is his home for the night") but, nonetheless, he's just one of the lads when he's with the Eagles, mixes in well with the leg-pulling team spirit ("[British] humour runs through our pits") and has absolutely no airs and graces. Jon views Nicki as a special talent and a gentle person "whose earnings might be right up there with the top sports people, but the fans are still able to share a beer with him afterwards or to be in the same room because, like the sport, he's approachable and you don't need to be one of the chosen few to get access – like in football, for example". He believes the fact that both Trevor Geer and himself are ex-riders ("I made my debut at the old Berwick track with Eastbourne") helps with the understanding of the riders and that this in turn aids team spirit and bonhomie. However, even Eastbourne Speedway has slightly lost the camaraderie gained when they "used to tour together as a team" but, unfortunately, the changed nature of the presently smaller Elite League means that is no longer the case, since they only ever "go for the night and then return". Nonetheless, Eastbourne under Jon's management and promotion still strives to retain the visibility of the riders in the community, their understanding of the local area and the fans and thereby retain the "lovely feel" of the club and the sport of speedway.

Another benefit of a predominantly British or English domiciled team is that, as Nigel Wagstaff pointed out to me about the Eagles, it keeps costs down that otherwise might have to be spent on airfares, hotels and accommodation for foreign-based riders. These costs have to be borne by any club that chooses to look outside the UK for its riders, irrespective of whether they ride at reserve or are the team's best rider. Cost control is also an issue for a team like Eastbourne which finds itself out on a limb in East Sussex, unlike many other Elite League clubs, when it comes to nearby large-sized conurbations from

which it might attract regular or floating support.

Jon believes that while speedway is a minority sport in this country as a percentage of the total population and, for that matter, when judged against the size of its attendances; it, nonetheless, still engenders strong personal feelings among the fans and enables close links and connections with the performers. To maintain this it's Jon's idea to have an open pits policy before every meeting for the general public at Arlington, so the fans can meet the riders in their place of work on a regular basis; though sometimes the riders "don't like it" and this level of close interaction can have unintended consequences. Earlier in the season, one fan innocently and in an attempt at encouragement, said to David Norris "good to see that you actually got going [last week]" which was a well-intended point that nonetheless upset Floppy. However, on balance, Jon views it as "the beauty of the sport where fans have the contact and feel that they can share an opinion". He also highlights that the down-side of this accessibility, particularly because speedway is such a community-based sport, is that fans can have the opportunity to take against riders, often for the most minor, innocuous and "personal reasons". He believes that if the fans didn't have the expectation of being able to interact with the talent, then it's highly unlikely that they could ever fall out with a rider because they once ignored them or spoke to them rudely.

Not that Jon is a great fan of interaction when it concerns speedway forums on the Internet. "I don't tend to look at it, except very occasionally when things have gone well. I'm the promoter and the team manager, so why bother to read about it when I'm the one who has to do it, along with Trevor? Some of the people who give their opinions you wouldn't take seriously in person, so why bother when they're in writing?"

Technology has had a big impact on the visibility of the sport and nothing has had greater recent impact than television and the Sky Sports television contract. This season the BSPA had organised a seminar for the promoters about "how to properly present yourselves on the telly" which Jon felt was "strangely timed" given it's the sixth season of live coverage. However, laudable though the aim of this coaching was, Jon believes that a key reason the Sky programmes have worked in the past is precisely because speedway has "endeared itself to the viewing public by being off the cuff and often cringeable – the still 'untouched' and 'real' feeling appeals when so many other things are false or scripted". Jon tries to avoid appearing if possible, but realises that along with the print coverage in *The Argus* that "people do notice locally more and appreciate what my job is" as well as what the club does and he takes pleasure in their pride in that. He does wish that people would come along more consistently to watch the Eagles at Arlington; though he believes that their absence is more of a function of "their available free time rather than the importance of the meeting". The lack of attendances is a problem that the sport has in general, though the lack of new fans coming into the sport is the real concern. Jon affectionately mentions the "eclectic group of fans at Eastbourne speedway", which he thinks is the case with the diehard supporters round the country, though he also believes that "some of the newer tracks get a better cross section and representation of the general public". The sport desperately needs to find ways to "appeal to a new group of supporters who don't usually attend to improve your crowd". How this might happen is open to debate and no one has yet to find the magic solution. Anything that increases local awareness should be embraced and even rider selection can play a part. For example, he thinks that both Coventry and Wolves missed an opportunity when they failed to sign Antonio Lindback, who might have attracted more new fans within their catchment areas than in the more 'blue rinse' area of Poole. Though, in many respects, Jon believes that "speedway has an identity crisis – what is this Team GB nonsense? It's an English team – the Swedes and the Poles are proud of their country and identity and so should we".

When it comes to the regulation of the sport there are always lots of theories about what could be changed to make things better. These debates often create more heat than light though Jon thinks that it's self-evident that there should be an immediate change to ensure that "BSPA rules should ban promoters from betting as they can influence the result". Apart from that, decisions are taken collectively and should be lived with on that basis, even when these decisions don't necessarily benefit your team.

After all my discussions with Jon, I'm especially excited about the prospect of the next Elite League visit of Wolverhampton since it means that I'll finally get to speak with their team manager, Peter Adams. He's kindly taken the trouble to consider the questions I sent to him, after our failed initial attempt to talk before the fractious May Bank Holiday Monday between the two teams in Wolverhampton. Since then, the return Arlington fixture had been rearranged to the comparatively rare race night of a Friday.

Because I don't want to delay Peter's preparations for the evening I've turned up hugely early at the riders' entrance at the back of the pits area. It's the first time I've been here and I take full advantage of the opportunity to sit and watch all the activity. It's a strange place littered with the accumulated detritus of many meetings over many years, most noticeably a huge pile of discarded tyres stacked by the exterior fencing of the stadium. There's already quite a collection of white transit vans, which belong to the riders although there's a couple of other mysterious ones with trailers. You can't help but notice quite a sharp contrast in the age and quality of the cars parked among the trees; many have seen better times whereas some are the obvious gleaming symbols of wealth and power. The contrast is very marked and runs from the jalopy to the other extremes with smoked glass or personalised number plates.

It seems sensible to stand with Sid Shine who must ensure that the riders, mechanics and personnel for each team sign in before they enter the stadium. It's a legal requirement that everyone be properly insured for his or her evening in the Sussex countryside at Arlington. The atmosphere is completely different around this side of the stadium and it feels much more a works car park and, as with any place of work, the staff have a variety of outlooks and emotions to being there. Some are excited and pleased to be here, whereas others have the more careworn and tired attitude of people who resentfully endure another day at the office.

Sid travels down from London for each meeting, just like he has done for the last eight years. Like many throughout the country with a position of responsibility at speedway tracks, he is now retired and therefore has the time and inclination to contribute some dedicated effort to his passion. His involvement obviously means quite something to him and his overall demeanour radiates considerable enthusiasm. Sid also likes to compile statistics on the sport, a common vice, and has latterly compiled all the relevant stats for both the Pedersen and Shields websites.

With him at the gate is Martin Smith, whose son Desmond sponsors Eastbourne's Adam Shields. Martin explains that

there's a hierarchy of sponsorship ("there's sponsors and sponsors") from the minimal to the all-embracing. The riders usually welcome any level of support on offer. The ideal form is "proper sponsorship where the sponsor should really be there for the rider, to look after them if they need something" though the most common type of support tends to involve "the van, oil, tyres and kevlars". Martin knows from bitter personal experience that "it's not cheap", from when in the early 1980s he sponsored his own son's ambitions to succeed in the sport, "I used to keep him when he rode and I've never been so poor in my life as I was then!" When you stand season in and season out at the back gate you can often see the people involved in the sport as they really are – whether it's the riders, mechanics, sponsors, promoters, or team managers: "we see the lot really". All sorts of attitudes and behaviours can be found in the sport. It's a very rich tapestry of life and humanity, much too complex to describe even if they were prepared to break someone's confidence (which they're not). Martin taps his nose meaningfully before he notes, "suffice to say there's arseholes in every sport and every walk of life, there's just less of them in speedway!"

Before we can carry on this conversation any further Jon Cook arrives at the gate from inside the stadium to say that Peter Adams has already arrived. He's come in another gate and so has eluded me while I waited for him. I walk with Jon who mentions "I want Belle Vue in the play-offs" before I get to join Peter in the pits. We adjourn to the wooden benches near to the hut that houses the bar and the nearby snack bar. The tables are just outside the pits gate and there's already a crowd of people picnicking at the many tables or eating the excellent baked potatoes from the snack bar. People affect not to recognise Peter Adams or if they do, at least, leave him in peace to enjoy a snatched cup of coffee and a few well-deserved cigarettes.

Peter answers thoughtfully and deliberately throughout our conversation in his strong Midlands accent (I hesitate to try to guess exactly from where as there are so many subtle distinctions locally). He's a very calm, unflustered man with a quick, analytical mind. Peter's earliest memory of speedway is from 1962 or 1963. After he heard about the thrill of the sport at school, he'd continually badgered his father to go until he finally relented, "we arrived too late for the meeting, I can remember exactly where we stood on the fourth bend to watch the second-half handicap races. My abiding memory is that they played Frank Ifield's 'I Remember You' from the charts non-stop!" Like many people he was attracted to the "noise and spectacle of it all, I couldn't believe how fast they went". He believes once it's got into your blood, you always go. His earliest hero as a rider was Peter 'Speedy Pete' Jarman at Wolves. Peter wistfully recalls that he was "fantastic to watch", inevitably slow out of the starts but he always eventually caught and passed them all. Peter believes that speedway's appeal is not only that it's a safe environment, but also that you can witness the entire spectacle of the race and not just the merest glimpse of it as you might in many other motor sports. He also believes that another important factor is that "the winner of each race is concealed at the outset" and is inherently unpredictable.

Away from the sport Peter is a successful businessman and has already satisfied his desire for material success. However his involvement in speedway gives him "an outlet" he couldn't find in business or in any other walk of life, particularly since he relishes the chance to "be competitive, think analytically and regularly pit my wits against those of my peers". Of course, there are areas where he feels that the sport could improve; most notably, the need for a "better hierarchy, as presently management from the top overrides everyone else". However, the most urgent need is for a regulatory mechanism to "maintain a team's parity [with others] when they fall into misfortune". He believes the fact that the present system doesn't discourage disparities in strengths between individual teams, brought about by events beyond the control of the team managers – most often through happenstance or foul riding – and should be rectified, particularly since it often diminishes the sport in Peter's eyes. It's a theme he returns to repeatedly during our conversation with numerous examples. He cites the recent heat 3 clash during Peterborough versus Wolves, where Jensen "wipes out Howe" and is excluded from the race. However, Howe is injured as a result of Jensen's actions and Wolves are thereby disadvantaged, since they don't have dispensation under the present rules to track adequate replacements to substitute for him during the rest of that fixture or, indeed, at subsequent meetings. The unfairness of the situation is compounded by the fact that Jensen can then continue to ride in his next races in the fixture, without further penalty when really "he should have been removed from the meeting for parity to be maintained and for it to be equitable".

Like all people of his generation, Peter prefers the one-off World Final, although he can see the value of the present cumulative system because it's "better able to reveal the true champion". The best rider he ever saw ride was Ole Olsen whereas the contemporary rider he most admires and enjoys watching is Tony Rickardsson. "I like seeing master craftsmen at work; it's not just skill, it's the combination of ability and machine as you can put a poor rider on a rocket and he'll still finish last". Peter admires skilled practitioners wherever he finds them, and speaks highly of Bob Dugard at Eastbourne also as a "craftsman" who always prepares a consistent and race-worthy track. If Eastbourne is his favourite track to visit, then Peterborough is the least because it's a "soulless place lacking in atmosphere".

If Peter could wave a magic wand, he'd try to address the chronic and critical issue of declining attendances. Rather than retrace our steps or demand more action from the promoters themselves ("the existing promoters have already spent enormous sums and, after all, where should it be advertised?"), Peter feels that the power of personal recommendation through a sustained campaign of "word of mouth" should be zealously exploited by all the sport's fans. "Ninety percent of anyone who watches speedway was brought by someone else, those who profess to love speedway should try to attract new people to watch by bringing them to watch". Unlike rugby and soccer, which recently started to exclude fans by over-charging their traditional working-class support and thereby have drifted off from their original roots and constituency, Speedway has retained its cloth-cap supporter image. It's still a welcome environment for its traditional fans; which is something to be proud of, fought for and preserved. It's a safe environment for spectators and it's also become safer for the riders with the advent of the air fences ("which makes the racing more exciting as the riders take more chances"). After he has identified some ways in which the product and attendances could be boosted, Peter admits that his own personal motivation within the sport remains to win more meetings for his club Wolverhampton. His interest in the sport from a purely results perspective means that he rarely attends a meeting where he isn't involved to a large degree ("how many ex-footballers go to watch from the stand if they're not still employed by the club?"). Peter's many years within the sport have left him with a wealth of stories, mostly repeatable, which he is often pressured to transform into a book, but he will hold off from committing pen to paper for a few more years yet as "there are a few more chapters yet to unfold!" After graciously spending some considerable time with me, Peter travels the short distance back to the pits to supervise the last-minute preparations for yet another test of his wits and ingenuity. It's been very enlightening for me to listen to one of the sport's most articulate proponents range widely across so many aspects of the sport that he's, very obviously, considered deeply

and thoughtfully.

Back on the terraces the chatter is mostly about the impressions that the Eastbourne management have created among this section of the supporters. Not many people really know anything much about Terry Russell, owner of the promotional rights at Eastbourne, along with Swindon, and has a brother that owns another rival Elite League club, Arena Essex. Between them, the Russell brothers own 30 percent of the highest-level speedway league in the UK. As a reflection of this state of affairs, but much more likely his acumen as a businessman away from the track, everyone has noted that they don't always notice his car in the car park for every fixture, but that he is definitely around on the rare nights when the television cameras are in attendance for their live coverage from Arlington. In the popular speedway imagination he's forever linked with Sky Sports, since he was instrumental in the negotiation and agreement of the Sky Sports deal with speedway. Speculation about his personal financial benefit that resulted have become the stuff of folklore with completely unsubstantiated figures bandied round authoritatively ("a man who's in the know told me ...") that range from a king's ransom to the totally stratospheric. That's business or rather his business and no one else's, though it's only human nature to guess and gossip. Much more factually based is the question whether "Jon Cook is the Alex Ferguson of speedway – as he's a much better manager than he was a rider?" It's a claim given some weight and credence since Jon is seen as "lanky and dangerous as a rider but completely something else as a manager, arguably one of the best that there is!" Comparisons, though, are often invidious; but there's no doubt that his experiences as a rider contribute to his skill and respect as a manager.

His programme notes for tonight's match covers the usual rich mix of topics that include promotional activities, bereavements and the renowned annual club dinner-dance. There's absolutely no mention of Steen Jensen in the notes, although he is riding tonight. Most in the crowd around me, expect him to ride to another faultless three-ride maximum, albeit of the wrong non-scoring kind, based on his previous performances and his subsequent lack of confidence. Also, on the track, Wolves will present extremely tricky opposition as they haven't lost at Arlington for two seasons and Eastbourne appear to have run over a black cat when it comes to the injuries that have recently beset their riders David Norris, Adam Shields and Trevor Harding.

It's quite a record around Arlington and one that inspires some pessimism among the home fans. This continues after Peter Karlsson flies from the starting gate tremendously fast in heat 1. He does so quickly that our ever-wily campaigner Deano is left looking completely silly when he attempts to tactically elbow Karlsson aside as he comes into the vital first turn, only to find himself waggling his own arm into thin air. Luckily Jon Cook has selected two superb guests to ride for Eastbourne, Mark Loram (of whom Cookie notes later, "he never lets me down and always does all that I ask of him when he rides for us") and the very in-form Chris Harris who demonstrated considerable sympathy for the circuit as a visitor the last time Coventry were here. Strangely, the key rider in the early stages isn't a guest, but Deano. After he wrestled with thin air in his first ride, Deano won heat 3 after the visiting Steve 'Johnno' Johnson had done all the hard work before he disastrously locked up when in the lead to throw away all his hard work. Out again to ride in heat 5 as well, Deano submitted a superb and quixotic entry for the most *Bizarre Incident of the Season* award on the very first bend of the race. After he roars from the gate, Deano decides to indulge in a bit of solo wrestling with his machine which bucks and rears like a demented bronco at a rodeo. Deano struggles manfully to control the energetic beast of his bike, even after the other riders have long since departed. Initially astride the bike he soon finds himself standing off the back of the machine before he eventually grapples it to the ground in the style of a circus ringmaster flinging a lion to the sawdust. He then stands looking at the fallen bike in bemused fashion as the race continues, though he wrestled with his machine for so long on the bend that the referee nearly had to call a halt to the race to avoid the riders as they came round on the next lap.

Heat 6 sees another incident, this time at high speed and without any humour, when Lindgren falls heavily on the last lap. How, after such a heavy fall, Lindgren hasn't sustained a broken collarbone or any other injuries is a complete mystery; Watt narrowly manages to avoid him through sheer skill and quick reactions. The bike travels a considerable distance without its rider, which complicates the situation for Watt, making his control all the more impressive.

By the interval, Steen has raced to a three-race zero while Deano has stopped wrestling his bike long enough to scorch to a hard-ridden two points in his next race. The interval allows resident master of ceremonies, Kevin 'KC' Coombes, to conduct a master class in track maintenance for the waiting fans. Not everyone appreciates that while the racing surface, prepared by Bob Dugard and Roy Prodger, is justifiably renowned for the quality of its surface and preparation, it's also completely removed after every speedway meeting for the stock-car racing with which it shares the circuit! The continual laying and lifting of the whole track surface gives Bob and Roy considerable practice at their art, but is also a logistical headache throughout the summer. The preparation for last Monday's meeting against Ipswich, according to KC took 12 hours. They worked on Friday, Sunday and another 8 hours before the meeting and didn't stop until 1 a.m. on Monday. It's a huge effort, completely unseen, and only really noticed and appreciated by the fans due to KC's intervention.

The resumption of the racing sees Johnno and Deano, despite or maybe because of their friendship off the track, in an intensely aggressive race against each other in heat 12. After they ride extremely close to each other, Deano eschews any bike wrestling but fails to catch a determined Johnno. Ironically, given Peter Adams's claim to enjoy the tactical cut and thrust of team management, heat 14 provides the sort of fiasco that can delight or frustrate you about the laws of speedway depending on your point of view. Peter Karlsson was nominated for a tactical ride 15 metres back from the tapes. Any points he gains in the race will then count double. Following some skilful riding he eventually finishes second but is subsequently, after some delay, disqualified for wearing a yellow helmet, whereas the correct helmet colour is black and white for a tactical substitution ride. There was considerable delay before this adjudication was announced that leads many to assume that Peter Adams put his thoughts on the matter strongly to the referee. Fired up and after receiving insightful tactical advice from their manager, Karlsson and Lindgren rode to the 2-4 race win needed to tie the meeting and force a run-off for the bonus point. This then saw a head-to-head encounter between Karlsson and Loram that went to the Wolves rider after the race ended in some controversy. Loram fell when close to Karlsson on the second lap and was adjudged by referee Barry Richardson to be the prime cause of the stoppage and therefore excluded. This handed the overall victory to the visitors. Peter Adams had pitted his wits against his opponents (and the helmet colour rules!) and emerged victorious.

12th August Eastbourne v. Wolves (ELB) 49-41

Showered in Shale

SKY CHATTER

"We've had it all – close racing, controversy and even some crowd abuse. When you get a bit of argy bargy it tends to galvanise the away team, developing a bit of a siege mentality" Gary Havelock

RANDOM SCB RULES

3.1.3 Competitors and licenced Officials renounce their right to all legal proceedings before a civil court until such time as the procedures outlined in these regulations are exhausted.

The wonderful city of Newcastle upon Tyne is a great place to visit and spend some time, particularly if you're keen on going out to enjoy yourself socially on an evening. They take a zealous approach to relaxation and there's an enviable choice of places to go. This is especially so in the centre of the city and the regenerated quayside area by the river Tyne, where the recent years of social and cultural renaissance are most spectacularly visible. On the Sunday early afternoon that I visit, the centre is strangely deserted and there is a subdued atmosphere about the place. This isn't caused by the heavily overcast skies but due to the city's main passion, focus and, almost, its religion because its beloved football club starts another campaign of Premiership football with a televised lunchtime encounter with Arsenal. Expectations are at their usual exaggerated Olympian levels based on faith and belief rather than the actual record of results in terms of trophies and championships of the last five decades. Pretty well everyone who doesn't have a ticket for the match chooses to watch on TV in one of the many bars or at home. On any normal day the cultural, commercial and social vibrancy of this city would immediately stand out to any visitor.

The home of the Newcastle Diamonds Speedway Club at Brough Park is located over two miles away from downtown in one of the area's most famous locales, known as Byker. What an appropriate name for the part of the city in which to run speedway events! Since I am a regular visitor to this part of the country, I make a point to take full advantage of the excellent metro transport system, a sort of under- and overground train-cum-tram, that stretches in all directions throughout the area and as far away as the airport or Sunderland, the other nearby city that is sadly forlorn and neglected in comparison to Newcastle. In the course of the train journey to Byker station it bursts out from its underground tunnel into daylight to bestow a wonderful elevated view across the buildings at the core of the city, one that almost competes with the spectacular vista when the metro crosses the bridge over the Tyne. Once on foot, the walk to Brough Park takes you past the swimming pool, some newish blocks of flats built in the current brutalist style of fashionable hotels or offices, before you discover the more traditional terraced houses of Grace Street which then lead to the stadium's impressive perimeter fencing.

On an overcast and cloudy afternoon, I arrive at the stadium to meet with George English, the cheery co-promoter of Newcastle Diamonds Speedway. A small group of volunteer staff have already arrived but they find themselves locked outside the fortified fencing, since they're unable to gain access through the padlocked main entrance. The locked gates are the responsibility of the landlords, William Hill, and these dedicated volunteers all have to wait patiently to get on with the tasks that George so values their help with every week. I leave them to wait for William Hill to fulfil their responsibilities and double back on myself to enter Brough Park through the open pits gate entrance. The car park just inside the gate entrance is already crowded with riders and their, mostly white, vans. The Somerset Rebels team, this evening's opponents for the Newcastle Diamonds have arrived early since they're already in this part of the world. Tonight is the third leg of their 'Northern Tour'; a trip on which they have already suffered defeats on successive nights at Edinburgh and Berwick. Just inside the gate Peter Toogood, the promoter of Somerset and Chairman of the BSPA, pulls out his briefcase from the boot of his car, unfastens it and then puts his tie on to add the final touch to his smart attire of collared shirt and trousers. According to his stepdaughter and co-promoter Jo Lawson, it's a compulsory SCB regulation for officials to look smart and present themselves well on race day. Later she leaves to go to change out of her own casual travel clothes. Peter looks slightly distracted when I greet him but he hopes for a closer meeting than the previous evening at Berwick, especially since Somerset have a good chance of gaining the bonus point due to the 24-point advantage they obtained through a 58-34 home triumph against the Diamonds in June. I pass an armada of riders' vans that includes Paul Fry's transit, whose side door is open to reveal his wife in a deep sleep on the specially customised bed, while their children play contentedly in the front seat. As I head off to meet George English in his office I stroll through the pits area, which looks out across the track itself and the stadium grandstand, which is filled with riders and mechanics who busily prepare the bikes for tonight's racing.

The track itself, located inside the tarpaulin-covered greyhound track, undergoes some last-minute preparations supervised by the club's experienced track manager, Robbie Best. These attentions mostly involve watering of the surface using the aged fire engine that serves as the bowser at Newcastle. Robbie has the weekly problem to attempt to prepare an ideal racing surface. He works within some very restrictive conditions that necessarily result from the speedway club's status as the mere one-day-a-week tenant of William Hill, the company who own and run this greyhound stadium. Though Robbie has the dispensation to spend the odd hour here and there during the week, he basically only has access to the track on the day of the actual meeting. Therefore, every Sunday during the season he arrives at first light to do everything he can to ensure the track is the best that it can be before the traditional start time of 5.30 p.m. George later pays tribute to his skills, "he's so dedicated and spends an awful lot of time here" and praises the work of the regular track staff volunteers. Often this work is of a remedial nature, since the intensive use and maintenance of the dog track on the other six days of the week regularly results in damage to the speedway track surface; particularly troublesome is the sand leeched by the water drainage trenches from the dog track onto the shale race surface. These tribulations and the severe time constraints they all work under are part and parcel of the difficulties the Diamonds speedway staff face on a weekly basis.

George already waits for me in the Speedway Office, which is housed in a slightly dilapidated building that also has the home and away riders' changing rooms in it, and a small kitchen area where somebody's grandmother cheerily washes the dishes and prepares the tea. George welcomes me into his office, surely one of the few speedway offices in the country with a comfy sofa, and we quickly start to discuss his life in speedway and some of the history of the club. He first visited the speedway at the age of four, brought by his mother Joan and father George who'd been "fanatical all his life" about speedway since he first began to go in the 1940s. Joan English is the very sprightly lady you usually see at all of the Diamonds away meetings thoroughly absorbed in the racing, who often urges the Newcastle riders on in her broad Geordie accent while she displays levels of energy that would be enviable in a considerably younger person. At Brough Park Joan has many tasks and responsibilities on race night ("I'm general dogsbody"), often in the office or at the turnstiles, so she has to take her racing pleasures where she can, "I love going away, it's when I get to see all me races, as I don't get to see a whole match here anymore, just the odd race". Speedway prides itself as a sport with a family emphasis, which is something that appeals to Joan who enjoys the "family orientation and involvement" among the spectators, staff and riders. I first encountered Joan accidentally at a Newcastle away meeting in Workington and, once you've noticed her, she cuts a very distinctive figure at the tracks she visits and is always notable for her energy, commitment and keen support of the Diamonds. This close-knit social emphasis you get at speedway is illustrated by today's contest between the Diamonds and the Rebels, which matches mother and son of Joan/George English for Newcastle versus the father and stepdaughter combination of Peter/Jo for Somerset.

The day-to-day experience of speedway promotion at Newcastle has, however, over the last few years been quite a struggle financially and throughout its existence the club has had a chequered history that has involved intermittent closures. George notes, "I've been here all my life, it's in my blood" but as a track it's "an outpost or feels like an outpost", both geographically and in the sports imagination of the city itself. George became a promoter when Newcastle joined the newly formed Premier League in 1997 and it won't be long before he overtakes Ian Thomas (1975-84) as the longest serving boss in the club's history. Every promoter at the club has made a virtue of Newcastle's limited finances, the club has had to discover and develop young riders, so consequently is renowned for its rich tradition and a selection policy that uses mostly unproven "foreign riders" before they, hopefully, develop into successful exponents of the sport. Each era has attracted different nationalities to Newcastle, in "the 1960s it was the Aussies and lately it's been the Danes". The list of famous riders who've successfully worn the distinctive black-and-white team race bibs is a roll call of speedway's great and good. It includes: Ivan Mauger ("my favourite and idol; from the age of four I was lucky to watch him go all the way through the sport to winning six World Championships"), Ole Olsen, Anders Michanek ("not my favourite as he hardly ever turned up"), the Owen brothers (Tom and Joe) as well as more recently the Pedersens (the unrelated Bjarne and Nicki) plus the diminutive Kenneth Bjerre. Though these riders and the teams they rode in have provided lustre to the great history of the club, George nowadays describes himself as "very much a Premier League person, full stop" and it's at this level they have enjoyed some recent notable success. The last triumph for the club was when they won the Premier League Championship in 2001 followed up with, George is keen to assert, a repeat "moral victory" in 2002 where they won more meetings than the eventual champions Sheffield (who apparently won with their significant "home-track advantage"). George stresses, "while we lost out on race points difference, I look on ourselves as the rightful winners".

It's a truism, but correct nonetheless, that supporters in all sports are much more attracted to success than failure, so it's hardly a surprise that crowds at Brough Park fell dramatically the previous year when the team endured a shocker of a season and found themselves rooted last in the league. While this season the league position is slightly healthier and performances are much improved, the low crowd numbers still reflect the recent legacy of last season's poor results. George is characteristically phlegmatic if not quite able to solely blame the Diamonds' own performances, "our crowds aren't good this season but then we're also being squeezed on the one side by the Elite League and TV coverage and on the other by some not true Conference level sides". Newcastle ran a team for three years at a Conference level to develop young talent and refused to use experienced riders ("old hands") because it went against the ethos and true spirit behind the inauguration of the league, never mind the cost implications of having to pay too much.

The Diamonds also remain saddled with a very high rent for the use of the stadium and its facilities. Especially as it now uses only a small proportion of the terraces compared to when it attracted 10,000 spectators to a fixture and now the situation is further exacerbated because they cannot even generate any additional revenues through the sales of refreshments and at the bars, since the landlords William Hill own these facilities. To compound this difficult situation, in the local area it's also "an unbelievably difficult job to bring in sponsorship", particularly when compared to local rivals Berwick[1] or tracks like visitors Somerset where "sponsorship levels are excellent". It is difficult to attract major financial support in Newcastle, which George notes, "is down to the place itself, as it's a major struggle to keep the sport going

---

[1] Though, in contrast to this opinion, parsimonious Berwick promoter Peter Waite claims it's impossible to attract high levels of sponsorship never mind to avoid running the Berwick club at anything other than a loss.

in the city, if your names not Newcastle United Football Club" where George himself, for his sins, is a season ticket holder! The speedway club attempt to compensate for this dearth of sponsors and interest by running lots of local promotions in an attempt to try to attract more people to visit the track with discounted tickets, school visits and, even that day, they'd been leafleting at an important motorcycle rally in Durham. These activities are not a magic solution, since the situation with school visits is extremely competitive and the speedway club finds itself disadvantaged in comparison to the school visits arranged by other local sports teams. The basketballers, for example, can easily put on a full display of their skills in a restricted space whereas the Diamonds can't even play their trump card – for understandable health, safety and noise reasons – because they daren't start up their demonstration bike at the school.

More resilient than downcast, George has high hopes for the next season when it's rumoured that speedway might restart at nearby Middlesbrough. This would provide a much-needed fillip to the interest of the fans as the club could, once again, race in local derby fixtures. It's an attraction and rivalry that doesn't exist with Berwick, presently the speedway club closest to them, which "technically isn't classed as a local derby". No matter whom the Diamonds are racing against, the "social element of the sport is fantastic" and George is fulsome in his praise of the "ability, skill and bravery of the riders". It's an admiration that's always there for George despite his caveat, gained through many years' work with riders in his official capacity as co-promoter, "even if you're dealing with them on a day-to-day basis". However, he does not doubt "their dedication", particularly as many of the riders are employed in full-time jobs away from their racing at the track. Throughout the country and particularly outside the Elite League, many riders are really only semi-professional participants in speedway, who all have to find the time and money to purchase and maintain their equipment. It's a lifestyle that contrasts markedly to those riders fortunate or skilled enough to ride full-time professionally and remains in sharp contrast to, and some wayward Newcastle players immediately spring to my mind here, "other pampered sports stars". I'm grateful to George for his time, consideration and courtesy on another busy evening for him at Brough Park. I've just thanked him, when Somerset promoter Peter Toogood arrives in the office for a pre-meeting chat, but then apologises for his interruption, "oh, sorry, you're doing your thing, going down in history".

I leave the office and retreat briefly to the Somerset side of the pits where Jo Lawson, the Somerset co-promoter, chats with Sean Stoddart the 18-year-old Armadale rider, who clutches a Tesco's carrier bag. He's been drafted in for this fixture to help with the Somerset injury crisis that's already eliminated Chris Mills and Trevor Harding from reserve. Sean has been recommended as an exciting prospect to team manager Mick Bell by the referee who officiated at their Saturday night meeting at Berwick, when their ongoing injury jinx this time struck their replacement reserve Benji Compton. Sean is keen and hopes to impress as well as not succumb to the Somerset injury curse. He's very personable but dedicated to his long-term goal to try to "reach the top in speedway". Sean comes from Edinburgh, relishes the chance to ride for his local club at Armadale and is very definite that he's "always wanted to do this". He claims another stage in his long-term aim to pursue a successful career in the sport starts tonight, when he hopes to ride well and score points for Somerset in this Premier League meeting ("my ambition for tonight"). Sean has ridden for six years, although his advancement has been slightly hampered by the closure of Linlithgow after he had two seasons there, and the general "lack of tracks up north", though he practises wherever practicable and even goes for occasional spins on the beach at Portobello. He wouldn't have got to where he already is in speedway without "my dad and my mechanic", nonetheless, he remains a keen student of the sport and tries, wherever possible, to apply what he observes in the other riders around him in the pits and at meetings around the country. The riders that have most influenced him and fired his enthusiasm for the sport have been Hans Nielsen, Les Collins and, most recently, Rory Schlein. Just the experience to ride alongside Rory is education enough and, allied with Rory's real desire to educate and mentor Sean, it's all been really useful. "I think he's brilliant, a really nice guy and very helpful which says something about him, I think", declares Sean as he goes off to continue his education in the form of some last-minute instruction and individual advice from the experienced Somerset team manager, Mick Bell.

As a former rider, Mick knows the outlook and approach of riders, which helps him to motivate his own team as well as being able to pass on the many tricks and tactics of the trade. He appears a jovial presence in the pits and, when I pass a

few minutes after he's offered some encouragement to Sean, he strolls round to speak to each Somerset rider in turn. His favourite initial question to them appears to be, "you been here before?"

The home grandstand and terraces begin to fill out nicely with quite a crowd of people, in eager anticipation of the fixture due to start in 45 minutes' time. There's also a gaggle of interested fans that crowd the white picket fence for a close look at the increased activity levels in the pits area. On the steps of the covered section of the terraces, in front of the steps that lead to the bar area, someone has hung a highly visible large Somerset flag. The marker pen text on the Rebels flag proclaims the undying allegiance of the flag's owners to the team and helpfully lists a few of the individuals who transported this flag to Newcastle. The Somerset fans have been on a road trip with the team and have suffered defeats at Edinburgh and Berwick, so far, but their enthusiasm remains undimmed. There are around 25 of them on the trip, who either stay on the caravan sites they booked in February or, if they're really lucky, at the same hotel that the team uses for the tour. Consequently there's great camaraderie among the contingent of riders, mechanics, co-promoters and fans as well as ample opportunity for them all to let their hair down together after the night's racing. Each night everyone has congregated in the pub by the *Holiday Express* in Berwick where the riders and some fans were billeted throughout the tour. In fact the Somerset riders, along with riders everywhere, are a sociable lot who are more than happy to spend some time to chat with their fans, even those riders who travel with their wives and children though these, perhaps, haven't had the same levels of resilience or availability when it comes to staying up to carouse the night away. The flag itself has travelled well and has held pride of place on the front of one of their caravans as they travel across the country. The sight of the flag has attracted considerable interest from other motorists on the road, who try to read it when it passes them ("it's getting the bus lots of looks"), and it has been a frequent talking point in the car parks and laybys that are an inevitable part of the numerous comfort breaks that long-distance journeys inevitably require. The flag continues to work its magic as it has now drawn my attention to the group of Rebels fans that loosely cluster around it.

There's quite a friendly, mixed group of people that includes 'Tim the Hat' – a large, very affable and knowledgeable man who wears the sort of magnificent hat that wouldn't look inappropriate on Screaming Lord Sutch. Away from the speedway he's a bookmaker and claims to be one of the (few) "honest ones", he says this so sincerely that you can't help but believe him. With him by the flag, rather territorially, are his friends from Taunton, notably 'Speedway Dave' – who jokes that he travels to "get away from the missus, but don't put that in or I'll be in trouble" – and the unmarried 'Jonny Sometimes' who, as the only member of the Caravan and Camping Club in the group, researched and booked the caravan sites in February when the 'Northern Tour' away fixtures were initially announced. The consensus is that they've "had a great time" and have only been too pleased to literally and metaphorically fly the flag for the club. They've had their photo taken in the pits with the riders (and the flag) "to show the boys we support them" and they hope this photograph will shortly appear in all its glory in a home match programme just to "show other people that there's fun to be had". Jo Lawson, the co-promoter, adds "we've had a good crowd with us on tour including a few Swindon ones, as they don't have a Northern Tour anymore". Despite the defeats, it's been an eventful and memorable trip with plenty of incidents and talking points to debate. The Edinburgh meeting featured ten fallers that included Paul Fry's spectacular doughnut fall in heat 7, executed with such aplomb that he still had the time to signal a congratulatory thumbs up to Ritchie Hawkins, who laid his bike down so promptly behind him. The young, rising Premier League potential star of the future Ritchie has one special fan on this trip, Margaret Hallett, who hails from near Andover but "always went to Swindon". She says simply, "Ritchie knows me as Supergran". She's absolutely besotted with him "he's my boy, my best friend" and has followed his career from the outset "since he was 15". He's patiently but skilfully worked his way up through the ranks after he started to ride competitively in the Conference League, so far with Mildenhall, Swindon, Berwick and now Somerset serves as the latest step on the route of his personal speedway apprenticeship.

The Somerset fans are a pleasantly mixed group of ages and gender which includes Di, who runs Magnus 'Zorro' Zetterstrom's Testimonial Stall and the 50/50 draw back at the track in Somerset, and Elaine who's been coming to speedway for 45 years. Di has really enjoyed the tour, "we've had a wonderful time and have laughed from the moment that we got in the car", plus there's been some enjoyable quality time spent with Zorro. He's "such a gentleman" although this is a view not held by the Berwick fans following "a coming together" with Tom P. Madsen last night. Everyone only has positive words about Zorro as a person, a rider and for what he's brought to the club this season. Di is positively evangelical on Zorro's behalf, since she views him as a "real team man" and, most significantly, as "one of speedway's nice guys". Events on track later in the evening would have most Newcastle fans question that analysis, but Di genuinely speaks as she finds based on considerable experience of the man on and off the track. 'Speedway Dave' interrupts loudly and mischievously to accuse Di of being overly obsessed with Zorro "every time he wins, you have an orgasm"; she smiles good-humouredly and replies with equanimity, " I'm just going to have to take him home with me".[2]

Di started going to speedway in 1960 when her "first boyfriend" was mechanic for Poole's captain Geoff Mudge. The relationship fizzled out but her love of the sport endures undimmed, which she puts rather elegantly, "the boyfriend lasted three months and the speedway 45 years so far". She has personally witnessed many changes to the sport she loves in the many intervening years from the heady time of her first love. The men in her own life may have come and gone, but the men racing on the track have been an abiding passion and always thrilling for Di. There have been considerable changes in the ranks of the riders and a huge shift in their approach and attitudes to the sport during this time. Contemporary speedway is "very much more professional"; the most notable change is that "gone are the days when they just threw their gear into the back of the truck and left it there until the next week". The riders themselves have always been good with the fans but, hand in hand with the decline in popularity of the sport, "you can now get closer to the riders than you could years ago". There's still a lack of "prima donnas" and, almost to a man throughout the sport, they're all great with the fans, "especially the Somerset riders". But amid all the praise, frivolity and bonhomie of the tour, it's also a trip heavily tinged with sadness – for Jo, Supergran and others – due to the premature death from cancer earlier in the week of Barbara, a dear speedway friend of the travelling Wiltshire contingent. The previous week at Somerset, Jo Lawson had spoken to me extremely glowingly about her friend and the sad news of her recent rapid decline in health. It was only a few days later that Barbara sadly passed away as a result of her illness, but only after a long and tenacious fight. The shock of her loss was still very raw to them all but it was clear that although she was gone from this earth, those who'd travelled away this weekend from Somerset on a tour of the northern speedway clubs did not forget her, let alone undervalue the good times

---

[2] I must stress that Di is not a Zorro groupie at all. In fact afterwards, Di is very keen that I clarify that she is "just someone who likes to get involved with speedway and help the riders by, for example, doing match reports for Zorro's website among many other things". I am very happy to make/agree with this clarification.

they had enjoyed with her. They'd stood on the terraces with Barbara so often in the past; her absence in the future was going to be a continual reminder of her, just as it already was on this evening.

Since I'm at Brough Park to experience all things Newcastle Speedway, I soon leave the Somerset contingent to their own devices in order to sample the true flavour of the local fans that follow the Diamonds. I decide not to watch from behind glass in the tiered main grandstand and instead decide to view the meeting from near the back of the standing terraces surrounded by the many fans of the Diamonds.[3] The crowd around me features a general mix of ages with a noticeably high number of young women in addition to the usual preponderance of older males. I finally choose to stand by the steps that lead up to the bar, sandwiched between a middle-aged couple in front of me and another small group of 'typical' fans on the step behind me. There's the pensioner of the group, snappily dressed in a blue zip Regatta sweatshirt over his matching but unbuttoned collared shirt. Next to him is a tanned man who wears sunglasses throughout the meeting, despite a conspicuous lack of sunshine at the outset of the evening, which starts in some warmth under dull, overcast skies, and a smattering of darker rain clouds. Beside him is a blonde-haired young woman, dressed in pink sweatpants and Nike trainers, with a pink swoosh, offset by her NUFC replica shirt underneath her black sweatshirt and with an anorak tied around her waist. She's in her mid to late teens and I assume she is the daughter of the man in glasses and the granddaughter of the pensioner. Throughout the meeting they're all extremely vocal and keenly absorbed in the changing dynamics of each race, and their comments leave you in absolutely no doubt that they passionately want the Newcastle riders and team to prevail at all costs.

The Diamonds team has seen lots of recent changes in personnel. Following the acrimonious departure of Richard Juul from the side the week before, he's been replaced in the team not, as stated in the match programme, by Danish rider Henning Loof (who sounds like he's ready for use in a bathroom) but by Kristian Lund. His appointment captures the innate complexity of the rules and regulations that beset your average speedway team. It's a level of complexity that usually quickly defeats, forever, the attention span of even the most-determined novice spectator. In this case Kristian is a "Newcastle asset", which means that the Diamonds own his registration contract in the sport but, for the 2005 season, he'd already been loaned to Newport. The Wasps, according to the helpful explanation provided on the tannoy by announcer and co-promoter Barry Wallace, have kindly granted Newcastle permission to use their own rider as Juul's replacement for the rest of the season, since Newport no longer required Kristian's services. Even in a soothing Geordie accent, the minutiae of these rules remain shrouded in some confusion and mystery but this doesn't bother the young lady behind me. She enthusiastically screams her encouragement throughout each race to the home riders, but is particularly vocal with her shouts of "go on Kristian, go on, go on, Kristian". Her participation starts vociferously from heat 1 onwards. Not that you could miss Kristian when mounted on a speedway bike, as he appears a much 'bigger lad' than many others especially in comparison to the usual "70 to 80 kilos when wet" diminutive and jockeyesque stature of many speedway riders. I'm surprised he can't hear her shrieks of support, as she bounces from foot to foot, above the roar of the bikes and the muffling effect of his helmet. The pensioner with her adds his own repeated mantra of "get stuck into them, lad!" which he equally vehemently suggests albeit at a much lower decibel level.

Heat 2 witnesses the on-track re-appearance of former Diamond Rob Grant, who'd been loudly booed by the crowd on the

---

[3] At this point I must emphasise that Newcastle Speedway Club have always stood for something special in my view of the sport. Not only have I encountered George's mother Joan at away meetings in the past, most often at Reading, but also it was a fixture that featured Newcastle a few years ago at Workington that had the biggest impression on me. I particularly remember that day because there were a huge number of Workington fans as well as a large group of away supporters on the terraces. But, even more notably, there were a few fans of Newcastle Speedway Club who wore the usually hated red-and-white stripes of Sunderland Association Football Club and were able to mingle unselfconsciously among them without the inevitable rancour, bother or comment that this would usually attract. Though this might not be possible at home fixtures nor sensible to parade through the streets of Byker on the way to the meeting; it was, nonetheless, the ultimate counter example to the type of behaviour often experienced at football matches. It also exemplifies the fantastic behaviour and friendliness of which the sport of speedway is so justifiably proud. Large crowds of traditional (true) speedway fans exchange all the usual banter and criticism associated with passionate rivalry without the need to resort to violence or the need for police supervision, no matter how big the crowd or important the meeting. The sight of these Sunderland shirts was, for me, symbolic of the prevalence of a general 'live and let live' attitude within speedway and stood in sharp contrast to the narrow tribalism of contemporary football fanaticism which wouldn't tolerate this combustible combination of deeply held allegiances without the swift resort to violence.

introductory parade of the teams. He rides this race with his distinctive leg-trailing style that, though unusual, doesn't prevent him from remaining at the back of the race throughout this heat. In fact Rob, rather unfortunately but consistently, rides all three of his races badly trailed off at the rear. Heat 3 hears the announcer name-check the race sponsor (*LH Pianotuning Ltd*) with the touchingly old-fashioned observation that "if you need any tuning or repairs to your piano then the number is there to call". I'm sure that the general incidence of piano ownership has declined, in parallel with a similar deterioration of speedway attendances, since the height of its heyday and popularity in this country. Even if we assume there's still a burgeoning or latent demand for repairs, I'm not sure that the demographic of any speedway crowd would be your most obvious choice should you wish to target the remainder of the country's keen pianists. I admire the sponsor's optimism and continued support of their local speedway club though!

We often boast that speedway is a family sport and the group close by to me supports this claim with an accomplished display of coordinated family screams and shouts of "go on, go on" for Jamie Robertson in heat 5, perhaps they hope to watch a repeat of his wheelie celebration at the end of heat 4. The race line taken by Jamie Smith for second place, as they rush to the line from the final bend, provokes a hysterical reaction from granddad who howls "you'll have him in the dog track you freaking dirty bastard". A few heats later one of the track staff also feels granddad's ire, who volunteers to freaking place a flag where the sun doesn't shine, for his tardy use of said flag when he eventually deigned to stop heat 7. The level of anger the OAP possesses is almost palpable, unable to be held back from frequent eruptions start and are triggered by the most innocuous incidents. The start marshal is next to receive some harsh advice on his competence in heat 8, which sees the OAP freaking fulminate, once more, at Smith's lack of track etiquette when up against Robertson. "That's freaking twice Jamie boy" was the printable gist of his outburst. Just before the interval break, we're treated to Glenn Cunningham bravely pass Lubos Tomicek on an evening throughout which, as they say in match reports in the *Speedway Star*, 'passing was at a premium'.

Some of the small details I observe during the interval, I believe illustrate the essential charm of the sport. There's the young woman, Montana Jowett, who is the Diamonds' team mascot and I spot her when she clacks down the stairs from the bar in her steel shoe and red kevlars while she eats her interval portion of chips with gusto. We're informed by Barry, the Geordic announcer, that Roy Clarke, mechanic for the Diamonds' heat leader James Grieves, has a spare place in his van for Thursday night's trip to Sheffield, leaving from Palmerston, should anyone wish to make themselves known to him at the pits gate to make arrangements during the interval. Barry even has the time to wonder aloud whether Andrew Dalby, the Sunderland AFC season-ticket holding centre-green announcer, will have the time during his busy interval schedule to snatch a well-earned interval cuppa? We then learn from Andy that, while he mostly tries to live life on the edge, he "can't stand coffee flavour and has only had two cups of tea in 16 years!"

Immediately after the interval, the meeting quickly moves onto a more controversial plane with the events of the very next heat. Even before it has started, granddad vociferously advises Grievesy with some slightly obtuse and unorthodox tactics – "go on Jimmy put him on the freaking green grass!" – to deal with the threat posed by Zorro in this race. The whole thing kicks off and anger levels rise exponentially when Zorro, who trails in this race by some distance in second place behind Christian Henry, appears to decide to deliberately knock him off with a charge on a straight line that takes him directly underneath him on bends 3 and 4 of lap 3. In my view, it's a manoeuvre that was never likely to result in anything other than its actual outcome, which is that Henry and his machine smash dramatically and painfully into the wire safety fence. James Grieves skilfully lays down his bike to avoid the fallen riders ahead of him before he immediately jumps to his feet and, in the heat of the moment demonstrates the skill that indicates some boxing prowess, when he punches Zorro in the face a few times through the narrow gap provided for this very purpose at the front of his helmet. The track staff just about manage to hold the riders back from further violent confrontation, with Zorro particularly keen to break free of his handlers to effect some swift retribution on the always-up-for-it Grieves, while the medical staff crowd round the stricken Henry. The partisan crowd of locals have gone ballistic while granddad, rightly for once, fulminates to all and sundry around him as he repeatedly shrieks, "he had freaking ne' chance of getting past him there". Grieves ostentatiously apologises to Zorro with a proffered handshake as they depart via the centre green on the long trudge back to the pits from the bend on the far end of the stadium. Henry still continues to lie prostrate on the track as the medical staff and ambulance crowd round him in attendance. His injuries could have been much more serious than they were, nonetheless, it's still an incident that ends his season for 2005 there and then. The crowd hasn't had this formally confirmed at the time, but it's a reasonable assumption given the severity with which he hit the fence, which is a particularly galling outcome when his recent improved form on the track is considered. Subsequently we learn that the injuries Christian sustains from the crash result in a huge gash on his thigh, right through to the bone, which is then initially stitched together albeit with the strong possibility of future skin grafts if it fails to properly heal.

The SCB referee, Workington-based Stuart Wilson, summons the riders, Grieves and Zetterstrom – and the team managers, English and Bell – to the changing rooms for an impromptu emergency discussion. The crowd has massed by the pits fence where they bay for retribution and, to be polite, are calling provocatively to everyone involved with the Somerset team. The atmosphere has taken on a nasty, violent edge – restricted to verbal threats but that I sense would quickly translate to physical action, if further 'provoked' – while the pits wall provides a welcome barrier for the Somerset riders still stuck in the pits. Peter Toogood forlornly stands alone. He looks completely downcast and nonplussed. It's a tricky situation for him, politically and presentationally, since he's both the co-promoter of the Somerset team as well as being Chairman of the BSPA, speedway's governing body. He resolves the dilemma of his position through a sustained campaign of total inaction and remains apparently completely detached on the periphery of the incident and its aftermath throughout the rest of the evening. It's as though he's not there or just an accidental bystander in a bad dream. We're all interrupted by the announcer who ecstatically proclaims that Christian is "back on his feet and able to walk past the ambulance" apparently intent to walk back to the pits unaided before, after a few tentative steps, commonsense prevails and he's helped into the ambulance. The crowd by the pits fence continue to bate the Somerset riders and go deliriously potty with extended jeers, when Zorro emerges, or more accurately, storms from the changing rooms to animatedly speak with Peter Toogood in a flurry of ferocious waves and assorted other arm gestures. No further details have been confirmed about the referee's decision on this incident, other than his initial award of the race to Henry and Zorro's subsequent exclusion, to loud cheers, for "foul riding" although the fact that Zorro immediately and angrily starts to pack his equipment away seems to speak for itself. The announcer Barry tries to restore calm and counsels the still wild home crowd with a peculiar choice of advice, "a message to Newcastle fans: don't take it out on the Somerset fans as, whatever you thought you saw on the track, wasn't them and isn't the sort of behaviour we want at a speedway meeting". Soon after we learn, to a roar of approval from the Diamonds fans, that there has been a "rare referee's decision to exclude him [Zorro] from the rest of the meeting".[4]

I leave the still angry crowd by the pits fence to rejoin the group of Somerset fans who stand on the grandstand terraces to establish their impressions on this train of events. When I arrive Tim the Hat, the most visible fan in their group, informs me that he was disturbed to be approached immediately after the incident, by an extremely angry man in a black-and-white cap (whom he points out to me staring back at us from about 10 yards away and I'm relieved to notice isn't the perpetually angry pensioner I stood with) who threatened him with violent retribution. Tim rather plaintively asks if I "saw the abuse we were getting?" or was close enough by to have possibly heard the threat of "I'm going to shank you afterwards" from the brute in the cap. The threat of violence, compounded by the broad Geordie accent of the very intimidating man as well as anxiety over the specific intention behind the forceful use of the word "shank", is an extremely worrying development for the visiting group of Somerset fans, who huddle still closer together as a group. Tim assumed these comments specifically

<hr>

[4] A few days later I'm told anecdotally that Stuart Wilson, the referee in question, had previously witnessed, in his capacity as a spectator, Zorro's involvement in a similar incident when he "accidentally speared" a rival rider, after he had inadvertently crossed the grass of the bend. The decision of the referee that day, unlike at Newcastle, was to put all four riders back in for the re-run of the race. The subsequent print and Internet furore that surrounded this episode in Newcastle was exacerbated by a debate as to whether referees should punish apparent unfair or rough riders and their riding with fines and exclusions or ignore these incidents as just part and parcel of a dangerous sport. It is a debate that will continue. Though, equally, I imagine that now the metaphorical dam has been breached, that we will see more SCB referees take strong, decisive action to exclude recalcitrant riders in the future.

referred to a definite intention to threaten his person afterwards, though whether the man was to punch or stab him no one could accurately predict but, nonetheless, everyone had a reasonably good idea that a post-meeting cuddle hadn't been proposed.

Rather than pour oil on already troubled waters, Tim sensibly sought out Barry the announcer to inform him of what had been said, if not so far transpired. Barry, with commendable alacrity, promptly tried to calm things and assuage the heightened tension of the situation among some members of the home crowd, when he broadcast an appeal for general tolerance ("the Somerset fans aren't responsible for what goes on out on the track and shouldn't be held responsible by anyone"). Di, the big Zorro fan, is outraged by the decision of the referee about this "racing incident" and indignantly says, "I've never heard of that before, I don't understand that – we should withdraw". Di's considered opinion of the event we'd all witnessed was very definite, "Magnus would never take a fellow rider out on purpose, he's not that kind of rider, riders have to take split-second decisions and he took the wrong one". Beside her, Margaret is more philosophical, "well it gives us something to talk about going home" but, then, she can comfortably say that since it's an incident that doesn't involve her beloved Ritchie. Speedway Dave believes that the ref is a confirmed practising onanist and another Somerset fan says "we all have a word for him". While co-promoter Jo looks to the practical implications of events and feels that this rare decision has "taken away the chance of a bonus point". The remainder of the Somerset fans in this small group also appear to be completely nonplussed by this surprise turn of events. Despite a couple of centuries' speedway attendance between them, no one can recall any other rider ever being thrown out of meeting in modern times for such an incident, especially for an occurrence that isn't exactly uncommon within the sport. The jungle drums continue to still beat strongly and the collective memory has been consulted, which is illustrated when a text message to Elaine arrives from the former Rebels' team manager Ray Dickson. He now organises the juniors in the second halves at Somerset and, Elaine reports the gist of his text message, namely that as an "ex-Monarchs' supporter" he's "never seen (sic) such a thing since Charlie Monk and Doug Templeton were thrown out at Edinburgh in the 1960s".

By the nominated race of heat 15, a 5-1 would give Newcastle the opportunity to win by 24 points and thereby force a run-off for the bonus point. Josef 'Pepe' Franc falls on bend 1, apparently without help, but the referee calls all four riders back, due to his view that it was an unsatisfactory start. It's noticeable throughout the meeting that while Franc's name is spelt in a way that would lead you to think that you should pronounce it like the coin, his surname is actually pronounced like the country at Brough Park and, subsequently it transpires, in Josef's home country of the Czech Republic. Whatever the pronunciation it makes no difference because 'Pepe' storms to an easy victory in the re-run of heat 15, followed home in second place by his team-mate James Grieves. On his subsequent victory celebration lap, Franc delightedly stops in front of the home grandstand and takes a theatrical bow. Almost simultaneously, the third-placed Somerset rider Paul Fry reacts dramatically to physically attack James Grieves just at the moment when he arrives at the pits gate after his celebration lap. The crowd storms *en masse* over towards the pits area for a better view of this altercation and in the ensuing confusion it's difficult to see or establish what exactly is happening. Although it's clear that there's an almighty rumpus and that the barney mostly involves Fry and Grieves who ferociously attack each other with considerable gusto. When the dust of another fight finally settles, Grieves returns to his section of the pits to receive, what is effectively a victor's welcome from the nearby, baying Newcastle fans. Despite his diminutive stature, Grieves (who used to train to improve his upper body strength with kick boxing) strides with bantam-like confidence around the pits area, even though he has a remarkably prominent lump on his forehead – reputedly sustained as a result of a kick in the head from Paul Fry's mechanic. Which, if this was achieved while he was still astride his bike, signals a possible impressive alternative career in ballet should a ban from mechanic's duties result from these (alleged) actions.

Whatever has prompted these scenes – rumoured to be Paul Fry mistaking Grieves's "innocent celebratory hand gestures" as a deliberate and provocative form of personal insult – it's obvious that tensions continue to run extremely high on both sides of the pits. A Newcastle fan close by suggests that the only sensible option is to "give 'em boxing gloves and let them settle it on the centre green" Diamonds co-promoter George English sensibly swiftly steps in to admonish Grieves

and to instruct him to stop playing up to the assembled crowd at the pits fence perimeter; while his mother, Joan, restores a good degree of order with her loud instructions to the many trespassers to relocate themselves with considerable speed or risk injury and expulsion. Although she is small and much older than everyone who surrounds her, Joan quickly restores a semblance of order and control with her powerful presence and voice. The referee Stuart Wilson again returns to the pits area for another long discussion with Mick Bell, this time in full view of the crowd rather than hidden away in the intimate privacy of the dressing rooms.

While tensions still run high on both sides, there's still the final drama of the run-off for the bonus point to unfold between the riders nominated by the rival team managers. In this instance, we are to see a match race between Josef 'Pepe' Franc and Ritchie Hawkins. The tension is all too much for Supergran who tosses her programme board to the floor and shoots off saying, "I just can't watch it, I just can't watch it". Tim the Hat is the voice of understanding and compassion, when he sweetly says to her in a calm voice, "come on Nana, come on Nana". We gather that Supergran is anxious that if Ritchie were to win the run-off (which as his staunchest supporter she deems highly likely), she fears that this might spark further aggravation in the pits and on the terraces.

The selection of Pepe is not a surprise choice, since he has remained completely unbeaten by a visiting rider all night. Before this decisive race can even start, the Newcastle start marshal decides to indulge himself in some apparent last-minute gamesmanship, when he unnecessarily harasses Hawkins at the tapes about the inaccuracy of his starting position on the recently repainted white lines of the start grid. Again George English intervenes, in his role as co-promoter, mediator and true sportsman, when he runs over to overrule these petty concerns, and thereby enables the race to start and Pepe to zoom away confidently to win in untroubled style. Just as the race finishes, the Newcastle riders run on the track in celebration to give Pepe the bumps for his performance and also an early, very unexpected bath, to judge from his reaction, when they duck him in the handily adjacent centre-green pond. Announcer Barry, for once without the hyperbole that naturally afflicts the species, intones his closing summary of events, "an extraordinary last hour or so at Brough Park for one of the most eventful meetings I've ever seen at a speedway track!" before he finishes with considerable understatement, "so, in the light of circumstances, there won't be a victory parade". Supergran has finally returned to the Somerset group, while they pack away their flag, flasks and sandwich boxes in preparation to leave the stadium, with tears in her eyes from the emotion and upset of it all which, culminated for her, in the drama of Ritchie's run-off race. She's in determined and ebullient mood about his career prospects though, despite the set back of the last race, "I've seen him get a maximum in the Conference League, I've seen him get a maximum in the Premier League and I'll be on my Zimmer frame when I see him get a maximum in the Elite League!"

The home crowd cheerfully swarms to the bar, continues to mill and mass round the pits area or streams out of the stadium. I catch a preoccupied but satisfied George English for his immediate thoughts a few minutes later. "All I will say is that personally I thought Zetterstrom totally deserved to be thrown out. However, I want a definitive list of fines from the referee before I comment further, as fines were being dished out all around earlier". In front of the grandstand I chat to Paul and Karen Brown from Northumberland who are one of many groups who hang around and talk about events animatedly, in their case with their children. They've "never seen anything like it before" but don't really wish to be drawn on any specific comments, though there's absolutely no doubt that they hold Zorro completely to blame for the fights that marred the meeting (even though he'd left in his van before the second contretemps). They watch all the speedway that they can as family, on TV, at Brough Park or at the British Grand Prix in Cardiff. Their daughter Lauren, and her friend Bethan, are both professed James Grieves fans and appear quite shocked by events that involved their hero. The unusual events of the evening haven't in any way deterred her brother Sean, who "likes everything" about the sport, from the desire to fulfil his ambition to "become a speedway rider". His dad prefers to sound a note of caution and concentrate on matters that specifically impact the current form of the Diamonds, since he believes that "George needs to think long and hard" about rider selection, particularly since "he's dropped a few clangers recently". Paul hopes that the poor crowds might pick up in the future, especially if there was a more attractive team to watch race at Brough Park. He welcomes the increased TV coverage on Sky Sports, but it doesn't, to his mind, change the fundamental fact that, "it's never been a big sport, it's always been a poor man's sport". His wife Karen nods her approval throughout as she listens to her husband, though she personally loves the atmosphere and the thrills of speedway. As they leave the stadium, Paul declares, "if I won the lottery I'd take over Newcastle!"

I wander back off through the deserted stadium and join the many fans already in the glass-fronted grandstand bar, who animatedly relive the evening's events in blow-by-blow fashion over a pint. I wave to George and notice that the referee, Stuart Wilson, sits completely isolated and alone in another deserted part of the stand, while he painstakingly completes his official report for the SCB on the night's tumultuous events. Given all that we witnessed, you just know that he's going to struggle to describe all the incidents and list all the fines never mind finish the remainder of the paperwork quickly!

Just after 9 p.m., I trundle off into the dusk of the evening that envelopes the Byker estate, with the sky decorated with wisps of glowing red clouds, many hours after the start of a memorable meeting that will be talked about for years afterwards, particularly when it becomes ever more dramatic in the recollection. A short distance away at Byker Metro Station, unusually to my mind, there are two police squad cars with flashing emergency lights parked directly outside on the entrance concourse. I worry that there has been some kind of emergency or terrorist incident. But, instead, more mundanely discover that the vestibule of the station is guarded by three policemen, well, one of them was actually a policewoman, each of them dramatically armed with a sub-machine gun (!) and they are spread out across this part of the completely silent and deserted station. I'm concerned enough to ask, "Is there something wrong, officer?" "No, it's just a bit of high visibility policing to reassure the public." I'm not convinced as just the mere sight of these impressive guns makes me nervous. To disguise my anxiety, I inform them that we could have done with their armed presence at the speedway fixture at Brough Park tonight. The tallest policeman replies, without discernable irony, "I thought they always knocked seven bells out of each other on the track and then had a punch up after!" before he adds, " Are you saying it's not like that every week at the speedway?" Just for tonight, I can't possibly disagree with him.

14th August Newcastle v. Somerset (Premier League) 60-36

Chapter 29: End of an Era in Ull
17th August Hull v. Workington

SKY CHATTER

"We all race together, live together, travel together" Sam Ermolenko

RANDOM SCB RULES

15.3.1 All starts shall be by clutch start, with the rear wheel in contact with the track surface and stationary.

The drive from Brighton to Kingston upon Hull, to give the city its proper name, is a long one. And it seems even longer than it actually is due to the amount of motorway driving it entails, after you negotiate the various M's 23, 25 and 1 before you then find yourself on the comparatively exotic tarmacs of the M18 and M62. To any self-respecting southerner this would definitely count as being a trip 'Up North', mainly because you must drive somewhere north of the Watford Gap service station. To any self-respecting native of Yorkshire, this is merely the eastern reaches of God's own chosen county. But, as we all know, God works in mysterious ways his wonders to perform, and once you leave the certain certainties of the M62 for the long straight road of the A63, except for the contra-flow system through the road works a few miles out that is the latter stages of the highway, you find yourself very conscious of driving to "a destination".

It's a fairly far-flung destination by the standards of English geography since this route eventually leads directly to Kingston upon Hull, the banks of the Humber and the North Sea. In the general geographic imagination of the public, the 'Kingston

The impressive Craven Park © Jeff Scott

Some of the start line girls cum dance troupe. © Jeff Scott

View of the track from the main Roger Millward grandstand. © Jeff Scott

Upon' dropped from Hull a long time ago, no doubt for complex and interesting historical reasons. This process of abbreviation and denial of its full name has now reached its logical conclusion, since its known locally as "Ull". When you drive into the city, one of the nine largest in England, you can't help but notice the imposing structure of the Humber Bridge, so impressive in scale that it distracts you as you drive under it. I missed the chance to drive over it but, even so, from ground level you can still appreciate the majesty and size of the gigantic river it crosses, the Humber estuary. No doubt when you live in Ull you no longer notice the river or its incredible width that dwarfs that more famous and paltry London stream, the river Thames. No wonder people say that someone has a mouth the size of the Humber when they wish to draw attention to a particularly large orifice. When you drive into the city for the first time you are immediately struck by the continuous line of moderately sized buildings – including numerous warehouses, office and factories – that line the river as you travel into the city centre. As well as the strong pungent smell of something, along with the sea air, which you would hope to be fish, and the proximity of the brand new football ground to the dual carriageway on the outskirts of the city.

The ever-helpful Tourist Information Office recommends that I stay at a bed and breakfast located in what they call the "picturesque Avenues area" of the city. A lush, green verdant city oasis, it apparently welcomes the casual visitor, impresses with its yuppie regeneration, ongoing gentrification, restaurants and comes recommended as "safe for your car". Please note that "safe for my car" is usually not in my Top 50 criteria for how I choose where to stay on my trips to the speedway stadiums around the country. After all I have one of those lock things for the steering wheel, which I struggle with even when I actually own the key that unlocks it. But the chap at the tourist office laid great stress on this, and I agree it's important, so I take his advice to try to diminish the increased possibility of car theft that might have resulted if I'd chosen a B&B close by the rugby-cum-speedway stadium. I admired his honesty but I question if this is the best way to present your town to complete strangers.[1]

Before I can get to the stadium, it appears everyone in the city has joined

[1] The official website of the city takes a somewhat different approach to highlight the town's attractions, with a definite Big Push on Civic Pride – that I'm sure, most likely, comes with lots of proud local councillors and a mayoral chain and gown to die for – along with its key claim to be a "city of contrasts". The casual visitors attention is directed to the attraction of 'The Deep', and we're then instructed to admire the 'depth' of this local sea-world attraction, as well as drawn to the Museum quarter. Absolutely nothing mentions, subtly rebuts or even tangentially refers to the inaugural award of 'Britain's Crappest Town' bestowed upon Hull in 2004. Notice I said Hull not Hell, a more accurate description if you care to give credence to those inane, witless public schoolboys who compiled the first *Crap Towns* book. These people deserve to be the first against the wall come the revolution, primarily for their gratuitous insults to so many people in so many towns, but also for their banal negativity and pathetic attempts at humour. With the arrival in 2005, of the imaginatively titled sequel *Crap Towns II*, Hull had climbed to a more exalted 19th crappest town in the country. Of all the mostly provincial towns that host speedway in this country, only Glasgow and Edinburgh (joint fourth) were mentioned besides Hull's entry in this pantheon. This says more than money ever can about the duff selection criteria this book employs. The editors condescendingly note the improvement in Hull's ranking, which they ascribe to an "impressive email campaign from its residents" that praises 'The Deep', oak-beamed pubs and an historic old town. They still can't resist a reprise of their previous slander that Hull "smells of death" and also charge that there is a "silent threat of violence hanging in the air". They also note the 2004 crime statistic of 15.3 per cent, or 3,427 crimes in real money, in a population that now totals 224,000 people. No mention is made of how many of these were car crimes, but now I'm curious. It's all you need to hear before I visit the speedway track for tonight's Premier League meeting against the Workington Comets.

some general citywide campaign of concern about car safety and about my car's safety in particular. The reception lady, at my bed and breakfast, lays great stress upon the private car park at the rear that is locked promptly at 11 p.m. and closed, without exception, until 6 a.m. I have a family room with four beds at the top of the house, always handy for the lone traveller who anticipates a quick change of bed in the night or hopes to find new friends that evening. None of these beds is at all comfortable and they all look as if they've done previous sterling service with extremely heavy but fidgety guests. If only they could speak, the stories they might tell would be an education in itself. However, I'm anxious to check if the car is still there so I can begin the final part of my journey to Craven Park, the shared home of Hull Kingston Rovers Rugby League club and also of the Hull 'CPD' Vikings Speedway. I also want to try to spot the distinctive cream telephone boxes of the Kingston Communications Company for which the city is renowned. And I promise not to cite the subsequent disastrous catalogue of mismanagement, vanity, schoolboy errors and bungles that led the local council to fritter away the windfall profits generated through the privatisation of this telecommunications company. At least the distinctive phone boxes reputedly remain untouched, even if I can't manage to find one during my visit.

More roadworks on the way to the stadium enable me to get an even better sense of the city's geography on my winding detour in the rush hour traffic. Craven Park is situated towards the end of a long road that passes through a large council housing estate laid out in the old style with a big-tree lined central reservation that separates one side of the street from the other, the new Arcadian look for the masses during the 1960s. I notice quite a few unbranded off-licences and supermarkets, convenience stores as we prefer to call them nowadays as the gradual Americanisation of our vocabulary steadily increases, with a smattering of other businesses that includes a fish and chip shop, which has the only visible queue of people. I'm pleased that this isn't the usual 'anywhere street' of national brand name shops, although I'm sure the city centre will reek of these pseudo-aspirational zones that frame so much of the modern consumer experience.

As you arrive in the large car park in front of the main Roger Millward Stand you can't help but be impressed with the apparent stadium facilities that Hull Speedway share with the Hull Kingston Rovers Rugby League club. I notice too, that the stadium itself is ringed with the sort of barbed-wire-topped fencing that wouldn't disgrace a prison, as is the car park. Reassured that my car will survive the duration of my visit to the club, I park close by where all the riders have left their large vans. I note that Shaun Tacey's van has already arrived along with many others of the visiting Workington riders. I also observe that Hull's captain and veteran rider, Paul Thorp, appears to have bucked the current trend of speedway riders' vehicles since he drives a T-registration Turbo diesel VW Sharon Estate, one of the VW brands that doesn't quite have the cachet of the Golf or the Passat. That also makes me think that he must be a committed family man or else he owns a very small bike that he brings to each meeting from his home in Macclesfield. Off track, despite not being 41 until September, he dresses younger than his years, and favoured (when I saw him) the smooth Simon Templar 'Saint' roll-neck sweater, albeit with a gold chain. I enter through gates to the left of the main grandstand with the track and rugby pitch in front of me. The relationship between the clubs at this stadium has suffered, especially since the speedway tenant's track circles the playing area of the pitch with an additional sandy covered track that in turn circles the shale racing surface. Tensions have risen in recent months with the lease due for renegotiation and renewal. Rumours, as ever, abound on the speedway Internet forums – some supposedly involve large unpaid outstanding debts – while the *Speedway Star* reports the official club line that the negotiations are complex, involve disagreements about restrictions to the size of the pitch and racing surface and are complicated by reneged council promises about the stadium's redevelopment. This is a great tangle of affairs, very complex and it creates great uncertainty within the local speedway community.

To the left of the entrance a pathway leads past various blue portacabins that house the Speedway Office and the track equipment, but not the St John Ambulance facilities which are housed in the swish rugby medical room underneath the main grandstand. The very large pits area is located in the lee of one of the stadium's massive fence-encased floodlights. Some metal steps lead up a steep, grassy hillock that is roped off in a manner that suggests that it's the riders' viewing area. Because all of this is located on the fourth bend it provides a great vantage point from which to view the entire track, particularly along the home straight in front of the grandstand. A vast, impressive multi-tiered all-seater affair; the

grandstand must create a great atmosphere when full, and vertigo in the minds of those who suffer from a fear of heights. It houses the rugby club offices, modern changing rooms, bars and a restaurant. While the stand opposite is very impressive by the usual standards of speedway stadiums, but in comparison to this imposing edifice, it is an altogether simpler affair that provides covered standing terraces for a sizeable crowd, should they turn up to watch. Although it's a sunny day there's already quite a strong, cold wind and a contingent of young women cheerleaders shelter behind the wall of the entranceway to the stairwell, where they patiently wait dressed in their matching, bright white, short-skirted uniforms. They're happy to pose for photographs and to confirm to me that they're part of the dance-cum-cheerleading troupe that, every week, provides pitch-side entertainment for the Hull speedway fans. They're also just about to leave and have a lengthy pre-meeting final rehearsal to perfect their overall technique and ensure that all their movements and routines, rather complicated ones it transpires, meet their usual demandingly high professional standards.

As they leave for the pitch, the size of which dwarfs their small group, I head for the doorway of the Speedway Office. The Hull Speedway promoter Paul Hodder, who started in 2003 when Nigel Wordsworth got into a financial pickle, is there but unable to find the time he'd promised he would have to speak with me. He appears extremely preoccupied, noticeably nervous and he believably cites the urgent need to sort out staff wage payments as the primary reason for his sudden unavailability. It's always very sensible to pay outstanding monies, especially if one believes the unofficial Internet forums, to ensure the smooth administration of the club on race night. But Paul's affable and friendly co-promoter Dave Peet is only too happy to step into the breach for a chat with me about the club and its future prospects. Dave has watched the sport for 44 years since he began to go to his local club, Sheffield, in 1961. His connections actually go back further than that, because he was christened in the church directly outside the Owlerton Stadium in Sheffield and lived just across the road from it. He rarely misses any Sheffield meetings and views it as his speedway home. He's also passionate about the other popular Sheffield sporting passion – football – since he states, "there's only two football teams in Sheffield: Wednesday and Wednesday reserves". However, just this season, Dave has paid a substantial sum of his own money to become the co-promoter and team manager at Hull after he had spent nine years as a popular, well-respected and successful speedway referee. Neil Machin, the Sheffield promoter, emphasised that I should make it a point to meet Dave on my visit to Hull; since he was a good bloke, well informed and was very knowledgeable about the sport. Quite a recommendation and pointedly not one he made about Paul Hodder. Neil worried that Dave's promotional association with Paul possibly might have negative consequences and may result in damage to his reputation and savings account should things go awry. But then, Neil also noted, he's a grown up! Dave Peet has quite a pair of shoes to step into as Hull team manager because he has replaced the legendary Eric Boocock, who surprisingly retired from these duties just after the end of the triumphant 2004 season. It's not only a hard act to follow in management terms but also because 2004 was one of the most successful seasons in Hull's history because they were Premier League champions, as well as winners of the cup and the Young Shield. It's been a very mixed season so far with many home meetings cancelled because of the weather, a dispute ongoing with the stadium landlords and rumours of financial difficulty, which swirl on the Internet forums. To compound it all, the team has just been royally thumped every night for the last three nights before this home fixture with Workington. They've managed to lose successively at King's Lynn, Reading and the Isle of Wight by a combined aggregate of 181-101. It would be understandable if Dave Peet wondered what on earth he'd let himself in for in his first season as co-promoter at Hull!

Still, hope springs eternal and, like religion and politics, I decide to avoid the topics of money and landlords unless Dave brings them up. He suggests that we retire to the privacy of the empty Roger Millward grandstand; so we climb the many steep stairs to the seating area where we have a wide choice before we decide on some of the empty front-row seats. From this high up, these seats afford a fantastic panoramic view of the track and the pitch as well as the various buildings that surround the Craven Park stadium. These buildings include a number of warehouses along with a huge array of cranes which tower in the near distance and that indicate that we must be very close to the sea and the port facilities. Since I spent my childhood summers watching with interest the teaming banks of the river Wear; this evokes pleasant memories and it's not a sight that you can see very often in this country any longer, especially given the criminal demise of our ship-building and fishing industries. As the nearby sea-based economy declines, so too has the speedway at Hull. However, there are still relics from every era all around. In fact, as we speak, on the track, the tractors busily continue with their last-minute grading activities. Indeed, there's quite a selection of tractors at Hull as well as a large yellow water bowser that slowly sprinkles its contents on the dry-looking track. In the distance, a solitary crane in a landscape dotted with a swathe of similar-sized cranes, painstakingly lifts some large metal containers.

Dave informs me that this season crowds have declined by around 150 people per meeting from the peak attendances of the previous year when Hull swept all before them ("we won everything last year") and were crowned the Premier League Champions. This season the virtually identical team has struggled to regain these heights and has suffered numerous injuries to key riders at different points throughout the campaign. Dave believes they've been "plagued with injuries", particularly to loyal team men like Garry Stead, Emiliano Sanchez and Paul Thorp, but also to young Joel Parsons whose season-long loss from the team had a "huge impact" too. It's been a frustrating but educational time for Dave when he's tried to secure replacement guest riders for Hull and, so far, he has heard a litany of reasons not to ride that range from injury, to fatigue or a lack of equipment. It's all part of the job and he's philosophical "if it were that easy everyone would be a promoter". The net result has been some poor results and the team has "just been spanked" during their last three away meetings at King's Lynn, Reading and the Isle of Wight. The performance was especially poor at King's Lynn where "we were shocking: we were like a string of washing strung out at the back". Though, it is rumoured that, as a plain-speaking Yorkshireman, Dave has never been shy to tell his riders exactly what he thought of them and their equipment. On the basis of his honest communication, if nothing else, Dave hopes for better tonight but has begun to feel that perhaps his team are just "too nice". Many of the Hull riders hover around the broadly similar 7 or 8 point average whereas experienced riders like Craig Boyce or Shane Parker, who've raced in the Elite League, have pushed their averages to around the 10 point mark. These particular riders are very aggressive and competitive and "take no prisoners" whereas Dave believes "our riders are often more gentlemanly in their riding, using their heads because they're older" but just "missing that little bit". They can all earn good money in the Premier League, but the experienced Aussies, Craig and Shane, "take you all the way, are absolutely savage on the first corner having learnt that in the Elite League". Getting that little bit of difference is the key, you "just need that edge" of the extra two or three yards to win consistently. This problem of the necessary desire to win has been allied to all sorts of teething problems with the landlords of the stadium. There's been the problem of the stadium landlords who want to move the track, a dispute about the minimum number of customers

Pits view. © Jeff Scott

Team Giffard – Adam and Nicola Filmer.
© Jeff Scott

Graham and Denise Drury queue for refreshments.
© Jeff Scott

required (30) on a speedway night for the refurbished restaurant to actually open, and many other petty things that are the lot of a contemporary speedway promoter at Hull.

Not that he'd have it any other way though. He's delighted to have this job, especially as "it's something I've always wanted to do", particularly after he'd served a long apprenticeship in the sport. Dave has evolved from a fan, to riding second halves at Ellesmere Port in 1977, and then he was a mechanic for Jamie Young, the ex-Edinburgh, Stoke and Boston rider. By 1991 he worked with Neil Machin at Sheffield as "clerk of the course and various other things" before he decided to become a full-time referee when John Whittaker retired. As a referee he "had no illusions about what went on in the sport, nothing has surprised me as, with refereeing, you get to know all the pitfalls".

The referee's role has its own pace and problems, "it should be black and white, but it never is". He's noticed more frequently that some referees put themselves under a lot of pressure and, it's this self-inflicted tension, which makes a hard job harder. Dave has plenty of stories to tell from his refereeing days, most notably his run-ins with Hull's very own Paul Thorp who always used to complain to Dave about his "double standards" when he excluded Paul for moving but allowed other riders to get away with it. He ruefully admits that it's "only human nature to concentrate on one rider" which often, in his case, was Paul Thorp. Dave notices other referees continue to do this during the season to Hull and Paul's detriment.[2] A rider that inspires strong feelings and gets a lot of attention for his 'hard riding' on the track is Nicki Pedersen. As he recalls Nicki's Premier League riding days, when he was younger and wilder, Dave shares many stories. He recalls when Nicki once "twatted Paul Pickering big time", he "just looked at him, put out an elbow and back wheeled him". There was consternation among the watching riders, who were "all dying to jump over the fence and onto the track" to assault Nicki but couldn't, since they knew Dave could fine them from between £250 and £1,000, because it's illegal to jump onto the track.[3] Afterwards Jon Armstrong said, "in future we're all going to club together to pay the fine and one of us will run on and twat him". Back in the pits "there was afters, I knew that there would be". This mystified Nicki, "the mildest chap you could meet off a bike", who asked, "what was that all about? I didn't think that I touched him". Dave believes that while Nicki rode "on the limit", as a referee he always restrained his own treatment of Nicki

[2] Paul Thorp is notorious for the number of exclusions he's had at the tapes throughout his long career. The competitor in him always tries to gain an advantage over his rivals, wherever and however possible. When interviewed for the start of the 2006 season in the *Speedway Star* he commented, "I don't like getting excluded at the start, but I accept that it has happened a fair bit throughout my career. It's nothing intentional, I just try to anticipate what the referee will do at the start and I guess there are times when the referee tries to anticipate what I do!"

3 They were well aware that they couldn't go onto the track as Dave had warned both sets of riders before the meeting, the first of the season, that violence on the centre green or track wouldn't be tolerated. This instruction was partly because of a mass brawl at the Isle of Wight at the end of the 2002 season, but also because trouble would cause difficulties for Neil Machin with the council should it have flared up at Owlerton.

"because riding is hard when you come down to it".

Such stories aside, and even though he's moved on and is "not part and parcel of it anymore" he does remember the politics of the induction process. Dave still finds it hard to believe that some of those who have passed the exams have actually passed and formally qualified as a referee whereas, in his opinion, many of those training that have failed should not have done so. It's no longer a personal concern since as a promoter he has his own 24-7 demands rather than their routines, paperwork and travel schedules. He's delighted to have crossed the fence to the world of promotion but still manages to retain his joy for speedway, "I just love everything – the thrills and spills, the atmosphere and the smell". It's a passion helped by the fact that you can go for a pint with your rivals and staff, especially the riders who are "the most down-to-earth people and not prima donnas". Other promoters have been very generous with their help to Dave, while he finds his feet in the world of speedway promotion, "everyone to a man has helped me 100 per cent, they've been absolutely superb", and have often volunteered their help and advice. Dave attributes this to the collective survival instinct that the sport must have. Everyone wants to see the sport succeed, to help each other out and to try to protect the future. It's "always been a sport where the tracks are up against the world". He gets on well with many other promoters and, as if to prove it, rings one of my favourites, Stoke co-promoter Caroline Tattum on her mobile to have a quick joke, about life, speedway and the stories she told me for this book. He confesses "everyone thinks we're more than just good friends as we get on so well, she always jokes I'm too old for her and I joke she's too poor to keep me in the lifestyle to which I'm accustomed". The time Dave could just about spare has flashed past and I've enjoyed the experience with this courteous and passionate man, but his many duties call, literally, since his mobile rings continuously throughout our conversation. We leave the stand and walk back to the Speedway Office where the sun has weakened and the strong wind has now picked up strength to become almost gale force. It blows round the dust and swivels the loose metal sign on the side of the portacabins. Dave cheerfully notes "it's always really windy here in Hull 'cause we're close to the sea; luckily it's warm tonight though as it gets quite fresh sometimes". Fresh! I've already betrayed my southern roots when earlier I changed out of my shorts and collected my warm clothing from the car. To my mind, it's summer everywhere else in the country on this sunny August evening, but not in Hull.

Also up from the south coast this afternoon and in the queue at the snack bar by the side of the grandstand to purchase some chocolate to share is Team Giffard, in the form of brother and sister Adam and Laura Filmer. Both look rather smart in their matching Team Giffard gear, with Adam in a button shirt and his sister in a hooded sweatshirt. Both garments are black with the Team Giffard logo picked out brightly in dazzling green letters on the front, with other sponsors' details to ensure that everyone receives the appropriate name check. Adam is actually here in his capacity as Dan's mechanic and his sister is Dan's girlfriend; so, for once, any claim that our sport is like a family has a strong ring of truth about it. They are likely to repeat the long round trip journey up to Hull weekly in the coming weeks, since they tell me that Dan has just been officially confirmed as Hull's new reserve, to ride at number seven, for the rest of the season. It's a good deal for both parties, since Dan would welcome more Premier League riding experience in addition to his existing position as heat leader at Conference League Weymouth. Earlier as we chatted about the Hull squad, Dave Peet welcomed Dan's signing because "we can have a look at him and he can have a look at us, plus he can still come in on a three point average in 2006". The trip to Hull has taken about five hours in the van, which strikes me as making good time and, if they manage to pack up promptly after the meeting, they expect that they'll return home at around 4.30 a.m. It's a long day and then they have to get up promptly a few hours later to clean and maintain the bike for Dan's regular duties at Weymouth on a Friday. They live in a continuous cycle of driving, riding and cleaning throughout the summer months. Laura has, like myself, clearly underestimated the cooling strong wind, because she's failed to wear socks with her open-toed sandals. It looks like it will be a long cold evening ahead without socks for her, but then they are young, hardy people. I reflect that it's strange to meet Laura so often, all around the country, and yet I have never spoken to her boyfriend Dan Giffard. Maybe I'll get the opportunity to chat with him at some point tonight.

By now, speedway bikes litter the pits in all directions. Both sides overflow with riders, mechanics and a large number of bikes that spill over the pits margins to line up by the floodlight pylon. Everyone seems to have their spare bike with them tonight in Hull, and this observation discounts the large number that the Under-15 Academy League riders have brought with them that are presently lined up behind the portacabins in the adjacent secondary pits area. Graham Drury and his wife Denise, the joint Workington promoters and team managers, have just arrived inside the stadium after their long drive from Wales. As usual, Graham proudly wears his Workington Comets jacket. They immediately duck into the Speedway Office to catch up with Paul Hodder and Dave Peet before they get down to the nights activities in earnest.

The person in charge of all the hustle and bustle in the pits area tonight is the very cheerful 63-year-old Peter Morgan, who is clerk of the course at Hull. Peter has done this job for three years and it requires a 150-mile round trip every week from his home in Bradford. When asked what makes speedway special to him, he can only say, "God knows, there's a lot of answers to that!" Mostly though he believes "keeping this thing on keeps me going", apart, that is, from his other regular work at the plumber's merchants. As the clerk of the course, Peter is officially in charge of the pits throughout the meeting and is directly responsible to the match referee. He must be impartial and industrious with eyes in the back of his head to ensure that everything runs smoothly during the meeting. It's a position that he has earned and he proudly informs me that he's worked his way up to his present position from when he began his career at Halifax in 1964-65. Then he helped "with the making of Halifax" and he still laments the passing of the track at The Shay. For Peter there was "nowhere ever quite like it" with its distinctive banking, that caused the base of the fence to be at head height with the slope of the track. Any rider who arrived there for the first time was always intimidated and bamboozled because, "it was semi-frightening, looking like a wall of death, but once you got the hang of it there were so many racing lines". In his opinion, it's the speedway riders' and speedway fans' ultimate venue, but he also enjoyed his time at Odsal stadium when he subsequently moved on to work at Bradford speedway. Peter finds it hard to single out any one thing that represents the joy and the pleasure that he's found through his involvement in speedway. It's all been good, whether it's his 10 years as a mechanic for Ian Cartwright or his present work as the clerk at Hull; although 2004 was a special year with its "fantastic atmosphere when we were triple champions". He's witnessed a lot of major changes in the crowds during his time in the sport, but the biggest change was when the sport became "much, much more professional". In the past it was often a case that a rider "did speedway and had a job as well". Peter often laughs with his wife that "I'd have thousands in the bank if it wasn't for speedway", but he doesn't regret a penny of the expenditure since you could never "take the memories and souvenirs away!"

As I leave Peter to his memories, the Workington team manager Graham Drury politely but wryly enquires if I'm trailing him round the country, which he follows with a "you're everywhere, you are". He hopes for a good away performance from his Comets, despite the injury to the talismanic Carl 'Stoney' Stonehewer who has been replaced, this evening, by an experienced and very capable guest, Sean Wilson. For Graham, speedway is always sold as a family sport. As if to illustrate his point, he asks in what other professional sport would you expect to have such ease of access to key personnel? Just a few minutes later I see Graham and his wife Denise take their place in the queue for hot drinks at the refreshment stand. They just stand there like everyone else, nonchalantly, and talk among themselves or to the few passers by who stop to engage them in conversation. It's obviously the best way to get a hot drink at the stadium and completely without pretension. Certainly not the modest behaviour you'd expect from the managers in any other major sports, such as cricket or football. This complete availability of the sport's influential people is also encouraged at Hull by the lay out of the stadium, particularly as all the riders have to pass along the front of the stand to enter and exit from the pits, after they have changed into their racing gear for the evening's work ahead in the nearby grandstand changing rooms. A gaggle of keen and strategically well-placed autograph hunters lurk along this walkway, though most of them intend to speak with their local Hull Viking heroes rather than the more exotic visitors. All of the riders are happy to stop for a word, pose for a photograph or sign a few autograph books. And it's pleasant to see that some of the youngsters still travel to sports events with rather old-fashioned autograph albums, even in this modern digital hi-tech age! Two young women in particular appear anxious to fill their autograph books with every passing riders' signature and even the prized signature of Dave Peet! He stops to speak with them for a couple of minutes, laughs and jokes and seems impervious to the very cold breeze, dressed as he is in only a thin shirt and a flapping tie. The small crowd in the bar oversees the comings and goings of the riders as well as the dancers, who have continuously practised their elaborate moves for the evening, uninterruptedly for over an hour on the centre-green rugby pitch. The pitch is half bathed in sunlight. The large shadow of the main grandstand ever lengthens onto it and all the dancers formation work – they dance in unison, build human pyramids and towers as well as execute their graceful and ecstatic leaps – looks great exercise, illustrates their complete dedication, and would definitely keep anyone very warm. The dance troupe consists of ten dancers, eight of them young short-skirted women in white uniforms with blue pompoms accompanied by two pompom-less black-trousered, not-so-slim males. Their moves are complicated, energetic and well choreographed. They are the only really flamboyant dance troupe I will get to see at any speedway track in the country during my travels, though many have their own less energetic choreographed routines.

With the racing about to begin I return to the riders' hillock that overlooks the bowl of the track and all the activity in the pits. I find Laura Filmer there; she's decidedly cold in the strong wind that whips through this part of the stadium. I chat with local girl and Hull Vikings' fanatic Louise McLoughlin, who stands next to me in her official-looking blue anorak. She lives 20 minutes away from here and normally works on the checkouts at the local Morrisons supermarket, although I didn't notice any of these nearby, when I drove through the local housing estate on my way to the track. Her work at the stadium is, like everyone else's, voluntary and she's done it with great enthusiasm for two years. She used to stand by the pits gate when she first came to watch "Ull" race and would say to her friends, "I'll be in those pits one day, watch me". Her dream and forecast has come true, although it's slightly tinged with sadness. She used to help out at the speedway accompanied by her friend Lynn who has had to sadly stop coming along for health reasons. Louise helps all year round, even out of season, with the tasks that need attention about the place. In the winter months without racing, she helps paint the kickboards-cum-safety fence that lines the complete circumference of the track. This must be a marathon task, even in warm weather, never mind during the cold of the close season. Still, Louise is local and is no doubt properly acclimatised. On a racing night like tonight, it's her job to "look after the riders and sort the pits", whatever that might mean. Usually it's to help the track staff or to clean the pits. It's unpredictable but very intense, which is how she likes it, and always "in the thick of the action". Louise is a mine of information about everything connected to the club, which includes the mascot 'Ullvik', so called through a combination of the city name – Ull – and the team's nickname of the Vikings, which, obviously leads to the name Ullvik! Her biggest bugbear, if she has one in a job she loves, is that most Ull people appear blissfully unaware that the speedway team exists locally, despite the fact that in recent years they have raced on both sides of the city. Both at the present location Craven Park, since 1995 Louise thinks, and previously across the city at The Boulevard. Overall, she's delighted to actively participate with the club – in the pits – as well as travel round the country with her friends to watch the racing at other tracks and, most definitely, meet all the riders afterwards. Louise knows that she's lucky to have realised her dream and appreciates her good fortune. She looks over at the gaggle of fans who stand by the closed pits gate before she notes that "lots of girls would love to stand with the riders all night, like I am every week, but they have to stand behind the gates and watch me!"

With my pits pass I also get to stand with the riders and mechanics all evening and watch them from the hillock too; it's a place that overlooks the action on the track on one side and, on the other, the feverish activity in the pits below. Bikes rush in all directions; they leave for and return from races, are refuelled or have to have vital adjustments made to their gearing and set ups. In heat 1 Sanchez passes Wilson in exhilarating fashion on the back straight on the last lap to then race to a deserved victory. Adam Filmer pushes Dan Giffard away in heat 2 for his first outing of the evening. Hull has a peculiar shaped track with long narrow straights and what appears to be rather angular shaped contours that must trace the outer perimeter of the rugby pitch in its centre.[4] It's an added degree of difficulty for riders at this track, which Giffard negotiates well, since he uses his local knowledge to swoop past Aidan Collins to take third place. This bend isn't negotiated so well

[4] In his book *Wheels and Deals* ex-Hull promoter at the Boulevard, Ian Thomas, comments on Craven Park, "it's an unusual track because it's narrow and there's not much room for passing … but the riders seem to stay close, it always appears as if there is going to be some overtaking and, strangely, the racing looks good".

by Craig Branney in the next race. He crashes straight through the fence and doesn't appear to attempt to bother to turn, when all four riders arrive at the first bend in a tight bunch. The referee has all four riders back in the re-run, while Craig swiftly extricates himself from the wreckage of the safety fence that he has practically demolished. He strides back to the pits to prepare, while the announcer approvingly notes, "they make them tough in Cumbria". If Craig's reaction, or lack of it, is anything to go by, they certainly do!

In the pits I notice Newcastle's Kristian Lund, the present British Ice Speedway Champion, he's here to help Hull's experienced rider Garry Stead as his mechanic for this evening. After Garry has been pushed off to make his way to the start for heat 4, Kristian runs up the metal stairs to watch from the hillock. He stands in a large group of mechanics and riders who cluster and watch together along with the various team managers – Dave Peet and both Drurys.[3] He only watches a couple of laps of the race before he rushes off again to attend to his work with Garry and looks forward to seeing me again at Sheffield tomorrow night when Newcastle race there. I mention that George English has already warned me not to bother to go since Newcastle ride so poorly there. Kristian replies "its not one of my favourite tracks, as I don't ride Sheffield that well".

The announcer has somehow managed to find and collar veteran rider Ray Morton, who has come along to watch this evening's meeting. He's on holiday in the area with his family, which causes the announcer to question his sanity, "don't people look at you funny when you say that you're going on holiday to Hull?" Ray won't have any of it and he sincerely notes that his "kids love it up here" and that it's a great place to visit. He also stresses that so far he's enjoyed the meeting and the chance to mingle with the friendly Hull crowd.

For myself, I enjoy the chance to mingle with the riders who watch on the hillock and, as they talk so loudly, it's hard not to eavesdrop on their conversations. Stood directly in front of me, among a group of young riders and their friends, is the 15-year-old prodigy from Sussex who rides for Weymouth, Lewis Bridger, who is due to ride later in the second-half meeting in the Academy League fixture. He has an impressively large and angry looking abrasion on his left arm by his elbow which, because he's made of stern stuff, he affects not to notice. He must be a particularly hardy young man since he finds a T-shirt sufficient protection from the freezing cold wind, while he stands there and chats to his granddad, while they both survey the racing. The heat they watch on the track features his Weymouth colleague Dan Giffard, his friend and rival, who he sees regularly those days when he's at Dan's father's motorcycle shop and workshop. Lewis hasn't ridden at Hull before but confidently notes, "it doesn't look that quick, does it?" While Dan rides a steady race, stuck in third position, as he rounds each bend Lewis exclaims, "he's doing that freaking leg trailing thing again?" Granddad has no easy explanation about this distinctive style but, instead, calmly notes that Dan has improved enough this year to begin to ride once more in the Premier League and advises the youngster, "you want to watch his averages this year at Weymouth". Lewis responds with a blunt "it dun't matter".

After the race, Dan Giffard rejoins this small group and proceeds to immediately rather aggressively take the mickey out of Lewis, who no longer has his granddad by his side since he's gone to work on Lewis's bike. They must banter on a lot, since Dan delights to regale the group with story after story of Lewis's supposed idiocy, "he's such a thicko, his sponsor bought him a new bike and when he's interviewed about it he doesn't name them but says 'my sponsor is a building company, they do digging' – what an answer!" Lewis is having none of this abusive banter and defends himself, "they do

[5] Earlier in the evening, before the racing started, I had taken the chance to ask Kristian about the recent extraordinary fracas at Newcastle during the Somerset match. He diplomatically notes with admirable understatement that "there was a lot going on!" To his mind, events got out of hand as "there were too many people in the pits" which wasn't helped by "Paul Fry's mechanic kicking James Grieves in the head" after heat 15. I share my view that the only person who really established any control over the situation was 70-year-old Joan English who, belied her advanced years, calmed the large angry crowd with her strength of personality and voice. Kristian smiles, and says, Joan loves her speedway and is a great woman, something he experienced first hand when he once stayed with her for a few days. He's keen to stress the upturn on and off track this season at Newcastle, with racing results markedly improved and increased numbers of fans in attendance as a result. Kristian enjoyed the opportunity to throw the fully clothed, well-kevlared, 'Pepe' (Josef Franc) in the centre-green pond after the traditional bumps were administered in celebration by the team and track staff for his full maximum at the meeting. He claims it's the sort of thing the fans enjoy, which diverts attention away from the fact that the riders enjoy it too!

do digging, I looked it up on the web, but it was just before my heat and I was nervous, so I said that". Then, self-consciously, he plaintively adds as a form of extenuation, "he's got one GSCE and I ain't got nothing yet". Meanwhile Shaun Tacey has fallen in heat 5 and got stuck under his bike. This allows Lewis to attempt to deflect attention from himself with a shout of "get up you freaking prick!" I leave the lads in their T-shirts on the hillock to their relentless mockery, while a bored Lewis loudly but accurately imitates the strangulated roar of the bikes at full revs, just before the tapes lift on heat 6. I mention the noticeable lack of warm clothes in a cold wind to Louise, who shrugs and says speedway riders are a tough lot known for never complaining. Recently she'd seen Ross Brady stripped off topless with his kevlars around his waist, which I gather she'd enjoyed; but she couldn't help but notice that his chest was pitted with dents from where the shale repeatedly flies up and hits his body at great speed while he rides. Between the races, Louise then rushes to get on the centre green to watch the racing continue from a much more exhilarating vantage point. The scores remain close until around heat 6, after which Hull begin to establish a decent lead over Workington that they never look likely to relinquish.

Someone who hasn't enjoyed his visit to Hull is Shaun Tacey. He returns to the pits area with mechanical difficulties and proceeds with his mechanic to try to fix his bike. All the while the two-minute time allowance ticks down, which prompts his promoter and team manager, Graham Drury, to rush down the steep metal pits stairs as he repeatedly shouts very loudly, as if talking to the deaf and retarded, "you can't do it, you can't do it, get another bike!" He's completely correct, albeit impatient but then maybe that's what you have to be as team manager; it's a role that requires a strange mix of mentor, advisor, but above all, a somewhat militaristic and often demanding Sergeant Major figure. It's a role Graham plays well and is temperamentally suited to in his attitude and demeanour, although others ascribe the more patrician and instructional aspects of his temperament and character to his normal day job as a magistrate. Shaun is not at all happy that three races have given him zero points and two exclusions, so far. What particularly galls him is that since he used to ride here for the Vikings, he already very much knows his way round this awkward shaped circuit. He's warmly polite towards me, as ever, despite his annoyance at the evening so far and kindly enquires about my recent travels for my book. I tell him that I've just been to Newcastle at the meeting where Zorro was thrown out. He jokes, "I'd love to be thrown out of the meeting there just so I could pack my van and leave before the crowd does", or, at least, I think it was a joke. Despite the fact that this is the first night Sanchez has raced since his return from injury, we then watch him continue his inspired evening of fast rides with yet another win in heat 10. Well, to be exact, Shaun watches the first lap where Sanchez overcomes a poor start to power superbly round the outside of all the riders on the first bend in to the lead. Before he's seen enough already, though not the actual heat victory itself, and retreats back down to the pits to mount his bike in preparation for his next race in heat 11.

I also wander off from the riders' hillock, since I've decided to experience the rest of the meeting from the main grandstand. I want to take advantage of the rather unique and superb view it provides of the track, and arrive there to find the surrounding area bathed in the bright light of a large three-quarter moon, which shines onto the nearby water, cranes and warehouses. It's also appreciably warmer in the grandstand since it dramatically shelters you from the bitter cold of the strong wind, despite Dave Peet's earlier bizarre claim that it's a "warm breeze" tonight.

It also gives me the chance to sit down and properly study the match programme. They say that the advertisers, whom you trust to have a good handle on these things, will often give you a good insight into the readership of a programme or magazine. If that's the case, then the audience that comes to watch the speedway and that reads the Hull match programme must be both patriotic but pretty keen for even more excitement and thrills. I make this assumption on the basis of full-page adverts, not just for one service, but for each of the armed services. It's certainly a group of advertisers unique to the Hull programme and a smart idea by the people who sell the advertising space to get all three of the services to compete for their readers' attention. In these adverts, the Army and the Navy both congratulate the recent success of the team in 2004 and then advocate enlisting: possibly because the average length of an enlistment will approximate the number of years that it'll take Hull Speedway to triumph once more. The Army chap looks wistfully into the distance out of the open

doors of a military plane and might have been attracted by the offer of six weeks' holiday and £219 per week in the "16 to 27 club". In their advert, the Navy decides to showcase a boat (possibly a frigate), a torpedo and a helicopter all apparently involved in the protection of the country and who work to bust drug rings (?) while they also boast of a "training everyone is envious of". The RAF go for a full-page colour advert that bizarrely features someone on a toboggan, which itself might indicate severe military spending cut-backs? Their motto is 'Rise Above The Rest' which appears difficult to achieve when you're shooting down the Cresta Run on a toboggan. They don't picture the vehicles of any other rival service, such as ships or tanks though; instead they stress the sports and fitness angle invariably attached to RAF service. I presume the person pictured is a man as the advert states that they're a non-discriminatory organisation, but with the important caveat, "however for reasons of combat effectiveness, women cannot join the RAF Regiment". A quick glance around the stand for a visual straw poll of likely candidates who might be tempted to enlist for any of the armed services after the meeting isn't promising. There are a number of older people with their grandchildren on the nearby seats – those who've already served their country with those who are too young – along with a couple who enthusiastically snog to my left who already appear too old to enlist but, at least, they are passionate.

The sponsors of the Hull team itself, 'CPD: Cleaning and Paper Disposables' with the great mission statement of "one source, many solutions" – how many types of toilet paper do you need? – look much more likely to have identified some potential customers among the traditional speedway audience. I decide to keep a weather eye out during the evening for anyone who abseils down from the stand rather than uses the stairs but forget this when I become distracted by the rest of the evening's racing. From this imposing grandstand, not only do you get a superb aerial view of the start and the race itself, but also the cavernous shape of the stand amplifies the noise of the bikes tremendously. I like this very much, because the roar of the machines vibrates in the air and provides a cacophony appropriate to the spectacle. Heat 12 produces another easy win for the rejuvenated Sanchez that leads the announcer to ponder aloud, "I don't know what Emiliano Sanchez is on, but I want some of it!" The meeting closes when Sanchez finally loses to a rider from the opposition in heat 15 but, despite this, Hull win comfortably with a final score line of 55-40.

The action hasn't finished though, since there is still a fixture from the Under-15 2005 British Academy League to be run. It pits a team called Buffalo against a team called Dinosaurs. All these Academy League fixtures were arranged to take place in the school holidays so that they didn't distract any of the young riders from their important studies. It's rather incongruous to notice that Lewis Bridger will race in this fixture. It might be appropriate to his age, but it's no longer appropriate to either his skill level or the continued development of his already considerable abilities. When I return to the hillock I put this question to Lewis directly. He answers that he's here to support the league and as "it's my first time at this track" so he prefers to look forward to the valuable experience of riding it, which he otherwise wouldn't get. Compared to the conversations I overheard with his granddad or his mates, Lewis is understandably much more guarded when he speaks with me but, nonetheless, goes out of his way to praise his erstwhile 15-year-old rival, Josh Auty. With a slightly backhanded compliment Lewis mentions, "he's very good but sometimes tries too hard". Prior to the season, Josh had garnered the most press attention as the young rider identified with the greatest potential for the season. As it turned out, Lewis has subsequently excited everyone with his bravado and ability throughout this season.

Nonetheless, Josh really looks the part when he races against Lewis in the first heat, and he is extremely noticeable with his very brightly coloured bike and kevlars. As if to illustrate Lewis's point, Josh falls in the race and is excluded by the referee. On the hillock, the guiding force behind many of the recent events for young riders in this country, Peter Oakes, the British Under-21 and youth team manager, marshals the youngsters that eagerly throng around him. Otherwise he dispenses words of encouragement, praise and advice in the pits or when surrounded by the clamouring young riders on the hillock. I watch Peter closely throughout, he's totally absorbed and engaged in what he's doing, with an air that communicates that he's very much in his element but not to be interrupted. We don't get any chance for a chat other than when he copies the winning times for the Academy League races from my programme towards the end of the meeting. Everyone from the Academy League rides with great enthusiasm and surprising aplomb, though sometimes the youngsters can look a little shaky or tentative in their riding. This is totally understandable and just as it should be, since these riders are here to gradually improve their overall skills. The only rider who stands out, riding at a superior level of skill and style considerably above that of his contemporaries, is Lewis Bridger. Although, that said, Josh looks very composed on his bike as well. The racing comes thick and fast, as does the Bridger-Auty re-match. This results in another win for Lewis in a time that is, amazingly, only half a second outside the slowest winning time achieved by the riders in the Premier League meeting that had just preceded it. This result, achieved on his second-ever race on the Hull track, underlines Lewis's ability and potential, though his skills would be obvious even to someone unfamiliar with the sport. The next time these two stars of the future meet Josh beats his rival, which thereby indicates that the gulf between them isn't so great that it can't be bridged on a race-by-race basis. Ultimately, the comparatively equal chance of victory in each and every race is one of the essential appeals of speedway. However, Josh's victory only comes after the heat is stopped by the referee in the interests of safety, because of a dramatic fall, on the second bend, by Gary Irving. Josh greets the decision and result with some exultation as he returns triumphantly to the pits area.

Sadly no more racing is possible, since the time curfew in operation at the track is reached and so we have to prematurely conclude the Junior racing with two heats still unraced. The Buffalos win 21-15 against the Dinosaurs. I believe that it's increasingly rare for Lewis to have the time with his other riding commitments to compete at this level of racing so, at least, I can say I saw him ride Junior Speedway in years to come! The real winners are all the youngsters who participate and will possibly become the future of the sport itself. Peter Oakes makes an especially valued contribution to that hopefully not too distant future with his time, dedication and enthusiasm. The riders and their parents and helpers start to pack their bikes and belongings away into their waiting vehicles for the journeys home.

My intact car still sits in the car park and, after I leave and get lost, I head off for an extended tour of the city centre's one-way systems and pedestrianised precincts. By the time I return to the B&B, the secure car park is already secured and the couple in the room next door have begun to spend the remainder of the night on the edge of loud ecstasy.

17th August Hull v. Workington (Premier League) 55-40

Chapter 30: Something Special in Sheffield
18th August Sheffield v. Newcastle

"If you're sitting at home with a pizza takeaway and the food has gone all over the floor due to the excitement of that race, please forgive us" Nigel Pearson

9.1 A Track Homologation Certificate will be valid for 3 seasons, detailing information on the Track, including its size, construction, safety fences, zones and lighting and detailing any dispensations given, including those applicable when used for a Training session only.

It's the sort of summer day that starts for me in the warm sunshine of Hull, and the journey from there to Sheffield, while not the most prepossessing still makes you consider living in God's own county, Yorkshire. My journey took me through a rich mix of the beautiful and the industrial. We're supposed to call this a heritage nowadays. It's something to marvel at, in some places; but, in others, it still leaves a scar that remains long after the industry has departed, no matter how much money and effort has been spent to restore the area. If I lived hereabouts I'd thank my lucky stars for the down-to-earth, friendly bluntness of the locals, if only because of the brainwashing I received from my father who was evacuated to Yorkshire during the war, although that was in the north of the county[1] and it's definitely a county whose citizens pointedly preserve such geographic considerations.

[1] The Reverend Sydney Smith (1771-1845) – a 19th century writer and humorist (born in Essex but sometime vicar in North Yorkshire) – once commented: "Never ask a man if he comes from Yorkshire. If he does he will tell you. If he does not, why humiliate him?"

Mick Gregory in the Sheffield Track shop. © Jeff Scott

Roughed up shale at the start line. © Jeff Scott

The Diamonds prepare in the pits. © Jeff Scott

I wouldn't go and see most of the football teams round here even for free but, for the cricket and the speedway, that would be a different matter. If you lived here you would have the chance to enjoy successive nights of speedway racing during midweek. If you only kept to all the events within the county boundaries of Yorkshire, it would still involve one night at Hull and the next at Sheffield. And with a bit of effort and a few hours driving in any direction, you could probably watch speedway every night of the week, except Tuesdays, when a trip to the Isle of Wight would be a little too far.

This next leg of my trip requires a quick return visit to the Garrison Hotel, exceptionally near to the Owlerton Stadium in Sheffield. My excuse, as ever, is this book because I've had to return to try and actually see some racing on one of the country's biggest and fastest speedway tracks. When you quiz Sheffield co-promoter, Neil Machin, about the reasons behind the success of the club and the track, he highlights the excellent relationship with the stadium landlords, the strength of the bond with the sponsors Pirtek, and the business acumen of the owners. No less importantly, but useless on their own without these other vital ingredients, Neil praises the track and track staff, knowledgeable fans and a team of riders who relish the fast speeds that the excellent shape and condition of the track encourages. It's always been a fast track since it was built in 1928 with a unique D shape on the back straight. You can't really see this shape from within the stadium, but Neil assures me that, if you happen to view it from the impressively rural Parkwood Springs Hills that overlook this part of Sheffield, you can see this distinctive layout really easily. Neil delights in the quality of the stadium infrastructure when it comes to the enhancement of the spectators' overall experience at the speedway, whether they watch the meeting from the terraces or "the executive boxes that hold 72 people". That you can watch from the restaurant and have a "delicious, warming meal" is another additional benefit in its favour. Neil is keen to stress the quality of his restaurant is another key feature that contributes to the success of his club, particularly in comparison to many other British speedway tracks without the luxury of such a facility. Or, indeed, those clubs that are housed in stadiums, which are more decrepit, but that Neil diplomatically declines to specifically identify. Whatever the experience at Sheffield is like as a fan, it's definitely a track that intimidates the visiting riders and favours the home riders used to its particular contours, dynamics, grip and speed. Only the other day, tonight's visiting team manager, George English, specially advised me not to bother to attend this fixture in the expectation of witnessing anything like a competitive performance from his Newcastle team; who all profess to have a particular antipathy with the circuit and so, from a close racing perspective, entertainment values will be pretty poor. Not that this level of fear or intimidation among the visiting teams bothers Neil, who definitely relishes the high speeds that the home riders generate around Owlerton, both as a spectacle and as a benefit to sell to the public. These speeds were recently measured at around 76 m.p.h. and, never prone to understatement in his capacity as a promoter, Neil claims West Yorkshire born Sheffield rider Andre Compton is "probably as fast as anyone on the planet round here!" How to ride well here is apparently not a secret, it's "just a question of bravery and confidence to want to chase the dirt out on the kickboard".

It promises to be an ideal evening for racing. There's a weak late afternoon sun, less bright than in Hull because of the light cloud cover, but enough that it still almost passes for a summer heat wave in this part of South Yorkshire during August. By the time I've walked over the busy dual carriageway and crossed the impressively large car park, I'm just in time to join a queue of scouts who patiently wait with their scoutmaster to go through the turnstiles. Neil, the always ebullient Sheffield co-promoter, expects that I'll turn up at his office prior to the meeting and, as he chats on the phone, I overhear that he's already beside himself with anticipation at tonight's visit of Sheffield legend, Nigel Boocock. Both Booey and his wife Cynthia are over from their home in Cleveland, Australia ("level with Brisbane on the coast"), where they've been happily settled for years since they emigrated from England. Once he's hung up, Neil appears distracted and preoccupied with the last-minute work of a promoter, but he has a few people to help him in the Speedway Office tonight as well as a continual stream of visitors through the always-open door to contend with. Everyone but Booey turns up in the doorway. In the Owlerton office is Betty Wilson, who "just came down and helped on a Thursday" and has now done so for the 20 years ever since. The work involves various administrative tasks and Betty also helps with the production of the distinctive Sheffield race card that, uniquely within British speedway, you get free on admission to the stadium. Neil doesn't believe in programmes and, as with so many things, has his own inimitable approach. Nonetheless Betty helps with what she insists is a "programme" but most other people strongly disagree and call it a race card; which includes the anonymous reviewers of the *Speedway Star* who annually assess and compare every speedway tracks' programmes throughout the UK. I think it's exceptional value – it's free – serves its purpose, and definitely doesn't leave you with the sense that you've been ripped off, as you sometimes do at some other speedway tracks. It's all part of Neil's zealous pursuit of cost-savings and his mantra to provide good value to cost-conscious customers. After an initial marked reluctance to answer questions that would do any captured prisoner of war proud, Betty chats amiably about the era at Sheffield when she first began to attend; when her brother-in-law, Maurice Ducker, ran the speedway back then. The family connection still holds strong for her at Sheffield Speedway because her grandson, Ben Wilson, rides at the club and has lately received positive reviews for his recent performances on the track for the Tigers. Neil perks up at the mention of family connections, and he reiterates the longevity and loyalty of service displayed by so many of the people that help behind the scenes every week of the season at Owlerton.

Neil has many stories to tell about Booey, some of them printable but the majority not. He also has quite a repertoire that involves some of the more slapstick jokes that Booey has told him over the years, which are complimented by a rich fund of anecdotes and true stories. Neil particularly loves Booey's stories from an era when the Edinburgh Monarchs had a rider named Cox. When the rider was injured one week, the local paper had a report with the headline 'Monarchs take on Diamonds with Cox Out'. He had recovered sufficiently by the next week for the headline to read 'Monarchs take on Glasgow Tigers with Cox In'. Neil guffaws enthusiastically, but Betty only smiles weakly. A short while later, Booey says the Monarchs actually took on Middlesbrough with Cox in. There are hours of fun to be had with this joke and I resolve to keep an eye out for any teams with riders called Cox, just so I can make a prick of myself with this playful use of words. I won't repeat some of the other jokes in order to retain some level of decency for now, but instead leave the office for a wander round the stadium.

I've only reached the covered terraced grandstand on the home straight that's just around the corner from the Sheffield Speedway Office when I join the crowd that's gathered round the well-stocked tables of the track-shop stall run by the affable Derby County supporter, Mick Gregory. He has legions of Brian Clough stories which he repeats, while we commiserate on the death of the maestro some 11 months previously. Mick only has time to chat in the seconds he snatches between the demands of an armada of fastidious customers. All the usual items are on sale and the stall does a brisk trade in *Speedway Stars*, Sheffield pens and, while I'm there, photographs and miniature models of the Sheffield riders. Some customers even leave in disappointment and empty-handed after the last highly prized miniature model of Andre Compton had already been sold, just minutes before. While I observe the people studiously examine the features of the models, Mick affects to be slightly baffled at this sudden level of demand while he lets the disappointed customers down gently, "they've all gone, sorry, he's been the best seller this year surprisingly". The offer to buy a discounted photo of Andre "fastest rider on the planet around here" Compton instead doesn't appeal to any of them, but, it does stimulate quite a debate about his healthy and luxuriant eyebrows. The consensus after a few minutes' discussion, leans towards the declaration that he's a great bloke and team rider, but probably prone to a vanity that leads him to secretly dye his eyebrows. I'm not so convinced myself, but some fans are insistent but without corroborating evidence; while another lady imagines that he's so hirsute that he has to shave them for definition and to achieve the effect of a gap.

All the talk of depilitatory habits prompts me, inadvertently, to steal a glance at every passing Tigers' fan's eyebrows before Mick distracts the gathered crowd with a lament about the poor mathematical skills of modern youth. Only the other night he met "a young man of around 22" in a Thresher's off-licence who couldn't add £4.99 and £3.99 for two bottles of wine without the aid of a calculator. Mick then proceeded to amaze him with his mental maths abilities when he immediately predicted the answer without the use of a calculator. It's a story that almost achieves plausibility among the listeners, but then immediately loses credibility when the customer that Mick has been serving throughout this story points out that he has undercharged him for all the items he's just purchased. Mick, without missing a beat, says "that's what I mean about everyone being so honest at speedway", and thereby smoothly covers up his own inability to add £15 for the DVD and £2.40 for the *Speedway Star* correctly. Mindful of the need for accuracy, or pursuing his own agenda, he then adds the caveat "except for Newcastle, where it's the only place they're dishonest or that I've had trouble, though it's not surprising given the rough housing estate it's right next to".

I look vainly about for any Newcastle fans, who've travelled down to Sheffield for the evening, to gainsay the calumny of these observations. There aren't any nearby and, in fact, I struggle throughout the evening, outside the pits area, to find anyone who wears any form of clothing or insignia that indicates they follow Newcastle. Maybe they all share the same fatalism as their promoter, George English, about their team's limited prospects of success in the City of Steel or, perhaps, they have already heard George's prophesies of doom about this fixture first hand.

Meanwhile, as all things Sheffield Tigers continue to fly off the stall – clocks, key rings, pens, models and photos – Mick and I return to the rich vein of history that are his many recollections of Brian Clough. He has many funny stories but, now that he's passed on, Mick regrets that "I never had the courage to speak to him".

Over by the first bend, quite a crowd of people gathers in their favoured positions for an evening of speedway. Given the notorious speed of the racing at Sheffield, a couple of people inform me that it's their favourite place to stand since you get a great view of the vital first-corner action. With the voice of hard-won experience, they say if a rider springs ahead of the others here, it's often very difficult for his competitors to make up any ground throughout the rest of the race. Conversely, if they make a forced or unforced error in the first bend, it's statistically unlikely that they'll ever get back on equal terms. Some people do occasionally manage to bridge this gap, usually the home riders or those who know the track well, but most don't manage it. While I'm on the bend, I chat with Steve Darning and his son Rob who are just the sort of Sheffield speedway supporters to affirm Neil's faith in the usefulness of his many marketing activities and promotions on behalf of the club. They began to come to the track regularly some years ago, "after Wednesday went down", when the then 12-year-old Rob came on a "freebie ticket". From then on they'd caught the bug and they've since graduated to become season-ticket holders for these last four years, thanks to that initial 'free' night. In reality Steve was already a member of the vast legion of lapsed speedway fans, since he began to attend with his dad when he was six years old. He would sit on the wall outside the third bend bar, while his dad had a pint. "It was called 'Clive's Corner' 'cause Clive Featherby used to knock them off there!" He also recalls an "old chap" who always stood on that bend with a "tiny programme board and a tiny pencil, which had started out as a full-size one in 1949". By the late 1980s and early 1990s, it had become just a sliver in the shaking hands of an old man. Apart from these fond recollections, Steve also remembers "before we had the barrier, I got shale in my hair every week, even though I had a parka; my mum used to have to comb all the shale out".

Over in the cosily compact pits area by the fourth bend, both teams of riders busily make their last-minute preparations for the meeting that starts in just under 30 minutes' time. I can't see his mother, Joan, but George English, Newcastle's avuncular team manager and co-promoter, assures me that she's around here somewhere. Unfortunately the crowd they attract at Owlerton are loud and noisy, because otherwise I'm sure that later we'd probably be able to hear Joan loudly encourage her beloved Diamonds to greater efforts. When the crowds are smaller, as they often are at other tracks, her keen vocal support matters. George has the sort of cheerfulness you affect before a major hospital operation, studiously upbeat but, nonetheless, he obviously fears the worst. After the tempestuous meeting with Somerset five days ago at Brough Park, he jokes, "I hope that you're not going to cause problems again!" For the rest of the season, as a result of a bad run of injuries, he's drafted Sheffield asset James Birkinshaw into the Newcastle side. It's his debut tonight and this could prove significant since he'll have something to prove to his former club Sheffield and, also, because he knows the racing lines round the circuit. In an ostentatious but genuine show of promoterly co-operation, Neil Machin is happy for his rider to ride for his opponents. Given this and what I know of Birkinshaw's recent form, I'd be more than slightly suspicious myself. George isn't, but clearly he has his eyes wide open since he notes, all too accurately it happens, "Birkinshaw goes well round here but nowhere else". With the timing of a comedian George phlegmatically reviews this evening's prospect of a surprise win with practised scepticism: "in order to beat them you have to actually catch them, particularly here!"

A short step away in the pits is Ken Alvy, the track-gate operator at Sheffield for the last 20 years, who also doesn't expect to see any flying pigs tonight, "to lose we'll have to have a hell of a lot of bad luck and all of our bikes will have to break down!" He should know. He's here every week and he's been a fan ever since 1945, when he used to regularly go to watch Sheffield, Bradford and Long Eaton. On race night though, he concentrates on the tasks at hand to make sure that things run smoothly and he also tries to ensure that only legally insured and registered personnel are allowed on the hallowed surface of the track. However, it isn't always possible to stop people who wish to expose themselves to significant danger. Only last week, a parent invaded the track after one of the riders from the Under-15s Academy League got "seriously injured with a badly smashed up hip, but how can you stop a parent following their instincts?" Luckily, I have signed in and have the insurance and the permission to be able to go on the track or the centre green, so I won't be feeling the sharp

side of Ken's tongue myself this evening. Ironically though, the first time I try to cross the track to the centre green, I do manage to wait until the bikes are safely back in the pits but forget to check for tractors and so I'm very nearly mown down by a particularly silent one, as it passes by for some essential track grading!

Just at that moment, Neil appears by our shoulders and excitedly invites me upstairs to the renowned Owlerton stadium restaurant to meet tonight's legendary guest of honour, Nigel Boocock, for a few snatched minutes before the racing starts. The guests of honour have all just sat down to choose a slap-up meal from the menu and already there's quite a lively crowd on the centrally positioned table of honour, that includes Booey, his son Darren, and wife Cynthia. Booey suggests we grab a few minutes to ourselves at a slightly quieter and much less lively nearby table. He's a stocky, very friendly man in a dark suit with a very firm handshake from a hand with a very obviously missing finger. Neil informs me later that Nigel lost it after a crash at Exeter, when he had the choice to either wait three months for it to heal naturally or "only three days if he takes it off" before he can ride again. It's the sort of decision you make in haste but repent at leisure and Neil notes sympathetically, "I think he regrets it now as it means you lose 20 percent of your grip forever". Neil can empathise since he has his own rogue finger, which he then proudly shows me and quickly waggles, but he has avoided the perils of amputation by his sensible decision to just live with this peculiarity.

While he toys with what to choose from the menu, Booey speaks with the speed of a racing commentator and I listen to a stream of stories that would invariably delight any after-dinner audience. Throughout our conversation, he's very blunt, down to earth, matter of fact, and often very modestly makes light of his considerable achievements within speedway. Booey appreciates how well life has treated him and, from his praise for and descriptions of his life in Australia, you'd think that he also moonlighted as a publicist for the Aussie Tourist Board. He's a few days away from his 68th birthday and is proud to be happily married, have children, and to have emigrated to Australia. He notes, "I don't miss a great deal about England". Booey attributes this to the quality of life he enjoys because he lives in a large house on land that overlooks the sea and has the luxury of his own swimming pool ("with cover"), though he immediately stresses, "I don't sit at home doing nothing all day". He spends some of his time in paid work and he looks after 141 plots of land for around five hours a week ("not an enormous job", but one that does involve the use of a pressure water blaster, which I gather Booey enjoys using) and also "a local MP pays me to clean his offices and car park".

All this talk of Australia gives him a few moments to remember some things he'd like to tell me for my book. He laughs and says, "I must think of freaking something I can rubbish for you to make it interesting". Booey is President of the Veteran Riders Association of Australia ("an honorary position") and is convinced that in the UK the sport is "on the up". Particularly so at Sheffield, where he has "huge respect for Neil – he invests a lot of effort into the speedway, it isn't just the riders that work blooming hard you know!" But, Booey despairs of the "politics of the sport, I could say freaking more but it's best to be polite". He admires Neil for the way he has built up his club, while he steers his way around some of the crazier aspects of the sports internecine politics. Beside their friendship, mutual respect and admiration, they clearly have a lot in common which manifests itself with characteristically blunt opinions that they're unafraid to share. Maybe that's a characteristic Yorkshire thing too?

One thing is certain, Booey has looked forward to watching some speedway, while he's here in England. He's here tonight and, like myself, at Coventry tomorrow. The sport has changed dramatically since his day, "thank freak I'm not riding, I couldn't go that fast". He thinks that technical advances might have gone too far when it comes to the power of the machines on the modern slicker-surfaced tracks, "I'm cringing at the speed of the sport, it frightens me, when we were a bit slower there was more overtaking".

It's a topic he'd memorably addressed earlier in the day, live on the local radio station BBC Sheffield, when he'd commented, "freaking hell I really do think they go too fast". Later in the interview when asked, "what about Newcastle?" Booey bluntly replied, "I've had better bloody trips to the toilet". Which, if nothing else makes good radio, was typical Booey, but maybe was just a bit too frank and his language too industrial for the afternoon audience.

 I compliment Booey on his legendary status in the sport, while he orders from the menu with the very attentive waiter, which further confirms the sort of deluxe restaurant facilities they have at Sheffield speedway. After he has placed his food order, Booey admits "I'm the highest ever scorer in the British League" before he pauses momentarily and adds with modesty, "only 'cause I freaking rode more than anyone else!" His modesty means that he fails to mention that between 1958 and 1976 he scored an incredible 7,739 points in 748 team matches for Coventry!! He also literally introduced a splash of colour into the sport with his dyed pale-blue leathers with white belt, boots and gloves during an era when everyone else wore regulation black racing leathers.

To his mind, Owlerton is "a proper race track, with excellent preparation and a real racing surface – very few can compare to Sheffield for the competitive racing and overtaking taking place". It was always a contrast to other places, the very thought of which makes Booey shudder, "when you think of the bloody, crappy little tracks I used to ride; it's hard to adapt to grotty surfaces on bumpy fart arseing little tracks". He lists a few examples, which I tell him I won't mention, which incites him to again ponder, "I must think of someone to insult for you".

Booey doesn't, of course. It's all talk as the flood of affectionate memories drowns out the need to manufacture any hurtful or critical comments. He's shocked that I haven't watched any racing at Sheffield before. Living a couple of hundred miles away in Brighton is apparently no excuse, when you can witness overtaking and excitement like they have at Sheffield. However, any thrill at the spectacle of daredevil overtaking manoeuvres at high speed isn't going to happen "if the track is as flat as arseholes, like many are!" He leans back to wistfully think aloud, "I've had my good days here …" just as Neil passes and interjects, "usually injured though". The talk of injuries provokes another trip down memory lane and fond recollections of his races and many travels with his "good friend Barry Briggs".

They had many escapades together and, like all speedway riders, suffered an unenviable catalogue of injuries. These they tended to ignore or tried to work round as best they could. He recalls an International meeting at Wolverhampton where Briggo got "knocked off" and broke the stirrup that holds your thumb in place. He'd no sooner got to the pits than he had to exclaim, "hold up they're carrying Booey in as well". It transpired that Nigel had just broken his collarbone after a crash with Anders Michanek. Their journey home in the car that night required some memorable coordination and teamwork, while one of them changed gear and the other pushed the clutch down; which gives a whole meaning to the concept of team riding. By the next Thursday they'd patched themselves up sufficiently for the British championship semi-final. Briggo had made revolutionary but practical use of a knobble from his tyres to function as a kind of compress, which he adapted as a tube round the thumb held in place with a gauze bandage. Booey rode with his broken collarbone strapped up but was soon on the floor after he crashed on the pits bend. The "ambulance was freaking about so much I thought I'd put my collarbone through my lung". Despite the injuries, they managed to finish first and second in that particular meeting. Booey's eyes dance and he's completely animated as he relates all the injuries and how they coped, ignored the pain or generally tried to ride on despite them. For example, another time Booey had broken his left ankle[2] but "tied a strap from me toe to me knee so I couldn't put my foot down riding, as I kept forgetting it was broken". It makes me wince just to listen to the descriptions. Booey's on a roll and tells a whole series of sadly unrepeatable but hilarious jokes without any apparent concern with or awareness of political correctness, before his scrumptious meal arrives and we have to say goodbye.

I rush down from the grandstand dining area to just catch the start of the first race and watch it from the crowded terraced area they have within the pits, which any of the pits personnel may use. However, both teams' riders prefer to crowd together by the safety barrier to watch most of the race before they dash back to their bikes, just as the race draws to a close. Sean Wilson, the diminutive Sheffield captain, stands on some steps to get a better view of the action and throughout the meeting always claps Sheffield riders on the back, just when they head back through the pits gate. Most of this congratulation is well deserved because the Tigers have usually just finished first or second in their race. It also has sufficient effect to gee them up again, since effort levels understandably diminish when it quickly becomes clear, almost from the start, that they'll not face any real opposition on the track from the Newcastle Diamonds team. The only visitor to actually win a race is James Birkinshaw (in fact two, but one of them was awarded to him in contentious circumstances, after he took a rather theatrical fall in heat 8) who, along with Josef 'Pepe' Franc, provides the only real opposition in a rather pitiful Newcastle performance. It's so one-sided that the scorecard soon records a score of rugby-style proportions though, to be fair, the Diamonds might have had another heat winner if Kristian Lund hadn't suffered an engine failure when he led in heat 5.

Still, the racing does have lots of incident and interest. From wherever you watch: the stands, the pits or the centre green the sheer speed of the riders here is phenomenally quick. They achieve terrifying speeds on the straights, test their skill and nerve by riding very close to the safety fence, and negotiate the corners at breakneck pace. A few heats watched from the centre green makes the racing look even faster and, for most of the meeting, the Newcastle riders perform as though they know they're already beaten before they even arrive at the tapes. The races glide by in orderly fashion as I stand and sip a cup of tea made by the pits tea lady, Catherine, and savour the atmosphere of the floodlit stadium. From trackside, it appears a magnificent facility and, when viewed from the centre green, the grandstands and terraces are thoroughly packed with fans.

Kyle Legault enlivens the fixture early on when he clips the fence at speed, but still manages to hold on to his bike sufficiently well to continue and go on to win the race. He overtakes brilliantly the next time he rides and the DJ celebrates with the theme from *Hawaii Five-O*. The commentator at Sheffield is the always-bubbly Nigel Pearson, the BSPA press officer and ubiquitous Sky Sports commentator. If anything he is slightly restrained tonight in his announcements, compared to what I would have expected based on his television commentary work. But then it wasn't the sort of meeting where you could inject too much bravura or verbal fervour into what was always a very one-sided but often exciting meeting; though lack of entertainment rarely prevents Nigel's voluble excitement on the television. When Jamie Robertson hits the fence with an audible thump in heat 8, Nigel understatedly notes, "it looks very, very uncomfortable that one". Neil kindly introduces Nigel to me during the interval and he's only too keen to help[3].

---

[2] The foot riders use, with a steel shoe on, to help them negotiate round corners.

If the meeting had been a fight, the referee would have stepped in long before the end, which Sheffield win exceptionally easily 63-29. The Sheffield team and mechanics rush onto the track after heat 15 to enthusiastically administer the bumps to both Andre Compton and Ricky Ashworth, both of whom have remained undefeated by Newcastle riders throughout the fixture. The team then rides off on a victory lap of celebration loaded onto to just three bikes. Neil Machin would have joined the frenzy of reciprocal enthusiastic waving, hollering and punching the air between the riders and the crowd, but is just a fraction too slow to arrive on the track and cram himself onto one of the heavily laden bikes. Instead, he settles for a more regal wave. By the time the delighted Sheffield riders have exhausted the adulation and returned to the pits the Newcastle team have almost completely packed up their bikes and gone, like criminals all too keen to rush from the scene of the crime. George English is happy to talk though; as is Josef 'Pepe' Franc who slowly and meticulously cleans practically every detachable piece of equipment he can find from his bike before he carefully packs them away with equal precision. When I mention that he rode well, Pepe pulls a face as if he's eaten something unpleasant, "You think? It's very hard here!" He's happy though to solve the mystery that surrounds the pronunciation of his surname, "in Czech we say 'France'" before he returns to some more earnest TLC of his equipment. The only other Newcastle rider that remains in the pits is Jamie Robertson; he's not overwhelmed by admirers but appears reasonably pleased with his own performance and is certainly the only member of Newcastle staff who smiles afterwards. The Sheffield side of the pits is still thronged with smiling riders, who laugh, joke and converse with each other loudly, secure in themselves and the moment of victory surrounded by contented but noticeably industrious mechanics.

The Diamonds co-promoter, George English, has a litany of comments on the events of the evening but mainly looks forward, very sensibly as you wouldn't want to look back too much on tonight's performance. The return fixture between these teams is the next weekend at Brough Park, "we just want to win at our place, though it'll be hard as Andre and Richard used to ride for us and Sean was a track record holder". On the positive side, George feels "Robertson rode his heart out, Birkinshaw rode well and Lund, who'd never scored a point here before, blew an engine when leading and then had to ride his other bike which is set up for a small track". He is disappointed not to have matched the 30 points target he'd set for the team beforehand — coincidentally also the total that League leaders Rye House managed on their visit to Sheffield — which I assume is code for 'It's a difficult track for any team to visit no matter how good they are' without actually uttering the phrase. When I ask where everyone has gone, George shrugs theatrically and says with resignation, "there's a bar beckoning" which causes Jamie to interject, "I'm not going, I'm a professional", something that his broad smile appears to contradict.

Neil Machin pointedly nods over to the work his riders are still around to perform on their bikes, despite the adulation of the crowd and although the meeting has ended in an easy victory for them. To his mind, fundamentally, "the difference between the good kids and the others is that you've got to want to learn." Every young rider dreams of speedway glory, "they all want to do the Hollywood part but it's workshop points that are absolutely crucial!" Neil maintains that it's the many hours of preparation away from the track, the mental aspect, the diet, training and conditioning, plus the maintenance aspect on your bikes and assorted equipment, which ultimately makes the key difference to the level of success that a rider enjoys in their career. "Every level you move up it becomes harder and harder in the first turn, by the time you get to the GPs it's just savage". As we leave the pits, Neil invites me to join him in the Sheffield riders changing room for a celebratory beer, well a bottled drink with a Budweiser label that passes itself off as beer. I dither in the doorway as Neil cheerfully enters and playfully calls back, "don't be shy, there's nothing you haven't seen before". He then knocks loudly, with a sense of theatre, on the door and then opens it to bellow inside, "what's going on in here then?"

A few minutes of motivational banter and brief celebration later, Neil strides across the tarmac to his lair in the Speedway Office. Two youngsters, aged eight and five, stop him for a very passionate chat about the prevalence of and consequences

---

[3] Particularly with access to any club in the country where I encounter difficulties. I'm very far advanced in my travels so I'm unable to avail myself of his kind offer, although when he learns how far I've already got, he does instead volunteer to help with information on key journalists he knows that I should try to contact when I publish the book in 2006. It's a relief to have finally made some personal contact, particularly since he'd never returned my calls in the spring when I left messages about my book.

for "cheats". They're outraged and incredulous at the behaviour of James Birkinshaw in heat 8. They're so upset that they've been to grill him about it, after the meeting, by his van and they claim, "Birko admitted he just fell off and no-one touched him". They really just can't believe the audacity and iniquity of it. Neil courteously listens to all they have to say, in a manner that would lead you to think – particularly if you were those young boys – that he's just heard the most amazing revelations ever told to him in his life. After he patiently considers their thoughts and weighs their evidence, he settles for mature diplomacy and then sagely observes, on a night when it's easy to be magnanimous, "it's how the ref sees it, isn't it boys!" It's not how these zealous youngsters see it and they wander off to mutter further at the iniquity of the decision and the mystery of Neil's professed equanimity in the face of this daylight robbery.

Safely back in his counting house, Neil's immediate question, when he's barely got through the door, is bluntly directed to his business partner and the co-promoter Malcolm Wright is "how many came in on giveaways?" It's a question that Malcolm has already asked himself and it appears the management team is anxious to establish the exact scale of the impact of their marketing activities; as measured through the members of the crowd that came to the stadium for free tonight on "giveaways". There's definitely an impressive pile of clipped-out coupons – 84 in total – the recent holders of which Neil hopes will have been so entertained that they'll think about a return to the stadium to watch the speedway on another night in the near future. It's a proven and cost-effective promotional tool at Sheffield. "10,000 leaflets cost £350, of which we gave out 200 in the town centre on Saturday, 800 at the grass track on Sunday and 500 for the summer holidays with [the local paper] *The Star*". In a flash of mental maths that Mick in the track shop would be proud of, Neil works out "that's a conversion rate of six percent for leaflets that costs just over £50". Neil and Malcolm both look satisfied before they leave straightaway for the grandstand bar to mingle with the fans, the sponsors and the riders at the end of another successful evening. As they leave I hear Malcolm ask, and inadvertently completely reveal his own priorities for the business, "what was the score so I know who to commiserate with?"

Still on the terraces of the home-straight grandstand, Mick has just about packed away all his merchandise and his small band of extremely youthful helpers carry away the tables or containers of speedway goodies ready for the next meeting. He stands and gossips with David Hoggart, who is one half of the speedway race-night presentation team at Sheffield. Usually he works with Shaun Leigh but tonight, for a change, it's been Nigel Pearson. There's quite a bit of talk about the recent incident with Zorro at Newcastle, which then easily turns into a brief but personal history of various controversial decisions by referees, managers and the BSPA in the last 40 or so years. Dave started to watch speedway in 1963 – "I've been on the inside since 1968" – and they both agree that they have both seen far too many meetings to be at all shocked by events at speedway any longer. Dave laughs at my naïveté, "I've always said that if the paying fans knew what really went on behind the scenes, they wouldn't come again". The talk moves to a discussion of lots of people and incidents I've never even heard of, so I don't get the chance to ask for an explanation of what he might possibly mean afterwards. As I walk back to the Garrison Hotel I decide it's nothing that I should bother to learn about, just in case it's true and I become disillusioned.

18th August Sheffield v. Newcastle (Premier League) 63-29

Chapter 31: Of Bees, Memories and Referees
19th August Coventry v. Arena

"Experienced ref Chris Durno regarded as a rules expert by all the refs" Tony Millard "I've just been assaulted by Scott Nicholls on live TV" Ian Thomas "@@@@ off out of it!" Colin Pratt (shortly afterwards, to Ian Thomas in Belle Vue pits phone box) "I did touch him, but not enough for him to fall off" Andy Smith (after taking off Scott Nicholls)

RANDOM SCB RULES

10.10 The fuel output section of the carburettor must be circular and be 34 mm dia. (max). This measurement must remain constant over a distance of 25mm (min) on the engine side and 5mm (min) on the air intake side. These measurements must be taken from the edges of the throttle valve or the throttle butterfly. The one carburettor must be normally aspirated; fuel injection or other systems are not permitted. Only ambient air may be mixed with the fuel as an oxidant.

A huge choice of roads will eventually lead you to Brandon Stadium, home of the Coventry 'Buildbase' Bees, in the quiet village of Brandon near Coventry. As a village and as a club they have excellent access to the majority of the UK's motorway network. Maybe there's no proper answer to the question 'how many roads must a man walk down before he's allowed to be free?' but when it comes to driving we're not so spiritually challenged and around the Brandon area you're spoilt for choice on the M front with numbers 1, 6, 40, 45 and 69 all in remarkably close proximity to the track. Not that this means that Coventry's star rider Scott Nicholls will arrive early for most home fixtures after his journey from the east of England; instead, he allegedly prefers to arrive in the nick of time for each and every meeting and so test the equanimity of the co-team managers, Colin Pratt and Peter Oakes. Peter Oakes is a comparatively new addition to team management at Brandon, one of the many changes made there since Avtar Sandhu – a man whose name is always prefaced with the phrase "millionaire owner" in the speedway press – and his family took control of the club in 2004. The club were League champions five times during the period from 1968 to 1988, but since then success in the League has been thin on the

View over the pits. © Jeff Scott

H & H with "The Crew". © Jeff Scott

The law arm of the law at Brandon – Keith Denton. © Jeff Scott

ground. There have been other trophies, of course, and numerous illustrious riders have worn the club's distinctive yellow and black "fighting bee" embossed body colours with pride and distinction. Like many once great clubs, the power of the Coventry name has survived but quite a bit of the sting has gone from the team's performances. Their domination of many competitions in the 1980s has diminished to such an extent that it's now the fifth season since they last won a trophy. The *annus horribilis* for the club was arguably 2004 when they finished bottom of the League, for what was only the second time in their 57-year history.

The decision to bring in Peter Oakes mid way through the 2004 season was a surprise within the industry, but has been widely attributed to be at Colin Pratt's instigation. It's Colin who I've journeyed to the stadium to meet hours before the Elite League 'B' fixture with the Arena-Essex 'Husqvarna' Hammers. Given the recent tremendous run of form that has seen Coventry climb from bottom of the league in April to challenge for a position at the top of the league, it's a meeting that Coventry would be expected to easily win. Particularly when Arena's form has seen them remain rooted in the basement of the league throughout the period of Coventry's dramatic improvement. The Bees will also have home advantage and, more importantly, a team of young riders who have gelled together well and have ridden into a purple patch of form. They're the least experienced group of riders in the country – the team has an average age of 21 years and 3 months – and have excelled under the Oakes-Pratt guidance and the captaincy of Scott Nicholls, despite the shock of the loss of their star Swedish Grand Prix rider, Andreas Jonsson, half way through the season. Andreas's resignation was caused by a mixture of illness and his weariness from the relentless travel, which is the lot of the modern gifted speedway rider. This situation ultimately caused Jonsson to reassess his life and reduce his speedway commitments and, in this instance, he decided to stop riding for Coventry.

Since I arrive five hours before the tapes fly up for the meeting, I'm allowed a tremendous choice of parking spaces in the huge car park in front of the impressive Brandon Stadium. At the time of the purchase of the club by Avtar Sandhu, the stadium and the possible redevelopment of the extensive grounds that surround it fuelled the love of intrigue and gossip that powers the speedway forums and Internet message boards. The more vivid theories had the land being developed for housing or other equally lucrative developments by Mr Sandhu[1], after he'd implemented the first stage of his master plan to close the club. Despite frequent denials, these rumours persisted throughout the winter that

[1] Though, at that time, if you did look at the Coventry official website and then look at the pen picture for Mr Sandhu, he did actually admit that he did purchase it with the intention of building on it.

followed the disastrous results of the 2004 season. These prophets of doom have erred in their forecasts of Mr Sandhu's intentions and, as the 2005 season has successfully progressed, their clarion voices have recently subsided to an inaudible whisper.

It is a short walk through the gates, after I persuade the ever-vigilant security guard Keith to let me through, and I then reach reception for my meeting with Colin. He's slightly delayed, since last night's torrential rain had lashed this part of the Midlands to such an extent that the stadium's management office had been flooded during the storm. A leakage made much worse in its effects by the natural internal slope of the building, according to Caroline on the reception desk. While I sit in reception, I get the chance to listen to various staff chat as they arrive and to savour the strong smell of onions that wafts in from the refreshment kiosk next door. I also observed in a prominent place a framed copy of an article from the local paper, headlined "Brandon Soars", which outlines Mr Sandhu's biography and his stated plans for the stadium. From this I learn that Avtar comes from Malaysia originally but arrived in the UK in 1969. It's apparent that there are very few sports that he hasn't participated successfully in as a player. He has enjoyed cricket, soccer, volleyball, badminton and demonstrated notable prowess at hockey. With bundles of energy evident from this impressive sports repertoire, the article describes him as a workaholic and sportaholic with extensive contacts in the Midlands area, but especially in Birmingham where he was educated at Great Barr. How Mr Sandhu found the time and energy to become a successful businessman and "millionaire" isn't explained in great detail, but along with Brandon he owns other stadiums – Henlow in Buckinghamshire and Ellesmere Port on the Wirral. It's Brandon Stadium that presently inspires his particular interest and is a property that he's repeatedly pledged to continue. Though as a successful businessman, he's keen to utilise his assets, maximise his returns and, therefore, has already introduced more sports to the Brandon Stadium complex. In this instance, greyhounds, which have returned to race at the facility after a 20-year absence to accompany the regular stock cars and speedway. He's invested over £2 million to facilitate a successful return of the dogs, which includes building a new, state-of-the-art kennel block. The stadium has been overhauled in general, but the most dramatic change for the speedway has been the switch of race night from Thursdays to Fridays[2]. This definitely angered traditionalists and those opposed to any change, but it emphasises his family credentials and it's a move that he hopes will attract more schoolchildren to the speedway.

In pride of place next to this article is a framed photograph with the legend 'The Crew' imposed on top of the image in 1970s hot rod style typography. It features a very young-looking Billy Hamill and Greg Hancock who kneel in its centre surrounded by a phalanx of cheerleaders. Everyone in the photograph smiles broadly as the girls pose around this pair of American riders, the major stars of this recent era of the racing at Coventry. The training, deportment and routines of their young women is something that's taken very seriously at Coventry which operates a training programme that makes it the equivalent of RADA for speedway cheerleaders. From other visits to the stadium, I can recall seeing a rather dictatorial lady who organises the girls in their cubbyhole-cum-waiting-area, located in the centre of the main grandstand. I also remember that, rather like the ball boys at Wimbledon, they have a number of separate teams who take turns to carry out their duties with military precision and aplomb during the event. It's become standard practice around the country for many tracks to have some sort of start-line or cheerleading presence and approaches vary from the naïve amateur to the polished professional. At Poole they all dress in specially designed uniforms that deliberately echo the riders' kevlar colours, albeit with crop tops that expose their flat, bare stomachs. At King's Lynn the young co-promoter Jonathan Chapman, perhaps reveals his own proclivities with his claims that his fans set great store that the start-line girls are legally consenting adults and thereby, theoretically, are comparatively available for the punters. Coventry, with perhaps the country's foremost troupe of start-line girls, has an atmosphere and approach that combines the application of ballet dancers with the showmanship of *Come Dancing*. In the photograph's era, this manifested itself as 10 lithe, young women dressed in bright yellow florescent jacket tops, tight black crop tops that expose their midriffs, very short black skirts, shiny stage tights and black ankle length boots. They all joyously clutch large white pompoms in each hand, which would have made changing the tyres or wheels in the pits tricky if they were ever called upon to help out. Immaculately dressed in the yellow and blue

[2] Though the switch that really caused the local angst was from Saturdays to Thursdays initially.

Chris Durno in the track shop. © Jeff Scott

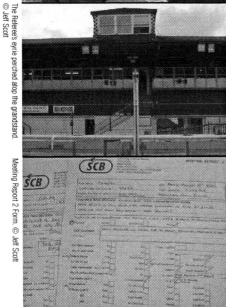

The Referee's eyrie perched atop the grandstand. © Jeff Scott

Meeting Report 2 Form. © Jeff Scott

Exide-sponsored kevlars of the time, Billy and Greg have the contented look of men with notably luxuriant hair who enjoy the weekly attentions of 'The Crew'.

Colin Pratt interrupts my study of the photograph when he arrives in the reception area. He's the sort of bluff, down-to-earth chap that you imagine would run a mile from any hint of the need to dress according to the dictates of fashion and who would cringe at the offer of a style makeover. This is confirmed later when, at the end of the season when he eschews the option to dress in drag as a woman, in contrast to his colleague and co-promoter Peter Oakes who seizes the opportunity to celebrate in this manner. During my visit, I had tried to think of which television characters the Pratt-Oakes partnership reminded me of most. At the time *Dads Army* sprang to mind, I placed Colin as Sergeant Wilson, albeit with a different accent, to Peter's Captain Mainwaring. Subsequently, I now realise though that their relationship is, perhaps, in the light of this further information more drawn from *It Ain't Half Hot Mum* with Colin as a mild-mannered, avuncular Sergeant Major Williams, albeit again with a different accent, to Peter's 'Gloria' aka Gunner Parkins. No sooner have I abandoned my 1970s TV reverie and sat in the chair on the opposite side of the desk from Colin than the sounds of his mobile ringtone of Abba's *Mama Mia* immediately interrupts us. Colin's answers to this weather query perfectly capture the difficulties that are experienced in the preparation of a speedway track, especially when one has to cope with all the weather variants that make up a typical English summer's day. "We were flooded this morning but now we're doing some watering as it's that dry on the track".

I'm delighted to have some of Colin's valuable time on a busy race day, particularly as he had been reticent to meet earlier in the season. We rather bizarrely start our conversation with a brief chat about Coventry speedways approach to their young mascots. There's a lot of demand for the position, so they invite applications from all interested parties before they make their selection for the whole season. Usually the chosen youngster is mad keen to succeed with his own speedway career and views this opportunity as a vital stage in their progression towards that goal. They are usually aged around 13 or 14 years old. The idea is that they will graduate from their mascot duties and then start to ride for the under-15s. Colin comes across when interviewed live on the television as a man who deliberately, wherever possible, shuns the limelight. He appears to prefer to leave these obligations to the more willing, media-friendly but equally telegenic Peter Oakes. When obligated to appear, Colin presents himself as shy, acerbic but extremely knowledgeable with a tendency to answer the exact question he's been asked rather than seek to address its wider implications. My own experience confirms that Colin is slightly shy but courteous and also very modest. He goes to great lengths to praise others while he remains humble about his own achievements or diminishes his own considerable knowledge and experiences. That said, if you persist, he slowly warms to his own reminiscences and recollections, and so a torrent of names and insights begins to flow.

If Colin ever writes his own book, a project he has started but never finished ("I'll do it when I'm no longer involved"), he'd call it *Both Sides of the Fence*. He has decided upon this because he has managed to achieve the comparatively rare feat to find success in the sport both as a rider and as a promoter. In speedway usually it's a choice of either a successful career as a rider or a successful career as a promoter and manager, and very few people have been similarly blessed in both respects. The earliest influence on Colin's life in speedway began when he was born within quarter of a mile of the Rye House track in Hoddesdon. As a child, Colin lived in Sheering and it's from this period that he fondly recalls Dickie Case, the old Aussie pub owner. In fact Colin has known a veritable mob of people that includes Mike Broadbank, Clive Hitch, the Jackson brothers, Gerald King, Brian Brett and Peter Sampson, among the many others he names too quickly for me to record. Proud of his Hertfordshire/Essex connections, Colin fondly recalls riding to Broxbourne on his bike to take part in the cycle speedway there. From there he naturally progressed to ride bikes with motors at grass track and then onto become a speedway rider. He remembers he watched speedway after the War; he was 9 or 10, when West Ham attracted crowds of 40-45,000 for a normal fixture. When Colin started to ride he didn't perform in front of such large numbers, since he rode for Stoke in the Provincial League before he moved onto Hackney and finally Cradley Heath in 1970. His career was tragically cut short by the infamous accident at Lokeren, an incident he avoids discussing since "you probably know all about that". I do, as it happens, because it remains one of the sport's darkest moments: a road accident on 14th July 1970 that involved a party of riders and mechanics travelling back through Belgium, as they had been touring Holland, which killed six people. Colin's riding career ended with this accident but he escaped with his life, despite a broken neck and severe internal injuries. As he reflects positively on his riding career – a very noticeable character trait – he displays intense pride in his achievements, "I achieved in 10 years what riders don't achieve in 20 years". He rode in nine World Championships and two World Team Cup finals, but views his most significant personal achievement as when he twice won the London Riders Championship. This was the oldest speedway trophy and he still feels considerable pride with his accomplishment and indeed he would have had a hat trick of London Riders Championship victories, but for a broken chain when he led on another occasion.

With his riding career over, he then embarked on the next stage – literally and metaphorically on the other side of the fence. This involved work on the mechanical side of riding, for example getting the bike set ups done for Terry Betts, the star rider at the time with King's Lynn. The person who changed Colin's future life was the "very influential Lennie Silver". At the time Silver promoted the famous Hackney Hawks at Waterden Road, and he gave Colin his first chance after the end of his riding career. Colin praises Len, as a man and for all that he taught him about the sport. Without Len, Colin believes he wouldn't have enjoyed his eventual success in the sport. He fondly recalls Len from many exciting nights of racing on 'Friday at Eight' as well as his undoubted showmanship accompanied by his trademark 'Magnificent Seven' theme music. It took little persuasion for Colin to jump at the chance to own 50 percent of the promotion franchise and partner him at Hackney from 1976-79. Afterwards he worked as team manager at King's Lynn under Martin Rogers before he took Peter Adams's place at Cradley Heath in 1984 when Peter moved onto Wolverhampton. Colin stayed there until "it shut down in 1995". He switched to Hackney in 1996 with the ill-fated London Lions, Bradford in 1997 under Alan Ham and then arrived at Coventry in 1998, where he's been ever since. He first worked for the legendary Ochiltree family, famously owners of the Coventry club for 57 years. After Charles Ochiltree it was Mrs Ochiltree and Martin who "kept it going" before Avtar Sandhu arrived to "put [his] money in". Mr Sandhu has "tried hard to get it back with big crowds" through investments in the team and the stadium complex, although it can be difficult at the stadium with so many greyhound meetings to run. Colin goes out of his way to compliment everywhere he's worked in speedway and everyone he's worked with, as "they were similar really but with different operations". I ask Colin what the secret of success as a team manager is and what he enjoys about the role. He replies, "I dunno" before he notes that, "it ain't always enjoyable when you lose". Speedway is the sort of sport that attracts well-informed followers; consequently you have terraces where "everyone is a team manager so you ain't going to please everyone all the time". He's pleased by how the present young team of riders at Coventry have

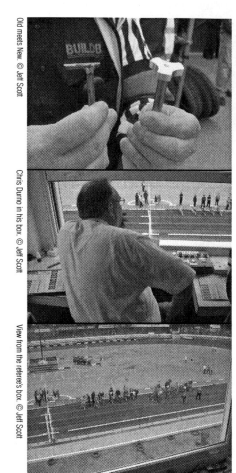

performed this season after a slow start. Colin mentions "the downfall of Andreas Jonsson, partly through travel and partly through not feeling well" before he notes that this situation has been more than compensated for by Nicholls, who has "led well", and Harris, who has "really come on". He's reluctant to single out any one person as the key to success, on or off the track, and notes that it's genuinely a team effort. He hesitates to predict the seasons results, but their form has come together so well that they want a top two place in the League, so as to race at home in the semi-final of the play-offs. Beyond that Colin "dunno" how the season will end but he will try to "work the oracle to win all the time".

Colin happily reviews the changes in the sport since his youth and riding days. Most importantly, the sport has actually survived through the decades since its heyday, especially "through the lean years". Nowadays he's pleased that the speedway is, once again, in the shop window with the live television coverage, although it attracts lesser crowds these nights because some fans prefer to stay at home to watch. The bikes have evolved from two to four valves and from upright to lay-down machines but he believes the "two valve remains the complete speedway machine". He broadly approves of new safety developments like cut-outs, chain guards and silencers. He also believes noise mitigation is essential everywhere, not only because it's a "big factor" but there's "always a house close by and someone will complain". Other environmental factors that have changed with the times is the modern requirement to collect and correctly dispose of all the waste oil, which wasn't done in the past, and indeed it was often blatantly poured onto the tracks to help bind the shale. As for the riders, Colin notes that they have bigger and better sponsors, more colour in their kevlars and racing suits, as well as operating with very hectic schedules for those who ride in the three main European leagues and the Grand Prix's. He concedes that they're "probably more money motivated" but some things never change and they still try to ride their best and enjoy it, just like they always did. The fans can still see into the pits and watch what's going on with the riders and mechanics. After the meeting, if they have time in their travel schedules, riders still go to the bar for a drink and to meet the fans. There's slightly greater social distance now between the riders and the fans than there was, but it's not insurmountable or not even noticeable compared to the separation you find between the players and the fans in many other sports.

Overall, speedway retains its timeless appeal with the excitement of the racing, the 15-heat package with its 60-second lap times, plus the gladiatorial nature of the competition. People may refer to the "good old days" but for Colin it's very hard to agree since the sport always drives itself into the next decade. He'll admit, "the good old days were good", but there are always "lots of theories of better!" Perhaps two-valve engines and grippier tyres were once the pinnacle of the sport, but when it comes down to it, such comparisons are irrelevant, since it's your enjoyment of the moment plus your memories and recollections that really matter. A special memory for Colin is his involvement with the BBC series *King Cinder* at Rye House in the late 1970s. They filmed after the meeting at Rye House and the riders wore specially made leathers. Other scenes were filmed along the River Lea on a houseboat and at Maldon in Essex. They made six episodes that finally were broadcast in a prime-time slot on the telly. I leave Colin with his happy memories[3] and this evening's work, as he starts to shuffle through a sheaf of faxes, to once again double-check the declarations of teams; but first he must call to check on the weather forecast for the evening.

I wander back out towards the car park where I've arranged to rendezvous with Chris Durno, the SCB match official for tonight's meeting, so that I can follow and shadow his every movement at the stadium. He's kindly allowed me this unique opportunity so that I can put to rest many of the commonly held opinions about the role of the speedway referee. Often fans on the terraces feel that they have a superior knowledge of the rules and regulations, while the referee just turns up at the last minute in order to make some mysterious but incorrect decisions to spoil the evening's racing. Given that the officials, like the riders, are only human, mistakes can always happen. While I wait for Chris, I take the chance to chat with the security man on the gate, Keith Denton, who has worked here for the last 38 seasons. He started out at the speedway as a car-park attendant, as a reluctant favour for an old friend who's now sadly passed away, although "initially I said you're joking it's a Saturday night, but you were finished by half seven". It was a wise decision and he's never looked back after he worked his way up through the organisation since then. He certainly appears to know all the riders, from both sides, as well as the various staff. Keith has a quip, a smile or a friendly word for everyone who passes through and clearly enjoys his work. He was born and bred in nearby Wolston and has been a Coventry speedway fan since it opened in 1948 when he was 9 years old. He recalls that Bob Fletcher was the club captain in 1948, but then there's so much to remember from his early years following the club – particularly the size of the crowds. There were special trains put on in those days that ran from Northampton via Buckby to the now defunct Brandon Holt station just down the hill. There were also lines upon lines of packed city corporation double-decker buses that filled the car park and the queues to get on them were so long that they were arranged in chicanes. He gained a lot of experience in the car park when he worked there as an attendant, marshalling the huge numbers of fans and vehicles. Every Saturday night, there were the cars (one shilling), the motorcycles (sixpence), and it was free for the coaches with complimentary entry for the driver and courier. It was "always full, gosh, yeah"; you couldn't even see a space in the crowd in those days. The riders of the 1950s had a major and enduring impact upon Keith; his memory's brief roll call of honour includes Derrick Tailby, Jim Lightfoot, Les Hewitt, Johnnie Reason and Nigel Boocock who they used to call "Little Boy Blue" on account of the colour of his highly polished pale blue leathers, in the days when every other racer was attired in standard black race leathers.

Nowadays they've altered the stadium and the buildings but it's still roughly the same old place. It certainly is one of the country's most impressive venues to regularly stage a speedway meeting but, for Keith, it's been the people – the owners, the staff, the riders and mechanics – that fascinate him. He remembers Martin Ochiltree as he grew up and, similar to changes in the rest of society, Keith notes that the club is run more as a business today. But then life off the track, like life on the track, moves a lot faster. The track record stands this evening at 57.4 seconds whereas it was 80.8 seconds when Keith first arrived to watch in 1948. Whatever the changes, he wants to carry on his work at the speedway. His reminiscences are interrupted when he spots Chris Durno, as he drives up, which prompts him to wonder aloud what it's like to be a referee, now that the speeds are so fast and that more much money depends on the referee's decision. He thinks I'll enjoy my evening with Chris as "he's approachable, a nice chap, very keen but hasn't been doing it that long".

Chris lives in Solihull and has been a lifelong fan of the sport. When he doesn't officiate he tries to attend as many other matches as he can in the UK, with his 8-year-old son Tom, just to watch and enjoy the sport away from the pressures of officialdom. Even last weekend he'd been with his son on a trip to Croatia, with that doyen of speedway referees Tony

---

[3] He makes no mention that *Blue Peter*'s Peter Duncan also starred in the series.

Steele, to watch a tri-nation international meeting at a newly opened track at Gorican. They'd had VIP passes that gave them access throughout the stadium and the welcome had been superb. Afterwards they went to a party in the mountains where, despite the lack of English speakers, they had a fantastic time late into the night. Chris saw this as another example of how the camaraderie, casual freemasonry and friendliness of speedway people always transcends the usual barriers of language and national pride.

Chris has arrived at the track before 6 p.m., which is over two hours before the meeting begins. He always likes to allow himself a couple of hours to prepare, a decision borne out of pragmatism and experience. Each referee has a different approach, though, and some only arrive an hour before the tapes are scheduled to rise. Chris is mystified how they can get all the essential checks done – which he will demonstrate to me shortly as I shadow him round the stadium on his duties – before the meeting starts, particularly if they only allow an hour for the completion all these tasks. The biggest factor to allow for prior to a meeting is the "protests that eat your time away". Protests are caused by a couple of factors. It's partly the complexity of the regulations – especially regarding guests, rider replacements, 'doubling up' riders and number 8s – but often calculated gamesmanship on the part of promoters and team managers. "It's a regular tactic with some promoters, they've been unhappy for a week though you walk in and wouldn't know anything about their grievance or contestation before they present it one hour before the meeting starts". He says I just wouldn't believe the number of occurrences of last-minute protests, "when everyone loses their temper", which always uses up many minutes of the referee's valuable preparation time while he resolves these, often illusory, issues. However, that's the modern way and, for officials that unlike Chris arrive late, it's very much their look out, since each takes his or her own approach to the job and its responsibilities. We make a brief detour to the track shop, which is littered, to the extent you can hardly get in the door, with large yellow circular laundry bags. These will be signed by the riders and sold in the shop as a unique item of gift merchandise. The club hopes they will become an essential purchase for all the mad keen, die-hard Coventry fans. The bags are all still scattered around the shop, since only two of the home riders have ventured along to sign them. The only autographs they have, so far, are from Chris Harris and Martin Smolinski. Luckily the turnstiles aren't yet open, since the fans definitely wouldn't easily be able to fit into the shop. The staff in the shop joke that if Scott Nicholls arrives at his usual time this evening then he won't actually get to the stadium until 7.45 p.m. Chris has called in to deliver 19 miniature models of the home captain Scott Nicholls sent over from Poland; it is custom and practice that referees are often used as the most reliable postmen in speedway because they travel so regularly around various tracks. Everyone is very familiar with each other in the shop, banter is exchanged and they all clearly get on well, Chris wryly notes that, "as usual everything is backwards at Coventry" while he waves at the room cluttered with laundry bags. Not that I ask but I understand from Eastbourne's film man, Ken Burnett, that Chris was a Coventry fan in his youth. He was a pen pal with Ken, when they were 12, a time when they regularly wrote and swapped Coventry programmes for Eastbourne ones.

The first stop for the match official is the Speedway Office to pick up some match programmes (four in this instance) as well as all the paperwork from the previous referee's visit. The referee then has to check this information, which will inform the match official of the fines levied at the last meeting, Chris notes "it's your job as the referee to pick these up at this meeting – plus any details on adverse comments on the track or the stadium". The official then has to check that the factors that caused these adverse comments to be reported have subsequently been rectified by the home club by the time of this visit or, if not, the referee would again report them for the next visiting official. When he glances through the paperwork, specifically the meeting report, Chris establishes that it's been three weeks since the last meeting at Brandon Stadium, and that the last referee issued only warnings but no fines so, in this instance, there are no monies to collect. Talk of the collection of monies allows Chris to tell me the most surprising fact, namely that, "as referees we make the biggest donations by a long way to the Speedway Riders' Benevolent Fund charity". The amounts collected each season from the referees are far greater than the track collections that take place throughout the country. Though without both sources of income, the SRBF would not be able to undertake all the good work it does. All fines levied by a referee during a meeting go to this charitable fund and these fines can be levied for a wide variety of reasons within the match referee's control. However, while these fines are capped at a maximum of £250 per offence, there is an inequality between the income levels of those who ride in the Elite League in comparison to those who ride in the Conference League. A maximum fine, say for a physical attack, would be significant in the Conference League where earnings can be as low as £5 per point, whereas in the Elite League £250 often represents, for some riders, less than the earnings for a heat win so isn't really a similar punishment. Some referees use their discretion when they levy fines whereas others issue the maximum fine irrespective of the earnings or League level of the rider.

However, all failed protest fees and fines levied by the Speedway Control Bureau are kept by the SCB and are, sadly, not donated to the SRBF. The fines levied by the SCB are for disciplinary infringements, walkouts and breaches of the code of conduct; though a significant and problematic grey area is the level of the fines issued when foreign riders fail to turn up at a speedway meeting. No-shows frequently irritate the fans and the perception exists that some foreign riders are tacitly encouraged by promoters to pick and choose the meetings they miss in the full knowledge that the fines issued by the SCB will be both derisory and confidential. When I have reviewed the speedway press and Internet forums, it's hard not to get the impression that the people who adjudicate on the SCB panel historically have a slight predilection towards leniency, if the frequency of the (re)occurrence is any standard to judge. This appears to favour the promoter's needs over that of the paying spectators who are deprived of the chance to see the foreign riders that in contemporary speedway form a significant component of most teams, particularly at the Elite League level. However, tonight Chris's main concern is to administer his specific responsibilities at the track and make all decisions based on the relevant rules as he understands them and the events as they appear to him. The work and procedures of the SCB remain solely within their own jurisdiction and, ultimately, solely their responsibility.

In the meeting report, there are no critical comments from the previous official about the stadium or the track; which doesn't surprise Chris, since the track at Coventry is widely known for its "excellently prepared surface". However, this reputation for quality will not influence the thoroughness of Chris's own imminent inspection of the track and the stadium, when he will vigilantly search for matters of concern. This routine is all part of the continuing campaign by the SCB to heighten/improve the importance of health and safety issues at every track in the country. At every meeting Chris carries with him all the paraphernalia and paperwork that comprises the lot of the modern referee. There is the rulebook itself, a small blue book filled with dense type, tables and diagrams plus a couple of thick lever-arch binders of information that covers everything from supplementary regulations and clarifications belatedly introduced over and above the new rulebook, rider averages, race-card layout and, even, environmental records. There are also the many different forms that every official legally must complete at each and every meeting where they officiate. The SCB has taken this increased and paperwork-driven approach, mostly fuelled by a desire for increased professionalism, greater health and safety rule compliance but also because of underlying insurance liabilities and fear of litigation. It's a fact of modern life and society that we are bound by ever more complex legislation, often health and safety based, and there is an increased willingness to litigate – rather than to mediate or accept – in all walks of life. Speedway as sport has yet to have a significant legal case brought by a rider or a spectator and sensibly tries to prevent this future possibility through its present actions. Indicative of this more careful approach is the legal requirement for each track, under SCB regulations, to have a 'circuit license' as well as a certificate of 'homologation'. This is, I must say, a new word for me, but basically it's a fancy way of saying that the SCB official Colin Meredith has reviewed and approved all the dimensions and features of the track itself along with a map of the circuit and centre green based on these measurements!

All very complicated stuff, which stands in contrast to the visit of the referee to the home team manager's office. Only a short while after I leave Colin Pratt's office, I return again, this time with the referee. Colin chats cosily and motivationally with a couple of the Coventry riders but breaks off to update Chris about the track and the weather. He informs him that the six-hour forecast is for no rain, but because of the torrential downpour overnight, "we've had to re-do the track – so you'll have to bear with me". Colin isn't quite sure what exactly will happen but his track preparation work will definitely involve a "half tidy up" and a spin of the special grading 'magic wheel' that they have as part of the essential equipment at Brandon, which is used to maintain the surface in its renowned premium condition. The overall message Colin communicates is that everything is in hand for the meeting, that the air fences are already successfully inflated and that there should be no surprises. Something Chris will soon judge for himself during his track walk. Colin then adds that tonight's meeting will feature an Elite League meeting of 15 heats, a special four-lap try out by a visiting rider, and six second-half races for the juniors. The whole discussion is very matter of fact, amiable and courteous. It's surprisingly far removed from the confrontational interactions with the referee that characterise the television coverage and its portrayal of the clubs' and riders' relationships with the referee. But then, I suppose, those heat-of-the-moment discussions are precisely the type of exchanges that Sky Sports relish to show, emphasise or engineer for the home viewers to keep them enthralled and entertained every week. Chris wanders back through the office to the general joshing of the Brandon Speedway Office staff, who mostly doubt his abilities to conduct the meeting but then close their jocularity with a "see you later, Hawkeye!"

Understandably, given what they do and the risks that they take, every rider has their pre-meeting superstitions and rituals. Among the officials this behaviour is the same. We leave the Speedway Office to put all of Chris's stuff in the referee's box. The box at the Brandon Stadium is located up some steep stairs in the main grandstand. This grandstand is arguably the most impressive of its kind in the UK and the referee's box is similarly well regarded; Chris immediately sings its praises as the best type of box to officiate from as a speedway referee. Mainly because the box provides an unobstructed, panoramic view of the whole circuit, there are no members of the general public in your eye line, nor can they mill about in the vicinity to distract you. It's so high up that you can see almost everywhere in the stadium with ease and, as a visitor, with considerable interest. The box has quite a few people in it during a race, apart from the referee. There is the announcer (David Hammond), soundman, incident recorder and time recorder (Norman), the scoreboard operator (Wally) and another Chris, who's in charge of the jingles from his laptop. There are some brief "hellos" before we then wander back down from our gantry box for the track inspection.

Chris clearly knows his way easily and quickly around the stadium having visited it many times before. For the novice or the experienced referee, just to find the various doors and gates that allow you access onto the track surface would complicate an otherwise already demanding job. Chris again praises the track as one of the best in the country because of the attention that is paid to safety, its organisation and preparation; this is primarily due to the valuable services this season of the highly regarded and skilled Terry Chrabaszcz, who is also the track curator at Wolverhampton Speedway. Chris speaks of Terry as "an excellent trackman who's deservedly very proud of his work". The purpose of the track inspection, for any official, is to establish the condition of the track, its general surrounds and other associated equipment as well as whether the track preparation conforms with the principle of safe riding. Chris doesn't anticipate that he will find an awful lot wrong with it but, then again, there are only a couple of hours to put any things right before the tapes go up. For major concerns they identify, the referee would itemise these in the 'green Track Record report' they have to legally complete as a mandatory requirement and the track would have seven days to correct them, before the visit of the next referee. There are no outstanding concerns to address; nonetheless Chris bears in mind, "they're telling me slick" will be the track conditions. This effectively means that they have recently pulled off the top surface of the track and have then packed down the shale. To Chris's estimation, the maintenance equipment here is superb with a "very good magic wheel that grades, mixes and breaks up the burr", which inevitably forms on the track as a result of the bikes racing round the circuit. His analysis translates to mean that one part of the track surface will be smooth and slick – the racing line that the majority of the riders will use throughout the meeting – while some of the looser shale will inevitably be thrown towards the fence, where it becomes deeper and grippier for the riders who venture onto the outside racing line of the track. The gap that separates the slick part from the deep part of the track has a raised area, or burr, which a responsible track curator will try his best to remove or mitigate.

We deliberately walk anti-clockwise round the whole track, which is wet and gooey enough under foot for the surface to immediately stick to your shoes. Our wander round in this direction enables us to more easily highlight errors with the wooden kickboards that surround the track. These kickboards should all fit together perfectly to provide a smooth outer surface to ensure that a passing rider isn't snagged. Chris notes that they still fit together well although, since it's midway through the season, they've become rather tatty where the tractors sometimes catch them. Checking the actual integrity of the fence is also crucial during this inspection. Chris notes that all referees once had to learn the dimensions of the various accoutrements of the track furniture but, as it's no longer listed in the rulebook, this has ceased to be a requirement for the referees to know[4]. However, like many experienced and conscientious people, Chris is 'old school' enough to still adhere to "the old methods and dimensions". Therefore, if only in his mind's eye, the kickboards should be 300 mm while the sectional fence should ideally be 1.2 metres high, constructed of 3 mm wire with holes no more than 50 mm square. Although he carries a lot of equipment with him to every meeting, Chris checks all these dimensions by sight rather than break out the tape measure he also brings with him to meetings. We zigzag around the whole circuit as Chris points out some newly laid top surface on the track. This has been placed horizontally with a view to fairness and consistency rather than in a manner that suggests it is what the home riders have requested. The preparation of a 'special area' for the home riders' advantage is much more prevalent than I naïvely imagine and usually takes place in and around the start area. This practice still continues and it's up to the referee to spot it during his inspection. It's also possible though for some alterations to occur while the track is graded throughout the meeting. As a spectator, Chris has seen what he considered to be incidents of doctoring at tracks that he requests that I do not name. Inspections are vital for safety, but this reconnaissance also allows the away riders the chance to identify the alterations and, thereby, potentially ride the circuit as well as the home riders.

During our inspection, Chris pays special attention to where the rainwater collects on the deflated airbags since, when they're inflated for the meeting, the water will naturally drain onto the surface of the track and create intermittent soft patches. There is often a substantial amount of water that accumulates during any week in an English summer, so the unpredictability of these soft patches can often cause havoc for the riders. Through experience, Chris knows that the majority of crashes at Coventry happen on the bend exits, which is a hazard that these soft patches can often exacerbate. He also notices that some of the white line that marks the inside edge of the track has become covered in shale at different points on the circuit. When he returns to the pits area, Chris informs the clerk of the course Graham Snookes of the damp patches, the covered white line, and an insecure gate on the back straight that Chris found when he shook the structure of the fencing, which he did regularly throughout the walk. The eavesdropping Peter Oakes immediately reassures him with a dismissive, "don't worry we'll see to that" before he quickly changes conversational tack to chat about a "missing SCB registration certificate", that the mystery second-half rider has yet to produce to be able to ride in the second half. All riders at a speedway meeting must have their National Federation and SCB registrations in good order to legally be able to ride and they also must have insurance before they can go and risk life and limb at the start line. Chris states that, in this instance, he will accept a fax copy of the rider's registration details from the PZM[5] and issue a 'one-day registration permit' for £10 and warn the rider to get a full SCB registration by his next meeting.

Contrary to popular belief, a referee doesn't just roll up on race day and press a few buttons that control the tapes and the lights. Like the bane of all modern office life, you have numerous forms, often in triplicate, to complete for everything. Chris endeavours, where possible, to do as much of his paperwork in advance so he can concentrate on his inspection, what actually happens around the stadium, on the track as well as in the pits. Consequently, he has already checked the probable team details in advance on the official websites and, now we've returned to the referee's box, so that he can get round to the vital work that is the double-checking of the programme. He checks everything from the basic to the sublime, which includes that the opposition, date and time are correctly listed along with the "important information" on track length, and the various standard statements with regard to public safety, "jurisdiction and safety certificate numbers". These are all vital, legal and necessary requirements should there ever be litigation as a result of events at a meeting. Chris

[4] It is unusual that a rule change from the SCB should simultaneously reduce the paperwork and effectively de-skill the officials in this manner. Particularly given their vigilance on other health and safety areas that might potentially lead to litigation.

[5] Polski Zwiazek Motorowy, the Polish Motorcycle Federation

then checks the race card against the official format in case of printing errors. Here the worst case would be that a meeting might need to be re-run should he fail to spot hidden or accidental errors. All referees also check the riders' averages against the "official 'green sheet averages'" to ensure that these and the subsequent team line-ups are correct for each team. It's something that becomes especially important, particularly to avoid unnecessary disputes when the inevitable rider replacement rides take place during a meeting. In this respect Premier League programmes, in contrast to the Elite League ones, are fractionally more useful since they helpfully print riders' averages on the race card, whilst the BSPA decreed that they for some reason should not be printed in the senior league. It's also a legal requirement that the referees complete the programme and the carbonated meeting results sheet. The design of this report is based on the old Cradley Heath and Long Eaton versions, which Chris notes with undisguised approval, are "a Colin Pratt design". Until just recently referees were still actually personally filling in three programmes during a meeting. The completed race meeting programme and form must be handed into the promoter's office at the end of the night. Each meeting also produces an Incident Report Sheet, in which all on track incidents are dutifully recorded. Other forms to be completed and sent to the SCB include the 'Meeting Report 1' that covers start/finish times, disciplinary matters, rider changes and the SCB obsession with dress/rider equipment standards. 'Meeting Report 2' covers the track, also there is the 'Referee's Supplementary Track Report' which covers some of these items yet again.

A casual glance at the Report 1 form explains the recent mystery of the increase in general smartness that is prevalent among speedway promoters – a sort of Rotary Club or Conservative Party members' club chic – since there is now a specific section that covers "non-conformance to the BSPA dress code" for the promoters, riders, team managers, machine examiner, clerk of the course, start marshals, flag marshals and the presenter! It's like taking part in a peculiar kind of fashion parade or a retro-themed episode of *What Not To Wear*. Chris also has to check that all the officials listed in the programme are currently licensed to fulfil their allocated programmed roles. If they do not have a licence, he can sell them a temporary version for £10 for the meeting that night. Competence and good citizenship are required for every licensed official.

The final preparatory checks in the box involve the test of the referee's control panel to ensure that the tapes rise[6] and that the appropriate lights

---

[6] There has been an intermittent but almost regular problem with the tape mechanism at Brandon this season, and Chris on one occasion assisted by twanging a piece of elastic to represent the starting tapes at Coventry, which allowed the meeting to be completed. Not that this is a problem solely restricted to Brandon Stadium, since Chris has had the misfortune to undertake this task on six separate occasions when he has turned up at tracks with the sole expectation that he will simply spectate at these meetings. In future, when the tapes malfunction at the meeting you attend, you would be advised to hopefully listen out for Chris or one of his colleagues, as they shout, "let me through I'm an SCB official".

come on when each button is pressed. Every referee's box differs drastically from track to track, as does the layout of the control panel. I am very surprised, almost shocked, that there is no standard version or configuration of this essential equipment and Chris admits that it's one of his own personal bugbears. In this instance a familiarity with your tools is vital since any fractional delay or hesitation by the referee, while they search the layout of the panel for the switch for the red 'stop' lights, can have severe consequences through the increase in danger to fallen riders. As with many things at Coventry, the control panel is just the ticket.

We again set off to the pits for some last-minute checks and instructions. On the way there, Chris readily acknowledges the existence of the "ref's grapevine" which swiftly communicates news among the referees. They try to avoid a siege mentality but there is sometimes hostility towards officials, which leads to a need for them to share observations and information as well as reinforce the camaraderie and support network that the isolation of their job makes so difficult to produce. The Coventry track is located very centrally in England, so Chris will officiate tonight in the full knowledge that his most insightful critics – his contemporaries – will also be here to judge his performance. Tonight's crowd heaves with referees, probably rather like policemen, never there when you need them but mob-handed the next moment. Lurking anonymously in the crowd is local man and referee par excellence Tony Steele and elsewhere in the stadium is Jim Lawrence, Dave Watters as well as Robbie Perks who's up from Worcester with his sons. When we leave the referee's box again and return the pits are thronged with riders, mechanics and machines as well as Coventry's famously experienced meeting presenter, the dapperly dressed Peter Yorke. In a very rare appearance, since he lives in Australia, the club also has Nigel Boocock as a guest of honour and he is in the pits. I instantly recognise him from our meeting last night in Sheffield, though Nigel is otherwise occupied, as he is warmly greeted by all and sundry, often in a star-struck manner. It's clear that he's held in great affection at Coventry who, as a club, are delighted to have his company again while he visits this country.

The riders and mechanics all look suitably busy with their preparations. Earlier in the week, live on television, controversy had raged about the alleged illegal size of Peterborough's Jesper B. Jensen's carburettor. The Poole Pirates lodged an appeal, widely viewed as both unnecessary and sour grapes (though subsequently denied by them), in the light of their impending shock home defeat, for a retrospective examination of his equipment. The subsequent examination by the SCB official, Jim McMillan, revealed that the carburettor was perfectly legal. Consequently, the issue of carburettor sizes and their pre-race measurement by the referee is very much a matter of the moment and visible in the public eye. Ironically, as luck would have it, Jim McMillan is the machine examiner at Coventry, as well as being the nominated British licensed representative for FIM events; therefore Chris informs him that he will randomly check the carburettors of riders from both teams. As an ex-international rider and now as an SCB official, Jim is quietly sceptical of the potential benefits to be gained by tampering with your carburettor. If riders seek to gain any advantage from alterations to their equipment, he feels that they'd much more likely try something that would be undetectable under the present regime of testing and examinations. This could, for example, involve nitro loaded into the air filters which, when dragged through the engine, would allow a rider to gain a significant speed advantage to the first bend but, on return to the pits, would leave no trace. Though Jim stresses that this is much more probable in high profile and important races rather than an 'ordinary' Elite League meeting like tonight's. Jim then emphasises that he doesn't claim this actually happens, but it is just a technical possibility. Nonetheless, much as I believe him, I make a mental note to watch the performance of riders who very slowly idle around to the start line in future and who then, apparently fortuitously, roar away at an incredible pace during their initial journey from the tapes.

Whatever the ingenuity involved in engine tampering, on principle and as a deterrent Chris is determined to select a few riders at random to test their carburettors. On the Coventry side of the pits, he asks the American Billy Janniro if he could test the width of his carburettor. Billy tuts but obliges, as he pulls his bike cover aside and allows Chris to insert his measuring device. This is hardly the most high-tech or sophisticated implement in appearance, as it's basically two pieces of metal brazed together in an 'L' shape. While it looks particularly scraggy, the base of the 'L' is the exact 34 mm width of a 'legal' carburettor inlet and outlet port. Billy takes one look at this measurement tool in Chris's hand and hoots with disbelief and laughter, "look how freaking professional our sport is! How freaking professional is that? You might just as well go to freaking McDonald's and use their stuff!" Chris shrugs in a 'what can I do' manner before he then looks for another rider who doesn't appear that busy on the Arena side of the pits. He advises in a stage whisper that the "one person you definitely don't ask is 'Havvy' [Gary Havelock] who'll always give you a real mouthful of abuse". Instead, Chris decides to examine the ever-affable Mark Loram's machine. Mark staggers back in a pantomime version of horror at the temerity of the request, before he mentions that it was also checked last night at Ipswich, "so it's okay and anyway we'll just put another one on later". The final victim is Arena's pony-tailed rider, Adam Skornicki, who shrugs at the request. All three riders machines pass the rigorous examination that the insertion of this tool provides.

Not that examinations are solely limited to only this aspect of all the various bits and pieces of equipment that are piled into the narrow confines of the pits area on race night. Chris also checks for marked tyres and to ensure that the 14 sets issued to tonight's 14 riders have been fitted to the bikes. He then pays a lot of attention to the rider's crash helmets. I didn't realize that, like fresh eggs, they can go off when they go past their expiry date; never mind that he's also keen to establish which manufacturer's brand is being used by each rider. Chris stresses that the crash helmet is THE essential and most often overlooked item of safety equipment in the sport. Speedway is a dangerous sport and it is important that every possible safety precaution hasn't been skimped over or sold short. Chris fastidiously examines a few of these randomly chosen helmets and looks whether they have a 'British approved' ACU kite mark or sticker on them. We're probably all patriots here and we just know that British is best! Of course, we affect not to notice that this no longer applies to the nationalities of the riders themselves who are in the pits this evening[7].

All of this becomes irrelevant as we gather by Peter Oakes who, like Billy Janniro, feels that the referee's carburettor measurement tool isn't the best advert for the sport in the 21st century. I suggest that I'd just made it in my metalwork class and he sarcastically notes that, in that case, "it would fail". Jim McMillan then brandishes the modern state-of-the-art version of this tool with a more elegant head designed to look like a three-pronged lost puzzle piece. The joint team managers, as I realise I should call them given their official although awkward titles in the programme, Peter and Colin advise that they intend to grade the track regularly tonight, after heats 4, 7, 10 and 14. Chris nods and reassures them that "I'll blitz the first four to six heats". As a fan, I'm surprised to hear the matter-of-fact way the meeting dynamics are discussed and agreed to among the various officials.

Our inspection continues along to the Medical Room, which Chris praises in front of the doctor there, as clean and well run. This is due to the huge amount of "pride" that Dr Kenyon has in his work and the facilities themselves. He inherited the medical work at the Coventry Speedway from his father, who had practised here before him, since the club began in 1948. Chris assures me that these facilities are among the cleanest and the best in the country, "some of them are so dirty you wouldn't want to even go in them, never mind be treated there". The room still looks rather spartan to my untutored eyes; maybe the pain is so great that the riders don't notice the lack of hygiene or creature comforts, if they're unlucky enough to get injured at tracks that don't have Coventry's high standards. The next stop is the Arena Essex changing room where all the riders have gathered for a motivational team talk just before the meeting starts. As a fan, you're naturally curious as to what happens behind the closed door of the riders' changing rooms. The hidden mystery of the tactical conversations always intrigues, but the reality is somewhat different and altogether more prosaic. The actual talk isn't from

[7] Now is not the time to rant on about where all the British riders went. It would take too long to discover why, let alone apportion the blame or agree an explanation, never mind find a solution. The reasons are complex. It's partly attitudinal because the contemporary youngster has so many other distractions or exciting entertainment options, they have little time and lots of pressure, or they are spoilt for choice when it comes to other more lucrative alternative sporting careers. Most relevantly, there has been a systemic failure by the BSPA to construct and manage a consistent system that supports the discovery of young talent and systematically treats them as a vitally necessary part of the racing scene in this country. In Poland and Sweden, they patriotically look after their own. They go so far as to restrict or exclude foreigners, or at least severely limit their use in favour of homegrown talent. They also provide regular training opportunities away from race night and have competitive racing at every age level for most levels of ability. Strangely, the governing bodies in this country have historically preferred to serve the vested interests of those who own or rent our temples of worship, and allowed them to trouser the cash, rather than invest to ensure a steady stream of future disciples and servants. Before I get too biblical or apocalyptic, tonight's line-ups actually have a higher proportion of British riders (6 out of 14) than you often find in the pits on race night. Most of them ride for Arena who, coincidence or not, have found themselves rooted to the bottom of the Elite League table for the majority of the season.

the expected Alex Ferguson Hairdryer School of Encouragement, although Arena's recent form might suggest that this approach could be worth a go. When we walk through the door, the club's promoter and team manager, Ronnie Russell, as the quintessential Englishman he is, talks about what's been on the telly that week. Albeit speedway on the telly, about which he speaks with particular admiration of David Norris in his commentator's capacity, "wasn't Floppy's quotes on Sky the best ever?" The response from his team ranges from non-committal to uninterested but then that's probably the impact a referee's sudden entrance has in a speedway dressing room, especially when he's apparently shadowed by yet another over-eager, wet behind the ears trainee with a clipboard. It will hardly quicken your pulse, set your heart soaring or, probably for that matter, increase the referee's credibility or engender respect. Our popularity seems to hover slightly above that of a rattlesnake in a lucky dip. With some instant but crafty psychology, Ronnie tries to establish a level of authority over Chris the referee that if judged by recent results he appears to lack with his team, when he jokes, "will it be 1-2-3 tonight?" How long the referee actually holds or intends to hold the tapes before they release them is a dark secret that the officials guard jealously and the riders try to subtly or not so subtly outwit in every race. Chris shrugs this off with a practised but sharp, "I can't count" before he reverts to that other, oh so English, staple of conversation – the weather. Well, the possible threat of rain forecast by the local Met Office, which he explains means that he will try to run through the meeting quickly. Part of the reason for Chris's visit is that he is looking for co-operation from the visitor's team. Havvy breaks off from his menacing glower long enough to dismissively utter a curt, "suits me", and so acknowledge the referee in the manner of a petulant teenager. Mark Loram, ever the gentleman, empathises in his gentle country burr with the local threat of precipitation with reference to his home in Suffolk, "it's raining in my neck of the woods". We exit promptly to allow Ronnie's easy conversation and tactical master class to resume. If this turns out to be my one and only opportunity ever to be a fly on the wall for those mysterious speedway changing-room conversations, they are not quite what I expected. Instead with Arena, it's the sort of mundane topics of everyday life that you'd expect to hear away from the cauldron of competition that is modern racing – the weather, the telly and the stamina of the ref on the button.

All that remains before we return to the referee's box is for Chris to collect a couple of signed certificates from Clive Raven, the pits and environmental marshal. Legally required documents, these are the 'meeting certificate' and the 'doctor's certificate', whereby the doctor certifies that all the required medical equipment is in place. By the time we leave the pits Coventry's star rider Scott Nicholls has finally arrived. Chris laughs at Scott's reputation for lateness, "but if I was team manager I'd be tearing my hair out – in a nice way, he's the original East Anglian bumpkin, so laid back he's horizontal". At least that's the case until Scott gets onto a speedway bike. Just as we're about to leave the pits, Chris turns back to have a few words with a speedway hero of his childhood, in the form of ex-rider Nigel Boocock. The mask of authority is thrown aside for a few minutes as Chris joins in the gaggle of people – Peter Yorke, Jim McMillan and Peter Oakes among them – who hang on Nigel's every word and opinion.

Chris takes the chance to explain his own philosophical approach to being an official, as we pass back through the bar and exit it again via a nondescript door you could easily miss before we climb the steep stairs that will take us back to the panoramic view of the stadium that the referee's box affords. In essence, he always tries to apply the many rules sensibly and fairly. He uses the example that some policemen will book you for doing 33 m.p.h. in a 30 m.p.h. zone, whereas others won't. Chris belongs to the more lenient, common-sense school of refereeing. He also notes that criticism is part and parcel of the job but like the riders, promoters and the managers, "no one likes being criticised". As a measure of his dedication, Chris is so nervous before each meeting he referees that he finds it difficult to eat and drink or nip to the loo, since he concentrates all his attention on the races.

In the crowded box, he briefly and good-humouredly chats to everyone while he sorts through the various pieces of his paperwork. Some of the paperwork he piles on his impressively large lever-arch file, while other bits he keeps close by to fill out as he goes along and the meeting progresses. On the dot at 8 p.m. he sounds the two-minute warning to gather the riders at the start line for the first race and then finally scans that "everyone's in place". To the untutored eye, the centre green seems very crowded with track staff and the initial team of the start-line girls. The girls have run out in front of the fans a few minutes before the racing starts from their cubbyhole in the grandstand, like a team of lithe but slightly earnest majorettes. This post Hancock and Hamill generation of start girls appear to have abandoned the mandatory use of pompoms, but then maybe the dressing room is actually littered with them for use in carefully choreographed dances on really special occasions. Another modern innovation appears to be very skimpy, tight pants in the team's helmet colours of red, blue, yellow and green. After every few heats or so, a fresh but substitute team of start-line girls, one of many it appears, replaces the original girls for a short interval under the watchful eyes of their strict but no doubt charming choreographic trainer. Their effect on the pacemakers and heart rates of the many older males in the crowd can be imagined; while it creates the impression that there is a tardis-like room of mystery filled with scantily dressed girls located within the interior of the grandstand. The height of the referee's box gives a great view of everything that takes place at Brandon, but is much too high to properly study the start girls directly below us.

Clusters of men in orange overalls with yellow fluorescent sleeveless tops are stationed on each of the bends as well as men in blue overalls who stand with the start marshal. I'm not sure what the colour-coded overalls signify, but it all adds to the air of professionalism you experience at Coventry. Chris will check that everyone is in place and that the pits gate is shut before each and every race. Then the start marshal must cajole and persuade the riders into their final start positions, almost but not quite touching the tapes. When all are in position and stock still at the gate, the marshal moves away, Chris presses the green button on his control panel to signal to the riders that they are under starter's orders before he then releases the tapes seconds later. The amount of time between the moment the green light is illuminated and the tapes are released varies slightly throughout the meeting (and from referee to referee). This ensures that the start remains comparatively unpredictable and, hopefully, stops the riders from anticipating the exact moment the tapes will be released. Throughout the whole process, it's vital that Chris vigilantly watches all four riders for any signs of movement prior to the tapes' release. If he spots any movement, a difficult task despite the ideal placement of the referee's box, he will immediately stop the race by hitting the red lights button on the control panel, before then publicly identifying the culprit and ordering a re-run of the race.

My instant impression is the difficulty, even with a panoramic view, that any referee will have as he tries to watch all the riders, often scattered some distance apart, throughout any four-lap race. It's a task that requires exceptional concentration allied to an ability to visually interpret the potential moments of danger and collision that four men riding high-performance machines without brakes and suspension will inevitably create during a race. It's a skill that you have to hone and continually refresh and one that definitely comes from the experience of watching many races over the years as a fan, spectator or referee. From the first race, it's very clear how closely everyone in the box works together as a team. They all follow their lead from Chris, who shouts, by helmet colour, the official order of the riders as they cross the finish line. The time is called out and Chris fills out his official documentation, while the announcer then relays the official details of the race over the tannoy system to the fans throughout the stadium. The fans in turn also fill out their own paperwork in the form of the race card in the centre of the match programme.

Another surprise is the very regular communication that the referee has by phone with the clerk of the course. It is the clerk's responsibility to relay all the referee's comments onto the appropriate parties in the pits area, in person or via walkie-talkie. There is also some communication with the start marshal as well as any riders or team managers that use the pits phone to call the box to dispute or clarify decisions.

Chris prefaces each call to the pits with "ref to the clerk of the course". Heat 2 has a call to the pits requesting that they "tell Rymel that the ref prefers he wears a clearly distinguishable red helmet colour" rather than the peculiarly semi-red painted item he's just worn in that race. He also reminds Adrian Rymel that, "he can't have his back wheel spinning at the line". Heat 3 perfectly illustrates the contention and controversy that the role of referee attracts. The race is re-run after Chris adjudges the rider in the red helmet, Billy Janniro, has moved. There was definitely movement but I would have said that this was the rider in yellow, Adam Skornicki. Given we were both looking at the same event from exactly the same position, this difference is significant although, obviously, the referee's decision is final and the only one that counts! Others in the box apparently think that the rider that moved was Skornicki but remain silent. Janniro clearly isn't a happy camper and, rather touchingly, argues his point from the track way below us when he returns to the start line.

It's characteristic of Chris's demeanour and handling of the meeting throughout the evening that he never fails to be polite and witty with everyone he speaks with. Before heat 4 he asks the clerk of the course to pass on a message to Janniro, "tell him to sit still and not to make the start look like a McDonald's drive-through". While the tractor grades the track after heat 4, Chris calls down to say, "please ask Scott politely and respectfully to put on a red helmet colour" – a suggestion that is made because his helmet is only predominantly red. Chris takes the opportunity of the brief respite provided by the track grade to file and consult records as he notes, as if it needed further explanation, "it takes lots of housekeeping to keep up with all the paperwork we get". Despite the grading, Chris points out that we can still clearly see, even from this height, the damp patches on the apex of bend 1 and the exit of bend 2 that we originally noticed on our earlier track walk.

My strongest impression of the evening is Chris's enthusiasm for speedway. After he starts each race seated, he then immediately stands over the control panel for the rest of it, his body slightly twists and turns in sympathy with each exciting manoeuvre or pass. He also calls the results out throughout but also peppers the races, or the intervals between them, with the insightful comments of the true aficionado. Heat 5 he notes that Janniro, "is clearly faster but he's just too heavy to catch them". In heat 6 his whole body moves involuntarily, but with appreciation, when Harris superbly passes Loram and Povazhny through the tiniest of gaps on the third bend of the third lap. He also gasps with excitement during the hard riding duel of Hurry and Harris throughout heat 8.

During the interval, Chris tries to catch up with the avalanche of text messages that have been sent throughout the evening on his phone. They all come from the other referees at tonight's meeting, who now all call Chris to offer their feedback. They're the refereeing equivalent of the Midlands Mafia, and they definitely look after one of their own. The entire battalion of off-duty referees has each watched from different vantage points in the stadium and Tony Steele has called to say he saw a decision differently from Chris on the first bend. Chris is unfazed and philosophical, "your perspective all depends on where you are in the stadium, and I've called it as I saw it from here". Tony arrives in the box with many photographs of last weekend's trip to Croatia, which he shares excitedly with Chris. Everyone in the box gets on with their own tasks but, among the referees in the box, all the talk is about the new Croatian stadium at Gorican, the racing, the remarkably friendly people, and partying until the early hours in the mountains.

The meeting resumes after the interval and immediately Nicholls's pass of Darkin on the first lap of heat 11 causes Chris to loudly exclaim, "whoa, you just can't do that!" After all the formalities are concluded for that race, Chris enjoys his immediate recollection of the race we've just witnessed, the brilliant skill of the rider before he replies to absent, imaginary critics of the sport with, "and they say that speedway has no overtaking". Heat 12 has Janniro engaged in complex mechanical adjustments by the start line that causes a slight delay as the riders set up at the tapes. Chris informs the start marshal by phone, "tell BJ – it's not a good time for him to start stripping his clutch down". After the race he requests that the clerk inform Billy that he should come to the phone, because the referee wishes to speak with him. Rather laconically Chris then politely admonishes Billy for his on-track repairs, while Janniro takes the opportunity to protest about his rankles with regard to the heat 3 re-run. We can only hear one side of the interchange with Janniro, which goes like this:
"Eh, Billy Bob, are you a special child or something? You're not even good at hiding it."
"You bloody did!"
"You definitely did!"
"I definitely saw ya".

After the call Chris says, "He's a lovely bloke, a bit of a good-time Charley; hasn't got the hunger of a Hancock or a Hamill but has the ability."

Thus all the racing passes off safely, the primary consideration of any referee at every meeting, and the meeting is declared over at 22.23 p.m. It's been a long evening's work as a referee. Coventry have won 52-42 without really breaking sweat, while the second-half youngsters have mostly wobbled their way round the track for some further experience. There has been no real controversy of note, although there were a number of re-run heats. Chris efficiently completes his paperwork and collects the rest to hand in at the Speedway Office or post to the SCB. Part of the paperwork involves his selection of his top three riders of the night. He chooses Nicholls, Harris and Kylmakorpi – I'd have chosen differently, but what happens in the eye of the beholder is part of the appeal of most sports. Chris is still on a high from the successful management of the meeting and slowly recovers from all the "self-pressure and the fear of failure". He is happy that it's gone well but most of all, that it's gone safely. He wouldn't like to identify his own officiating style – I'd characterise it as efficient, knowledgeable, involved and witty, while Chris throughout remains approachable but most of all enthusiastic. Typical of the man he finally says, "other refs would have gone away with a couple of hundred quid tonight at £50 a time for every time they moved but, it's their living, so I don't!"

At the bottom of the steps, we go through another door and find ourselves in the crowded bar. Chris immediately says "hello" to quite a few people and two Solihull-based Coventry fans particularly delight in telling him, "we liked the way you kept re-running it until we were ahead!" By the time he's been round the pits and back to the Speedway Office, it's just on 11 p.m. when we finally get back to his parked car. It's been an intense five hours for Chris as well as an extremely insightful and privileged experience for myself. I'll never criticise another referee again or, at least, until I forget this promise the next time. Chris reckons I should try to see some other meetings with some other referees to understand the contrast in their different approaches to the same task. Some of them are real characters, each has their idiosyncrasies and whose abilities run in the range from 'could do better' via 'interesting' to just plain 'weird'. Ever keen to learn but also true to himself and genuinely modest, Chris stresses, "look I'm just learning and still want to improve. We all want to be like Steely – sincere, not hassled or flustered. He's a mediator, communicator and man manager". And with a quick wave, he's reversed his car and he heads off into the darkness home, not so far tonight, to Solihull. Judged by what I've seen, I can't help but think that with his list of Steely's qualities that he's just as easily described himself and not just his career aspirations.

19th August Coventry v. Arena (ELB) 54-42

Chapter 32: Televising the Aces on their Dirt-Naked System Track

22nd August Belle Vue v. Eastbourne

Jonathan Green (x1000) "Over to Sophie in the pits" or Jonathan Green "Sophie has just caught up with XXXX" Sophie Blake (to XXXX) "How did it feel to win that one?" XXXX (to Sophie (flirtatiously if Deano)) "It was fantastic/it was just what we needed etc"

3.5.4 The basic protest fee is £250
3.6.3 The Appeal Fee is £250 (£500 in the case of an appeal to the ACU)

The city of Manchester has a great industrial heritage that has gradually started to undergo a regeneration programme appropriate to its status as a major 21st century English conurbation. It also has a rich sporting tradition and a wealth of famous clubs that immediately spring to mind across a whole variety of sports disciplines. I've travelled up early on the train through rain for most of the journey to arrive on a glorious afternoon of sunshine into Piccadilly Station in the centre of Manchester. The station, along with many other areas within the centre of the city, has had a stylish makeover and now boasts the light, spacious and airy concourses of steel and glass beloved of modern architects and airports throughout the world. It's remarkably crowded though it's not yet the rush hour and looks fetchingly continental in the sunshine. I walk to Piccadilly Gardens for my bus to the Old Trafford Lodge, the functional hotel superbly located within the grounds of Lancashire County Cricket Club that overlooks the hallowed turf, scene of many triumphs for the county and the England team. Until you visit, it is hard to appreciate just how close the two Old Traffords are to each other. The more commercially successful stadium that houses the iconic Manchester United Football Club almost casts a literal and metaphorical shadow

over the County Cricket Club. However, I eschew the delights of an afternoon spent watching Lancashire easily lose a one-day match against Gloucestershire, which some of the more expensive hotel rooms look directly out onto, to journey across the city for my meeting with Ian Thomas. He is the promoter and team manager of the notable and legendary Belle Vue Aces Speedway Club.

I follow the instructions of the Polish receptionist, who's distinctly underwhelmed by my prospects for the night ahead at the speedway ("it bores me but not the men"), when I travel by bus to the stadium. I enjoy another chance to savour my Manchester surroundings as the number 53 bus slowly snakes through areas of the city that have yet to, and are unlikely to, undergo any further significant level of redevelopment since the original slum clearances of the 1970s, let alone a style makeover. This journey mostly takes in large estates of houses, arterial roads and parks surrounded by busy streets of restaurants and shops. All of which juxtaposes with the slightly eerie mid-afternoon atmosphere of calm that hangs over these decaying, long rows of suburban houses in the late afternoon heat. It's much more the Manchester I recall from my student days in the late 1970s, albeit bathed in bright sunshine not the frequent rain of the autumn. After I purchase a ticket to "Belle Vue", rather than Gorton as I request and the driver pointedly corrects me, the journey initially takes us away from the cricket club and the selection of large corporate headquarters type offices for famously branded companies, such as Centrica and Kelloggs. We pass the Royal Brewery, known in the region for both its lager and beer, which is surprisingly active if judged by the large clouds of white smoke that belch from its chimneys. The sight of an active factory in a smoke-controlled city-centre location is unusual for someone based in a seaside town and is strongly reminiscent of the traditional mills and factories of yesteryear that the popular imagination invariably associates with the north. We also have our own accompaniment of smoke on the bus, since a group of dissolute teenagers drink cans of Tennent's and ostentatiously smoke reefers of skunk. The few passengers that were already on board either quickly get off the bus, open the windows or, like the driver, studiously ignore them and thereby avoid any possible confrontation.

The loud chatter but dour party attitude of the youths provides an interesting counterpoint to the scenes outside the bus, as we slowly skirt by the infamous Moss Side residential estate, still notorious as one of the more deprived areas of the city. Shortly afterwards we pass what have now become two universities – Manchester and Manchester Metropolitan, respectively – while we snake by Whitworth Park and then trundle slowly in thick traffic through the intense ethnicity of what is the Rusholme area of the city. A huge concentration of the student population lives cheek by jowl in this varied area that is home to a thousand excellent curries (Wilmslow Road aka Curry Mile), saris and a richly diverse mix of very individual shops, urban housing and a variety of temples. As we approach Belle Vue, we noticeably lurch away from the buildings of worship of the Muslim faith back towards the Christian faith, albeit it's more esoteric manifestations as our bus passes 'The Church of God of Prophecy' close by to signs that advertise the 'Reorganised Church of Jesus of the Latter Day Saints' or the 'Sharon Church'. I get off the bus by an austere-looking hotel that wouldn't have been out of place behind the Iron Curtain, if it were judged by its exterior decoration and security measures. A short walk away from this 'Belle Vue' bus stop, through the entrance gates of a high blue security fence, is the Speedway and Greyhound stadium located in Kirkmanshulme ('Kirky') Lane, the latter-day scene of worship for all committed fans of the Aces.

Belle Vue hold the record for the most Division 1 titles won by any team in British speedway – 12 in all – with most of them gained before World War II with the latest victory tasted by the club in 1993. Since Armistice Day there has been a surfeit of World Champions who rode for the club. It's a list that reads like a veritable Who's Who of the last 50 years – Peter Craven, Ove Fundin, Ivan Mauger, Peter Collins and, now, Jason Crump. Their latest venue is very noticeably no longer the famous Hyde Road stadium with its stupendously large crowds attracted by the lure of success as well as the nearby thrills of the racing, the circus or the drinking and dancing. The present incarnation of the club shares the facilities within the GRA-owned Greyhound Stadium on a large site with ample car parking and the sort of impressively high, sturdy-looking perimeter fences that wouldn't disgrace a Borstal. It is, however, a club on the rise once more that befits its rich tradition and history within the sport. This reinvigoration comes after a few recent years in the comparative wilderness of low investment and, in 2004, abysmal performance with a rain-affected season that found the team rock bottom of the Elite League. Last season the club was in the hands of fast-food entrepreneur John Perrin, but now, to the relief of the local fans and many within the sport, he has sold his interest in Belle Vue to Tony Mole the entrepreneur, successful businessman and speedway fanatic. Tony already has a proven record of achievement away from the track in the aggregates business, plus he has a demonstrable record of enthusiastic support for the sport through his various speedway investments, which includes his ownership of the Workington Comets. They race in a different league to the Elite League level the Aces compete at, but it's similarly blessed with fanatical supporters. Tony is reputed to have invested heavily in the facilities, the team and the staff after he straightaway brought in the hugely experienced speedway impresario Ian Thomas as co-promoter, who is also well renowned as a shrewd showman, entertainer and magician. Colin Meredith has also been employed as the club's track curator to resolve the endemic and reputedly intractable (no pun intended) problems that have beset the racing surface at Kirky Lane over recent years.

The season so far has gone fantastically well for the club who sit comfortably at the top of the league table. This is an ideal position from which to, hopefully, secure a possibly advantageous home fixture in the semi-finals of the end of season play-offs that determine the final whereabouts of the championship. Tonight's clash has the Aces due to compete against one of their erstwhile competitors, the fourth-placed Eastbourne Eagles, who are keen to consolidate their own qualification for the play-offs. It's the return 'B' fixture between the two sides that immediately follows Belle Vue's narrow three-point away defeat at Arlington two days beforehand. A home victory is expected but is not a foregone conclusion and the contest is an exciting enough prospect to have attracted the welcome attentions of Sky Sports to televise this particular Elite League meeting for their regular Monday night live speedway feature. Despite the wonderful form shown by the Aces all season so far, it's only the second visit of the cameras in 2005 to the Gorton area of Manchester for a speedway meeting held at Kirky Lane. Conspiracy theories abound among the local fans and on the Internet message boards about the real reasons behind the comparative lack of attention paid by the cameras to what the locals rather self-consciously and rhetorically style "one of speedway's most exciting teams". Whatever the reason, the full panoply of equipment required for a live outside sports broadcast is parked outside in the car park, and spread all round the pits area. This includes the hallmark presentation booth that the enthusiastic and avuncular Jonathan Green – along with his usual perspicacious but often somewhat mardy sidekick-cum-expert colleague, the former grass-track world champion Kelvin Tatum (MBE) – occupy throughout the live broadcast. It looks rather forlorn when it stands empty in the bright light that reflects off its many shiny metal surfaces.

Mechanics prepare the helmets. © Jeff Scott

Some admiring Jason Crump fans rubberneck. © Jeff Scott

Sophie poses with admirers. © Jeff Scott

Jonathan is clearly an enthusiast for all things motorcycling and has an infectious presentational style when he's on the television that draws in the viewers, which just about sustains viewer interest levels throughout even the most turgid of meetings. Every single meeting is relentlessly plugged and billed as a potential "cracker", but tonight these plaudits will be well observed and almost sincerely meant[1]. At the moment, however, Jonathan isn't anywhere to be seen but all the paraphernalia is in place, which includes the camera on the dizzyingly tall crane gantry suspended high above the pits bend along with other cameras positioned at key vantage points — by the referee's box, the start line and the bends. When I arrive, in the absence of the show presenters these are being thoroughly checked by the sound and vision backroom staff from Sky. The microphones are also in place throughout the stadium to capture the atmosphere and noise of tonight's action as it unfolds. There's no doubt that the live coverage by Sky is done extremely professionally and, often, innovatively with the overall aim to engage and fascinate its armchair audience at home, and thereby content its advertisers. If there were any cause for complaint about the Sky Sports coverage, it would probably be the frequently shouty and frantic commentary, which often operates, with some commentators more than others, at a default setting of over-excited and histrionic, irrespective of the actual action shown on the track[2]. Sky Sports use of technology, in terms of missed action, occasional clunky editing and the excessive use of the helmet camera, often leaves something to be desired when it comes to the enhancement of the overall experience of the home viewer. Overall, these quibbles aside, Sky Sports usually provide a great-looking package that, in many respects, has been a huge boon to the public's and sponsors' perceptions of speedway; particularly after a long period of decline that has driven spectator numbers and the awareness of the sport among the general public into the doldrums. It's a great shop window for all its participants — clubs, riders, officials and advertisers — though only for the partial subset of British speedway that it features, namely those solely drawn from the Elite League. It's not for nothing that the sport is, reputedly (and impressively, if true), the third or fourth most popular sport on Sky after football and cricket coverage.

Many people argue that the sport is always best watched and often appreciated better at the track itself. But you're demonstrably, as the

[1] Jonathan also popularised the most notable speedway phrase of recent years with his slightly hyperbolic claim that "Tony Rickkardsson is the Schumacher of the shale". If it has a ring of truth, then it is a great pity that Rickardsson no longer chooses to compete full time in this country, but prefers instead to only use the Elite League as a form of glorified pre-season warm up for his other campaigns. Tony has for some time opted out of Britain, since he primarily saves his energies for Swedish and Polish League fixtures or, sensibly, to ensure that he continues his domination of the contemporary Grand Prix World Championship.

[2] This relentless 'excitement' ultimately bores the viewers and makes it almost impossible to distinguish the real skill and panache exhibited by some gifted riders (and commentators!) from its mundane opposite. Which, when push comes to shove, if you claim everything is perpetually a "great race", demonstrates "brilliant action" or constitutes "sublime skill" then this will, over time, necessarily devalue the overall product. It also sells the sport remarkably short when it comes to its campaign to achieve wider credibility as a serious endeavour, particularly with major advertisers in the UK, rather than appear as a gimmicky, circus-like activity, which is the perception that this bombastic style of cartoon commentary commonly inspires. Even committed speedway fans could cease to be converted by this ceaseless onslaught of ecstatically enthusiastic piffle.

recent years have painfully illustrated, not going to attract new and larger audiences unless you put on an impressive show in every avenue available. The Sky opportunity is, in some ways, still a work in progress for the sport to put its best foot forward and a boon. However, in the total absence of substantiating facts and figures, there is no way to accurately or independently corroborate these frequently advanced claims of a huge impact. Belle Vue of all the country's speedway clubs, especially after they appointed Ian Thomas as their promoter, should be able to seize and maximise the opportunities presented by the medium of television. Not only is there the Belle Vue name itself with all the strength, resonance and reputation that its rich tradition of brilliant riders and track success brings; but there is also his much-vaunted speedway experience, show-business background, connections and credentials of their promoter. I'm very excited about the chance to meet the man himself and to learn more about the factors behind his success in the sport in general, specifically how he applies these skills at Belle Vue but also, when allied to his show business publicity skills, to learn about his vision of the future for speedway, the Belle Vue brand and this club.

When I spoke with Ian the previous week, I quickly learnt that he was in the process of writing a book but, other than that basic piece of information, he refused to talk any further about the nature of his top-secret project[3]. When you meet him in person Ian is smaller than I expected, especially since he comes across on television (and in the press) as a larger-than-life, albeit combative, character. I'm keen to get some insightful answers and useful information on all things Belle Vue during my pre-arranged visit to his office.

Ian's office is located inside a portacabin close to the riders' changing rooms, the pits area and the access route out onto the track. When I arrive he has an already full office, since he's already inside with two of the casually dressed stars of his team. The well-established, young but diminutive heat leader, Kenneth Bjerre, is in the office along with the very promising reserve rider Russell 'Rusty' Harrison. Both clutch envelopes with their names on, which I assume are their pay packets from the previous week. This is a very visible sign, if any more were needed, which indicates the healthy financial situation the club has now achieved under the auspices and guidance of their new owner Tony Mole. This even keel is a marked contrast in comparison to the florid but unsubstantiated rumours of financial instability of the previous ownership regime. The tall, slim Sky commentator Kelvin Tatum is also in the office, and as he leaves I enter and I hear him say that he "felt sorry for Jesper"[4] I gather Jesper is quite a topic of conversation between Ian and the riders. Whatever the exact nature of the topic, Ian lays great stress on the public recognition of the integrity and veracity of his opinions. "I'm an honest man and straightforward as you know" he prefaces his remarks to Kenneth before he makes some observations and plans of action that I have redacted from this account. You only have to listen to their conversation for a few minutes to gather the tight-knit nature of the world of international speedway riders and the extensive travel that these star riders undertake, means that they frequently congregate together at a variety of tracks throughout Europe. It's a world where everyone knows each other and each other's business, never mind that you can usually resolve real or potential difficulties on an informal basis. I also quickly gather that they've either finished their conversation or can't really talk openly while I'm in the office, so almost immediately the riders leave to carry on with their pre-meeting preparations.

---

[3] The book is published in association with Pinegen Ltd, the company behind the *Speedway Star*, entitled *Wheels and Deals*. It's Ian's autobiography and covers, the adverts inform us, 57 years in the sport from a man "who has seen it all and done it all", when he "teams up with top journalist Richard Frost to bring you the complete lowdown". The impending publication of his own book could have been a factor behind Ian's guarded approach, circumspection and reticence to provide any real meaningful insight when we met in his office. I'm sure that if I had Ian's extensive experience, I'd be reluctant and wary, so perhaps he took this approach just in case he accidentally let out some of the many speedway stories and anecdotes that would soon grace his own book. He was also keen to guard against inadvertently revealing too much insight into Belle Vue's 2005 season, as I'm sure he was still confident that the Aces would eventually triumph and be crowned champions of the Elite League, which would thereby increase the potential sales and importance of his reminiscences on the 2005 season. Sadly, the expected hat trick of trophies ultimately didn't transpire for the Aces. Also a couple of hours before an important race night isn't the best time to speak to any promoter, never mind someone so busy. Nonetheless, the book is a real page-turner and I'd wholeheartedly recommend that anyone interested in speedway should read it. It covers his many eventful years in the sport as well as all the famous and notable people, and many others besides with whom Ian has worked. You learn of some of his many "spats" and "strokes", as well as that Ian is definitely his own man and doesn't suffer fools gladly or beat about the bush. Best of all there are some laugh-out-loud funny stories. I highly recommend it as book, never mind a speedway book.

[4] I take this to be the end of a conversation that concerned the unfortunate denouement to the previous week's live televised meeting on Sky during which Poole suggested that the secret of Jesper Jensen's success for Peterborough that evening had possibly been down to an illegal and oversized carburettor.

Throughout our conversation Ian is seated behind his desk, often with his arms folded, except when the phone rings. Which it does endlessly with callers who enquire whether tonight's meeting will actually go ahead, despite the severely overcast conditions in the local area. When we get time on our own together, except for the interruptions of the constantly ringing phone or a brief visit of the club's experienced Australian rider Jason Lyons who pops in to collect his pay envelope ("I'll give you some money"), I try to take full advantage of the opportunity Ian has kindly provided before he and his team appear in front of the cameras before a national audience on television.

Ian Thomas has been a competitor throughout his career and, just like C.J. in 'Reggie Perrin', he 'didn't get where he is today' without being competitive in some fashion or other. If judged by my own experience of him, this is especially true once Ian has his 'game face' in place for the work night ahead. They also say that you only get one chance to make a first impression and, for whatever reason, I don't think that mine was the best. I was respectful throughout but clearly, as it was our first ever meeting, I was never going to be admitted into his charmed circle (or in Ian's case magic circle?) for him to relax enough to be candid or share any real insights gained through his many years within speedway. Everyone who really knows him within the sport can't speak highly enough of him and his many qualities, both for his straightforwardness and his sense of humour. Sadly our interview was rather snatched and had a slight 'walking-in-treacle' quality but then it was not long before race night at, arguably, the country's top club. For all my research interviews for the book, I have a prepared list of 20 or so questions, which I have covered to some degree during my interviews with managers and promoters. These questions serve as an *aide memoire* since most people I spoke with tend to reminisce, have strong opinions or want to just talk about whatever comes into their head. Ian's approach was to limit himself to brief and often staccato replies to the questions, as though he were speaking with someone not very quick on the uptake, and throughout which he was content to keep his fabled sense of humour well hidden. To some extent, our interview turns into an exercise like trying to box my own shadow during which I fail to ask a question that really loosens Ian's tongue or reveals any of his vast wealth of insights and speedway stories. He answers all questions in a manner that suggests that they might be taken down and could be used against him as evidence in some yet to be convened speedway show trial. Also very sensibly he was determined to keep his own tinder dry for his not yet published, partially ghosted autobiography. If he was keen to scrupulously guard against inadvertently letting anything of real note or interest escape his lips, and in this he was extremely successful.

Nonetheless, we both persevered in that polite British way to try to get the most out of the meeting and we superficially covered a lot of ground in a very short space of time. My questions, which usually served well enough to provoke some form of discussion, were quickly exhausted. Some of our exchange went as follows:

Me: "How do you see the season going for Belle Vue?"
Ian: "I'll tell you at the end of the season, I don't make forecasts."
Me: "You've had a long and varied career in speedway?"
Ian: "I have."
Me: "What do you most remember?"
Ian: "There are too many things to pick just one."
Me: "You had some time away from speedway before coming back, why was that?"
Ian: "I just fell out of speedway."
Me: "Having come back, what were the positive changes you noticed?
Ian: "There have been some strange things about coming back but it's the same really."
Me: "What are these things?"
Ian: "There's been two changes, one is fixed gate positions, which we never used to have in the 1970s and 1980s, and the other is aggregate bonus points."
Me: "What do you think of these changes?"
Ian: "They've happened, haven't they? So we have to live with them."
Me: "What about changes for the negative that you've noticed?"
Ian: "I can't think of any."
Me: "How do you think the sport could be improved?
Ian: "There's not much to improve. It's a simple sport – riders are still doing four laps and turning left."
Me: "Anything else?"
Ian: "Freak knows, I wish you'd sent me these questions beforehand."
Me: "There have been a lot of changes round here since you arrived; what have they been?"
Ian: "We brought in Colin Meredith 'cause the track was awful. We put in 270 metres of drains and it's been totally re-laid. Speak to Colin, he'll tell you more; he's the man in red overalls outside."
Me: "You obviously like it, being a speedway promoter here?"
Ian: "I do."
Me: "Why?"
Ian: "Well, there's the promotion and showmanship aspect; then there's the show business and magician aspect, I know lots of people, which comes in handy in this job."
Me: "What are the major differences between promoting Workington in the Premier League and Belle Vue in the Elite? What do you miss?"
Ian: "I spent a long time at Workington. So I miss the riders and the fans and I knew a lot of people there, so it was wrench to leave. But if you're offered a job like this you have to take it ..."
Me: "But what do you notice?"
Ian: "It's still speedway. The sponsors are different – we have Fonestyle here, they're great to work with! There's the quality of the riders, they're a couple of seconds quicker. And the first 50 yards out of the gate is harder but it's still four laps in both leagues."
Me: "What's your favourite speedway story?"
Ian: "Where from?"
Me: "Anywhere."
Ian: "They'll be in my book."
Me: "What's the secret of your success here this season?"
Ian: "We put the right team together and stayed away from injuries, though they're just starting now, so I can't say what'll happen yet."

Me: "Like Joe's?" [He'd dislocated his shoulder two nights previously at Eastbourne, though he 'popped it back in' to continue to ride that night he, sensibly, won't ride tonight]

Ian: "He rode on adrenalin that night – he had flu as well, so he's not here and we've got rider replacement."

Me: "How do you see tonight going against them?"

Ian: "I'd have preferred that we had no points difference between us.[5] I have to go in a minute, is that all your questions?"

Me: "Mostly."

Ian: "You should have sent them before – what's your book about anyway?"[6]

Me: "It's about what I see and hear when I visit the tracks – including meeting people like yourself and others from behind the scenes or in the crowd. It's a mostly affectionate but general look at speedway in Britain, really."

Ian: "How come you're doing it?"

Me: "It's a labour of love"

Ian: "When's it coming out?"

Me: "Early next year, hopefully."

Ian: "How many pages does it have?"

Me: "Not sure."

Ian: "How much will it cost?"

Me: "Between £15 and £20. I won't know until I know how many pages or if it's coming out in hardback or paperback. Most likely paperback."

Ian: "Who's the publisher?"

Me: "I'm doing it myself."

Ian: "How come?"

Me: "I used to work in publishing and now do book publicity so I can do a lot of things myself. Hopefully I'll get some coverage, as it's my job. If you'd like my help or advice on publicity for your book, you have my contact details so please let me know if you do?"

Ian: "I'll be fine, thank you. Will it make any money?"

Me: "No, most likely a loss, but you never know."

Ian: "Why are you doing it then?"

Me: "I felt I had to; it's a labour of love as I mentioned [pause] what's your book about?"

Ian: "I can't say it's a secret."

Me: "I can keep a secret."

Ian: "You'll find out when it comes out."

Me: "When's that?"

Ian: "Next year."

Me: "Who's the publisher?"

Ian: "I can't say and I have to get on, let me know if you need anything else."

Me: "Can I wander around the pits?"

Ian: "You can do what you like, just don't get in the way."

And with that our meeting is definitively over. I can't say that I felt hugely comfortable or relaxed during it and Ian made little attempt to pretend to be interested any more than he had to be or to hold his natural irascibility in check. I really admire him for just being himself, for not affecting to be nice or falsely emollient and for the courtesy of giving his time. With Ian, I quickly gathered, what you see is what you get and, given he doesn't know me from Adam, was probably more than I merited or deserved.[7] As I leave I pass Colin Meredith who heads towards the office and he suggests that I wait for a few minutes, since he'll be free to talk after he's spoken with Ian.

---

[5] The score at Arlington was 46-43 to the Eagles.

[6] Ian was suddenly much more curious, inquisitive and engaged during this part of our meeting.

Outside in the warm sunshine, I relax for a moment and sit on the corner of the distinctive interview stand that Sky Sports use for their outside broadcasts at speedway. It's empty apart from a backdrop of the Sky Sports logo and the black box of the monitor the interviewers use to review replays of the action on the track to interviewees. Away to my left a steady stream of Eastbourne mechanics wheel the bikes from the riders' vans up the slight slope into the pits. Everyone is casually dressed for the warm weather and the atmosphere appears extremely relaxed in a lull before the storm fashion. Some of the Belle Vue riders emerge already dressed in their black and red kevlars from the changing room, apparently already to race while others still remain in their shorts. While I wait, I get to feed the talking and sleeping 'dolly' owned by Tony Mole's precocious and friendly young daughter Emily.[8] According to Zanna, her mother, she began to go to speedway at four months old. Now Emily is three and a half, I'm told "she loves all the riders and she's happy at speedway". As if to demonstrate this, a few moments later she says hello to Jason Lyons as he passes and then asks her mother, "who's that?" as Russell 'Rusty' Harrison passes in the other direction on his way to get changed. Moments later, Emily then runs off towards the grandstand with her mother, who trails a few yards behind in her wake. Nearby, while I wait, Kenneth Bjerre watches the track staff and bemoans the probable track conditions they will probably create for later, "he's putting too much freaking water on". The mechanic is unsympathetic, and laughingly replies in a broad Mancunian accent, "come off it, with the money you're making riding here, Poland, Sweden and the GPs – you're loaded and you can ride anywhere!"

The red-overalled Colin soon emerges back out into the warm early evening sunlight and is more than happy to chat affably about his career and work at the track. He appears trim and athletic in his overalls, maybe aged around 50, though he looks younger than that. Like many in the sport, Colin has watched speedway for over 40 years and has been actively involved, in a variety of capacities, for over 30 years. He's participated as a rider, a team manager and most recently, as a track curator. Colin is acknowledged to be one of the best, if not the best, trackmen in the country by many of his contemporaries; indeed his great aptitude and skill with shale has been formally recognised by the sport's governing body, the Speedway Control Bureau. He works for the SCB throughout the UK, after they appointed him as a 'consultant track inspector', and also independently advises many UK promoters on track and fence design, preparation and care. He modestly, but correctly, insists that he admires other UK track curators such as 'Doc' Bridgett and Bob Dugard, "if we've got a problem, good track men can sort it out, whereas the less able just stand there while it goes to pot". He started to watch Belle Vue as a 10-year-old and "never missed a meeting until 1970". Colin relishes "having been involved since school" when he embarked on a successful riding career that took in Wolves, Bradford, Stoke and Oxford. He stopped racing prematurely, in 1980, after he badly broke his leg at Oxford. He has always retained a fascination with speedway bikes though he notes, "sadly I only rode standard equipment"; nonetheless, he still paid great attention to "engine speed and engine tuning". However, contemporary speedway has altered dramatically since he rode competitively, most notably with the increased speed and sophistication of the modern bikes, to the extent that if "you're without top equipment, you're not competitive". When he looks back on his career, "the racing side was always brilliant and there's nothing better than riding for your club and country, as I was lucky enough to do". When he retired, Colin was fortunate enough to "know a lot of people" and thereby kept involved in the sport by "just doing tracks". He began at the old Blackbird Road track in Leicester, then owned by the Ochiltree family, "doing odd jobs" though he eventually progressed to manage all aspects of the track, when Phil Storey retired in 1986-87. He then remained working with the Ochiltree family and had 18 years at Coventry with his last couple of years in the position of team manager. Colin Pratt's arrival as speedway manager "around 1997" lead to slight differences of opinion that saw him then spend, "three good seasons, and included winning the league in 2000, at Oxford" working under the promoters Steve and Vanessa Purchase.

---

[7] Michael Payne, my American Editor, who has read the drafts of this manuscript says in his margin note, "Ian is a competitor who has always has to compete, he's competing with you here. You Brits are too false and polite. He's not. It's a backhanded compliment really, but get over it". Afterwards, in a very kind letter to me later, Ian Thomas said "I'm sorry I seemed to give you a hard time when we met, even my wife does not come near me on race day afternoons".

[8] I'd previously seen her play around at the Waverley Hotel in Workington where she had rather sweetly tested her own boundaries and the calm equanimity of her father Tony Mole and joined in with the breakfasting riders in her own inimitable fashion. Emily was a bundle of energy and curiosity then and later that evening when she played contently in the Stoke pits and, rather dangerously given the bikes that hurtled around at speed, in the pit lane. She was without a care, completely absorbed in her conversation with dolly, and totally doted on by her besotted father, Tony, who held her closely while she slowly tired.

With Tony Mole installed as the owner at Belle Vue, Colin didn't hesitate to accept his invitation to be the curator of the Manchester track. Though he "knew it was in a very poor state of repair", he also knew that Tony had the determination to succeed and the "finances to buy the correct equipment". It's essential at all tracks to get the "drainage right, then the water will never settle", particularly in an area like Manchester that is reputedly prone to wetter weather than other tracks around the country. Colin spent all winter working hard on the track, "getting the levels right" and things quickly improved after Tony "spent nearly 20 grand on equipment", which includes his curatorial pride and joy the "Volvo power blade" that has been put to good use to create a completely new track surface. The frequently mentioned stock-car track bricks of the last few seasons still remain at the stadium but are now buried "six inches below", rather than dangerously penetrating, the racing surface.

The relationship with the riders at any track is a vital and peculiar relationship for any curator. It's always advisable to "work with the riders and ask them what they want". For the 2005 version of the Aces, what they want are "slick starts and a smooth track" with the additional possibility, if required, that Colin uses the "spike and harrow to generate dirt" during the meeting. It's a job where you get rapid negative feedback, "if the track's good nobody praises you but, if they don't score points, it's the track". On that basis, for any track curator silence is golden, "if they score a lot of points it's because they're good" and therefore the condition of the track is taken for granted. Colin prefers to just get on with his work quietly, "I like things to be clean and tidy", though he modestly attributes the secret of his success to the "dedication and pride" of his staff. In his ideal world to "take speedway forward" he thinks "steps are needed on the presentation side" and a good model for the future could come from the world of Formula 1 with staff in overalls with racing gear on display that looks "all clean and tidy". He's also of the opinion that the "only people in the middle of the track during a meeting should be the medical and track staff". Not that this would be the only change if he were to find himself in control of speedway's future, since he'd straightaway introduce "standard equipment with every bike the same" then it really would be "up to the skill of the rider" rather than the present situation which favours those fortunate enough to have the greatest finances through sponsorship and are, thereby, able ride on the best equipment.

Since he retired through injury, Colin strongly favours the safety benefits gained by the installation of air fences as standard equipment, which he unreservedly views as a "good invention as the solid fences I've hit were very hard". Despite the fact that they are "so expensive" and at some speedway clubs the "nature and width of the track can't accommodate them". Colin notes that the limited number of air fences installed at UK tracks have usually been paid for by the "riders themselves with their services given for free" in a couple of early season meetings to raise the necessary funds. While it's fun to put the world to rights, Colin has to get on with the day job. I leave Colin to his last-minute ministrations to the smooth and slightly wet-looking Belle Vue track for its next grand appearance on live television in an hour or so. Though he arguably fates himself for the evening ahead, when he notes, "watering and track preparation are a fine art, yeah, everyone makes mistakes but they should be less as you get older". In passing as he heads off Colin advises I watch out for Andy Smith tonight "Smudger's excellent round here, even if he misses the start he doesn't panic" since he then applies his many years of riding experience to skilfully pass the opposition riders.

As the start time draws near, the pits throng with keenly interested spectators and riders happily sign autographs or pose with young fans for photographs with their idols. I chat with Trevor Geer, the joint team manager of Eastbourne and I quickly gather, before he wanders back off to the pits, that he's rather optimistic about the possibility of a result against the league leaders "we're one of the few teams that's a danger to them around here". By the side of the track, I wait for a few moments while tonight's referee Stuart Wilson confirms the programme details with a Sky Sports researcher. Stuart is a keen but recent follower of the sport and now, since he qualified in 2002, a respected referee who hails from Workington. I wish him a controversy-free evening on national television before I enquire about his views, as the referee involved, on the recent hullabaloo that affected the meeting at Newcastle with Somerset.[9] Rather than dwell on past meetings, we chatted about the racing prospects ahead tonight, particularly because it's a meeting that Stuart thinks will be an exciting encounter and one he relishes officiating at. Every time I speak with an SCB referee it never ceases to amaze me how enthusiastic they all are about speedway; it's also an enthusiasm that appears to increase rather than become jaded the more they get to watch! With that Stuart is off towards the pits to start with the many activities and meticulous checks that form an essential part of the activities of being a Speedway Control Bureau referee on any evening. With the presence of live national television, like everyone else he's keen to ensure that everything proceeds professionally and smoothly.

The ubiquitous sombrero-wearing Belle Vue fans haven't yet arrived but others have unfolded their garden chairs or already stand on their boxes in anticipation of the start of the fixture. Sky Sports presenter and proprietor of his own successful independent television presentation company, Jonathan Green is sat on one of the benches, where he relaxes with a friend and a last-minute cup of coffee before another evening where he has to think on his feet, while he broadcasts live to the nation. A short distance away, his glamorous co-presenter, Sophie Blake, patiently poses for photographs or signs autographs for a steady stream of delighted but keen male admirers, while she slowly picks her way towards the pits gate entrance. Shortly afterwards the show for the fans in actual attendance at Kirky Lane is off and running with Brendan Kearney, the centre-green announcer, who informs us all "we're starting early 'cause Sky are here". Significantly, we also learn that despite the overnight torrential downpours, which continued unabated until 10 a.m. that morning "we've even put water on the track tonight as it was so bone dry we had to put three tanker loads on". It's the sort of additional information that's given out at meetings and is usually just vaguely informative to know. Tonight, however, as soon as the racing gets underway, it will seem of much greater significance to everyone. Recalcitrant youngsters slightly delay the riders' parade and their practice laps when they obstinately sit on the safety fence but soon feel the full ire of the announcer's threats, which take the form of "we won't start until everyone is behind the safety barrier".

When the meeting finally gets underway in front of the watching nation, Eastbourne's David Norris swiftly grinds to a halt after his back chain snaps within yards of his departure from the start, which establishes the tone and direction throughout the rest of the evening for the Eagles team. The sombrero-wearing Aces fans whoop in delight and wave their distinctive hats in celebration as the home team roar into a comfortable lead. Their boisterous celebrations are definitely significantly bolstered by the amplifier that the fans have brought into the stadium for this purpose, which allows them to 'comment' on events as they unfold and, mostly wittily, abuse any of the opposition riders that it takes their fancy to berate. Despite the ease of their first heat win, the home riders visibly struggle with the very slippery track conditions and the experienced Andy Smith takes a heavy tumble in the next heat. This results in the first of many frequent remedial sessions of track grading for Colin Meredith and his track staff team; who thereafter repeatedly come out at the end of each heat to give the surface some further care and attention. Kelvin Tatum, never one to eschew stating the obvious, informs the armchair viewers that "conditions are tricky" and he also then insightfully observes, "they're working really hard on the track".

With the benefit of interviews and behind the scenes footage that's unavailable to the fans crowded within the stadium – in my opinion, the real and incontrovertible innovation of the Sky coverage – the viewers at home hear a considerable amount of detail about the changing state of the track conditions for the rest of the evening. The home side's confidence of victory is already so great at this early stage in the meeting, that they decide to use James Wright, their number 8 rider, in heat 3 to give him additional and valuable riding experience at this level. He is an up-and-coming young British star of the future who 'doubles up' from Premier League Workington. James has a number of important connections to Belle Vue speedway club, particularly since former Aces rider, Jim Yacoby, is his grandfather as well as the fact that he rides for clubs that are both owned by Belle Vue's proprietor Tony Mole. Despite his pedigree and connections, he finishes the race

---

[9] It was a meeting in which the clerk of the course urgently called him after the end of heat 15 to say, "it's got out of hand here". This fracas happened after Stuart had rather boldly thrown out the Somerset captain Magnus Zetterstrom for an earlier racing incident during the meeting. Stuart is unequivocal in his comments, "I was very disappointed by the reaction of Mick Bell but thought Peter Toogood reacted correctly by keeping low key". He has no regrets about the Zetterstrom incident, as he felt that 'Zorro' was clearly "intent to take out the rider", when he started from 20 feet away with "absolutely no justification from coming from behind like that". "It was a bad injury and not one I wished to see personally". Stuart supports the idea advanced by the experienced Australian rider Shane Parker in his capacity as chairman of the Speedway Riders Association, "about starting a yellow and red card" disciplinary system for the sport. "It's been overdue for a year or two" and would have helped that night as "we should hit offenders in the pocket with a ban for a few weeks" which would, in Stuart's view, quickly stamp out the problem. However, before he goes off, Stuart unequivocally states, "whatever comments you read otherwise in the speedway press – that was my decision and it was the correct one!"

in last position; while the winner Jason Lyons, the club's experienced Australian rider and the only surviving member of the 1993 league winning team, really isn't happy with the track conditions, despite the comparative ease of his victory. In the strange world of live television coverage, it's possible for the riders and mechanics to crowd round the telly located at the pits area entrance to watch the various interviews that take place only five yards away in the Sky interview booth or even, watch replays of the race action that takes place on a track located only 15 yards away. I watch Jason get interviewed, fresh from his last triumph, when he's asked, "what's gone wrong out there?" Jason then provides detailed insights into the continuing work of the track staff that wouldn't be out of place in an agricultural college lecture or during a gardening programme, "he's [Colin] put a bit more dirt back in there which is the clay that's hard to water, though he's made a bit of a mess of it".

Greeted with the ritualistic boos that greet him at practically every away track he visits in the UK; Nicki Pedersen, in his role as public enemy number 1, struggles to adapt his skilled and aggressive race technique to the slippery conditions in the next heat 4. He's beaten by Belle Vue's veteran reserve Andy Smith to the uproarious delight of the waving hordes of Aces fans in the main grandstand. The ease with which the home team dominates effectively ends the meeting as a competitive event at a very early stage.

It's so protracted and one-sided that, despite the fact that I actually watch the meeting live, I'm reduced to occasionally loitering by the television for some additional information. The races have been so predictable and processional that even the normally pathologically ebullient commentary, for which regular commentator Nigel Pearson is renowned, has (very unusually) been so severely dampened that as a spectacle he can, for once, only claim – with complete accuracy – that it's been "a meeting that's had a sprinkling of reasonable racing". The TLC the track receives creates many longueurs and thereby dominates televised discussions, since it leaves them with considerable time to fill with little or no action to show the armchair viewers. There is the appearance of Colin Meredith to issue his *mea culpa* to the armchair nation when he apologises "for watering the track too late". And Sophie Blake reports that Nicki Pedersen claims, "I hate this track". Added to this rich mix, there is another of Sam Ermolenko's trademark gems of enthusiastic but inevitably awkwardly phrased insight, when he praises Simon Stead as "very good on dirt-naked system tracks". Though it is true that Stead quickly adapts to the conditions to put in the most assured performance of any rider on the night. When interviewed, Eastbourne's Trevor Geer can only sheepishly admit to Sophie that "I thought we'd run 'em close but the track has caught us out and freaked a few of the boys out".

Far more excitingly, the actual crowd on the stadium terraces creates their own fun through wild celebrations of every Belle Vue triumph or indulge themselves liberally with their witty and abusive amplified comments about the visiting Eastbourne riders. Just before heat 9, Nicki Pedersen is regaled with a loud and blunt "Pedersen is a turd" as he lines up at the starting gate and afterwards is greeted with a joyous chorus roughly indicating to him that "you're [excrement] and you know you are!" Dean Barker is mercilessly lampooned throughout and is usually greeted with an amplified serenade of "Deano Barker, Deano Barker's eaten all the pies". David Norris has an unfortunate evening plagued by mechanical problems and still suffers from the neck problems that have disrupted his riding throughout the season. Not that this gains him any undue sympathy from a partisan crowd who delight in relentless pokes of fun at his poor fashion sense. It's a perception apparently generated by his decision to have blond highlights in his lightly permed hair style; though chants of "David Norris why have you come dressed as Neil Collins?" enlists no response from the object of their taunts. They also elicit no reaction with their playful and witty chants of "David Norris – are you Keegan in disguise?" It's a comment that, among Manchester residents, skilfully links criticism of Norris's chosen style of coiffure and, at the same time, associates him with hysterical over-reactions as well as creating inflated expectations that ultimately are never fulfilled.

The centre-green announcer Brendan Kearney tries to inject an element of excitement into proceedings through the introduction of the few celebrities that there are in attendance at tonight's meeting. First we are all treated to some laborious comments and platitudes from the very tall visiting Manchester City goalkeeper, Nicky Weaver (whom Sophie "I'm friends with many footballers" Blake introduces live on television as playing for Manchester United). It goes downhill as an interview, almost immediately after Brendan greets him with an excited cry of "Nicky Weaver is here!" The crowd react with the odd sarcastic jeer but mostly bored indifference to Nicky's 'insights' on speedway or his reaction to it as a sport. Brendan makes it a point to be completely unprepared to extend any form of a helping hand to improve the celebrity novice's appreciation and enjoyment of the evening "don't ask me to explain the rules to Nicky, there's too many of them". Later, during another gap in proceedings, Brendan interviews eight-times Isle of Man TT winner and current track record holder on the island, the very engaging John McGuiness. Despite having braved the 38-mile TT course at an average speed of 127.68 m.p.h., John modestly notes that he's lucky enough to ride bikes with brakes, before going on to be very appreciative of the sport "it's 60 seconds of action, it's great! I'd love to have a go on a speedway bike". Brendan wonders about John's health following his recent fall at 130 m.p.h. at Silverstone before he then moves on to have must more fastidious enquiries about his bank balance. John admits that he earns over £100,000 a year "it's a lot of money to some people but I think I deserve every penny as I've lost a few friends to the sport". The crowd listen patiently to John, most likely because of his enthusiasm and interest in speedway but, also, because he's a member of the loose fraternity of motorcyclists of which speedway is the brakeless chapter, "I do something similar only at higher speed but with brakes!"

Arguably these exchanges are the highlights of an evening that lumbers to its protracted foregone conclusion. The Aces thump the Eagles comprehensively in a manner that would have had the referee stop the fight long beforehand if this had been a boxing match.[10] Leavened by an easy victory, Ian Thomas is conspicuously light-hearted and evangelical about his side and its prospects in front of the cameras, "I think we might make the play-offs" said *sotto voce* with a sly smile and a level of bonhomie that apparently initially surprises Sophie at the televised heat 15 coin toss. When pressed, he also makes light of the difficulties with track conditions.[11] With victory assured, it's good to see the pressures of office fall temporarily from Ian's shoulders to reveal (albeit only to the armchair fans and to his friends in private, I'm sure) a more light-heartedly, whimsical side to his character that wasn't noticeably evident a few hours earlier.

[10] Jon Cook wryly observes a few days later at Oxford that it's "typical we should save our worst performance of the season for in front of the TV cameras".

[11] When I bump into him working on the Oxford track a few days later, Colin Meredith has the final word when he admits, "I did over water it but sometimes you just can't win". Despite the fact that he provided a track that the home riders won easily on, they still complained about it anyway; thereby instantly disproving his theory that you only get complaints from your own riders when they lose. "Reading the Internet" Colin has been astonished at the ill-informed criticism of his skills and performance as a curator. Some correspondents have lost all sense of proportion "you'd have thought I'd murdered someone!" but he's resisted the temptation to reply, mostly because, " they're just not worth it".

When I make my way to the crowded pits area immediately following the ecstatically greeted victory parade by the Belle Vue riders who salute the jubilant crowd from their bikes, Sophie kindly poses for yet more numerous photographs by the pits gate entrance, haloed by the frequent flash of cameras and new fangled phones. A crowd of eager sombrero-wearing fans surround her, while Sophie good humouredly poses at length at the centre of her giant huddle of admirers (wearing a sombrero herself), before she immediately rushes off to the taxi she says that already waits to whisk her away from Gorton. The fans loudly serenade her with a rousing rendition of the "she's just the Queen of Speedway" as she rushes off into the dark of the night. By the time they gleefully disperse, Jason Crump is the only rider from either side to remain to still chat amiably in the pits. Though the Belle Vue side of the pits is still crowded with mechanics, hangers on, bikes and machines but no riders, except Jason. In total contrast the Eastbourne side is already forlornly deserted, scattered with the usual detritus of their recent participation in a speedway fixture, with a bin full of discarded dirt-deflectors all that remains to signal their attendance. The Eagles have flown, even quicker than the brief time it took for Sophie to pose for her gaggle of admirers and then get to her taxi, onto their long journey home to the south coast.

22nd August Belle Vue v. Eastbourne (ELB) 59-35

Chapter 33: The World According to Waggy
25th August Oxford v. Eastbourne

"He's prepared to do anything to win, including taking other riders off" Gary Havelock (on Nicki Pedersen)

RANDOM SCB RULES

17.1.4 A Rider may have:
a 2004 Elite League CMA only
a 2004 Premier League CMA only
both a 2004 EL & PL CMA (gained as a consequence of Doubling-Up).
both a 2004 EL & PL CMA (as a consequence of transferring Clubs/Leagues) during the 2004 season
a 2004 EL CMA & a 2003 PL CMA (as a consequence of transferring Clubs/Leagues during the 2004 season or as a consequence of Doubling-Up/Down)
a 2004 PL CMA & a 2003 EL CMA (as a consequence of transferring Clubs/Leagues before the 2004 season).
an Assessed CMA (see 17.3 below)

After a few calls to Nigel 'Waggy' Wagstaff's office and conversations with the man himself I wasn't sure that if I turned up early at the Oxford Silver Machines' Stadium in Sandy Lane it would result in the promised interview. There's a lot to get done on a race night and, everything he is required to do in his capacity as a promoter during that evening must be done; so Nigel was understandably reluctant to definitely commit to meeting me. He suggested I call once more on the morning before the Elite League 'A' fixture with the visiting Eastbourne Eagles to make sure. If I turned up three or so hours before the start of the meeting Nigel would kindly find the time to spare a few words.

I have lived in Oxford, I have previously visited the track on and off so consequently it's a familiar place that I know well. The city itself appears to become more and more gentrified all the time, especially in the centre around the colleges, but also in North Oxford.[1]

One thing that hasn't changed though is the reputation and pariah status of the Blackbird Leys estate, at least in the minds of the so-called or self-styled Oxford intelligentsia. All the usual stories apply – if your car is stolen you will find it on the Blackbird Leys estate or its converse: if you want your car to be safe you have to park it on the estate, etc. There are bored, disgruntled and dispossessed young people throughout the country and Oxford is no exception[2]. The Blackbird Leys estate is still one of the largest council estates in Europe never mind England, so large that it's a civil parish. It's one of the most deprived estates in the country with its residents prone to poor health, reduced life expectancy and, compared to the notional average, generally low socio-economic status. However, despite the ethnic mix of a white and African-Caribbean population, there is and has been historically very little racial tension. The new investments in buildings and infrastructure throughout the Oxford area have brought the arrival of the new football stadium, the development of Oxford University's Science Park and a leisure complex. Over the years a number of superstore sites have sprung up round the Blackbird Leys area, which is the closest, many of the Oxford city-centre residents get to the estate but, overall, this part of the city has resolutely remained under-resourced.

It's on the outskirts of the estate, close by the ring road, railway line and retail park that Oxford Stadium is located. In publishing circles, the idea that I would voluntarily visit the area to watch either the greyhounds or the speedway was snobbishly received as though I'd publicly acknowledged that I was a child pornographer, wished to start a regular car boot sale in my front garden, or had become part of the Oxford branch of Al Qaeda. Obviously, my experiences when I visited over the years indicate that this reputation is completely unfounded and is a massively exaggerated form of snobbery and class demonisation.

A cursory visit quickly shows that Oxford Stadium is primarily the home of the dog track and that it secondarily shares its facilities with the

[1] It hardly seems possible that it could take on more airs and graces or achieve a higher level of poshness, but it has. The city still reeks of history, privilege and property, but now much more noticeably, money. Oxford has always had its various but distinctive estates that surround the city centre of the famous colleges and river that the tourists visit. The wave of increased gentrification has visited many of the outlying estates around the city but others still remain stubbornly unreconstituted and resistant to this change. One city-centre enclave and a tremendously vibrant pocket of resistance, albeit it has become a very 'done up' area, is the culturally rich locale of the Cowley Road, surrounded by lots of lovely houses, which still just about retains its uncouthness and proud defiance. As you journey further along the Cowley Road and away from the fields and meadows of the colleges, you run towards the ring road that circles the city and the whole area that used to be the site of the old Cowley car plants and its associated buildings. These have been demolished, but the car industry still remains in the city. Though, it's now foreign owned, the sale was a national scandal or should have been, and the whole area has rapidly changed its outward appearance with factories replaced with smoked-glass office developments and retail shopping parks that increasingly dot the whole perimeter of the city. These sleek buildings house all the usual suspects – pharmaceutical companies, insurance companies and publishers. It's a bookish city with an incredible concentration of publishing or publishing-related employers that inevitably results in many dinner parties, huge sales of *The Guardian* and a big demand for organic produce. Even the publishers have begun an exodus from the centre to the outskirts of the city (or, heaven forefend, Abingdon!), which has fundamentally changed the socio-economic profile of the area, at least during the daytime.

[2] When I lived there, more-confident joyriders would circle the police station until the police finally deigned to emerge and vainly chase them around the city in the early hours of the morning. Despite their superior equipment, training, advanced driving skills, state-of-the-art cars and communications devices, the police were no match for the dangerous idiocy, skills and local knowledge of drivers too young to hold a driving licence. The police coped with this epidemic of bravado by pretending not to want to chase the 'twockers' – taking away without consent – until the disaffected youth became bored and slowly settled back into the more manageable but predictable routines of high unemployment, crime, alcohol and drug abuse, often allied to their single-parent families.

speedway club. Promoter Nigel Wagstaff is in the final year of a three-year lease agreement with Steve Purchase, the speedway licence owner, to manage the sport at the stadium. Nigel arrived at Oxford after he previously had been the promoter of King's Lynn. One of the first changes Nigel made was to the name of the club, which he altered from the traditional moniker of the Oxford Cheetahs to the Oxford Silver Machine. After you walk through the pits gate towards the Speedway Office, you can see a few of these distinctive looking silver machines lined up on the home side of the pits area. Well, they're ordinary speedway bikes really – just decorated with futuristic looking, stylised silver and green liveries that add a real touch of class to their appearance. Unfortunately, while the bikes look incredibly good, the results on the track haven't been all that the management, riders or fans were expecting at the start of the season when everyone's hopes ran high. The team has since suffered debilitating injuries, which has forced some early changes to the line up of the team. With these initial changes forced upon him, 'Waggy' then appeared to get severely bitten by the bug and continued to regularly introduce new riders into his team. By the time of my arrival at the stadium for the meeting with Eastbourne, the Oxford Silver Machine had tracked an incredible and mind-boggling 17 different riders for the club, many of whom were unheard-of riders from outside this country. Most of these riders have gone as quickly as they arrived, but not before they have been introduced to the fans and their team-mates as the great silver hope for the search for glory and the future continued success of the club. Often the justification employed by Nigel in his announcements, for the more comparatively unknown riders, has been that he wants to discover new talent and give it a chance to develop and, hopefully, achieve future success. At other times the introduction of these different riders has been presented as thrust upon the club by the need to find 'temporary cover' or to bring in an experienced (foreign) rider 'to do a job'. Whatever the justifications, reasons, or spin no one could deny that the frequent alterations to the team didn't help to foster a collective spirit that consistently translated into victories on the track.

Just to briefly attempt to keep track of all these personnel changes was both a challenge and entertainment in itself. The frequency of the riders' arrivals and departures often had the intense, banal complexity of a soap opera. Many of these riders had no sooner come on to the Oxford scene than they left it again. If it were actually a proper television soap opera, viewers would long ago have switched off due to lack of proper character development and the frequency of plot changes.

Let's review the highlights, as early as April we have Nigel Wagstaff "slamming his Internet critics" for their attacks on his policy of using Conference League youngsters. He makes a good point about the need for the development of British youngsters and, since Oxford is the only Elite League club to officially participate in the Conference League, it seems churlish to question his commitment on this score. By late May, Waggy's concern over Jesper B. Jensen's form when he's been signed on a "short-term contract" clearly signals that he's already started to search for replacements. When Nigel signs the "Russian star Renat Gafurov" on June 15, he provokes widespread mystery among the fans but Waggy isn't perplexed and he predicts that Renat will "accumulate lots of points, initially perhaps on bigger circuits". Just after mid-summer, June 27 to be exact, staff problems have developed on another front within the club that indicate they're soon to announce a "new signing" to replace the "disappointing" Pole Tomasz Bajerski. And Waggy then promises yet another "new signing", hopefully to quickly become the talk of the Cowley terraces, after "complications" beset the all-too-brief career of Renat Gafurov at the club. Luckily, like London buses, if you miss one "signing" another one will be along in a minute, and so the next day deliriously excited fans soon learn that the club has captured the services of another Polish youngster, this time in the form of Pawel Staszek. Say what you like about the necessity or advisability of this approach, there's absolutely no denying that as team manager and promoter Nigel Wagstaff is completely unafraid to make radical changes to his team.

His unique approach has generated huge amounts of wry comments from the supporters of other clubs and has provoked frequent critical comments with regards to Waggy's supposed competence to run Oxford Speedway Club. Internet forums and their comments appear to be something that promoters across the country are unduly sensitive to and I suspect that Waggy has good reason to have a similar reaction. The BSPA website, as early as April, had him "slamming" his Internet critics – or genuine Oxford fans, it all depends on your point of view – about their ignorance of the difficult work of being a

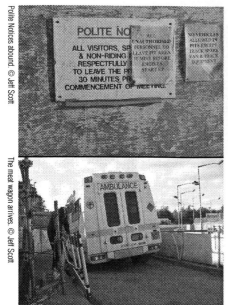
Polite Notices abound. © Jeff Scott

The meat wagon arrives. © Jeff Scott

Floppy meets his admirers. © Jeff Scott

promoter. But comments in the area of team selection matters also prompt his anger and lead to his further outbursts on the BSPA site, "I only go on the Internet because some people tell me to have a look and unfortunately some of the comments come from my club as well as others. They really need to get a life and understand what British speedway is all about and these people simply have no idea". It's the sort of perspective that makes you curious, if you weren't already before, about what exactly these people have to say.[3]

Unfortunately for Waggy, the team steadfastly has remained rooted to the bottom of the Elite League for the majority of the season, so far, and this has especially emphasised its lack of cohesion and results. Although that said, it is undoubtedly a sport where teams can greatly suffer in their performance because of injuries and no one can deny that this has also contributed to this season's struggle for success. In my daydreams, I have half-expected that if I'd brought a bike and had been able to actually ride reasonably competently, and could pretend to be Polish or Eastern European, I might thereby have had an outside chance for consideration for selection for the Oxford Silver Machine myself.

When I arrive at the stadium, it's a warm summer's afternoon, although some black clouds threaten rain. Waggy is dressed casually, for the sunshine or the beach rather than the speedway track. He wears a T-shirt, shorts and sandals. He's always cut a notable figure in the sport with his blond highlighted hair, cut and styled in the 1980s look favoured by Duran Duran, with a penchant for suits beloved of 'The Wide Boy' look prevalent from that era. He's clearly very much in charge as he marches about the pits area and the stadium grounds. Waggy has a word for everyone as they arrive or he passes them – riders, mechanics, track staff and backroom staff – I'm sure that this would include the fans if we had reached the time for them to gain admission to the stadium. He invites me into the inner sanctum of the Speedway Office, which is opposite the increasingly busy home team section of the pits. It's a small, cluttered dingy room without windows with an impressively paper-strewn desk that Waggy immediately sits behind, for reasons of space and authority. There are some visitors' chairs plus copious piles of boxes that are filled with programmes, sponsors' literature and the dust of ages. Waggy thrives in this element and lair, since he confidently multi-tasks and promptly deals with a steady stream of people who arrive in the office with queries about programmes, expected arrivals of

[3] Luckily, given his reluctance to soil his dignity or to welcome challenges to his own point of view, Waggy already had help waging a cyberspace war of correction against the great tide of the ill-informed. This often takes the form of Bryn Williams, Oxford's Conference League team manager, programme editor and Elite League assistant team manager, who regularly finds the time to contribute his own opinions, be an arbiter of 'what is right' and often chides those of dissenters who fail to appreciate this on the speedway forums. Bryn is usually very helpful and informative, but when it comes to the Oxford club that he's closely connected with, he can become a little more peevish and so resorts to his default position that people shouldn't criticise if they don't have all the "facts" – usually information to which only the promoters, Bryn or well-connected people will be privy – or if they don't invest in the clubs they comment on. Given that these "facts" frequently aren't available; not everyone can become a promoter, even if they have the finances to want to be; or that the internal workings of most clubs in the country are deliberately shrouded in a mystery, obfuscation and silence; this becomes a pretty incontrovertible defence with which to try to unfairly stifle criticism.

visitors and sponsors, and the other race-day minutiae that is the lot of a speedway promoter but remains invisible to the majority of fans. Our meeting starts inauspiciously when, like John Louis at Ipswich, he immediately asks to be sent a copy of this chapter but unlike John doesn't demand copy approval. Initially he has the querulous, put-upon look that P.G. Wodehouse described as the typical facial expression of an Englishman in the instant before he's about to attempt to speak French.

My opening 'warm up' question about 'how did he get involved in speedway' elicits the weary response of "I've already said this a thousand times!" I hadn't heard the story before and fortunately, with little further prompting, Waggy quickly warmed to his many themes and, you couldn't help but sense we were now onto one of his favourite topics of his conversation, 'The World According to Waggy'. And what a surprisingly happy and wise place it is too, in contrast to the naysayers in the ether, on the terraces or at other clubs. In life it's always good to make a dynamic impression, often better still to inspire strong emotions rather than measured indifference. Waggy definitely doesn't disappoint in this respect at all. He comes from a motorcycling-mad family. His parents carried him as a baby, maybe even in swaddling clothes, to his first grass-track meeting in Northampton. From then on his early childhood in Northamptonshire was a blur of scramble meetings throughout the country, chucked in the back of the works van as part of a veritable crush of kids with their crisps and sandwiches. He'd been completely absorbed in attending motorcycle events right up until the end of his teenage years. On the speedway front, his father took him regularly to Coventry Speedway in the late 1960s when his idol of the time was Nigel Boocock. Waggy then had some years away from all motorbikes until he got married and then he returned to his old stamping grounds. His fascination grew once more at Mallory Hill as he watched cars and motorbikes or attended various club days. At the Berks Bonanza, which Waggy recalls as being in 1980 or 1981, he saw the late Simon Wigg ride and soon got to know him. It was to be a significant meeting for Waggy, who soon followed "Wiggy" round the grass-track circuit and watched him ride speedway for Weymouth. Simon moved on to ride for Cradley Heath before he arrived in Oxford in 1984. By this time Waggy had ended up as Wiggy's sponsor through his Northampton-based company Houghton Hams, who uncontroversially enough manufacture hams. They ended up "becoming very, very close and friendly". During our conversation, Waggy repeatedly emphasises his experience and credentials as a supporter of Oxford speedway. He watched throughout their British League championship and Knockout Cup winning season of 1985 and continued to stand on the terraces "just as a supporter" for another League triumph in 1986 and a trophyless 1987. It was a golden era to be an Oxford supporter with ambitious promoters prepared to invest hugely in the world-class riders of the era. In that era, of the club's history Northern Sports Ltd expensively bought in a dual spearhead that comprised the legendary Hans Nielsen for £30,000 from Birmingham and Simon Wigg for £25,000 from Cradley Heath. It was an approach to team creation, development and investment that Waggy omits to compare to his own present approach. But then it was a different time for Oxford, whose success then was acknowledged as being built on financial investment but also through the stability of their team, which featured the consistent support of Andy Grahame and Marvyn Cox on the track.

Waggy stresses that irrespective of fortunes at Sandy Lane, he continued to travel all over the UK and Europe to grass-track and long-track meetings with Wiggy until Simon finally stopped riding in the late 1990s. Waggy started his association with speedway promotion through another of Wiggy's sponsors, Brian Griffin. He eventually joined him as a co-promoter at King's Lynn, where he stayed for three years from 2000-02. The next stop was Oxford in 2003 and Waggy is convinced that Oxford should have won the League title that season. He brought in Jason Crump early on in the season and, with five Australians in the team, a "wonderful team spirit" developed. They won lots of meetings, but "stumbled on the telly" when they lost the last meeting and the chance to win the championship. For Waggy, it's an achievement that the Oxford fans underestimate and have started to forget all too soon. Especially since, in his opinion, the "League was stronger then" with higher team averages and every meeting involved strong riders from the opposition to race against the Oxford Aussie quintet of Crump, Adams, Boyce, Parker and McGowan. Across the League, every team was comparatively stronger than now and Waggy mentions many examples that includes, to name just one, the Ipswich team with their triumvirate of Gollob, Louis and Nicholls.

The move from outside on the terraces to inside behind the promoter's desk involves a sharp change in perspective, since it's "very, very tough" and the work, unfortunately, "diminishes your love and affection for speedway and the riders". When you don't spend your time having to deal with the riders and the vexatious sports authorities, then you have the fans that "query and question what you do continually" and only see things from a black-and-white perspective. They seriously underestimate what's involved in the promotion of a club, particularly since they usually "only see the glossy finished article" and are oblivious to all the hard work that happens behind the scenes. Lots of people think that they could do the job of a speedway promoter with ease and aplomb, "I'm sure that they think we just open the gates at 5 p.m. and then bring out the bikes". The reality, of course, is very different and Waggy would be very happy for any erstwhile promoter to share the everyday tasks – to paint the lines, maintain the fences, clear the drums or inflate the airbags – with him. It's also work that takes its toll on your personal life away from speedway. Waggy completely doubts the claim made to me by Workington's Graham Drury, that he often spent 70 or so hours a week on his work as a promoter ("when would he find the time to sentence all those people as a judge?"), but the time he does spend involved with the club is seriously underestimated by his critics. His business, and particularly his family, would like much more of his time and attention, especially his youngest daughter and son. To succeed in all aspects of the work requires extensive travel, administrative work, working weekends and overall is a "massive strain" with a huge impact on everyone connected to Waggy. All this comes with the territory but is singularly unappreciated by all those on the terraces who think that they can do his job much better than Waggy.

Relationships with the riders take a high degree of management too as the sport has evolved so much, especially when it involves the star riders. They no longer live in the town as they once did, but now instead travel from country to country throughout the week to race in the various European leagues or the Grand Prix series. It's no longer a parochial and provincial sport for the most gifted riders and many of them have four different bosses, so often to them it is a transitory experience since a race day is "just another track and another payday". With this 'another day, another dollar' attitude gaining prevalence, the element of loyalty between clubs and riders has almost completely disappeared and the problem of sufficient club finance has been thrown into sharper relief. Oxford's problems with attendances started with a change of the regular race night ("which was a massive gamble") and with Waggy's decision to sign "two flamboyant world stars who are not cheap". While the gates were okay to begin with they have dropped off dramatically with the team now stuck at the bottom of the league, albeit with fixtures in hand. Waggy stresses that gates aren't fantastic, even if you actually win everything. He believes that to really maximise attendances and revenues, the ideal position for any team to aim for would be to challenge for everything, have last-heat deciders but still manage to be placed second or third in the league.

On the subject of television coverage Waggy notes, "while you have to say Sky was the shot in the arm we all needed, as promoters we haven't been able to hang onto the money, as we've paid it to the riders". For Waggy, the main reason that the Sky Sports coverage has worked is that television has been able to show the behind-the-scenes activity and controversy among the riders and referees. These are all the parts of speedway that the ordinary fans on the terrace are curious about but can't usually get to watch. But the problem endures for promoters that this activity still remains invisible on a normal race night without the cameras present. And so television coverage doesn't then regularly attract these 'armchair' fans that want to gain this level of insight and perspective to proper live-in-the-flesh speedway on race night.

 For Waggy the future of speedway doesn't look rosy and he feels that the sport "needs a massive kick up the arse". Specifically, in his opinion, we need a sport where the majority of the team's riders are British or, if they're not, that they're committed to the team rather than themselves. This would thereby enable the promoters to showcase a consistently good quality product throughout the season (injuries notwithstanding), which would in turn enable the fans to commit to the team as supporters and have greater empathy with the exploits of the riders in their local team. Without this they run the chance that they will not inspire the loyalty that they could and will, in some quarters, always be seen as mercenary. Waggy praises Eastbourne as a speedway club that exhibits loyalty to its mostly British team of riders and, thereby, through this consistency retains loyal support from its fans. Sadly though, while the need for a reinvention of the sport might be urgently required "very, very quickly", as he reads the runes Waggy sees no sign of imminent change.

If Waggy were given permission to implement some immediate changes in the sport he'd seek to cover the surface of every track in the UK. He doesn't see why it couldn't be done and the reduction in cancelled meetings would benefit everyone from the promoters to the riders and the fans. Another essential change would be a switch to a squad system, where each team has a previously declared roster of riders from which to select their team, "so we all know where we stand so that we can promote and push it". Finally, as in Poland and Sweden, he would require all teams to have a couple of British Under-21 riders to ride at reserve all season (barring injury), no matter how well or badly they performed. It would benefit the sport overall through the development of the young riders' skills but also help to reduce the expenses presently spent on flights, immediately and over time, for riders not domiciled in this country. In this respect he's always looked at the constituency of tonight's visitors, the Eastbourne team, who have for years mostly tracked a local and British team, and thereby operate with comparatively lower expenses than their rivals, while "enjoying more than their fair share of success".

As our interview draws to a close, Waggy alludes to but refuses to divulge any of the quirky stories that his time in the sport has created. He has met many people with interesting and complex personalities and has "all the stories" but these tales will have to remain secret until his involvement in the sport has finished – when they'll appear in his own book, that he jokes is most likely to be called *Fuck British Speedway*. However, if there's one thing that he won't be sad to see the back of, it's all the derogatory comments on the Internet, "I freaking hate it!" Waggy despairs of the damage these comments inflict, with all their ill-informed views and opinions, often from people who he claims don't regularly attend speedway fixtures at Sandy Lane or who are just young kids. Waggy removed the forum from the Official Club website in a bid to stem the tide of opprobrium that flowed his way over the perceived inadequacies of his management of the club. He doesn't see this as censorship, but rather his prerogative and a sensible way to protect his commercial interests and to guard the reputation of the Oxford Silver Machine. He feels that while everyone is definitely entitled to his or her opinion but they're often uninformed. As a case in point, even the report in tonight's local paper *The Oxford Mail*, written by John Gaisford, who is arguably a staunch supporter and friend of the club, disappoints Waggy. "I struggle to get a half-decent crowd anyway and then the bloke in the local paper has gone on about the missing would-be superstars, putting people off coming tonight rather than stressing us taking the chance to help develop riders like Chris Mills".

In an almost Shakespearian turn, Waggy stresses that everyone in speedway does a job and are all too human. Speedway riders especially are seen by many fans as a breed apart, somehow gladiatorial and superhuman; whereas "we all have to live our own lives, often doing things that we shouldn't in private". Waggy brushes aside my curiosity, as to exactly what he has been up to himself and the dark secret nature of the skeletons in his cupboard. Instead he prefers to recall another story about Wiggy, "Simon always said about one of his sponsors that when he discovered that we weren't superhuman but just got up in the morning and had a shit like everyone else, he never got over his illusions being shattered!" Waggy breaks off his wistful reminiscences when his mobile rings. It's the local bookmaker. A unique and distinctive feature of Oxford speedway is that you can actually have a bet on the result at the track. The bookmaker has called to discuss the odds he proposes to offer on the point's spread of the final score for tonight's meeting. Afterwards, when he's given definite advice, Waggy complains that the bookmaker is misguided in his assumptions and has little real insight into the possible range of results that could occur in tonight's fixture with Eastbourne. It's something that Waggy simultaneously despairs of, since it's an ongoing sign of his battle against a tide of ignorance and ill-informed opinion, and yet at the same time he clearly enjoys; in instances when the power his words of advice have influence, like with the odds and the livelihood of the bookmaker. Though typically, Waggy makes a joke of the situation and playfully suggests the odds are now so attractive – after the bookmaker acted upon his considered advice – on a narrow win or a massive defeat for the Silver Machine that he later might well be tempted to have a bet himself.

As Waggy leaves for his duties elsewhere at the track, he emphasises that he prefers to speak to fans directly and try to respond to them in person rather than via the press or the Internet. For that reason, he's made a point of holding press conferences straight after every meeting in the bar with his riders to discuss the events of the night and other news from the club. He believes that these are generally well received and that people might start to appreciate that many of the team changes at the club have not only been made with an eye to the present season but also to develop the riders concerned for future seasons. Waggy claims that riders like Tobias Kroner will benefit from both the experience and a sensible future average based on his actual ability rather than a level determined by his nationality.[4] If there were promotion and relegation in the Elite League, then Waggy would have to concentrate his efforts to ensure that Oxford remained in the league, but instead he claims he is glad to "develop rider assets" so that "in six years' time someone else can inherit my work". He doesn't mind the play-offs that have been deliberately created to heighten the interest of Sky's television audience right until the final fixtures of the season. Success in the league for the Silver Machine, this season, would be not to finish bottom. This remains a real possibility with all the fixtures they still have to ride, though, Waggy still holds out the highest hopes for Oxford's potential in the forthcoming Craven Shield. The team is now settled and injury free, plus basic economics dictate that "more meetings for the club mean more pay days for the riders" as well as additional gate receipts for the promoter. Waggy rushes off in his shorts and sandals to motivate his staff and continue with the task to stage another good show for the crowd tonight. He smirks, when he leaves me, at the thought that "you never know we might still surprise a few of the people who have written us off!"

Outside the office, the Oxford area of the pits has now completely filled with riders and machines, literally Silver Machines with their distinctive livery of silver with green and black borders. By the office door two more 'ordinary' speedway bikes stand ready but displaced from the ritual of being loudly revved to warm them up. Next to them also stands a forlorn airport luggage trolley that advertises 'Team Monarch'. It's some distance from any airport, never mind the airport that this particular piece of equipment was liberated from. The match programme gives no indication that Monarch Airlines sponsors the club, and given the season's performance so far they're still perhaps too grand a company to deliberately associate themselves with the team, despite being a low budget airline. Perhaps to accidentally load a luggage trolley into the back of your van, rather than, say, an object from yesteryear such as a tomato ketchup dispenser borrowed from a transport café, symbolises the dominance that air travel has in the lives of the riders on the contemporary speedway scene,

[4] The BSPA runs a system where the averages of the seven riders that make up a team must add up to a cumulative number that is below a pre-agreed limit. All new riders to this country initially receive a high 'assessed average', comparative to their actual abilities or their worth to the team, unless they have ridden here previously.

with so many of the modern star performers much more likely to be frequent fliers rather than habitués of transport cafés.

Whatever its significance, or otherwise, a group of older-looking staff sit on the bench outside the next door office as they drink tea, read the programme or chat among themselves dressed in their tribal uniform of a brightly coloured speedway anorak or the brown overalls of those who will soon do some of the more hefty work around the track. The office they sit by houses the rather poshly designated Medical Officers Room, which already has many of its yellow fluorescent jacketed staff in attendance, who stand and wait outside it. Diagonally across from the bench, by what appears to be a tyre dump area, there's a child who is clearly the team mascot. He's dressed in kevlars, while he melodramatically and earnestly revs his mini-bike, and very much looks the part; resplendent as he is in a small but full-face crash helmet decorated with a bright red home-team helmet cover.

I stroll through the tunnel that separates the pits area from the track on to the boards laid over the tarpaulin that covers the dog track and bump into Belle Vue's track curator, Colin Meredith. He tells me that he'll help out with the track at Oxford for the next month. It fits well with his work at Belle Vue, since that's on a Monday and Tuesday whereas this lasts from Thursday to Friday lunchtime. There are some problems with water that drains across the surface of the track from the deflated airbags, but apart from that he tries to prepare the surface to meet the Oxford riders' requests. The track has a reputation for always being rough and he's tried to remedy that, only to be mystified by the Oxford riders who then request that it needs "roughing up on the outside". Even if he doesn't understand it, Colin follows their request nonetheless "even though they don't go out there! Anyways, by heat 6 or so, the dirt's moved out to the fence anyway". Colin and I laugh about when he inadvertently jinxed himself when we spoke about track preparation before the televised Belle Vue meeting earlier that week. He admits that he did make a mistake "but reading the Internet you'd have thought that I'd murdered someone!"

It's already that track-walk time of the evening, the obligatory ritual when the riders ostentatiously go round in a group to study the handiwork of the track staff, in this case Colin's. The Oxford team are first out. They mooch around the track, stop for a minute to chat and laugh or kick the surface in desultory fashion. They linger by the start line, adjacent to the glass-fronted home-straight grandstand with its empty terraces in front, for quite some time. The discussions are led by the experienced Billy 'Bullet' Hamill, who is casually dressed in that speedway rider's uniform of shorts, sweatshirt and Aussie-style sunglasses worn jauntily on top of his head. All the other riders wear shorts and baseball caps, while Niels-Kristian Iversen savours some gulps from an energising can of Red Bull. Given how ubiquitous this drink is among speedway riders – I see them drink it before the races at every track around the country – the company should definitely think about the sponsorship opportunities the sport offers for their brand. However, it is pretty well the only stimulant that the riders are permitted to indulge in prior to a meeting, apart from wild sex, under the strict regulations that govern the use of stimulants and medication within the sport.

The track itself is surrounded by a dog track covered in the traditional manner by a tarpaulin weighed down with tyres. You see this covering throughout the country, but it still does not effectively ensure that pieces of shale don't end up on the sandy racing surface of the dog track. The shale often compacts the sandy racing surface to the detriment and damage of the dog's feet and that's quite a serious problem under the new Animal Welfare Bill. Hopefully, it's another one of those hidden complexities that Waggy has in hand but for which he berates the average fan for knowing nothing about. Unconcerned, the riders return to the pits and they pass the Eastbourne team who wander up the planks on the slope that leads up from the pits across the dog circuit to the track itself. It's a sunny afternoon and a smooth-looking racing surface lies before them. The oval-shaped circuit surrounds the centre green with its distinctive but tortuously shaped tarmac go-kart circuit. The first spectators have now begun to file into the stadium and rush to the best parts of the various terraces from which to watch this evening's fixture. There aren't any places for the public to watch from at all on the back straight, so the initial crowds hurry to places on the banked open terraces that overlooks the apex of bends 3 and 4, which also allows them a view of the bikes as they travel to and from the pits area. A gaggle of youngsters, four girls and a boy, who chat together easily, strategically place themselves by the brightly coloured crash barrier that divides the riders' and guests' viewing area from the rest of the crowd on the terraces.

Tonight the Eastbourne team line up is without their star rider Nicki Pedersen; while the club captain, Dean Barker, so far appears not to have arrived at the stadium. However, they do have their talismanic Eastbourne-born and Hailsham-based rider, David 'Floppy' Norris, who has now returned to the team on one of his many comebacks during his own personal season to forget that has been continually plagued by the recurrence of the early season neck injury he sustained at Swindon. The ramifications of this mysterious neck injury has damaged his surprisingly delicate and finely calibrated equilibrium. He's fine when on terra firma but in agony when astride the vibrating machinery that is his speedway bike and the essential equipment of his self-employment. He appears cheerful enough, though.

He's dressed in his trademark black jacket and cap that covers the strong blond highlights that he's adopted for his hair during his recovery. Eastbourne team manger Jon Cook, intently studies the track as he stands literally head and shoulders above his diminutive riders Andrew Moore, Olly Allen and Davey Watt. On their return to the pits the team meander past the waiting fans and elicit no reaction from them, except to clamour for David Norris's autograph. Floppy has a slightly aloof attitude that's matched with a sharp and acerbic wit, particularly handy as he reputedly doesn't suffer fools gladly, no matter how well intentioned. He also has a reputation, often comparatively secret except among those who really know the 'real' him, for considerably helping young riders develop their talent and young fans develop their interest. Whether as they practice on the junior track at Eastbourne where he always has time for words of advice, encouragement and support, or when they gather in the pits, by the pits gate or, in this case, are a small group of admirers who loiter to meet with him on the terraces. He appears far more open, relaxed and at home with them than he would be if they were adults. He diligently signs their autograph books and programmes, conscientiously asks if any of them want him to pose for their cameras, only to have them sheepishly admit that they don't own one. One teenage girl seems particularly bashful and blushingly declines Floppy's offer to sign his autograph. He smiles and asks, "you're sure?" as she waivers, and then says, "last chance?" when she haltingly but definitely declines. But as he turns to go, she feels confident enough in his company to cheek him and retort "can I phone a friend?" which gets a laugh and a broad smile from Floppy. Once he's out of sight they cluster round together to excitedly compare the handiwork of his signatures and say that he's "even nicer" than they already thought when you really get to speak with him.

A few minutes later Jon Cook quickly returns to hang over the safety fence, while he watches Colin Meredith drive the tractor round the track for some last-minute grading. He's not happy at what he sees. Colin roughly gouges the outside of the track with the equipment he trails from the rear of the red tractor. "What's he freaking cutting it up for now, just after our track walk?" Jon asks rhetorically before he wryly adds, "maybe he's creating the usual Oxford track as they're well used to riding really rough tracks!" We carry on and chat generally about speedway and photography, as I've now taken many pictures throughout the country – so many I intend to do a book of them – and it's something that Jon has a family interest in, since his wife is a photographer. We've both been very impressed by the work shown on BBC2's *Digital Britain* project and his wife is just about to begin her involvement in a similar programme on the Discovery channel under the guidance of a full-time professional photographer. When Jon enquires about my book and whom I've met on my travels, we have quite a discussion about the complexity involved to stage a live Sky Sports outside broadcast at a speedway fixture. I'd been surprised at the amount of equipment it required and the complex logistics involved for Eastbourne's visit to Belle Vue earlier in the week. Jon had kept himself occupied with team matters and I gather doesn't exactly rush to be interviewed on live television, despite his earlier season media-training course. He speaks admiringly of their professionalism but, away from the screen, he hasn't really had much to do with the interviewer Sophie Blake or the presenter Jonathan Green, reputedly an Eastbourne fan, of whom Jon notes "he doesn't know much either, does he?" Our talk ranges widely about the

[3] The start-line girls were known as the Workington "Start Tarts" until Graham and Denise Drury arrived as the promoters at the club. They are now more sophisticatedly known as the Workington "Brolly Dollies". They are by brolly colour – Red: Catherine McEuan; Blue: Charlotte Hayton; Green: Adele Rodgers and Yellow: Kayleigh Boag.

Elite League situation but then moves onto Wimbledon Speedway's possible stadium lease problems with their landlords, the GRA – Jon knows the team manger, Dingle Brown, but hasn't met the promoter and Wimbledon PLC Chairman, Ian Perkin – so notes he hasn't benefited from his insight on this situation. What he has seen of this Conference League incarnation of the venue though is enough to feel that "it's a shame about Wimbledon, if they'd laid the track properly it could have by now been a neutral, prestige venue for the whole sport, which we're crying out for".

With the meeting only 40 minutes from its scheduled start time, Jon's biggest concern is that his captain Dean 'Deano' Barker has yet to arrive at the track. He mildly notes that, "it would help if he were here!" It's vital that the whole team has prepared their mental approach and equipment for a fixture that Eastbourne must win to cement their place in the Elite League play-offs and to try to secure the important home advantage. Deano has already rung in from his van to explain that he's been delayed by "accidentally driving along the M4 by mistake", rather than the M40, to get to the stadium. Jon raises his eyebrows when he relates this explanation but offers no other comment. Given that Deano has rode in the past for Oxford, and still visits regularly, as an excuse it probably ranks well below 'the dog ate my homework'. As if by magic, all is not lost as Deano bounds up the planks from the pits to trackside towards Jon. They exchange a few words before Deano insouciantly observes, in his lilting London accent, "the main freaking thing is I'm here!" before he makes a quick exit back to the pits to change. Jon phlegmatically shrugs, and then ambles off with his distinctive lope to join the team as they warm up their bikes in the pits. Floppy, as usual, conducts his energetic pre-meeting almost gymnastic routines and, already, has started to wave his arms around in a manner that, if it were a drama class, would be much more 'I'm an aeroplane' than 'I'm a teapot'. Davey Watt fusses over some last-minute adjustments on his bike, while Andrew Moore sits astride his steed, wears super-sized ear defenders, and creates prodigious quantities of exhaust fumes that catch the back of your throat instantly, as he revs his machine. Glenn, Deano's mechanic who just recently celebrated his 32nd birthday says, "I think Deano is the key to tonight's result, they're bottom and we should beat them". He's pretty confident that "if we stop Hamill, and he's flying, we should be okay".

I've arranged to meet an authentic speedway novice, my Welsh friend Alastair Lewis, at the track this evening for his first-ever speedway fixture. Therefore, I spend the evening trying to simplify and explain the complex rules and scoring of the event. I also try to give some insight into the riders, the tactics and what we actually witness on the track. He arrives just in time to hear the Hawkwind tune 'Silver Machine' blare out over the speakers of the stadium tannoy system. After the initial rider parade, we decide to watch the fixture from a variety of places in the stadium and begin by the start line before we move to the Apex of the bends 3 and 4. Al is immediately impressed by the speed of the racing, the passion of the fans as well as slightly mystified by the idea of high-powered bikes without brakes or suspension. He's enthralled to notice the sheer number of spectators we encounter obviously without a full set of teeth ("it's literally a toothless crowd"). But it's the crowd-at-prayer moment that follows each race, normal behaviour to any regular attendee, which most obviously stands out to him. The sight of the fans, almost in unison, as they fill out their programmes remains the strangest and most peculiar spectacle to him throughout the evening.

Eastbourne gain a shock early lead in heat 2, but after that it's pretty well all Oxford who look sharp throughout the team in contrast to Eastbourne's rather sluggish overall performance. Deano, as Glenn predicted, is the key rider for the visitors. He's the top scorer as well as involved, with Oliver Allen, in a mini fightback in heat 8. Floppy scores in every ride, four Eastbourne riders win heats, and Oliver Allen wins twice, but the team appears consistently second-best throughout this fixture. Steve Boxall has replaced Nicki Pedersen and he races to an unenviable but experience-boosting zero score from four rides. Oxford, who also miss their star rider Greg Hancock, ride in a manner that suggests they really want to win and, with the trio of Iversen, McGowan and Hamill, they dominate all the key races. With the result never really in doubt, we ask Glenn what's going wrong tonight, after heat 9 when Eastbourne trail 31-23. He succinctly sums up Eastbourne's evening with, "it's shit, isn't it?" We encounter the man himself, Waggy, who's on walkabout aboriginal style, at least in the sense that despite the increasing chill of the evening he's still dressed for hot weather. It's definitely a night that he can venture out to meet the fans on the terraces – adoring, or otherwise and even his Internet critics – with full confidence that the

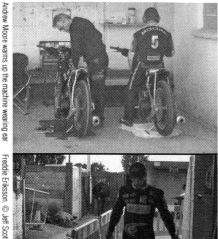

Andrew Moore warms up the machine wearing ear defenders (pardon). © Jeff Scott

Freddie Eriksson. © Jeff Scott

Tyre heaven. © Jeff Scott

result tonight will ultimately go Oxford's way and salve their anxieties. I ask him why tonight's the night, and he responds with a smile and a thumbs up before he advances the opinion, "if they've taken our shale we want it back!" My visitor Al seems impressed that we can actually meet and chat on the terraces with Oxford's equivalent of Barry Fry, but Waggy's practised and mysterious sound bite in reply to my question leaves him totally nonplussed. This image conjures up, for the novice visitor, visions of the playground or sand castles on the beach, albeit shale ones, rather than the exciting handlebar-to-handlebar racing and desire to get ahead that Waggy really intended to allude to.

The crowd goes wild with delight and is ecstatic in their appreciation of each and every Oxford race win or heat victory. And tonight, for once, there are a lot of these for them to celebrate. Later by the start line, we encounter a large gaggle of excited people who are tonight's visiting sponsors. Well, to be exact, the announcer informs us that they're "the finance teams from the Oxford, Swindon and Gloucester Co-ops". If the shrieky, enervated manner that this group exhibits when they stand by us is anything to judge them by, it's already been an excellent team-building exercise for them and a night out of great entertainment. As is the way with visiting sponsors at most speedway tracks, they revel in their mandatory visit to watch the fixture from the centre green. While it's chilly, temperatures aren't so cold as to freeze them in their office clothes, as they stand on the exposed open space that is the go-kart track on the Oxford centre green. Enthusiasm and accountancy conspire to have common sense desert them, while they collectively try to climb the obstacle course that are the safety fence steps on to the track in order to cross it, just after the race finishes. Clearly they haven't paid close enough attention to spot the dynamics of a speedway race, so the subsequent celebratory victory lap by Travis McGowan nearly mows down a few stray members of the finance team. I bet that they didn't budget beforehand for such a surprise high-speed encounter with a speedway bike, and fortunately they narrowly avoid a real night to remember at Sandy Lane.

So, overall, for Al it's not exactly the greatest introduction to the thrills and spills or cut and thrust of an all-action speedway meeting. However, you must go to a tremendous number of meetings to ever watch a repeat of anything like the unique cameo that McGowan and Norris provided in the first running of the nominated heat 15. It's the most definitive handlebar-to-handlebar race ever ridden! The race starts traditionally when Norris races from gate 2 and McGowan from gate 3. They negotiate bends 1 and 2 with aplomb before they manage to get their bikes completely jammed together, just when McGowan tries to sneak past Norris, close by the fence on the back straight. Both riders then struggle to separate their machines and themselves from this tangle with the other, while the bikes grind to halt almost in slow motion. Their attempt at modern sculpture, a mobile installation as it would doubtless be called at Tate Modern, results in the exclusion of McGowan by the referee, just as the mangled but sculptural remains of their joined bikes are carried back to the pits. Since he has just witnessed this collector's item of a race, my visitor Al is then blessed by another extremely rare occurrence – the referee who changes his decision at a speedway meeting. You'd have to travel a good few country miles to witness such a retraction; in this instance brought about by the good offices of Waggy and Cooky, who jointly appeal to the referee to reinstate McGowan. In that sense, it's not quite the collector's item that a spontaneous retraction by the referee would be, but it is close enough to be very notable. McGowan returns to the fray on another machine to win the re-run closely followed by his partner Billy Hamill. Norris finishes third while Davey Watt finishes a distant last as he continues his recent performance levels which have seen him renamed as Davey Who after spending most of the season riding like Davey Wow!

They say that all things happen for a reason, so to test the theory and take the chance to see an ebullient Waggy give a press conference with his riders in the bar is difficult for anyone to resist. By now Waggy has made a concession to the elements and the dress requirements of his press conference by donning shoes and socks instead of sandals. When it comes to formal presentations to the fans, the only other track that I have so far witnessed such an event at, on my travels, was in the bar at Peterborough. After a rare but well-deserved victory I imagine Waggy will have to be held back from his attendance and I presume he will be even more ebullient and better value to listen to and watch perform tonight than after a defeat. Not usually prone to modesty in his public pronouncements when he appears in full on 'Promoter Waggy' mode, Waggy has had his hyperbole chip disabled for tonight. The press conference itself takes place over the far side of the bar, against a backdrop covered in sponsors' names, as if it will also be televised like post-match interviews in football's Premier League. These events are obviously very popular with the Oxford crowd since it's packed throughout and the fans listen attentively as they hang on every word. And there are many words, enough to satisfy even the most information-hungry Oxford Silver Machine fan, of which there seems more in the bar than on the terraces earlier. No topic or cliché is too outré to offer in response to the astonishingly gentle and anodyne questions posed to Waggy by the Oxford announcer. While he does the vast majority of the talking, Waggy also gives the riders time to speak before he continues with his extensive insights, comments, digressions and much convoluted detail.

Waggy is quizzed about Chris Mills – star of Oxford's Conference League team, who arrived at Oxford after earlier season problems with Reading in the Premier League. Chris rode in place of Greg Hancock tonight, for 3 points (paid 4) from four rides. So it's been another "invaluable experience" in his career for Mills to race for Oxford in the Elite League this evening, and Waggy mercilessly expands upon its significance when he claims, "he was one of those that grew tonight, he wears the Number 1 jacket with pride!" The magical properties of the jacket or his increase in height and stature aside, Chris himself is overwhelmed with delight at his race victory over Eastbourne's Andrew Moore. Like that song in *Evita* where she sings, "he's just a man", Mills declares, "he's just a rider – I've beaten him before and I can beat him again", before he gets really carried away with the microphone in front of him that he adds, in a fashion Waggy would be proud of, "I've gated Rickardsson before so I can out-gate anyone!" It's a start, literally it seems, and somewhere to progress your career from; but since I actually witnessed the race in question myself[5] Mills should know, and his team-mates would be able to verify (in the event that any of his team mates from that evening still ride for the club!), that it's probably only really worth remembering if you actually beat Rickardsson to the finish, or for just a lap rather than over congratulate yourself on the one time that you've actually managed to exit the tapes ahead of him. Still I can't deny that ambition and pride, much more than skill, are often key components to a successful career, whether or not it's in speedway, and Mills excels already in this respect. Travis McGowan, Waggy's most dedicated and loyal rider throughout his career as a speedway promoter, has a typically laid-back Australian manner, although even his nonchalance had been tested by the unexpected entanglement of his bike with Norris's. He's pleased at his good fortune, "I've never seen that happen before and never will, I was lucky to pull my leg out". So delighted in fact, that he playfully admits "it's not often I want to cuddle another man!"

[5] Heat 4 of the encounter with Arena Essex in 2005 at Sandy Lane on April 21st.

It's not long before Waggy is once again back on the microphone, while he holds forth to an apparently rapt audience of Oxford partisans. Without a trace of irony or self-consciousness, he informs the assembled fans that "I don't rule out changes or trying to do things". I'd be shocked if this came as a surprise to any of the fans of a team that has so far already this season featured 17 riders arranged in a mind-boggling variety of team permutations that would test even advanced computational abilities. As he gives us insight into his man-management skills and team-building prowess, Waggy just about leaves his onion in his pocket when he discusses Henka Gustafsson's absence from the team in the manner strongly reminiscent of a sketch from the *Fast Show*. "Unfortunately, we've had to report Henka as 'withholding his services', which automatically results in a massive fine". This decision ensured Oxford could definitely use rider replacement to their advantage tonight, though Waggy touchingly claims, either as an eternal optimist or with faux naïvety, "where this leaves us with Henka I'm not sure"[6]. It's got very late, not that far from last orders, when my friend signals that he'd like to draw his first experience of a speedway meeting and its post-match press conference to a rapid close. While we run down the stairs and out onto the edge of Blackbird Leys estate to find the car, Al wants to return to see Oxford race again but can't help but observe, "that bloke, what's he on? He can't half talk, can't he? Though he doesn't actually say much."

25th August Oxford v. Eastbourne (ELA) 50-41

---

[6] I think we all know really.

Chapter 34: Something Special in Buxton
28th August Buxton v. Scunthorpe

"I look so smooth when you watch it on TV, on the bike I feel like I'm everywhere" Andreas Jonsson

RANDOM SCB RULES

18.7 Heat 15 is the Top Scorers race and the qualification is to be:
• top 3 points scorer (exclude any rider who has already taken 7 rides)
NB. All Rides, Points and Bonus Points to count
• a Rider in the Top 3 of the team (by CMA)
NB. In the CL any Rider can be nominated

I arrive in Buxton the night before the meeting after I drove across the fells from Wigan Pier, well the JJB Stadium really. The scenery is spectacular and I would have appreciated it even more if I'd been the passenger. The town itself nestles in the Derbyshire Peak district and, as you might imagine, there are all the undulations you could possibly need throughout the general area. Steep ones in all directions at that. I'd only really ever known of Buxton because of its famous 'Natural Spring Water', which the cynic in me anticipated wouldn't actually be from the town and would inevitably come from some grotty industrial estate that the marketing department liked to keep quiet about in their bucolic adverts. The only thing I'd ever consciously learnt about the town was from a mutual friend at Brighton Art College who relished his time in the larger, more fashionable East Sussex place in contrast to the supposedly monotonous life that he'd led in his small hometown Buxton.

So, really nothing prepared me for the beauty of the drive through the magnificent landscape of the Peak District, an area

that's often been overshadowed in the popular imagination by its relatively near neighbour the Lake District. Save for a brief trip to the Styper Stones, I had just not visited or appreciated how spectacular, barren and unspoilt it really is. I blame the English Tourist Board or anyone but myself for not communicating this message more widely. Nor was I prepared for the substantial and classical magnificence of the centre of the town or the pleasant promenades in its lush park, never mind verdant atmosphere created by all the trees or the encroachment of the nearby Peaks themselves[1].

In 1993 even the famous Buxton Water, by then part of the derided Perrier group, was bought by Nestlé. Less than a year later the first speedway meeting ever held at the Hi Edge track took place on August 24th 1994, when Stoke visited to take part in a drawn meeting.[2] Until my visit I'd always thought that Eastbourne probably had the most beautiful area in which to base a speedway track and stadium or maybe Workington, if you count the spectacular scenery of the drive towards the coast. As you travel up the steep road from Buxton towards Axe Edge just outside the town, it's quickly obvious that no other track in the country has any realistic chance to snatch the 'most beautiful area' accolade from the 'Home of the Hitmen'. As you follow the signs to the speedway along the Dale Head Lane towards the village of Dalehead, you're struck by the immensity and desolation of the hills. You feel like you share the area with only a few hardy walkers or the sheep that are keen to escape over the cattle grids towards freedom. If you were to accidentally leave the windy single-track road at any point, there is the ever-present promise of substantial damage to your car and, for once, I regret that I don't drive a vehicle more suited to the challenges of this rugged terrain. The sort of vehicle that's most often seen on the school run in urban environments would be ideal for these rough, narrow and hilly lanes. After I reach the end of Dale Head Lane, I park the car in the huge flint-covered car park and push through the strong, blustery wind towards the Buxton speedway track with its superb vistas of the national park in which it's located. There's no sign of permanent stadium

[1] A classic joke when you study history is to pose the question "what did the Romans ever do for us?" To answer with a "nothing" is to be both xenophobic and ignorant, since they were hugely influential upon what we consider as many of our typically 'British' characteristics throughout our culture, country and society. Everyone knows the Romans brought many gifts of civilisation to our shores, built many of our important roads and also built the spa town of Bath (*Aquae Sulis*). The only other British town to receive the desired *Aquae* designation was Buxton, or *Aquae Arnemetiae* (literally 'the waters of the sacred groves') to give it its proper Roman name. The Romans arrived in the town in AD 70 and thereafter put it on the map, both as a destination and a spa town. From that period onwards it attracted visitors to its waters, even though it had actually been a settlement since the Stone Ages, a considerable time before the clump of Roman sandals were heard in the area. The town received its present name – from a combination of Buck and Stan (stones) – reputedly from when the stags from the Royal Forest used to regularly visit to drink from its warm waters. In the 16th century it was a place of pilgrimage for the healing power of its waters with Mary, Queen of Scots, the most notable visitor before developments by successive Dukes of Devonshire in the 18th and 19th centuries ensured the town's place as the most fashionable spa in Europe. Quite an achievement given its remote location, especially throughout the Victorian and Edwardian eras when the importance of the spa town saw the rise and development of many, equally attractive, rival towns scattered throughout the Continent. On my stroll around the centre of the town, like many visitors, I can't help but be impressed by The Crescent, the Pavilion Gardens or the many other stunning buildings. Inevitably the fashion for spa visits would pass and the decline of the town was never adequately compensated for with the arrival of the railways, the traditional benefit of Victorian ingenuity, or electricity and the telephone at the start of the 20th century.

[2] However, the initial meeting took place on a different track inside the adjacent stock car circuit but didn't have a conducive shape for good racing, so Ken Moss took it upon himself to build a new bespoke track and stadium. This is the track that the club still uses to this day.

buildings in the form of a grandstand or other such fripperies, but you can see the referee's box perched on a black sea container and to the right of that a number of other buildings coloured black, green and blue.

These buildings are either single-storey portacabins or other converted sea containers that abut the track itself and the pits area; with its small, roof-covered sections for each team that you imagine would only provide minimal protection from the elements throughout most of the year. One of the most notable things about the track – apart from the incongruity of how it stands alone in acres of wild countryside and instantly appears redolent of its glamorous name 'Axe Edge' – is the colour of its racing surface, which looks grey-black from a distance. It is even more striking that the track exactly mirrors the contours of the landscape so, in keeping with everything else, it has a pronounced, almost steep, slope from one side to the other. Which must, surely, provide some sort of advantage to the home team riders once they've become familiar with this unique feature of their own circuit. The track has its own safety fence with a small gap between it and the wire fence that serves to separate the action on the track from the hardy band of spectators that travel to this barren but beautiful landscape to watch speedway. There are no floodlights but there are speakers for the tannoy system dotted around the perimeter. I know from having read about the club beforehand, that many fans take advantage of the fact that it is one of those rare tracks where you can sit and watch the action from the secluded comfort of your car. I don't quite understand the appeal of viewing any event from your own vehicle; particularly at speedway, because the smell and the noise of the meeting is a vital and essential component of its fundamental appeal. But then again, different strokes for different folks is the English and the speedway way, so why not if that's how you prefer to enjoy the proceedings? As the wind blows so strong and cool for a late August noontime, Buxton greets you with scudding clouds and bathes you in intermittent weak sunshine; so I start to understand the appeal of the protection and warmth provided if you decide to remain inside your car. As there are no floodlights here, the meetings must always take place at Buxton during daylight hours, which must keep the temperatures some way away from the worst excesses of such an exposed area. I hope to meet Jayne Moss, co-chairman of the club and wife of the owner and co-chairman Richard Moss. I soon find her at work in the small hut that serves as the gateway post that all arrivals have to pass on their way into the stadium grounds proper.

The stringency of the wind ("yes, it's breezier here today") is matched by the nonchalant calm and warmth of Jayne, who's happy to chat to me about the club, while she works. Throughout the time I'm there, she works in the multi-tasking fashion supposedly beloved by the fairer sex. She cheerily supervises the many and varied last-minute behind-the-scenes details, whether she chats to the riders and their helpers who arrive for the meeting or laughs with the many fans who tail back in a queue of cars eager to enter and to park up inside. It quickly appears that Jayne knows absolutely everyone who arrives and greets them with warmth, calm equanimity or genial bonhomie. The only distraction to the smooth running of the operation is the harmless but bewildered presence of a cranefly that frightens Jayne much more than you imagine it should. Jayne runs the track as a family business with her husband, Richard, who's "harassed as usual" and, as we speak, currently sits on his tractor grading the track. According to her, Jayne's job at the track apparently "involves doing everything" which roughly translates to mean working as chairman, secretary, administrator and odd job person. The club is in its twelfth season after Richard's dad, former rider Ken Moss, who is "sadly no longer with us", started it. The track moved from where the stock-car track is now to its present location 10 years ago, and all the work required to build it was done by members of the family or dedicated friends. Richard's mum is the incident recorder and, if the team manager is away, then Richard or Jayne automatically step into the breach. Jayne has watched speedway all her life, well since she was three years old when she went to the Perry Barr track in Birmingham. It's 32 years later and she's keener than ever; along with her work at Buxton, she always attends Belle Vue every Monday, and travels to many other tracks, whenever possible, besides that fact that she keenly follows James Wright at Workington and throughout Europe in his quest for success in the Under-21 World Championship. James, his brother Charles, his mum Lynn and the rest of his family are closely allied to all things Buxton and Jayne tries to go to as many of his meetings as she can possibly fit in, wherever they happen to take place. The last week before we met saw Jayne's speedway travel itinerary include: Sheffield, Weymouth, Rye House, Boston, Workington, a rare night off and then Belle Vue. It's difficult to imagine when any of the family actually finds the time to run the family business of Buxton Dairy Supplies. This sounds as though it would be a demanding

business to run in its own right; with the dairy and the milk rounds to go along with the papers and groceries involved in their general store. But then, as at the speedway, they all muck in together.

When it comes to romance, speedway has been a catalyst throughout the Moss family, with visits to Odsal to watch speedway of particular significance ("we all met through speedway at Bradford really"). In 1993, Jayne went to the World Championship final in Pocking, won by Sam Ermolenko, to support her hero and idol Hans Nielsen. Her future husband, Richard, was on the same trip and romance blossomed from there. When it comes to love on the terraces there's a family 'double header' as Richard's sister also met her husband through going to the speedway. Hopefully, with all this romance in the air at speedway tracks, the love of a lifetime will be just around the next bend during my travels, although as I'm nearing the end of my trips there seems no sign of this so far.

Jayne believes that "speedway is just something you love or hate" and doesn't think "there's an awful lot wrong with it". In speedway, as in life, "you just can't please everyone all the time". If she has any gripe with the present organisation and structure of the sport, it's with regards to the riders that make up the teams in the Conference League. She feels it should only be full of young, inexperienced riders trying to learn their skills and find their way in the sport. She believes older, more experienced riders should be barred from the Conference League competition. That way, the younger men will get the opportunity to hopefully gain the skills they will need to eventually make the big step up to the Premier League and they might thereby avoid the "norm of getting a year, not setting the world alight and then getting dropped". An alternative approach, to serve the same end, might be for these young riders to get a two-year deal at reserve in the Premier League to allow them the time to gradually develop and show some improvement. Jayne is keen to stress that James Wright's experience when he quickly stepped up a league from the Conference to the Premier is "the exception not the rule".

At Buxton, they practise what they preach with a team composed of young people, all keen to learn their trade. This isn't necessarily the best business decision as "speedway fans are very fickle, always seeing the riders as only being as good as their last ride". Without regular victories it's widely acknowledged "you do notice a difference in your crowds" so, from a financial perspective, the temptation is to track more experienced riders in the short term to retain crowd enthusiasm and numbers. In order to continue their commitment to young rider development as well as to overcome tight finances, the Moss family "do everything ourselves" in order to keep costs to an absolute minimum and "just about break even". Elsewhere in the Conference League though, "some tracks pay riders a lot of money, so some of them ask for a silly amount of money which we can't afford to give".[4] Jayne believes that "people always appreciate riders who try hard", irrespective of their age or abilities. Conscientious effort and an attempt to try hard will always entertain and, if you can link this with skill, you have an unbeatable combination that fans everywhere will relish the regular chance to watch. Talk of entertainment leads her to spontaneously mention some riders whose appearance usually guarantees this on the track, Paul Clews and Moggo (Alan Mogridge) from nearby Stoke spring to her mind as competitors that she always appreciates to watch race. When Jayne looks back over the many years she has spent following speedway, she identifies her all-time idols to be Arthur Browning and Hans Nielsen "since then there's not really been anyone after him". In contemporary speedway her favourite is definitely James Wright, although with him it's a unique situation because "we support him as a person as well as a rider, so he's a bit different!" But, then, it's clearly a relationship built on mutual respect since "James is always here in the pits with them – home and away". His younger brother Charles rides but James "helps them all, he walks the track with them, tells them how to set their bikes up and just generally gives advice". Just as we speak about her son his mother, Lynn Wright, arrives at the entrance gate office to help Jayne. She admits she's "very proud of both of them both" although "sometimes it's frightening but I'd rather be here than not!" Lynn's Dad, Jim Yacoby, rode for Belle Vue and she "went in a trolley before I could walk at 12 months old in 1962"; since then she's "always enjoyed the sport and the racing, as it's exciting to watch". Charles Wright, at 16, already capably follows in his brother's tyre tracks at Buxton, whereas James has now moved onto ride full time for Workington in the Premier League and intermittently for Belle Vue in the Elite League. According to his mum, James has "always been keen" and "wants to go all the way, that's his ambition". To further his career goals, he's "very dedicated and very professional", both on and off the track and, Lynn proudly stresses, "you hardly ever see him in a bar".

All the while I chat to Lynn, Jayne handles the steady and impressive stream of fans that arrive in their cars. All of them appear keen to part with the extra £1 that is required to watch the meeting from the warmth and comfort of their cars. Despite the proximity of the track to the town of Buxton, Jayne believes that the majority of fans that attend travel to watch the speedway from outside the local area. They come from many places in the general vicinity and include Leek, Macclesfield, Glossop, Stoke and Manchester.[4] Jayne estimates that they are all roughly located within an hour's travel of Hi Edge, not immediately local, but handy nonetheless for a journey to this beautiful and remote destination with its own uniquely special speedway track. It sounds peculiar to me but Jayne shrugs, just as a fan interrupts to ask, "are they working on that bend over the summer?" to which Jayne retorts, "what bend?" The subsequent answer of "you know the one where they have all the problems" has Jayne quickly mount a stout and indignant defence, "there is no problem other than they're out of control; anyway we passed our official SCB track inspection by Colin Meredith with flying colours!" The punter goes off apparently unconvinced, but Jayne and the family are pleased with all the positive feedback they get on the track and the club. They particularly appreciate praise from referees, who are always keen to officiate at the track, plus the various riders and fans, which is "always nice to hear as it makes it all worthwhile". Jayne mentions that they have the advantage that the track is not clay based, so even when it's not windy "it dries out very good". If I want to find out more comprehensive details about the track then "Richard will be all technical with you!" The queues of cars lengthen further, as I decide to leave Lynn and Jayne to supervise arrivals and to resolve the lack of catering for this afternoon's meeting, since the lady who usually runs the burger van is in the midst of a crisis. There are also some girls outside the office and they clutch a number of birthday cards because they're very keen to find Scunthorpe rider Danny Norton, though they refer to him with the nickname "The Italian Stallion".

I stroll round to the metal container that serves as the track shop, which inside boasts a wide variety of merchandise to quicken the heart of any speedway fan or Buxton devotee. It's run, on behalf of Dave Rattenbury, by the ever-friendly John Rich, who wears his trademark blue apron with the word 'speedway' embroidered in bright letters on the front. He's busy as usual with a travel schedule that takes him from track to track. It's an itinerary that saw him at Stoke last night, for their

[3] The official BSPA Conference League pay rates are £5 a point and 10p per mile travel expenses.

[4] There are no local services whatsoever to allow people from Buxton to travel to the track. So it's a case of drive, share or hike.

Close to BethHELL. © Jeff Scott

Pits gate crowd. © Jeff Scott

The experienced Kenny Smith. © Jeff Scott

meeting with Rye House, at Buxton this afternoon and he will return again to Stoke later this evening. There's a small crowd of punters inside the container and he chats affably with the bearded pits marshal from Sittingbourne, Dick Jarvis, who reminds me to make a point to speak with Steve Ribbons when I visit the Kent club in September. After much chit chat, I learn that while some footballers and pop lotharios allegedly keep their own 'little black book' of information, John has his own equivalent in the form of a big "yellow book" in which he conscientiously records all the results from every speedway meetings he attends. It's getting to be a very long list in a large book with all his years of experience watching speedway, but he modestly wears his authority very lightly with characteristic understatement.

In the pits the riders and mechanics of both teams attack their last-minute preparations for the meeting with gusto, particularly since it's only a few minutes away. There are lots of familiar faces from my recent visit to Scunthorpe, which includes Scunny's friendly team manager Kenny Smith, with his strikingly distinctive and patrician grey hair, who bobs all about the pits area. He's from Yorkshire, used to ride speedway himself and is also the assistant team manager at Newcastle, so he definitely doesn't lack experience. Years of speedway have taught him "never to go to any speedway meeting feeling confident of the result" and today is no exception, since Kenny limits his remarks to a rather guarded, "we're up for a good meeting and for trying our best". Scunny co-promoter Rob Godfrey is in the pits with his son Paul, who is Scunny's machine examiner and informs me his brother Michael won't ride today, as he's "bust his wrist" since my last visit to Normanby Road. This happened in heat 13 of the August meeting with Sittingbourne while he rode against Gary Phelps, who also broke his thumb in the crash. He mentions that Michael, unsuccessfully, tried "scaring him by taking him wide" but instead they both ended up through the fence. By the pits exit onto the track is clerk of the course, Clifton Mould, who also works as pits marshal at Stoke, when he's not involved at Buxton. Clifton is full of praise for the track and its miraculous absorbency qualities, apparently the track dries out so quickly that it can easily withstand any deluge from a thunderstorm, although "lack of vision" for the riders would, nonetheless, still force the abandonment of the meeting. Luckily, he doesn't anticipate storms today, despite the clouds, but does expect Scunny to be too strong a team for Buxton. Clifton has been at Buxton for nine years now and "loves it all, it's a privilege to do!" Elsewhere in the pits we have another notable speedway figure in the distinctive form of Peter Oakes, who is here to supervise and watch the Under-15s Academy League fixture which follows the Buxton versus Scunthorpe clash.

A group of four young, start-line girls wait patiently for events to get underway. They chat among themselves or make last-moment adjustments to the clothes that they wear for their work at the start line, to entertain the crowd and guide the riders to the appropriate start position at the tapes. They help each other to tie coloured ribbons that match the riders' helmet colours tightly around their waists or fiddle nervously with the red and yellow pompoms that they each loosely hold. They're happy enough to pose for photographs but seem reluctant to talk too much, though they do giggle and cackle among themselves in response to anything I say. They don't offer any predictions about the match result but, instead, chat among themselves about what else they've been up to that weekend. I later discover that this group of young women are known locally as the Buxton Babez and I imagine that the 'Z' indicates that they're all still at school but, then again nowadays, I can never tell.[5] Nor is it best to make any assumptions out loud. It's pleasant to find that the Babez all wear what is, by modern speedway standards, quite modest and comfortable clothing. Again this is most likely to be a practical factor, which is not usually the key criteria when it comes to the choice of clothing for start girls round the speedway tracks of the country. However, given the location of this track on picturesque but, most likely, normally very windswept hills I'd have thought that the chilly or 'fresh' conditions would still dictate the choice of articles of clothing with greater potential for warmth rather than comeliness. Still, as local girls, they probably don't notice the chill or, at least, affect not to.

After I signally failed to engage the Babez in witty repartee, I decide to watch the races from the other side of the track from the pits area. Subsequently I find myself walking round the perimeter of the track circuit with Scunthorpe presenter Roger Westby, along with his wife, and they helpfully highlight the unusual downwards slope of the Buxton track, since it mirrors the contours of the hill we look down from. It definitely must be the only track in the country where the riders go downhill into turn 2 before they find themselves heading back uphill in turn 4, but "then it is a National park". They're both mad keen followers of speedway in general and Scunthorpe in particular, a hobby which fits well with Roger's regular column in the Scunny programme, his work as a presenter at the track as well as his normal job at Radio Humberside. We chat about the events that presently beset Hull Speedway and its probable demise. Roger worries that Dave Peet, who's only arrived in a position of responsibility at the club this season, might well get tarred with the same reputation Paul Hodder allegedly has in relation to finances should the club finally, as looks highly likely, go under.

By the time the first race starts, I have just managed to find myself by the fourth bend, where I stand with keen speedway photographer Steve Dixon – who is up his stepladder – and his partner Debbie who remains on terra firma. There was no need for me to hurry as three of the four riders in the race get in touch with the terra firma too, when they fall on the first bend, and the race is then ruled an 'unsatisfactory start' by the referee. Steve sardonically remarks, with the careworn manner of a long-suffering Scunthorpe fan, "Benji likes to get his compulsory fall out of the way as early as possible". The riders dust themselves off and remount for the Scunny pair to then roar off from the tapes for an easy first-heat victory. The next race features the reserves and, in which, Joe Reynolds and Scott Richardson appear to have an almost irresistible attraction to each other from the start. In the first attempt to run the heat, Richardson is apparently attacked by the safety fence one yard away from the start line, which thereby initiates a weird series of events that has Reynolds fall on the first bend, for the referee to again rule for yet another 'unsatisfactory start'. The re-run of the race just about reaches where we stand on bend 4, when Reynolds and Richardson flirt with disaster just before they thump into each other but still manage to stay on their bikes, to the accompaniment of loud collective "oohs" from those members of the crowd who have braved watching outdoors. The Buxton riders narrow the aggregate points deficit with an eventual 4-2 victory in the race and the crowd goes absolutely mental. Or, at least, I think they must be going mental, albeit in the comfort and warmth of their own cars that completely line the race circuit, if the concerted beep and cacophony of their horns, all with weirdly different pitches, is any indicator of the collective delight. The sound of the racing at Buxton is generally all rather surreal because the sheer vastness of the surrounding hillsides disperses the sound of the bikes as they roar past; and the noise effectively just disappears with the bikes themselves as they again shoot away from you into the distance. It's a most abnormal lack of sound; a peculiarity that's emphasised by the rustle, slap and scatter of the flying shale, as it hits the kickboards at the bottom of the fence, momentarily after the bikes surge past. The announcer fills the silence when he mentions the

[5] When I look at their website, I learn that most of them are, in fact, now at college. The Babez line up comprises Kelly, Helen, Sarah, Amy and Jen.

noticeable lack of the burger van to the assembled hungry hordes but tantalises us when holds out the prospect that "we might kill a few sheep later". Steve clambers down the few steps of his mini-stepladder to comment on the apparent "ongoing competition among the riders to see who can get the dirtiest kevlars the quickest!" We haven't even got to heat 3 yet, whereupon current form is discarded since the race is completed without the need for a re-run. But also, however, without all four riders as Benji Compton suffers an engine failure that signals the start of a lengthy and difficult afternoon's endeavours for him in the Peak district.

Heat 4 has Richardson excluded and in heat 5 there's yet another faller, which this time features the alliteratively named Byron Bekker. The wind has picked up strongly by now, which Debbie assures me is usual around these parts. In fact, Debbie notes, "you can get sunshine, hail, rain and sleet all in the same meeting along with a very cold wind" but sadly there's "only so much room to shelter in the track shop if we all try to crowd in there at the same time". It begins to become clear to me why so many of the fans desire the comfortable surroundings of their own cars, even on a summer's day like today.

On the subject of kevlars, dirty or otherwise, before heat 6 Jonathon Bethell lingers by our position long enough for the pithy message on his pair to finally grab our brief attention. He's club captain and it's his third year at Buxton, since he switched to speedway after he used to ride motocross. His bottom is adorned with the phrase "close to [Bet]HELL" which is perhaps a tad overwrought but a none too subtle warning for any sharp-sighted rider who unfortunately happens to trail along behind him. At the start line, Bethell dispenses with any nuance to his psychological tactics to upset or put off his rival riders, when he leans over from gate 4 to deliberately rest his arm heavily on the opposing reserve rider, Grant Hayes, before the race starts and just as Hayes tries to line up on gate 3. All of this after Bethell has already deliberately encroached on Grant's personal space and signalled that he initially appears to intend to line up way too close to him for comfort or safety. Upset achieved, Bethell then moves away to line up in the correct position and to leave a more sensible but legal gap between them at the start line. However, this respite only precedes his intended manoeuvre to violently cut across the unfortunate Hayes, almost within a yard of the start and with great ferocity and venom. A bit excessive for a race against a rider that, by all accounts and experience, Bethell was bound to beat easily but perhaps, it shows a commendable tenacity and huge desire to succeed. However, the race is stopped when Danny Norton falls and is excluded. Bethell then wins the re-run without the need to indulge in any more gamesmanship. The next race, heat 7, has Benji Compton gain an exclusion; while the next two heats pass off without incident, but do feature an imperious win for Charles Wright in heat 9, to take the aggregate score to 32-22.

Back in the comparative shelter of the pits, I catch a few more words with Jayne, who wants to highlight Buxton's need for a "major financial backer". The club survives on its attendances and the club has "to pay all our bills from the gate money" and this afternoon's visit by Scunthorpe is very welcome, particularly as they "have fetched a lot of people" in a coach to the meeting. But apart from the 'Superbikes' sponsorship of the riders' fuel and oil, everything else that is done at the club comes from extremely limited funds. It's surprising how quickly costs mount up on mere "incidental expenses" like the body colours, the artwork for these or the wayside caravans. While these financial challenges are undeniably "hard work" sometimes, Jayne's family and everyone else involved is delighted that "lots of riders have gone onto better things which is what we're all about really". Jayne mentions Lee Smethills, Simon Stead and the apple of her eye, James Wright. What is especially rewarding "is when you see the progress James has made!" Jayne is interrupted, by the appearance of her genuinely cute son Joshua, who arrives at her side insistent to gain her attention. Apparently "he's 5 going on 15" and he's totally set on becoming a speedway rider when he gets older. Joshua has grown up around bikes since he was a toddler, loves the noise and the smell and has all his own speedway gear, right down to a miniature body colour and kevlars. Jayne informs me that Joshua has all the mannerisms and confidence, even to the extent that he always digs out his own racing line at the start line, just like all the other speedway riders. He appears to be a bottle of pop and his lively nature then takes him and his mum away to the edge of the pits to watch the racing over the safety fence together.

The last race before the mid-match interval has Benji Compton fall, once again, and then get excluded from the race. Rob Godfrey loudly approves of Compton lying on the track long enough to halt the race ("at least he's done summat right"), a decision which was strategically sensible since Scunny's tactical substitute Byron Bekker was placed in last place behind the home riders. In the re-run of the heat, an incident between Bekker and Belfield causes heated controversy in the pits, after Belfield is excluded. The Scunny team manager, Kenny, is less than pleased with the decision. "It's freaking shite, I look on it as an ex-rider, it was a good challenge and my rider was ahead". The second re-run of this heat results in an unopposed 5-0 victory for the Buxton riders and almost effectively ends the meeting as a contest with the score 38-22 at the interval. Lynn Wright fusses around Belfield when he returns to the pits and he mournfully repeats his belief that "he just totally took my front wheel". I compliment Lynn on the performance, so far, of her youngest son Charles but I also mention that her sons look exactly alike each other. Lynn isn't convinced "I don't think so, and they have such different personalities". James has helped throughout and is in the thick of the action over the far side of the pits, where he works on some of the Buxton riders' bikes before Lynn kindly volunteers to fetch him, so that we can have a brief chat during the interval.

After James has finished some more emergency maintenance, he walks over to join me, just outside the pits, where we try to shelter from the wind. He's tall and fair haired but a quietly spoken, polite young man; though earlier his mother had already mentioned, "when he puts the helmet on he grows horns, they just can't believe it's the same James but, then, he's got to be forceful to succeed!" James is in his fourth season of racing speedway and, before he took up the sport, he rode grass track. On the bike, he looks very composed and has a comfortable and stylish appearance when he races. This season he has rode with greater confidence and aggression, which makes it easy to forget that he's still a teenager. He sometimes finds the travel from home near Stockport hard, "if you're having a good evening it's fine" but knows he's lucky to have his family drive, escort and support him at his many meetings. In fact, he's very keen to stress that the support and advice of his family contributes an essential component of his recent success but, as ever, It's also what actually happens on the track that really counts in the end. He's quite measured in his outlook but still very determined to succeed, though he prefers to "take it as it comes" with the ultimate aim to gradually improve over time. Although that said, in some ways, he views himself as "everyone's target", which is definitely a perspective that will always keep him on his toes. He's delighted he decided to concentrate "full time" on speedway to build his professional career and that he's already experienced Elite League racing with Belle Vue (which is good "since it's a lot harder than the Premier League"), all this along with his regular appearances for Workington. He quite baldly, and almost confidently states, "I know what I have to do"; which he then informs me is mostly to make the starts and try to learn from all his races. But, he also takes the opportunity to learn from others around him, like the Jasons – Lyons and Crump – "you're always learning something off them, tips and the like". James also tries to emulate his all-time speedway hero, Mark Loram, since he's "always passing and making everything exciting!" James has been slightly held back with injuries this year; but when he rides he hasn't changed his basic approach of "trying to get talking with everyone", particularly since he finds inactivity in the pits tends to cause him to lose his concentration. In the Elite League, James believes that there is no pressure on him, mostly because his goals are straightforward " I just try to get my points" and to best riders that he hasn't beaten before. He's pleased with his recent "scalp" of 'Deano' (Dean Barker) but mostly he tries to be as keen as he can, "you've got to want it all the time!" He's added a bit of steel and determination to his armoury this year, "last year some of the riders used to boss me about as reserve, but this year they know who I am". This season's injury was a bit of a set back and he had a short-term blip in his form, "I can't explain why, I started changing stuff and I wasn't so hard in the corners but I got my confidence back once I started scoring". I mention his mother Lynn's comments about his horns that grow, whenever he reaches the track; but James, matter of factly, notes that it's the same with all the riders because "they're all nice off the track!" Before he quickly adds, " the good ones just keep coming and coming".

Speedway is a team sport so it's not just about your own personal performance. The combination of individual prowess melded together within a team environment is part of the undoubted appeal of the sport to many speedway fans although this season, in the case of Workington, it has been pretty difficult to get the levels of team motivation and performance that

is traditionally required for success. According to James, some of the team have been a "bit down", which is partly due to team changes but mostly brought on by injuries to different riders at different points during the season. For James, it just goes to confirm that when you're on a roll no one can beat you and when the opposite is the case, you really struggle. While morale has suffered at times, he's keen to stress that to be in the same team with Shaun Tacey is fun ("he's a real jester") and that everyone, including himself, have really missed Carl 'Stoney' Stonehewer because "he's so important on and off the track to Workington".

The key to success though, for James, is just as much what is done off the track as on it; and he prides himself that he puts in many significant hours of preparatory work behind the scenes. Everything needs to be "spot on" because "if your equipment isn't right, you don't go right". It's also very important to avoid the twin distractions of "women and beer", although James does grin sheepishly when he notes these dangers. In fact, throughout our conversation he's friendly and personable and extremely modest about his abilities or even about the help he provides ("whenever I can, I do") to the other riders in the pits at Buxton. James is proud to have rode for Buxton but claims he's not sure if he has provided any real help to the newer riders, "it's hard to tell, they're all learning and if they ask I'm there". He's pleased that he "gets on well with most people" and he still remains quite close with Ben Wilson who he's known since 14, when they rode second halves together. The bikes start to rev up again and, as the second half of the Conference League fixture is just about to get underway, James politely excuses himself to rush back off again to help in the pits, but not before he remembers to politely wish me well with the research for my book.

The remaining heats of the fixture are packed with incidents galore and the trend for numerous falls by the riders continues unabated for the duration. Of the last five heats, the most peculiar was heat 13, where we had both a fallen rider and another rider was lapped, which thereby produced an unusual score of 2-3. Sadly we get to see no more of Benji Compton;[6] but, instead, we get to enjoy the wild but enthusiastic racing style of Byron Bekker for Scunny and to an exhibition of smoothly controlled riding skills from Buxton's Charles Wright. Buxton win easily on aggregate 54-38 to the delight of the home fans, who either frantically honk their horns from the comfort and warmth of their cars or loudly cheer from the sidelines and hang over the safety fence. The spirit of loud congratulation has particularly seized those fans that stood outside in the wind throughout the afternoon, although may be it's also partially a way to keep warm?

[6] The referee Paul Ackroyd was so concerned at Benji's 'out of control' riding style that he even requested Benji demonstrate that he was safe to compete with other riders, through an additional four-lap practice on his own after the meeting. This request was impolitely declined.

It has stayed dry all afternoon, which is the main thing, and finally the sun shines brightly to make the surrounding countryside appear even more spectacular, when bathed in a picturesque combination of brightness and shadows. The Buxton team goes back on the track to ride round on their victory parade with little Joshua Moss, mascot and rider manqué, all too keen to celebrate along with the rest of the riders. In fact, he's probably the most enthusiastic in his celebrations while perched on Charles Wright's bike. The announcer reveals the "Men of the Match" as Charles Wright and Scott Chester before he notes, "it's getting a bit of a habit for Charles Wright, just like his brother". Mother Lynn beams in the pits with pride, while simultaneously all around her in the pits, Conference League equipment is packed away, just as the Academy riders, mechanics and helpers begin to push their bikes onto the track for the start of the Academy fixture. Completely in his element, Peter Oakes enthusiastically shouts instructions, waves his arms and offers advice to a steady stream of youngsters almost every time you glance in his direction. The fixture pitches the Rhinos' team up against the Bulls and, if anything, the actual fall count decreases though the possibility of a dramatic crash or an impending fall appears to significantly increase with a display of very tentative riding by some of these youngsters. The first heat has Gary Irving fall twice but he still manages to get a point, in an awarded race, by dint of his determination to remount his machine twice. Tim Webster wins heat 2 after a brief but dangerous flirtation with the fence, at one stage. It's very much a delight to watch the keenness and commitment of the Academy League riders as well as the equal enthusiasm of their parents and helpers.

I head to the Speedway Office to thank Jayne and find her swiftly completing some of her usual match-day administration, while she's surrounded by yet more members of the Wright family. "They're all here" she says and introduces me to another member of the family, James's grandmother Eva Yacoby. At the other extreme, also in the compact but crowded office is sister-in-law Sarah Rawnsley with her 16-week-old baby Keth; while club mascot and speedway rider of the future, Joshua, runs excitedly into the office just as I leave. Going back out via the pits, I find that Clifton Mould, the clerk of the course, has enjoyed Buxton's win but reminds me that every rider that competed today is "something special, you know they are if you stand in the middle to watch, 'cause you realise how mad they are". He appears to have really warmed to the visiting Scunthorpe rider, Byron Bekker, the most this afternoon. Clifton predicts a great future for him, based on the raw skills he's witnessed that afternoon, "sure he's wild and out of control but all the great riders are to start with, once he figures it though, he'll be really something!"

As I drive off, on a short cut across the fells on narrow windy roads towards Dalehead, that pass through the open countryside and near to the occasional isolated house or small farm building; I realise that not only is Axe Edge Britain's most picturesque location for speedway, but it's also arguably illustrative of what speedway is really all about. A family sport where young people get the chance to try to live out their lives, dreams and ambitions in a supportive but competitive environment. Skill levels and experience may differ but you can't help but notice that everyone seems equally part of the experience and comfortably at home or at peace with everyone else's participation, no matter how big or small. It's been a real pleasure to experience this outlook and atmosphere first hand!

28th August Buxton v. Scunthorpe (Conference League) 54-38

Chapter 35: The Pride of the Panthers
1st September Peterborough v. Eastbourne

"Peter Karlsson's no shop egg... He's 150% every race he rides in, he wants to win" Gary Havelock

12.10 Spectacles, if worn, and goggles shall be made of shatterproof material.

After my last rained-off visit to watch Peterborough race, their co-promoter Neil Watson suggested that I could return for any future fixture at the East of England Showground (EOES) to watch them in action. With my complex travel schedule to visit other tracks throughout the country, this eventually turned out to be the re-staging of the rain ravaged fixture against Eastbourne. Though, since it was near to the end of the season cut-off date, I had the good fortune to turn up when the re-arranged meeting had been changed into a double-header fixture, which would comprise both of the outstanding Elite League matches between the clubs. Since the American Independence Day postponement, there has been a massive transformation in Peterborough's fortunes for the better. The team had really started to rack up an impressive run of results to charge up the Elite League table and push themselves into strong contention to win the forthcoming play-offs. Eastbourne though, since early July, had a stop-start season that has been closely tied to the health of the Hailsham based David Norris. He had determinedly tried but struggled to fully overcome his early season concussion and neck injury or return to the proper form that had set the league alight the previous season. An injury sustained in Sweden days previously

by the Eagles talismanic Dane, Nicki Pedersen, along with the absence of their recently inspirational captain Dean Barker, has left them with a truly makeshift team for the evening's encounter.

Unlike my previous visits I arrive on a pleasantly warm evening that has no forecast threat of rain. Wayne Swales, assistant team manager for the Peterborough Panthers and son of Trevor, is in a buoyant mood about the team and their prospects as we grab a few minutes' conversation in the busy pits, just before the riders' parade. He has come to the speedway at Peterborough for 24 years, ever since he was a very small child; "Gran has a picture of me when I was four standing with three riders" one of them was the "Mr Peterborough of the time" Brian Jones who "lives in the same village as me". Wayne's interest in speedway was almost inevitable given his "dad used to ride", so there was little surprise when he "started as track photographer" before eventually trying his hand at team management at Mildenhall prior to his move back to Peterborough. Wayne relishes his involvement and enjoys his life in the sport, though he recalls as a teenager people "took the piss out of me for liking speedway" but perceptions recently changed "when they saw you on the telly". These same people who used to point the finger and make fun of his interest, now "even stop dad in the street to discuss speedway".

At the moment, there's a lot to talk about the Peterborough team enjoying a great run of recent form after six of the last seven meetings have resulted in a win. Wayne believes that there are a number of factors behind this success: an "awesome team", a "decent track" and suddenly "everything's clicked, it's all come together". The major factor behind the change in outlook and fortune also appears to have had its roots in the early season ownership transfer between the Horton brothers, from Mick to Colin. Under the old regime there were "so many little games" whereas Colin enthusiastically runs Peterborough Speedway as a business. The club is back on a firm financial footing, it has started to properly invest in the fabric of the club and there has been a firm delineation of job responsibilities on and off the track. Peter Karlsson, the club captain, has taken responsibility for the organisation of the team with the happy result that Peterborough enjoys the "best team spirit where everyone helps one another". Trevor is also full of renewed vigour in his work, since the changes have "made dad's job much easier". The club have also found motivation from the description of their prospects for the 2005 season, particularly those made by the Sky Sports pundits Jonathan Green and Kelvin Tatum, who viewed them as "a team of people nobody wants" who "couldn't get team places" elsewhere. Wayne believes this commonly held opinion had the happy result meant that the team felt, "no pressure on the riders as nobody expected anything of us". The impact of this has been tremendous with all the riders going out to enjoy themselves and performances have improved to such an extent that "plenty of teams would swap us for them". Typical of the resurgence throughout the team is Lukas Dryml, "he came here last year low on confidence, with stiff body language and people hammered us for signing him". However with faith in his abilities and some words of encouragement he's undergone a transformation as a rider, he oozes confidence and "is funny as you like and brilliant to have in the pits". If success is part inspiration and part perspiration, then Wayne prides himself on the secret weapon that is the comparative statistical information provided by Peterborough supporter Dick Butler. This analysis has been utilised to great effect to provide additional information and insight into the teams performances and is much more useful than the similar figures CMA (Calculated Match Average) produced by the BSPA. Just as Wayne praises these statistics, the latest version arrives with Dick and they immediately go off to discuss their direct import for tonight's fixture with Trevor.

Standing close by is Eastbourne's manager Jon Cook, who's in downbeat mood about this season's turn of events at the club. They haven't recently enjoyed much good fortune, while the various twists and turns lead Jon to claim, "you could write a book just about our season and no one would believe you". The double-header fixture tonight is crucial to Eastbourne's chances of success in the league this season. They require at least a bonus point from an aggregate victory in one of the two matches to leave them with a realistic chance of qualification for the all-important end-of-season play-offs. Jon is often plainly spoken but still friendly and well deserves his reputation as one of the country's most thoughtful managers, though the search to find suitable replacements for his absent or injured riders has tested his patience and proved extremely difficult, "it's a bloody nightmare getting someone". Tonight the Eagles are without the gifted and combative Nicki Pedersen and the experienced Dean Barker, who has confounded expectations with some inspirational captaincy for the Eagles since he took over the position from David Norris, at short notice, earlier in the season. However, the rush of speedway fixtures at this time of year, since all Elite League teams have to hurry to complete their campaigns before the official fixture cut-off date of September 8th, has stymied Jon's choices because of the dreaded "eight-day rule". This has severely limited Eastbourne's options, "Belle Vue was the only team we could choose [guest riders] from, well, until midday when Oxford and Wolves got cancelled, so we could choose from them too". An additional problem has been that, at this stage of the season, many riders are reluctant to ride because they carry injuries, are keen to rest or, more likely, they've been instructed not to help a rival team during a vital stage of the year. Whatever the reason, replacements have proved elusive, "first Simon Stead said he'd ride, then said he wouldn't" while "Rusty [Harrison] packed up all his stuff and left work to come here so I'll be giving him a ride".

As I leave Jon to weave his motivational magic on the depleted squad he has tonight, he despairingly notes, "it's all bollocks now, mate!" On the Peterborough side of the pits, there's a real contrast in atmosphere since it's all laughs and smiles among the riders, staff and mechanics. Trevor Swales dashes about but isn't complacent or that happy, even when you consider the recent results and robust camaraderie of the squad, mostly because his ambitions to finish in the top two places in the Elite League remain thwarted, "we just can't get where we want to I don't think – which is second".[1] Though to have great expectations is, perhaps, the necessary and motivational role of any team manager. In sharp contrast to Trevor's desire for yet greater achievement, the club chaplain, the Reverend Michael Whawell, as you'd expect, takes considerable delight in "those six consecutive victories in what must have been the most remarkable week in Panthers' history".

I wander over to the pleasant grassy area in front of the first bend bar for a bite to eat and to watch the crowd fill the main grandstand or bask in the late evening summer sunshine. There's a group of Eastbourne-shirted fans, each with their own garden chair,[2] who have staked a claim to this prime position on the apex of the first bend. Apparently they all go regularly to Arlington and always try to tie their holidays in with the Eagles' away fixture list. Fortuitously their holiday in Great Yarmouth, along with late season fixture changes, has allowed them to come along to support the Eagles tonight, while last

[1] In order to get the benefit of a home tie in the initial knockout phase of the Elite League play-offs.

[2] The deluxe, more modern and comfortable type with the dark green camouflage colour webbing material and drinks holder. This version has gradually colonised the terraces at speedway meetings throughout the country, in contrast to the more basic version favoured by fans everywhere for many years.

year a holiday in the Norfolk Broads coincided with the Eagles fixture at Ipswich. The consensus among them is that the Eagles will get a result or at least a bonus point tonight, though their mood is somewhat sombre when you consider that they should be full of the holiday spirit. Later I notice that they quickly move position once the meeting starts because they get sprayed in shale, well, to be more accurate, pelted by industrial quantities a great speed. They beat a hasty retreat to a much safer distance away on the lawns, to the amusement of the locals which explains the lack of rivalry for what otherwise would be an excellent vantage point from which to enjoy proceedings on the track.

With 30 heats to be raced by the 10 p.m. curfew time, Trevor has enlisted the additional help and expertise of Steve Brandon from Sky Sports. He regularly supervises the prompt departure and return of riders to the pits throughout the country for the live Sky televised meetings, where the need to get everything completed in a timely fashion and, more importantly, fit in all the commercial breaks, is essential for their schedules and revenues! To this end, Steve already has all the riders for the first four heats lined up, ready and waiting by the pits in almost military fashion. Consequently the meeting starts at a cracking pace, as do the races, which all look frighteningly fast on this massive circuit suited to riders with a high-speed, full-throttle technique. Heat 2 is won by a young rider with a mythical sounding name, Troy Batchelor, who we learn from the announcer was only, a few days previously, just 18. He's resplendent in some smart but slightly garish new kevlars with 'Troy' emblazoned across his bottom, which he'd just given the other riders, if they were sharp sighted, a good chance to admire when he romped to victory by some margin in the reserves race. He's young but the youngest person already gurgles contentedly and plays with her toys in the pits. She's Olivia Armstrong, the eight-month-old daughter of Mildenhall rider Jon Armstrong, who's been brought along in her pram with her mother and father. Jon chain smokes throughout and rightfully basks in the glory of his hard-won but successful previous night's performance – "you were a hero", he's told by one of the pits staff when they congratulate him – for Peterborough when they unexpectedly won away at the league leaders Belle Vue.

Heat 5 indicates the first signs of a possibly mixed night ahead for David Norris, when he retires very early from the race. This leaves the recently rejuvenated Sam Ermolenko to stalk, as they say, Adam Shields for two laps, while he bides his time before he generates the speed to superbly pass him on the last lap. The announcer, Edwin Overland, is delighted "all I can say is wow!" A comment that appears to unnecessarily restrict the possible range of his future vocabulary choices to describe any subsequent but similarly exciting race. It's a spectacle that has clearly got him going as Edwin christens it "vintage stuff, brilliant stuff, the smoothest overtake of the night", excitable comments though we still have 25 more heats to go. At least Edwin Overland turns out to be a real and very enthusiastic person. The Peterborough match reports, filed under his rather unusual name in the *Speedway Star*, had aroused my suspicions that it was a nom de plume to disguise the fact that the report was really written by the home promoter. That said, you really couldn't wish for more favourable comments on the microphone throughout the night, since Edwin very clearly and very often holds the Peterborough team in exceptionally high regard. Oblivious to Edwin's continual aural paean to all things Panthers, back in the pits Trevor Swales remains mystified as he ruminates with Jon Armstrong, about the lack of demand for his services as a guest, "I just don't know why more people haven't booked you as a guest?"

If the 'A' fixture had been a boxing match the referee would have definitely stopped the contest a long while before we arrived at heat 15. Had this happened it would have deprived everyone in the pits of the opportunity to witness the bizarre but wildly delirious celebrations of Peterborough track staff member, Dean. I know this is his name since it was clearly emblazoned in large letters on the back of his bright red boiler suit cum overalls. In fact, in a visible concession to razzmatazz or increased professionalism, all the Peterborough track staff wore these rather natty red work uniforms, albeit mostly without the words 'Dean' on the reverse. Between dances, Dean's official task is to monitor the air pump of the inflatable safety fence and to ensure it's constantly refuelled, particularly as it's a small, thirsty beast. Unofficially it appears, his role is to leap and dance around the pits with the vigorous ecstasy of a lottery winner; something he very capably fulfils whenever he celebrates each Panthers race win or heat victory with ever greater displays of unbridled joy and delight. Ales Dryml's overtake past erstwhile Sky expert pundit-cum-commentator Steve Johnson, the combative guest rider for Eastbourne, provokes a celebratory jig that wouldn't look out of place in Rio at Carnival time. Neil Watson passes by and clearly is infected by the same bug, that has undeniably infected Dean, but without the jigs and dances.

A jubilant Neil Watson believes that the arrival of Colin Horton in charge of the speedway club resulted in a greater professionalism and a much-improved relationship with the Showground's management. So much so that they've lent the club an extra tractor for the evening to ease the burden of the frequent track maintenance that 30 heats of racing require. This unexpected but gratefully received loan of a tractor and driver, along with an agreement on a regular race night for the club next year, are just some of the many helpful but symbolic signs of the rekindled understanding between the landlords and their speedway tenants. Neil then evangelises that this is the "fastest track in the country" with "a racing "shape that suits the riders, particularly if they're on form and firing, they can go really well". I mention that, to my untutored eye, the surface looks much smoother than for the last Eastbourne visit, when Deano had good cause for complaint. Neil laughs and admits, "it's all part of the black art of track preparation" and that there's "no point in playing into the hands of the opposition". In fact practical consideration behind the need to run 30 heats dictates "we had to be slick tonight, in case it rains, so it would run off". However, for the visit of Poole the next night, "it'll be much rougher than this as it'll only be 15 heats and on a smooth surface Poole might beat us!"

Tonight's track is definitely prepared to the considerable liking of the home riders who've already raced away into a considerable lead by the time that David Norris repeatedly delays the attempted starts of heat 9. First of all, Floppy is excluded for a tapes infringement, which thereby requires him to start in the re-run with a 15 metres back from the start line. He's then excluded again, this time from the re-run, under the two-minute time allowance regulation. Edwin Overland then informs us over the tannoy that, "Norris has been reinstated at 15 metres at the discretion of the referee and with the agreement of the two team managers". It's the sort of common-sense decision that says more than money ever can about Peterborough's confidence and their justifiable expectation that they will easily win the match anyway. David then nearly misses the repeated re-run heat again, under the two-minute allowance, and only just makes it to the start line in time after he's accompanied and rather wittily serenaded by specially chosen music from The Kinks, which blasts from the tannoy with a brief chorus of "Tired of waiting for you". After such a protracted palaver, Norris finishes last and looks far from happy as he returns to the pits. This is further confirmed when, in a state of considerable frustration, he gets quite stroppy and shouty with his equipment in almost Basil Fawlty fashion.

By the time they've won heat 10, Peterborough captain Peter Karlsson and his race partner Lukas Dryml take the chance to exuberantly pose on their bikes with some wheelies and another much more peculiar, choreographed and elaborate leg-trailing celebrations, to noisy approval from a packed and delirious grandstand. Dean dances, Neil laps it up but quickly acknowledges the fickle finger of fortune, "it's a winning team that makes all the difference, if we were bottom of the league you wouldn't see this attitude". Home track knowledge and the advantage of familiarity has become very evident on the track and in the scoreline, most notably when Ales Dryml confidently finds the grip required for some huge acceleration to pass David Norris on the back straight during heat 11. It's often said, but Dryml really did appear to ride past him as though he really were stationary. By me in the pits, Dean smiles broadly and hops manically from foot to foot as though he's St Vitus. By the usually crucial heat 13, a completely absorbed Dean indulges himself in an impressive repertoire of stretches with a series of flexibility and bending exercises as if he's just received word that he'll be called up to actually ride in the next race. Instead, he merely refuels the air pump and follows that with some brief callisthenics and a few more mini leaps in the air.

All is clearly not well with David Norris on the Eastbourne side of the pits, not only because of his continued aggravation with his injuries, but also through the psychological upset and mental havoc it has wreaked on his often fragile confidence. Before heat 13, David remains rooted to his seat, with his back to prying eyes for the duration of the two-minute time allowance. Throughout this 'sit in', the clerk of the course, Dick Swales, peers over and offers a running commentary to co-promoter Neil Watson. It's not hard to gather that Dick isn't overly surprised or impressed with David's level of interest and dedication, "he's doing his usual trick of just sitting there, the only time he's ever rode well here was last year". Throughout this minor distraction Dean remains focused and carries on with his elaborate routine of warm-up exercises. Dick believes, "if you've got a dodgy head you'll really notice it on a large track, so you shouldn't freaking ride; plus, he's a danger to himself and everyone else – they shouldn't let him ride at all!" I'm not sure whether the "they" Dick holds responsible are the authorities, the doctors, the referee or the Eagles' team management but, whoever they are, he blames them for this "fiasco". The inclusion of Andrew Moore as a replacement doesn't hold back the Karlsson/Dryml (A.) pairing that, once again, the crowd roars on delightedly as they perform their elaborate choreographed duet of leg-trailing celebrations. Dean whoops when they cross the line and simultaneously performs a Morrissey-like wave of the arms (without the bunch of flowers) in combination with a superbly executed pirouette while the music on the tannoy loops endlessly with the chorus of "That's the way I like it". My selection as the race of the night would be the next one, which features a duel between Davey Watt and the flying Sam Ermolenko. It's a thrilling spectacle and one where they race almost wheel-to-wheel and shoulder-to-shoulder throughout, for all four laps as they pass and re-pass each other with "no quarter given", as Edwin Overland announces afterwards. Dean dances in a comparatively restrained manner, but still lives every turn of the wheels for the remainder of the fixture while he hops around, with almost ballet-like grace. It's practically a cricket score, 62-31, by the end of the meeting. The Eagles' wings have been clipped by an all-round team effort from the Panthers. However, it's Sam Ermolenko who has really impressed. He has ridden in the manner of a man possessed with great skills and boundless desire to compete that belies his age and his early season scores, but not his extensive experience.

Before the second half starts I grab a few words with the new 43-year-old owner of the Panthers, Colin Horton. He's clearly very enamoured with the sport and his team; he appeared fully involved in the pits area during the first half of the meeting and repeatedly offered thumbs-up gestures to his victorious riders when they returned through the pits gate. Colin comes across as very down to earth, pragmatic and confident of himself when you talk with him. He's optimistic that "commitment, loyalty and trust" allied to "getting behind them with a little money" will make all the difference and give everyone at the club "a new lease of life". You know that it's not an idle boast when he compares his squad to others and states, "we've got riders that cancel theirs out and that little bit more". He's particularly impressed with the "awesome" Peter 'PK' Karlsson though he hates to single out any one person, since there is now a "real buzz" about the whole club.

He's had a long involvement in speedway, which began when he "watched it as a kid", as just another six-year-old fan at Wembley and White City who "always loved it, the smell, everything". The "opportunity came along" at Peterborough so he's "having a bash and giving it a go". The landlords have given him full support and "everything I want", while the response of the fans has been "tremendous" in the stadium and "on the forums". Colin modestly admits, "maybe I saved the day", and believes "we're back fighting fit" with the "fans enjoying their speedway; when all's said and done, all that matters is the speedway, really". Not that Colin contemplates resting on his laurels, "I can't wait for next year as I still want to crank it on some more". He appears genuinely delighted to have the privilege to control the destiny of Peterborough Speedway, which means he's in demand with everybody, "you'll have to excuse me, I've got to go and meet the people here, it goes with the territory, they like it and I want to hear what they think, at least while we're winnin'!"

In among the crowd is the friendly, laconic but always quietly assured Tony Steele, fresh from his 50th birthday and he's returned to the scene of the crime (in terms of his start marshal's career rather than his referee's one!). He chats affably and delights that his Leicester home finds him "within 100 miles of 15 or 16 tracks", which allows him to get full value from his referee's pass, since it enables him to watch as many speedway fixtures as his limited free time permits. Tony speaks exceptionally highly of Colin "he loves the sport, goes to all the GPs and has quietly sponsored Lee Richardson for years". Sadly he can't stop and talk all day, but smiles conspiratorially before he rushes off to carry on with the casual freemasonry that is top-flight speedway. I'm not sure if it's a case of Chinese walls or Chinese whispers but Tony is already on his way, "because I'm just trying to see Trevor to tip him off about something".

I'm delighted to be invited to watch most of the second match from inside this huge racing circuit on the centre green with all the sponsors, riders' girlfriends, photographers and the St John Ambulance crew. I'm also a lot closer to the black-kevlared young woman who is working as the start marshal at the meeting. Unusually, compared to the marshals at many other tracks I've visited this season, she seems scrupulously fair and keen to ensure that all the riders (not just the visiting riders) line up properly at the start gate. The propensity to only really hassle and harass visitors is very noticeable at many tracks but not at Peterborough. I learn later that this conspicuously impartial and even-handed young lady is Colin Horton's daughter, Marni. For this approach and attitude, I believe she should be applauded and her approach copied at some other tracks I could, but won't, name! While I watch from the huge centre green, not only do the races appear stupendously fast and tremendously exhilarating but you really realise how committed the riders are to even race! You soon get dizzy with all the repeated swivelling round and round to try to catch the action as the riders fly past on their bikes. The chance to watch from this prime position, makes me think that I suddenly live in the parallel universe, since it gifts me the same point of

view and perspective that the *Speedway Star* regularly portrays in its photographs!

The second meeting is a lot closer, surprisingly so after the withdrawal of the often talismanic David Norris from the Eastbourne team. Yet another race of the night, definitely THE race of the night in heat 9 sees a neck-and-neck race with pass after pass throughout along with wheel-to-wheel action from start to finish that involves Ermolenko, Watt, Batchelor and Jensen. You could have thrown the proverbial blanket over them at almost any point in the race. However, two races later, the spirit of fair, safe and competitive racing appears to be thrown to the wind by Jesper B. Jensen, which results in a very painful-looking crash, for the vastly improved and competitive Troy Batchelor, who hurtles into the bend 2 air fence which results in a broken arm for the young rider. Viewed from my position directly by the incident (I was stood next to Neil Watson at the time), it appeared as though Batchelor – who had consistently pressured Jensen and had frequently attempted to manoeuvre past him round the outside – misjudged the space available to pass Jensen. Though it was a misjudgement that the wilier and more experienced Jensen could, in my opinion, have mitigated if he had chosen to ride a slightly different racing line and thereby not narrowed the gap as quickly as happened, that then caused Batchelor to hit the air fence at speed. Perspectives on incidents like these in the immediate aftermath usually divide down party lines. Just as one person's terrorist is another person's freedom fighter, so it is with the conundrum of when is it 'dirty riding' and when is it just 'hard riding'? In this specific case, the incident was viewed by some people as "just showing him his back wheel" and by others as "deliberately sticking him in the fence". It all depends on your point of view and, given the high speeds the riders reach, it all takes place in a fraction of a split second. Neil Watson, a short while later, defended Jensen when he observed, "Troy said they're riding too hard but these youngsters should learn to shut off; it's time some of these young lads learnt that they can close the throttle as well as open it, before complaining". Eastbourne's Jon Cook avoided the relative merits of the throttle control debate and preferred instead to sarcastically advise upon the need for an urgent eye test for Jensen. Jon also pointedly drew a comparison between the "racing room" left by the experienced Sam Ermolenko a few heats earlier in an aggressive, excitingly competitive but "fair race" and what he saw as in marked contrast to the "lack of space Jensen had left Troy" to safely race in. Without the benefit of an adjudicator for these diametrically opposed perspectives, we can all agree that the net result was a premature end to Troy Batchelor's season; to the great disappointment of the rider, Eastbourne on the night but, most of all, his parent club King's Lynn. The crash also ended the Eagles' resistance in this fixture. In the re-run of the race Rusty Harrison fell and was excluded, which resulted in yet another re-run with only the Peterborough riders. The subsequent 5-0 extended the Panthers' lead on the night to the nine points that were required to ensure an easy aggregate victory in the fixture. After literally not being at the races in the first 15 heats, Eastbourne then got remarkably close to nearly causing an upset. Though the bonus point was only secured in heat 15, the suspicion remained that the Panthers had coasted for the remainder of the meeting without any real fear that they might lose their winning position.

Immediately afterwards all the Peterborough riders retire straightaway from the pits area to the bar for an extremely crowded post-match press conference. The confidence of the team is completely obvious as is their team spirit. Captain 'PK' talks of the "team spirit" in his, always amusingly incongruous, perfect, broad Black Country accent; gained through years of loyal service for Wolverhampton. 'PK' also has a very good line in dry, self-deprecating humour, which he uses wittily to discuss his colleague Lukas Dryml's recent excellent performance at Belle Vue, despite his long-standing deep distrust and sincerely held dislike of the track. "He talked himself into liking it" PK wryly observes before he adds, "but then Lukas kept saying it's sunshine even when it was clearly pissing it down!" It's smiles all round for the riders and their audience. PK then hands the microphone over to Sam Ermolenko, who is well practised in either being the interviewer or the interviewee through his regular appearances over the years on Sky Sports television. This experience, let alone the skill with words and self-presentation that derives from his American heritage, all stand Sam in good stead when it comes to well-practised observations and plausible sound bites. He doesn't disappoint with "we're serious about it, this team just clicks without trying. I've never been in a team that's been this easy. We're laid back and focused when on the track. We're peaking at the right time and all riding for maximums". Sam speaks for probably most members of the unfeasibly packed room when he concludes with "I wish I'd put a bet on us!"

Shortly afterwards the victorious Panthers' riders rush en masse from the heaving bar and pile into their vans to make a quick getaway. The life of the modern speedway rider is, reputedly, to be forever on the move — from track to track, airport to airport or other similar permutations that involve service stations, families and groupies. Since I've already become lost in the pitch darkness on the many dead-end roads that characterise the EOES and that only lead to the perimeter fence, I decide to follow these vans to finally find my way out. No sooner have the vans shot off at speed from the grandstand area with confidence and, more importantly, local knowledge along the narrow roads of the showground, all easily exceeding the strict 10 m.p.h. speed limit that apparently applies, than they almost immediately grind to a halt again. They have stopped outside what turns out to be the changing rooms. I'm not sure who's more surprised, the riders at my following them at break-neck speed (though I'm sure they'd welcome a car full of young female admirers) or myself at the sudden halt. They all noisily pile out of their vans, still in their dirty kevlars and boisterously good spirits, as I plaintively enquire, "I'm lost, how do you get out of here?" Ever the gentleman, Sam Ermolenko sympathises before he very patiently provides clear and concise directions to the exit. I thank him and he calls back, "No problem, drive safely buddy!" as the group of them proceed to yelp away together towards the changing rooms.

1st September Peterborough v. Eastbourne (ELA) 62-31
1st September Peterborough v. Eastbourne (ELB) 52-43

Chapter 36: The Penultimate Evening of the Racers

19th September Reading v. Isle of Wight

Jonathan Green (to Kelvin Tatum, every week, who holds a slightly vacant but quizzical expression throughout): "You know it's really strange it just keeps getting more exciting/this is a really vital meeting for both sides/they're both going to want to do really well here etc"

Despite all my travels round the country I've hardly managed to attend any Reading Racers' fixtures during the 2005 season. In an attempt to correct this state of affairs, I have come along to watch the Premier League fixture with the Isle of Wight. It's a meeting that has the potential to generate a lot of heat, at least in the minds of the fans if not the riders, after the controversial Spring Bank Holiday fixture earlier in the season, which saw Danny Bird badly injured in a crash with Jason Bunyan. It is fair to say that the explanation "it was a racing accident" without malice or premeditation hasn't gained increased acceptance in the subsequent months among the Reading faithful. Pat Bliss's match programme notes covers many topics that includes the news that the Jackpot Raffle now has a prize £750, but she is the model of brevity when it comes to comment on this fixture. She welcomes the visitors and notes that "the home and away contests" between these two teams are traditionally "some of the best of the season". It's a pretty anodyne and irrefutable claim since these judgments are invariably subjective. The phrase of her welcome that could possibly allude to the early season meeting is "we are sure no one is likely to give an inch". However, it's also fair to say that the embers of resentment have already had

A lorry that's seen better days. © Jeff Scott

Tractor with working bowser. © Jeff Scott

Matej works conscientiously on his bike. © Jeff Scott

the chance to burn themselves out during the club's next encounters in the late summer, when Reading won easily at Smallmead to eliminate the Islanders from the Knock Out Cup.

By this stage of the season, there is still some slight doubt about the destination of the Premier League title, though it's strictly a two-horse race between Rye House and Berwick to become champions. Reading has endured another disappointing season after very high pre-season hopes, which were dashed and effectively ended by the aforementioned Bunyan crash with Bird. In contrast the Islanders have demonstrated admirable form on the Island where they have been pretty invincible, often easily win their fixtures and have drawn only the once, with Workington. On their travels it's been a different kettle of fish, although they have managed to do well in the south-west with wins away at Newport and Somerset. Though they did win the controversial encounter at Smallmead in March, by a single point, it's highly improbable that this feat would be repeated since the Bird injury and subsequent mid-meeting withdrawal was the essential difference between the teams on that particular night. The difference between the two racetracks is another significant factor since Smallmead is much smaller and slicker than the huge banked circuit of Smallbrook Stadium. These differences will get a quick and thorough examination when tonight's Smallmead encounter will be followed the next night, weather permitting, with the return fixture on the Island.

However, in the tall, slim person of Matej Zagar the Reading Racers have this season's best and arguably the most exciting rider in the Premier League. He's won plaudits everywhere he has ridden, from rivals and fans alike, and around Smallmead he has become practically invincible. The most likely person to threaten his relentless form is the vastly experienced Australian Craig Boyce, a rider who will be expected to demonstrate Brer-Rabbit-like cunning, rather than all-out speed, to impede and beat the fast Slovenian. The Reading fans have quite rightfully warmly embraced the latest young speedway superstar to excel while he wears the famous winged wheel of the Racers. There has been a rich tradition of exceptional riding talent that entertained the gradually diminishing crowds during the 30 years that Reading have raced at Smallmead. There's also a strong sense that the Racers fans should savour the skills of Zagar, while they can, since such talent is rumoured to want to pit itself against the best riders in the Elite League from next season. But then rumours are the lingua franca around this Berkshire outpost of speedway. There have been the many years of talk about the move of the club to a nearby new site, something that's long been required due to the continued decline and dilapidation of Smallmead;

[1] It's a position on the race card that means three of Steen's four programmed rides will be before heat 9, which thereby gives the riders Dave chooses to use as 'replacements' an early chance to experience track conditions and then adapt the set-ups of their equipment to that night's vagaries of the track surface for their own programmed races.

indeed, in recent years, the likelihood of the move has also contributed to this atmosphere of dilapidation and decline. More recently, there have been strong rumours that Pat Bliss, the long-time promoter at the club, might sell the club and thereby severely reduce the number of women involved in the almost exclusively male preserve of speedway promotion. The gossip authoritatively claims that Pat would have already sold out her interests in the club last winter, if the offer had been more acceptable. Rumours are rife as to the likelihood of a more lucrative offer being made during this winter that anyone, including Pat, would be foolish to resist. So then, the end-of-term feeling at the club, with only one more home meeting to race before the season ends early and prematurely at Reading, also has an even stronger end-of-an-era atmosphere about it. It's an uneasiness that isn't calmed when Pat Bliss offers the constant "no comment" rejoinder to questions with equally unconvincing vague visions of the future.

Whatever the future holds for the club, I'm truly honoured and delighted to be invited to spend the evening as a guest of the club and watch the action from the pits during the penultimate meeting of the season. After 30 years of watching the Racers I've finally made it to the other side of the wire fence to hang out, by the third bend, with the riders and their mechanics on the raised area that they always stand on. Even tonight, when the crowd looks quite sparse, though there's a large congregation of fans with their faces pushed against the fence who look down over the industrious activity in the pits area or observe the riders who themselves watch the racing from the rough hillock that is the ideal position from which to view events as they unfold on the track. After I exchange a few words with Pat about the prospects of the visitors this evening ("they often go well here") she has to rush off back to the office to attend to some emergency with the stadium lights. She leaves me in the capable hands of Paul Hunsdon, the club's commercial manager. I gather that he's had quite a bit of success in his time at the club in this role, which is primarily to attract sponsorship for the Racers. Until a few years ago, Reading were one of the few clubs in the country that was completely unable to attract any form of major team sponsorship. It was an astonishingly poor performance given the location of the club in one of the country's fastest growing cities with many new industrial developments; particularly so, given that numerous businesses had also relocated their company headquarters to the burgeoning estates that lined the important M4 corridor. It must have said something about the perceived unattractiveness of the sport itself, but possibly also more about the manner in which the club presented itself to prospective sponsors. Recently the club was sponsored by Euphony, who I believe had a fanatical Reading speedway fan as managing director. Fortunately for the club, he was also in charge of the purse strings. Unluckily, the telecommunications industry, like many others, is beset with mergers, takeovers and consolidations, which sadly resulted in the loss of office for Reading's main supporter and advocate within the Euphony boardroom after they were taken over. This season the club are sponsored by Ideal Video, who straddle the domestic and commercial video production markets, to such a level of business success that they feel it's worthwhile to sponsor the Reading Racers to boost their local and national profile. Paul professes himself "reasonably pleased" with his impact on commercial activities, as we wander on the tarpaulin-covered dog track round to the pits gate area, but admits "you always want more in my job". He lives reasonably locally in Tadley, the village that I grew up in as a child. He's one of the new arrivistes that populate the village in executive housing estates that have gradually turned the place into a small but still staid town. He has much to attend to, so he leaves me to fend for myself in the pits after he ensures I've signed in to be insured and have my valuable, access-all-areas, pit pass for the night.

There's not long before the meeting will start, so the preparations of both sets of riders are already very well advanced. On the visitor's side of the pits the 'Two Daves' are conspicuously in charge, promoter Pavitt and manager Croucher; they stand together and survey their riders who presently busy themselves with last-minute adjustments. The ebullient Dave Croucher is much happier with the team's recent form, which has recovered from the early season "stumbling block" of Jason Doyle's injury. With a consistent team line up comes form with the result that, "our boys are dialled in at our place now". He expects the Islanders will run the Racers close at Smallmead but doesn't publicly expect victory, though he also rather disarmingly stresses, "this really doesn't matter much anymore". The only absentee tonight is Steen Jensen who has his broken right hand in plaster, but has come along to Reading to offer the team help and moral support. The Islanders will operate the dreaded 'rider replacement' for the injured Steen, which, Dave believes, still leaves any astute manager with

many tactical options to explore and exploit, especially since Steen was programmed to ride at number 2.[1] Over by the pit gate, Pat Bliss has finally broken clear of her office with all the paperwork, hassles and administrative duties that this inevitably brings her way on race night. She still looks remarkably stressed but, instead, I compliment her on her smart look tonight, "oh, I always dress up for meetings". Not that her sartorial elegance is of any real help with the electrical problems that they repeatedly continue to experience at the track. Last time I visited Smallmead, there were severe problems with the water and equipment that steadfastly defied repair. Today it's an electrician that has been here all day without success. It's the second week of electrical problems for the club, though this week it's much more serious, "last week it was the green light not working, this week it's the red". In a nutshell, at the last meeting it was hard to start the race, whereas this week it will be hard to stop a race! It's a situation that has even greater implications for rider safety, should one of them fall or crash and require the race to be stopped. Pat bustles away to try to find a resolution to the situation.

Tonight's match official is the legendary Frank Ebdon, who officiated the last time I visited Smallmead and I encountered him later outside the stadium when his deluxe motor badly cut me up on the approach road to the M4 roundabout, as he hurried to get away from the stadium, after a protracted meeting, without due consideration for other road users. I'm not sure if he, or his driver, has again driven like Toad from *Wind in the Willows* on his journey to the stadium tonight, but Frank has dressed in an executive manner with jacket, collared shirt and trademark "modest, slim handle-less document case (£4.99)". His approach to meetings he officiates at remains resolutely 'old school', but consultative. As usual, he calls all the riders and team managers together for an impromptu briefing in the pits, just 10 minutes before the 7.30 p.m. start time. He stands on the edge of this large group and I witness first hand his exaggerated schoolmasterly manner and wry humour of his monologue to the intently listening assembled teams. "Tonight we have a problem, apart from me being the referee, the red lights aren't working properly on the first bend [waves arm expansively in the direction of Reading Town centre] so we've got eight red-flag marshals instead. So do expect to see them waving a flag!" There are bemused looks all round among the riders and, just like as if they were all still at school, nobody says a thing. There's not even a murmur, as Frank pauses for further effect and to let it all sink in for a few moments, "right, does anyone have a problem with that?" After a further silent pause and a few nodded heads, "if anyone does have a problem please speak to me now or on the phone later, thank you". With the talk over Frank strides away with a patrician almost military bearing – head held high, shoulders back and apparently aloof – at military medium pace back onto the track towards the referee's box perched above the grandstand. The riders disperse and chat among themselves about almost everything but the red-flag wavers. Matej Zagar doesn't talk to his team-mates but immediately returns to his section of the home team pits and gets back to his extensive warm-up exercises for the meeting; which involves him in a rather gymnastic range of exaggerated callisthenics as well as some elaborate stretching exercises that also look frighteningly energetic. At the other end of the exercise spectrum, Dave Croucher overlooks him from the hillock by the pits with a look of bemused puzzlement on his face. It turns out, though, that this isn't surprise at the intensity of Zagar's exercise regime, but a much more mundane matter because he turns to me, holds out his wrist and asks, "Is my watch fast?" The riders are soon all back together in a group, when they climb onto the waiting truck to parade round the track in front of the fans on the sparsely populated terraces and grandstand. As always, the riders are serenaded to the strains of 'Monday, Monday' that inconsistently blares from the tannoy system, which itself is another item of equipment that invariably needs some TLC and attention.

No sooner has Frank Ebdon drawn the competitor's attention to them, when the red-flag marshals get an immediate test of their reactions and flag-waving skills, after Jason Doyle falls heavily on the apparently lightless first bend. In the re-run Doyle is second by well over a quarter of a lap, with Boyce further behind still, as Zagar wins with consummate ease and in celebration the tannoy crackles with the sounds of the Undertones 'Teenage Kicks'. Matej is so fresh faced that he looks like a teenager, although he's already 22. With the rare privilege to actually stand on the hillock by the pits to watch the racing, I'm intermittently joined throughout the fixture by a variety of the riders, mechanics, other guests and sponsors. Very noticeably, the only rider on both sides keen enough to closely study every single race that he doesn't ride is Matej Zagar. He studies it with an intensity that leads you to think that Frank Ebdon will be checking his observational skills afterwards with an exam or, at least, a few penetrating questions. Zagar always stands on his own, usually in exactly the same spot, a narrow block on the edge of a sheer drop to the pit lane exit to the track, and stares out towards the start line. Already very tall, where he stands exaggerates his height still further, since he likes to utilise the time to either stretch, stand on his toes or drink repeatedly from his bottle of still water. He cuts a solitary and intense figure, much more concentrated rather than content. He only appears to speak to issue instructions to his mechanics throughout the evening, rather than his team-mates, and very much keeps himself to himself.

In contrast the injured Steen Jensen is happy to chat inconsequentially about anything to those near him. In fact, he's only ever briefly there as he continually rushes back down the steep steps to the far side of the pits where the Islanders are based, to excitedly gather round the riders who are next due on to the track. I can only guess that he passes on last-minute words of advice, instruction or motivation. This also appears to be the role of captain Craig Boyce and co-promoter Dave Pavitt who, when he doesn't watch from the back of the hillock, cuts an imposing figure on the periphery of the pits before he occasionally darts forward for a few brief words with the riders. The other Dave (Croucher) spends the evening rushing about frenetically; as one minute he watches the race and the next he gesticulates wildly, points to the programme race card or issues final instructions in his trademark geezerish fashion.

After he became more familiar with the track during his additional 'rider replacement' first heat ride, Jason Doyle displays the tactical advantage Dave Croucher shrewdly alluded to, when he easily wins the next race with considerable aplomb. When you stand on the opposite side of the stadium almost for the first time in 30 years, you can't help but get a totally different perspective on the track and the stadium. The grandstand looks sort of quaint and appears crowded from this distance, though in reality I know that there will be considerable empty gaps in the seats. From this hillock in the pits, I also have a great view of the beautiful orangey red low moon that's visible behind the grandstand roof. Back on the track, in his keenness to extend the Islander's early lead, Ulrich Ostergaard inadvertently bursts through the tapes, is penalised by referee Ebdon and has to start 15 metres back. The stadium announcer is very philosophical about misfortunes that befall the opposition riders and notes, "going off 15 metres is the more exciting option, probably". The key word was definitely "probably" as Ostergaard trails in a comprehensive last position as a result of this additional handicap. The Racers take full advantage with a 5-1 heat advantage in that race which they repeat in the next race as well, to take an early 15-9 lead. It was an unusual race in itself since Zagar didn't win but, instead, contented himself by shepherding his less experienced team-mate, Richard Woolf, to victory.

With the lights problem among others, it's definitely an all-hands-to-the-pump kind of evening for the speedway club's staff and management. The announcer clearly relishes one aspect of the situation, as it applies to his fellow announcer Martyn Dore, who suffers ribald comments when he has to temporarily become a trackman for the evening. He's on duty directly in full view of the pits gate so we can see him clearly. He cuts an incongruous figure dressed like a referee in smart jacket, collared shirt, tie and trousers; something of a leap away from the usual boiler suit most track staff favour. Well disguised or not, there's a primal desire to take joy in another person's suffering. Schadenfreude is a basic human characteristic and flaw from which the all-too-human announcer definitely isn't exempt, "I'd just like to draw your attention to Mr Martyn Dore, stadium manager, on the third bend working up a sweat raking the track, oh, and just a reminder that there's no alcohol allowed on the centre green". The Isle of Wight 'Two Daves' both stand deep in conversation and ignore Martyn Dore's clear discomfort, while the announcer fills in the time that the track maintenance takes with some information about the fancy dress competition for all the children at next week's final meeting of the season at Smallmead.

When the meeting continues again, four of the next five heats are drawn. The only things of note are an "all Czech pairing for Reading" in heat 8, along with Zagar who wins his next by the proverbial mile; eventually the string of draws is relieved by a race that features Appleton and Simota for a Racers 5-1. The large points deficit provokes Dave Croucher to indulge his options under the present rules when he brings in Ostergaard for a tactical ride that results in a 3-5 race win for the Islanders to slightly narrow their points gap with the Racers. The announcer has become almost joyous as he celebrates the Reading aggregate lead but this rule isn't one that meets his favour, "I've been watching speedway 43 years and the tactical ride rule is the most ridiculous I've ever seen!" Instead, he prefers to talk about a highlight of the final meeting next week, which will be the annual presentation of the RAFA (Royal Air Force Association) Trophy to the rider of the season. There's an illustrious list of previous winners that reads like a role call of the Reading Racers' favourite sons. "Per, Armando, Shaun Moran, Jan, Jeremy, Todd to name but a few" says Pat in her programme notes, while she rather contentiously misses some key riders and notable names from her brief list! In advance of next week's presentation, the announcer needs no second invitation to launch his 'we will fight them on the beaches' history mode for the younger listeners in the crowd, on the off chance there are some who listen, with a rabble rousing, "there's a collection for the RAF tonight, it's 60 years since VE Day and they've given 59 years' loyal service to their country since peace broke out!" It could almost bring a tear from your eye and money from your pocket, as well as a lesson in maths for the announcer, but before we become all misty eyed the racing resumes with another Boyce-Zagar clash in heat

11. It doesn't resume for long when the enthusiastic and aggressive riding Ostergaard falls heavily and is excluded from the re-run, though the announcer offers his "congratulations to Chris Johnson for the way he laid down his machine". That's as much involvement as Johnson gets in the race since, in the re-run, he's a virtual spectator stuck a long way at the back behind the other two riders. Boyce himself doesn't get that close to Zagar, after the first lap when he initially makes a lightning start from gate 4 to completely block Zagar's rush up the inside. It's only a temporary set back as Matej powers easily round the outside of Boyce as he enters turn three and streaks away for an easy win.

The next heat Woolf crashes painfully and is excluded besides spending some considerable time trapped beneath his fallen machine. Or, as the announcer would have it, "he's just emerging from under it, thankfully, so he'll be battered and hopefully not too bruised". Throughout each race Zagar stands beside me and watches – intense, impassive and completely expressionless – and only returns to the pits when he has to ride. In heat 13 he again beats Craig Boyce, who this time manages to hold the lead for one complete lap before Zagar bravely powers through an apparently non-existent gap by the fence to escape and win easily. Once again, the announcer's delight is without parallel.

No sooner has he completed a few wheelies on his celebratory lap, than Zagar dismounts and again stands next to me, drinks from his bottle of water while he waits and mentally prepares for the next race. Overcome with the exhilaration of the sheer brilliance of this latest manoeuvre and his riding in general, quite apart from the fact that he's my favourite Racers' rider of the last few years, I stupidly let my emotions run away with me. Well, only in that very guarded 'English way'; when I turn to enthusiastically address him directly with "that was an amazing ride again, Matej!" Maybe there's some etiquette here I'm not fully aware of or an invisible line that you're not allowed to cross? Whatever, Zagar just stares at me with undisguised contempt while he ostentatiously swishes water round in his mouth in a manner that would be viewed as over thorough even at the dentist. With his mouth thoroughly swished, Matej noisily spat this mouthful of water onto the floor before he very slowly averted his staring eyes from my face to pointedly resume staring at some invisible point on the far horizon across a track still devoid of riders.[2] I'm sure that Matej Zagar is lauded every time he sets foot into a speedway stadium and has to endure fans and sponsors that fawn over him like a superhero, just when he needs to concentrate fully and uninterruptedly. To excel in the brilliant manner he does on the track must require considerable preparation, concentration and focus. I'm sure even to try to speak was to transgress but it still seems slightly shocking and ignorantly impolite to behave in this manner without even a nod or a polite but dismissive 'thank you'. It's not the behaviour I've experienced when I visited his country or, I imagine but can't confirm, how his mother brought him up. Nor is it an attitude or approach that seems to exemplify the friendly and modest attitude of the majority of speedway riders within the sport. Luckily, I'm already a committed speedway fan as younger, more impressionable people might find this attitude would dampen their enthusiasm. Equally, they might also be more respectful of his workspace, and possible shyness, to a far greater extent than I was for that brief moment.[3]

From my perspective, as a long-time Reading Racers fan, the meeting closes in typical fashion when I watch an easy victory and large lead suddenly and disappointingly get frittered away by the home side. The Islanders take advantage of the announcer's pet hate once again, the tactical rules, and an engine failure for Zagar in the last heat finally enables Boyce

[2] I'm reminded of Jon Cook's prescient words, earlier in the season, when he talked about the fragility and dangers of the close access that speedway permits and that allows the fans get close to the riders. It's a relationship that can become tedious and lead the fans to be presumptuous and rudely invade the personal space of the riders. It has a cumulative impact upon the riders, and often makes them guarded and wary if not a little abrupt, so that "fans often take against riders for what are completely individual and personal reasons, when they've refused to give an autograph or been spoken to rudely, not knowing that the riders are often bothered all day every day, though it is part of the job".

[3] When I was 19, I sat next to a scruffy and unshaven Jack Nicholson at a Wimbledon tennis match on Court 1. After an hour or so of trying to pluck up the courage to say something I eventually blurted out, "you're Jack Nicholson, aren't you?" He slowly turned his head to face me and said, "freak off!" Because I was young and impressionable I almost immediately did what I was told and, in fairness, it was a day off when he was notionally a private person keen to relax. Matej Zagar appears to hold himself in similar high regard, without yet having displayed an Oscar-winning performance at the sport's highest level. I sincerely hope that Matej does achieve great things within speedway, since he is a prodigious talent and a delight to watch, but those few seconds completely shattered my regard for him as a person. I have subsequently heard rumours that he is known not to be a modest man, if you compare his attitude with his achievements so far within the sport.

to beat him. The meeting ends with a much narrower victory margin and a final score of 50-45, much closer than the ease and quality of the Racers superiority merited. Given how poorly Reading traditionally perform on their travels, even after the comparatively short distance to the very different Smallbrook stadium racetrack, this small margin doesn't bode well for the possibility of an aggregate victory.

Minutes after the riders return from their victory parade, Pat Bliss arrives through the pits gate with a very large wodge of the proverbial cash-filled brown envelopes beloved of crooked MPs and businessmen. She proceeds to dish them out to the riders before she rather assertively tells Matej that he should "get ready" to be presented with a flag from his loyal supporters and sponsors. The very obviously home-made flag, with his name on it in large letters and the traditional winged wheel of the Reading Racers team logo, arrives with its proud makers and owners excitedly in tow. With the meeting over and in the company of his young fans, a markedly different and diffident Matej briefly emerges; one who smiles and almost contentedly poses for photos and signs autographs on the centre green with his admirers. I watch this other Matej: warm natured; so easily courteous, charming and considerate. Pat also looks on in the manner of a proud parent who watches her offspring find their feet, confidence and métier, as Zagar holds the homemade flag as if it were a rare artefact or had the complex, crafted handiwork of the Bayeux tapestry. Pat praises his riding this evening to me, though she is pragmatic enough and has been in speedway long enough to identify his faults, "he'll have to improve his gating if he's going to make it at higher levels as he won't be able to come from the back like he does here!"

I leave Matej diffidently charming his admirers, to wander round to the away side of the pits. The area is almost empty of the visiting riders already. All the younger riders have packed away their bikes and equipment into their vans, all except for the veteran Craig Boyce who industriously works on both of his machines. Dave Pavitt glad hands some die-hard fans that have made their way round to the pits to survey the scene and exchange opinions. Since he's been round the houses a few times, Dave isn't one to get carried away with the result of one fixture and therefore contents himself with, when we speak, "it's turned out to be quite a good meeting, after all, I suppose".

19th September Reading v. Isle of Wight (Premier League) 50-45

Chapter 37: The Magic of the Island
20th September Isle of Wight v. Reading

"There's not a lot of people in the world of speedway of who you can say the older they get the braver they get." Gary Havelock (on Sam Ermolenko)

2.1 Exclusion: A penalty which may entail exclusion from a meeting, a race or a number of races or from its results of a competitor or machine.

There's something really delightful about sailing from Portsmouth to the Isle of Wight. It's another beautiful, bright and warm day. The sun lights the water and the contours of the Island in the distance as the ferry steams across the short distance from the mainland. Since I have sailed earlier than I expected, I have some time to kill while I wait for the special bus service that runs on race days from the bus station where the ferry lands. In fact when you arrive there, it appears that there's pretty well every type of land and sea vehicle near by; you can sail on a ferry, ride on the SeaCat, get a bus, train or taxi all within yards of each other. I decide to use Shanks' pony for a walk on the esplanade while I wait for the 'special' bus to turn up. For quite some time it appears that no fans will actually turn up for tonight's meeting either, since the bus station is very low on passengers and staff. It's noticeable that all the drivers lock their buses with alacrity and head straight for the old fashioned smoke-filled canteen for some well-deserved respite from the passengers. The few people there are at the station, all eventually end up in a queue at the kiosk-cum-newsagent that serves various ice creams. The most popular variety is the '99' ice cream cone, which the seaside holiday atmosphere of this part of the Island encourages,

and then people eat while they savour the late evening sunshine on the nearby seats. In fact, despite the sunshine, there's a real end of season feel about the place. The arrival of the next ferry provides enough fans to form a decent-sized queue of 10 or so people for the special bus. Since we're British, the chance to have a good but totally pointless queue is just too much temptation to resist. Silly really, as there's definitely no danger that we all won't fit on the rather worn-looking double-decker bus, which has "Special" advertised as its destination on the front sign above the driver.

In the queue the conversation is very much self-consciously macho. Despite the massive beer bellies, tight-fitting shirts and anoraks that most of the men favour, they all appear to have the illusion that they are irresistible to every woman. Luckily only a few of the local women are unfortunate to have to pass by at this time of the evening and, to a woman, all of them maturely and wisely ignore the suggestions about what they might like to do then or later. Though they don't look ideal relationship material and despite the fact that they have the physiques that suggest they would probably fail to muster an erection between the lot of them, all the blokes still delusionally compete to brazenly shout out graphic suggestions. After the potential object of their affections has walked purposefully and quickly away, the graphical content of their imaginations receives an even greater public airing. Maybe it's some form of therapy or a weekly but very public self-help class in sexual dysfunction. Fortunately, before the talk becomes too surreal, the bus driver arrives to unlock the bus and we can then all mostly go upstairs to wait for the next ferry to arrive. Without the distraction of the opposite sex walking by, talk turns to the perceived shortcomings of the typical Reading Racers fan. In an unironic inversion of received wisdom about the effects of too much time spent on the Island, the general consensus appears to suggest that the Berkshire area is rife with the various suspect types of family relationship that wouldn't meet the approval of the average *Daily Mail* reader. A consequence of this alleged behaviour is a severely reduced cognitive capacity that manifests itself in many characteristics and behavioural traits, not least among which is a fickle loyalty to the Reading speedway team.

Discussion also centres on the need to restrain themselves from critical comments when the Racers' fans actually arrive on the bus as well as the mode of transport that they will have chosen to get here. One hunk of man says, "careful the Reading fans'll soon be here — all four of them" to which his portly friend answers with lightning-quick repartee, "will they be coming in their own rowing boat?" Logically, obviously, this can't be the case as we sit here and wait for the ferry to arrive, but still it passes the time. As does filching a football chant and adapting it to "shit track, no fans!" This chant dies in the mouths like a strangulated scream when an impressively muscular Reading fan sneaks up the stairs from apparently nowhere and nonchalantly wanders to the back seat of the bus to relax. He's quickly joined by an assortment of men, children and lads of various ages, many who wear the Reading Racers' winged-wheel logo and insignias on their clothing or headgear; and who have, for once, apparently managed to leave their blood relatives back at their illegal campsite. A quick glance at the Racers' fans' physical features appears to confirm that only the superior specimens have been allowed to travel on this trip, since there's no telltale sixth fingers or knuckles that trail the floor among them. A keen speedway fan, David Wallis, sits next to me for the duration of the windy and hilly journey to the track, undertaken by the bus driver at a speed that indicates that he may be on a promise later back at the bus station. David's 67 and has followed speedway since he began to watch the Plymouth Devils in his native Devon in 1946. Since then he's moved around the country but has always followed speedway wherever he's lived, so consequently he's supported a catalogue of teams that include Wimbledon, Hackney, White City, Eastbourne and, for the last 12 years, Reading. David aims to see every single club in the country ride a home meeting each season, which means that beside watching the Racers he estimates that he watches around 80 fixtures a season. His current favourite track is Berwick but he's strongly predisposed to any venue that echoes or imitates the black shale and "solid wooden fencing" of his beloved Plymouth, "I feel at home at Berwick, like, but I like Exeter as well, like, with its iron girders for a fence too!" He's driven to all these meetings, by his equally fanatical son, Mark, from his home near Heathrow or "London Airport" as he quaintly still refers to it. Dave is quite pleased with Reading's form this season and feels that "we've gone up a notch" though he needs to be convinced that Matej Zagar is quite the finished article that so many people claim that he is already, "if he woke up at the start gate, he'd be good but at the standard he's riding to at the moment he should stay at Reading another year". David isn't confident about the result tonight except that he knows Reading will "definitely lose, probably by 10 to 15 points". Just as we get off the bus, right by the turnstiles to the stadium, other than his many memories, he mentions his special, unique and most irreplaceable speedway treasure: "I've still got my mother's and father's autograph book with over 2,000 photos and autographs in it".

There's actually quite a lot of Reading fans on this bus and in the queue the voluble Islanders fans of earlier are noticeably reticent in their opinions. In front of me is another old-stager, Buzz Terry, who is 77 and has followed teams in the south since 1947, previously he supported Southampton and then Poole but now he only has eyes for the Racers, who he expects might pull off a shock this evening.

Inside the Smallbrook stadium grounds, it's already crowded with less than 30 minutes to go before the tapes go up on the return fixture from last night. The track shop has its table outside and Dudley is there but can't really spare the time to talk, since there's a crowd of fans eager to handle if not buy the merchandise. I make my way round the grass banks of the first bend, then along behind the back of the main stand to the fenced-off pits area. Like at many speedway tracks, the fans have an enduring fascination and compulsion to watch the riders and mechanics prepare themselves and their equipment for the meeting. There's always a hint of a trip to the zoo about these spectacles, mainly because there's always some fencing, though, in a departure from the norm, it's the spectators and not the animals that cluster close to the fence desperate for attention. All the beasts that we've come to see studiously ignore us, except for when they emerge from the enclosure to retrieve something from their vans or to use the 'riders and officials toilet'. There's a slight feel of a scrap yard about this area of the stadium, since it's obviously been well used and there are random piles of old and superseded equipment whose actual use remains unknown. Preparations for the meeting are well advanced and Dave Pavitt strides about the place and ensures that the riders and mechanics have everything in hand for the meeting. He's kindly agreed to let me spend the evening in the pits or on the centre green. I have to sign in, for insurance purposes, like everyone else in a small hut by the edge of the pits area, adjacent to the access pathway that, in turn, leads to the pits gate and the track. The kindly older gentleman in charge remembers me from my only previous visit and again issues his standard words of advice when he warns me, "though you're insured, try not to get knocked down as it hurts".

I'm keen to get back out onto the centre green to experience the thrill of watching the races from there once again. The track looks particularly well watered and extremely grippy as I pick my way gingerly across it. The various mechanics wheel the bikes down to the start gate area and line them up in preparation for the riders' parade. I bump into Dave

Croucher, who waits by the start marshal's flags and bikes for the riders' parade and introduction to the healthy-sized crowd to start. We discuss last night's meeting at Smallmead and he's of the rather honest opinion that, "we were lucky to get eight points we shouldn't have due to their engine failures". This good fortune makes the likelihood of victory tonight that much more certain although the need to gain the aggregate bonus point is just as important. With rider replacement for Steen Jensen again "running at number 2" (his favoured tactical option), and the riders all "dialled in", he sounds pretty confident of victory. Particularly with the team captain and talismanic leader Craig Boyce who is so dominant at Smallbrook and where he regularly demonstrates that "he's still one of the best that there is". Dave, though, is much more preoccupied about the future prospects for the sport since Exeter and Hull will both close down, while his old stamping ground Wimbledon find themselves with dwindling crowds and financial trouble "with a 25 percent rent increase it will definitely close"; his lament that "we need more clubs not less" sounds really quite forlorn.

I base myself right by where the riders enter the first corner after they shoot from the starting gate. I still haven't got over the sheer speed and excitement of the sport when you watch from the centre green, so the fixture just can't start soon enough for me. To watch from the inside of the track is a completely different experience from the terraces. The racing appears much faster and dizzying, plus you're even more aware of the sheer nerve and bravery of the riders as they all arrive at high speed into the constricted area that is the first corner. The battle for position is really quite something to behold and I'm again privileged that the kindness of the Islanders' promotion has given me this fantastic opportunity. The first bend is the area that the Islanders' club photographer, David Valentine, prefers to stand at every week to take the best action shots of each meeting. Even after so many years on the centre green as a photographer, David has still got all the enthusiasm and respect for the skill of the riders and the joy in his appreciation of their riding still signals the continued presence of the long-time fan in him. He's also very knowledgeable about the riders, promoters and many others involved in speedway, so he knows much of the gossip, but sadly keeps it to himself.

Matej Zagar is introduced to the crowd in an end-of-an-era fashion, "it could be the last-ever Premier League meeting appearance for this superstar of the future". The various introductions are all pretty standard stuff; though Krister Marsh is introduced as "the females' favourite", as one by one the riders don their helmets, sit astride their bikes and ready themselves for a few quick practice laps. They each have a mechanic to push their bikes off to get the machines going. It's a process that's all part and parcel of the experience, for spectators and riders alike. It's one that I always relish no matter how many times I see it, since it provides a potent atmospheric mix that combines the anticipation, the noise of the bikes, and especially the smell of the fuel together. The track definitely looks very slippery tonight, which is confirmed when the very large mechanic with a beard who pushes Craig Boyce almost immediately struggles to remain on his feet, but still just about manages to do so, to the great disappointment of the jeering grandstand crowd.

Photographer David has seen many changes to the team and the overall facilities during his time at Smallbrook stadium. Something that has definitely changed dramatically is the surface of the track itself, though the improvement in this regard has been a mixed blessing because David believes, "we've lost home advantage since we got rid of the bumps on the back straight". According to him, Reading's Andrew Appleton used to ride extremely well at Smallbrook due to his "long track experience with bumpy surfaces which worked well here, but he'll struggle tonight now it's smoother". Another obstacle tonight will be the impact of the slowly changing seasons, with the peculiar climactic conditions of the early autumn a significant factor at Smallbrook as it always affects the track surface at this point in the campaign. While the riders come to the start line as 'Born to be Wild' plays in the background, David explains, "we have the dew coming through the surface which will keep it wet all night, it'll be sticky and wet making passing difficult once someone's made the gate".

It's difficult to establish the truth of this statement on the basis of heat 1 alone. In this race Zagar gates quickly to block Boyce on the first corner before he easily pulls away at great speed to win by a country mile in a race time that's only 0.1 seconds away from equalling the track record of 67.7 seconds, jointly held by Krister Marsh and Craig Boyce. We both stand transfixed on the first corner bend, where the sheer speed of the riders looks enormous as they flash past. This happens even during heat 2, the reserves race between the notionally slowest and least experienced of the riders. Though this race does appear to bear out David's contention that whoever gates first will most likely win on tonight's wet and sticky track surface. The Islanders' pair of Phillips and Doyle win very comfortably, though the race for third place between Reading team-mates Jones and Johnson provides some last-gasp excitement. They're so close on the line that, without a photo finish, the referee has to decide the final race order and, more importantly to them, who actually earns the points money for third place. David's 'no overtaking at this time of year' theory appears to only have some limited validity until heat 3, when Ulrich Ostergaard rather magnificently overtakes the race leader, Reading's Mathieu Tresarrieu; when he skilfully uses his home track knowledge and track craft to go up the steep bank of the final bend to swoop past his victim. The announcer is delighted at the determination shown by Ostergaard for his victory ("Ulrich was having none of it") over Tresarrieu. The Frenchman is a comparative rarity within the sport, since British speedway hasn't historically seen many successful French riders. Despite the clichéd but apparently characteristic French national love of suicidal overtaking on the roads, in all forms of transport but particularly cars and on mopeds, this just hasn't managed to translate itself into success on the speedway track. The Tresarrieu family has quite a history on the Island with the elder brother Sebastien, who enjoyed some years here on the wide-open spaces of the banked Smallbrook circuit. Even Mathieu had ridden a few times for the Isle of Wight before he continued to pursue his racing career at Reading. The smoothness of the track did also appear to hamper Andrew Appleton who finished last in this race. Based on the evidence of my own eyes, David's other theory is much harder to verify; namely that to become a speedway rider, which therefore requires you to race bikes without brakes at breathtaking speed against other like minded individuals, incontrovertibly demonstrates, "you can't be the full shilling to do this!"

Another big difference tonight compared to my last visit is the pungent aroma that assails your nostrils on the centre green – the strong sulphuric smell of rotten eggs that wafts about the place. At first I'm sure that I've imagined the smell, but David confirms that it's the problematic drains at the stadium. I recall Dave Pavitt mentioned that sorting the drains was on his list of tasks to do at the stadium, but was presently held up by administrative red tape for which he held the council completely responsible. It definitely needs attention too, since it's enough to make your hair curl and is another, albeit very minor, unexpected hazard that the riders encounter when they race here. David warns that I should also look out for the low-lying mist that can start to fog up the final corner during the early autumn evenings. I've never seen speedway riders race in light fog, let alone the predicted "fog that always comes in on bend 3", so it would be another first (In a year of firsts) during this season of visits to all the various tracks around the country. The next heat provides the opportunity to witness another flawless exhibition of high-speed skill from Zagar, who wins so easily that he can slacken off on the final lap without danger from the chasing pair of home riders. It's a drawn heat, which takes the cumulative score to 15-9 and retains the Islanders' initial comfortable lead.

This comfortable margin and the confidence it instils immediately goes out of the window when Simota and Appleton combine to win easily, ahead of Ostergaard. The race after only gets as far as the entry for the first bend turn when Boyce falls, just as all four riders arrive at the same point simultaneously. The referee excludes him and does not declare the incident as the usual 'first bend bunching'. It's not a popular decision by referee Jim McGregor, and Boyce and the home supporters in the crowd greet it with a mixture of derision, disbelief and visible incredulity. It is also a disappointing decision for neutral and partisan spectators alike, since it instantly deprives us of the evening's next exciting instalment of the Boyce-Zagar saga. From my centre-green vantage point on the first bend, I get a ringside view of the incident, which appears just to be a normal racing occurrence. Throughout both my visits I've been constantly amazed that more riders don't get thrown from their machines when they enter the corner at speed together. Predictably enough, Zagar wins the re-run with some ease, and with Jones taking third place the race score of 2-4 levels the overall score at 18-all. This excites the fans, especially the visiting Reading Racers' ones, but I've realised during the writing of this book that the score is almost completely unimportant to the riders. They are, obviously, interested in the points they score individually in each race because they get paid per point won. This issue of the cumulative or overall score is comparatively of negligible interest to them in comparison to the pound in their pocket. Stirred into remedial action, the Isle of Wight riders bang in consecutive 5-1s in the next two races to extend their lead back to expected proportions at 28-20.

During these heats I have watched proceedings across from the start line where I chat with the very affable and extremely sprightly Roy Collins. He wears many hats at the speedway club, since he's "one of the directors – technically the commercial director"; he also has charge of car parking and tonight he's also temporary clerk of the course. When I'd rung the afternoon previously, Roy had answered the phone at the club but had omitted to mention his additional responsibilities as a part-time telephonist among his extensive list of influential duties. I point out the prominent 'Ryde Barber Shop' sign on the grandstand and remark that there can't be many barbers who sponsor speedway clubs throughout the UK! (Though Mildenhall spring to mind) Roy believes that trying to drum up sponsorship for a speedway club is an unenviable task, even when you have strong local connections or loyalty towards a club. As a case in point, at the Island they'd had a "young lady who did well attracting sponsors but not enough to keep her on – what she didn't know, that I did, is that 50 percent of people hate motorbikes so it's hard to start with!" Our conversation is cut short when we both become dimly aware of the announcer saying on the tannoy, "the ref is calling Roy, the ref is calling – will someone get a message to him out there?" In fact the hotline phone by us at the starting gate hadn't rung but Roy swung effortlessly back into action.

Shortly afterwards it's the interval and the photographer David takes me under his wing, "shall I show you where the tea and cakes are?" It's a welcome suggestion since it's distinctly very cool on the centre green, if not almost very parky. Good as his word, David then leads me across the congealing thick mud of the damp track, steps over the kickboard through a tiny gap in the safety fence by the start gate, and then up through the fans in the grandstand to the hidey hole that is the secret canteen. To be exact, it's "Doreen's Teashop for Riders and Track staff", or that's how it's described on the sign above the small kitchenette serving area, where a lady already industriously serves drinks to a large crowd of track staff. I imagine the "Riders and Track staff" bit of the sign is mentioned both as a badge of pride – it's spotlessly clean, which isn't the norm at speedway tracks, but is among ladies of a certain age – and as a reason not to serve stray members of the public who wander in and might expect to be served. Maybe it's the cramped size of the room, but there appears to be more track staff in to have their tea and cakes than I saw at work outside just a few moments earlier. During the short walk there, David's descriptions of the homemade cakes at Doreen's made me salivate, but my taste buds remained unslaked as everyone else had arrived early enough to decimate whatever selection there was on offer. To judge by the gusto with which these cakes were eaten, they came in very large but extremely tasty varieties: chocolate sponge, ordinary sponge and many others. It was just like a childhood tea at a distant auntie's house, except we were at a speedway track. Everyone had settled down for a rest and was deep in conversation on the seats that lined the wall of the hut, with an air of long-standing familiarity, before I'd even managed to collect a scolding hot cup of tea. It was difficult to drink this in the time that remained before we were quickly summoned back to the action and the rakes, though I did have time to burn my tongue. It was a bargain, at 50p, and I'd relish the chance to sample the cakes in the future.

Back out on the track, the "fog" that David promised has materialised but only as a rather delicate, wispy mist easily picked out in the glare of the floodlights. It would disappoint any American visitors raised on a diet of images of bowler hats, pipes and pea-souper style fogs from the films of the late 1940s and 1950s. But then, if these images held true, we'd all still wear these hats and travel on steam trains with loud whistles. After the racing has resumed, Reading trail by eight points at 37-29, so they decide to enter Zagar in heat 12 as a tactical substitute. This means that he has to start the race 15 metres back from the other riders but that any points he scores count double. With such a handicap, it's an exciting spectacle to watch him race to attempt to catch up all that distance in an effort to win the race despite the poor odds; though if any rider can succeed in this challenge, Zagar with his present form looks most likely to. When the tapes fly up, Matej passes his team-mate Appleton easily, who subsequently manages his third last place in five rides, before he is held up sufficiently by Glen Phillips, so that this delay prevents him from catching the reputed ladies' favourite Krister Marsh. Zagar is out again in the next race where he, once again, beats Boyce and, with Simota who finishes third, Reading win 2-4 to narrow the score to 43-37. That leaves the aggregate scores delicately poised, with the Islanders just a single point ahead, with just the last two races to be completed.

It's widely acknowledged that the best plan, when you leave the Smallbrook stadium on the double-decker buses provided to take you to the penultimate ferry of the night, is to watch the last race from the upstairs window of the bus. Due to the tightness of the travel time and the staggered nature of the late-night sailing schedules, the riders have almost no sooner passed the finish line than the bus starts its engine and leaves at breakneck speed through the darkened winding streets. This overcomes, what is also unofficially common knowledge within the sport, the deliberately planned nature of the finish times at Smallbrook designed to maximise bar revenues. Later Dave admits, "we always try to finish after 9.30 p.m. so they can't get the 10 o'clock sailing and have to go to the bar". With this need for a quick getaway in mind, I've made my way to the other end of the centre green to the fourth bend from where I will watch heat 14. This gives me the chance to watch the penultimate race with the 'Two Daves' – Pavitt and Croucher – which to judge by their accents and choice of language is to be instantly transplanted from the streets of London to the green, open but misty spaces of the Island.

Heat 14 turns out to be one of those races that will be remembered for a long time, but not only because the match, aggregate result and therefore the destination of the league points still remains undecided. When the race eventually started satisfactorily, Ashley Jones fell as the riders jostled for prime position on the first corner. As he has for the last two nights, Ostergaard rides in a firm, confident and aggressive manner; though the net result of his style of riding in this race was his exclusion for "unfair riding" by the referee. It would be safe to say that this decision gasted the flabber of the 'Two Daves' and the air turned remarkably blue. Both Daves are no longer quite built for gazelle-like running and therefore resist the impulse to run back across the track, through the pit gate and up to the pits phone pretty damn quick to add their thoughts to the, no doubt, vigorous complaints of the team manager Martin 'Mad Dog' Newnham to the referee. The protests from the pits are to absolutely no avail, while I was left to marvel at what excellent eyesight both Daves possessed given the considerable distance we were from the incident. Dave Pavitt is mystified and nonplussed, "that's the freaking first exclusion I've seen for unfair riding this season". The riders eventually start to journey back out to the start line with Jason Doyle as the sole representative of the home side. The 'Two Daves' work themselves up, while they consider the full range of all the various possible scoring permutations in the last two races. I gather they're not that confident that their riders will manage to stop Zagar from winning the final race; so it's clear that a win or a second place is definitely vital for Jason Doyle in this race, if they're to retain a chance to win the aggregate bonus point. As mentioned earlier, most riders pay little continuous attention to the match score during a meeting (and even less afterwards, except for the purposes of their pay!) but do usually know what is required of them individually in the heats that they race in. The realisation of this fact hits the two Daves simultaneously as Croucher shouts across the track to the gate marshal and to the other Dave "the whole freaking meeting rests on Doyley, does he know? Does he know?" Whether he does or doesn't, it's not possible to check this fact at this point since the riders make their way back to the tapes.

In the re-run Doyley and Tresarrieu indulge in four laps of very aggressive racing for second place. While Ashley Jones wins easily, the other two riders continually try to battle past the other with no quarter given on each corner or along the straights. Doyley eventually gets past Tresarrieu as he swoops up the final bend banking at great speed before he dramatically cuts down in front of the Frenchman. It's an effective and aggressive manoeuvre that gains Doyley the vital second place. With the race over, it's also time for me to rush from the centre green via the pits gate as soon as the riders have left the track. Tonight, however, I'm unable to do so since feelings run extremely high and tempers fray almost immediately when Doyle and Tresarrieu decide to carry on with their confrontation by the pits gate. If it were a boxing match, then the two riders would have been difficult to split in a points decision. With the enthusiastic intervention of many other assorted personnel from the pits, though it very quickly became difficult to establish who was doing what to whom or, indeed, who was trying to fight and who was trying to stop it. Many tempers were lost and punches thrown. Some were, without any noticeable success, trying to hold the angry riders apart. Fights at speedway often appear faintly ridiculous, particularly while you still wear your crash helmet, never mind you are astride your bike or trying to dismount. It definitely restricts the chance to land any meaningful or effective punches, since your choices are only really limited to the visor area through the open-fronted part of the helmet. Like the claim that wrestling matches are fixed or that physics proves that fights on ice skates at ice hockey matches are all show and no power, it's an opinion you keep to yourself in case these 'facts' turn out to be inaccurate. In fact, I decided that to observe the ruckus was the more sensible option than to try to pass at its height in order to ensure I caught the bus. By now, I had become used to fights at the speedway – it was my third or fourth of the season so far, which just depends on how you count the two separate incidents at Newcastle. Not that I had become inured to these, but, with helmets still worn, this fight didn't have the ferocity and brutality of the affair that involved the man mountain that was the Wolverhampton security man. Nonetheless it was serious, hostile and lengthy enough to bring referee Jim McGregor scurrying from the security of his box to the Wild West frontier that was the pits gate area. He's a no-nonsense kind of chap, albeit in a slightly Mr Mackay (chief prison warden from *Porridge*) type way. He asserts his authority on the spot, when he immediately and dramatically throws both riders out of the meeting, fines them both £150 and loudly informs all and sundry that he will report the incident to the SCB. Woo, woo. There is also a school of thought that says that admonishments afterwards are always a bit like childhood threats from the Sunday School teacher to discuss your errant behaviour with your parents at an unspecified date in the future. I'm sure that the SCB will have their all-purpose carpet ready to immediately sweep the incident under and use the standard denial that the matter was fully dealt with by the referee on the night. The widely acknowledged public image of the 'light touch' of their governance will doubtless be further confirmed in a conspicuous lack of public statements on the matter and its resolution.

Whatever the effectiveness of the punishment, it's safe to say that neither rider would have featured in the nominated final race, but the referee, on principle, has to be seen to be doing something to subsequently re-assert his authority. It's also safe to say, preferably from a considerable distance, that things really kicked off disgracefully, in a big way, for a minute or two. It doesn't reflect well on the oft-mentioned family credentials of the sport or the mentality and actions of some people involved at speedway, who were only too keen to get involved in the fight or any fight. The riders could, perhaps, be excused for their age and for getting caught up in the drama of the situation after their adrenalin was pumped up by the events of the race. The same can't be said of the bystanders who got thoroughly involved and indulged themselves with more than a few thrown punches. I have to admit that I had a ringside view of the whole thing and wouldn't usually have seen things so clearly from the grandstand. Given the comparatively small number of fans at the meeting, perhaps the long-term repercussions and general damage to the sports reputation isn't that significant. Nonetheless, it's speedway racing we're here to watch, not boxing and wrestling.

With the fracas over but with feelings still running very high, I leave the pits and run round to the double-decker bus, where I luckily get one of the few upstairs seats that remain with a good view of the track for the last race. In fact, on a freezing cold day, it would be an ideal raised vantage point, especially since, once inside the bus, you're positioned on the apex of the bend with an uninterrupted view of the riders as they race from the start line into and round the bend. It's also reassuring to know that we'll probably make the SeaCat sailing, although the driver appears keen to worry us that he might have to leave before the race starts because he repeatedly revs the engine. What you gain in perspective from the height of this view, you definitely lose out on the atmosphere created by the noise of the engines and the smell of the bikes. However, the bus buzzes with the drama of the events of the meeting, particularly the previous heat, the subsequent fight and various opinions on the likely result of the last race.

The tapes rise and Zagar picks this race to resume his renowned habit of slow starts from the outside gate position. Next to him and on his inside, from gate 3, is Craig Boyce; who has endured two nights of being thoroughly beaten and outclassed by Zagar. By all accounts a proud man, a patriotic Australian as well as one noted for his committed or some would say 'hard riding', Boyce finds himself ahead and on the inside of Zagar. Predictably, as he has done repeatedly all season after slow starts, Zagar accelerates and attempts to regain the lead by passing round the outside of his opponent. Boyce waits his moment, until Zagar is committed, parallel with him and at speed, to then deliberately guide him into the fence. I could say brutally put him in the fence, but I can't guess Boyce's intentions and this is only the way it appeared to me (and most other people on the bus if gauged by their reaction). The thump into the fence by Zagar is dramatic; though there is sometimes a tradition in speedway of the older, more experienced riders teaching the younger more naïve riders a lesson in manners, track craft and etiquette by choosing to introduce them, at some point, to a taste of the fencing or the shale. In my opinion, as I sit directly adjacent to the incident and therefore I am far better placed than the referee some considerable distance away in his box, it appeared that Boyce 'fenced' Zagar deliberately. To my mind, for this action, he should have been excluded from the re-run of the race. But, this is only an opinion and the only important decision-maker, the referee, gives him the benefit of the doubt. Or, more likely, according to some on the bus, since the official was already put off his stride by the fight and his subsequent disciplinarian reaction to it; he thereby wished to avoid further controversy and so took the safe option when he declared 'an unsatisfactory start' with 'all four back'. The entry to the second bend is some way from the start line and a very unusual location to ascribe the often-used reason for a re-run of 'first bend bunching'. However, these things are all in the eye of the beholder. One person's "dirty riding" is another person's "hard but fair riding"; just as an alcoholic is just someone who drinks the same amount as you, but that you don't like. I must stress on the basis of his constancy and effort that I'd like to have Craig Boyce ride for my team any day. Though I also remember that Boycie has already had some involvement in controversy, when he had a riding 'incident' with Stoney at Workington earlier in the season that provoked strongly differing opinions. Still, as they often say when nothing else can quite cover it, "that's speedway!"

After he stays down for some considerable time, Zagar gingerly gets back to his feet and goes back to the pits to join his wrecked machine. The bus buzzes with excited conversation and then echoes to the sound of loud shushing when some people try to continue to talk throughout the race. In the re-run, Reading can still win the bonus point if Zagar shows his usual form. However, the incident appears to have had the desired psychological effect, since Zagar has learnt his lesson and merely just goes through the motions to finish in third place and so avoids any further unnecessary contact with the safety fence or Boyce. It's taken two whole nights and many races between them but Boycie has given his own very clear message to Zagar that I'm sure will form part of his continuing education as a rider. Just as the race ends and Boyce starts to celebrate his team's victory, the bus pulls out from the car park and proceeds to hammer along the roads at great speed, as though the driver is really a frustrated rally driver who likes to take the chance to occasionally practise by racing double-deckers through some quiet residential streets at night.

The many Reading fans on the bus are pretty subdued and when we arrive back at the combined bus station, railway station and ferry terminal, there's only a few minutes left to make the connection and get on the SeaCat in time for its final sailing of the evening. The more regular punters eschew the wait for the train and instead walk at speed down the wood-floored road that takes you to the terminal. I accidentally find myself at the front of the queue when the gates open for embarkation, so I take the chance to rush to the front seats of the SeaCat to look out the windows. It's a pretty pointless decision as I'm not exactly going to see a tremendous amount in the near pitch darkness of the harbour, never mind the complete darkness of the crossing. Two Reading fans occupy the seats next to me. It's the traditional speedway combination of fans – the pensioner with his grandson. I know that I'd have been excited just to travel to an away meeting, let alone one with a complicated journey that involved a car, bus, ferry and a type of passenger speedboat all just to watch a speedway fixture. I fall into casual conversation with John "they call me Jesse James" about the evening's events and speedway in general. Eventually our talk turns to why I supported Reading as a teenager and, therefore, where I come from originally. It turns out it's a small world since I come from Tadley and he comes from the nearby village of Pamber Heath, where his dad used to be the blacksmith, though he now lives nearby in Bramley. He'd first started to watch speedway in 1946 when he used to cycle to California[1] from Tadley. Further conversation establishes that he worked locally all his life in the atomic weapons facility at Aldermaston, so it's vaguely likely he might know my parents who also both worked there, though along with thousands of others.

---

[1] California is a hamlet in the parish of Finchampstead in Berkshire approximately 2 miles south of Wokingham. Best known for its Country Park. It was once a famous holiday camp, complete with glass-floored pavilion and speedway racetrack. Tadley to California about a 15 mile cycle ride.

Jesse asks me, "Where did your dad work?"

"He used to work in the active areas, A14 I think."

"So did I – what's his name?"

"Alan Scott."

"No, you're not Alan Scott's son. No, you look nothing like him (I do). We worked together for years in A14.10 yard; he often mentioned football and Sunderland but we never spoke about the speedway. Well I never, what a really small world!"

His grandson looks on nonplussed as we almost journey down memory lane by discussing the peculiarity of coincidence, but not much about Aldermaston since, like my dad too, he always says "I signed the Official Secrets Act so I can't talk about it". It might be exciting secret agent stuff or maybe that's just the glamour and mystery it held as a child. While the reality was probably altogether more mundane for any adult who worked at Aldermaston, since it probably just remained plain old demanding and dangerous manual work within an added possible nuclear radiation-poisoning context. Speedway would have been a relief from all that, not that my dad was interested since he much preferred golf to properly escape. Jesse walks on the gangplank and off the boat as he holds his grandson's hand to complete the final leg of their journey to the other end of Hampshire. I think we're both a little stunned as we go our separate ways.

20th September Isle of Wight v. Reading (Premier League) 50-42

"And Elvis has just left the building" David Norris

15.8 The referee only is empowered to stop a race.
15.8.1 It is an offence for a competitor failing to observe the "stop" signal.

From all that I'd heard when I travelled to other tracks around the country, I didn't exactly look forward to my trip to Sittingbourne Speedway Club. People had disparaged the facilities and the welcome that you supposedly encounter at this club. I had tried to visit the club in July but this was during a period when they had often struggled to run their home fixtures. I'd received a voicemail message from long-time track owner, Graham Arnold, who said that the fixture in question had been postponed, primarily due to a lack of the staff needed to do all the organisational tasks required on a race day. When I set off from Brighton, to visit the last unique league track in the country that I had yet to watch a fixture at for the purposes of my book, I was cheered by the prospect of a double dose of racing that afternoon. The home fixture pile up from earlier in the season meant that the Sittingbourne Crusaders would race in the Conference League, first against the Armadale 'Dale' Devils and subsequently against the Boston 'Barracuda' Braves. The Crusaders had yet to win a home fixture this season and, after they had already suffered almost equally terribly on their travels, they understandably found themselves firmly anchored to the bottom of the league table. Not that this would be of great concern to the Sittingbourne club members, since they primarily view themselves as a training track that exists to develop young riders rather than achieve short-term team or league success. Nonetheless, I still secretly hoped that I would actually witness the Crusaders ride to their first home victory that afternoon.

It depends on your point of view, whether the town of Sittingbourne is either, as the council would claim it to be, "a modern day market town with a sailing barge past history" or, an industrial town eight miles east of Gillingham. This part of North Kent, with its close proximity to the so-called Thames Gateway, always appears somewhat otherworldly to me when I visit the area. You have all those strange flat areas of land close to the water's edge that aren't quite farmland and aren't quite beach. In fact, you can find these salt marshes and their associated flatlands all along the coastline in this part of England, which thereby creates a peculiarly in-between landscape located eerily close to the water of the nearby Thames or the sea. The settlement of Sittingbourne has a rich and varied history that stretches back to medieval times when it was a regular staging post for pilgrims on their way to Canterbury. Technically the town is located beside the Roman Watling Street off a creek on the Swale, which itself separates the Isle of Sheppey from mainland Kent. After I got lost in the town centre, quite an achievement in a place so small, I then managed to miss the turning for the Old Gun Site – the home of the training track formerly known as Iwade Speedway but now known as Sittingbourne Speedway Club. While I was confused about my exact whereabouts I'd also luckily avoided a visit to the Sittingbourne branch of Sainsbury's, which is notorious locally for the manner in which it mysteriously disables your car's central locking system or, at least, sends it haywire. The only significant landmarks to orient myself by were what I took to be a large canal and an even larger monument that was a partially finished white bridge, which dominated the skyline for miles beforehand, as I drove past the flat fields of the landscape that surrounds the town. Without adequate signposts, it appeared that you really did have to be a local resident to even find the speedway club.

With a new set of directions to the Old Gun Site from a kindly pensioner, who hadn't ever heard of the speedway despite the fact that he'd lived in the town all his life, I doubled back on myself, as directed, past one of the many relics of the area's recent military history. A relatively recent wartime past has left the countryside littered with fortified pillboxes, which used to form the outer perimeter of the military camp that for many years stood just outside Sittingbourne. Built to repel a German invasion that never materialised, or only really got as far as the Channel Islands, the area had been much more deeply affected by the loss of its menfolk, the 'lost generation', during the earlier 'Great War'. The memorial to the many dead from the town (and its near neighbour Milton Regis) was considerably renowned in historical circles.

Eventually, I head down Old Ferry Road, which eventually runs into a rough and ready road, at times almost like a dirt track, before it finally arrives at Sittingbourne Speedway fence. I then find myself in what appears to be a scrap yard in the making or the sort of place the *Daily Mail* would have you believe is an ideal location for an invasion of rapacious gypsies. Admittedly there are quite a few caravans but these have seen better days and are permanently located on this site. I park my car in a field that a helpful man on the other side of the impressive fence that surrounds the speedway stadium and its environs, assures me is the car park. Given my choice of wherever I would like to park within this completely empty field, I make the wrong choice and have to return almost immediately to remove my car to a location more suitable to the tight formation of parked cars that the attendants prefer and skilfully manage on race day. A sign belatedly advises drivers to 'Drive Carefully' as there's an uneven road surface, which even if you'd arrived in a 4-by-4 vehicle you'd definitely already have noticed! There's quite a crowd of men of a certain age already congregated inside the fence, who direct me circuitously to the entranceway track that leads towards the stadium buildings, the pits and I assume copious amounts of staff car parking. The man on the gate, dressed in woolly hat, fleece top and jeans, interrogates me about why I want to see Graham Arnold before he finally points in the direction of the buildings with instructions to specifically look for "an older man dressed in green overalls".

I search without success for Graham in a long hut-like building by the edge of the home straight that serves as the supporters' club and tearoom. Inside there are already some ladies and young helpers who have begun to lay out tables of supporters' club merchandise, a petition to 'Save Wimbledon Speedway' and some raffle tickets plus cold refreshments in the form of fizzy soft drinks and a good selection of sweets. The room has large windows that with the elevation of the building provide an excellent view across the track and the flat lands beyond. The track is surrounded by rather old-fashioned traditional white wooden safety fencing, still extremely effective in comparison to some of the more modern constructions you find in this country, held in place by metal posts surrounded by an impressive cushion of tyres. On the back straight, there are a couple of adverts that stand forlornly on their own and proclaim the merits of reading the local papers *The East Kent Gazette* and *The Faversham Times*. In the near distance you can see a large container vessel as it navigates its way along a narrow waterway that might be the Swale. Large electricity pylons stretch into the distance to the horizon, where a good number of flat-roofed factories belch out the copious quantities of smoke that you wouldn't usually associate with this apparently rural location. I imagine that these might be the famous cement manufacturing plants that this part of North Kent is known for throughout Europe, which are located here because of its geologically chalk-rich soil.

The track itself shows no hint of chalk but looks smooth and well kept although it appears that the start line and the finish line are, rather unusually, separate from each other. So not only is the meeting a double header but we get to see the riders race for four and 1/16th laps! When I head back outside, I notice that the stands on the home straight are empty, but are both constructed from scaffolding poles and planks with three tiers for the fans to perch on during the racing. The referees box is a multi-windowed affair modelled on a cross between a garden shed and greenhouse, located parallel to the finish line on top of a large blue metal container normally used for cargo shipments, but that here serves as a makeshift building. There's a crowd of men in the pits, mostly helpers it appears although there are a smattering of riders who attend to their bikes with the inevitable ritual, repeated everywhere, that involves much pre-meeting fiddling, general checks, fuelling and some vital last-minute tuning. Just as I give up hope that I will ever find Graham, he appears from nowhere (well, from grading the track), resplendent in faded lime green overalls offset with grey sleeves and the obligatory (brown) baseball cap beloved of track staff everywhere.

He's a man who looks to be in his late fifties with a tanned face, firm handshake and compact build. In his overalls, he has a look that appears to be a cross between *Top Gun* and the sensible attire favoured by paramedics, but not the St John Ambulance service, who seem congenitally unable to abandon their fluorescent jackets at any of the country's speedway tracks. He's a man with a dry wit, who is exceptionally dedicated to Sittingbourne Speedway. Graham spends many hours per week working at the track, in order to get all the maintenance done that the track requires. It's an unusual club in that not only do they field a Conference League team but they also run a motorcycle club for their members, who range in ages

between 5 and 70 years old. The training track is well known and even better used, which means that the level of maintenance it requires is significantly greater than that at many other tracks, irrespective of the Leagues they compete in. Familiarity might breed contempt, but in this case it contributes to the club's comparatively poor home record because many of the visiting riders have cut their teeth practicising in this corner of North Kent. Consequently, with the varied mix of users, Graham admits that he doesn't know how to properly prepare the track to suit all their requirements. He's definite that for this afternoon the "second meeting will be better than the first meeting when the track will be very slick". Although he heavily watered the track last night, early this morning, and just a few minutes ago, it's highly likely it will be dusty throughout for the riders and fans alike. Since the wind blows in the direction of the estuary, it means that those hardy spectators that stand on the back straight will get a liberal dose of dust all afternoon.

Graham will, most likely, give up or severely reduce his huge commitment to running the club at the end of 2005, since his general health and the discs in his back have begun to suffer from the long hours. Despite these hardships, voluntarily undertaken, he has really enjoyed his time serving the club and is very proud of the variety of people that the club caters to during the 140 days that it is open throughout the year. The challenge to run the speedway team is a huge responsibility and the additional demands placed on all the staff, because Sittingbourne have entered a team in the Conference League, has contributed to the prevalent sense of jadedness and a desire to reassess the future aims of the club. Graham waves his hands at the group of men who stand idly in the pits area and wryly notes, "we get hundreds of volunteers, we just don't get enough paying!" although, last week's meeting against the Stoke Spitfires was the first time that the club had recorded an actual loss when they have staged a league fixture.

The ethos of the Sittingbourne club coincides with what they view was the original intention and purpose of Conference League racing; namely, to give up-and-coming young riders the chance to practise and hone their skills during the white heat of racing and team competition. Sadly, some Conference teams have been prepared to fund a move away from the initial ethos of "one old hand and six novices" to more of a win-at-all-costs situation where "they're having to buy a winning team". Graham worries about Wimbledon since they're going to win the league but also have problems that threaten to curtail their involvement in the 2006 Conference League. "They'll have the trophy, but nowhere to parade it and no one to defend it in front of next season!" Many experienced riders, as self-employed people, have asked themselves "why race at the Premier League level when you can earn excellent money, if you score ten points every week against the kids at Conference level?" Each to their own approach though, since Graham believes that, irrespective of pay rates, the racing at Sittingbourne has been generally acknowledged to be "out of this world, we've had some cracking meetings even though we've always been on the receiving end all year". The club has helped develop the skills and potential of many young riders, although it's then struggled to retain them when they then get lured away by the higher wages offered by rival clubs. The club also has a problem with the motivation of some riders, notably Shane Colvin, "who's decided he ain't coming today" as he'd prefer to ride grass track. Graham has too many other things to get on with, so he suggests that I go back to the entrance gate and look for the man I met earlier in the woolly hat, Steve Ribbons, since he has many firmly held opinions.

Steve is still there to supervise arrivals and is, as Graham, suggested, a man who has considerable recent experience in speedway promotion and many strong and colourful opinions. He certainly doesn't disappoint throughout our discussion, which mostly involves Steve offering his opinions on the sport and its people. He has little regard for many contemporary promoters or, indeed, those within authority with positions of responsibility for the management of the sport in this country. Steve believes Peter Morrish, the man in charge of the administration and management of the present structure of the Conference League, does not adhere to the spirit or the letter of the original goals of it, namely to encourage rider development; but has instead fostered a situation where the present 'win at all costs' attitude has gradually come to prevail. He doesn't have a high opinion of other promoters – "most are chancers" – apparently due to a couple of negative personal experiences through his involvement in the return of speedway to both Rye House and Wimbledon. With Sittingbourne he hopes it will be third-time lucky and he intends that the difficult transition from a passionate fan on the terraces to a speedway promoter is, this time, successfully accomplished. He pointedly claims that "I was stitched up twice but the people here are decent and I'm not giving up".

Without any real invitation, Steve then launches into a passionate account of his involvement in a venture to restart Wimbledon at Plough Lane with Dave Croucher. The Dons have such a huge name within the history of the sport and the re-launch at Plough Lane attracted huge interest as well as first-night crowd of 3,500. The roar of speedway bikes was, once again, heard at a venue within the capital and Steve played an instrumental role with Dave Croucher in ensuring that this happened[1].

Though, for Steve, it didn't prove to be a case of 'once bitten, twice shy' when it came to his involvement in attempts to rejuvenate a defunct track. Next up for him was Rye House in Hoddesdon in Hertfordshire, which had one incarnation from 1977 until its closure in 1993. It's an area that Steve loves, not least because it's where he was "born and bred". He recalls that in 1998 he called a public meeting to discuss various ways to reconstitute the speedway club at Rye, "we were just a bunch of supporters and I use that term loosely". The club reopened initially as a motorcycle club based at Mildenhall before it explored the option of a complicated ground share agreement back in Hoddesdon. The supporters group then brought in Len Silver ("as a figurehead") for his promotional expertise and experience, both of which would be fully required to achieve their plan of laying down a track for a Monday night and then removing it immediately afterwards.

Again there was an unfortunate breakdown in relations, this time with Len Silver, after Steve had been instrumental in the resurrection of another defunct speedway club. I have redacted the majority of Steve's comments on the situation. When I put it to Steve that Len has an excellent reputation within the sport as well as a track record as an innovative promoter and investor in the facilities at Rye House Speedway, where he runs an excellent team at what is a well-respected club, he shrugs before he then gruffly notes, "I look on myself as an ideas man that's moved on".

If Steve spoke bluntly about his version of the events that led to the end of his involvement in the renaissance of speedway at Wimbledon and Rye House, he is equally forthright with his opinions with regard to contemporary British speedway. He

[1] After the inaugural meeting, there was a subsequent complicated dispute and fall out between Dave and Steve. I have redacted Steve's many comments but suffice it to say that they no longer exchange Christmas cards.

Chelsea (future lady World Champion) and Shannon Lee-Arnies. © Jeff Scott

Earnest discussions by the pits gate. © Jeff Scott

Adam Lowe and Scott Campos watch the racing. © Jeff Scott

believes that the current problems that afflict the sport are systemic and derived from the inadequacy of the strategic vision and supervision provided by the sport's governing authorities, particularly the BSPA and the SCB.

He readily acknowledges that his contention that "speedway as a whole is badly run" is a personal opinion and partially based on his own negative experiences when he opened a number of tracks. However, when doing this he found that "you're 100 percent on your own until you dig your first spade into the ground". Steve believes that the problems faced by new and existing tracks throughout the country are often broadly similar but, despite this, the BSPA provides "no expert advice to deal with spurious objections from local councils; especially as practically every council in the country is anti-speedway". He sincerely believes that the BSPA should try to pool its expertise and resources to ensure that would-be promoters or existing promoters could consult expert planning consultants, barristers or solicitors. To be fair, he notes, the BSPA have invested in medical expertise and that of skilled machine examiners. But Steve then highlights that skill in these peripheral activities doesn't help overcome various objections (planning, environmental etc.) or ensure any long-term ownership of the actual staging stadia infrastructure, unlike the outcomes that many other national sports associations in this country have managed to ensure over time. Instead the speedway authorities in the UK are content "for the sport to be parasitic", in the sense that it mostly survives utilising existing stadia that run dogs, stocks, soccer and other sports.

Steve believes if there had been strategic thinking and competent forward planning the BSPA could have, historically, invested financial resources to purchase stadia leases, as they became available, to thereby safeguard the sports continuity and its survival at existing venues. This would have resulted in the benefit of the actual ownership of some tangible assets for the sport to hold onto rather than follow the present strategy of primarily placing their "emphasis on the ownership of rider assets". To Steve's mind, this surely raises the sensible question of "would anyone in their right mind invest £50,000 in an asset that could break its leg tomorrow?"[2]

Our conversation has taken an unexpectedly frank and pessimistic turn. It's a perspective that Steve sincerely holds and the net result, he believes, is that speedway is a "sport not built on any solid foundations at all because everyone in this sport has something to hide!" Whether it's the non-publication of attendances or, at the highest level, the lack of transparency and independent verification when it comes to the articles of the association. Steve spoke about what he claims is the mystery that surrounds various important aspects of governance by the UK governing body before he fulminates and rails against many of the major and significant figures within our sport. I have redacted these since Steve offers nothing but his own view of his personal experiences within the sport and various other assertions to corroborate his claim that he represents, "the unheard view from the terraces, as it's where I'm from". Ultimately he bemoans the "veil of secrecy" that the ruthless pursuit of money in UK speedway engenders with many people "really just being in it for themselves as individuals". To step back from this welter of unsubstantiated allegations and if you look at it simply, Steve has alleged that speedway suffers from a lack of strategic vision that has, to choose one example, failed to ensure the development of an infrastructure at a stadia level. Which, when allied to a lack of transparency and the haphazard approach to continuity at the club level, makes it hard for the sport to plausibly substantiate its claims of professionalism to independent, outside organisations. He believes that this is particularly important when speedway seeks to attract significant interest from major UK sponsors and, thereby, hopefully increases the awareness of speedway among the general public for the long term benefit of the sport.

Steve much prefers the situation at Sittingbourne, the "true grassroots of the sport where the only person getting paid today is the referee", rather than attempt to track down and worry about where all the various revenues in the sport go. He is pragmatic enough to realise that it goes in part to the performers who make the sport what it is to watch, especially the star performers, as he acknowledges that "you've got to be a hard bastard to be a world champion". He then randomly identifies many past and present riders (names redacted) as "dour characters that knew the value of a quid".

It's a pretty unrelenting and critical perspective on the sport; in sharp contrast to practically everything else I've heard on my trip around every track in the country. I try to ignore for a few moments his continuing diatribe about the present "climate of fear" in the sport he believes that has been engendered by the deleterious impact of the pursuit of money on the sport. He also worries that there are many people who donate their time, effort and lives to the sport who do not realise that "someone somewhere is having a fortune". Whatever the reality of the situation, the disparity between "more and more people giving up so much for the sport" and the idea that "someone's having you over" very much angers Steve. He concedes that "maybe that's life" but won't let his disgruntlement rest as "the more I know the angrier I get".[3]

Quite a queue of cars have built up for the car park and some of the afternoon's riders have still to arrive, so it seems the best time to leave to meet some more of the other staff and fans who are already in the stadium. With a long queue of arrivals, Steve no longer has time to talk but I'm definite that he still has the inclination. He is clearly a passionate and committed man about speedway who has been deeply angered by the real or imagined slights that he's experienced in his attempts to make the transition from the terraces into the world of promotion. While I'm walking away but still in earshot, he mentions a catch phrase that I've never heard before but in many ways, brilliantly captures the modern reality of our sport at many clubs, "speedway is the sport of five hundreds – 500 people and 500 cc engines!"

Back at the nearby track, quite a crowd has developed in the open grandstands that line the perimeter of the track. Many people sit on the assorted garden furniture that they've brought with them for the purpose, while others stand around and talk in anticipation of the meeting that's just about to get underway. There's quite a queue at 'Leo's Snack Bar' that is housed in an odd-shaped van-cum-caravan with a personalised number plate (9159 PF) that defies any easy interpretation. They do a brisk trade at what, according to the sign at the front of the van, is an establishment that's very proud of its

---

[2] A number of brief investigative articles by accountant and Wimbledon fan Sue Jackson-Scott (no relation) in *The Voice: the Official Journal of the Friends of Speedway* (Issue 20 Spring 2006/Issue 21 Summer 2006) attempts to investigate the finances of the sports governing bodies. There was confusion over names but, nonetheless, this article raised more questions than it answered but immediately led Sue to her initial methodological question of "who really runs speedway in Great Britain? Is it the Speedway Control Bureau, the ACU or the British Speedway Promoters' Association?" When Sue looked at the BSPA, she found it to be "not registered in any way, either under its initials or its name" at Companies House. "On to the Speedway Control Board and yes, it's listed as the Speedway Control Board Limited, a private limited company, limited by guarantee with no share capital. This is exactly the type of organisation one would expect, all above board and open to public scrutiny, just how things should be. However, the last accounts noted as submitted were to 30th June 2003 and this company was dissolved on 17th May 2005. This was when a change of name was announced to Speedway Control Bureau, but this is not a company and no accounts are therefore submitted." This leads Sue to ask, "Who decided this change?" In the absence of accountability or other concrete evidence, Sue postulates "my belief is that everything is handed over to the BSPA with its self-appointed committee" which raises a further question for Sue "why close down a proper company and run behind closed doors?"

[3] Michael Payne, my editor, has a margin note here that says 'don't conspiracy theorists drive you nuts? Typically when what they don't know, only suspect or isn't true seems to fuel their anger'

culinary expertise 'You've tried the rest, now eat the best'. It's almost too much to resist, but since I brought my own sandwiches I do myself the favour of a trip to the track shop instead. It's located in a converted metal container and stocks all the usual paraphernalia, which includes numerous pin badges, pennants, adhesive stickers for the car or caravan and programme boards; but is notable for its large displays of a great many speedway items and memorabilia from years gone by. It's an obscurely located but veritable treasure trove for the interested speedway fan but, most unusually, it's run by the charming Sirirat and Kannika Batham. They are a very polite and demure mother and daughter from Thailand, transposed into this part of the Kent countryside and who've lived here for five years since Sirirat married an Englishman. The lucky man in question arrives shortly after I do, but then adamantly refuses to give his name, so he'll always have to remain the mysterious Mr Batham to me. Though he shouldn't be too hard to identify because he quickly then admits that he's been in the track-shop business for years but has in recent years, since 2000, taken a step back from the industry. He believes that it's all become too competitive, especially in comparison to the halcyon days when he used to compete with Alf Weedon for track-shop franchises. They fell out years ago over a disagreement about the Coventry track shop even though "he'd had the cream for years". Alf was upset by the promoter's decision to choose the rival but better financial offer from Mr Batham – "promoters always take the more money" – and they didn't speak for years; until Alf kindly reconciled them again when he got back in touch after the death of Mr Batham's first wife. The final straw that hastened his exit from the industry to this shop and his decision to no longer actively source new merchandise was, he claims, being "stitched up" over the King's Lynn and Peterborough track-shop franchises. This thereby prompted him to decide to liquidate his own stocks of his "superior quality" merchandise without thought of future replenishment. The roar of the bikes on the track for the first race allow me to make my excuses and reflect on the considerable difference between the warm friendliness of the ladies in his life and Mr Batham's barely suppressed anger at the track-shop world and even his apparent slight resentment at unexpected visitors to his shop.

I have time for a brief word with the affable speedway referee, Chris Durno, who will officiate at this afternoon's double-header meeting along with another colleague; a friendly female trainee referee called Christina Turnbull. She will look after the second meeting on her own later under the watchful tutelage and guidance of Mr Durno. It will be the first time she's ever officiated at a meeting and she looks forward to the chance to put her knowledge and the long hours of her studies into practice. Albeit that Christina also confesses that she now feels slightly apprehensive at the thought of the impending public scrutiny and examination of her capabilities. This is perfectly normal, as I know from when I watched Chris officiate at Coventry recently; he more or less rides every inch of the track in his mind. As a result he finds that his nerves and concentration becomes so intense that he mostly forgets to eat or drink for the duration of the meeting. As ever, Chris is a great enthusiast for all things to do with speedway – just to be at a meeting, in another location in the country and to savour the thrill to be at another venue – never mind that he truly enjoys his work as a referee. We can't really chat, since he has to rush back to the official's box perched high above the finish line with the start line to its right.

Sittingbourne and Armadale both will operate 'rider replacement' this afternoon and I quickly gather from the ferocity of the competitive racing that both teams are keen to enjoy a victory. The first heat is drawn and the passing riders already whip up clouds of fine dust from the track. It drifts away in slow motion on the wind towards the spectators who stand on the back straight. I've decided to stand on the grass area of the first bend with a crowd of other interested fans. The most notable and distinctive of these fans is a man, away to my right, who stands out like a sore thumb because he wears a brightly coloured jester's coxcomb along with a badge-encrusted Wimbledon scarf. I can't resist discovering some more about this unique figure and quickly confirm that he's a committed but recent Wimbledon fan called Mark Drewell. Although he's only supported them for the last few years, he's been well and truly bitten by the speedway bug to the extent that he follows the Dons at home, around the country whenever he can, and, out of curiosity, also tries to visit as many other teams' home tracks as he can manage. When he's not doing this or bending everyone's ear that stands close by to him about the need to sign the petition to try to help ensure Wimbledon's survival at Plough Lane, he works in the distribution department for Tesco in Weybridge. He's keen to inform me that "everywhere I go, my Wimbledon flag goes!" He proudly points to it, the distinctive Dons' red coloured flag with a yellow star, tied to the wire fence behind us, although the wind has already severely crumpled its shape. Because of this, he descends a small steep bank to ensure that it's unfurled correctly to show its full glory and I capture the moment with a photo of Mark as he proudly holds its edge. This small burst of concern for the flag attracts Mike Moseley with his camera from a nearby garden chair, who's here today to follow Boston's match and wears a blue tracksuit top that features their logo and name. He's also keen to have his photograph taken by the flag, since the Dons were originally his first love in speedway, after he began to watch Wimbledon at Plough Lane in 1958. He's been involved with speedway for many years as a fan, track-shop manager and author. When he's not watching racing or speaking in his capacity as the founder member of the Boston Branch of the Dons' Supporters Club, he regularly contributes his thoughts in the Berwick programme or supplies the statistics as co-author with the famously prolific speedway author Robert Bamford. He's a charming and courteous man with a wealth of stories. More disturbingly for me, since it highlights the very small world that is British speedway, Mike recognises me from my recent trip to King's Lynn as the budding author who has travelled to every UK track in the country, although I didn't actually meet him when I was there. However, before his knowledge spooks me too much, he admits that he did overhear my conversation with Jon Barber in the track shop about my book. But with this, we all rush away from the attractive Wimbledon flag to resume watching the close contest that's in progress on the track between the Crusaders and their initial visitors this afternoon, the Devils from Armadale.

When I return to the stand near the finish line, I begin to chat with the Lee-Amies family in the form of mother Helen and her three children Chelsea (12), Shannon (7) and the baby of the family, Mercedes. What great contemporary names they have! They've keenly followed the Crusaders' on-track exploits throughout the season and hope to finally see a home victory this afternoon. It certainly looks promising as a close contest between the two evenly matched sides fights itself out on the track before us. All of the riders seem dialled in and capable, while the heats crack along at a good pace under the watchful eyes of referee Chris Durno. The occasional 'wobblers' you anticipate at this level are almost completely absent, but the meeting is plagued with an epidemic of fallen riders and incidents. Although many riders remount, Chris Durno is ever vigilant, and he puts on the red stop light so often during the races that you begin to feel that you're at a nightclub. Heat 6 sees the retirement and subsequent withdrawal from the meeting of the Sittingbourne captain Chris Hunt; this is after Sean Stoddart found some dirt that accidentally accelerated his bike painfully into the side of Hunt. Sportingly Sean slowed to gesture an apology for this racing incident before he then continued on for a deserved race victory. Another of the fleet of different vehicles at the Sittingbourne Club made its way onto the track, in this case the ambulance, to remove the stricken Hunt. Earlier I'd noticed that Chris cut a slightly incongruous figure in the pits, since he's quite a large but nonetheless compact 41-year-old man, a very distinctive sight when you consider that he's completely surrounded by the other speedway riders who are, as you'd expect, all athletic, wiry and young enough to be his children.

Oblivious to everything but the racing, Chelsea intensely watches each race; though she is only happy to chat about speedway when the bikes idle in the pits, she is incredibly reluctant to have her photo taken. Chelsea is exceptionally well informed about the sport and likes everything about the Sittingbourne Crusaders Speedway Club, especially watching or when she can help out at the tables in the supporters' clubroom, where I'd noticed her earlier in the day. She's keen enough to have ridden a speedway bike since she was nine at the smaller training track they have specially out the back for this very purpose at the club. I walked past it earlier but it was deserted in favour of the racing on its larger version a few yards away. Chelsea becomes very animated when she talks about her riding and, since it's a gender-stereotyped world in the playground, she struggles to make the boys take her seriously or believe that she's really not lying about her skills on a speedway bike. As soon as they ride against her, they quickly revise their opinions when she "beats some of them". It's presently her main childhood obsession, hobby and leisure activity although she only modestly claims to be "sort of good at it". This is despite having recently won a trophy for her victory in a meeting against all the peers in her age group. I imagine the boys involved would no longer need any persuasion that she really "doesn't lie" when she says she "rides a speedway bike". When Chelsea is not enthralled with the races or loudly cheering the successes of the home riders, she confides to me that her ultimate ambition is "to be the first woman speedway world champion!" Apart from her pride in her own riding abilities she delights in the fact, and if she mentions it once she proudly mentions it numerous times, that her dad Stuart ("they call him Rat, everyone does") works at the track as a training instructor. That's when he's not driving past us in a specially adapted van, while he grades the track surface to broad, toothy smiles from his very proud daughter.

At the centre of another group of cheering kids on this stand is little Alex Baseby who, while only small and six, has a larger-than-life personality. He shoots about the place as if powered on his own high-octane fuel and is energetically everywhere at once. He's also here with his mum, Jackie, his younger brother James while his father, Paul, also helps out at the track with some of the building work and general maintenance. Even as we speak, according to his son Alex, he's doing something necessary or vital for the club, somewhere close by the stand. In fact Paul Baseby spent 20 years riding sidecar grasstrack, so bikes have always run in the family, but since his retirement in 1999, he's turned his attention to help his elder sons' attempt to succeed at speedway. Oblivious to family history, but absorbed by his interest in his brothers' riding for Sittingbourne, Alex proudly wears a Mark Baseby T-shirt. He's delighted every single time his eldest brother takes to the track for Sittingbourne. He unfailingly and doggedly answers "yes" to my endlessly repeated question as to whether that is really his brother riding. Alex is even more ecstatic when his other brother Aaron, already over six feet tall at 15, gets to ride in heat 11 with his elder brother Mark. Alex squeals with glee when Mark wins the race, while his mum repeatedly urges "go on, Mark" throughout; but the whole family seems frozen when Aaron falls heavily, remounts before he falls again, just to then be excluded by the referee for his troubles. It's been a real full-on Baseby experience for me and the club announcer is pretty keen on Mark Baseby too, since he urges the crowd on with a "let's hear it on the back straight for Mark Baseby". His word isn't law because there's only a rather half-hearted ripple of adulation. Jackie reiterates that her husband always rode grass track before and so, as a result, the whole family has always been "all very bike orientated". Jackie tries to be involved as much as possible too, except when she has to look after the little one at home, since she knows that for her husband Paul "it's his life really, it's their lives".

Jackie is reassured by the knowledge that Paul has taught the boys to ride intelligently and safely, to always "ride with their heads not the throttle". Consequently, because he's such a methodical person, he's a much calmer spectator than Jackie when either of his sons happens to fall during a race. Luckily his practical skills come into great use at home in Sevenoaks as well as at the track. When he's not building and maintaining the bikes, he instils in the boys the care and effort that they will need to compete successfully on a bike. Without his skill and dedication, the cost for both boys to compete would be prohibitively expensive rather than just "really expensive" as it presently is. When the boys don't ride they spend countless hours at work on the bikes. As the mother of teenage boys, Jackie is grateful for this since it keeps them away from some of the other more dangerous but familiar temptations of youth. Though she's quick to admit that, for her entire family, "speedway is like a drug, once you're involved you really like it and get hooked". The only recent problem has been the poor results on the track for Sittingbourne, which she blames on a lack of consistency in the make up of the team, "from one week to the next you don't know who's going to be riding". With four boys of her own, it's possible, at some point, that her family could even form a considerable part of some future Sittingbourne team. Jackie doesn't have time to discuss my fantasy of a future Baseby speedway dynasty; it's enough to just look after Alex and James in the stands never mind will her older sons (safely) to victory.

Back on the track, heat 11 represents the high point of the Sittingbourne effort from the point of view of their score. For the remainder of the races of this fixture the Crusaders gradually fall behind the superior efforts and experience of the Armadale riders. This tendency to fall away during the latter stages of a meeting has been a problem throughout the season, particularly because Sittingbourne don't have the strength at the top of the team that their rivals usually have at their disposal. The structure of any race meeting scorecard inevitably means that, in every speedway fixture, the 'strongest' riders from each team will compete in heat 13 and also usually in the nominated heat 15. The visiting Armadale team has the greater overall comparative strength and, in the form of Derek Sneddon, they have a top performer, who is a confident and fast rider who has previously had experience riding in the Premier League. He's used this experience well throughout the 2005 season for his Conference League club and, this afternoon, is no exception. My favourite Armadale rider, the extremely polite and conscientious Sean Stoddart, also rides excellently. Today he really appears to have further improved his speed, composure, riding style and track craft in the few months since I last saw him ride, and he looked very good then. This afternoon though, unlike last time, his mother and sister haven't made the long journey down from Scotland to the south to cheer him on. It's worth noting that excellent performances by Sittingbourne's top-scoring duo of Mark Baseby and Jordan Frampton still weren't enough overall to ensure the victory that would end Sittingbourne's record-breaking run of meeting losses.

There's only a brief interval between the afternoon's two consecutive fixtures. The spectators stretch their legs, purchase refreshments or chat among themselves; while the referees Chris and Christina depart from the eyrie of the officials' box for a quick look around the pits area. The first meeting was packed with incidents and there were four races awarded by Chris after riders had fallen. Sittingbourne is the last UK track where he had yet to officiate at as a referee. As a huge fan of the sport, he's typically delighted by what he's just witnessed, "what a fantastic meeting, I really enjoyed the racing and how close it was!" Christina admits to a few more butterflies and nervous excitement at her own imminent opportunity to completely control a meeting. But she's still relaxed enough to be able to take the mickey out of Chris's earlier officiating skills, "I'm sure that I can do better than running a meeting in two hours".

At the pits exit, an extremely hot-looking Sean Stoddart wheels his bike away to be loaded into his van before the team travels over to Oxford for a meeting the next night. I compliment him on his performance, which he's having none of, but prefers instead to concentrate on where he could still improve his skills further. He praises the track and the weather, especially since he much prefers to ride in warm and dry conditions rather than the wet or the very cold ones that the microclimate at his home track in Scotland usually provides. Finally when pressed further, with a shrug of his shoulders, he does admit that he feels he's improved. Basically, he explains that his approach is to ride as often as he can, in order to do well at the Conference league level, and thereby get more chances to ride as a guest reserve in the next tier of racing, the Premier League. Since I last saw him ride for Newcastle at that level, he proudly informs me that he's also had additional guest bookings at both Stoke and Glasgow. Like many riders but unlike many fans, he has no idea of his actual average, since he just tries to win and do his best each time he rides. Sean confides that if he's to succeed in his dream to become a successful rider then he has to choose between riding and his education at college. With some understatement he notes that, "it's difficult to study and ride" – the books keep falling off for one thing. Participation in the sport is extremely time intensive and "very expensive", so he needs to find work in other paid employment to enable him to "survive and compete". A short while later, after the obligatory mobile phone calls that all young riders appear compelled to make immediately after the finish of a meeting, I spot Sean in the crowd with the other Armadale riders, as they soak up the sunshine and watch the next meeting. My impression is that if dedication and commitment are the key ingredients to drive success in this sport, then Sean will definitely go very far! He'll be helped along the way in his career by his warm, friendly but refreshingly diffident manner, which compliments his parents and reflects well upon himself.

Since I am fortunate to have a pits pass, I decide to take advantage of the privileges it offers to watch the next meeting from the riders' viewing area, well, riders' hillock would be more accurate. From there, you get an excellent view of the peculiarly positioned start line and the adjacent pits area. It's crowded with riders, mechanics and parents who watch the meeting before they all rush back to attend to their bikes. Or, perhaps, to push their bikes out to the little ginnel where they patiently wait while the track clears of the previous heat's riders. I met the very pleasant and up-and-coming rider Simon Lambert on my visit to King's Lynn, and so it's a pleasant surprise when his father Stephen takes the trouble to go out of his way to introduce himself to me and wish me well with my book. When he's not dedicating a huge number of hours to help and support his son, he works for his own transport and warehousing company in Spalding. Stephen is keen to check on how much I have already written for this book and also points to the Boston team manager, Malcolm Vasey, who is on the track to provide some last-minute words of encouragement to Jeremy Pestell. Away from the track, Malcolm spends much time on research for his own book that he's writing on Boston speedway and speedway in East Anglia. I'm curious to read his books and talk with him about the work involved, but the pressure of his team management duties keep him fully occupied all afternoon.

Dust billows. © Jeff Scott

Urgent bike repairs. © Jeff Scott

Graham Arnold in action. © Jeff Scott

We all concentrate on the fixture at hand, and what a controversial and incident packed afternoon of racing it actually turns out to be. An exclusion, that immediately follows his fall in heat 2, causes the promising Jordan Frampton to return to the pits extremely angry with himself. Rather like a friend of mine whose son, Luther, fell so often she taught him to kiss himself better; Jordan motivates himself by giving himself a severe and loud telling off. After he has remonstrated with his alter ego for a good minute, he calmly watches the re-run of the race; which Mark Baseby wins, followed home by Boston's Scott Campos who confuses identification matters because he has 'Bird' emblazoned on his bottom, since he wears Danny Bird's old Euphony-sponsored kevlars in the Reading Racers' distinctive blue livery. Simon Lambert, to his dad's chagrin and disappointment, has an engine failure in his first race which helps Sittingbourne stretch their early lead to 15-9. The racing is competitive and often thrilling, especially the encounter between Darren Mallett and James Theobold in heat 6. They spend three exciting laps locked together, in handlebar-to-handlebar action, with only inches to separate them, before Mallet just wins on the line.

A Sittingbourne win still looks a possibility throughout most of the afternoon, especially when they hold an eight-point lead by the end of heat 9. However, the riders prefer to concentrate on the matters in hand, and both teams intently watch the races, while they cluster closely together in the bright August sunshine on their hillock. In the case of the announcer, he advertises the availability of the collector's item of ponchos with the Sittingbourne logo for £10 from the track shop or else he congratulates the crowd on their generosity in collecting £112 worth of donations for the speedway museum. Apart to confirm the race results, the announcer also reads out the Conference League table, albeit with the unnecessary caveat that "it doesn't make such good reading for ourselves". Throughout the afternoon Steve Ribbons energetically appears here, there and everywhere within the stadium – the pits, the terraces, and the centre green – living each moment of the racing with characteristic intensity and involvement. The exclusion of Mark Baseby in heat 11 irks him so much that he invades the track itself, to loudly shout his objections, with many accompanying arm gestures, to the referee perched above him in her box. I'm not sure what fines the referee has at her disposal for such comments, but I can't help but be struck by the lack of similar such vocal on track objections being directed towards male referees during my travels. Obviously, I'm not privy to conversations that team managers have on the phone with the referee, but Steve's reaction does appear both disproportionate and extremely chauvinistic.

As Boston draw level on 36 each, heat 13 sees controversy and anger reign throughout the ranks of the Sittingbourne riders and officials in the pits, on the track and centre green. These reactions definitely aren't motivated by latent sexism but are founded upon a strong sense of injustice and bluntly expressed doubts with regard to the referee's competence and understanding of the rules. I saw the disputed situation as follows – Sittingbourne's Dan Blake fell and Boston's Jeremy Pestell laid down his bike, which caused Sittingbourne's trackside flag marshals, *without* the referee's permission, to unfurl their red flags to signal that the race should stop. This was an instruction from the marshals that Sittingbourne's Andre Cross obeyed until he realised that Pestell had remounted to continue and that the race leader David McAllan had also resumed racing, after he initially slowed due to the signals of the flag marshals. However, because the referee did not stop the race by putting on the accepted signal of the red warning light, though technically the marshals reacted to ensure what they saw as rider safety, they crucially and erroneously acted without the referee's instruction or permission. The race time of 72.1 seconds was ten seconds slower than any other time throughout the day and reflected the confusion that the sincere use of these flags created. A wave of anger and annoyance then moved throughout the stadium among all the Sittingbourne riders, staff and supporters who were keen to dispute the fact that, rightly or wrongly, the referee always remains in charge of the meeting and his/her decision is final. The outcome of that contentious race also saw Boston take the lead for the first time during the meeting and then extend it for an easy victory in the remainder of the fixture.

The sense of injustice and disappointment still pervades the pits as I leave, although I linger by the home-straight grandstand to hear what the announcer suggests will be a special and pertinent announcement by Graham Arnold. While I wait, I listen close by to Steve Ribbons who is deep in earnest conversation with another Sittingbourne fan. He explains at length that other clubs' excessive payments have forced up costs and severely limit Sittingbourne's ability to attract or retain key riders. He acknowledges that it's only human nature for the riders, as self-employed workers, to try to maximise their earnings and to go where they'll be paid the most. In contradiction of his earlier claim to occupy the moral high ground, when he discussed this subject with me, Steve now says, "I'll stake up, if they do the business; but if they don't, I can't afford it, as we need crowds of one thousand here to do so". The fan listens to some more despairing comments on the spiraling costs of speedway at the Conference League level before he phlegmatically observes, "you'll have to have a good think about things over the winter, then". Seconds later Graham's voice is heard as it echoes laconically over the tannoy with his interpretation of the afternoon's major incident, "I never thought it would ever come to this, but after 11 years, I am for the first time going to have to lodge an official protest". He explains that he believes that the flag marshals have a duty and responsibility to always, where possible, ensure the health and safety of the riders and will, therefore, produce the red flags if their judgement dictates that they should do so. A rather peeved Graham continues, "as far as I am concerned, if a marshal puts out a red flag – even if by mistake – the race must be stopped!" It's always been a sport rich in opinions, drama and controversy but you can't help but think that Christina shouldn't expect to receive a Christmas card from Graham or any of the disgruntled Sittingbourne fans. If she passes her exams to become a qualified referee, when Christina next officiates here she can expect a warm welcome from the Sittingbourne management and staff.[4]

It was a shame that this one race should overshadow what was a superb advert for the sport as it is practised at any level of racing in this country. Sittingbourne is a track built and managed for many purposes other than just running speedway meetings. The people are very committed and take the time to be inclusive and friendly. Prior to my visit, others disparaged Sittingbourne as "just a training track" when, in my experience, it represents all that is good about the original hobbyist, 'make do and mend' roots of speedway in this country. It's a club with a vital part to play in the motorcycling community. A facility that provides valuable time on the track for people of all ages, from very young to 70, isn't something that many other clubs can boast they accomplish so successfully, if at all! The clouds of controversy in which the meeting ended and

[4] As a postscript to these events, a few weeks later I ran into Chris Durno who said that he couldn't agree with all of the opinions Graham gave out over the tannoy. He sympathised with Graham's point of view as well as his obvious disappointment at how some of the decisions might have contributed to the final result of the match, especially when the Sittingbourne team looked so close to gaining their first success of the season. However, he strongly disagreed with the Sittingbourne interpretation of the afternoon's events – for both meetings – as they appeared in the news section and the reports section of the *Speedway Star*. Chris stressed that while he might not have made all the decisions exactly like Christina did that afternoon "you have to admire her determination to stick to her guns once she'd made her decision as, under the rules, only she can make the decision to stop the race whether or not a red flag is shown".

Graham's comments made in genuine frustration shouldn't obscure the fundamental value and integrity of this club. It's a down-to-earth, come-as-you-are type of place, lovingly tended and cared for by its mostly indefatigable club chairman, Graham Arnold, along with a trusty cadre of willing helpers on and off the track. It's possibly an example of what it perhaps means to be part of a British community. A club with passion but without pretension, that welcomes all comers while it remains unafraid of disagreements through speaking bluntly or out of turn in the heat of the moment. Whether anyone really cares enough to copy this model, listen to their philosophy, give some of the more contentious remarks credence, or act upon any of these is altogether another matter.

25th September Sittingbourne v. Armadale (Conference League) 43-47
25th September Sittingbourne v. Boston (Conference League) 42-48

Chapter 39: The Sheer Power of the Thing
25th November Referee's Practice Day

SKY CHATTER

"If it's a green light I'm cheating" Billy Janniro

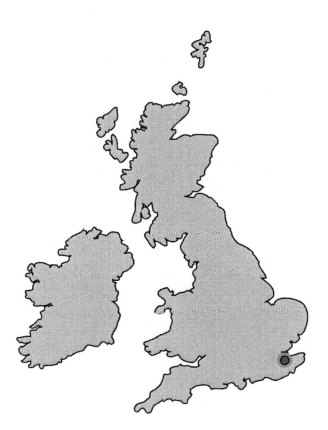

RANDOM SCB RULES

12.5 The part of the neck between the Helmet and the suit should be covered. Scarves or neckerchiefs must not trail so as to be a source of possible danger. Hair should be covered by the Helmet and suit.

The season has only been over for a few weeks and already going cold turkey from speedway can force me to drive considerable distances on a Sunday morning for just another quick fix. The chance to observe the men and women from behind the buttons in action would be pretty difficult to resist during the close season, but after some recent deprivation it's definitely irresistible. Plus, it's another chance for me to visit Sittingbourne – one of the country's loveliest clubs, quite an accolade in a sport packed with so many friendly and welcoming people at so many different venues.

I'd heard from Chris Durno about the referees' meeting, which is primarily to enable them to practise on full-sized speedway bikes and to get some experience of what the riders go through most nights of the week. He wasn't able to attend this year and was disappointed that he would not get on a bike once more, though not sad to avoid a painful reacquaintance with the Sittingbourne safety fence. Last year there had been a referees' meeting that had run to a Grand Prix format. The *Speedway Star* gave it excellent build-up publicity and the Speedway Riders Association was amongst

those who generously sponsored the event. Although the referees had much help and co-operation organising the event – they also learnt a great deal about the various aspects, hassles and occasional controversy inevitably involved in speedway promotion.

The meeting was covered as though it was a 'proper' speedway meeting with photos and a thorough match report in the *Speedway Star*. It attracted quite a crowd, eager to enjoy the refs' travails on a speedway bike and to raise money for charity. Though it was supposed to just be a bit of fun, it was inevitable that talk of a "Champion" and the fickle finger of fame and pride would add some zest to the races. In the first race to establish the first Champion Referee, Dale Entwhistle and Chris Durno got caught up together as they came into the bend. Dale found himself excluded by referee Paul Hurry – a definite case of gamekeeper turned poacher. As noted afterwards by Mr Sittingbourne, Graham Arnold, "it was a slow motion crash – with their inexperience they didn't know how to get out of trouble – it looked worse than it was but could have been avoided". It was a crash that Chris Durno well remembers since it left him to nurse rib and hand injuries for months afterwards. In true speedway tradition, Chris continued to ride in the event. Unfortunately, the eventual winner Gloucester-based Rob Smith won't be able to practise this morning because a burst pipe prevents him from leaving his house, so we will miss seeing his expertise on a bike.[1]

This year the meeting is deliberately a much more low-key affair and has received no public advertising, since it's a 'private' practice day just for the referees. Sittingbourne exists primarily as a club to develop the motorcycling abilities of riders of all ages, irrespective of gender, on the junior practice track and on their full-sized circuit. The referees have hired the facilities for the day, which includes race suits, bikes, appropriate insurances and the tuition for the day from the very experienced Paul Heller from the 'Fast Track Club'. He is a teacher with an excellent reputation and proven track record when it comes to the coaching and development of riders of all ages. A few days beforehand I call Graham to find out if it's okay that I come along and attend as well as to find out the details of the day's scheduled agenda. He informs me that the refs are all due to arrive around 10 a.m. to don their race suits and generally psyche themselves up. All the nervous novices will begin the day on the 125 cc bikes of the junior track so they can learn the basics of how to ride and control a speedway bike. They will hopefully master the difficult but essential art of how to slide a bike into the bends and, if the tutors think so, they might then progress to the "bike track". Those that are more confident will immediately start on the regular Sittingbourne speedway track. This is the larger circuit where the

[1] The inaugural referees' day in 2004 raised £4,000 through individual sponsorship raised by each of the referees who competed. The organiser Chris Gay presented the cheques on behalf of the ASR (Association of Referees) to the Speedway Riders' Benevolent Fund and this donation was by far the biggest donation received that season from the traditional track collection method.

speedway meetings are held, where the referees usually officiate, and there will be fully powered 500 cc machines available for them to ride.

Graham is "looking forward to the visit of Christina" with glee, since it will be her first return to Sittingbourne since her previous rather controversial visit late in the season. "We'll have a red bike and a red race suit ready for her, we'll take the mickey and have got lots of red flags which we'll use lots – she'll remember that afternoon definitely on Sunday". Not that it's an afternoon that will be forgotten by anyone in a hurry. Graham was so irked that he even wrote his first letter of complaint to the governing authorities. Not that he got any joy: "Graham Reeve wrote back saying she was correct, I still think that she was wrong but that's the past now though she'll always remember that afternoon whenever she comes across something similar as a referee, so I suppose it's done some good".

Since it runs all year round as a club, the end of the Conference League season isn't as significant a milestone at Sittingbourne as it is for practically every other club in the league. However, the end of the 2005 season has left the exact make up of the Conference League shrouded in uncertainty with many rumours of track closures. Armadale will definitely close and there are question marks against the continued participation of Weymouth and Oxford, while Wimbledon are definitely without a track to race on after they were evicted from Plough Lane[2]. If all four clubs fold, "there could be as many as 40 riders without tracks". It's a worry and a problem that bothers Graham. One possible solution Graham has considered, if that is what transpires, is "we're thinking of running our own league for them with home and away meetings under the authority of the BSPA with refs and so on".

In reply to my question, "won't that cost a lot?" Graham retorts, "we don't care about that, all we bother about is rider safety!" For each meeting you run at Conference level, "the BSPA charges £100 in advance of which the ref gets £10 plus their petrol money". Given these pay rates, a referee's job is definitely a labour of love for them to do, like so many other people who voluntarily give up their time to be involved in some way with speedway clubs around the country. In respect and acknowledgement of this dedication, the Sittingbourne Club were only too happy to involve themselves and stage the referees meeting last year or to help with the unofficial practice day this year.[3]

When I arrive at the stadium, most of the referees have already arrived. They drink warming cups of tea or think about changing into their race suits. It's sunny but very cold and the home straight of the big track is covered in frost. This straight rarely gets the sun and looks like it would be much better suited to the discipline of ice speedway rather than the dirt variety. They also say that Sittingbourne has its own mini-weather system and to judge by the strong but very cold wind that blows from the estuary, just visible in the distance, it's in full force today. The view from the track has the Sheerness docks in one direction and the large clouds of smoke that billow from the cluster of plaster factories in the other. Between these two compass points the half-built support arches of the new bridge under construction can be clearly seen in the distance along with numerous electricity pylons that stud the marshy flatlands.

A small crowd of helpers stands round the edge of what serves as the home team's part of the pits area during the season. They watch a couple of speedway bikes being revved, warmed and tuned up in preparation for the referees. Everyone

[2] Graham believes that it's very unfortunate that Wimbledon's revival hasn't lasted as long as it should have. Speedway at Plough Lane in the Conference League was originally revived by Steve Ribbons, who now helps behind the scenes at Sittingbourne, along with Dave Croucher, who is now team manager at the Isle of Wight. "Steve was the worker and got slammed, and Dave was the man who put the money in. They couldn't make a go of it and Perkin then took over".

[3] Graham is keen to stress to me that he truly respects the very experienced referee Frank Ebdon as a person and as an official. Graham has known him since 1994 when Sittingbourne started and Frank has been supportive ever since. Frank owns a restaurant ("he invited us all for a meal once") and hotel – guests have ranged from one extreme to another and have included Status Quo and Margaret Thatcher – 10 miles from Cambridge, but his occupation is actually as a chartered surveyor. According to Graham, "he uses reffin' as a hobby to relax". Not only does every meeting Frank officiates run quickly ("they run as sweet as a nut") but he's also really appreciated because "he chats to everyone individually beforehand – riders, paramedics, mechanics, machine examiner and so on – explaining his approach and inviting questions". Unfortunately he won't ride today and didn't ride last year ("though he sent a card wishing us well") because previously sustained injures prevent him from doing so ("he suffered 26 dislocations of the shoulder at cycle speedway"). Graham believes "he would have attracted a massive crowd if he'd rode in the refs' race last year!"

The youth of yesteryear. © Jeff Scott

Dick Jarvis, machine examiner. © Jeff Scott

Chris Gay in kevlars. © Jeff Scott

dresses in clothes appropriate to the sport, though there appears to be very little concession to the biting cold wind that's whips through the open spaces of the trackside. There are a few beanie hats which I feel is much more of a speedway fashion item, given the number worn by mechanics and riders during the warmer summer months, than something worn for protection against the elements. I stand on the periphery of the group and listen to the conversation. Some of this involves queries as to the exact whereabouts of the referees who've arrived or those that are expected to arrive. There's much jollity about the difficulty they predict that some of the referees have when they try to fit their less than svelte physiques into the confines of their race suits or, for that matter, when they eventually venture out onto the track on their bikes. The general consensus is that kevlars offer excellent protection against abrasions brought on by the anticipated high number of falls expected and also that they will mostly stretch, albeit not flatteringly, to accommodate the vagaries of the flesh. Apart from this, the talk is mostly of the future prospects of teams and riders that will make up the Conference League next season. Dressed in his standard dress of green overalls, Graham believes that the league is "gonna be a mess". It's a situation he expects will be exacerbated by the large numbers of riders who won't be able to earn a team place in the reduced sized league that will inevitably happen in 2006. The lack of teams will not only result in riders who won't be able to ride ("someone like Dan Blake, who rode well here this year, isn't even gonna get to sit on a bike") but the "standard is gonna go way up and costs are gonna go way out of the window!"

Discussion moves onto what's been reported in this week's *Speedway Star*, which, almost immediately, brings up the issue of the future of Wimbledon Speedway. One of the group says, "Perkin wants to know about sharing as soon as possible so plans can be made for the future"[4]. Another man rhetorically asks, "how are they gonna get the fans here?" before he continues, "there's talk of bringing them over in mini-buses, though they brought so few the first time they came here they'll only need a taxi!"

First out of the changing rooms and down to the pits are Tony Steele and Chris Gay. Both clutch cups of tea and pay very close attention to the bike preparations. Quite aggressive-looking blokes in clothes more suited to a summer's day still enthusiastically rev these up. Chris sports a rather elegant-looking neckerchief or bandana. On closer inspection, Chris really isn't that fashionable since the neckerchief turns out to be a scarf worn as a badge of allegiance to his beloved but proudly provincial

[4] The actual piece they refer to in the *Speedway Star* reads: "Meanwhile Dons' Chairman Ian Perkin should know by today (Thursday) the reaction of Sittingbourne in regard to a track-share scheme for next season. He said: 'We need to know something soon and to make it clear to our riders before Christmas what the options are in regard to the 2006 campaign. We cannot leave them in limbo too long. That would be unfair'. I have redacted all comments but definitely gathered that this suggestion would not meet widespread approval at the Sittingbourne Club, if this cross section of their members were any indication.

soccer team Southend F.C. Supporting the Shrimpers is often a guilty secret, but one that Chris feels great pride to publicly acknowledge, particularly this season when they are doing so well. Whether it's a real or imitation bandana, no one can deny that this look was popular among speedway riders in the 1970s, but now appears to have died a death within the much more studiously fashion-conscious generation of modern riders. Not that this puts off Chris, who strides round the pits area with the air of a man in charge of his own destiny and supremely confident in his abilities. These have yet to be tested or demonstrated on the shale this morning, but dressed in predominantly black kevlars with green trim, Chris exudes great assurance. Dressed for action and shaped as he is, Chris bears a striking resemblance to 'Buzz Lightyear', though he affects to have no idea of the film or figure of fun that Buzz was in the film *Toy Story*. Shortly later, once he dons his helmet, Chris morphs even more uncannily into an even more Buzz-like appearance; though he doesn't exhibit his rather vainglorious character and, in fact, is himself the very capable organiser and instigator of this referees' practice day. Tony Steele is altogether more nervous and much less confident, though his default personality trait of extreme modesty and friendliness makes his true feelings hard to detect at the best of times; except, of course, for his casual use of ironic comments. Tony stresses to me that while he's an enthusiast for everything to do with speedway, when it comes to riding he's just here for the experience. In fact he frequently stresses, "I'm only here for a laugh – I'm totally crap on a bike so I'm here to make up the numbers and I'm certainly not going to be a hero". Initially reluctant to identify the latent abilities of his fellow officials, he does then confidently predict that the best rider of the day will be Lee Coleman. But then he's not actually a referee, but used to be a speedway rider until he broke his back over ten years ago. Ironically, he sustained his injuries at a training school run at Peterborough by Vaclav Verner and, up until that point, he was a promising reserve rider for Coventry[5].

Referee Phil Griffin also intends to ride on the big track. He has come along with his brother Paul 'Gansta Man' Griffin as well as another referee Jim Lawrence. Out at the smaller novice track will be all the speedway bike virgins – Robbie Perks, Barbara Horley, Christina Turnbull and her partner Mark. Of this group, only Robbie Perks confidently claims he is determined to master the basics of control and sliding sufficiently so he can progress to have a spin on the bigger track on the much more powerful bikes. He intends it "to be my first and last time here"[6].

According to the organiser of the day, Chris Gay, the referees want to have fun as a group and "to get an idea what it's like to ride a bike, in our case poorly, to help us with our jobs as referees". Tony Steele is happy to clarify that "even the Conference riders ride at a completely different level". The sheer power and vibration of a speedway bike surprises even those people well used to riding a road bike. At last year's meeting Tony stresses, "we gave it everything – I tried really hard and afterwards my wife said 'were you having some trouble with the bike?' because it looked like it was going so slowly".

Training people of all ages and sizes to learn some basic skills on a speedway bike is meat and drink for everyone at Sittingbourne. In fact, it's the club's raison d'être though, with some pride, Graham puts it more bluntly, "we've done 600 people through here since we started with around 100 this year". On the 'big' track each of the referees take a turn to ride round the track individually. The slow motion effect of gravity Tony mentioned appears to weigh strongly on all the riders with the notable exception of Lee Coleman. Just a casual glance confirms that he feels very confident on the machine and that he is really prepared to attack the bends with the bike since, compared to all the others, he slides the machine at some considerable speed, as well as riding on the 'correct line' round the circuit. Everyone else is understandably much more reticent or, when they're astride the bike, have the sensation that they travel much more quickly than they actually are. Tony suggests that I should try it myself next year, when they come back, to get my own experience of "the sheer power of the thing". Between practices the referees all stand around to watch or discuss the sensation of hanging onto the machine for

[5] When Lee met Vaclav years later, the trainer pointed out that he was the only rider to ever injure himself during one of Verner's many successful training school days.

[6] Robbie is the step-brother to the old Long Eaton and Cradley Heath rider Dave Perks and, contrary to his claim to be a true speedway 'virgin', had a go at speedway in the 1980s without the success he hoped.

grim death. Robbie Perks who has practised sufficiently to now venture onto the big circuit believes, "you just hang on though we're all so tense holding on tight, it's knackering". With each progressive ride they take, the referees become more exhausted and generally marvel at how speedway riders manage to become inured to the effects of riding four or five races every night of the week. The riders also have the added complication of additional riders who compete with them for a few vital inches of space and so don't have the luxury to ride the track 'solo' like the referees. The greater confidence that Lee Coleman exhibits on the bike, and his natural ability to move about the machine to get into the best riding position to attack the bends, becomes more and more obvious as the morning progresses. Tony Steele is wary of the effects of over-confidence that the increasing familiarity of practice inevitably breeds; as he discusses his experience with Robbie I overhear him confide, "that last time out I almost felt that I was going to go – I could feel the back wheel starting to move!"

 Chris Gay is a man of a few words, but strides masterfully around the pits when he doesn't throw himself round the track with some determination, if not great speed. He continues to look more and more like Buzz Lightyear as the morning progresses. His father Gordon has come to watch the racing with his son. He's a charming man with a wealth of stories about sport in general, particularly his twin passions of speedway and football. Though in his retirement, he likes to travel round the country with Chris as much as he can to watch speedway in as many different stadiums as possible. It's a privilege he relishes and savours. The experience of all those meetings is (I gather without him specifically saying) enhanced by the paternal pride he feels at his son's involvement and his contribution.

Gordon first took Chris to speedway at Halifax in 1966 when they won the KO Cup and Championship. Chris was three and a half years old. They also went to watch speedway at Belle Vue before they moved down south in 1974. They then started to go to watch Hackney on a Friday night and Rye House on a Saturday night. It's an era that Gordon remembers with some nostalgia, but he doesn't denigrate the modern version of the sport as many people from his generation often do. Through Chris's work as a referee, Gordon has some additional insight into the inner processes of the sport unavailable to the average fan on the terraces; but, nonetheless, he still manages to remain an enthusiastic fan. He does mourn the fact that "all the tracks that I have loved have now closed – Odsal, Belle Vue, Bradford – and we've sadly lost the quiet and competent Colin Hill at Exeter". Not that he wishes to stand in the way of inevitable change, though he does wonder at the lack of racing lines that have increasingly become the norm because of the contemporary trend to prepare slicker tracks more suitable to the needs of modern engines. It's delightful to chat with Gordon with his many keen insights into so many things[7].

Round at the junior track Barbara and Christina have benefited from lots of individual tuition and appear to have progressed very well in a short space of time. They have the possible added embarrassment that they've attracted quite a crowd of onlookers – mostly young lads with their fathers, who are themselves dead keen to get out onto the track. Unfortunately I have to leave before the practice day is finished and won't be able to have lunch with the referees as they, in the style of anglers in the pub, discuss what might have been – the speedway equivalent of the one that got away. I find Graham in his office with Stuart 'Rat' Lee-Amies, the man in charge of the many aspects of track maintenance at Sittingbourne, whose wife and family I met on my last visit. I tell him what a lovely enthusiastic girl his daughter Chelsea is about her speedway and her sincerely held ambitions to become the first lady World champion. Rat is a friendly man of action rather than words and so appears proud of his daughter ("she's very keen") but protective all at the same time. Graham says, "she is a one, she often beats the lads". The office they're in is extremely cluttered with accumulated bits and bobs from over the years, while the desk is piled high with papers. It's clearly a room that serves it's necessary purpose as a place to store the paperwork while most of the real work, the practical work, takes place outside on the tracks.

After he rustles about on his desk, Graham eventually finds a photocopy of the completed scorecard for the 'Clubman Championship' and the 'Ernie Edwards Memorial Trophy' held at Sittingbourne on November 12th. "I like to do these properly as so many of the riders and the people working here don't get the chance to do them on the day", explains Graham. The Ernie Edwards Memorial commemorates the fact that Ernie was the former landowner of the site upon which the speedway now takes place. The programme notes identify Ernie as "our much-loved former landlord" and it was a meeting won by Mark Baseby ("Mark rode really well, he's a good lad who's really come on a lot"). The speedway regulations administered by the BSPA are such that the club was not allowed to advertise the meeting ("even though the entrance was free, if we advertise the BSPA will charge, which is mad really when you think about it"). As well as a copy for myself, Graham is very keen that Rat should have a completed copy of the scorecard. Rat studies it very briefly before he folds and puts it into his pocket with a quietly murmured "thanks"[8].

Graham and Rat make quite a pair together in this office with years of dedication and selfless service to the sport in general between them both. Graham talks about the contributions of others and the role of Sittingbourne Speedway as "the grassroots of the sport" with touching modesty. You can't mistake the fire of his commitment or how his eyes glow when he talks of the "community ethos we have, by that I mean non-payment I suppose really – we do everything properly and we treat the riders too good. So good that when they go to a commercial track it's usually much less well maintained. Ours is always good to race on safely, you have to do it for love, as you don't get paid in amateur sport. So many riders have come through here I've lost count. Many have gone on to be successful. We had the last British World Champion, Mark Loram, who started here – and Paul Hurry and David Howe. Now David is a good example of what I mean, he's always always giving back – often here advising the young ones and not forgetting where he started and where he came from!" Graham searches the drawers on one of the old-fashioned metal filing cabinets that the office houses, since he's keen to find the original plans for the land. As the postal address of Sittingbourne Speedway Club suggests (the Old Gun Site), the track is built on land that was originally used for military purposes. It's hard not to almost straightaway notice the peculiar

[7] He also robustly defends his son when I ask why Chris is notorious, as a referee, for holding the tapes for so long at the start of many of the races where he officiates? Gordon emphasises the need for vigilance to ensure that no one gains an advantage through cheating. He also reminds me that the rules state that riders should be motionless at the start line and Chris merely applies the rules correctly and, more importantly, applies them "consistently and fairly". You may infer that the belief in and need for respect, equality and fairness are definitely qualities that Chris Gay has inherited from his father Gordon.

[8] Later, when I study it closely, I notice that in capitals at the bottom of the scorecard it reads, "SPECIAL THANKS TO RAT FOR DONATING PLAQUES FOR ALL OF TODAY'S RIDERS" and elsewhere it emphasises "Trophies For Finalists Donated By Rat". The scorecard has been painstakingly completed in the neat, slightly shaky handwriting of an older person – most likely Graham I imagine. Number 16 is Stuart Lee-Amies who is Rat himself. He finishes second in a couple of his races riding the bike he "received as a gift" on his 44th birthday. It's the first time he's ridden a "competitive speedway meeting since a horrific accident motocrossing back in 2000". The programme notes explain that Rat is "Mr Sittingbourne Speedway himself...well-known to all at the Old Gun Site as the Club's Training Instructor and in charge of all sorts of maintenance around the circuit". This echoes almost exactly what his daughter, Chelsea, proudly told me about her father on my previous visit to Sittingbourne.

shape of the building outside the office or the incredible thickness of its walls. If you walk very close to it, as you pass by to the pits area or when you stand in front of it to watch the racing, you could be forgiven if you don't gather that it's actually one of the old gun turrets of the old military base. As you look at the detailed surveyor's plans Graham eventually locates in the drawer, it's clear that this was quite a significant establishment. It dates from 1933 though it was adapted during the Second World War to become a vital part of the coastal defences in this part of Kent. There is a rich tradition of service for your country from the nearby villages in both World Wars. The plans, entitled ' Iwade HAA Site TS2 Chatham', cover the surprisingly wide geographic area occupied by the base. The four substantial gun turrets and pillboxes are clearly marked, though I gather they weren't put in until 1944. Graham and Rat excitedly identify which gun turret on the map is the office we're stood in as well as the other turret near the first bend of the circuit. As part of the hidden history of this conflict, the base housed over 800 people at the height of the militarisation ("mostly women" according to Graham) before the numbers gradually declined, until the 'peace dividend' closed the base in 1956. It was eventually de-commissioned in 1959. Both men study the maps with great intensity, while Graham identifies the current usage of each and every one of the landmarks identified by the map. The English Heritage people visit the site every year and "check up on things, particularly the gun turrets and pillboxes, just to make sure that we're looking after it right. I reckon they'd like to buy it one day but they don't have enough money so they're just keeping an eye on it till they do!"

It's still bitterly cold as I make my way over the partly frosty grass that the sun has still yet to reach. Most of the referees still roar round the main track (at least in their imaginations), while the youngsters itch for the lady officials to conclude their practice for lunch, and Gordon Gay watches his son from the home straight, oblivious to the wind. Graham and Rat remain inside for a little while longer to pour over the large strangely discoloured surveyor's chart in the cluttered Speedway Office. Judged by this day at this club, the community spirit and grassroots of the sport of speedway appear very healthy for the future, although they exist on love and a shoestring budget. Like on so many of my journeys to meet people at speedway tracks throughout the summer of 2005, it makes me feel good to be alive when I find myself surrounded by so many sincere and decent human beings. It's been a privilege to meet so many committed people.

On the weirdly touching travelogue *Searching for the Wrong Eyed Jesus*, about the people, atmosphere and Pentecostal religion of the sometimes forgotten Deep South of America, the narrator and guide Jim White says, "they don't know it's a real place, it's just a place they go". He also says, when he deliberately chooses to echo the sentiments of the *Wise Blood* novel by Flannery O'Connor, "they have the wise blood – the blood rules them, they don't rule the blood". While these thoughts are from a different place and context, they are sentiments that sum up my overall experience of speedway this year better than I possibly could or have managed in this book.

25th November Referees' Practice Day

Chapter 40: Behind the Scenes at the Bonanza
11th December Brighton Bonanza

Graham Flint (ref): "Who is this?" Jon Cook: "Jon Cook" Graham Flint: "You're not the team manger, do not call the box again!" Jon Cook immediately calls back. Graham Flint: "You have not signed on the Meeting Signing on Sheet as the team manager so do not call back again" Jon Cook calls back again "Trevor Geer here" Graham Flint (looks at TV monitor) "no it's not!" (Hangs up in exasperation)

RANDOM SCB RULES

7.5.2 In respect of Out of Season Meetings (indoor or outdoor), the SCB will grant a maximum of 1 permit per month (November to February inclusive) for which the appropriate fee is payable.

When I graduated from university I invited my parents to the ceremony held in the Brighton Centre on the seafront. It had the all the atmosphere and charm of the 'Golden Egg' restaurants of the period and was the antithesis of any place to celebrate anything. It's a multi-purpose venue designed as both a concert hall and a conference centre. It was built, I imagine, in the 1970s as part of the Churchill Square shopping development, and for its day was state of the art in its choice of design and materials. Although its time has in some respects passed, that has not stood in the way of it as a venue for an incredible variety of events including the indoor speedway meeting known as the *Brighton Bonanza*. Though the fabric of the building has begun to show signs of its age, the speedway event promoted by Martin Dugard and Jon Cook has become a key occurrence on the winter calendar for speedway fans and is always enthusiastically attended by fans from all over the country. In fact after the close of the official season and the onset of cold turkey, this is the first chance that the fans will have to get their regular fix – although in the cut-down indoor version of the sport which, to echo Spock on *Star Trek*, is speedway, but not as we know it. The winter rest the riders have already had or the lack of one of the

sport's major trophies to strive for doesn't adversely affect the keen competitive approach taken by the riders on this small but tricky indoor circuit. It's definitely a unique event, which, as Jon Cook informed me in the early summer, the Brighton Centre classifies as generating the "second *strangest* crowd they attract here after the snooker crowd". It's a claim based on the serial non-responsiveness of the speedway punters who, despite repeated mailings to invite them return to watch other attractions, steadfastly refuse to darken the Centre's door again. Most likely, this reflects the specialised tastes of the speedway audience but also, since the event attracts comparatively few local residents, the distance the vast majority of the crowd must travel to watch the *Bonanza*.

In order to get the full experience of the event Jon Cook has kindly allowed me to spend time behind the scenes to watch the Brighton Centre transform itself from the empty shell of the multi-purpose venue that it remains in reality without stage, ice rink or bowls 'green'. Last night it was the venue for a concert by 1980s Norwegian pop rockers 'a-ha'; throughout the day it will be an indoor speedway track; and tomorrow it will host the Stereophonics in concert. It's an auditorium that can serve a multiplicity of purposes but, perhaps, none so peculiar as the site of the *Brighton Bonanza*. I'm sure that it's undoubtedly the smelliest event they stage here, the dog shows excepted perhaps, but it isn't the noisiest by a long way, even though the sound of the bikes indoors creates quite a roar. In fact, not only has Jon Cook allowed me to watch the event from behind the scenes, he's also "volunteered" my help to work on whatever odd jobs need doing throughout the whole manic 24 hours that he estimates it will take to transform the venue, stage the event and return it, once more, to its almost pristine state. He brushes aside the news that my practical skills are poor and that, according to my mother, I was behind the door when common sense was given out. Jon is very definite, "we'll always find something that needs doing that you can do!" So now that I've failed to convince him that I am a liability and how useless I'll be if I help them, there's nothing for it but to throw myself into the experience of the event, all in the interests of research for this book. In reality though I do have one practical skill, namely that I'm actually a highly proficient user of a broom, whether soft- or hard-bristled with a small head or large, from my time as a temporary groundsman at the Wimbledon Tennis tournament at the All England Tennis Club. I convince myself that like swimming or riding a bike that it's a skill that, once you've learnt it you can never forget, though time and gravity affect the girth and size of your stomach and so might make wielding the brush just like a wand a fraction of a second slower and the trajectory of those elegant strokes more ungainly. With approximately 120 tons of dusty and dirty shale due to arrive, I decide that it's best initially to keep mum about any skills I have with a brush.

After I agree to help, Jon then hits me with the kicker that I will have to turn up by 1 a.m. on the Sunday morning to help with the layout, installation and fit out of the track. This all sounds well and dandy, when you say 1 a.m. quickly it sounds early but not that deadly. The day before it sounds horrendously early, but after a few fitful hours in an attempt to get some sleep, it's just not the way to contemplate the start of Sunday morning. Though we're at the seaside in Brighton, the so-called warming effect of the sea isn't apparent since a bitter temperature with a biting cold wind makes the trudge down to the Brighton Centre a character-building exercise. My journey there takes me down from the station along Queen's Road, past the restored and now shiny Clock Tower, towards the central party zone of the city that you access via West Street. Any self-respecting adult over 25 years will leave this street to the younger element or the tourists on most nights, but especially over the weekend. It has a deserved reputation for high jinks, carousing, revelry, doorway sexual encounters and drunken violence. It's not a scene that the locals feel especially proud of; most avoid it or consider that it has no real connection with their lives. For the younger people though it's a complete magnet with its cavernous bars, popular nightclubs, amusement arcades and fast-food outlets that prove an always-irresistible attraction. This snobbishness about the West Street area of the town is quite an achievement in a city enamoured of it's own self image as a city known for its escapism, dirty weekends and an all-round 24-hour party experience.

As I get much closer to the seafront and the Brighton Centre, two worse-for-wear young women in crop tops, short skirts and high heels stagger about, screech loudly as they struggle to carry a large red 'For Sale' sign up the incline of the hill by the army recruitment office. They're just not dressed for the cold in their skimpy clubbing clothes, though the effort to slowly weave along the street with a sign of this size that advertises the opportunity to lease some superbly located office space, might warm them up. It definitely draws attention to them and their inebriation, something that their lurid loud discussion of a quick visit to a nearby ex-boyfriend to offer him sexual favours ("it's gotta be worth £1.50, at least") to raise the necessary funds for the taxi fare home doesn't undermine. I feel totally ancient and out of place, when I pass the first night club on West Street with its extremely loud thumping music and, on the subject of thumping, two security men unceremoniously heave a drunken and rowdy punter out onto the pavement. There he sprawls, almost oblivious, before he gingerly rises to his feet and heads off towards the Kentucky Fried Chicken shop that's crushed with hungry young people and is guarded by two, very burly, security guards. Security guards for a fast-food establishment say it all about this street, modern contemporary life and the violent nature of crowds fuelled with alcohol. But then so do the five bright yellow police vans with their rather futuristic and ostentatious cameras perched on their roofs. Lest we mistake them for anything else, each has large red fluorescent lettered signs that say 'Police CCTV'. It's typography that clashes garishly with the fluorescent yellow but, though they're in plain view of the marauding punters, they don't appear to have any calming effect on overall behaviour. Though, perhaps, they are? Just by their presence the number of fights and stabbings that traditionally might happen on this street are possibly held in check or, at least, documented. By the time I get there, it's definitely a relief to find myself at the back door loading bay and bulk deliveries entrance of the Brighton Centre, where there's already quite a hive of activity as the auditorium prepares for the speedway.

Despite the bustle all around me, inside the Centre there's a strong sense of purpose that contrasts sharply with the drunken chaos outside less than 100 yards away. Though I've yet to spot her high up in the grandstands at one of her many fixed camera positions, a text message sent at 12.52 a.m. from Julie Martin arrives, "where are you? Have you overslept!" Jules has come along to photograph from the start the various stages of the process of the installation of the equipment and the track as well as to capture almost every turn of the wheel that 16-year-old Lewis Bridger will make during his *Brighton Bonanza* debut later. It's all part of her ongoing campaign to preserve the whole of the Bridger career on film for future posterity. It's a project that nicely compliments her infectious enjoyment at her involvement with his progress and her chance to live practically every moment so far of Lewis's meteoric rise and impact upon British speedway. She's just driven over in the thick, freezing fog from Hastings – from the home of Tony, Nan and Lewis – to capture the whole thing from the very start to the finish of the meeting. She makes no secret of the fact that she hopes that she'll see Lewis get presented with the winner's trophy for the Pairs and the Individual event.

Hopefully Jules has a wide-angle lens, because she'll need it to capture all the tasks that happen simultaneously on the auditorium floor. Jon Cook and Martin Dugard arrived before midnight and by 1 a.m. the mini-army of helpers, the majority of them familiar faces from the meetings each week at Arlington, industriously work away. I report into Jon Cook who puts me to work on various duties necessary to help erect the wooden safety fence. Laconic as ever, he is sensibly dressed in his usual Eastbourne promoter's race-night garb of anorak cum jacket top, casual trousers and trainers. Since he has produced the event every year since 1997[1] when they'd had a real struggle with the logistics of staging and managing the event. Jon nowadays has the quiet confidence of someone who knows how everything should run smoothly, "there's approximately 25 people helping out and I think we all know what we're doing". Many things have changed or been refined over the years, but the need to spend the morning before the meeting working feverishly to get everything just right has become a fixed tradition among the organisers and helpers. Jon believes, "it's great nowadays, knowing what we know and what with the convenient start times [of the meeting] it all goes much smoother and easier compared to before". As I look around, it certainly appears that everyone knows their tasks and their place in the complicated set up and installation process. There's even a specially recruited posse of workmen who assemble the special fencing to protect the bank of seats that will house the spectators who'll be closest to the track and start line. Wooden boards are fitted in front of this large bank of red seats. A gantry is used to install the start gate mechanism as the electricians run their cables throughout the perimeter of what will become the track surface when the shale is eventually transported from the depot via the loading bay and onto the surface of the auditorium floor.

The task of getting 120 tons of shale into the Centre, laying it all out and then rolling it into an almost pristine state to provide a competitive racing surface, is a considerable feat in itself. In the comparatively short window of opportunity actually available, it's an even more logistically impressive feat – one that requires considerable planning, ingenuity and skill for the entire event to run without a hitch. At one point the redevelopment of the Churchill Square shopping area threatened the event because it was to include the temporary closure of the facility for its complete demolition and subsequent reconstruction as a modern state-of-the-art amphitheatre. The shopping centre design was appropriate for its time; and the consensus eventually became that it had not only passed its best, but was no longer suited for the various roles placed on it by the contemporary demands of retailing and consumption. Therefore it had to be rebuilt. The same fate awaited the Centre but, in a

<hr>

[1] Jon and Martin have also staged the *Bonanza* in Bournemouth and intend to run another indoor event in the North England in February 2007. To all intents and purposes, the *Brighton Bonanza* is the contemporary home of indoor speedway racing in Britain and follows on from the indoor tradition represented by the event at the Wembley Arena during the sports heyday.

victory for pragmatism and an acknowledgement of the huge revenues it generates annually for the owners, it gained a reprieve[2]. Instead of actually rebuilding the entire structure a new floor was laid in the auditorium at a cost of £250,000. This is the Centre manager's pride and joy, and he regards the floor with a devotion usually only granted to religious artifacts. Consequently there's huge and widespread paranoia to ensure that we don't damage this floor during our time in the Centre.

This new faux white marble floor is not the only new factor that affects the layout and installation of this year's event. The rampant anxiety of the Centre's management and the promoters about the possible damage that 120 tons of shale could wreak on this surface has resulted in the floor being covered with thick plastic sheeting rather than the wooden boards that have previously been used to cover it in recent years. On this additional plastic protective layer, the shape of the track has already been clearly marked out and surrounded with two complex oval shaped rings of wooden boards and slats. These inner and outer rings delimit what will become the tracks perimeter and what will form the centre green. The need for careful plans and measurement to the nearest inch in such a confined space is paramount and even with hardly any equipment installed, I can't help but marvel at how they will manage to use this severely restricted space and such a large volume of shale.

In a building filled with feverish early-morning activity a key point to note, as throughout the season at every speedway track in the country, is that practically everyone who is at work in the Centre does so on a voluntary and unpaid basis. Obviously, Jon Cook and Martin Dugard have a financial interest and stake in the success of the event and its organisation. Apart from them, it appears that you either work for the Eagles' sponsors and shale suppliers – Robins of Herstmonceux – or you work at Arlington stadium, in some capacity as track staff or in the office. To be at work at this time of the morning without payment necessarily marks you as both a volunteer and an enthusiast. Like the sport itself, it's a predominantly male environment and only Kath from the Eastbourne Speedway Office (who lifts many heavy objects with greater strength, dexterity and skill than myself throughout) and Jules the photographer represent the fairer sex. What is immediately noticeable is the energy, zeal, commitment and application that everyone brings to their various tasks. Many people are keen to inform me that they have worked on the *Bonanza* "every year" since it began in 1997. The idea sprang from a bet made during a local television studio appearance by Martin Dugard. It was a brief brush with fame that required him, while live on air, to manage to kick footballs while he rode a bike In a small studio. This in turn provoked discussion about the possibility of holding an indoor speedway meeting. Martin, with a confidence derived from his father Bob's expertise at staging speedway meetings at Arlington, was seized by enthusiasm but without much real thought for the full implications and complex logistics required to stage such an event. A speculative phone call by promotional partner Jon Cook to the Brighton Centre manager revealed, "he was up for it". The rest they say is history. Well, it is if you chose to ignore the initial wrinkles that have beset the meetings, but now have been gradually ironed out over time through experience and hard learnt lessons. Jon is supremely confident that the 2005 staging of the *Brighton Bonanza* will be a comparative doddle since "there's more people than usual, we just need to get in the 120 tons of shale, four lorry loads, flatten it out, roller it and then we'll be finished by 6 a.m.!"

It's a confidence that initially doesn't appear misplaced after the first lorry load of 30 tons of damp shale has already arrived in the loading bay and is being unloaded. One current version of what people imagine a speedway rider's life is like is that you turn up to the track, hop on your bike to ride a few races at great speed with aplomb and bravado before you retire to the bar where your supporters will buy you drinks, or, even more likely in the popular imagination, you will exhaust yourself with some wild post-meeting sex with a troupe of nubile and voracious young women. Apart from this, it's just a question of banking some sponsors' cheques, sleeping late before you clean and maintain your bike for a bit, then sleep again in the van or plane on the way to your next meeting. The true shape of the reality of any ambitious young British speedway rider's world was already being staged in miniature in the loading bay where last year's Individual Champion,

---

[2] Never one not to strike when the iron is hot, Jon and Martin have already signed a contract to stage the *Bonanza* at the Centre until 2009.

Edward Kennett, was very hard at work in the back of the shale lorry with a shovel. He'd already done a few hours work before I spotted him just after 1.30 a.m. as he worked very industriously along with his Liverpool FC supporting colleague and 'Robins of Herstmonceux' lorry driver Lance Wyman, Edward's task was to break up the shale so that the earth mover could drive into the back of the lorry and shovel out scoops of shale. Each individual load of shale would then be dumped and spread out inside the designated track shape marked out on the plastic-covered floor. It was a task that was repeated endlessly throughout the morning, continuously, relentlessly, and without a break except for when there was a slight delay for the next lorry load of shale to arrive at the loading bay. It was freezing cold with a very chill wind throughout the loading bay area, though Edward and Lance were oblivious to it as they both worked so energetically to lift and break up the compacted shale with their shovels.

Like everyone involved in the preparations, they worked dedicatedly and chat amiably. Edward works for Robins of Herstmonceux throughout the year and is sponsored by the company's genial owner and boss, Mick. Most of the actual work Edward undertakes for the company is during the off-season, mostly the winter months, and you quickly gather that Edward is sincerely and massively grateful for their support. Lance takes the mickey relentlessly out of his work-mate and affects to have little interest in speedway or Edward's successful track career. This appears partly true and partly an affectation. Lance informs me that Edward often practises on his bike during the summer out at the quarry site. Today promises to be a long day's work for Edward since he'll work here from around midnight, then ride in the Pairs and Individual event at the meeting before he again helps with some of the breaking down and packing away afterwards. With some understatement he acknowledges it's going to be a "long day" though he'll still be back at work as normal on Monday, "I'll probably go in tomorrow afternoon though, as I work for these anyway and they know what I've got to do and don't mind". Despite his busy shovel, Edward is happy to chat and remains extremely polite and friendly throughout. The 2005 season has been a good year for him on the track, particularly since Rye House won the Premier League and he won the British Under 21 Championship. Understandably he numbers the Hoddesdon track among his favourites, along with Poole ("a great place") and, slightly more surprisingly, Oxford. Lance berates him throughout about the quality of his work and the limited effort he claims that Edward puts into the shoveling of the shale. Edward shrugs this off patiently or replies in kind, as they continue the banter on to distract themselves from a particularly backbreaking and repetitive job. Later when I marvel to Jon Cook about the effort and hard work of Edward while he also has a very long day ahead of him, he shrugs and laughs, "he's young though in't he!"

Unloading the damp shale is an all-round family and team effort, which also features Gary Robins who drives the digger and his brother Norman who works on the track itself with another large machine. In such a confined space, they both exhibit very impressive control of their machinery. You'd expect this equipment to be used in a rough fashion that befits the heavy, often brutal, work involved with the shale, but they both use their tools with a confidence, delicacy and movement that constitutes its own industrial form of ballet.

Before they could demonstrate their capability and skills, I'd already mucked in when I helped to set out the metal frame stanchions that, when fitted with wooden boards, form the safety fence for this small arena. My impression, as a first-time visitor, was that everyone appeared to intuitively just know what to do, the order of what gets done when and exactly what tasks were expected of them individually. As I lean on the loose boards of the safety fence with another experienced old hand familiar with the staging of these events, Roy Prodger, and watch the feverish activity going on in front of us, he explains that to fit together all the various components is a bit like completing a giant jigsaw puzzle. But in this case, you have the added complication of considerable time pressure as well as the need to wait for some tasks to be completed so that others can begin. For example, "we don't know where all the boards go exactly yet". This will remain undecided until the shale for the track has been laid out, flattened and rolled. He's calmly confident that everything necessary will happen and that everything will be completed on time.

Apart from Martin Dugard who works and rushes about the place like a man possessed, there were many other very familiar faces from the Arlington race meetings. These included Roy Prodger (senior clerk of the course), Malcolm Cole (clerk of the course), Alan Rolfe (start marshal), Kath (of the Speedway Office) and various other actual or honorary members of the track staff. These range from John Strudwick, father of the up-coming Eastbourne second-half speedway rider Niall, who busies himself with the complexity of the centre green's wooden boards and electrics, to Neil Hollebon who works the car park before he rakes the track every week at Eastbourne. He's also an erstwhile speedway manager and a shrewd judge of speedway talent, given the fact he's the 2005 winner of Speedway's Clubcall Fantasy League organised through the pages of the *Speedway Star*. It's a very prestigious prize among speedway followers and an accolade to actually win it. The competition for the £1,000 prize is very intense among some very studious and well-informed fans. Neil is a man of action and few words who's very modest about his achievement. Later during a brief break in the work, while we wait for more shale-laden lorries to carefully wend their way along the foggy country roads, Neil explains the secret of his success. It quickly becomes clear that he has an encyclopedic recall of his team members as well as when and why he changed the composition of the team. When he chats about his fantasy team management philosophy, Neil rather modestly attributes his success to the "careful choice of riders and reserves" before he acknowledges that he has employed both knowledge and cunning, much too complicated to outline easily here[3]. Since Neil will be photographed shaking hands with Sam Ermolenko in the *Speedway Star* while he receives his cheque, Jon makes a point to remind him to spruce himself up "as you're representing the club". Jon even offers to lend him his shirt for the photo. Neil doesn't seem that keen to doll himself up and later is captured for posterity wearing the dusty but plain practical normal work clothes that originally prompted this suggestion.

During this break, the conversation among the volunteers illustrates that everyone is a fan of the sport first and an Eastbourne fan second. Though everyone is slightly tired and tries to preserve their energy levels, they listen with curiosity as Jon Cook chats amiably with all and sundry. He outlines the tasks still to be completed, some brief history of the event and excitedly talks about how he played for his football team yesterday. His team won 3-0 in the local cup quarter-final and he appears much more delighted at "making the first goal" than the morning's success in the Brighton Centre so far. When talk turns to preparations for the Eagles' team next season, it's clear that the recent influx of increased money into the sport, at the Elite League level, is often driven by vanity much more than financial returns or philanthropy. It appears that this is

---

[3] When I press him for more actual detail another time, Neil is much more guarded, "you pick seven riders for your team, hope they score well and don't get injured". With general comments like these Neil definitely showed his potential for speedway management.

an increasing trend and that the wealth required to run a successful team is no longer generated by traditional methods of robustly driving fans (and thereby revenues) through the turnstiles nor through major sponsorship deals or through traditional business fundamentals. Jon wryly notes, "the sport's getting that more and more glory promoters are arriving rather than running it as a business – soon all the fans will want you to run every club at a loss, just so that you can have all the best riders!" If the balance between fielding the best team and running a successful business has become even more skewed and out of kilter through the introduction of the welcome addition of the deep pockets of individual hobbyist benefactors, then – particularly if you ignore the Sky Sports payments to each club – it's logical to conclude that the structural organisation of the sport might not be so rosy or stable in the medium-term future, despite the apparent lustre and sheen of its contemporary appearance. Luckily another lorry load of shale arrives and so signals the end of our discussions and these revelations about the increasing preponderance within speedway of ego- and vanity-driven promoters.

As the event organiser, along with Martin Dugard, Jon Cook has to have foresight, experience, knowledge, shrewdness and adaptability in spades. Some of the casual talk during our enforced break illuminates the complexity and detail of all the things that you must consider or remain vigilant about as the event manager. For example, Jon worries about car-parking logistics in the light of the complications presented by the huge queues of Christmas shoppers that later will throng to the area along with an armada of riders' bikes and vans. If that and the need to ensure that the track is set up in time wasn't enough already, Jon now regrets the additional stress he has visited upon himself by his agreement, back in October, to also stage some Academy League racing during the *Bonanza*. Jon is completely in favour of youth development, indeed Eastbourne still regularly stage second-halves and successfully operate a junior training track, but he now realises that to fit all the bikes, riders, mechanics and parents into the narrow confines of the loading bay area "will be a nightmare!" I gather that his attitude towards the additional logistical complexity of his generosity has not been helped by the lack of reciprocity that his favour has elicited from Peter Oakes, the Academy League organiser, in the area of Elite League team building. I overhear Jon comment on a poaching incident, "I'm not happy as the England Under-21 team manager has just stitched me up over a rider – he knows he has 'cause he's been emailing me every day which he's never done before as he always calls". Though it's still very early in the morning, well-laid plans have just begun to unravel, and the prospect of possible additional problems ahead now bothers the equanimity of the ever-phlegmatic Jon Cook. I'm sure that these disruptions and complications will soon be resolved, forgotten or forgiven in the intense activity of the day, when Jon's usual levels of placid reserve and bonhomie return.

The most noticeable aspect of the preparations is the care and attention that the track itself receives throughout the morning. Obviously it's the essential component for the meeting and the installation of such a surface indoors is the unique selling point of the *Bonanza*. It astonishes me with how much careful fastidiousness the rough shale is slowly packed down by the staff to create the smooth racing surface. It's as though everyone were prize gardeners lovingly tending their favourite roses. By all accounts the track will be thicker when it's finally laid this year and the popular consensus is that it won't cut up this year. Norman Robins, who spreads the heaped piles of shale across the plastic sheets, is a true artisan with his equipment as he carefully redistributes the dark brown gravel of the shale in roughly even quantities throughout the auditorium. He's able to use the scoop arm of the equipment with such dexterity and precision that, if you took him to the nearby pier, you'd be certain to win many prizes from one of those glass cases with the hypersensitive and temperamental pincers. Once the shale is placed in position, it's packed down with the mini-steamroller, although the frequent journeys back and forth from the loading bay with shale in the dumper truck by his brother Gary also helps to compact the surface. The colour of the shale changes as it's compressed from a very dark brown to a lighter and more caramel hue. I am amazed how the sheer volume of 120 tons of shale is transformed into a racing surface, no more than a few inches thick when it's finally laid to everyone's satisfaction. But before you arrive at that stage there's a tremendous amount of attention lavished on the surface, not only from the workers but also from the number of unofficial observers who earnestly spectate throughout the process. The preparation of the surface not only requires large earth-moving machinery but also requires the ultimate in low-tech equipment – small red watering cans with which Jon Cook finesses the track. It's an implement of extremely modest proportions, tiny in fact when you contrast it to the enormity of the track or the weight of the shale that's required to construct the surface. The lure of the simplicity of the watering can technology exerts considerable magnetism throughout the morning and later in the day since everyone appears to briefly want to try them out at some point.

With all this heavy equipment shooting about in a confined space, spatial awareness is at a premium though, like the few building sites I've worked on, the majority of people here affect to have a casual almost nonchalant approach to the possible dangers. I'm sure that this confidence comes from experience and being comfortable in an environment where you create something from many disparate elements. This work is, in reality, similar to the weekly construction of the track at Arlington during the summer months except it's inside and it's still early morning. To have the strength to lift the heavy blue and yellow wooden safety boards around the place is also a prerequisite. Edward Kennett, who has switched to drive the forklift truck with a pallet of the boards balanced carefully on the forks, takes the boards round the circuit to their position. He's temporarily abandoned shale shovelling but hasn't stopped working, while he waits for another lorry to wend its way through the thick early morning fog from Hurstpierpoint to Brighton seafront. Much of the fixtures and fittings, the speedway furniture as it were, has been brought along from Arlington. As you unpack the huge number of stanchions you can't help but admire the handiwork of whoever packed them away the last time they were used during the season. It requires an eye for detail and an intuitive awareness of patterns that would serve you well at the entrance examination to be admitted to MENSA. It's also the particular kind of cognitive perception you need to be able to solve the metal Chinese puzzles you used to get out of old-fashioned Christmas crackers before their actual production in China and the contemporary need for cost control reduced them to meaningless husks of plastic. Inside the centre, it appears that every eventuality has been thought of and that everything is almost always to hand.

The work styles of the two organisers differ considerably and most likely reflect the different temperaments of Martin Dugard and Jon Cook. Jon is definitely more patrician and taciturn with a habit of appearing silently by your side just when you least expect it, to deliver a few words of banter, encouragement or direction. While he also does his share of the tasks, he clearly is the troubleshooter and facilitator, the behind-the-scenes fixer, with everyone from the Centre management to the riders' mechanics. I'm sure that Martin is equally involved in all this work, but during the morning he has delegated a lot of the hands on activities to himself, particularly if it involves vital speedway equipment like the starting gates mechanism tapes or the various lights that are required round the track and at the start line. Martin is extremely industrious and skilled after a lifetime spent in the sport and, more importantly, he learned all the many aspects of the job by his father's side at Arlington. Bob has reputedly forgotten more than most people know about speedway track preparation and promotion, since he seamlessly and professionally ensures that all the preparations to efficiently run a speedway fixture at Arlington happen. In this respect, Martin is definitely his father's son and his abilities around the place are a credit to his apprenticeship with his father. And is he ever energetic! Martin appears to be the equivalent of a DIY black belt – so, he uses drills, screwdrivers, drives vehicles, hangs off ladders and gantries and leads by example. Slightly less svelte than he was during the prime days of his speedway career, nonetheless he signals his seriousness and expertise by wearing carpet fitter's knee protectors. They're a very sensible choice of accoutrement with all the kneeling, bending, and earnest peering at the mysteries of the object in front of him that he occupies himself with all morning. I'm delighted with my own investment in equipment for the *Bonanza* – a pair of sturdy work gloves to protect my hands softened by years of office work. These are so evidently new and unused that they signal wussiness in stark contrast to the message delivered by Martin's kneepads. Nonetheless, they were a shrewd and invaluable purchase, even if they don't enhance my practical skills or strength.

Contrary to popular myth and the attitudes that newspapers like *The Sun* and the *Daily Mail* often promulgate about industrial and manual workers, there appears little time or incentive to have a well-earned tea break. The smokers do break off to have a roll up on a regular basis, sometimes inside the auditorium, until the Centre's facilities manager strikes and rather hysterically reminds the transgressors that it's a designated no-smoking area. Which is faintly ridiculous given all the dust and fumes that visibly swirl around in the increasingly polluted atmosphere of this enclosed space. Even the strong cold morning wind, drawn down the wind tunnel of the access road that continually batters the loading bay, doesn't shift the eddies of particles raised by all the work with the shale and the repeated trips of the various earth-moving equipment. Also there is a giant urn of hot water in the corner of the room though, sadly, the murky liquid it produces can only be described as dark and hot rather than specifically identified as tea or coffee. Still, it's the warmth that you want and the opportunity for a brief chat or sit down, though not for too long since fatigue soon returns your thoughts to why you're not still wrapped up in bed asleep.

It certainly does feel like an extremely early hour throughout the morning's activities though the intense nature of all the work gives little respite or time for contemplation. There are distractions, the most spectacular of which was the loud and boisterous arrival of the legendary Dean 'Deano' Barker, Chris 'Geernob' Geer and two other mates who have popped in from a Saturday night's birding and carousing to check on the present state of the progress. One of these mates is Scott Sullivan, the notorious roué whose chief claim to fame is that he's one of the many ex-boyfriends of the glamour model Jordan. She's reputed to have had enough of these that if they were all invited along later, then the Centre would be much fuller. Not content with romancing Jordan, Scott has also allegedly enjoyed some quality time with her pneumatic erstwhile rival Jodie Marsh. Happy in such company, despite the bracing cold, Deano is dressed in a somewhat ostentatious and strangely patterned pair of jeans set off with a tight leather jacket, which he wears unbuttoned to show off his plain white T-shirt. Despite the obviously half-made track, Deano's first question of Jon Cook and Edward Kennett is to ask, "alright who's got a bike I can ride then?" Edward and Geernob greet each other warmly with a complicated display of gestural handshakes that are common with young people. These peculiar handshakes always look like they would be much more at home in the Bronx than anywhere in East Sussex, never mind close to the border with genteel Hove. They're all warmly welcomed and, after he climbs into the driver's seat of the forklift truck, Deano quickly falls into an unduly loud but animated conversation with Cookie who warns him, "take it easy in case you have a heart attack".

Close by Jules sits trackside in the empty stand seats and holds her camera with the giant lens on a pole in search of another photo for her website. Geernob spots her and is plainly delighted to see her there unexpectedly. Geernob contentedly reports that he's been out on the lash to the Shore Bar, "a very posh bar where they bring the drinks over and you pay for them afterwards". He confides to Jules that they're "expensive but worth it – I don't do that in Hailsham".

Afterwards they'd all then gone along to the Lowlands Nightclub or Disco, I can't quite make out which, and, after it closed, they had decided to call into the Centre to catch up with friends and have a look at how things are getting on. Geernob appears slightly less able to take his drink than Deano, who is just far enough away that, as he talks ten to the dozen with Cookie, he almost sounds sober. Geernob is extremely animated but in an avuncular friendly manner apart from repeatedly suggesting to Jules that she might like to give him a kiss or immediately head back to his place. Not that it's his place really, "I'm living with Deano, and it's colder at his place than it is here!" When he learns that I'm writing a book he's only too keen to help with a raft of anecdotal detail and information about his life around the speedway tracks as a valued mechanic as well as his various impressions of the riders. He asks, "have you met my friend Deano?" before he calls, "Deano! Deano!" which only elicits a vague shrug of the shoulders from the man in question before Geernob tires of the idea and, instead, again playfully pesters Jules for a kiss or some romantic attention. They clearly get on well and spend quite some time in deep discussion about all the characters and salacious gossip from Weymouth Speedway Club. As I listen to some of what goes on, I realise that it sounds like the last days of Rome down there in Dorset. I'm surprised that the riders can barely manage to find the energy to get on their bikes never mind ride them, after all the intense extra-curricular activity that's apparently commonplace. It's a heady mix of adrenalin, glamour and youth that finds expression in some extremely licentious behaviour. It's a whole different side of life, as a travelling speedway rider or a speedway mechanic, that you definitely don't see written about in the *Speedway Star*. You should also add don't let your daughter become a start-line girl, keen fan or rider's girlfriend to the usual advice of not letting them go on stage, or, for that matter, even become a junior rider's mum. Especially since the devil always finds light work for the suitably inclined, if there's some spare room in the back of the van or an empty changing-room floor. No wonder so many speedway riders' girlfriends and wives take the time to make a point of travelling with their man.

Luckily, talk then turns to a topic always close to Jules heart, namely the likely impact of the talented Lewis Bridger at the *Bonanza* later in the day. They both believe that Lewis adapts to unfamiliar tracks very capably ("like Stoke which he hadn't seen but rode flat out"). Also, among such an august crowd of famous and experienced, Lewis will enjoy the comparative anonymity that will, hopefully, allow him to fully concentrate on the matter at hand, rather than have to weather the distractions of continual adulation from fans and admirers alike that he suffers when he rides for Weymouth. One thing that they both agree on is that Lewis wouldn't have had the chance to become the success that he might be without his innate natural ability, however, without the commitment, support and total belief of his grandparents, Tony ("Granddad") and Nan, it would have been a very different story. According to Jules, "everything Lewis's granddad earns he spends on Lewis". Tony works as an electrician, "he already does six days a week and would do nights if he could, only he has the bikes to do as well". The whole house is taken over with bits of equipment, "there's carbs all over the kitchen, and sometimes Nan can't even cook the food". Not that Tony's dedication leads him to get the respect that he deserves from the younger element at Weymouth. Geernob gleefully recalls, "I've had his pants down – we've gaffer-taped him to a pole and sprayed him". They both laugh uproariously at the recollection of Tony's struggle to resist and the memory of the look on his face.

Having literally discussed the ins and outs at Weymouth, Geernob's happy to talk about his life as a speedway mechanic. It's quite a hectic life which for him began in earnest when he became the "youngest person ever to be a mechanic at the Grand Prix when I worked there when I was 15 in 2002". He'd always been around speedway bikes and tracks because of his father Trevor's career in the sport, so it always seemed a logical choice for him. Since then "it's been a dream come true" with travel all round England as well as to Poland and Sweden practically every week during the summer. Mostly this has been with David Norris and Geernob has grabbed with both hands the chance to experience the world. Geernob doesn't ration his praise for those who've helped him, who he's enjoyed working with, or who've stood by him. In the past he's lived with Mark Loram ("I loved working with him and his manager Norrie Allen who's still the tops") who is one of his favourite riders, along with Dave [Norris], Deano and Joonas [Kylmakorpi]. He also speaks highly of Jon Cook, "he's given me good chances" and, unusually for some young people, lays great stress on doing a job conscientiously and with the pursuit of excellence strongly in mind. "I don't care if it takes two days to wash a bike, I just do it till it's right". Edward who passes close by on the miniature steamroller inadvertently interrupts us, "Kennett, you traitor you should've signed for

Eastbourne, your career would have gone a lot further!" Edward replies with a blunt gesture while Geernob mutters, "sometimes he just don't listen to advice".

Warming to his theme, Geernob again stresses his satisfaction at how things have turned out in his life, "it's the happiest I've ever been – speedway is my life, it's all I believe in". Many people don't appreciate the effort and difficulties one undertakes and overcomes as a rider or how good some underrated riders actually are in reality. Geernob muses, "Deano, I live with him so I know, that if he got it right in his head, if he really believed, he'd be brilliant – he's great now for his age with a seven average at 35 years old and still regularly pulling 19 year olds!"[4]

No discussion on speedway with Geernob could avoid the issue of his central role in the fracas at Wolverhampton when Eastbourne visited there. Geernob is matter of fact in his recollections of the evening. By now Geernob is tired and the realisation that Deano has gone home without him, and that he doesn't have any money for a taxi fare, does cause some concern. I leave him to Jules's company, as he still playfully makes offers that she can indeed refuse. As I cross the centre green, Martin Dugard chirrups, "I see you have had the misfortune to meet Geernob". We both agree that he's honest, engaging and enthusiastic, "he always is when he's doing nothing" says Martin enigmatically. Very close by there's quite a crowd of helpers who lean on the safety fence and study the track intently. John Strudwick rather earnestly tells me that he believes that, "this will break up badly tonight" but he's in a minority. However, they are all agreed that, "we just don't let Jon get on the rollers, as he falls asleep and demolishes the fence!"

Eastbourne's clerk of the course, Malcolm Arthur Cole, looks on with a furrowed brow. It's a name that must have been torture at the height of the popularity of *Minder*. He's a long-time speedway fan and began to watch 45 years ago at the "old Rayleigh and Romford tracks". Malcolm has been "involved over there" at Eastbourne "31 or 32 years, working on the track and working my way through to being the clerk". For him it's always been a very enjoyable sport and it still is, "though sometimes I think we had more excitement in the olden days with the olden bikes". Kath from the Speedway Office doesn't agree on the appeal of speedway in its historical or contemporary versions, whether live or on the telly. It's much more of a job for her, "when you work for the place, and I'm there all the time for the stock cars and the speedway, you don't want it when you go home as well".

By 5.30 a.m. Martin Dadswell from the Eastbourne track shop arrives to

[4] Maybe if the sport were to adopt the theme of this comment as slogan ('Become a speedway rider and pull a 19 year old every year of your life until you're 40 or retire'?) there would be many more youngsters only too keen to try out for a long career in speedway in preference to many other career options.

supervise the preparations for the popular collectors' fair area that's always set up in the foyer close to the revolving doors of the entrance. He's not especially happy that the security man at the Centre has rather inflexibly refused to unlock the front entrance way but instead has forced him to transport his stock circuitously via the loading bay area. Before he starts on this task, Martin is off to ensure that all the tables are laid out correctly for the many stallholders that will shortly throng the whole foyer area in the expectation of the large crowds of eager speedway fans out to purchase the ideal Christmas present. I always find it a real treasure trove and, undoubtedly, there will be a sufficiently wide range of speedway memorabilia and accessories to cater for every taste.

Shortly before dawn finally arrives I head off home for my breakfast, just as Jules wanders off with her camera to capture the light as it breaks over the sad sight of the derelict Victorian West Pier.

When I return later, it's still bitterly cold though there's a desolate feel as I pass by the nightclubs, fast-food joints and amusements arcades of the now deserted West Street. The contrast is thrown into sharper relief because while there's hardly a soul in West Street, though the loading bay area of the Brighton Centre now teems with people, vans and bikes. Everyone wants to unload their things immediately and the logistical nightmare that Jon predicted has come to pass. He's already roped in some volunteers, including Jules's affable partner John, who is prepared to drive the surplus riders' transit vans to a temporary car park outside the Dugard building in Hove. The hierarchy among the riders is visible for all to see. The actual *Bonanza* competitors all find the smallest of spaces to stand and maintain their equipment on the narrow walkway that is the loading bay. This position gives excellent access to the auditorium; via the main doors for the bikes and via the emergency exit doors for the crowds of mechanics, helpers and hangers on that form the inevitably large entourage at major meetings. The eager young men who are here in Brighton for their Academy League fixture all find themselves, along with their parents and helpers, bunched up at the bottom of the loading ramp in a temporary pits area that's fenced off from the yet-to-arrive public but exposed to the elements. I spot a harassed-looking Jon Cook and compliment him on how smoothly everything has actually gone, except for the delay in the shale deliveries earlier in the morning. That's not how he sees things as he waves his arms expansively towards the loading bay area, "not really, we have shortages of everything, mainly space, I just don't know whose freaking idea it was to run the Academy League – we have bikes everywhere!"

Though there's still the odd task going on, the transformation of the arena was completed while I had breakfast, when the auditorium was further tidied up and kitted out in the final splendor of its match-racing look. The track looks perfect and in pristine condition. The referee's panel is in the centre green along with all the various flags. The speakers are in position and so is a small table where the trophies stand to await the winners from today's meeting. Many of the track staff stand and lean on the fence rather contentedly as they admire their handiwork. In fact there's an understandable air of satisfaction among all the helpers, which contrasts with the feverish activity in the pits. A man who always appears extremely calm is start marshal, Alan Rolfe. He speaks in a deliberate almost contemplative manner about his life in speedway. "I've been over at Arlington since 1969 when I was running about in the car park doing silly things". He's been the start marshal since "around 1972-73" though he's not exactly sure how it came about, "dunno it just came naturally, it's just something you do and luckily I took to it like a duck to water". Alan certainly has a distinctive style and manner about him on race day when he cajoles the riders to line up correctly, hopefully motionless, at the start gate. It's a pleasure to watch all the distinctive twitches and mannerisms that he skilfully uses to communicate his instructions to the riders above the din of their engines. There is also a strong element of showmanship about his presentational style though Alan is keen to stress, with some pride, that his sole concern is to get each race smoothly organised and under the referee's control. The biggest change in his career was the elimination of the "old rolling starts" in favour of the modern and supposedly stationary "green light starts, which is the more natural way to do it". Often, after he has all the riders under orders at the line, the miniscule gap Alan then has to squeeze through, between the tangle of handlebars, looks from the terraces very hard to negotiate without the need to bump or jostle the riders, "I've never touched any of 'em since I began though sometimes it's close". Alan has helped with every *Bonanza* so far. He notes, "the track took longer to lay this time, it should have been down by 5 a.m. but

took till 7.30, so it's in the hands of God as to whether it settles". This is only a slight problem compared to the fun and games of the initial indoor meeting, "we just made it up as we were going first year – then we had the major problem of the fence moving and the track moving with it. Now we've done it so many times we've sorted all the problems out really".

In the loading bay area behind us, the various ages of the riders span 33 years from the suspiciously and luxuriantly brown-haired American Bobby Schwartz, who at 49 is the oldest *Bonanza* competitor to the youngest participant at 16, the highly fancied Lewis Bridger. As he stands up from a struggle with his helmet visor, Bobby greets the passing Edward Kennett, by now dressed in his speedway rider's attire of kevlars, with a jovial, "are you getting taller or am I getting shorter?" Later when he's being interviewed by the experienced *Bonanza* announcer, Kevin Coombes, Schwartz professes delight to be back in "Dugard country again". In contrast to the ambient air temperature, the atmosphere in the pits is warm and friendly among the competing riders. They're all here to win but there's an evident camaraderie and an out-of-season feel to behind the scenes. The narrow confines of the track make the set up of your bike and considerable delicacy in your throttle control essential prerequisites. A number of riders are highly favoured to do well in the Individual Championship. There's the defending champion Edward Kennett as well as previous year's winners Paul Hurry (twice), Brent Werner and Martin Dugard (twice) who will race along with many other possible contenders. Paul Hurry is especially keen to do well since over the years he has established a reputation as a real indoor-track specialist at Brighton. He's suffered from some injuries in recent years that have prevented him from further confirming this reputation but, according to all accounts, he is very keen to excel. So much so that the affable Dick Jarvis, who is machine examiner at Sittingbourne, mentions that Paul has practised in secret there on their junior track. It's a track normally only used to train novice riders and from which powerful, full sized 500 cc bikes are usually banned. Earlier in the week, as a special dispensation, Paul was given permission to perfect his technique on a 500 cc machine. This preparation, allied to his natural skill indoors, should be a considerable advantage against other riders who will be both a little race rusty and unused to the cramped confines of indoor racing.

There's still some time left to finish some last-minute tasks around the auditorium before the public is allowed into their seats. The doors to the centre opened at 11 a.m. and already the collectors' fair area is crowded with eager fans, as are the many bars and catering facilities. Many of the country's notable track shop stallholders are in attendance, including the always friendly and chatty Mick Gregory, the Derby County supporter who runs the Sheffield stall. Not too far away but with a different range of merchandise is John Rich who helps to run the Wolverhampton track shop along with the track-shop stalls at Buxton and Stoke. The knowledgeable Martin Dadswell, from the Eastbourne track, who supervised this collectors' fair area hours before anyone else arrived is now in situ behind the counter with the charming Barber brothers – Nick and Jon – who run way too many track shops to remember, never mind list them all!

There are a number of stands selling very specialist speedway or motorcycling-oriented merchandise that includes T-shirts, DVDs from T2TV (videos appear to have died a death even in speedway circles), body colours and, most bizarrely, a stall that sells slippers, awful shoes, sleeveless jackets and other shoddily made items. They look just the sort of quality that you'd struggle to sell at rock-bottom prices at a car boot sale. The friendly ex-Belle Vue and England rider Chris Morton has taken a stall to promote and sell his autobiography *Until the Can Ran Out*. He certainly hasn't run out of energy, stories about the olden days of his racing career, or his apparent determination to sell his book to every speedway supporter in the country. This isn't the first venue that I've seen him charm the fans.[5]

If you can't have the great man there in person on your stall, the next best thing to attract a good crowd at an event like this is to movingly evoke or resurrect memories. This isn't something that you need to tell Tony McDonald who has built an impressive and apparently robust publishing business upon nostalgia for past sporting glories in both football and speedway. At the *Bonanza*, he has a stall, placed in prime position, that sells back issues and subscriptions for *Backtrack*, the retro speedway magazine that covers the 1970-90 eras, as well as the books he has successfully published over the past year or so[6].

Pride of place in the stall is devoted to advertise their latest book on Simon Wigg. They have enough Simon Wigg memorabilia on display to satisfy the most ardent fan or collector, including a race jacket and leathers[7]. Publishing a tribute book, albeit this rather unique version, is a tactic Tony had already successfully employed earlier in the year with his unauthorised tribute to Brian Clough, ironically described as "not very good" by another stallholder, ardent Clough fan Mick, since it created expectations that it didn't fulfil. Apart from the production of speedway books and magazines tinged with nostalgia, Tony publishes similar material on football about his beloved West Ham[8]. Tony wants to learn more about the content of my book and my publishing plans. He's concerned to discover that I'm not writing a guide to every speedway

[5] The book is a sincere and chronological account of his career and has the added feature that it has many of his own words rather than being merely ghosted by someone else. His stall also attracts quite a number of passers by who idle the time away before the *Bonanza*, while they watch the video highlights of his racing career that are shown on a continuous loop on the large-screen television. As you glance at the images, they still definitely resonate though they come from a completely different era, which reminds you of what a star Chris really was in his own right. His long career at Belle Vue was lived in the shadow of his illustrious team-mate, compatriot and World Champion rider, the great Peter Collins. The lustre of Peter's performances, and the subsequent rose-tinted effect of distant memories of him, tend to make you forget that Chris was just as much a part of some key moments in that era of British speedway.

[6] The subscriber mailing list from his speedway magazines provides a ready-made and easily accessible market for his book publishing activities. These books include John Berry's *Confessions of a Speedway Promoter*, where he claims to tell it as it is but, often, is in fact how he saw it or would like to recall how he saw it. It's a strongly personal book written from a position of authority and it's a delight to read. The book, like the man, inspires strong emotions and reactions. It was the first book to really break away from some of the blandness that has traditionally afflicted speedway book publishing. The publication of John's next work by Tony, his path-breaking 'speedway novel', won't achieve similar sales success and is the sort of vanity project usually described in publishing circles as "brave", "unique" or "distinctive". It might possibly win an award though, as the Publishing Industry has a competition called the 'Bad Sex Award'. It's a hotly contested accolade given to works of fiction where the author has (unintentionally) written descriptions of sexual encounters that provoke derision and mirth. I decide not to enquire of Tony if he thinks John has some material in his novel that might merit his entry. Though again, some of the contest's submissions are so execrable but hilarious that they set a standard that it would be difficult to beat.

[7] Tony is a resourceful and clever publisher of book and magazines who is well aware of his audience and the different prices that different groups will pay. He's also canny at squeezing the most out of the material he has to work with. The Wigg book is a case in point. There he has made a virtue out of originally only having a half manuscript – a no-holds-barred interview with Wiggy that is presented as "forthright and opinionated" – since Simon's tragic death from cancer robbed him of the opportunity to complete his own account. However, Tony has supplemented this great material with a variety of other subsequently written material to bulk out the book. This includes "heart rending and in-depth accounts from Simon's widow Charlie and his elder brother and mentor, Julian," that cover the "*real* Simon". The book also features 200 photographs and "60 new and unique tributes" from many other people who knew Simon and, more importantly, thought highly of him so that the tributes are thoughtful, compelling and sincere. As if these already weren't reasons enough to purchase a copy, altruism should influence the few remaining waiverers left, since a "donation from every copy sold will go to Simon's young children, Abi and Ricki".

[8] Tony had stressed to me before that, in his experience, speedway fans will always pay higher prices than football fans are prepared to pay. Though this could be a self-fulfilling prophecy, the specialist nature of speedway compared to football intuitively makes this statement appear true.

track in the country as he'd previously thought, which would have appealed to him as a publisher, but rather I've taken a more personal and discursive approach. "I thought that you were going to do something lasting more than just one season – it'll date very quickly"[9].

They say if you sit by the river long enough you will see your enemy's body float by. More pleasantly, if you hang around the collectors' fair long enough you get to meet or, at least, wave to many of your old speedway friends and acquaintances. At the bottom of the stairs stands Tony Steele, the sport's number-one referee, who chats animatedly with a large group of like-minded, similarly aged gentlemen. The programme tells me that, heat 7 of the Individual meeting has been dedicated to him by the promoters Martin and Jon, "Tony Steele – valued friend of the *Bonanza*". Typically of the man, when we speak about this dedication later, Tony is tremendously touched by this public display of respect. Dave Fairbrother from the *Speedway Star* lurks over on the far side of the fair. He's lucky enough in his work to travel to every major meeting that there is in the sport in the UK and throughout Europe as he follows the Grand Prix series from venue to venue throughout the summer. He also has behind-the-scenes access and privileges that most fans would kill for. We catch up ("I didn't realise how serious you are about this book") before Dave envies my independence as a writer in the same way I envy his access to all and sundry as a staff member of the *Speedway Star*. I mention to him that my experience was that some promoters I interviewed were highly cautious or sometimes suspicious to the point of condescension doesn't surprise Dave. He informs me that in the past journalists have deliberately misquoted some promoters, plus the conscious and unconscious self-censorship of the specialist reporters in the speedway press corps has tended to reduce the level of critical questioning promoters actually receive, or expect to receive, to a bare minimum. So, if their opinions are ever challenged they tend to be extremely shocked, hypersensitive and angry. On the whole, as a response, they maturely tend to keep their own counsel rather than indulge angry denunciations or heavy-handed threats of litigation since they respect the close community of which we all are a part. Many of the top riders will only submit to be interviewed by Richard Clark, the editor of the *Star*, since they trust him to understand them and keep to the party line when he reports on them and to always present their comments favourably. Not only is Dave a good bloke, but also he's a key person to know if you're keen to make your way and boost your profile as a photographer. I make a point to rush off to find Jules to introduce

[9] My hope that my work will say something about social history, people as well as speedway in general and every British track doesn't convince him. It's an approach and a perspective that he describes as "a serious mistake" which to his mind typifies the "hobbyist author or publisher". It's a mistake that he predicts I'll compound by publishing a book with too many pages ("the maximum should be 256 pages") at too low a price compared to the cost of production. Since I have 20 years' experience in publishing I know much of his perspective is accurate but they do say publish and be damned, though they rarely add the silent caveat, and be broke! It's worse than Tony thinks as I'm also prepared to compound my possible commercial mis-step through a donation to the Speedway Riders Benevolent Fund for every copy sold. Tony shrugs in a 'what can you do' type manner, though we do agree that an advert in his magazine *Backtrack* would make sense. It's a magazine that I personally relish reading almost as soon as my subscription arrives. Tony sensibly refuses to disclose the number of subscribers on the grounds of business confidentiality.

her to him to cement the working relationship they've started to create via phone and email.

Next I also bump into Jurgen Gilsdorf who's come to the *Bonanza* from his home in Germany along with his mother! I'd met him years ago at Eastbourne and had been impressed with his knowledge of British speedway. Even more impressively, not only does he like to spend some of his summer holidays travelling round Britain to a different speedway meeting each night, but he'd also been to every track in the country. It was an achievement that had stuck in my mind for a few years and in some ways influenced my decision to visit them all myself. Like all true obsessives, at the time I met him he had just visited the country's newest track, the unique Trelawny circuit. It was lucky Jurgen took the trouble to do so promptly since it didn't remain open for long and is now defunct, though recalled fondly. I leave Jurgen to talk loudly in German with his mother while they linger over the speedway memorabilia. No meeting would be complete for me this season without a serendipitous encounter with Nicola Filmer, the extremely pleasant and dedicated girlfriend of Dan Giffard. They've travelled the short distance within Sussex to both, for once, attend a speedway meeting together as ordinary spectators rather than as participants. Although I've spoken with Nicola many times, Dan remains a stranger to me.

Just before the racing is about to commence I wave my backstage pass at the ladies on the door to make my way round to watch the meeting from the prime position of the pits area. My excitement is short lived as Jon Cook politely but pointedly asks me to leave the area and, instead, go to watch from the stands, "don't stand there Jeff, you'll get hurt!" Unlike everyone else involved in the preparation of the track since 1 a.m. that morning, or some roped in later, who remained but apparently oblivious to the dangers[10].

Now that I've been dismissed to the stands, I decide to make the best of it and take advantage of my pass to sit wherever I choose to watch the afternoon Pairs meeting. Initially, I decide to watch from the East Stand where I'm surprised to see that Deano, Geernob and their mates are already there, all apparently as fresh as daisies, after their late night. Unlike the night before they are also accompanied by some girls. To be honest, throughout the afternoon they often appear distracted by the jollity of their own conversation as much as the *Bonanza* itself. No sooner have I sat down than all the lights inside the centre go out, a fanfare plays extremely loudly and the riders enter the arena very theatrically picked out by bright spotlights. We're invited to applaud and greet the riders enthusiastically as a pre-recorded introduction in an American showbizzy accent plays before we're reacquainted with the distinctive dulcet tones of Kevin 'KC' Coombes. Prior to the start, KC has already tried to work the crowd into a frenzy with his demand to know which teams the members of the audience support. After naming each team in the country, often without any reply for those located a considerable distance away, KC then offers a few summary words of insight about their club. When the name Sittingbourne gets a warm cheer, KC tactlessly but accurately notes, "you had a bit of a rubbish year".

The shortness of the circuit and the compactness of the bends inevitably means that all four riders cannot negotiate the initial turn at the same time, as there just isn't enough room for them all. Though they don't get up to the usual speeds associated with racing outdoors, they're all very determined to get the advantage of the lead position, since the opportunity to pass other riders is extremely limited. Even to stay on the machine requires great skill and careful throttle control to ensure that the sheer power of the machine itself doesn't catapult you through the fence. Consequently, the dynamics of the track combined with a determination to win or establish an advantage means that, understandably, there are an inordinate number of first bend crashes at the *Bonanza* (even more than at the dusty and protracted Conference League Pairs Championship 2005 meeting staged at Wimbledon in the summer). Since it's notionally a fun event or, more accurately, not

---

[10] Though I actually had already purchased a ticket to watch the event in October from the stands, I had, until that moment, felt privileged and fully part of the *Bonanza* team. It was definitely a shame, since I had hoped to be allowed to watch trackside; as well as take part in the preparations, to continue my unique perspective, though it still was an insightful way to experience the *Bonanza* for my book. Then again, I wouldn't like to get injured and the wooden safety boards wouldn't provide that much protection if a speedway bike unexpectedly hurtled towards me. Also I can understand that presumptuous strangers like myself, would clutter up the place or get under people's feet in the cramped space back stage during show time.

subject to the usual stringent rules and regulations that traditionally govern a speedway meeting, the crowd is often consulted to adjudicate on the final decision after crashes. They do this by waving either the red or yellow portion of the centre of their match programmes. If the majority of the crowd wave yellow then the rider is re-instated, whereas when a majority wave a red that results in an exclusion. This level of participation has worked successfully for the past few years and certainly provides a sense of personal involvement for those in the stands.

The racing gets faster and faster throughout the afternoon as, with each ride, the riders gain more confidence. The experienced pairing of Paul Hurry and Roman Povazhny is viewed by many spectators as the pre-meeting favourites for victory in the Pairs event, though there are many other strong pairs that include Schwartz-McConnell, Werner-Correy, Kennett-Bridger and Dugard-Tomicek to name but a few of the others in an evenly matched field of riders. Sadly for Paul and Roman, the weight of expectation about a possible probable triumph is dashed straightaway in their first ride together, albeit in bizarre circumstances, when they crash into each other on the very last bend of the race. Not only did they lead easily but they also somehow contrive to crash within a tyre width of the finish line, after Hurry accidentally picked up acceleration and violently removed his partner from his machine. Conditions are so tricky for Jordan Jucynski and Vladimir Dubinin that they both separately manage to crash before the start of the race! It's quite an achievement though, in extenuation, this is the first time they've ever ridden on a circuit like this in their short careers. When the riders acclimatise to the circuit, the racing noticeably increases in ferocity. Janniro particularly suffers some very hard-riding manoeuvres from both Werner and Correy on successive laps in heat 10. The invitation nature of the event is captured in the next race, when we witness the strange sight of all three riders race wearing a white or a predominantly white helmet colour. We have Dugard officially in white, McConnell officially in blue but wearing white, and Schwartz officially in red but who wears a helmet where white not red is the dominant colour.

Throughout the afternoon the Pairs meeting is interspersed with heats that feature the under-16 riders from the British Academy League Grand Final. It's a match that pits the Buffaloes against the Cobras, teams of young men who will hopefully be the stars of the future for British racing. It's a sign of his rapid development this season that Lewis Bridger also rides in this event. It gives him the chance to well and truly become used to the peculiarities of racing on this indoor circuit. While there are a few falls among these inexperienced riders, though not as many as the doom-mongers predicted, the racing is extremely close and competitive. Between all these races KC takes the chance to interview the various riders including the meeting co-promoter and old Eastbourne favourite, Martin Dugard. Like Edward Kennett he has worked at the

Centre since midnight and will now ride in both events. Since he's Martin, this also means he will expend lots of energy dashing here, there and everywhere to sort out last-minute problems. Martin outlines to KC the logistical problems of the event's management and the logistical difficulties behind importing a track indoors. Though he tries to make light of it, he describes a difficult task made all the more complicated because of the expensive floor, the late finish of last night's a-ha concert, the curfew because of the Stereophonics concert tomorrow and the need to use protective plastic sheeting this year. He's pleased with how the track has held up, considering the volume of races, "the track takes a lot more and everyone is out to win so it really takes a beating". Martin is keen to do better than last year when he had a disastrous meeting, "you're only as good as your machine when you no longer ride regularly and the bike I borrowed from Deano didn't work out". KC then interrogates Martin further:

KC: "What's it like coming back?"
MD: "Well, I've put on a stone since I raced and have a cold."
Crowd: "Aaahhh!"
KC: "Yes, but do you still get excited?"
MD: "Do you want the truth — yes!"
KC: "Do you miss it then?" [KC asks quickly since he hopes for exclusive news of Martin's comeback]
MD: "No!"

Despite the number of races, the track has indeed held up extremely well although there is a short interval for it "to receive some TLC". This involves a wheelbarrow of shale, a shovel and the compacter that works on the damage at the apex of both bends. And, of course, the small red watering cans. The work is supervised under the expert tutelage of Bob Dugard who mentors everyone with calm capability. The racing resumes with some aggression and after a keenly contested heat 14, KC enlists the crowd as they get to pass judgement on the fate of Billy Janniro, "yellow he's back in, red he's in the showers!"

In an afternoon characterised by bizarre crashes, Jucynski achieves the apparently impossible when he falls off his machine in heat 15. Without its rider, his bike manages to land upside down perfectly balanced on its seat and handlebars. The crowd so relishes the chance to intervene that they vote to penalize Pecyna with a 15-metre handicap in the re-run of heat 16, because of his lengthy lay down on the track surface after he fell. Heat 17 witnesses an incredibly painful and unfortunate fall for Billy Janniro who gets walloped by an out-of-control Tomicek. Quirkily Janniro manages to crash his bike into the only very narrow space on the home straight where there's a gap in the wooden safety fencing. In fact it's the only gap in the whole fence; though, nonetheless, it's a mishap that obtusely leads KC to gleefully conclude that, "the safety fence is doing its job". Though to contradict himself, KC immediately notes, in his 'isn't it a funny old world' tone, that Billy has been perversely unlucky, "of all the places to find a gap in the safety fence, wouldn't you just believe it, the bike finds it?"

While the crowd waits patiently for the fence to be repaired, KC thrills us with some technical information on the tyres in use at the meeting. "The riders have a traditional motorway tyre on the back of their bikes to ensure they get grip appropriate to the size of the circuit". The re-run takes place without Tomicek, who has been summarily excluded by the referee without any pretence of consultation with the crowd, and without Janniro who nurses injured wrists from his crash.

At the end of 20 heats, the final of the Pairs Championship pits the young Kennett-Bridger combination against the Dugard-Tomicek partnership. Though Dugard wins, the unique scoring formulae ensures that Edward and Lewis win the final 4-5 and therefore the trophy, since they finish in second and third places. This didn't look likely until Lewis sneaked past the rather wild Lubos for third place on the fourth lap. The only other danger that would prevent the youngsters from lifting the trophy was Edward's initial determination to try to catch and overtake the race leader Martin. His initial zeal to actually win the race often left Edward on the verge of losing control and crashing. Just as they crossed the line to win the trophy both young riders celebrated exuberantly with some wheelies plus lots of waving and punching the air. I decided to

sneak back down to the pits area to view the celebrations first hand, especially as the danger of my imminent death had, hopefully, passed now that the racing had stopped for the interval. While I watched the centre-green presentations from behind, it was clear that Edward and Lewis were delighted with the outcome. Also beside himself was Lewis's granddad, Tony, and hopping about the place like a mad woman, as she tried to capture every possible angle and permutation of the presentation for posterity, was the energetic Jules. KC was also keen to quiz the lads with some typically anodyne but friendly questions as soon as they had the trophy safely in their hands. Lewis admits to KC that he was extremely nervous about competing in the pairs with Edward "as I just didn't want to let him down by messin' up". Submitting to KC's persistent questions, Lewis finally gives us some insight into the factors behind his success with the elliptical explanation, "the less throttle you've got the more you're ahead". When he summarises how things have gone during the afternoon, KC's speech imitates the racing which "just got quicker and quicker". Since Edward has now been at work at the *Bonanza* for over 14 hours already, both as track staff and as a rider, he is touchingly modest and bashful when he recollects the afternoon's racing. He thanks everyone and appears reticent to be at all self-congratulatory, he prefers instead to just be surprised. KC jokes with Edward, "you lay the track and then they have to give you the trophy".

In keeping with tradition, Martin Dugard also receives the Dick Bellamy Trophy, which is presented to the winner of the Pairs Final each year. The trophy exists in memory of Dick Bellamy, one of the sport's pioneer riders who rode at the first meeting in this country at High Beech in 1928. When Martin gets backstage with the trophy, both of Martin's sons rush up to him and excitedly ask, "Dad, dad, can we hold the trophy? Dad, dad, can we keep the trophy?" Keen to instill respect and ambition in his boys, Martin passes the trophy over to them with the words, "you can hold it for a bit but be careful with it – you can't have it though, you have to go out and win your own!" A short while later I watch him give the trophy to his mechanic. When I ask him about this afterwards he explains, "it really means something to my mechanic, whereas it'll just go in the corner of their bedroom". Martin looks much more on the pace at this year's *Bonanza*, despite not riding regularly, and appears all the happier for it. Like all true competitors, he looks for an explanation outside himself and, in this case, the unforeseen events like last year's bike problems and the scapegoat of the bike's owner. "Deano gave me a bike that he said was great when he knew it wasn't, then Deano likes to be top dog but pretends he doesn't".

Near by, people close to Lewis delightedly celebrate with him. Jules looks close to tears and his granddad Tony has swapped his traditional slightly put-upon expression for an extremely sunny disposition. As ever, Jules has been nervous on Lewis's behalf throughout the event, "I was too nervous to take my photos and I'm still shaking". Never one to miss the chance to hug Jules, Tony believes, "it was fantastic, really fantastic! You've had a perfect weekend Jules – you've groped me and Lewis has won".

The crowd empties from the auditorium and chooses to either hang about the Centre bars and cafés or go outside. Once outside they temporarily join the eager throngs of Christmas shoppers, while they search for the ideal snack from the huge number of choices of different cuisine on the nearby surrounding streets. When I return to the collectors' fair later, Mick from the Sheffield track shop believes that "Sheffield is the best track in the country by a mile". He's not at all surprised by this week's revelation in the *Speedway Star* that Sean Wilson won't ride for the club next season. He claims that Neil Machin has wanted "to get rid of Sean for a while 'cause he's awkward, no longer good away not just 'cause they were a mile off in wage valuations". There's no chance to quiz him further on his opinions of the season ahead, mainly because the fans have besieged his corner stall eager to take advantage of his 'Winter Sale' and to snap up some last-minute but essential presents.

I re-visit the pits area, which heaves with riders and mechanics of all ages. I decide not to hang around, since the meeting is just about to start and the threat of imminent death or injury is just about to return. In addition to the injured Russian rider Sergei Darkin who has his arm in a sling, it's very noticeable that, rather unusually, there are a couple of one-armed men in the pits area. Later I learn that one of these men is Mick Robins, Edward Kennett's sponsor-cum-employer in Herstmonceux as well as the provider of the 120 tons of shale and the staff required to get the shale down for the *Bonanza* to be able run in the Centre. When I quiz him about his lost arm later, he matter of factly says, "I did a stupid thing and lost my arm climbing an electricity pylon when I was 12 – I wish I hadn't but you get on with it!"

On the stairs as I make my way back to my balcony seat from the pits, I pass Deano, Geernob and the girls they were with earlier, who all clutch drinks. They now look a bit more bleary eyed and Deano tells the young bloke closest to him, "You'll have to cover for me tomorrow 'cause I dun't think I'm goin' in". The other mystery male conspiratorially exclaims, "Oh, he's just gotta get fired soon, ain't he?" behind me I can hear Deano saying, "I really hope so!"

As the final few stragglers in the crowd take their seats we learn from a jovial KC that "we're just waiting for the speedway riders to come back from McDonald's". The evening Individual meeting starts with more of the special effects that involve the usual fanfare of music and bright spotlights that interrupt the almost total darkness of the auditorium, just as the riders troop out to the start line to be presented to the crowd. Before the introductions or the meeting starts, there is also a scrupulously observed one-minute silence in memory of the young Australian King's Lynn rider Ashley Jones who was tragically killed in a track crash in November after he had returned home for the winter to Australia. After the silence, KC reminds us that, "all these riders are putting their lives on the line to entertain you". Since I had just seen him earlier with Nicola when he clearly just expected to be a spectator at the *Bonanza*, it is peculiar to have KC introduce "Dan Giffard who's riding for the first time ever at Brighton". Dan had answered the last-minute emergency call from Jon Cook to his father's mobile with the request that he replace the injured Billy Janniro. KC claims," Dan's been thrown in at the deep end on his way to get a burger and chips". KC's obsession with speedway riders' burger diets isn't strictly accurate, since it later transpires when interviewed that Dan was actually on his way "for a pizza with my girlfriend".

KC introduces the last rider in the line up, Ronnie Correy, with the words, "he might be one of the shortest men in speedway", which is quite a claim to fame in a sport not known for its tall, gangly riders and where riders with the build of a jockey often excel. Eventually the crowd is introduced to the VIP guest of honour who'll present the trophy, 70-year-old former World Champion Barry Briggs. It's an apposite choice since Briggs, with Ian Thomas, was one of the promoters that initially pioneered indoor speedway in England with the Wembley Arena meeting in December 1979.

The first race of the night has Lewis Bridger quickly storm into the lead before that wily indoor campaigner Martin Dugard easily overtakes him on the inside, a very rare occurrence on the tight indoor circuit at Brighton. The introduction of Dan

Giffard could definitely be said to add a bit of colour to the meeting in the form of the bright florescent orange tassels that he sports on both arms of his kevlars. This heat also saw the Individual championship come to life, albeit in controversial circumstances after McConnell falls in the first running of the race. The referee immediately excludes McConnell only for the rider and the crowd to protest loudly that the cause of the crash was Chris Neath. The upshot of this raucous intervention by the fans is, instead, Chris Neath's exclusion for unfair riding. The tidal wave of red cards throughout the auditorium matches the predominantly red background of the grandstand seats. It's safe to say that Neath also saw red, though in his case through anger and frustration. Ever topical KC, and for a change courting controversy, immediately interviews Neath who is still busily throwing his toys out of his metaphorical pram, "what's the point of racing if the crowd are going to kick us out for nothing – it's my living and I know it's a bit of fun and I'll look bad for saying it, but what's the point of coming if I'm going to be kicked out like that?" Throughout this simultaneously rather passionate defence cum gripe, the crowd boos Neath in pantomime fashion. He definitely doesn't want to enter into the spirit of things, when he almost bellows, "Shawn McConnell agrees with me that it's ridiculous that the crowd not the referee decides," before he strumps back to the pits. His mood isn't helped when he's booed continuously in his next race, heat 5. It clearly affects his approach and he finishes forlornly in last place, thereby his challenge for the title is effectively at an end with 16 races still to go. Labelled as the villain in this melodrama, an outlook KC deliberately plays to in his commentary, the crowd greets his failure with cruel delight.

The first Academy race of the evening session, heat 6, has Brendan Johnson indulge himself in some wildly excitable celebrations that really wouldn't be out of place at a Grand Prix event. The next race of the Individual meeting, also slightly confusingly heat 6, immediately follows this rather charming display of youthful exuberance, and features two riders who both wear a red helmet colour. It's an improvement on the confusion of watching three white helmet colours race each other, but you start to wonder where it will all end? And more importantly (as they normally appear to be the sole instigator and ultimate judge for all inexplicable rule changes and head gear alterations within the sport) what would the visionaries at Sky Sports make of it all? Paul Hurry's chequered meeting goes from bad to worse when his Pairs partner, Roman Povazhny, ensures that he's the meat in the sandwich in the heat of the red helmet colours. It results in a nasty fall and crash for Hurry, whose career has suffered in the last few years while he's slowly recovered from significant injuries. Paul takes a considerable time to show even any sign of movement on the track, never mind get up, and you can't help but fear that he's done himself some serious damage. Bobby Schwartz confirms shortly afterwards "his left shoulder has popped out, we're going to keep an eye on Paul, hopefully he'll soon have his shoulder popped in". Casual as ever in the face of rider injury, KC informs us that the injury resulted from the fact that "it was the old bumper cars out there on bend 2".

It definitely appears even more congested on the first corner now that everyone competes for himself rather than as a team. The race is re-run without Paul Hurry who has withdrawn from the meeting as a precaution ("he's gone for an X-ray on his arm and shoulder") and thereby misses out on even more bump and grind on the first corner. Povazhny is again the instigator but some justice is done when he grinds to a halt shortly afterwards, while he is in the lead. The surprise late entrant Dan Giffard rides impressively well for successive second places in the space of three races. He's especially pleased to renew his friendly rivalry with Lewis Bridger when he decisively relegates him to third place in their only encounter. Heat 11 sees the young American rider, Chris Kerr, make the pass of the night when he manages to squeeze through a gap that isn't apparent to any of the watching fans. KC comes over all biblical with talk of Kerr threading his bike "through the eye of a needle".

The next race up is another Academy League encounter. Before the race starts, Ben Thompson's father, acting as his son's mechanic, falls over embarrassingly when he tries to push start Thompson's bike and so moves KC to sympathise "sometimes you pity the parents" when the bike then fails to start. The race is a bruising encounter that would make any nervous parent hide behind their hands. Most painfully affected is Ben Hannon who takes evasive action on the last bend to avoid a wildly spinning rider and consequently crashes into the safety fence with a tremendous thump. KC gleefully comments, "they certainly know how to entertain, these lads!"

With no bikes likely to run me over, I venture down to the pits during the interval. I have my first-ever conversation with Bob Dugard while he leans on the safety fence and watches the riders sign autographs for the crowd on the other side of the track. A man of action rather than words, Bob believes that the *Bonanza* is "going well" and that his son, Martin, is also "doing well".

A few minutes later Lewis's granddad Tony explains to me the thinking behind the open secret of the decision that Lewis will ride for Eastbourne in the Elite League next season. "I didn't want him riding on all those rough Premier League tracks with the dodgy safety fences – I told him we should take the risk as he'll beat a lot of the three-point riders". There is a possibility that the competition will be too intense but Tony is philosophical, "he might struggle but he'll learn, I said 'the money don't matter' – not that we have any – so I was pleased to get a guarantee". Jules had sent me interesting photos of a topless Tony to present to him at the Eagles Dinner Dance. He didn't attend so was unable, until now, to appreciate the difference between the original and "the one where Jules said she'd airbrushed out my gut".

Lewis arrives back from his autographing duties and looks none to happy with life. Granddad Tony nods at him and explains, "Lewis is not happy to be beaten by Giffard but he's taken a good few scalps already – mostly using his intelligence to get round this track, rather than the throttle, which I'm really pleased with". Lewis, however, remains apparently inconsolable when I chat with him. "I've lost some silly points, points I shouldn't have lost tonight, to riders like Giffard". It's a point of view not borne out by a close reading of the race results – Lewis has "lost" so far to experienced riders like Kennett (twice), McConnell, Schwartz, Giffard and Correy but has beaten Werner, Neath and Povazhny. A perfectionist attitude and a desire to learn from your defeats is a commendable attitude that must surely stand you in good stead for your future career.

After the interval, Dan Giffard continues with another barnstorming ride that includes a brilliant overtake before he falls very heavily on the third lap. KC is very appreciative of Giffard, "he really showed some courage carving his way through on that lap". It's a fall that ends his evening, since he has to withdraw from his final race and thereby deprives the crowd of a final glimpse of his flying fluorescent tassels. The final races of the evening result in a Grand Final line up of Dugard,

Kennett, Schwartz and the surprise rider of the evening, Kerr. To further highlight the fun nature of the event, Martin Dugard joins the rider parade to the start line for choice of gates in the final wearing a Superman outfit over his kevlars. In this version, Superman doesn't look so svelte as in cartoons or on film, but the crowd really appreciates it. Edward Kennett caps off a superb *Bonanza* when he wins the six-lap final race from Superman/Dugard, and it thereby enables him to win his second trophy of the day. It's a fantastic achievement for one so young but especially so in the light of the fact that he had already worked at the Centre since midnight. Apart from Martin Dugard, all his other rivals were tucked up in bed getting some well deserved rest in preparation for the demands of the racing ahead.

Barry Briggs presents Edward with the trophy in the centre green as the cameras flash to capture the moment. The epitome of modesty, in his acceptance speech Edward downplays his own achievements and prefers instead to thank all those people who have helped him retain the Individual trophy and win the Pairs trophy with Lewis.

All that now remains is for us to pack up and go home. For the crowd this is simple, although many of them remain like stalkers in the auditorium for the last possible glimpse of the riders. The riders, mechanics and parents pack away the bikes with their customary zeal and speed, no doubt aided in their desire to leave by the cold wind that blows through the loading bay.

Martin and Edward swiftly change from their kevlars back into their work clothes to join the crowd of helpers that remain to pack the show away. Jon Cook, along with all the other experienced hands at the event, have all assured me that everything gets packed away much faster than the early morning construction of the *Bonanza*. The meeting has finished on time and given that it's only 8.45 p.m., we have an absolute eternity until our agreed curfew time of 3 a.m. Around this time, the Centre staff will re-purpose the grandstand seats and their layout, construct the stage and so complete preparations to enable the early morning arrival of the equipment for the next night's Stereophonics concert. From an operations management point of view, the level of planning and co-ordination required to stage so many varied events at this venue is extremely impressive. Everyone on our breakdown team reckons that, if things proceed as usual, then we should be packed up and away within a couple of hours or, by midnight at the latest, if there's any unexpected delay.

While the various items of speedway furniture are quickly dismantled, it's soon apparent that the decision to place the shale on a protective layer of plastic to safeguard the faux marble effect floor will cause us a major problem. With huge but typical understatement Jon Cook explains to me that, "it hasn't gone to plan with the shale".

Basically, what hasn't gone to plan is that the shale can't just be quickly scooped up off the floor by the digger arm because the plastic immediately rips. When wooden boards form the base of the track, as they had every other year, the shale surface could be easily scooped into a dumper truck and then efficiently shifted into the back of the lorries that waited in the loading bay for its transportation back to Herstmonceux. But because the plastic tears immediately, and despite the great control and extreme delicacy with which the scoop is operated, the result is an unacceptable mix of shale and plastic. For some time, while this complex problem is pondered, everything else continues to be dismantled. This includes the safety fencing, the wooden floor, the electrics, the start gate along with all the other weird and wonderful paraphernalia required to construct a seamlessly organised speedway meeting. The only other small delay is caused by the monkey-puzzle conundrum of how to stack the safety fence support barriers into a neat and stable pile on pallets. It's a situation that is compounded since Martin Dugard is THE expert when it comes to carefully packing away practically every object of equipment and, sadly, he can only be in one place at one time doing one task at a time. We all have an attempt to stack the barriers on the pallet but it defeats Kath, Alan, Neil and myself when we all separately attempt the impossible. And though everything else is smoothly dismantled, packed away and disappears out the door, the shale track remains stubbornly and very obviously in position.

They say that success has many fathers, but failure is usually a solitary activity. In the case of the *Bonanza* track, there's quite a gaggle of interested and capable men who all offer their ideas as to the best solution to the shale removal problem. In the next hour or so, no matter how complicated, all these suggestions are tried, but without any hint of success since the track remains resolutely in position.

Now that the rest of the elements of the furniture are more or less packed away, the track appears to grow in size and the problem of its removal appears hopelessly intractable. I'm not sure who exactly identified the solution to the problem but whoever it was deserves a lifetime's free admission to the event. Of course the solution would not be anything other than extremely painstaking to execute because it would involve a laborious and repetitive procedure. It also requires extreme skill with the forklift and copious amounts of patience. Basically the solution is for the forklift forks to drive wooden planks into the narrow gap between the shale surface and the plastic floor covering. Each plank has to be carefully placed in position by hand before the forklift could drive it. This has the immediate effect that it broke the compacted shale into huge but more moveable lumps and so – plank by plank, yard by yard – separates the compacted shale from the plastic. These heavy lumps of shale then have to be shovelled by hand into piles sufficiently large to enable them to be picked up by the scoop. The scoop then fills the front hod of the dumper truck before that in turn transports the shale into the waiting lorries. All 120 tons of the shale track have to be picked up in this painstaking and laborious manner.

To say that this is backbreaking repetitive work would be a huge understatement. Also to break up 120 tons of compacted shale is an extremely dusty and messy business. It would choke you if you did it outside in a breeze, but it's quite a different kettle of fish altogether when you do it indoors. Everyone's humour (well, mine and a few other people's) isn't helped by the fact that it has already been an extremely long day after our early morning start. When Jon agreed that I could get some real and memorable behind the scenes experience of the *Bonanza*, I didn't for one minute imagine that this would be it!

It is a situation that is exacerbated by the clear hierarchical division of labour that becomes apparent – which I hadn't fully appreciated earlier that day – between those people who work on the track and those people with responsibility for the other equipment. This distinction becomes very noticeable after the numbers of staff that remain in the Brighton Centre to work on the track, massively dwindles to the basic hard core of us by around 11 p.m. or so, after the others leave for some deserved respite and beauty sleep.

By this point, it disillusionally seems that we have hardly lifted and shifted any of the track surface. At the present rate of progress, with only a small portion of the widened corner removed, it appears that we might work until day break tomorrow. Early in the track-removal proceedings Jon Cook emphasises to me that "we really need you to stay and help until the end!" and I am willing and happy to contribute my small part in the drama. Like practically everyone else who works there, I am a willing volunteer (only less capable), but unconnected with either Eastbourne Speedway or the sponsors, Robin's of Herstmonceux, from whom all the other volunteers are drawn.

The tedium, brutality and glacial pace of the work involve a real concerted team effort. It takes mental and physical determination to get it even half done, never mind completed. It feels like the sort of work that God would ordain as punishment for your sins in your present and previous lives. It also seems the sort of soul-destroying task that the Conservative press would advocate as the ideal solution for young offenders to try to teach them some decent values and respect. It certainly teaches *me* respect. Respect for anyone who has to do this type of manual work regularly and respect for all those who had volunteered to do this work year in and year out in the full knowledge of what it really entailed.

They say in artistic circles that you have to suffer for your art. I've never quite seen it myself, and have thought that they protested too much. I can now honestly say that I've at least made some small sacrifices for my writing and research for this book. My natural inclination on the night is to run away, to hide or to burst into tears. But no one else does and so we stick with it as a team. I'd go so far as to claim that we work extremely tenaciously and industriously. After all, we have a shared interest to accomplish the task as quickly and competently as possible, so that we can go home. Jon and Martin had the extra concern of the 3 a.m. deadline by which, I understood, they'd contractually promised that they'd have the Brighton Centre empty of any last hint of shale or their presence.

Despite my comparative lack of any real degree of physical strength or manual dexterity, especially compared to everyone else in our (chain) gang, arguably my best practical skill for this situation is with a broom. Once you have the skill and technique with a brush, you never really forget it. Not that I ever quite progressed to a level of proficiency that would allow me to be able to balance a brush on my chin like the real experts I worked with at Wimbledon every year. But I do still have a level of proficiency and skill – with brushes large and small, soft-bristled or hard-bristled – that sets me aside from the run-of-the-mill sweeper or wannabe sweeper. It's an ability that doesn't exactly rank up there with the more complicated of the apprenticed trades, but comes in extremely useful at the *Bonanza* where there is a lot of dirt and dust, a huge auditorium and enough work to keep you going for a month of Sundays. And a good bit of Monday morning it turned out – though it feels like a lifetime.

Still a promise is a promise and, in retrospect, it was a privilege to help and to be part of the final team that managed to clear up the track at the *Bonanza*. Also, Jon Cook has been unfailingly kind and helpful to me throughout with my book, never mind that he looked well panicked when the shale didn't look like it could be shifted at all. It was a worrying situation made all the more difficult by the limited number of helpers for the difficult final stretch.

After we get down to the hard core of shale shifters prepared to work late into the early hours of the morning, the hidden hierarchy among the members of the group becomes clear. Jon and Martin both have regular managerial type tasks to accomplish, which often require them to be elsewhere, though both of them do regularly return to help with the shale shifting. Jon is distracted throughout by his concerns about how long the clearing away will take. He frequently looks very pensive, whereas Martin appears less anxious and distracts himself with many tasks. The auditorium itself fills with a choking cloud of dust raised by hacking the compacted surface of the track into many pieces. All this activity produces a light film of dark dust that coated the faux white marble effect flooring and every other surface in the Centre.

The staff hired by the Brighton Centre, who arrive en masse near midnight, all wear safety masks throughout our work. They are employed every night to clear the seating of litter before they do a variety of other cleaning tasks. By 1 a.m. this independent team of cleaners have enjoyed themselves in that most thankless and pointless of tasks – the attempt to clean the floor of the dust that we've created when we cleared that part of the auditorium. Like an attempt to hold back the tide, it is soul-destroying work. Though they are diligent enough, no sooner have they pronounced an area of the floor dust free, then more of the dust we continue to generate wafts down to stick even more resolutely to the damp floor. An unsmiling and rather charmless man of diminutive stature, with a strong sense of his own unquestioned authority, supervises them throughout the night. When he doesn't issue orders aggressively to his staff, he contents himself with watching them or us do our work. Jon and Martin have to speak with him throughout the night, as they update him on the progress of our efforts that he could witness with his own eyes.

Right until we've almost finished, he remains a watchful, brooding and slightly malevolent figure that lingers around the periphery. When it is clear that we will almost be finished in time to meet the 3 a.m. curfew, his mood lightens and so indicates that his demeanour had, perhaps, been influenced by his own anxiety. The cumulative fatigue of the under-pressure late shifts of supervision – the dismantling, clearing away and building up again of the equipment every night at the Brighton Centre – would take a toll on anyone's sense of humour or bonhomie. Our own sense of bonhomie as a team just about remains intact throughout, helped in no small measure by the calm presence of Mick Robins. Though he has his own successful business and is the boss of practically everyone present, he manages to carry his authority lightly and motivates us with a gentle human touch.

When it is all over, I feel a real sense of elation and pride at our team accomplishment – as many of the others say they do every year – and everyone permits themselves some sort of smile at the end. For many of the people who remain working at this hour, however, there is still much more work to do elsewhere to unload the shale; and it will be many hours before they find the comfort of their beds.

Jon Cook had said he "could promise me an experience that I'd never forget". He definitely kept his word, though not quite in the manner I'd anticipated![12] As it was, hard work, tenacity and diligence won out along with all the dexterity and skills that everyone else took for granted because they see it all the time. They might just expect and assume it but, to a novice like myself, all these people were very impressive in their skills, teamwork and work ethic. Even the smokers rarely stopped grafting. Together we overcame the real enormity of the task to completely shift all the shale from the Centre in the time allowed. In retrospect I can definitely say it was a privilege.

11th December *Brighton Bonanza*, Edward Kennett and Lewis Bridger/Edward Kennett

[11] The roll call of workers on our chain gang was: Mick Robins (supervisor, enthusiast and one of the lads); Gary Robins (brilliant operator of the yellow loading shovel); Norman Robins (brilliant driver of the mini-digger); Lance Wyman (hard grafter) and his son Jamie (who worked well but managed to be more morose than me); Eric Dugard's son Matt (with a sunny disposition and extreme skill on the fork lift); Dougie Ballard (hard grafter); Edward Kennett (hard grafter allowed to go home early but only after he'd won every trophy on offer at the event); Ashley Wooler (hard grafter and charmingly enthusiastic bloke; loves life); Martin Dugard (tireless man, hard worker, brilliant rider and down-to-earth bloke) and Malcolm Arthur Cole (hard grafter, stoical and serial smoker of roll ups). Plus, last but not least, Jon Cook whom I'd describe similarly to Martin except, by all accounts the brilliant rider description would stretch things way too far and I'd add – owner of a wry, self-deprecating sense of humour and a sincere supervisor with a motivational but light touch. I'd like to claim that Jon remained calmly taciturn throughout, but I'd be lying, though Jon's version of a severe panic is everyone else's studied nonchalance. But, by his own calm but exacting standards he was positively a headless chicken when the 3 a.m. curfew deadline looked hopeless.

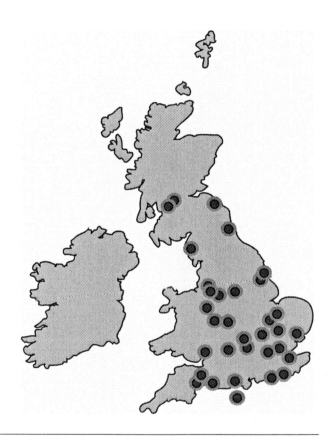

I hope that you enjoyed the journey.

Phew! What a fantastic year I had and what a brilliant experience. I was genuinely overwhelmed with the kindness of strangers and amazed how people went out of their way to help me.

The marathon task of writing up my travels has meant that events have moved on at every speedway club I visited and often dramatically so. I'd like to look briefly at what has happened.

In the Conference League, the lifeblood of the sport, many teams have disappeared from the competition in 2006; notably Armadale, Oxford, Sittingbourne, Wimbledon and Weymouth. Fortunately they have only scaled back activities at

Sittingbourne to run as a training track but still intend to compete in occasional fixtures later in the season, while Weymouth have a new owner and are trying to satisfy the local authorities about noise objections. Wimbledon continue their search for a new venue and welcome news or developments, which at the time of writing, are publicly thin on the ground. In case you wondered why I didn't include a chapter on the Dons in my book – I had actually written three – I'm afraid that Wimbledon club management, as is their right, chose to rattle litigious sabers in lieu of reading and commenting upon the chapters I devoted to the Dons. What a shame. This was the only club to take this approach. Unfortunately this meant that many interesting people I met with at Plough Lane were excluded from this account including the lovely story of the shale collector who has a collection of said material from every past and present track! Maybe I can tell this and the other stories another time. Much more positively, a new track has opened in Plymouth and I can't wait to visit.

In the Premier League, Hull folded before the season closed with outstanding debts and their fixtures uncompleted. Exeter also finally closed. Already, phoenix-like from the flames, Hull have been reconstituted under Dave Peet and will compete in a variety of friendlies, while Exeter are widely expected to return when they can find a suitable venue. Fortunately, Mildenhall have joined the Premier League (and big cheers to them for also still running a Conference League team, though this is tinged with sadness at the death of Brian Snowie who so fervently believed in youth development). Even better there is a new track at Redcar and again I can't wait to see the racing there. Less positively, the PL promoters in their (financial) wisdom have sadly seen fit to introduce the dreaded play-offs to decide the final destination of the championship. There will be benefits we're widely told but, to my mind, this doesn't really improve the situation.

In the Elite League, Reading have made the step and joined, albeit as the all-new Bulldogs rather than the Racers, the upper echelon. Pat Bliss has left and I feel something has been lost, if only a link to my childhood or a certain atmosphere about the place. The new owners are BSI with John Postlethwaite at the helm and I wish them every success at Reading. They have set about professionalising operations at Smallmead, often innovatively, and presently look likely to cut a swathe through some of their erstwhile competitors. I wonder if they are trying to rapidly turn themselves into the Chelsea of speedway (albeit a slightly less pecunious version)? I was also sorry to learn that Neil Watson has left the Panthers.

I'm sure that there's much more that I have missed out here and in the book in general. Obviously all mistakes remain my own and I apologise if I have accidentally upset anyone. If you have any comments, of either persuasion, please get in touch via my website on www.methanolpress.com

There will also be some more books very shortly.

Every effort has been made to get in touch with all copyright holders and many people featured in the photos but, again, I would be delighted to hear from you to make the appropriate credits or acknowledgements.

This book would not have been possible without the help of the BSPA – particularly the kind offices of the Chairman, Peter Toogood, along with the office staff – and all the promoters throughout the country. Many decry their efforts (including me sometimes in this book) but where would we all be without all their long hours of effort? Luckily they do what they do and so we still have a sport to watch and enjoy.

I mentioned earlier that I have been overwhelmed with help and kindness. I hesitate to name everyone as, inevitably, I will make a mistake and miss someone I'm extremely grateful to, so, with apologies for those I do manage to miss out I would like to thank the following people: Peter Adams, Graham Arnold, Jon Atkins, Mike Bacon, John Barber, Nick Barber, Dudley Barnes, Dick Barrie, Norman Beeney, Seth Bennett, Pat Bliss, Brian Burford, Ken Burnett, Sarah Chrisp, Kate Clanchy, Peter Clarke, Paul Clews, David Crane, Dave Croucher, Buster Chapman, Jonathan Chapman, Debra Davison, Gordie Day, Steve Dixon, Kevin Donovan, Graham Drury, Neil Dyson, George English, Joan English, Sam Ermolenko, Dave Fairbrother,

Nicola Filmer, Ben Findon, Richard Frost, Chris Gay, Arlette Gelphi, Arnie Gibbons, Rob Godfrey, George Grant, Mick Gregory, Andy Griggs, Rumana Haider, Tim Hamblin, Greg Hancock, Ross Heaton, Paul Hodder, David Hoggart, Colin Horton, Mike Hunter, Billy Jenkins, Chris Kinsey, Sheila La-Sage, Hywel Lloyd, Gary Lough, John Louis, Michael Max, Ian Maclean, Marian Maclean, Neil Machin, Geoff Maloney, Dennis McCleary, Ella MacDonald, Tony McDonald, Louise McLoughlin, Allan Melville, Colin Meredith, Karen Mosman, Tony Mole, Jayne Moss, Peter Oakes, Brian Owen, Dave Pavitt, Nigel Pearson, Dave Peet, Di Phillips, Matt Pitman, Graham Platten, Andy Porkpie, Andy Povey, Colin Pratt, Dave Rattenberry, Steve Ribbons, John Rich, Ronnie Russell, Graham Reeve, Nicola Sands, Neil Street, Tim Stone, David Short, Tony Swales, Trevor Swales, Wayne Swales, Peter Toogood, Tom at the Arena track shop, Sean Tacey, David Taylor, Dave Tattum, Caroline Tattum, Ian Thomas, Tim the Hat, David Thompson, Pam Thompson, Chris Van Stratton, David Valentine, Margaret Vardy, John Walsh, Neil Watson, Paul Watson, Nigel Wagstaff, Peter Waite, Alf Weedon, Ros Wesson, Brian White, Derek Wood and James Wright.

To pick out anyone in particular would be invidious. However, I owe so many 'thank you's'. The book wouldn't look as lovely as it does without Rachael Adams's brilliant design and artistic skills, along with her persistence. There would be many more errors than there are without the proofreading of Caroline Tidmarsh and Graham Russel has shown tremendous pedantry and knowledge to wrangle with my words into some sort of sense. Before Graham even got to manfully struggle with the manuscript, the gifted Michael Payne had suffered tremendously as my editor and without him there would be no even vaguely coherent book. Jules Martin has been my skilled photographic adviser and, so, on her advice I won't be giving up my day job. I am also particularly grateful to Jon Cook who has been supportive and sincere from the outset as well as to speedway referees Tony Steele – what a sensible and considered man – and the kindly, conscientious but always informative Chris Durno. I have luckily been touched by kindness and help from Jo Lawson. The Reverend Michael Whawell has been a credit to himself, the sport and his faith. Anne Brodrick has encouraged me for years to write and has shown much perspicacity in many things. Even more insightful, my true friend Sue Young has encouraged me often in so many things and really saved me when I needed that most – for which she has my eternal gratitude. Another real friend in this respect and so many other things since 1980 has been Dr. Edwin J. Jones. Of course, without the love and guidance of my parents – Mary and Alan – none of this book or so many other things would have been possible. Finally, you can never have too many teachers and I was lucky enough to have been inspired by a truly great teacher, poet, musician and funny bloke – Michael Donaghy – to write. Any book really! And it turns out to be this one. He was sadly taken away prematurely but not before he had touched so many people.

A donation for every copy sold will be made to the Speedway Riders Benevolent Fund.

Finally, if you go to speedway already why not make a point of taking even more friends this year and if you haven't been for a while or have never been, now's as good a time as any to start!

Obviously, I will continue to go along no matter, to still love my speedway, while I savour the people, approach to life and places that make it what it is. If I can compare the sport to London buses, I prefer my speedway as the old Routemaster bus version rather than the bright, new bendy bus variety. I'm constantly told it's modern, more practical, it's progress and that everyone loves it now, but it still really isn't comparable or the same.

Then that's speedway!

Thank you for getting this far.

25th May 2006 Brighton

Acknowledgements

Books and magazines

I have quoted with kind permission from the following sources:

The Evening Argus (2005)

The Speedway Star (2005) For subscriptions call 0208 335 1113

Backtrack (2005) For subscriptions call 01708 734 502

The Voice: The Official Journal of the Friends of Speedway (Spring 2005) For subscriptions call 0208 397 6599

Wheels and Deals by Ian Thomas (Pinegen, 2005) For orders call 0208 335 1113

The Speedway Regulations, Speedway Competition Rules and Sporting Code 2005 (SCB, 2005) For orders call 01788 565603

I also enjoyed these books:

Stoney (a real laugh and typifies speedway people) <tonyjackson@cometseh.freeserve.co.uk>

10th yer Baws! By Gary Lough (2004) For orders call 07718 909343

A Ref's Tale by Dave Osborne (2005) <ozzymike0412@hotmail.com>

Photographers

Julie Martin <http://www.juliemartinphotography.co.uk>

Steve Dixon <http://www.stevedixonphotography.co.uk>

Graham Platten <http://www.grahamplatten.co.uk>

Accommodation

All the following warmly welcome speedway fans and have special rates

Cara House, Berwick-upon-Tweed

01289 302749 <http://www.carahouse.co.uk>

Waverley Hotel, Workington

01900 603246 <http://www.waverley-hotel.com>

Garrison Hotel, Sheffield

0114 249 9555 <http://www.garrisonhotel.co.uk>

Showered in Shale

A fascinating book that holds up an illuminating mirror to both the sport and the community as a whole… Scott's pithy turn of phrase helps him to capture accurately a whole raft of personalities – his description of Arena Essex promoter Ronnie Russell is simultaneously laugh out loud funny and hugely respectful… through it all – and this big format softback runs to 500-plus pages – Scott's love of the sport and his fellow man shine out. Highly recommended.
Tim Hamblin, Wolverhampton Express & Star

It is very different from any other speedway book, the nearest comparison I can make is *Fever Pitch*, Nick Hornby's famous football book… I think it is likely to end up as one of the best speedway books I've ever read.
Arnie Gibbons, British Speedway Forum

It's all here, in almost soap opera style proportions… this is British Speedway stripped bare, this is how it really is and some of it isn't pretty… many years into the future, historians will gladly hold this book to their bosom for its insight… what the author has achieved – and it will be interesting to see how many people really take this on board – is that he's provided a book that will stand-up as a fly on the wall type narrative of where and what our sport really is in the early millennium.
…*Showered in Shale* is a quirky book, it's different and off-the-wall… it should find its way onto any true speedway fan's book shelf.
Brian Burford, Speedway Star

Jeff has a nice turn of phrase, doesn't pull his punches and isn't scared to offer critical observations when he feels the need! A new style of speedway read.
Dick Barrie, 'Straight Talking' in Berwick Programme

A superb new book chronicling speedway across the length and breadth of Britain… Dozens of quirky stories make the book as enjoyable for non-fans as those likely to be found near the third bend of any track… after reading Scott's chronicle, Wildcats fans will be hoping even more speedway in Weymouth has another chapter to run.
Matt Pitman, Dorset Echo

It really is a fascinating book and I hope fans don't miss out on the opportunity to read not just about the tracks, but also the characters behind them.
Chris Gay, SCB Official

A completely refreshing book to read. Totally different from everything else out there. Everyone should read it, especially every promoter, so that they can understand the complexity of our sport from a unique perspective – how the fans really see it!
Graham Drury, Workington Promoter

A refreshing change... Scott is not coming at the sport from an anorak-type perspective, but a far more open mind and he finds out plenty of information on the way.
Mike Bacon, East Anglian Daily Times

I don't know how the freak you did it!
Dave Fairbrother of the Speedway Star

A very worthy effort by this very candid author... supplemented by 409 interesting – if rather small – offbeat black and white photographs. Liberally laced with Scott's dry humour and pithy observations, *Showered in Shale* is a thoroughly absorbing travelogue that presents a whole new angle on the sport – from a fans perspective. Never afraid to ask a loaded question and attempt to get to the bottom of everything, Scott seeks out promoters, staff, supporters and a host of characters up and down Britain. The result is an entertaining read... it's unique and refreshingly honest.
Tony McDonald, Editor, Backtrack

A simply fascinating and unique observation of speedway in Great Britain in the early 21st century, described with a unique and entertaining use of the English language... it is simply a pleasure to read.
Mark Poulton, letter to the Speedway Star

Readers will find plenty to reward them.
Brian Owen, Brighton Evening Argus

A fascinating speedway travelogue.
Berwick Advertiser

Better than the usual boring speedway book full of stats or races from long ago.
Trevor Geer, Co-Team Manager, Eastbourne Eagles

If you have read any football books then you'll appreciate the difference between the typical Keeganesque "I were as sick as a parrot..." type autobiography and the works of authors such as Hornby, Davies, McIlvenney and Garry Nelson who have taken football writing to a new level. Well this book does this for speedway, it's thoughtful, intelligent, witty and interesting and takes the viewpoint of the people on the terraces rather than disappearing up its own bum the way too many of the books by riders, ex-riders and promoters have a tendency to. Due to the way it's written you can read it cover to cover or you can dip in and out...
Neil Dyson, Sheffield Speedway Fans forum

Definitely a must-have for any speedway fan – it is a detailed and informative, but amusing and off-beat, look at what goes on before the turnstiles open (and after).
Neil Watson, ex-Peterborough Promoter, British Speedway Forum

Some speedway books can leave you feeling quite cold and uninspired, but this one you can really relate to because a lot of what Jeff writes is what we all think as fans, naturally opinions can differ, but reading through this book is like chatting away to your mates on the terraces!
British Speedway Forum

Printed in the United Kingdom by Lightning Source UK Ltd
110956UKS00001B/3

Printed in the United Kingdom
by Lightning Source UK Ltd.
114959UKS00001B/71-76